The Classic of Changes

TRANSLATIONS FROM THE ASIAN CLASSICS

The Classic of Changes

A New Translation of the **I Ching** as Interpreted by Wang Bi

Translated by Richard John Lynn

Columbia University Press
New York

Columbia University Press
New York Chichester, West Sussex

Library of Congress Cataloging-in-Publication Data
I ching. English
The classic of changes : a new translation of the I Ching as interpreted by Wang Bi / translated by Richard John Lynn.
p. cm. — (Translations from the Asian classics)
Includes bibliographical references.
ISBN 0–231–08294–0
I. Lynn, Richard John. II. Wang, Bi, 226–249. III. Title.IV. Series.
PL2478.D48 1994
299'.51282—dc20 93–43999
CIP

∞

Casebound editions of
Columbia University Press books
are printed on permanent
and durable acid-free paper.

Printed in the United States of America
c 10 9 8 7 6 5 4 3 2 1

Contents

Acknowledgments

The idea to prepare a new English version of the *Book of Changes* originally came some years ago from Bonnie Crown, director of International Literature and Arts in New York, who also provided much assistance in planning the venture in its earlier stages. She convinced me that a new version was needed, that it would find an audience, and that I was the person to do it. Initially, I was skeptical on all counts and reluctant to get involved in such a complex and massive research and translation project, something that then was rather far removed from the usual areas of my scholarly work. Now that the book is finished, I thank her for all that good advice and encouragement, without which it would never have happened. David Knechtges and Kidder Smith served as readers of the manuscript for Columbia University Press; their reports contained numerous helpful suggestions, many of which I was able to incorporate into the amended and corrected version. I am grateful for their comments and criticism. I also thank Sarah St. Onge for her fine contribution as manuscript editor. Her unflagging energy and zeal for consistency and clarity greatly improved the manuscript, and the patience and good humor she showed in carrying out this complicated and demanding task was most remarkable and very welcome.

The

Classic

of

Changes

BARNES & NOBLE
STORE #1944 SAN JOSE, CA 408-984-3495

REG#05 BOOKSELLER#144
RECEIPT# 31207 11/23/94 11:17 AM

S 0231082940 CLASSIC OF CHANGES
LIST PRICE: 19.95 1 @ 15.96 15.96

S X1 MAGAZINE
1 @ 4.99 4.99

SUBTOTAL 20.95
SALES TAX - 8.25% 1.73
TOTAL 22.68
CHECK PAYMENT 22.68

LIST 24.94 SELL 20.95

YOU SAVED 3.99

BOOKSELLERS SINCE 1873

BARNES & NOBLE
STORE #1944 SAN JOSE, CA 408-984-3495

REG#05 BOOKSELLER#144
RECEIPT# 31207 11/23/94 11:17 AM

5 0231082940 CLASSIC OF CHANGES
LIST PRICE: 19.95 1 @ 15.96 15.96

5 X1 MAGAZINE
1 @ 4.99 4.99

SUBTOTAL 20.95
SALES TAX - 8.25% 1.73
TOTAL 22.68
CHECK PAYMENT 22.68

LIST 24.94 SELL 20.95

YOU SAVED 3.99
BOOKSELLERS SINCE 1873

Introduction

The *Classic of Changes* (*Yijing*) or *Changes of the Zhou* (*Zhouyi*) was originally a divination manual, which later gradually acquired the status of a book of wisdom. It consists of sixty-four hexagrams (*gua*) and related texts. The hexagrams, formed by combinations of two trigrams (also *gua*), are composed of six lines (*yao*) arranged one atop the other in vertical sequence and read from bottom to top. Each line is either solid (yang —) or broken (yin --). For example, Hexagram 59, *Huan* (Dispersion), is represented with the hexagram ䷺: First Yin, Second Yang, Third Yin, Fourth Yin, Fifth Yang, Top Yang—the bottom trigram being *Kan* ☵ and the top trigram being *Sun* ☴. The combinations are determined by the numerical manipulation of divining sticks, originally yarrow stalks (*Achillea millefolium*, also known as *milfoil*) or, later, by the casting of coins. In the translation, each hexagram graph or schema appears at the head of the section devoted to the particular hexagram, immediately below the hexagram number.

It is likely that, by the time the *Changes* was put together as a coherent text in the ninth century B.C., hexagram divination had already changed from a method of consulting and influencing gods, spirits, and ancestors—the "powerful dead"—to a method of penetrating moments of the cosmic order to learn how the Way or Dao is configured and what direction it takes at such moments and to determine what one's own place is and should be in the scheme of things. By doing so, one could avert wrong decisions, avoid failure, and escape misfortune and, on the other hand, make right decisions, achieve success, and garner good fortune. What exactly the Dao was in the thought of traditional China—at different times and with different thinkers—is a complex question. It was generally held throughout traditional Chinese society that Heaven was good and that human beings lived in a morally good universe—however it operated. Beyond that, it can only be said that a spectrum of opinion existed, at one end of which, the Dao—especially when it was understood as the manifestation of the will of Heaven—was seen as an unconscious and impersonal cosmic order that operated purely mechanistically, and, at the other, as something with a consciousness that heeded the plights of both humankind as a whole and the individual in particular and could answer collective and individual pleas for help and comfort. Although intellectual, elite culture tended to hold to the former view and popular culture favored the latter, much ambivalence concerning this issue can be found in the writings of many a sophisticated thinker.

Each hexagram is accompanied by a hexagram name (guaming), a hexagram statement (guaci) or "Judgment" (tuan), and line statements (yaoci) for each of the six lines. The line statements have a sequential or associational organization based on the general topic given in the Judgment; each states a specific, differentiated instance or variation of the topic, which in complete line statements (many statements seem to be fragments) is followed by a charge or injunction that one should take some action or refrain from it and a final determination ("misfortune," "good fortune," etc.).

The hexagrams, hexagram statements or Judgments, and line statements are the oldest parts of the *Changes*. The names and statements probably date from the ninth century B.C.—the hexagrams themselves may be much older—and constitute the first layer in what appears to be a three-layered text. The second layer consists of another two parts: commentary on the Judgments called Tuanzhuan and commentary on the abstract meanings or "Images" (xiang) of the Judgments and the line statements called Xiangzhuan. The Judgments have "Great Images" (Daxiang)—the abstract meanings of hexagrams as whole entities—and the line statements have "Little Images" (Xiaoxiang)—the abstract meanings of individual lines.

The traditional format of the *Changes* divides the Tuanzhuan and the Xiangzhuan each into two sections; together, they form the first four of the so-called Ten Wings (Shiyi) of the exegetical material included in the *Classic of Changes*. All Ten Wings are traditionally attributed to Confucius (551–479 B.C.); however, individual Wings actually date from different periods, with some predating his time while others date from as late as the third century B.C. Only the Commentaries on the Judgments and Commentaries on the Images, which for the most part seem to date from the sixth or fifth century B.C., appear to have been the direct product of Confucius's school, if not the work of Confucius himself. The remaining Ten Wings consist of later materials, which may contain some reworking of earlier writings—even from before Confucius's time. These constitute the third layer of the *Changes*.

The fifth of the Ten Wings comprises two fragments of an apparently lost commentary on the hexagrams as a whole called the *Wenyan* (Commentary on the Words of the Text). Only those parts attached to the first two hexagrams—*Qian* (Pure Yang) and *Kun* (Pure Yin)—survived into the period of textual redaction, which began with the early Han era in the third century B.C. The Commentary on the Words of the Text actually seems to be a borderline text that contains elements of both the second and the third layers. It deals with the philosophical and ethical implications of the Judgments, line statements, and images—all very much in a Confucian vein.

The sixth and seventh Wings are formed by the two sections of the so-called Commentary on the Appended Phrases (*Xici zhuan*) or Great Commentary (*Dazhuan*). This commentary seems to consist of fragments of two different texts, one a general essay or group of essays dealing with the nature and meaning of the *Changes* in general and the other a collection of specific remarks about the Judgments and line statements of individual hexagrams (not all are discussed).[1]

The eighth of the Ten Wings, Explaining the Trigrams (*Shuo gua*), consists of remarks on the nature and meaning of the eight trigrams (*bagua*), the permutations of which form the sixty-four hexagrams. Much of this is couched in terms of yin-yang dualism and the theory of the *wuxing* (five elements) and so probably dates from the early Han era (third century B.C.). It is among the latest of the exegetical materials included in the *Changes*.

The ninth Wing is Providing the Sequence of the Hexagrams (*Xugua*), a collection of remarks on each of the hexagrams that attempts to justify their order in terms of various etymological and rational considerations—often extremely farfetched. This also seems to be quite late material.

The tenth Wing, the Hexagrams in Irregular Order (*Zagua*), is a collection of brief remarks that attempts to define the meanings of individual hexagrams, often in terms of contrasting pairs—another late addition to the text of the *Classic of Changes*.

Traditionally, the hexagrams are thought to have been developed by King Wen of the Zhou (reigned 1171–1122 B.C.) out of the eight trigrams invented by the legendary culture hero and sage Fu Xi of remotest antiquity. King Wen is also supposed to have composed the Judgments. The line statements are attributed to the Duke of Zhou (died 1094 B.C.). However, the assertion that historically identifiable sages are responsible for the origins of the hexagrams and the composition of the first layer of the material in the *Classic of Changes* has been questioned throughout the twentieth century, both in China and abroad, and more recent advances in archaeology, paleography, and textual studies, which compare the earliest textual layer of the *Changes* with roughly contemporary inscriptions on bone, shell, metal, and stone, as well as with other ancient writings that exhibit similar syntax and vocabulary, have thoroughly discredited the myth of its sagely authorship. Modern scholarship has also discovered that the original meaning of the Judgments and line statements—as they were composed sometime probably during the two or three centuries preceding their compilation and final editing during the ninth century B.C.—is radically different from what the earliest layer of exegesis took it to be and that it often has very little to do with the values and ideals of Confucian morality and ethics. Either the writers of the *Tuanzhuan* (Commentary on the Judgments) and the *Xiangzhuan* (Commentary on the Images) were ignorant of this original meaning—concerned largely with the mechanics of divination and (often) its amoral consequences—or they knowingly suppressed it in order to replace it with a Confucian (or proto-Confucian) reading. However, with this first layer of exegesis, the collection of texts, which eventually developed into the *Classic of Changes* as we know it, was given a Confucian slant that shaped all subsequent interpretation—right up to modern times. This largely Confucian reading required a radical revision of syntax and the meaning of individual words—even the way the texts are divided into phrases and clauses. Therefore the original meaning of the earliest parts of the *Changes* is not represented in the commentary tradition—except perhaps, distantly, in some

Qing dynasty (1644–1911) philological approaches to the *Classic of Changes*—and thus plays no part in this translation, either of the *Classic of Changes* itself or of the Wang Bi commentary.[2]

The Translation

This work consists of an integral translation of Wang Bi's (226–249) *Zhouyi zhu* (Commentary on the *Changes of the Zhou*), including Wang's interpretations of the sixty-four hexagrams (Judgments, line statements, Commentary on the Judgments, Commentary on the Images, and—for the first two hexagrams—the Commentary on the Words of the Text) and his treatise on the *Changes*, the *Zhouyi lueli* (General Remarks on the *Changes of the Zhou*). The work also contains the commentaries of Wang's latter-day disciple, Han Kangbo (d. ca. 385), on those parts of the *Changes* not commented on by Wang himself: the *Xici zhuan* (Commentary on the Appended Phrases), the *Xugua* (Providing the Sequence of the Hexagrams), the *Zagua* (The Hexagrams in Irregular Order), and the *Shuo gua* (Explaining the Trigrams). Han was not an original thinker, but his remarks consistently seem to reflect Wang's approach, and so, while in no way as vital and interesting as Wang's own commentary, they probably are reasonably close to the kinds of things Wang himself might have said if he had chosen to comment on these parts of the *Classic of Changes*.

All translations are based on texts included in Lou Yulie, ed., *Wang Bi ji jiaoshi* (Critical edition of the works of Wang Bi with explanatory notes), 2 vols. (Beijing: Zhonghua shuju, 1980). Some passages in Wang Bi's commentary are dense, cryptic, and difficult to understand. Also, Wang did not comment on a few passages in the *Changes*, and it is unclear how he might have read particular phrases and sentences. Where I was uncertain or Wang was silent, I referred to the commentary on the *Changes* written by Kong Yingda (574–648), the *Zhouyi zhengyi* (Correct meaning of the *Changes of the Zhou*), largely a subcommentary to Wang's *Zhouyi zhu* (which is also included in the *Zhouyi zhengyi* in its entirety). Kong's commentary is often wordy and redundant, but he seems to have tried to read the *Changes* as he understood Wang to have read it, so his remarks are often the only guide to understanding the more cryptic passages in Wang's commentary and how Wang might have read passages in the text on which he did not actually comment. References to and translated excerpts from Kong's *Zhouyi zhengyi* are included in endnotes, along with other explanatory materials. I have used the text of the *Zhouyi zhengyi* that is contained in the critical edition prepared by Ruan Yuan (1764–1849) of the *Shisanjing zhushu* (Commentaries and subcommentaries on the thirteen classics) (1815; reprint, Taibei: Yiwen yinshuguan, 1955).

As this translation of the *Classic of Changes* is based exclusively on the Wang Bi/Han Kangbo commentary and the subcommentary of Kong Yingda, it is significantly different in many places from other translations, which for the most part are principally derived directly or indirectly from some combination of the commentaries of the Neo-Confucians Cheng Yi (1033–1107) and Zhu Xi (1130–1200). The most important of these are James Legge, *The Yi King; or, Book of Changes* (Oxford: Clarendon Press, 1882); Richard Wilhelm, *I Ging: Das Buch der Wandlungen* (Jena: Eugen Diederichs, 1924), translated into English by Cary F. Baynes as *The I Ching or Book of Changes* (Princeton: Princeton University Press, 1950); and *I Ching: The Book of Change* (New York: E. P. Dutton, 1968), translated by John Blofeld. Except for works that attempt to reconstruct the so-called original meaning of *Zhouyi* as a western Zhou document,[3] most modern editions of the classic published in mainland China, Taiwan, and Hong Kong, which often include translations or paraphrases into modern Chinese, also closely follow the commentaries of Cheng Yi and Zhu Xi. Modern Japanese and Korean studies and translations of the classic do much the same thing.

All this means that the contemporary reader of the *Changes*, regardless of the language in which it is read, will usually know it in some version largely shaped by Cheng Yi and Zhu Xi. Therefore where my Wang Bi version differs significantly from the readings of Cheng and Zhu, I include appropriate references to and translated excerpts from their commentaries in the endnotes to the passages concerned so that the reader may compare the different readings. Cheng's commentary is called the *Yichuan Yizhuan* (Yichuan's Commentary on the *Changes*) and Zhu's is called the *Zhouyi benyi* (Original Meaning of the *Changes of the Zhou*). Both these commentaries are included in Li Guangdi (1642–1718), editor, *Yuzuan Zhouyi zhezhong* (Compiled upon imperial order: Equitable judgments on interpretations of the

Changes of the Zhou) (1715; reprint, Taibei: Chengwen, 1975); all references to Cheng's and Zhu's commentaries are to this edition.

Wang Bi may be said to have written the first philosophical commentary on the *Changes*—that is, apart from those sections of the classic that are themselves commentaries. His approach synthesizes Confucian, Legalist, and Daoist views, with Confucian views predominant. His version of the *Changes* was extremely influential and became the orthodox interpretation during the course of the pre-Tang and Tang eras (fourth through tenth centuries A.D.) and was finally canonized in Kong Yingda's *Zhouyi zhengyi*. Although the commentaries of the later Neo-Confucians largely eclipsed Wang's interpretation, much of what he had to say was incorporated into what eventually became the official Neo-Confucian orthodox view of the *Changes*, and what they rejected also helped to shape that view. A comparison of Wang's commentary with those of Cheng Yi and Zhu Xi reveals how carefully Cheng and Zhu must have read Wang's remarks and how his arguments tended to shape theirs, whether they agreed with him or not (the disagreements largely result from their rejection of what they perceived to be elements of Legalism and Daoism in Wang's thought). The synthetic Neo-Confucian version of the *Changes* that emerged after the thirteenth century would have been very different if there had been no Wang Bi commentary first.

A comparison of Wang's interpretation with those of Cheng and Zhu also helps to emancipate the *Changes* from the notion that it can only be understood and appreciated as a timeless book of wisdom that somehow came into existence and maintained itself outside history and that there is one perfect and unchanging meaning to be extracted from it, if we only knew how. The "book of wisdom" approach to the *Changes* in modern times is, of course, extremely prevalent, and, although we can credit it largely to the great popularity of the Wilhelm/Baynes version, which interprets the *Changes* in such terms and includes an enormously influential foreword by Carl Jung, it also derives from the fact that the *Changes* was canonized as one of the Confucian classics at the beginning of the tradition and that throughout the centuries commentators, Wang Bi among them, attempted to wrest from it some kind of perfect meaning that could serve its readers for all time.

In my view, however, there is no one single *Classic of Changes* but rather as many versions of it as there are different commentaries on it. The text of the classic is so dense and opaque in so many places that its meaning depends entirely on how any particular commentary interprets it. Some interpretations, especially those of Cheng Yi and Zhu Xi, have become standard and orthodox, but the authority they carry, it seems to me, was derived not from any so-called perfect reading of the text but from the fact that the Cheng-Zhu version of Neo-Confucianism became the cultural and intellectual orthodoxy of traditional China; thus their commentaries, including those on the *Changes*, had to be correct. My approach to the *Changes* is entirely different. The commentary of Wang Bi is the historical product of a certain time and place—as are those of Cheng Yi and Zhu Xi or anyone else—a product that can tell us much about the development of Chinese intellectual thought during a particularly creative period of the tradition. It stands in great contrast to the later commentaries of the Song Neo-Confucians, the products of a different but equally creative age, and its presentation in the form of an integral English translation—with comparisons with the commentaries of Cheng Yi and Zhu Xi—should, it is hoped, reveal how much variety and vitality traditional Chinese thought could achieve.

In preparing this translation, I have tried—as much as it is within my capabilities—to be true to the literal meaning of the texts involved and to re-create the original tone of discourse that pervades them. Thus there has been no attempt to modernize what is being said, no effort to avoid offending contemporary sensibilities and values shaped by democracy, egalitarianism, individualism, feminism, or any other movement that might affect the way we think, feel, and express ourselves. There is much in the way Wang Bi and the other commentators cited here approached the *Changes* that can offend contemporary values and sensibilities, for what they said was the product of a culture that took for granted certain things that now largely do not go unquestioned:

1. Human society is *by nature* hierarchical.
2. The state is the family writ large, and the family is the state in miniature.
3. Both state and family are *by nature* patriarchies.

4. The universe is dualistic *by nature*; everything in it has either a yin or a yang character and exhibits—or, more precisely should exhibit—either yin or yang behavior.
5. Human society—as a *natural* part of the universe—is also characterized by yin-yang dualism.

Superiors are yang, and subordinates are yin, and they should fill their respective roles accordingly. Yang is the hard and strong, the assertive, the authority, the initiator, the male; yin is the soft and yielding, the submissive, the one subject to authority, the follower, the female. Political roles are conceived analogously: rulers are like fathers, the ruled masses like children; the sovereign is to his minister as a husband is to his wife; a senior official is to his subordinate as an older brother is to a younger brother; a subordinate should be submissive and loyal—that is, exhibit "female" behavior, and so on. Such assumptions are readily apparent throughout the commentaries; any translation that attempts an accurate reconstruction of the original tone and meaning could not possibly ignore or suppress them. For instance, when choosing equivalents in English, the use of gender-neutral terms for such a patriarchal mode of discourse would be entirely out of place.

How then should one read this translation of a Chinese classic and its commentaries, rooted as they are in value-laden assumptions that many may find, if not alien and offensive, at least out of date and superfluous? The work is so rich in meaning that it should be read on several levels. To get at this richness, I suggest that the reader accept the historical reality of the text's assumptions, let them inform a historical appreciation of traditional Chinese society, and then bracket or put them aside and allow the work to address the primary issues with which it is concerned: the interrelatedness of personal character and destiny; how position defines scope of action; how position and circumstances define appropriate modes of behavior; how the individual is always tied to others in a web of interconnected causes and effects; how one set of circumstances inevitably changes into another; and how change itself is the great constant—and flexible response to it the only key to happiness and success. There is a core of insights here concerning the structure of human relationships and individual behavior that can, I believe, speak to this and any other age—if we but allow it to do so.

Wang Bi

Wang Bi (226–249) lived at a time of great social and political uncertainty and military strife, marked by rebellion, usurpation, civil war, invasion, desperate economic conditions—all the elements that contribute to the precariousness of life. It was the beginning of that time of disunity in China between the great Han and Tang dynasties—initially, the period of the Three Kingdoms; later, the Six Dynasties Era or Southern and Northern Dynasties—a disunity that lasted nearly four centuries. Wang's own short lifetime coincided with the middle years of the Wei Kingdom (220–265), which had been founded on the chaos accompanying the disintegration of the Han dynasty. The Han general Cao Cao (155–220) usurped power in 220, and his eldest son, Cao Pi (187–226), became the first emperor of Wei.

During its existence, the Wei had to share the territory of the once-unified empire with two rivals, the later Han state in Sichuan, which occupied the southwest, and the state of Wu, which controlled the southeast. Even within its own polity, the Wei was far from secure. The imperial Cao family was quickly losing power to another clan, the Sima, which was packing both civil and military offices with its own members. The Sima, led by Sima Yi (179–251), eventually carried out its own usurpation of power in 249, the year of Wang's death. It held de facto state power, the Wei emperors mere puppets, until 265, when Sima Yan (236–290) became the first emperor of the Jin dynasty (265–420). Before this, from 240 to 249, the imperial clansman Cao Shuang dominated the government, and it was under him that Wang Bi served his stint at court. Sima Yi murdered Cao Shuang in 249 and ordered the execution of most of Cao's coterie. As we see from a biography of Wang written by He Shao,[4] Wang escaped execution, apparently not close enough to Cao and not a perceived political threat, only to die of disease later in the same year.

Wang Bi was not only in the middle of all this political and military turmoil, he was also right at the center of the major intellectual currents of the day, a fact that is immediately obvious from a reading of He Shao's biographical essay:

> Wang Bi revealed his intelligence and wisdom even when still a child. By the time he was only about ten years of age, he had already developed a liking for the *Laozi*

[*Daode jing*], which he understood thoroughly and could discuss with ease. His father was Wang Ye, a Secretarial Court Gentleman [*shangshu lang*]. At the time when Pei Hui was serving as Director of the Ministry of Personnel [*libu lang*],[5] Wang Bi, who then had not yet been capped [i.e., had not yet reached the age of maturity at twenty *sui* (nineteen years)], went to pay him a visit. As soon as Pei saw him, he knew that this was an extraordinary person, so he asked him, "Nonbeing [*wu*] is, in truth, what the myriad things depend on for existence, yet the Sage [Confucius] was unwilling to talk about it, while Master Lao expounded upon it endlessly. Why is that?" Wang Bi replied, "The Sage embodied nonbeing, so he also knew that it could not be explained in words. Thus he did not talk about it. Master Lao, by contrast, operated on the level of being [*you*]. This is why he constantly discussed nonbeing; he had to, for what he said about it always fell short." Shortly after that he also came to the attention of Fu Jia.[6]

At this time, He Yan [190–249] was president of the Ministry of Personnel [*libu shangshu*], and he too thought Wang Bi most remarkable. Sighing in admiration, he said, "As Zhongni [Confucius] put it, 'Those born after us shall be held in awe.' It is with such a person as this that one can discuss the relationship between Heaven and Mankind!" During the Zhengshi era [240–249], the position of Director of the Chancellery [*huangmen shilang*] became vacant a succession of times, and He Yan had managed to fill it with Jia Chong [217–282], Pei Xiu [224–271], and Zhu Zheng; now he also proposed Wang Bi for that office. However, it was then that Ding Mi and He Yan were vying for power [within the Cao Shuang clique], and, when Ding recommended Wang Li of Gao District to Cao Shuang, Cao appointed him to that position, in consequence of which he made Wang Bi a Court Gentleman [*tailang*]. When Wang Bi first took up his post and paid his ceremonial visit to Cao Shuang, he asked for a private interview. Cao dismissed his entourage, and Wang Bi discussed the Dao with him for an exceedingly long time, giving the impression that no other could equal him in explaining any aspect of it—so Cao jeered at him.

It was at this time that Cao Shuang monopolized political power at court and formed a clique whose members recommended one another for office. Wang Bi, unconventional and brilliant, did not concern himself with high office and reputation. Shortly afterward, when Wang Li suddenly died of illness, Cao Shuang appointed Wang Chen to take Wang Li's place, and Wang Bi failed to find acceptance with him. This made He Yan sigh with regret. Not only was Wang Bi now limited to superficial duties at court, even before that, it had not been his forte to accomplish anything of merit, a goal to which he paid less and less attention.

Liu Tao, a native of Huainan, was good at discussing the science of political strategies and alliances [*zongheng*], for which he had quite a reputation at the time, but on every occasion when he debated these matters with Wang Bi, he was always defeated by him. The talent with which he was endowed by Heaven made Wang Bi an outstanding figure, and what it allowed him to achieve, no one could ever seize from him.

By nature gentle and reasonable, Wang enjoyed parties and feasts, was well versed in the technical aspects of music, and excelled at pitching arrows into the pot.[7] In his discussion of the Dao, he may not have been as good as He Yan was at forcing language to yield up meaning, but, in his handling of the natural [*ziran*], his unique insights often excelled anything He Yan could come up with. To some extent, he used the advantages with which he was blessed to make fun of other people, so he often incurred the enmity of the scholars and officials of his day. Wang Bi was, however, good friends with Zhong Hui,[8] who was an established expert in disputation, thanks to his well-trained mental discipline, but he was always vanquished by Wang's high-flying élan.

It was He Yan's opinion that the sage is free of pleasure, anger, sadness, or happiness, and his discussion of this issue was meticulously argued. People such as Zhong Hui transmitted what he had to say, but Wang Bi took a different position from them and thought that what makes the sage superior to people in general is his intelligence [*shenming*] and what makes him the same as people in general is his having the five emotions [happiness, anger, sadness, pleasure, and desire]. It is because his intelligence is superior that he can embody gentleness and amiability and, in so doing, identify with nonbeing. It is because he is the same as other people in having the five emotions that he is unable to respond to things free from either sadness or pleasure. Nevertheless, the emotions of the sage are such that he may respond to things but without becoming attached to them. Nowadays, because the sage is considered free of such attachment, one immediately thinks it can be said that he no longer responds to things. How very often this error occurs!

When Wang Bi wrote his commentary to the *Changes*, Xun Rong, a native of Yingchuan, found fault with Wang's *Dayan yi* [Meaning of the great expansion],[9] to which Wang made a general reply, drafting a note that teased him:

> Even though one may have intelligence sufficient to delve into the most profound and subtle things, such a person will still be unable to distance himself from the nature he has thanks to his natural endowment [*ziran zhi xing*]. Whatever capacity Master Yan[10] had, it was something already realized beforehand in Confucius, yet when Confucius met him, he could not but feel pleasure, and, when Confucius buried him, he could not but feel sadness. Moreover, we often belittle this Confucius, considering that he was someone who never succeeded at pursuing principle [*li*] via the path of the emotions [*qing*]. But nowadays we have come to realize that it is impossible to strip away the natural. Your capacity, sir, is already fixed within your breast, yet here we are parted only about half a month or so, and you feel the pain of separation as much as all that! Thus we know, when we compare Confucius to Master Yan, that he could not have surpassed him by very much!

Wang Bi wrote a commentary to the *Laozi*, for which he provided a general introduction [*zhilue*] marked by clear reasoning and systematic organization. He also wrote a *Dao luelun* [General discussion of the Dao] and a commentary to the *Changes*, both of which frequently exhibit lofty and beautiful language.[11] Wang Ji [ca. 240–ca. 285] of Taiyuan was prone to disparage the *Laozi* and the *Zhuangzi*, yet he once said, "When I saw Wang Bi's commentary to the *Laozi*, there was much that I became enlightened about!"

However, Wang Bi was shallow in his personal behavior and obtuse concerning how others felt. At first, he was good friends with Wang Li and Xun Rong, yet when Wang Li stole his chance to be Director of the Chancellery, he came to hate him, and he did not manage to finish up with Xun Rong on good terms either.

In the tenth year of the Zhengshi era [249], Cao Shuang was deposed, in consequence of which Wang Bi was dismissed from service at court. In the autumn of that year he fell prey to a pestilence and died, then twenty-three years of age. He had no son, so his line stopped with him. Concerning his death, when Prince Jing of the Jin dynasty [the posthumous title of Sima Shi (208–255)] heard of it, he sighed and moaned over it for days on end; regret at his passing was felt as keenly as this by those of the intelligentsia!

Wang is commonly referred to, because of his famous commentary on the *Laozi* and other discussions of the Dao, as a "Neo-Daoist" thinker, an adherent of the so-called *xuanxue* (studies of the mysterious) that so characterized intellectual thought during the Wei-Jin era, when so many sought to penetrate the realm of spontaneous creation and uncover the mysterious constants that ruled both the natural and human worlds. However, as we see from He Shao's biography, this does not appear entirely accurate. Whereas Wang certainly contributed to the development of the *xuanxue* tradition in a variety of ways, it is also readily apparent that he had an intense interest and commitment to Confucian values and principles. Note that he seems to have regarded Confucius, at least at times, as superior to Laozi, as Confucius had "embodied nonbeing" and Master Lao had not. By "nonbeing" (*wu*), Wang seems to have meant the undifferentiated unity of things ontologically prior to their phenomenal existence, the permanent—indescribable and unnameable—reality underlying the "being" (*you*) of the phenomenal universe.[12] It requires a sage—Confucius, for example—to achieve a state of mind or spirit that allows the recovery of that sense of unity in the here and now—to obtain mystic insight into the equality of all things. If Wang had written only or primarily about such things, we could place him simply in the Neo-Daoist camp, but he also had a great deal to say about the real sociopolitical world of statecraft and military strategy, of personal and public ethics and morality—all of which suggests that he was a multifaceted thinker about whom we should keep an open mind. Most germane to our purposes here, we should note that whereas his commentary to the *Changes* at times refer to nonbeing and other Daoist concepts—especially when he attempts to explain how and why change itself occurs—the text as a whole focuses on the phenomenon of human existence and is in the main a Confucian statement.

Wang Bi's Approach to the Changes of the Zhou

The best introduction to Wang's approach is his own *Zhouyi lueli* (General Remarks on the *Changes of the Zhou*), and anyone who consults his commentary is advised to read this essay first, for without a basic understanding of how Wang himself interpreted the classic, much of what he says in the commentary will not be immediately accessible. I shall attempt to summarize its main points here.

In the first section, Clarifying the Judgments, Wang asserts that each hexagram is a unified entity and that its overall meaning or "controlling principle" is expressed in its name, which then is amplified in the hexagram Judgment. Moreover, the controlling principle usually resides in the master or ruler of the hexagram, one line that is sovereign over all the others. Rulership differs from hexagram to hexagram, but we can know what kind of rulership is involved by referring to the Judgments. He also notes that some hexagrams are exceptions to this general rule, as their meaning derives from the relationship between the constituent trigrams.

The next section, Clarifying How the Lines Are Commensurate with Change, Wang states a basic principle: change occurs because of the interaction between the innate tendency of things and their countertendencies to behave in ways opposed to their natures. "Things" include individual human beings, and the lines of a hexagram represent—either directly or through analogy—different kinds of people in different positions and different situations. In fact, Wang often describes the action and interaction of the lines as if they were people all involved in some particular set of circumstances. Some lines respond to each other and resonate together—signifying harmonious relationships—and some lines repel and clash—signifying opposition and divergence of interests—and this resonance or clash produces movement and change. By understanding this principle, one can know the innate tendencies of things—"how things are going"—and, by adjusting one's behavior accordingly, success can be had.

The third section, Clarifying How the Hexagrams Correspond to Change and Make the Lines Commensurate with It, explains how certain hexagrams signify moments of either obstruction or facility and thus serve as indicators that one should either refrain from action or engage in it. It is also here that Wang sets out his scheme of yin and yang lines, yin and yang positions, congruent and incongruent relationships between pairs of lines, and the mechanics of resonance and discord. Yin lines are soft and weak; yang lines are hard and strong. The positions of a hexagram are calculated from bottom to top. The odd number places—first (bottom), third, and fifth—are strong yang positions, and the even number places—second, fourth, and sixth (top)—are weak yin positions.[13] Yin and yang lines form resonate pairs; yin and yin or yang and yang lines form discordant pairs: the unlike attract; the like repel. Proper resonate relationships can take place between lines of the lower and upper trigrams—one with four, two with five, three with six—but each must pair with its opposite: yin with yang or yang with yin. Secondary harmonious relationships can also occur between contiguous lines when "yang rides atop yin" or "yin carries yang" but never when the reverse occurs, for this is an unnatural, discordant relationship—as, for example, when a superior supports or "carries" his subordinate. The sixty-four combinations of yin and yang lines and yin and yang positions schematically represent all the major kinds of situations found in life. One must know how to cast the hexagrams and how to understand the texts of the *Changes*, for if one can determine which situation prevails at any given moment, what one's place is in that moment and situation, and how one relates to the other major players involved, as Wang puts it, "change will yield its all."

The fourth section, Clarifying the Images, deals with the images formed by the hexagrams, expressed by the Judgments and line statements and amplified by the "Great Images" and

"Little Images" commentaries. Here Wang argues that the images of the *Changes* should be understood as vehicles of abstract meaning and not be taken literally or as symbolic representations of numbers. In doing so, he breaks completely with the earlier Han era *xiangshu* (image and number) approach to the *Changes*, in which interpreters combined and recombined standardized images, using various arcane mathematical operations, to generate new trigrams and hexagram relationships out of original hexagrams. By freeing the *Changes* from such calculations and from confusion with cosmological and calendrical considerations, Wang Bi allowed it, aided by his commentary, to become a literary text rich in metaphysical, political, and personal significance. He, more than anyone else in the commentary tradition, made it into the classic of philosophy that so attracted the attention of the Song era (960–1279) Neo-Confucians and continues to this day to fascinate readers in both East and West.[14]

The fifth section, Considering the Line Positions, reiterates and expands on things said in the third section. As first (bottom) and sixth (top) lines are at the beginning and end points, respectively, of hexagrams (and thus signify the beginning and ending of the situation involved), they are at the junctures of what precedes and what follows a given situation, and so "neither of these positions has a constant status." The other four line positions are either yang and "noble" (three and five) or yin and "humble" (two and four). Yang lines "should" be in yang positions, and yin lines "should" be in yin positions, for this results in hexagrams that generally indicate facility and harmony. Lines "out of position" (yin in yang positions, yang in yin positions) result in hexagrams that generally indicate obstruction and disharmony.

The sixth section, entitled simply General Remarks, Part Two, and the seventh section, Cursory Remarks on Some Hexagrams, expand on things said in earlier sections and illustrate the principles and issues raised by reference to specific hexagrams.

One principle of understanding the *Changes*, which is often cited in Wang's commentary but is not discussed in his General Remarks, is the special role of the middle positions in trigrams—positions two and five. These middle positions indicate "centrality" and "the Mean" (*zhong*)—the territory of proper and balanced behavior and action. The middle position in the lower trigram is a yin position (two), and in the upper trigram it is a yang position (five), so, very often, regardless of other considerations, the line in the fifth position—whether yin or yang—turns out to be the ruler of the hexagram as a whole, for it is the "most noble" place, the "exalted position."

Another assumption underlying Wang's approach to the *Changes* is, of course, that the casting of hexagrams is an absolutely sure and accurate method of determining the character of moments of time. This is alluded to throughout his General Remarks and in many places in the commentary, but it is an issue that he never goes into in any detail—he probably did not think it was necessary, since he could not have conceived of anyone challenging its validity. This is true of all traditional commentators on the *Changes*: the way the yarrow stalks or coins fall—the particular configuration that results—is indicative of the shape of that particular moment. This supposes that everything that occurs in a given moment is interrelated and that all such events somehow share in the same basic character. In other words, as far as the *Changes* is concerned, the casting of stalks or coins, when properly done, is the key indicator of the shape of moments of time—which restates, in very simple terms, the way C. G. Jung explained how the casting of hexagrams is supposed to "work."[15] Jung states that his explanation, based on his theory of synchronicity, "never entered a Chinese mind" and that the Chinese instead thought that it was "spiritual agencies" (*shen*) that "make the yarrow stalks give a meaningful answer." I do not think this was always necessarily so, for it brings us back to a consideration of whether people in the Chinese tradition, especially those of Wang's own day, thought Heaven operated impersonally and objectively or consciously and in sympathy with humankind. Wang himself, from various things said in the commentary and in the General Remarks, seems to have been ambivalent about this—as were so many before and after him. My general impression of what he may have believed is that the Dao for him was *largely* impersonal; it had to be because it operated on such a grand scale. Whether or not he thought gods or other "spiritual agencies" had anything to do with how the yarrow stalks behaved is an impossible question to answer with any certainty. My impression is that he did not think so and would have said instead, if he had been asked, something to the effect that the yarrow stalks manifested the workings of the Dao.

How to Cast a Hexagram

THE YARROW STALK METHOD

Various methods of yarrow (milfoil) stalk (*Achillea millefolium*) divination had been developed since the Han era—all apparently based on the brief description provided in section nine of the Commentary on the Appended Phrases, Part One, and commented upon by Wang Bi and Han Kangbo. The reasons for various steps in the process are given there.[16] Extant written versions of these methods were critiqued in the twelfth century by Zhu Xi, who then wrote his own account of what he thought the correct method should be.[17] Zhu's composite or reformed method became the standard way of yarrow stalk divination for the rest of the traditional era and is still the one most generally used today.

The casting of a hexagram requires fifty stalks, manipulated in four stages or operations. These four operations are repeated three times to form a line (one operation set), and, since there are six lines, six operation sets are required for the whole process. However, before these operations begin, one stalk is set aside, which leaves forty-nine.

To complete the first set:

OPERATION ONE: Take up the forty-nine stalks, and divide them randomly into two bunches, placing them down one beside the other.

OPERATION TWO: Take one stalk from the right-hand bunch, and place it between the ring finger and little finger of the left hand.

OPERATION THREE: Grasp the left-hand bunch in the left hand, and, with the right hand, take bundles of four stalks from it until four or fewer stalks remain. Set this remainder aside. Then count off the stalks from the right-hand bunch by fours until four or fewer stalks remain, and set this remainder aside as well.

OPERATION FOUR: Place the remainder from the left-hand bunch between the ring finger and the middle finger and the remainder from the right-hand bunch between the middle finger and the index finger of the left hand. The sum of all the stalks now held in the left hand is either 9 or 5 (either 1 + 4 + 4, or 1 + 3 + 1, or 1 + 2 + 2, or 1 + 1 + 3). In this first set, the first stalk—held between the

> ring finger and little finger—is disregarded in counting up the stalks, so the sum is adjusted to either 8 or 4. The result 4 is a single unit and has the numerical value of 3. The result 8 is a double unit and has the numerical value of 2. Therefore if the sum of the first counting is 9, it counts as 2, and if the sum is 5, it counts as 3.

This completes the first set, and the stalks that make up the sum are now set aside.

The second and third sets are identical, the third being performed with the stalks left over after the second set has been completed:

> OPERATION ONE: Take up the remaining stalks, and randomly divide them into two bunches, placing the bunches next to each other.
>
> OPERATION TWO: Take one stalk from the right-hand bunch, and place it between the ring finger and little finger of the left hand.
>
> OPERATION THREE: Grasp the left-hand bunch in the left hand, and, with the right hand, take bundles of four stalks from it, until four or fewer stalks remain. Set this remainder aside. Then count off the stalks from the right-hand bunch by fours, until four or fewer remain, and set this remainder aside as well..
>
> OPERATION FOUR: Place the remainder from the left-hand bunch between the ring finger and the middle finger and the remainder from the right-hand bunch between the middle finger and the index finger of the left hand. This time, the sum of the stalks is either 8 or 4 (either 1 + 4 + 3, or 1 + 3 + 4, or 1 + 1 + 2, or 1 + 2 + 1); again, an 8 has the value of 2, and a 4 has the value of 3.

It is from the sum of the three values that result from the three sets of operations that a line is formed. If the first set results in a 5 (which becomes a 4, with a value of 3) and the second and third sets each result in a 4 (value 3), the sum value is 9, which defines an "old" yang line—one that is about to change into a yin line and so warrants separate consideration when the hexagram is interpreted. If the first set results in a 9 (which becomes an 8, with a value of 2) and the second and third sets each result in an 8 (value 2), the sum value is 6, which defines an "old" yin line—one that is about to change into a yang line and, again, warrants separate consideration when the hexagram is interpreted.[18] The other possible sum values arrived at by adding the results of the three sets will either be 7 or 8. Sevens result from the following combinations: 9 (i.e., 8, value 2) + 8 (value 2) + 4 (value 3); 5 (i.e., 4, value 3) + 8 (value 2) + 8 (value 2); 9 (i.e., 8, value 2) + 4 (value 3) + 8 (value 2). Eights result from these combinations: 9 (i.e., 8, value 2) + 4 (value 3) + 4 (value 3); 5 (i.e., 4, value 3) + 4 (value 3) + 8 (value 2); 5 (i.e., 4, value 3) + 8 (value 2) + 4 (value 3). A 7 is a "young" yang line, and an 8 is a "young" yin line. Both these are "at rest" and not about to change, thus they are disregarded when the individual lines of a hexagram are interpreted. One repeats this procedure six times (6 × 3 sets) to form a hexagram, working from the first line at the bottom to the sixth line at the top.

When a hexagram consists entirely of "new" lines, one should only consult the Judgment, the Commentary on the Judgments, and the Commentary on the Images. However, if there are one or more "old" lines in the hexagram, one should consult the Line Statements and the Commentary on the Images for such lines. Also, one must consider the "new" hexagram that results from the movement or change of the "old" lines and should consult its Judgment, Commentary on the Judgments, and Commentary on the Images. For example, in casting Hexagram 36, *Mingyi* (Suppression of the Light) ䷣, if one were to come up with an "old" yang for the third line, it would mean that this line was about to change into a "new" yin—which would result in Hexagram 24, *Fu* (Return) ䷗.[19]

THE COIN METHOD

Given the great complexity of the yarrow stalk method, it was inevitable that some other simpler and easier method of casting a hexagram would develop. Of uncertain time and authorship, such a method did, in fact, come into being—the coin method. This may have had origins in popular culture, for it involves the manipulation of coin money—hardly something that one would expect to come out of an elite literati culture. Traditional Chinese coins were made of bronze, had holes in the middle (so they could be strung together), and an inscription on one side. The method is very simple. One takes up three coins and throws them down together; each throw forms a hexagram line. The inscribed side of a coin is yin --, with a value of 2, and the reverse side is yang —, with a value of 3. If all three coins turn up yang, the sum value is 9, which defines an "old" yang line; if all are yin, the sum value is 6, which defines an "old" yin line. One yang and two yin result in a 7, a "young" yang line; two yin and one yang result in an 8, a "young" yin line. From this point on, one proceeds as for the yarrow stalk method.

NOTES

1. An alternate tradition has the Commentary on the Appended Phrases as the fifth and sixth of the Ten Wings. Richard Wilhelm's translation, for instance, follows this order.

2. The great pioneer in recovering the original meaning of the earliest layers of the *Changes* is Gao Heng, whose *Zhouyi gujing jinzhu* (Modern annotations to the ancient classic, the *Changes of the Zhou*) was first published in 1934. Two recent works in English revise Gao's findings, summarize and develop more up-to-date Chinese scholarship, and make new advances of their own: Edward Shaughnessy, *The Composition of the Zhouyi*, and Richard Kunst, *The Original "Yijing": A Text, Phonetic Transcription, Translation, and Indexes, with Sample Glosses.*

3. See note 2 above.

4. He Shao, a prolific essayist on the people and events of his own times, was the son of He Zeng (199–278), high official under both the Wei (220–265) and Western Jin (265–317) courts. This notice on Wang Bi is appended to the biography of Zhong Hui (225–264) in the *Weizhi* (Chronicles of the Wei) section of the *Sanguozhi* (Chronicles of the Three Kingdoms; see Lou, *Wang Bi ji jiaoshi*, 2: 639–644). Most of the information provided by He Shao's biography is also found in Liu Yiqing's (403–444) *Shishuo xinyu*, divided among a number of entries, often in passages worded differently from those in He Shao's biography of Wang. Liu's work also contains a few other details concerning Wang's life. See Richard Mather's translation of Liu's work, *Shih-shuo Hsin-yü*, "Biographical Notices," p. 593, and index, p. 722.

5. Pei Hui was the father of Pei Kai (237–291), who also rose to high office. Hui gained a reputation for his expertise in the *Laozi* and the *Classic of Changes*.

6. Fu Jia (205–255) was a member of He Yan's circle of friends dedicated to "pure conversation" (*qingtan*) but broke with He and joined the Sima party in 249, thus avoiding execution. He authored one of the essays in Zhong Hui's *Siben lun* (Treatise on the four basic relations between talent [*cai*] and human nature [*xing*]). See note 8 below.

7. *Tou hu* (pitch [arrows] into the pot) was an elegant game played at formal or ritual feasts.

8. Zhong Hui (225–264) was the editor of the *Siben lun* (Treatise on the four basic relations between talent [*cai*] and human nature [*xing*]) and a strict Confucian who was opposed to the subversive (as seen by the Sima forces) Daoist-based "pure conversation" (*qingtan*) circle. He was an ally of the Sima party at the Wei court, but when the Sima usurped power in 264, Zhong attempted a countercoup against his own troops, which had joined the revolt, and was killed.

9. Part of this work seems to have been incorporated into Han Kangbo's commentary on section nine of the Commentary on the Appended Phrases, Part One; see note 36 there.

10. Master Yan, Yanzi (also called Yan Hui or Yan Yuan), was supposedly the most virtuous of Confucius's disciples. See *Lunyu* (Analects) 11:18.

11. For a discussion of extant, reconstructed, and lost works of Wang Bi, see Lou, *Jiaoshi shuoming* (Collation and annotation: An explanatory note), in *Wang Bi ji jiaoshi*, pp. 11–17.

12. See Bodde, "Harmony and Conflict," in *Essays on Chinese Civilization*, pp. 275–276.

13. The first (bottom) and sixth (top) positions are problematic. Wang tells us in the fifth section of the General Remarks that there do not seem to be hard and fast rules for these positions—yin or yang lines might both be suitable for either.

14. See Smith et al., *Sung Dynasty Uses*, pp. 18–19 and 22–25.

15. See Jung's foreword to the Cary Baynes English version of Richard Wilhelm's translation, *The I Ching or Book of Changes*, pp. xxiii–xxv.

16. See note 36 of that section.

17. Smith et al., *Sung Dynasty Uses*, pp. 188–189.

18. I avoid the term *moving line* to designate "old" yin and yang lines that are about to change into their opposites, because this term is used a number of times elsewhere in the translation to refer to any hexagram line (*yao*)—the attribute *moving* meaning "alive" or "numinous." Cf. section ten in the Commentary on the Appended Phrases, Part Two. The Wilhelm/Baynes translation of the *Changes* does, however, use *moving line* to designate an "old" yin or yang line; see *The I Ching or Book of Changes*, pp. 722–723.

19. Derivation of a second "new" hexagram from the "old" yin and "old" yang lines of a first hexagram is not mentioned in Wang Bi's writings on the *Changes*, so the method described here may not have been part of how he approached the *Changes*. However, as this became the standard way of interpreting hexagrams from Zhu Xi's time on, I include it here. See Smith et al., *Sung Dynasty Uses*, pp. 176–177.

General Remarks on the Changes of the Zhou [Zhouyi lueli], *by Wang Bi*

Clarifying the Judgments [Ming tuan]

What is a Judgment? It discusses the body or substance of a hexagram as a whole and clarifies what the controlling principle is from which it evolves.

The many cannot govern the many; that which governs the many is the most solitary [the One]. Activity cannot govern activity; that which controls all activity that occurs in the world, thanks to constancy, is the One.[1] Therefore for all the many to manage to exist, their controlling principle must reach back to the One, and for all activities to manage to function, their source cannot but be the One.

No thing ever behaves haphazardly but necessarily follows its own principle. To unite things, there is a fundamental regulator; to integrate them, there is a primordial generator. Therefore things are complex but not chaotic, multitudinous but not confused. This is why when the six lines of a hexagram intermingle, one can pick out one of them and use it to clarify what is happening, and as the hard ones and the soft ones supersede one another, one can establish which one is the master and use it to determine how all are ordered. This is why for mixed matters the calculation [*zhuan*] of the virtues and the determination of the rights and wrongs involved could never be complete without the middle lines.[2] This is why if one examines things from the point of view of totality, even though things are multitudinous, one knows that it is possible to deal with them by holding fast to the One, and if one views them from the point of view of the fundamental, even though the concepts involved are immense in number and scope, one knows that it is possible to cover them all with a single name. Thus when we use an armillary sphere to view the great [heavenly] movements, the actions of Heaven and Earth lose their capacity to amaze us, and if we keep to a single center point when viewing what is about to come to us, then things converging from the six directions lose their capacity to overwhelm us with their number. Therefore when we cite the name of a hexagram, in its meaning is found the controlling principle, and when we read the words of the Judgment, then we have got more than half the ideas involved. Now, although past and present differ and armies and states then and now appear dissimilar, the way these central principles function is such that nothing can ever stray far from them. Although kinds and gradations of things exist in infinite variety, there is a chief controlling principle that inheres in all of them. Of things we esteem in a Judgment, it is this that is the most significant.

The rare is what the many value; the one that is unique is the one the multitudes make their chief. If one hexagram has five positive lines and one negative, then we have the negative line be the master. If it is a matter of five negative lines and one positive line, then we have the positive line be the master. Now, what the negative seeks after is the positive, and what the positive seeks after is the negative. If the positive is represented by a single line, how could the five negative lines all together ever fail to return to it! And if the negative is represented by a single line, how could the five positive lines all together ever fail to follow it! Thus although a negative line may be humble, its becoming the master of a hexagram is due to the fact that it occupies the smallest number of positions. And then there are some hexagrams for which one may set aside the hexagram lines and take up instead the two constituent trigrams, for here the substance of the hexagrams involved does not evolve from individual lines.[3] Things are complex, but one does not worry about their being chaotic; they change, but one does not worry about their being confused. To tie things together, thus preserving the broad significance involved, and to bring forth the simple nature of things, thus being up to dealing with their multiplicity, there is indeed only the Judgments! To deal with the chaotic and yet manage to avoid confusion and to handle change and yet manage not to drown in it, only it [the *Changes*], being the most profound and subtle device in the whole world, could ever be up to doing these things! Therefore if we view the Judgments in the light of this, the concepts involved should become clear.

Clarifying How the Lines Are Commensurate with Change [Ming yao tong bian]

What are the hexagram lines? They "address the states of change."[4] What is change? It is what is brought about by the interaction of the innate tendency of things and their countertendencies to spuriousness.[5] The actions of this tendency to spuriousness are not to be sought in numbers [i.e., they are beyond count]. Thus when something that tends to coalescence would disperse or when something that tends to contraction would expand, this runs counter to the true substances involved. In form a thing might seem inclined to agitation yet wants to be still, or a material though soft still craves to be hard. Here, substance and its innate tendency are in opposition, and material and its inclination are in contradiction. Even the most meticulous reckoning cannot keep track of the number of such things, and even the most sage of intellects cannot establish standards for them, for change is something that laws cannot keep pace with, something that measurements cannot assess.[6] Of course, to happen, these things need not be caused by something great![7] A leader of all the armed forces might be frightened by the etiquette of the court, and a merciless and mighty warrior might come to grief in the pleasures of wine and women.

Contiguous lines are not necessarily well disposed toward each other, and distant lines are not necessarily at odds. "Things with the same tonality resonate together," yet they do not have to have the same pitch. "Things with the same material force seek out one another," yet in material substance they do not have to be equivalent.[8] That which summons the rain is the dragon.[9] That which determines the *lü* note [i.e., in a yin or minor key] is the *lü* note [i.e., in a yang or major key]. Thus two women are beset by contrariness, but the hard and the soft unite to form one body. Drawn-out sighs on lofty heights are sure to fill distant valleys. If [troops] throw down their arms on dispersive ground, even the six relations [i.e., closest relatives] will not be able to protect one another,[10] but if they were to share the same boat to cross a river, what possible harm could happen to the men of Hu and Yue in spite of the treachery they feel for each other![11] Thus if people recognized the feeling [or "innate tendency"] involved, they would not grieve at contrariness and distance, and if they understood the inclination involved, they would not bring trouble upon themselves by trying to settle things through the force of arms.[12] To be "able to delight hearts and minds," to "be able to refine concerns,"[13] to see how things in opposition still yield knowledge of their kinds, and to see how different things still yield knowledge of their continuity,[14] is this possible for anyone who does not understand the hexagram lines! Therefore if one has goodness for the near, those far away will come to one;[15] if one fixes the note *gong*, the note *shang* will respond to it; if one cultivates and nourishes those below, those in high positions [nobility, state officers] will submit, and when one gives to them [those in high positions], they from whom one takes [those below, the common folk] will be obedient.

And so lines that indicate true innate tendencies and lines that indicate spurious countertendencies react with each other; distant lines and contiguous lines pursue each other; lines that attract and lines that repel provoke each other; and lines that indicate contraction and lines that indicate expansion induce each other to action. One who perceives the innate tendency involved will be successful, but if he just goes after something abruptly, it will go against him. Therefore, by forming analogous models, they [the sages] captured the change and transformation involved,[16] and "this means that only when one has developed his instruments will he have the capacity [for action].[17] They [the myriad things of existence] do not understand how it [change] is the master, but when it provides a beat for the dance, all under heaven follows; this is what appears in the innate tendency of things.[18]

This is why they [the hexagram lines] "perfectly [emulate] the transformations of Heaven and Earth and so [do] not transgress them . . . [follow] every twist and turn of the myriad things and so [deal] with them without omission . . . [and have] a thorough grasp of the Dao of day and night . . . and change is without substance."[19] There are only one yin line and one yang line, but they are inexhaustible. These [the lines] have to be the most facile [i.e., capable of the utmost change] things under Heaven, for what else could ever be up to this!

This is why the hexagrams are the means to preserve moments of time, and the lines are the means to indicate the change involved.

Clarifying How the Hexagrams Correspond to Change and Make the Lines Commensurate with It [Ming gua shi bian tong yao]

The hexagrams deal with moments of time, and the lines are concerned with the states of change that are appropriate to those times. Moments of time entail either obstruction or facility,[20] thus the application [of a given hexagram] is either a matter of action or of withdrawal. There are hexagrams that are concerned with growth [of the Dao], and those that are concerned with decrease [of the Dao], thus the texts for them either impart a sense of danger or impart a sense of ease.[21] The constraint appropriate to one moment of time can undergo a reversal and turn into an occasion to exert oneself, but the good fortune of one moment of time can also undergo a reversal and turn into misfortune. Thus hexagrams form pairs by opposites, and the lines involved also all change accordingly. This is why there is no constant way with which application can comply, and there is no fixed track for affairs to follow. Whether to act or remain passive, whether to draw in or extend oneself, there is only change to indicate what is appropriate. Thus, once the hexagram is named, either good fortune or bad ensues, depending on the category to which it belongs. Once the moment of time is posited, one should either act or remain passive, responding to the type of application involved. One looks up its name in order to see whether the hexagram means good fortune or bad, and one cites what is said about the moment involved in order to see whether one should act or remain passive. Thus, from these things, it is apparent how change operates within the body of one hexagram.

Resonance provides an image of shared purpose, and the position taken provides an image of what it means for a line to be located there.[22] *Carrying* and *riding* provide images of incongruity or congruity, and *distance* and *proximity* provide images of danger or ease.[23] The *inner* and the *outer* provide images of going forth or staying still, and the first line and the top line provide images of beginning and ending.[24] Thus the fact that, although distant, a line indicates that one can make a move is due to its having acquired a resonant partner,[25] and the fact that, although in danger, a line indicates that one can occupy a position is due to its having achieved the right moment to be there.[26] To be weak yet unafraid of the enemy is due to one acquiring a place where one can entrench oneself,[27] and the fact that, though anxious, one should not fear the rebel is due to managing to have someone to attach to for protection.[28] To be soft yet free from distress about carrying out judgments is due to acquiring the wherewithal to exercise control.[29] A line that though in the rear yet dares to get in the lead does so by resonating with the beginning line [of the upper trigram].[30] A line that abides quietly alone while the others wrangle has summed up what the end will be.[31] Thus one's observation of the actions of change should be focused on the resonances between lines, and one's examination of safety and danger should be focused on the positions of the lines.[32] Whether change operates congruently or incongruently is a function of how lines carry and ride on each other, and the clarification of whether one should leave or stay depends on the outer [upper] and inner [lower] trigrams.[33]

Whether to distance oneself or draw near, whether to heed the ending or the beginning, in each case this depends on the opportunity involved.[34] To avoid danger, it is best to distance oneself, and to take advantage of the moment, it is most preferable to draw near.[35] *Bi* [Closeness, Hexagram 8 ䷇] and *Fu* [Return, Hexagram 24 ䷗] have the good involved at the first place. *Qian* [Pure Yang, Hexagram 1 ䷀] and *Zhuang* [i.e., *Dazhuang*, Great Strength, Hexagram 34 ䷡] have the bad involved at the head [i.e., the top place]. *Mingyi* [Suppression of the Light, Hexagram 36 ䷣] has one strive for obscurity, and *Feng* [Abundance, Hexagram 55 ䷶] has one regard the growth of his glory to be best.[36] Good fortune and misfortune have their moments that one must not violate, and activity and repose have their appropriate occasions that one must not overreach. The taboo against violating the moment is such not because the transgression involves something great but because it misconstrues what the moment offers; here overreaching does not have to be involved with anything profound, either. One might be tempted to make the world tremble and dispose of one's sovereign, but one must not fall into such danger. One might be tempted to humiliate one's wife and children and make a show of one's anger, but one must not let himself be so lax in behavior. Thus once one's rank is established as either high or low, one must not act contrary to his position, and once one encounters occasions where one should be anxious about remorse and regret, even small matters must not be treated lightly. If one observes the hexagram lines and ponders change, then change will yield its all.

Clarifying the Images [Ming xiang]

Images are the means to express ideas. Words [i.e., the texts] are the means to explain the images. To yield up ideas completely, there is nothing better than the images, and to yield up the meaning of the images, there is nothing better than words. The words are generated by the images, thus one can ponder the words and so observe what the images are. The images are generated by ideas, thus one can ponder the images and so observe what the ideas are. The ideas are yielded up completely by the images, and the images are made explicit by the words. Thus, since the words are the means to explain the images, once one gets the images, he forgets the words, and, since the images are the means to allow us to concentrate on the ideas, once one gets the ideas, he forgets the images. Similarly, "the rabbit snare exists for the sake of the rabbit; once one gets the rabbit, he forgets the snare. And the fish trap exists for the sake of fish; once one gets the fish, he forgets the trap."[37] If this is so, then the words are snares for the images, and the images are traps for the ideas.

Therefore someone who stays fixed on the words will not be one to get the images, and someone who stays fixed on the images will not be one to get the ideas. The images are generated by the ideas, but if one stays fixed on the images themselves, then what he stays fixed on will not be *images* as we mean them here. The words are generated by the images, but if one stays fixed on the words themselves, then what he stays fixed on will not be *words* as we mean them here. If this is so, then someone who forgets the images will be one to get the ideas, and someone who forgets the words will be one to get the images. Getting the ideas is in fact a matter of forgetting the images, and getting the images is in fact a matter of forgetting the words. Thus, although the images were established in order to yield up ideas completely, as images they may be forgotten. Although the number of strokes were doubled[38] in order to yield up all the innate tendencies of things, as strokes they may be forgotten.

This is why anything that corresponds analogously to an idea can serve as its image, and any concept that fits with an idea can serve as corroboration of its nature. If the concept involved really has to do with dynamism, why must it only be presented in terms of the horse? And if the analogy used really has to do with compliance, why must it only be presented in terms of the cow? If its lines really do fit with the idea of compliance, why is it necessary that *Kun* [Pure Yin, Hexagram 2] represent only the cow; and if its concept really corresponds to the idea of dynamism, why is it necessary that *Qian* [Pure Yang, Hexagram 1] represent only the horse? Yet there are some who have convicted *Qian* of horsiness. They made a legal case out of its texts and brought this accusation against its hexagram, and, in doing so, they may have come up with a horse, but *Qian* itself got lost in the process! And then this spurious doctrine spread everywhere, even to the extent that one cannot keep account of it! When the "overlapping trigrams" method proved inadequate, such people went on further to the "trigram change" method,[39] and when this "trigram change" method proved inadequate, they pushed on even further to the "five elements" method,[40] for once they lost sight of what the images originally were, they had to become more and more intricate and clever. Even though they sometimes might have come across something [concerning the images], they got absolutely nothing of the concepts. This is all due to the fact that by concentrating on the images one forgets about the ideas. If one were instead to forget about the images in order to seek the ideas they represent, the concepts involved would then become evident as a matter of course.

Considering the Line Positions [Bian wei]

Commentator's [Wang Bi's] note: The Commentary on the Images contains no statement to the effect that a first line or a top line is either in correct position or out of position. Also, the Commentary on the Appended Phrases only discusses how third and fifth lines and second and fourth lines "involve the same kind of merit but differ as to position,"[41] and it, too, never says anything about first and top lines. Why is this? The only thing we have to go on are the Commentary on the Words of the Text for *Qian* [Pure Yang, Hexagram 1 ䷀], Top Yang, which says "Although noble, he lacks a position" and [the Commentary on the Images for] *Xu* [Waiting, Hexagram 5 ䷄], Top Yin, which says "Although one is not in a proper position here." If we take the top position to be a yin position, then it cannot be said of *Xu*, Top Yin, that "one is not in a proper position here." If we take the top position to be a yang position, then it cannot be said of *Qian*, Top Yang, that "although noble, he lacks a position." Whether a yin or a yang line occupies this position, in both cases it is said of it that it is not in the right position. However, it is not said of first lines either that they "suit the position" or are "out of position." This being so, then lines in the first and top positions signify respectively the beginnings and endings of matters, things for which there are no definite yin and yang line positions. Thus when the first line of *Qian* contains the reference "submerged" and when the line past the fifth line is referred to as one that "lacks a position," these have never meant that, although located in a proper position, a line is still said to be "submerged" and that, although a top line is in a proper position, it is still said to "lack a position." I have looked at every hexagram in turn and discovered that all of them are similar in this way. That there are no definite yin and yang line positions for the first place and the top place should certainly be evident from this.

Positions are places ranked as either superior or inferior,[42] abodes suitable for the capabilities with which one is endowed. Lines should fulfill the duties proper to their position and should behave in accordance with their superior or inferior rankings. Positions are either noble or humble, and lines are either yin or yang. A noble position is one where a yang line should locate itself, and a humble position is one to which a yin line should attach itself. Thus noble positions are considered yang positions, and humble positions are considered yin positions. If we exclude the first and top places when we discuss the status of the positions, then the third place and the fifth place each occupy the uppermost position in their respective trigrams, so how indeed could we fail to call them yang positions? And since the second place and the fourth place each occupy the lowest position in their respective trigrams, how indeed could we fail to call them yin positions? The first position and the top position are the beginning and the ending of an entire hexagram and respectively represent what precedes and what follows a given situation. Therefore since neither of these positions has a constant status and since situations have no regular representation in either place, these positions are not to be designated as either yin or yang. Whereas there is a fixed order for noble and humble positions, there are no regular masters for the ending and the beginning positions. This explains why the Commentary on the Appended Phrases only discusses the general rules for determining positions by merit for the four middle lines and does not say anything about the first and the top lines being fixed positions in this way. However, since a situation cannot fail to have an ending and a beginning, so a hexagram cannot fail to have six lines. Although first and top places do not involve positions that are yin and yang by nature, they still are the places where hexagrams end and begin. If we discuss all this in general terms, then since where a line is located is called its position and since a hexagram has to have six lines to be complete, we cannot help but say of it: "The positions of the six lines form, each at its proper moment."[43]

General Remarks, Part Two [Lueli xia]

Whenever a hexagram embodies all the four virtues, they succeed one another with precedence going in turn to the more prevalent, and this is why it [the order of them] is stated as "fundamentality, prevalence, fitness, constancy."[44] The hexagram that has constancy take precedence over prevalence is the one that starts with constancy.[45]

All yin lines and all yang lines are entities that seek to form partnerships with the opposite kind. The fact that there are such lines that are contiguous but do not achieve partnership is due to the different goals toward which each line is directed. This is why any two lines, one yin and one yang, very often form contiguous pairs but do not resonate together, so even if they are contiguous, they will not find each other. However, if they do resonate together, even if they are far apart, partnership will be achieved.[46]

However, moments of time involve either danger or ease, and hexagrams involve either decrease or growth [of the Dao].[47] By practicing mutual cooperation, lines draw each other close; by practicing mutual avoidance, lines draw each other apart.[48] Thus sometimes there are instances that violate the general rule [that yin and yang lines seek to form partnerships with the other type]. However, if one examines such instances in the light of the kind of moment involved [one of danger or ease], it is possible to discover what the meaning is.

The Commentary on the Judgments always provides a general discussion of the hexagram as a whole. Each Commentary on the Images presents the meaning of an individual line. Thus, in *Lü* [Treading, Hexagram 10 ䷉], Third Yin is the ruler of the trigram *Dui* [Lake, Joy] and so in resonance with the trigram *Qian* [Heaven, Pure Yang]. The formation of the entire hexagram depends on this line. Thus the Commentary on the Judgments reports that, thanks to this resonance, although danger exists, yet prevalence will occur here. The Commentary on the Images, on the other hand, since it talks about the separate meaning of each of the six hexagram lines and explains how fortune or misfortune operates in it, here leaves aside the fact that Top Yang [of *Lü*] is responsible for forming the entire hexagram and instead indicates the virtue of this particular line. Thus, since there is danger, one will not reap prevalence here but instead will be bitten.[49] In *Song* [Contention, Hexagram 6 ䷅], Second Yang also has this same kind of meaning.[50]

The Commentary on the Judgments always provides a comprehensive discussion of the hexagram as a whole. When an entire hexagram necessarily depends on a single line, which is the ruler of it, it indicates and explains what the quintessence of that line is and thus provides an overall understanding of the meaning of the entire hexagram. Hexagrams such as *Dayou* [Great Holdings, Hexagram 14] are of this type. When a hexagram as a whole does not depend on a single line, then it uses the concepts embodied in the two constituent trigrams to explain it. Hexagrams such as *Feng* [Abundance, Hexagram 55] are of this type.

Whenever "no blame" is stated, all such cases actually involve potential blame, but because one is able to maintain the way [of the noble man], one succeeds in achieving no blame.[51] Whenever "good fortune, no blame" occurs, blame is actually involved also, but because of good fortune, one manages to avoid it.[52] Whenever "blame, good fortune" occurs, this means that one will first avoid blame and that good fortune will follow as a result.[53] Sometimes one is so situated that he can seize the opportune moment. Here the fortunate one does not have to wait for his achievement to occur to remain untouched by blame, and this is how he reaps good fortune.[54] Sometimes one has committed fault and brings it upon oneself, so there is no reason to resent the blame involved. This situation, too, is called "no blame." Thus *Jie* [Control, Hexagram 60], Third Yin, says: "As this one is in violation of Control, so he should wail, for there is no one else to blame." The Commentary on the Images says: "This one who violates Control should wail, for who else is there to blame for it?" This is exactly what is meant here.

Cursory Remarks on Some Hexagrams [Gua lue][55]

Zhun [Birth Throes, Hexagram 3 ䷂]: This hexagram consists of yin lines all seeking to pair up with the yang lines. *Zhun* signifies a world of troubles where the weak cannot take care of themselves, so they must rely on the strong. This is a time when the common folk long for a master. Thus the yin lines all first seek to pair up with the yang lines; without being beckoned, they go forth of their own accord. Although as horses they are "pulling at odds,"[56] yet they still do not give up. Unsuccessful at finding a master, they have no one on whom to rely. The yang line in the first place of the hexagram is located at the head place, positioned right at the bottom. One here is in resonance with what the common folk are seeking, in accord with what they hope for. Thus such a one "wins over the people in large numbers."[57]

Meng [Juvenile Ignorance, Hexagram 4 ䷃]: This hexagram also consists of yin lines all seeking first to form partnership with the yang lines. Yin is dark, and yang is bright, so as the yin lines are suffering from Juvenile Ignorance, the yang lines are able to release them from it. Anyone who does not know seeks to ask someone who knows. The one who knows does not seek out the asker, as the bright does not seek counsel from the dark. Thus "it is not I who seek the Juvenile Ignorant but the Juvenile Ignorant who seeks me."[58] This is why when *Meng*, Third Yin, sings out first [i.e., would take the lead], it is in violation of the female principle. The fourth line is far from a yang line, so it suffers ignorance and feels remorse. The first line forms a pair with a yang line, which in consequence releases it from ignorance.

Lü [Treading, Hexagram 10 ䷉]: The Hexagrams in Irregular Order says: "*Lü* means 'not staying in one's position.' " I also say that Treading means propriety. Modesty is the controlling factor in propriety. For a yang line to occupy a yin position, this is modesty. Therefore, in this particular hexagram, we always consider a yang line occupying a yin position to be a fine thing.

Lin [Overseeing, Hexagram 19 ䷒]: This is a hexagram concerned with the growth of hardness. With the triumph of hardness, softness becomes dangerous. But since softness here has its own virtue, it always manages to avoid blame. Therefore, in this particular hexagram, although the yin lines are in the splendid positions, they commit no fault and incur no blame.

Guan [Viewing, Hexagram 20 ䷓]: In terms of its meaning, *Guan* tells us that what one sees should be something beautiful. Therefore to be near what is noble is estimable [i.e., so that one can "view" it better], but to be far from it is base.

Daguo [Major Superiority, Hexagram 28 ䷛]: This hexagram signifies a world on the verge of collapse. Both major and ancillary joists are weak, and the ridgepole has already begun to sag. However, to try to maintain things as they are would be both dangerous and no help at all; it is the path to misfortune. For a yang line to occupy a yin position is a sign of the utmost softness and yielding. Therefore it is a fine thing here that yang lines all occupy yin positions. The only way to handle decline and deal with danger lies in shared devotion to the same goal, in consequence of which the situation may be saved and repairs done. Thus, since a Fourth Yang is in resonance [with a First Yin], this is why "there will be regret if there are ulterior motives." Since the Second Yang is not in resonance, this is why here "nothing done here fails to be fitting."

Dun [Withdrawal, Hexagram 33 ䷠]: This signifies the gradual advance and growing strength of the petty man. Such trouble resides in the lower trigram, but prevalence resides in the upper trigram. This hexagram is the opposite of *Lin* [Overseeing, Hexagram 19 ䷒]. In *Lin*, as the hard grows strong, the soft is placed in danger. In *Dun*, since the soft is growing stronger, the hard withdraws.

Dazhuang [Great Strength, Hexagram 34 ䷡]: It never happens that a person who violates modesty and exceeds the bounds of propriety is also able to perfect his strength. Therefore it is a fine thing here that yang lines all occupy yin positions. To have strength occupy a modest position will result in that strength becoming perfected, but to have strength occupy a position of strength will result in "butt[ing] a hedge."[59]

Mingyi [Suppression of the Light, Hexagram 36 ䷣]: The ruler of darkness here is located at Top Yin. First Yang is the farthest from it, and this is why it says: "this noble man on the move." The fifth line is the closest to it, yet adversity there cannot drown it. This is why [the Commentary on the Images for Fifth Yin] says: "The constancy of a viscount of Ji is such that his brilliance cannot be extinguished." The third line is located where the light is at its brightest [at the top of the bottom trigram *Li* (Cohesion, Fire)], the place from which is launched the expedition into the darkness [the upper trigram *Kun* (Earth, Pure Yin, i.e., the Dark)]. This is why it says: "On a southern hunt . . . he captures the great chief [Top Yin]."[60]

Kui [Contrariety, Hexagram 38 ䷥]: This hexagram shows how in Contrariety there is yet accord. If one looks at this hexagram in terms of the tops of its two trigrams, its meaning becomes most apparent. When the trigrams are at their respective limits of Contrariety, they come together, and when they are at their respective limits of disparity, they find accord. Thus both first suffer the accusations of the other, but once they form an agreeable union, such suspicions vanish.

Feng [Abundance, Hexagram 55 ䷶]: This is a hexagram that is concerned with how to act guided by brightness. It is one that places value on the manifestation of light, the bursting forth of an all-encompassing yang principle. Therefore it is a fine thing that all the lines that occupy yang positions do not resonate with yin lines. Their unity lies in nothing other than their common hatred of the darkness. Small darkness is called a "screening," and big darkness is called a "curtaining." When darkness becomes severe, brightness is all gone, but when it is not yet all gone, it is then "dim." When brightness is all gone, the Pole Star appears, but since the brightness is still faint, its appearance is "dim." If one is without any brightness at all, he will lack the means to interact with the world, and if he but makes a "dim" appearance, he will be incapable of accomplishing anything great. If one loses his right arm, although his left arm is still there, how could it ever be enough for his needs? If one does nothing more than appear "dim" in the peak brightness of the day, how could such a person ever be worthy of appointment to office?

NOTES

1. This line is a paraphrase of a passage in section one of the Commentary on the Appended Phrases, Part Two

2. This sentence is almost an exact quotation from section nine of the Commentary on the Appended Phrases, Part Two; see note 54 there.

3. Such hexagrams in particular include *Guimei* (Marrying Maiden), Hexagram 54, and *Feng* (Abundance), Hexagram 55, where the hexagram names and main concepts involved derive from the relationships between the constituent trigrams. See the remarks in the Commentary on the Judgments of these two hexagrams.

4. See section three of the Commentary on the Appended Phrases, Part One.

5. "The innate tendency of things and their countertendency to spuriousness" translates *qing wei*—that is, "things as they really are and their tendency to become what they by nature are not." *Qing wei* also seems to occur in this sense in section twelve of the Commentary on the Appended Phrases, Part One. However, Lou Yulie interprets *qingwei* as a single concept equivalent to "selfish desire" (*qingyu*) or the "cunning and deceit of 'wisdom.' " In support, he cites Wang's commentary on *Laozi*, section 18, "Thus wisdom appears and so great falsehood (*wei*) arises," and Xing Shou's (Tang era 618–907) commentary on this passage in the *Zhouyi lueli* here: "What *qingwei* tends to is the multifarious designs of cunning and deceit." See *Wang Bi ji jiaoshi*, 2: 598 n. 2. This alternate interpretation would result in a different translation: "It [change] is what desire and cunning produce."

6. Cf. section seven of the Commentary on the Appended Phrases, Part Two: "The hard and the soft lines change one into the other, something for which it is impossible to make definitive laws, since they are doing nothing but keeping pace with change."

7. Xing Shou's commentary says: "In innate tendency resides clever

deceit. The way that change happens and contrariness occurs has nothing to do with large things. Although sage intellect and meticulous reckoning might try to fathom it, it defies comprehension, so how could it ever have anything to do with grand matters!" See Lou, *Wang Bi ji jiaoshi*, 2: 599 n. 6.

8. The quotations are from a passage in the Commentary on the Words of the Text in Hexagram 1, *Qian* (Pure Yang), Fifth Yang.

9. Reference to the dragon here alludes to the passage cited in note 8 above.

10. "Dispersive ground" (*sandi*), i.e., where troops tend to break rank and run away, is an allusion to a passage in the *Sunzi bingfa* (Master Sun's [fifth century B.C.] art of war): "When a feudal lord fights in his own territory, he is in dispersive ground." Cao Cao's (155–220) comment on this passage reads: "Here officers and men long to return to their nearby homes." The translations are from Griffith, *Sun Tzu: The Art of War*, p. 130.

11. Cf. *Sunzi bingfa*: " 'Can troops be made capable of such instantaneous co-operation?' I reply: 'They can.' For, although the men of Wu and Yüeh mutually hate one another, if together in a boat tossed by the wind they would co-operate as the right hand does with the left.' " See Griffith, *Sun Tzu: The Art of War*, pp. 135–136. Hu can be identified with the state of Wu.

12. Xing Shou's commentary reads: "If one recognizes the feeling involved with a common purpose, why worry about the difference between Hu [Wu] and Yue, and if one understands the tendency to run away and disperse, one does not trouble oneself to use military force." See Lou, *Wang Bi ji jiaoshi*, 2: 600 n. 15.

13. See section twelve of the Commentary on the Appended Phrases, Part Two.

14. The last two phrases allude to the Commentary on the Judgments of Hexagram 38, *Kui* (Contrariety): "Heaven and Earth may be contrary entities, but their task is the same. Male and female may be contrary entities, but they share the same goal. The myriad things may be contrary entities each to the other, but as functioning entities they are all similar."

15. There is an allusion here to section eight of the Commentary on the Appended Phrases, Part One: "The noble man might stay in his chambers, but if the words he speaks are about goodness, even those from more than a thousand *li* away will respond with approval to him, and how much the more will those who are nearby do so." In Wang Bi's passage the implied sentence subject "one" seems to refer to one who would be a true sovereign.

16. This is a paraphrase of a passage in section eight of the Commentary on the Appended Phrases, Part One.

17. This alludes to section five of the Commentary on the Appended Phrases, Part Two: "The noble man lays up a store of instruments in his own person and waits for the proper moment and then acts, so how could there ever be anything to his disadvantage! Here one acts without impediment; it is due to this that when one goes out, he obtains his catch. What

this means is that one should act only after having first developed his instruments." Just as a hunter gets his bow (the instrument of hunting) in perfect working order, so the noble man perfects the instrumentality of his own person and accomplishes his affairs without hindrance.

18. This translation follows the gloss provided by Lou Yulie in *Wang Bi ji jiaoshi*, 2: 603 n. 22. However, another, more sociopolitical interpretation is possible: "Without anyone knowing how he [a true sovereign] has become the master, he provides the beat for the dance, and all under heaven follows. This is someone who has a perception of how the innate tendencies of things operate."

19. This is a quotation from section four of the Commentary on the Appended Phrases, Part One, where, however, the subject seems to be the sage who perfectly grasps the working of change rather than the hexagram lines—which, of course, "grasp" the workings of change as well.

20. "Facility" and "obstruction" translate *tai* and *pi*, which are also the names of Hexagram 11, *Tai* (Peace—i.e., interaction, facility), and Hexagram 12, *Pi* (Obstruction—i.e., stagnation).

21. This alludes to section three of the Commentary on the Appended Phrases, Part One: "There are hexagrams that deal with decrease and those that deal with growth [of the Dao], and . . . there are appended phrases that impart a sense of danger and those that impart a sense of ease." Han Kangbo's commentary says: "When this Dao shines brightly, it is said to be growing large, and when the Dao of the noble man is dwindling, it is said to be decreasing. If a hexagram is tending toward Peace [*Tai*, Hexagram 11], its phrases impart a sense of ease, but if a hexagram is tending toward Obstruction and Stagnation [*Pi*, Hexagram 12], its phrases impart a sense of danger." See Lou, *Wang Bi ji jiaoshi*, 2: 605 n. 3.

22. Lou Yulie comments: " 'Resonance' [*ying*] means mutual response [*xiangying*]. For example, the first line and the fourth, the second and the fifth, and the third and the top are in positions of mutual responsiveness. 'Position' signifies the second, third, fourth, and fifth yin and yang line positions." (We should note here that even-numbered line positions are considered yin and odd-numbered line positions are considered yang.) Lou then goes on to quote from Xing Shou's commentary: " 'When one gets a resonance, it signifies the mutual harmony of purpose shared. Yin positions are where the petty man should be located, and yang positions are where the noble man should be located.' " See *Wang Bi ji jiaoshi*, 2: 606 n. 8.

23. Lou Yulie comments:

> "Carrying" refers to a line below carrying the one above, and "riding" refers to a line above riding on the one below. When a yin line carries a yang line, this indicates congruity, but when a yang line carries a yin line that indicates incongruity. When a yin line rides on a yang line, this indicates incongruity, but when a yang line rides on a yin line, that indicates congruity. When a line is far from trouble, this indicates ease [smooth going], but when a line is close to trouble, this indicates danger.

Lou here cites a comment by Xing Shou: " 'In the hexagram *Xu* [Waiting, Hexagram 5], Third Yang is close to trouble, so it is in danger, but First Yang is far from the danger, so it is at ease.' " See *Wang Bi ji jiaoshi*, 2: 606 n. 9. *Xu* ䷄ consists of the trigrams *Kan* (Sink Hole) above and *Qian* (Pure Yang) below. The third line, right next to the water hole, is in danger of falling in, but the first line, far from it, is in no such danger and can remain at ease.

24. Lou Yulie comments: " 'Inner' refers to the lower trigram, which indicates a 'staying still' [remaining], and 'outer' refers to the upper trigram, which indicates a 'going forth.' " He also adds that, for the first (beginning) and top (ending) positions in hexagrams, "no distinction is made between yin and yang lines." See *Wang Bi ji jiaoshi*, 2: 606 n. 10.

25. Xing Shou comments: "Although the one above and the one below may be distant, yet the one that indicates action has a resonant partner [and so has support]. Although in *Ge* [Radical Change, Hexagram 49 ䷰] Second Yin is far removed from the fifth line, their yin and yang resonate together, so if one were to go out and do something here [at the second line], he would be without blame." Quoted in Lou, *Wang Bi ji jiaoshi*, 2: 606 n. 11.

26. Xing Shou comments: "In *Xu* [Waiting, Hexagram 5 ䷄], Top Yin is located at the top of danger, but one should not worry about falling into the pit [the upper trigram, *Kan*, Sink Hole], for here it has achieved the right moment to be there." Quoted in Lou, *Wang Bi ji jiaoshi*, 2: 606 n. 11. See also Wang's commentary on *Xu*, Top Yin.

27. Xing Shou comments: "[In] *Shi* [The Army, Hexagram 7 ䷆], Fifth Yin is the master of the entire hexagram; it is yin and weak. . . . Since it manages to occupy an exalted position, it thus can remain unafraid." Quoted in Lou, *Wang Bi ji jiaoshi*, 2: 607 n. 12.

28. Xing Shou comments:

> *Dun* [Withdrawal, Hexagram 33 a], Fifth Yang, states: "Here is praiseworthy Withdrawal, in which constancy brings good fortune." To be located in *Dun* means that the petty man's powers of encroachment are in the ascendancy and that the way of the noble man is in decline, so one should escape and withdraw to the upper trigram, where he may attach himself to the exalted position there [i.e., the yang line in the fifth position]. This always keeps the behavior of the petty man [the second, yin line] in correct check so he does not dare make rebellion.

Quoted in Lou, *Wang Bi ji jiaoshi*, 2: 607 n. 12. See also Wang's comments on *Dun*, Second Yin and Fifth Yang.

29. Xing Shou comments: "Even though the substance of a line is soft and weak, here one should not find making judgments a matter for distress, for good will come from the fact that a weak line is controlled by a yang position, and in the end one will have strength prevail. An example of

this is *Shihe* [Bite Together, Hexagram 21 ䷔], Fifth Yin: " 'Biting through dried meat, he obtains yellow metal.' " Quoted in Lou, *Wang Bi ji jiaoshi*, 2: 607 n. 13. See also Wang's own commentary on *Shihe*, Fifth Yin.

30. Xing Shou comments: "A first line occupies a position at the bottom of a hexagram and has resonance with the fourth line. This is why, although in substance it belongs in the rear, yet it still dares to get in the lead of the hexagram. An example of this is *Tai* [Peace, Hexagram 11 ䷊], First Yang: 'When one pulls up the rush plant, it pulls up others of the same kind together with it, so if one goes forth and acts, there will be good fortune.' " Quoted in Lou, *Wang Bi ji jiaoshi*, 2: 607 n. 13. See also Wang's own commentary to *Tai*, First Yang and Fourth Yin.

31. Xing Shou cites *Dayou* (Great Holdings, Hexagram 14 ䷍), Top Yang, as such an example. See Lou, *Wang Bi ji jiaoshi*, 2: 607 n. 14.

32. Lou Yulie comments: "The meaning of this sentence is: Observation of the actions of change should be focused on the resonance between lines. If they resonate with each other, this produces the action of change. Observation of safety and danger should be focused on the positions of the lines. If a line obtains a proper position, then there is safety, but if it is wrongly positioned, then there is danger." See *Wang Bi ji jiaoshi*, 2: 607 n. 15.

33. For the factors governing congruity and incongruity, see note 23 above. Xing Shou comments here on the inner and outer trigrams: "In *Dun* [Withdrawal, Hexagram 33 ䷠], the noble man stays in the outer trigram, and in *Lin* [Overseeing, Hexagram 19 ䷒], he stays in the inner trigram." Quoted in Lou, *Wang Bi ji jiaoshi*, 2: 607 n. 16. Where the noble man "stays" is apparently a function of the central yang lines.

34. Xing Shou comments: "To take proper advantage of the moment results in good fortune, but if one misses the essential opportunity involved, this will mean misfortune." Quoted in Lou, *Wang Bi ji jiaoshi*, 2: 607 n. 17.

35. Xing Shou comments: "*Dun* [Withdrawal, Hexagram 33 ䷠], Top Yang, says: 'This is flying Withdrawal, so nothing fails to be fitting.' This is an example of 'it is best to distance oneself.' *Guan* [Viewing, Hexagram 20 ䷓], Fourth Yin, says: 'Here one's Viewing extends to the glory of the state, so it is fitting therefore that this one be guest to the king.' This is an example of 'it is most preferable to draw near.' " Quoted in Lou, *Wang Bi ji jiaoshi*, 2: 607 n. 17.

36. For these characterizations of *Bi*, *Fu*, *Qian*, *Dazhuang*, *Mingyi*, and *Feng*, see their Judgments, line statements, Commentaries on the Judgments, and Commentaries on the Images.

37. This is a quotation from the *Zhuangzi* (fourth century B.C.); see *Zhuangzi yinde*, 75/26/48.

38. This refers to the doubling of the trigrams to form the hexagrams; see section one of the Commentary on the Appended Phrases, Part Two. The "strokes" are, of course, the hexagram lines.

39. The "overlapping trigrams" (*huti*) method and the "trigram change"

(*guabian*) method were popular ways to interpret the *Changes* during the Han era. Lou Yulie comments:

> The "overlapping trigrams" was a method used by the Han era specialists on the *Changes* to interpret the hexagrams. Wang Yinglin [1223–1296], in his preface to the *Zheng shi Zhouyi* [Mr. Zheng's *Changes of the Zhou*], states:
>
> Zheng Kangcheng [Zheng Xuan (127–200)] emulated Mr. Fei [Fei Zhi (ca. 50 B.C.–10 A.D.)] and made an annotated edition of the *Changes* in nine scrolls, which often frames its discussions in terms of overlapping trigrams. The practice of using overlapping trigrams to seek the meaning of the *Changes* has existed since Mr. Zuo [i.e., since the *Zuozhuan* (Zuo's commentary on the Spring and Autumn Annals), fifth century B.C.]. In all hexagrams, sets of the second, third, and fourth lines and sets of the third, fourth, and fifth lines mingle together but each set separately forms a trigram. This is what is meant in this practice by "one hexagram contains four trigrams."
>
> The "trigram change" method employs changes in the middle, upper, and lower trigram positions or changes in one of the lines to convert a trigram into a different trigram, and this consequently is supposed to explain the meaning of hexagrams and individual lines.

See *Wang Bi ji jiaoshi*, 2: 612 n. 20.

40. Concerning "They pushed on even further to the 'five elements' method," Lou Yulie observes: "This refers to the use of individual images to represent one or another of the five elements [*wuxing*] and then to use various theories of how the five elements sequentially generate and vanquish each other to interpret the hexagrams, something quite tainted with arcane mysticism [*shenmi zhuyi*]." See *Wang Bi ji jiaoshi*, 2: 612 n. 21.

41. See section nine of the Commentary on the Appended Phrases, Part Two.

42. This paraphrases section three of the Commentary on the Appended Phrases, Part One.

43. See Hexagram 1, *Qian* (Pure Yang), Commentary on the Judgments.

44. Hexagrams whose hexagram statements contain this kind of characterization are *Qian* (Pure Yang, Hexagram 1), *Kun* (Pure Yin, Hexagram 2), *Zhun* (Birth Throes, Hexagram 3), *Sui* (Following, Hexagram 17), *Lin* (Overseeing, Hexagram 19), *Wuwang* (No Errancy, Hexagram 25), and *Ge* (Radical Change, Hexagram 49).

45. This is *Li* (Cohesion, Hexagram 30). Wang Bi's comment on its Judgment says: "The way Cohesion is constituted as a hexagram means that rectitude is expressed by the soft and yielding [yin] lines, and this is why one here must practice constancy first, for only then will prevalence be had. Thus the text says: 'It is fitting to practice constancy, for then it will result in prevalence.' "

46. Wang Bi's comment on *Jiji* (Ferrying Complete, Hexagram 63 ䷾), Second Yin, illustrates an example of such partnerships:

Second Yin abides in centrality and treads the path of righteousness [it is a yin line in a central, yin position], so it occupies the highest point of civility and enlightenment. Moreover, it is in resonance with Fifth Yang [the ruler of the hexagram], which means that it achieves the greatest glory possible for a yin. However, it is located between First Yang and Third Yang, with which, though contiguous, it does not get along well. Above it will not give carriage to Third Yang, and below it will not form a pair with First Yang.

47. See note 21 above.

48. Xing Shou's commentary makes this cryptic statement intelligible:

[In] *Kui* (Contrariety, Hexagram 38 ䷥), First Yang and Fourth Yang do not resonate as a pair of yin and yang lines, but both are incompatible loners that occupy the bottom places in their respective trigrams. Engaging in mutual trust, they cooperate with each other and so manage to make remorse disappear. This is what "by practicing mutual cooperation, lines draw each other close" means. [In] *Kun* (Impasse, Hexagram 47 ䷮), First Yin has a resonance with the fourth line. It says that one should hide himself in a secluded valley, and Fourth Yang, having a resonance with this first line, says that one should come forward slowly and carefully and harbor doubts about the object of his ambition. In this way, they both avoid the metal cart and draw each other apart.

For an explanation of "metal cart," see the line statement for Fourth Yang of *Kun*. The text of Xing's comments is quoted in Lou, *Wang Bi ji jiaoshi*, 2: 617 n. 7.

49. See Hexagram 10, *Lü* (Treading), Third Yin, and the Commentary on the Images for that line, as well as Wang Bi's commentary on both.

50. See Hexagram 6, *Song* (Contention), Commentary on the Judgments, and Second Yang, Commentary on the Images.

51. Xing Shou comments: "*Qian* [Pure Yang, Hexagram 1], Third Yang, says: 'The noble man makes earnest efforts throughout the day, . . . no blame.' In this way, he takes steps to avoid losing the way, which would result in incurring blame for the faults involved." Quoted in Lou, *Wang Bi ji jiaoshi*, 2: 617 n. 13.

52. Xing Shou comments: "The Judgment for *Shi* [The Army, Hexagram 7] says: 'If an army's constancy is subject to a forceful man, there will be good fortune and with this no blame.' Wang Bi's commentary says: 'It would be a crime to raise soldiers and mobilize the masses and then have no success.' This is why the text says: 'There will be good fortune and with this no blame.' " Quoted in Lou, *Wang Bi ji jiaoshi*, 2: 618 n. 14.

53. Xing Shou comments: "*Bi* [Closeness, Hexagram 8], First Yin, says: 'If there is sincerity, joining in Closeness will not lead to blame. . . . So there will be good fortune brought on by others.' This provides an example of this." Quoted in Lou, *Wang Bi ji jiaoshi*, 2: 618 n. 15.

54. Xing Shou comments: "*Xu* [Waiting, Hexagram 5], Second Yang,

says: 'When waiting on the sand, it might slightly involve rebuke, but in the end, good fortune will result.' Wang Bi comments: 'Here one is close but not so close that he is oppressed by danger and far but not so far that he will be too late for the moment when it happens. He treads on a place of strength and abides in the Mean and in this way awaits the right opportunity. Although it might slightly involve rebuke, . . . in the end, good fortune will result.' " Quoted in Lou, *Wang Bi ji jiaoshi*, 2: 618 n. 16.

55. As they stand, a number of passages in the following section require elaboration in order to understand exactly what they mean. However, instead of burdening readers with a separate set of notes, I suggest that they compare Wang Bi's comments here about various hexagrams with the actual statements—and his comments on them—that make up the entries for the hexagrams themselves. Any notes that might be added here would consist of exactly those materials.

56. See Hexagram 3, *Zhun* (Birth Throes), Second Yin.

57. See Hexagram 3, *Zhun* (Birth Throes), First Yang, Commentary on the Images.

58. See Hexagram 4, *Meng* (Juvenile Ignorance), Judgment.

59. See Hexagram 34, *Dazhuang* (Great Strength), Third Yang.

60. See Hexagram 36, *Mingyi* (Suppression of the Light), Third Yang.

Commentary on the Appended Phrases [Xici zhuan], *Part One*

1. As Heaven is high and noble and Earth is low and humble, so it is that *Qian* [Pure Yang, Hexagram 1] and *Kun* [Pure Yin, Hexagram 2] are defined. {It is because *Qian* and *Kun* provide the gateway to the *Changes* that the text first makes clear that Heaven is high and noble and Earth is low and humble, thereby determining what the basic substances of *Qian* and *Kun* are.[1]} The high and the low being thereby set out, the exalted and the mean have their places accordingly. {Once the innate duty of Heaven to be high and noble and that of Earth to be low and humble are set down, one can extend these basic distinctions to the myriad things, so that the positions of all exalted things and all mean things become evident.} There are norms for action and repose, which are determined by whether hardness or softness is involved. {Hardness means action, and softness means repose. If action and repose achieve normal embodiment, the hardness and softness involved will be clearly differentiated.[2]} Those with regular tendencies gather according to kind, and things divide up according to group; so it is that good fortune and misfortune occur. {Thus similarities and differences exist, and gatherings and divisions occur. If one conforms to things with which he belongs, it will mean good fortune, but if one goes against things with which he belongs, misfortune will result.} In Heaven this [process] creates images, and on Earth it creates physical forms; this is how change and transformation manifest themselves. {"Images" here are equivalent to the sun, moon, and the stars, and "physical forms" here are equivalent to the mountains, the lakes, and the shrubs and trees. The images so suspended revolve on, thus forming the darkness and the

light; Mountain and Lake reciprocally circulate material force [*qi*],[3] thus letting clouds scud and rain fall.[4] This is how "change and transformation manifest themselves."} In consequence of all this, as hard and soft stroke each other, {That is, they urge each other on, meaning the way yin and yang stimulate each other.} the eight trigrams activate each other. {That is, they impel each other on, referring to the activation that allows change to fulfill its cyclical nature.}

It [the Dao] arouses things with claps of thunder, moistens them with wind and rain. Sun and moon go through their cycles, so now it is cold, now hot. The Dao of *Qian* forms the male; the Dao of *Kun* forms the female. *Qian* has mastery over the great beginning of things, and *Kun* acts to bring things to completion. {The Dao of Heaven and Earth starts things perfectly without deliberate purpose and brings them to perfect completion with no labor involved. This is why it is characterized in terms of ease and simplicity.}

Qian through ease provides mastery over things, and *Kun* through simplicity provides capability. As the former is easy, it is easy to know, and as the latter is simple, it is easy to follow. If one is easy to know, he will have kindred spirits; and if one is easy to follow, he will have meritorious accomplishments. {This is to be in accord with the innate tendencies of the myriad things, thus the text says, "He will have kindred spirits," and here one is in tune with the design inherent in all things in the world, thus the text says: "He will have meritorious accomplishments."} Once one has kindred spirits, he can endure, and once one has meritorious accomplishments, he can grow great. {With the virtues of ease and simplicity, one will achieve meritorious accomplishments that can endure and be great.} Being able to endure is inherent in a worthy man's virtue, and being able to grow great is inherent in the enterprise of the worthy man. {Because of the ease and simplicity of Heaven and Earth, each of the myriad things carries the outer form of what it is. The worthy man does not act with deliberate purpose, yet of all the methods he might employ, each and every one will bring about his enterprise. Once virtue is realized and enterprise accomplished, these then become translated into concrete form. Thus it is by means of the worthy man that we are allowed to lay eyes on the virtue and enterprise [of Heaven and Earth].}

It is through such ease and simplicity that the principles of the world obtain. {Every single principle in the world derives from ease and simplicity, thus each thing manages to behave commensurate with its particular position.} As the principles of the world obtain in this way, they form positions here between them [Heaven and Earth]. {"Form positions" means the way the images are perfectly constituted. Only something capable of the utmost ease and simplicity will be able to provide a channel for the principles of the world. As these [hexagrams] provide channels for the principles of the world, they are able to form images and so provide links to Heaven and Earth. As the text says "between them," such links are clearly to Heaven and Earth.}

2. The sages set down the hexagrams and observed the images. {This is the general summary [of what follows].} They appended phrases to the lines in order to clarify whether they signify good fortune or misfortune and let the hard and the soft lines displace each other so that change and transformation could appear. {It is by appending phrases that they clarified the good fortune and the misfortune involved, and it is by allowing the strong and the weak lines to displace each other that this good fortune and misfortune were brought to light. Good fortune and misfortune are inherent in the affairs of men, and change and transformation are inherent in how things go through their natural cycles.} Therefore, good fortune and misfortune involve images respectively of failure or success. {Because there is failure and success, good fortune and misfortune occur.} Regret and remorse involve images of sorrow and worry. {When the signs of failure or success are such that they do no more than cause sorrow and worry, the texts say "regret" and "remorse."} Change and transformation involve images of advance and withdrawal. {Going forth prompts a coming back and vice versa; this means advance and withdrawal in turn.} The strong and the weak provide images of day and night. {If it is day, then it is yang and strong, and if it is night, then it is yin and weak. The text here first provides a general discussion of good fortune and misfortune, change and transformation, and then after that separately clarifies what is involved with regret and remorse, day and night. Regret and remorse are the equivalents of good fortune and misfortune, and, for their part, day and night are constituents of the change and transformation that make up the Dao. As regret and remorse belong with good fortune and misfortune, they rely in the same way on appended phrases to have their meaning made clear,

and as day and night are constituents of the Dao of change and transformation, they equally become manifest through the strong and the weak. Thus the text begins with a general summary, then clarifies the difference between the greater and lesser types of failure and success, and finally distinguishes between the major and minor aspects of change and transformation. This is why the concepts involved are dealt with separately in this sequence.} The movement of the six hexagram lines embodies the Dao of the three ultimates {The three ultimates are the three powers [Heaven, Earth, and Man]. As the hexagrams are commensurate with the Dao of the three powers, they are able to reveal good fortune and misfortune and realize change and transformation.}

Therefore what allows the noble man to find himself anywhere and yet remain secure are the sequences presented by the *Changes*. {Sequences [*xu*] mean the succession of images [*xiang*] in the *Changes*.[5]} What he ponders with delight are the phrases appended to the lines. Therefore, once the noble man finds himself in a situation, he observes its image and ponders the phrases involved, and, once he takes action, he observes the change [of the lines] and ponders the prognostications involved. This is why, since Heaven helps him, "it is auspicious" and "nothing will fail to be advantageous."

3. The Judgments [*tuan*] address the images, {A Judgment sums up the concept of an entire hexagram.} and the line texts address the states of change. {Each line text addresses itself to the change involved with that line.} The terms *auspicious* and *inauspicious* address the failure or success involved. The terms *regret* and *remorse* address the small faults involved. The expression *there is no blame* indicates success at repairing transgressions. Therefore the ranking of superior and inferior depends on the positions. {Where a line is situated is called a *position*. Among the six positions, there are those that are noble and those that are humble.} Distinction between a tendency either to the petty or to the great is an inherent feature of the hexagrams. {Hexagrams are devoted either to tendencies to the petty or to the great. *Distinction* here means the same as "differentiation," which is what happens when "the Judgments address the images."[6]} The differentiation of good fortune and misfortune depends on the phrases. {"The phrases" are the line texts. This is what is meant by "the line texts address the states of change." It is by addressing the images

that the petty and the great are brought to light, and it is by addressing change that good fortune and misfortune are clarified. Therefore concepts of either pettiness or greatness are inherent to the hexagrams, and the states of good fortune and misfortune are revealed in the phrases. As for regret, remorse, and "no blame," they follow the same routine. Good fortune, misfortune, remorse and regret, "small fault," and "no blame" all are produced by change, but since affairs include both the petty and the great, the text later addresses the differences among these five in turn.} The means to make one anxious about regret and remorse depend on the subtle, intermediate stages [*jie*]. {*Jie* means "small matters." Wang Bi states [in section three of his General Remarks]: "Once one encounters occasions where one should be anxious about remorse and regret, even small matters must not be treated lightly." Thus, remorse and regret are addressed to small faults.[7]} The means to arouse one so to have "no blame" depends on remorse. {The reason one suffers no blame is that he is good at repairing mistakes.} *Arouse* means "to move." Thus to be moved so as to be without blame is inherent in the remorse one feels for one's mistakes. This is why there are hexagrams that deal with decrease and those that deal with growth [of the Dao], and why there are appended phrases that impart a sense of danger and those that impart a sense of ease. {When this Dao shines brightly, it is said to be growing large, and when the Dao of the noble man is dwindling, it is said to be decreasing. If a hexagram is tending toward Peace [*Tai*, Hexagram 11], its phrases impart a sense of ease, but if a hexagram is tending toward Obstruction and Stagnation [*Pi*, Hexagram 12], its phrases impart a sense of danger.} The phrases, in fact, in each case indicate the direction taken.

4. The *Changes* is a paradigm of Heaven and Earth, {[The sages] made the *Changes* in order to provide a paradigm of Heaven and Earth.}, and so it shows how one can fill in and pull together the Dao of Heaven and Earth. Looking up, we use it [the *Changes*] to observe the configurations of Heaven, and, looking down, we use it to examine the patterns of Earth. Thus we understand the reasons underlying what is hidden and what is clear. We trace things back to their origins then turn back to their ends. Thus we understand the axiom of life and death. {The hidden and the clear involve images that have form and that do not have form. Life and death are a matter of fate's allotment for one's beginning and

end.} With the consolidation of material force into essence [*jingqi*], a person comes into being, but with the dissipation of one's spirit [*youhun*], change comes about. {When material force consolidates into essence, it meshes together, and with this coalescence, a person is formed. When such coalescence reaches its end, disintegration occurs, and with the dissipation of one's spirit, change occurs. "With the dissipation of one's spirit" is another way of saying "when it disintegrates."} It is due to this that we understand the true state of gods and spirits.[8] {If one thoroughly comprehends the principle underlying coalescence and dissipation, he will be able to understand the Dao of change and transformation, and nothing that is hidden will remain outside his grasp.}

As [a sage] resembles Heaven and Earth, he does not go against them. {It is because his virtue is united with Heaven and Earth that the text says: "resembles them."} As his knowledge is complete in respect to the myriad things and as his Dao brings help to all under Heaven, he commits no transgression. {It is because his knowledge comprehensively covers the myriad things that his Dao brings help to all under Heaven.} Such a one extends himself in all directions yet does not allow himself to be swept away. {Responding to change, he engages in exhaustive exploration but does not get swept away by illicit behavior.} As he rejoices in Heaven and understands Its decrees, he will be free from anxiety. {As such a one complies with Heaven's transformations, the text says: "He rejoices."} As he is content in his land and is genuine about benevolence, he can be loving. {Being content in one's land and being genuine about benevolence [*ren*] are innate tendencies [*qing*] of the myriad things. If things are allowed to comply with their innate tendencies, then the good effects of benevolence will abundantly grow.[9]} He perfectly emulates the transformations of Heaven and Earth and so does not transgress them. {Being a perfect model means to model oneself on Heaven and Earth in such a way that one totally encompasses their principles.} He follows every twist and turn of the myriad things and so deals with them without omission. {As for following every twist and turn in this way, if one were to respond to things by keeping up with their changes and not being tied to them as they are found in particular places, he would indeed prevail over them!} He has a thorough grasp of the Dao of day and night and so is knowing. {As he thoroughly grasps the reasons underlying obscurity and brightness, there is nothing he fails to understand.} Thus the numinous is not restricted to place, and change is without substance. {Everything up to this point is addressed to how the numinous behaves. Regarding things in terms of either place or substance [*ti*] means to be tied to things that have concrete form [*xingqi*]. The numinous as such is something not to be plumbed in terms of yin and yang,[10] and change as such is something that one can only keep up with in terms of change, and neither can be clarified by reference to particular places or to particular substances.[11]}

5. The reciprocal process of yin and yang is called the Dao. What is this Dao? It is a name for nonbeing [*wu*]; it is that which pervades everything; and it is that from which everything derives. As an equivalent, we call it Dao. As it operates silently and is without substance, it is not possible to provide images for it. Only when the functioning of being reaches its zenith do the merits of nonbeing become manifest. Therefore, even though it so happens that the numinous is not restricted to place and change and is without substance, yet the Dao itself can be seen: it is by investigating change thoroughly that one exhausts all the potential of the numinous, and it is through the numinous that one clarifies what the Dao is. Although yin and yang are different entities, we deal with them in terms of the unity of nonbeing. When the Dao is in the yin state, it does not actually exist as yin, but it is by means of yin that it comes into existence, and when it is in the yang state, it does not actually exist as yang, but it is by means of yang that it comes into being. This is why it is referred to as "the reciprocal process of yin and yang."[12]} That which allows the Dao to continue to operate is human goodness [*shan*], and that which allows it to bring things to completion is human nature [*xing*]. The benevolent see it and call it benevolence, and the wise [*zhi*] see it and call it wisdom. {The benevolent make the Dao their resource and so see the benevolence in it, and the wise make the Dao their resource and so see the wisdom in it: each exhausts that respective portion of it.} It functions for the common folk on a daily basis, yet they are unaware of it. This is why the Dao of the noble man is a rare thing! {The noble man embodies the Dao and applies it as function, but if it is merely the benevolent and wise, then they are limited to just what they see of it, and if it is the common folk, then it functions for them on a daily basis, but they are unaware of it. Those who truly embody this Dao, are they not indeed rare! Thus, as it is said, "always

be without desire so as to see its subtlety."[13] This is how one can begin to talk about its perfection and address its ultimate meaning.} It is manifested in benevolence and hidden within its functioning. {"It gives succor to the myriad things";[14] this is why the text says: "It is manifested in benevolence." It functions on a daily basis, but they are unaware of it; this is why the text says: "It is . . . hidden within its functioning."} It arouses the myriad things but does not share the anxieties of the sages. {The myriad things follow it and so undergo their growth and transformation; this is why the text says: "It arouses the myriad things." Although the sages embody the Dao and apply it as function, they never are able to turn perfect nonbeing into this embodiment. Thus they may have success without hindrance throughout the whole world, but, as a consequence, there are always outward signs to the way they bring things to pass.} As replete virtue and great enterprise, the Dao is indeed perfect! {To make things go smoothly and to have matters unfold in accordance with their principles always entirely derive from the Dao. The sage is the mother of its function, since what he embodies is identical to the Dao. It is by means of such replete virtue and great enterprise that he is able to reach such perfection.} It is because the Dao exists in such rich abundance that we refer to it as the "great enterprise." {It is grand and great and complete in all respects; this is why the text says: "The Dao exists in such rich abundance."} It is because the Dao brings renewal day after day that we refer to it here as "replete virtue." {Things embody transformation and accord with change; this is why the text says: "The Dao brings renewal day after day."[15]} In its capacity to produce and reproduce we call it "change." {Yin and yang change from one to the other and, in doing so, bring about life as transformation.} When it forms images, we call it *Qian*. {Here Dao forms the images of *Qian* [Pure Yang, that is, Heaven].} When it duplicates patterns, we call it *Kun*. {Here Dao duplicates the patterns of *Kun* [Pure Yin, that is, Earth].} The means to know the future through the mastery of numbers is referred to as "prognostication," and to keep in step freely with change is referred to as "the way one should act." {When things reach their limit, they undergo change, and when change occurs, one should keep in perfect step with it. This is the dynamic that underlies the way one should act.} What the yin and the yang do not allow us to plumb we call "the numinous." {"The numinous" refers to the ultimate extent of change and transformation, the expression used to address the myriad things in terms of their subtlety, and is something for which it is impossible to formulate questions. This is why the text says: "what the yin and the yang do not allow us to plumb." I once tried to discuss it in this way: "Actually, how could there ever be an agency that causes the interaction between the polarity of yin and yang or the activity of the myriad things to happen as they do! Absolutely everything just undergoes transformation in the great void [*daxu*] and, all of a sudden, comes into existence spontaneously. It is not things themselves that bring about their existence; principle here operates because of the response of the mysterious [*xuan*]. There is no master that transforms them; fate here operates because of the workings of the dark [*ming*].[16] Thus, as we do not understand why all this is so, how much the less can we understand what the numinous is! It is for this reason that, in order to clarify the polarity of yin and yang, we take the great ultimate [*taiji*], the initiator of it, and, in addressing change and transformation, we find that an equivalent for them is best found in the term *numinous*. Anyone who understands how Heaven acts will exhaust principle and embody change, sit in forgetfulness and cast aside the things in his care.[17] As it takes the perfect void [*zhixu*] to respond perfectly to things, we equate this with the Dao. As it takes the complete lack of conscious thought to view things from the point of view of the mysterious, we call this the numinous. One who takes the Dao as resource and so achieves union with it derives his power to do so from the numinous but is himself more dark-like than is the numinous."}

6. Change is indeed broad, and it is great! When we speak of it as something far-reaching, then there is no stopping it. {It exhausts the most profound of profundities and plumbs the deepest depth; there is nothing to stop it anywhere.} When one speaks of it as something near, then it operates calmly and correctly. {Thus, as something close, it is fitting and proper.} When one speaks of it in terms of how it pervades Heaven and Earth, then it does so with perfect thoroughness. As for *Qian*, in its quiescent state it is focused, and in its active state it is undeviating. This is how it achieves its great productivity. {*Focused* means "to be perfectly concentrated," and *undeviating* means "to be impartial and straight to the mark."} As for *Kun*, in its quiescent state it is condensed, and in its active state it is diffuse. This is how it achieves its capacious productivity. {*Condensed* means "gathered in upon it-

self." When it is at rest, it condenses its *qi* [material force], and when it becomes active, it opens up and so brings things into existence. *Qian*, as the commander of Heaven and the initiator of things, is the primal mover of change and transformation and is omnipresent in what is outside physical form. As for *Kun*, it is through compliance that it takes up where yang leaves off; its efficacy is completely self-realized, and its function something that stays within physical form. Thus, when we deal with *Qian* in terms of its focus and nondeviation, we address its capacity to materialize, and when we deal with *Kun* in terms of its condensing and opening up, we address its capacity to provide physical form.} In capaciousness and greatness, change corresponds to Heaven and Earth; in the way change achieves complete fulfillment, change corresponds to the four seasons; in terms of the concepts of yin and yang, change corresponds to the sun and the moon; and in the efficacy of its ease and simplicity, change corresponds to perfect virtue. {The means by which change is conveyed correspond to these four concepts.}

7. The Master [Confucius] said: "The *Changes*, how perfect it is! It was by means of the *Changes* that the sages exalted their virtues and broadened their undertakings. {It was by exhausting principle and entering into the numinous that their virtues became exalted. It was by universally aiding the myriad things that their undertakings were broadened.} Wisdom made them exalted, and ritual made them humble. {Wisdom is esteemed for its capacity to make one exalted, and ritual has the function to make one humble.} Exalted, they emulate Heaven, and, humble, they model themselves on Earth." {In the exaltation of their perfect wisdom, they resemble how Heaven upon high has command over things, and in the application of their thoroughgoing ritual, they resemble how Earth so broad accommodates things.} With Heaven and Earth having their positions thus fixed, change operates in their midst. {Heaven and Earth provide change with a gateway or door. Accordingly, change in conceptual terms is something that completely encompasses the myriad things. This is why the text says "operates in their midst."} As it allows things to fulfill their natures and keep on existing, this means that change is the gateway through which the fitness of the Dao operates. {That things exist and fulfill themselves is due to the fitness imparted to them by the Dao.[18]}

8. The sages had the means to perceive the mysteries[19] of the world and, drawing comparisons to them with analogous things,

made images out of those things that seemed appropriate. {As *Qian* is hard and *Kun* is soft, so each thing has its substantial character. This is why the text says: "drawing comparisons to them with analogous things."} This is why these are called "images."[20] The sages had the means to perceive the activities taking place in the world, and, observing how things come together and go smoothly, they thus enacted statutes and rituals accordingly. {Statutes and rituals are to be employed at the times suitable for them.} They appended phrases to the hexagram lines in order to judge the good and bad fortune involved. This is why these are called "the line phrases."

These line phrases speak to the most mysterious things[21] in the world, and yet one may not feel aversion toward them; they speak to the things in the world that are the most fraught with activity, and yet one may not feel confused about them. {"As a book, the *Changes* is something that cannot be kept at a distance."[22] If one feels adverse to it, he will go against the flow of things, and if one regards it as erroneous, he will be in violation of principle.} One should only speak after having drawn the appropriate comparisons [as offered in the *Changes*] and only act after having discussed what is involved. It is through such comparisons and by such discussions that one can respond successfully to the way change and transformation operate. {If one only acts in consequence of such comparisons and discussions, he will perfectly grasp the Dao of change and transformation.}

"A calling crane is in the shadows; its young answer it. I have a fine goblet; I will share it with you."[23] {As a crane calls and its young answer, so if one cultivates sincerity, all others will respond to it. If I have a fine goblet and share it around, those I share with also will respond to me with goodness. To clarify how this Dao of comparison and discussion operates, the text continues on with this concept, which in fact takes good fortune and bad, success and failure, to inhere in how one acts. If one unites with the Dao, the Dao will provide him with success, but for one who unites with failure, failure will ensure that things go against him. Without exception, things comply with one another because of a common identity, respond to one another because they are of the same species. Whether one acts or whether one refrains from action, such compliance and response will come about, as with the crane who calls in the shadows: those who share the same *qi* [material force, i.e., "essential nature"] will answer. If one declares something for one's own household, there will be those who respond even from a thousand *li* away. As the effect of such utterances is already like this, how much more would be the effect if it involved major affairs! As there are already those from a thousand *li* away who respond, how much greater would be the response if it were from those nearby![24] "The means to make one anxious about regret and remorse depend on the subtle, intermediate stages,"[25] and he who has control over success and failure is one who carefully uses the door hinge and crossbow trigger.[26] This is why the noble man only acts in consequence of comparisons made and discussions engaged in and is someone who pays careful heed to the subtlety of things.}

The Master said: "The noble man might stay in his chambers, but if the words he speaks are about goodness, even those from more than a thousand *li* away will respond with approval to him, and how much the more will those who are nearby do so! If he stays in his chambers and his words are not about goodness, then those from more than a thousand *li* away will go against him, and how much the more will those who are nearby do so! Words go forth from one's person and are bestowed on the people. Actions start in what is near and are seen far away. Words and actions are the door hinge and crossbow trigger of the noble man. {The door hinge and the crossbow trigger represent the master control that governs action.} It is the opening of this door or the release of this trigger that controls the difference between honor or disgrace. Words and actions are the means by which the noble man moves Heaven and Earth. So how could one ever fail to pay careful heed to them!"

Tongren [Fellowship, Hexagram 13] says: "First howling and wailing, but afterward there is laughter."[27] The Master said:

In the Dao of the noble man
There's a time for going forth
And a time for staying still,
A time to remain silent
And a time to speak out.
But for two people to share mind and heart,
Such sharpness severs metal,
And the words of those sharing mind and heart,
Such fragrance is like orchids.

{The fact that fellowship eventually manages to end in laughter is all due to those involved sharing a resonance of the same heart and mind. But do not ever think that the way this sameness is achieved has to be tied to one particular way of doing things! Whether the noble man goes forth or stays still, remains silent or speaks out, he never violates the Mean. Thus, although the practical steps that such men take may differ, because they remain united in the Dao, resonance will result.}

First Yin of *Daguo* [Major Superiority, Hexagram 28] says: "Use white rushes for a mat, and one will be without blame." The Master said: "Even if one were to place things on the ground, it would indeed still be permissible, so if one were to provide matting for it with rushes, how could there possibly be any blame attached to that! This is the extreme of caution. As things, rushes are insignificant, but their use can be very significant. If one makes caution a technique of this order and subsequently sets out to deal with things, such a one will never experience loss!"

"Diligent about his Modesty, the noble man has the capacity to maintain his position to the end, and this means good fortune."[28] The Master said: "To be diligent yet not to brag about it, to have meritorious achievement yet not to regard it as virtue, this is the ultimate of magnanimity. This speaks of someone who takes his achievements and subordinates them to others. As for his virtue, he would have it prosper ever more, and as for his decorum, he would have it ever more respectful. Modesty as such leads to perfect respect, and this is how one preserves his position."

"A dragon that overreaches should have cause for regret."[29] The Master said: "One might be noble yet lack the position, might be lofty yet lack the subjects, and might have worthy men in subordinate positions who yet will not assist him. If such a one acts with all this being so, he will have cause for regret."

"This one does not go out the door to his courtyard, so there is no blame."[30] The Master said: "As for how disorder arises, well, what one says is considered the steps to it. If the sovereign is not circumspect, he will lose his ministers; if a minister is not circumspect, he will lose his life; and if the crux of a matter is not kept circumspect, harm will result. This is why the sovereign takes circumspection as a caution and is not forthcoming."

The Master said: "Do you think that the makers of the *Changes* did not understand what robbers were! {This refers to the fact that robbers, too, would take advantage of any rift to get at one.} The *Changes* says: 'If one bears a burden on his back yet also rides in a carriage, it will attract robbers to him.'[31] Bearing burdens on the back, this is the business of a petty man; a carriage, this is the rig of a noble man. When one is a petty man yet rides in the rig of a noble man, robbers think to take his things by force.[32] When the one above [the sovereign] is careless and those below are harsh, enemies will indeed think to attack it [such a state]. When one is careless about treasures, it invites robbers, and when one makes up to look glamorous, it invites licentiousness. When the *Changes* says that 'if one bears a burden on his back yet also rides in a carriage, it will attract robbers to him,' it means that this is a summons for robbers."

9. Heaven is one, and Earth is two; Heaven is three, and Earth is four; Heaven is five, and Earth is six; Heaven is seven, and Earth is eight; Heaven is nine, and Earth is ten.[33] {The *Changes* thoroughly grasps the virtue of the numinous and the bright through the mastery of numbers. Thus to clarify the Dao of change it first takes up the numbers of Heaven and Earth.}

Heaven's numbers are five, {These are the five odd numbers.} and Earth's numbers are five. {These are the five even numbers.[34]} With the completion of these two sets of five places, each number finds its match. {The numbers of Heaven and Earth are respectively five each. When these two sets of five match up, by joining together they form the five elements: metal, wood, water, fire, and Earth.[35]} Heaven's numbers come to twenty-five, {The sum of the five odd numbers is twenty-five.} and Earth's numbers come to thirty. {The sum of the five even numbers is thirty.} The total sum of Heaven's and Earth's numbers is fifty-five. These [numbers] indicate how change and transformation are brought about and how gods and spirits are activated. {Change and transformation take place in this way, and gods and spirits take action in this way.} The number of the great expansion is fifty [yarrow stalks]. Of these we use forty-nine. {Wang Bi says: "After expanding the numbers of Heaven and Earth, we find that the ones that are of benefit to us number fifty, and of these we actually use forty-nine, thus leaving one unused. Although this one is not used, yet through it the use of the other numbers becomes readily possible, and, although this one is not one of the numbers, yet through it the other numbers are formed. As this one represents the supreme ultimate of change, the other forty-nine constitute the ultimate of numbers. Nonbeing cannot be brought to light by means of nonbeing but must take place through being. Therefore, by applying ourselves constantly to this ultimate among things that have being, we shall surely bring to light the primogenitor from which all things derive."[36]} We divide these into two groups, thereby representing the two [i.e., the yin and the yang]. We dangle one single stalk, thereby representing the three [i.e., the three powers, or Heaven, Earth, and Man]. We count off the stalks by fours, thereby representing the four seasons. We return the odd ones to a place between the fingers, thereby representing an intercalary month. Within five years, there is a second intercalary month, so we place a second lot of stalks between the fingers; after that we dangle another single stalk [and continue the process].[37] {"The odd ones" are equivalent to the remainders that, after counting off the stalks by fours, do not leave enough to continue the process. Once the stalks have been divided into two groups, one takes the remainders left after the counting-off has been completed for each and dangles them together with the single stalk. Therefore the text says: "We place a second lot of stalks between the fingers; after that we dangle another single stalk." In general, for every nineteen years, seven intercalary months constitute one set; thus there are two successive intercalary months within five years. This is why the text gives an abbreviated version of the general rule in this way.[38]}

Thus the stalks needed to form *Qian* [Pure Yang, Hexagram 1] number 216, {There are six yang lines. As one line requires 36 stalks, so the six lines require 216 stalks.} and the stalks needed to form *Kun* [Pure Yin, Hexagram 2] number 144. {There are six yin lines. As one line requires 24 stalks, so the six lines require 144 stalks.[39]} In all, these number 360 and correspond to the days of a year's cycle. The stalks in the two parts [of the *Changes*] number 11,520 and correspond [roughly] to the number of the ten thousand [i.e., "myriad"] things. {The two parts contain 384 lines, with yin and yang lines each making up one-half; these combined together number 11,520.[40]} Therefore it takes four operations to form the *Changes*, {"We divide these into two groups, thereby representing the two": this is the first operation. "We dangle one single stalk, thereby representing the three": this is the second operation. "We count off the stalks by fours, thereby representing the four seasons": this is the third operation. "We return the odd ones to a place between the fingers": this is the fourth operation.[41]} and it takes eighteen changes to form a hexagram.[42] With the eight trigrams, we have the small completions. These are drawn upon to create extensions, {Their extension results in the sixty-four hexagrams.} and, as they are also expanded through the use of corresponding analogies, all the situations that can happen in the world are covered.

The *Changes* manifests the Dao {*Manifests* means "brings it to light."} and shows how its virtuous activity is infused with the numinous. {It is through the numinous that it [the Dao] perfectly fulfills its function.} Thus one can through it synchronize himself with things[43] and with it render service to the numinous.[44] {One can through it respond to the entreaties of the myriad things and assist in bringing to pass the good results of numinous transformation. *Synchronize himself with* means "to respond to."} The Master said: "Does it not follow that one who understands the way of change and transformation also understands how the numinous behaves!" {The Dao of change and transformation does not act out of a sense of purpose but behaves spontaneously. Thus one who understands change and transformation is someone who also understands how the numinous behaves.}

10. In the *Changes*, there are four things that pertain to the Dao of the sages. In speaking, we regard its phrases as the supreme guide; in acting, we regard its changes as the supreme guide; in fashioning implements, we regard its images as the supreme guide; and in divining by cracking shell and bone or by the use of stalks, we regard its prognostications as the supreme guide. {These four things belong to the concrete and perceptible world; they are things that one can seize upon and use.} This is why when the noble man would act in a certain way or would try to do something, he addresses his doubts to the *Changes* in terms of words. The charge that it receives comes back to him like an echo, with no distance or concealment to it. In consequence, one knows of things to come. The *Changes* as such has to be the thing most capable of perfect subtlety in the world, for what else could possibly be up to this!

It is by interspersing numbers[45] that change proceeds. The numbers are combined in the various ways, which exhaust all aspects of change, and, in consequence, the hexagrams form the patterns of Heaven and Earth. As they bring out all the potential of these numbers, they also establish images for everything in the world. As such, the *Changes* has to be the thing most capable of change in the world, for what else could possibly be up to this!

The *Changes* is without consciousness and is without deliberate action. Being utterly still it does not initiate movement, but when stimulated it is commensurate with all the causes for everything that happens in the world. As such, it has to be the most numinous thing in the world, for what else could possibly be up to this! {If it had not been something that had forgotten images, it would not have had the means to establish images. If it had not been something that discarded numbers, it would not have had the means to explore the ultimate significance of numbers. Being the thing most capable of perfect subtlety, it can avoid chaos without doing any planning. Being the thing most capable of change, it covers absolutely everything by embodying the One. Being the most numinous, it responds to absolutely everything while remaining completely still. All this means that it is the mother of all meritorious accomplishment as well as the means by which images and numbers are established. This is why the text says that if it were not capable of the most perfect subtlety and the most change and were not the most numinous, how could it have ever been up to such things!}

It is by means of the *Changes* that the sages plumb the utmost profundity and dig into the very incipience [*ji*] of things. It is profundity alone that thus allows one to penetrate the aspirations of all the people in the world; it is a grasp of incipience alone that thus allows one to accomplish the great affairs of the world; {"To plumb the principles that underlie the prephenomenal world" is what is meant by the term *profundity*, and "to be ready just at the moment when the imperceptible beginnings of action occurs" is what is meant by the term *incipience*.} and it is the numinous alone that thus allows one to make quick progress without hurrying and reach goals without forcing one's way.

When the Master said, "In the *Changes*, there are four things that pertain to the Dao of the sages," this is what he meant. {These four things are brought to pass through the Sagely Dao. This is why the text says "the Dao of the sages."}

11. The Master said: "As for the *Changes*, what does it do?[46] The *Changes* deals with the way things start up and how matters reach completion and represents the Dao that envelops the entire world. If one puts it like this, nothing more can be said about

it. {*To envelop* here means "to cover over," that is, since the *Changes* is completely commensurate with the aspirations of the whole world and because it represents how the affairs of the world reach completion, its Dao can be said to envelop the entire world.} Therefore the sages use it to penetrate the aspirations of all the people in the world, to settle the great affairs of the world, and to resolve all doubtful matters in the world.

This is why the virtue of the yarrow stalks resides in their being round and thus numinous, that of the hexagrams resides in their being square and thus laden with wisdom. {Roundness is active and something infinite, and squareness is static and something finite. This means that the yarrow stalk is an image of the numinous because of its roundness and that a hexagram is an image of wisdom because of its squareness. Change has only to indicate how the yarrow stalks should adapt themselves, and any number of them will perform perfectly. This is why they are referred to as "round." The hexagrams are arranged in terms of the way their lines are allotted, so each one has its own specific substance or character. This is why they are referred to as "square."} Meanings inherent in the six lines of the hexagrams are provided to us through the process of change. {*Provided to us* here means "announced to us." It is through changing from one into another that the six lines announce good fortune and misfortune to us.} The sages used these to purify hearts and minds. {This means they purified the hearts and minds of the myriad creatures.[47]} When it is retired, it becomes hidden among its secrets. {This means that the Dao that the *Changes* represents is so profound and subtle that the myriad creatures make use of it on a daily basis but cannot know the source of its workings. This is why the text says: "When it is retired, it becomes hidden among its secrets." This is like saying that "it is . . . hidden within its functioning."[48]} Through its pronouncements of good fortune and misfortune, it shows that it shares the same anxieties as the common folk. {It expresses images of good fortune and misfortune and thereby shares matters about which the common folk feel anxiety. This is why the text says: "Through its pronouncements of good fortune and misfortune, it shows that it shares the same anxieties as the common folk."} By virtue of its numinous power, it lets one know what is going to come, and by virtue of its wisdom, it becomes a repository of what has happened. {This clarifies how the functions of the yarrow stalks and the hexagrams are respectively identical to the numinous power and to wisdom. As the yarrow stalks determine the numbers at the beginning, they deal with the future in terms of the hexagrams [they create]. As the hexagrams form images at the end, they deal with the past in terms of the yarrow stalks [that determine them].[49] These functions that deal with the future and the past complete one another, just as with the numinous and wisdom.} Who could ever possibly be up to this! Were these not the intelligent and perspicacious ones of antiquity who had divine martial power and who yet did not indulge in killing![50] {They made the myriad creatures submit, yet they did not use military force or punishments.} They used the *Changes* to cast light on the Dao of Heaven and to probe into the conditions of the common folk. This is the numinous thing that they inaugurated in order to provide beforehand for the needs of the common folk. {It determines good fortune and misfortune at the start of things.} The sages did their fasting with the *Changes* and got their precautions from it. {"To purify the heart and mind" is what is meant here by *fasting*, and "to guard against calamity" is what is meant here by *precautions*.} They used it to make their virtue numinous and bright, did they not?

This is why closing the gate is called *Kun*, {The Dao of *Kun* [Pure Yin, Hexagram 2] enfolds things.} and opening the gate is called *Qian*. {The Dao of *Qian* [Pure Yang, Hexagram 1] stirs things into life.} One such closing and one such opening is referred to as a *change*, and the inexhaustibility of their alteration is called their *free flow*. What one sees of this is called the *images*. {What is brought to sight by augury is an image.} As these take physical shapes, we may say that they are *concrete things*. {Something that achieves a form [i.e., a phenomenal object] is called a concrete thing.} To make use of all this in a systematic way is known as its *method*. Taking advantage of and putting to use the ins and outs involved,[51] one provides all the common folk with the use of it, and this is called *the numinous*.

Therefore, in change there is the great ultimate. This is what generates the two modes [the yin and yang]. {Being necessarily has its origin in nonbeing. Thus, the great ultimate generates the two modes. *Great ultimate* is the term for that for which no term is possible. As we cannot lay hold of it and name it, we think of it in terms of the ultimate point to which we can extend being and regard this as equivalent to the great ultimate.} The two basic modes

[— and --] generate the four basic images [⚌, ⚍, ⚎, ⚏], and the four basic images generate the eight trigrams [by adding first one unbroken (yang) line — to each, then one broken (yin) line --]. {It is through the trigrams that change is provided with images.} The eight trigrams determine good fortune and misfortune, {Once the eight trigrams were established, good fortune and misfortune could be determined.} and good fortune and misfortune generate the great enterprise. {Once one establishes what good fortune and misfortune are, his efforts at the great and the grand will achieve complete success.}

Therefore, of things that serve as models for images, none are greater than Heaven and Earth. Of things involving the free flow of change, none is greater than the four seasons. Of images that are suspended above and emit brightness, none are greater than the sun and the moon. Of things respected and thought eminent, none is greater than rich and noble position; {It is through such a position that one [a sovereign] unifies all the activities in the world and brings succor to the myriad things}. Of those who made things available and extended their use to the utmost and who introduced ready devices and made them of benefit to all the world, none are greater than the sages. Of things that delve into mysteries [*ze*] and search out what is hidden [*yin*], that hook things up from the depths and extend a reach to the distances in order to determine the good fortune and bad in the world and to bring about the untiring efforts of all those in the world, none are greater than yarrow stalks and tortoise shells [i.e., instruments of divination].

Therefore Heaven produced numinous things, and the sages regarded these as ruling principles. Heaven and Earth changed and transformed, and the sages regarded these as models. Heaven hung images in the sky and revealed good fortune and bad, and the sages regarded these as meaningful signs. The Yellow River brought forth a diagram, and the Luo River brought forth writings, and the sages regarded these things also as ruling principles.[52]

In the *Changes*, there are the four basic images; it is by means of these that it makes its revelations. They [the sages] have attached phrases to it, and it is by means of these that it makes its pronouncements. It determines things to involve either good fortune or misfortune, and this is how it renders decisions.

12. The *Changes* says: "Heaven will help him as a matter of course; this is good fortune, and nothing will be to his disadvan-

tage."[53] The Master said: "*You* [numinous help] means 'help.' One whom Heaven helps is someone who is in accord with it. One whom people help is someone who is trustworthy. Such a one treads the Dao of trustworthiness, keeps his thoughts in accord [with Heaven], and also thereby holds the worthy in esteem. This is why 'Heaven will help him as a matter of course; this is good fortune, and nothing will be to his disadvantage.' "

The Master said: "Writing does not exhaust words, and words do not exhaust ideas. If this is so, does this mean that the ideas of the sages cannot be discerned?" The Master said: "The sages established images in order to express their ideas exhaustively. They established the hexagrams in order to treat exhaustively the true innate tendency of things and their countertendencies to spuriousness.[54] They attached phrases to the hexagrams in order to exhaust what they had to say. They let change occur and achieve free flow in order to exhaust the potential of the benefit involved. {They explored the ultimate significance of the numbers connected with change and its consummation and in consequence exhausted the potential of the benefit involved. This is why the text says: "As for change, when one process of it reaches its limit, a change from one state to another occurs. As such, change achieves free flow, and with this free flow, it lasts forever."[55]} They made a drum of it, made a dance of it, and so exhausted the potential of its numinous power.[56]

Qian and *Kun*, do they not constitute the arcane source for change! {*Arcane source* here refers to the deep, mysterious wellspring.} When *Qian* and *Kun* form ranks, change stands in their midst, but if *Qian* and *Kun* were to disintegrate, there would be no way that change could manifest itself. And if change could not manifest itself, this would mean that *Qian* and *Kun* might almost be at the point of extinction!

Therefore what is prior to physical form pertains to the Dao, and what is subsequent to physical form pertains to concrete objects [the phenomenal world]. That which transforms things and regulates them is called "change." {This is how the Dao that governs how things come together and go smoothly and comply with change is established.} By extending this to practical action, one may be said to achieve complete success. {When one who makes change his vehicle sets out in it, he will be able to go anywhere with ease.} To take up this [the Dao of change] and integrate it into the lives of the common folk of the world, this we call all "the great task of life." {It is by means of this great task that succor is brought to all things. Thus one takes it up and integrates it in among the common folk.}

Therefore, as for the images, the sages had the means to perceive the mysteries of the world and, drawing comparisons to them with analogous things, made images out of those things that seemed appropriate. In consequence of this, they called these "images." The sages had the means to perceive the activities taking place in the world, and, observing how things come together and go smoothly, they thus enacted statutes and rituals accordingly. They appended phrases to the hexagram lines in order to judge the good and bad fortune involved. This is why these are called "line phrases." These line phrases speak to the most mysterious things in the world, and yet one may not feel aversion toward them; they speak to the things in the world that are the most fraught with activity, and yet one may not feel confused about them.[57]

To plumb the mysteries of the world to the utmost is dependent on the hexagrams; to drum people into action all over the world is dependent on the phrases; {*Phrases* here means the line phrases. It is by means of the lines that people are drummed into activity; they provide models for all the activities that take place in the world.} to transform things and regulate them is dependent on change; to start things going and carry them out is dependent on the free flow of change; to be aware of the numinous and bring it to light is dependent on the men involved;[58] {To embody the numinous and bring it to light is not something that relies on the images. Therefore it depends on the men involved.} to accomplish things while remaining silent and to be trusted without speaking is something intrinsic to virtuous conduct. {*Virtuous conduct* here means the virtuous conduct of worthy men. As they have sufficient internal resources to comply [with the Dao], they accomplish things while remaining silent, and as what they embody is perfectly commensurate with principle, they are trusted without having to speak.}

NOTES

1. This and all subsequent text set off in this manner is commentary by Han Kangbo.

2. *Hardness* and *softness* here probably also refer to the yang lines and the yin lines of the trigrams and hexagrams. One should act only from a position of hardness and strength and refrain from action, remaining passive, when one's position is soft and weak. Such situations are indicated by the yang and yin lines, respectively.

3. Cf. section three of Explaining the Trigrams.

4. Cf. Hexagram 1, *Qian*, Pure Yang, Commentary on the Judgments.

5. Instead of "the sequences presented by the *Changes*," some editions read "the images presented by the *Changes*." See Ruan Yuan's (1764–1849) collation notes to *Zhouyi zhengyi* in *Shisanjing zhushu*, 7: 3a.

6. Kong Yingda comments:

> By saying that "the Judgments address the images," this refers to the fact that the images involve either pettiness [*xiao*] or greatness [*da*]. Therefore, the differentiation of things into the petty and the great is an inherent feature of the hexagrams—just as in [the Judgment of] *Tai* [Peace, Hexagram 11], when "the petty depart, and the great arrive, so good fortune will prevail," or in [the Judgment of] *Pi* [Obstruction, Hexagram 12], when "the great depart, and the petty arrive."

See *Zhouyi zhengyi*, 7: 8a. In this sense, *xiao* and *da* also refer to the decrease of the Dao (i.e., the ascendancy of the petty man) and the growth of the Dao (i.e., the ascendancy of the great, noble man).

7. Commentators interpret *jie* differently, usually either as *xianjie* (small or minor [matters]), as does Han Kangbo, or as *jiexian* (border, borderline). Cheng Yi interprets *jie* as Wang and Han do, as *weixiao* (small [trifling, subtle, suggestive] matter[s]), but Zhu Xi tries to combine both the "small matter" and the "border" meanings:

> Remorse and regret do not yet reach the stage where good fortune and misfortune are involved. When the first sprouts of action begin, they can develop into small [*wei*] states of good fortune and misfortune. *Jie* also indicate these small states involving remorse and regret. The word *jie* is like the *jie* in *jiezhi* or *jiexian* [border/limit/borderline]. It indicates the borderline where good and evil are first demarcated.

Wu Cheng (1249–1333) has a similar comment: "Regret and remorse interpose [*jie*] between good fortune and bad. If one is anxious about these interpositions, he will gravitate toward good fortune and not gravitate to misfortune. But another explanation states that this [*jie*] addresses 'small faults.' " See *Zhouyi zhezhong*, 13: 15b–16a. "Subtle, intermediate stages" attempts a compromise between these two interpretations. *Jie* is translated as "the interstices [between the lines of the hexagrams]" by Peterson in "Making Connections," 98, which also is possible, even likely, given the fact that the constituent parts of the hexagrams are being discussed here. However, unlike Peterson, who tries to present the Commentary on the Appended Phrases in its literal sense, unadorned by the later exegetical tradition (see "Making Connections," 68), I have tried to incorporate later exegesis into my translation when it seems particularly significant or influential.

8. "Gods and spirits" translates *guishen*. A more impersonal, mechanistic rendering would be "negative and positive spiritual forces."

9. "Being genuine about benevolence" (*dun ren*), a human characteristic, is here projected onto the larger world of plants and animals as a whole.

10. This seems to allude to a passage in the next section.

11. Since neither this passage of the Commentary on the Appended Phrases nor Han's commentary to it explicitly states what the general subject or topic is, it is possible to interpret them in different ways. I have chosen to follow the later commentary tradition, as represented, for instance, by Zhu Xi, and make that subject the "sage," with his numinous intelligence. (See *Zhouyi zhezhong*, 13: 20a–20b.) Peterson, who tries to eschew this later tradition, makes the *Changes* or, specifically, "the technique of the *Changes*" the general subject of this passage of the classic: the numinous powers reside in the way the *Changes* itself works (see Peterson, "Making Connections," pp. 102–104). In fact, the passage and Han's commentary both may be deliberately ambiguous here: the sages invest the *Changes* with their numinous power, which itself is one with the numinous power of Heaven and Earth, and other, later sages unite their numinous power with the power of the classic and, through it, with the powers themselves of Heaven and Earth.

12. Kong Yingda's subcommentary makes this difficult and cryptic passage readily intelligible. My translation follows his remarks. See *Zhouyi zhengyi*, 7: 11b–12a.

13. *Laozi*, section 1, p. 1. This interpretation follows Wang Bi's own punctuation of the text of the *Laozi* and his commentary. However, beginning with Wang Anshi (1021–1086), many editors and commentators have punctuated the text differently, which some modern translators prefer to follow, Wing-tsit Chan, for instance: "Let there always be non-being, so we may see their subtlety." See *Source Book*, p. 139.

14. *Laozi*, section 34, p. 89.

15. There is no explicit subject here; I have supplied "things" because the context seems to justify it. Kong Yingda construes it differently: "It is because the sage is able to be thoroughly commensurate with change, to embody transformation and keep in step with change, that his virtue increases and undergoes renewal day after day." See *Zhouyi zhengyi*, 7: 13b.

16. We should note that the compound *xuanming*, a common term in Daoist writings, is probably best translated as "the Noumenon." See Chan, *Source Book*, p. 788.

17. Kong Yingda says that this alludes to the Great Teacher (*Da zongshi*) chapter of the *Zhuangzi*, where Yan Hui is supposed to have achieved union with the Dao, "sitting in forgetfulness" and detaching himself from intelligence, body, and mind. In other words, one who has achieved union with the Dao will have transcended the need to maintain conscious control over things. See *Zhuangzi yinde*, 6/19/92–93. "Cast aside the things in his care"

translates *yi zhao*; this also follows Kong's commentary; see *Zhouyi zhengyi*, 7: 14a.

18. This essentially naturalistic interpretation by Han Kangbo stands in contrast with later Neo-Confucian commentaries that cast things here in terms of the moral nature and just behavior that men are endowed with and should aspire to, as in the following statement by Yu Yan (1258–1314): "Man's nature, being formed perfectly and naturally by Heaven, is something that is good throughout, and if one additionally makes the effort to nourish and cultivate it, it will be sustained. If so, then there will be nothing that one sets out to do that will not be the Dao, nothing that one sets out to do that will not be just [*yi*, that is, "fitting"]." See *Zhouyi zhezhong*, 14: 2a.

19. "Mysteries" translates *ze*, following Kong Yingda's subcommentary; see *Zhouyi zhengyi*, 7: 16a. Although most later commentators interpret *ze* in this way, Zhu Xi rejects this and instead glosses it as "confusion," that is, the sages had the means to perceive what occasions of seeming chaos or confusion in the world meant—its origin and causes as well as how to rectify it. See *Zhouyi zhezhong*, 14: 2b–3a.

20. "Images" here are the actual graphic representations of the trigrams and, compounding them, the hexagrams.

21. Or, following Zhu Xi, "the most confused/complex things." See note 19 above.

22. See section eight of the Commentary on the Appended Phrases, Part Two.

23. See Hexagram 61, *Zhongfu* (Inner Trust), Second Yang.

24. This paraphrases a passage in the following paragraph.

25. This quotes a passage in section three; see note 7 above.

26. The "door hinge and crossbow trigger" reference is explained in the following paragraph.

27. See Hexagram 13, *Tongren* (Fellowship), Fifth Yang.

28. See Hexagram 15, *Qian* (Modesty), Third Yang.

29. See Hexagram 1, *Qian* (Pure Yang), Top Yang.

30. See Hexagram 60, *Jie* (Control), First Yang.

31. See Hexagram 40, *Xie* (Release), Third Yin; the expression "attracts robbers to him" also occurs in Hexagram 5, *Xu* (Waiting), Third Yang.

32. "Think to" translates *si*, which is the way most commentators take it; however, the Qing era philologist and commentator on the Confucian classics, Yu Yue (1821–1907), thinks that *si* here should be read as a homonym *si*, a function word meaning "here" or "then." If this is correct, then the line should read: "If one is a petty man yet rides in the rig of a noble man, then robbers will rob him." The same possibility exists for the next sentence. See Yu, *Qunjing pingyi*, 192A: 15c.

33. This sentence, placed here at the beginning of section nine by Cheng Yi in the eleventh century, was originally at the beginning of the next section. Zhu Xi agreed with Cheng's rearrangement, and so this became the standard arrangement from the Song era on. See *Zhouyi zhezhong*, 14: 9a. See also note 37 below.

34. The five odd numbers are *one*, *three*, *five*, *seven*, and *nine*, and the five even numbers are *two*, *four*, *six*, *eight*, and *ten*.

35. Kong Yingda's subcommentary reads: "It is this way: Heaven's *one* and Earth's *six* combine to form water; Earth's *two* and Heaven's *seven* combine to form fire; Heaven's *three* and Earth's *eight* combine to form wood; Earth's *four* and Heaven's *nine* combine to form metal; and Heaven's *five* and Earth's *ten* combine to form Earth." See *Zhouyi zhengyi*, 7: 22a. This appears to be a reference to the way numbers and the five elements combine in the *Hetu* (Yellow River chart); see note 52 below. See *Zhouyi zhezhong*, 21: 28b–30a.

36. This passage may be a fragment of what was once an independent essay by Wang entitled *Dayanyi* (Meaning of the great expansion); see the section on Wang Bi in the introduction and note 9 there. The number *fifty* here is explained in various ways. The Han commentator Jing Fang (77–37 B.C.) says of it: "This *fifty* refers to the ten heavenly stems, the twelve earthly branches, and the twenty-eight constellations." See *Zhouyi Jingshi zhangju*, 3: 16a. Ma Rong (79–166 A.D.), a later Han commentator, says that this *fifty* refers to the *Taiji* (Supreme Ultimate), the two modes (i.e., yin and yang), the sun and the moon, the four seasons, the five elements, the twelve months, and the twenty-four subseasons (each of the four seasons has six such subseasons). See *Zhouyi Mashi zhuan*, 3: 62b. Zheng Xuan (127–200 A.D.), probably the most prominent of the Han commentators, thinks that the number *fifty* is the sum total of the numbers of Heaven and Earth minus the five elements—since they are already contained within Heaven and Earth. See *Zhouyi Zhengzhu*, 7: 89. A much later view, that of Zhu Xi, is that the number *fifty* is simply the product of the number *five* of Heaven and the number *ten* of Earth. See *Zhouyi zhezhong*, 14: 11a.

37. This paragraph originally came at the head of section nine but was moved to its present position by Cheng Yi. See note 33 above.

38. As there are two intercalary months for every five years, so there should be two bundles of stalks placed among the five fingers of the hand—each bundle between a different pair of fingers (the final pair of "fingers" being the index finger and the thumb).

39. For the mechanics of counting the yarrow stalks, see How to Cast a Hexagram, the Yarrow Stalk Method, in the introduction. These sums work only when old yang and old yin lines are involved. Kong Yingda comments here: "For a *Qian* hexagram that consists of old yang lines, one line results in 36 stalks, so six lines all together result in 216 stalks. . . . For a *Kun* hexagram that consists of old yin lines, one line results in 24 stalks, so six lines all together result in 144 stalks." See *Zhouyi zhengyi*, 7: 22a. That is, when an old yang line is formed, it requires 13 stalks ($5 + 4 + 4 = 13$), which, subtracted from 49 (the total number of stalks used), results in a remainder of 36, which, multiplied by 6 (lines), equals 216. When an old yin line is formed, it requires 25 stalks ($9 + 8 + 8 = 25$), which, when subtracted from 49, results in 24, which, multiplied by 6, equals 144.

40. This sum is computed as follows: One yang line requires 36 stalks, and, as there are 192 yang lines in the *Changes* (half the total of 384 lines),

the total number of stalks required to produce these 192 yang lines equals 6,912. Likewise, one yin line requires 24 stalks, and 24 times 192 equals 4,608. The sum of 6,912 and 4,608 is 11,520.

41. Apparently the counting-off by fours of both groups of stalks is considered the third operation, and the placing of both remainders between the fingers is considered the fourth operation, rather than the counting off and the placing for the one group being the third and the counting off and the placing for the other being the fourth—as Wilhelm understands it. See *The I Ching*, pp. 312–313. Zhu Xi and other commentators also understand it in the same way as Han Kangbo (see *Zhouyi zhezhong*, 14: 15a), so Wilhelm's interpretation seems to be without textual support.

42. If each cycle of four operations is defined as a *change*, then to determine one line requires three such changes. As there are six lines, it takes eighteen changes to complete one hexagram.

43. "Synchronize himself with things" translates *chouzuo*, literally, "host toasts guest (*chou*); guest returns toast (*zuo*)." By extension, *chouzuo* came to mean "harmonious relations," "relate harmoniously with," "be in step with things," etc. However, Willard J. Peterson translates *chouzuo* here as "recompense [such as those who sacrifice to divinities are thought to receive]." See "Making Connections," p. 105.

44. "Render service to the numinous" translates *you shen*. This follows the readings of most commentators who regard *you* as indicative and transitive and the phrase to mean "assist spiritual forces" or "assist the gods." Peterson translates *you shen* as *youshen*: "can be given a helping numinous quality [such as those who are protected by divinities are thought to receive]." See "Making Connections," p. 105.

45. Much effort has been made on the part of various commentators to interpret the expression *canwu*, which commonly means "to intersperse (interspersion)," "to shuffle together (shuffling)," or "to throw things together for the sake of comparing them," as *san wu* ("by threes and fives") and to relate these threes and fives to the actual numbers that occur in the course of yarrow stalk manipulation, the specific operations, the number sequences, etc. Both types of interpretation are provided by the commentaries in the *Zhouyi zhezhong*, and even Zhu Xi seems to have been of two minds about it. See *Zhouyi zhezhong*, 14: 18b–19a.

46. "What does it do?" translates *he weizhe ye*. This also could be construed as "Why did they [the sages] make it?" The commentary of Han Kangbo and the subcommentary of Kong Yingda (*Zhouyi zhengyi*, 7: 26b) support the former interpretation, but remarks by Zhu Xi seem to suggest that he understands it in terms of the latter. See *Zhouyi zhezhong*, 14: 22a.

47. Zhu Xi interprets this line differently; he thinks that the sages used the *Changes* to purify their *own* minds. See *Zhouyi zhezhong*, 14: 22b and 23b. Kong Yingda's subcommentary expands upon Han's remark: "The sages used the divinatory yarrow stalks of the *Changes* to cleanse the hearts and minds of the myriad creatures. When the myriad creatures had doubts about what they should do, then the sages divined for them, and this cleansed their hearts and minds of doubt. When good is done, good fortune is had,

but when evil is done, misfortune results. This means they cleansed the heart and mind bent on evil." See *Zhouyi zhengyi*, 7: 27a. Also note that Zhu Xi, as well as most Neo-Confucians of his day and later, interpret this entire passage in terms of the sages rather than the Dao of the *Changes* or the *Changes* itself. See *Zhouyi zhezhong*, 14: 22b–23b.

48. See section five earlier.

49. Kong Yingda's comment on this passage is worth quoting: "If we look at the hexagrams in terms of the yarrow stalks, we understand that the hexagrams provide images of matters that will occur in the future. . . . If we look at the yarrow stalks in terms of the hexagrams, then what is accumulated by the yarrow stalks provides images of matters that have already happened." See *Zhouyi zhengyi*, 7: 27b.

50. "Who had divine martial power and yet did not indulge in killing" translates *shenwu er busha zhe*, which Peterson renders as "and were numinous and martial but did not kill." He adds the note: "I speculate that the words 'but did not kill' are an allusion to the *Changes* being a divination technique which is not dependent on sacrificial victims, such as were employed in Shang times." See "Making Connections," p. 109 and p. 109 n. 59.

51. "Ins and outs" translates *churu*, which is likely to have the same basic meaning here as *wanglai*, "alternation," literally, "going back and forth" or "coming and going," i.e., the alternation of yin and yang that underlies change.

52. The Yellow River chart (*Hetu*) is supposed to have been inscribed on the back of a dragon-horse (*longma*) that emerged from the Yellow River at the time of the mythical sage-king Fu Xi, who modeled the eight trigrams on it. The Luo River diagram (*Luoshu*) was the design on the back of the spirit-tortoise (*shengui*) that appeared when the later sage-king Yu was controlling the flood and that Yu used as a model for the ninefold division of ancient China. For more about these legends and their later reception, see Smith et al., *Sung Dynasty Uses*, pp. 175–176.

53. See Hexagram 14, *Dayou* (Great Holdings), Top Yang.

54. See section two of Wang Bi's General Remarks, as well as note 5 there.

55. This quotes section two of the Commentary on the Appended Phrases, Part Two.

56. Kong Yingda comments: "This sentence sums up the beauty of how 'the sages established images in order to express their ideas exhaustively' and 'attached phrases . . . in order to exhaust what they had to say.' [By doing so] one may say that they transformed the hearts and minds of the common people, who then with such hearts and minds spontaneously fell into delighted compliance, as if it had been drumming and dancing." See *Zhouyi zhengyi*, 7: 31a.

57. This paragraph is almost identical to the first paragraph of section eight and the first sentence of the paragraph that follows it.

58. Kong Yingda glosses "the men involved" as "the sages." See *Zhouyi zhengyi*, 7: 33a.

Commentary on the Appended Phrases [Xici zhuan], *Part Two*

1. When the eight trigrams formed ranks, the [basic] images were present there within them. {They provide all the [basic] images in the world.[1]} And so, when they [the sages] doubled these, the lines were present there within them. {Although the eight trigrams provide all the principles of the world, they do not extend to cover all the change connected with them. This is why they [the sage] doubled them so they could provide images for all the activities involved. They used comparisons with analogous things so they could clarify what was appropriate for bringing order to disorder. They observed how correspondences took place so they could bring to light the merit that results from achieving synchronicity. As a consequence, the way concepts are contained in individual lines and the way they are contained in whole hexagrams differ. This is why the text says: "The lines were present there within them."} When they let the hard and the soft [i.e., the strong and the weak, the yang and yin trigrams] displace each other, change was present there within them. When they attached phrases to the lines and made them injunctions, the ways the lines move were present there within them. {"The hard and the soft displace each other"—this is equivalent to "the eight trigrams activate each other."[2] This means either obstruction and stagnation or ease and success. They [the sages] attached phrases to them so as to make judgments about good fortune or misfortune. This is comparable to how the movement of the six hexagram lines is always in step with the moments of time.[3] The concepts involved in the way the hexagrams are set up are to be seen in the Commentary on the Judgments and in the Commentary on the Images, and the efficacy with which the lines

stay in step with moments of time is to be seen in the line phrases. Mr. Wang's General Remarks deal with all this in detail.}

Good fortune, misfortune, regret, and remorse are all generated from the way the lines move. {Only with this movement does indication of good fortune and misfortune appear.} The hard and the soft constitute the fixed bases, {The "fixed bases" are equivalent to the trigrams.} and change and consummation are represented by those entities that are in step with the moment. {"Those entities that are in step with the moment" are equivalent to the trigram lines.} Thanks to constancy, either good fortune or misfortune prevails. {*Constancy* means the correct and unified, the One. No act ever stays completely clear of entanglement. One may sacrifice oneself to good fortune yet in doing so never stay free of misfortune. It takes someone who makes perfect use of change, as it governs how things come together and go smoothly, to avoid becoming entangled in good fortune and misfortune, for who else could ever achieve real constancy! The *Laozi* says: "A prince or noble who obtains the One uses it to provide constancy for the entire world."[4] Although the myriad ways that things undergo change are all different, it is possible to control them all by cleaving to the One.} Thanks to constancy, the Dao of Heaven and Earth reveals itself. {How clear Heaven and Earth are, for of the myriad things, not one of them fails to sustain the constancy they [Heaven and Earth] provide and, in so doing, [the things] perfectly fulfill their functions.} Thanks to constancy, the Dao of the sun and the moon makes them bright. All the activity that takes place in the world, thanks to constancy, is the expression of the One. *Qian* being unyielding shows us how easy it is; *Kun* being yielding shows us how simple it is. {"Unyielding" refers to the hard aspect of the one, and "yielding" refers to the soft aspect of the other. As *Qian* and *Kun* both constantly keep their single virtues intact, things draw on both to achieve existence. Thus the one is easy, the other simple.} The lines reproduce how particular things act, and the images provide likenesses of particular things.[5] As the lines and images move within the hexagrams, {This refers to the mantic signs or numbers that show themselves in the hexagrams.} so do good fortune and misfortune appear outside them. {This refers to the failure and success that one experiences in matters.} Meritorious undertakings are revealed in change, {It is due to change that meritorious undertakings manage to flourish. Thus they "are revealed in change."} and the innate tendencies of the sages are revealed in the attached phrases. {Each of the attached phrases indicates the direction a sage would take. This is why the text says "innate tendencies."}

The great virtue of Heaven and Earth is called "generation." {It gives life but makes no purposeful effort to do so. Thus it is able to bring about life constantly. This is why the text refers to it in terms of its "great virtue."} The great treasure of the sage is called his "position." {If something is of no use, there is nothing about it to treasure, but if it does have a use, there is something about it to treasure. Nothing is more marvelous than the Dao when it comes to being of no use and as such being always sufficient unto itself, and nothing is greater than position when it comes to being of use and as such augmenting the Dao. This is why the text says: "The great treasure of the sage is called his 'position.' "} The means by which such a one preserves this position we call "benevolence"; the means by which he gathers people to him we call "resources." {*Resources* are the means by which one provides for the subsistence of things.} The regulation of resources, the rectification of pronouncements, and his preventing the people from doing wrong we call "righteousness."

2. When in ancient times Lord Bao Xi[6] ruled the world as sovereign, he looked upward and observed the images in heaven and looked downward and observed the models that the earth provided. He observed the patterns on birds and beasts and what things were suitable for the land. {When the sage made the *Changes*, there was no great thing he did not explore to the utmost and no small thing he did not thoroughly investigate. For great things he took images from Heaven and Earth and for small things he observed the markings on birds and beasts and what things were suitable for the land.} Nearby, adopting them from his own person, and afar, adopting them from other things, he thereupon made the eight trigrams in order to become thoroughly conversant with the virtues inherent in the numinous and the bright and to classify the myriad things in terms of their true, innate natures.

He tied cords together and made various kinds of snare nets for catching animals and fish. He probably got the idea for this from the hexagram *Li* [Cohesion].[7] {Here *Li* means "cling to." For a snare net to work, one must carefully examine to what places creatures cling. Fish cling to waters, and beasts cling to mountains.}

After Lord Bao Xi perished, Lord Shen Nong[8] applied himself to things. He hewed wood and made a plowshare and bent wood and made a plow handle. The benefit of plowing and hoeing he taught to the world. He probably got the idea for this from the hexagram *Yi* [Increase].[9] {By creating implements he brought about abundance and in so doing increased the myriad things.}

He had midday become market time, had the people of the world gather, had the goods of the world brought together, had these exchanged, had them then retire to their homes, and enabled each one to get what he should. He probably got the idea for this from the hexagram *Shihe* [Bite Together].[10] {*Shihe* means "come or bring together." It refers to how he gathered the people of the marketplace, to how he had them come together from all different directions, and to his establishment of laws that governed the assemblage of goods. This is the basic concept inherent in *Shihe*.}

After Lord Shen Nong perished, the Lord Yellow Emperor, Lord Yao, and Lord Shun applied themselves to things. They allowed things to undergo the free flow of change and so spared the common folk from weariness and sloth. {As they allowed things to undergo the free flow of change, they made the use of these implements a delight, so the common folk did not become apathetic about them.[11]} With their numinous powers they transformed things and had the common folk adapt to them. As for [the Dao of] change, when one process of it reaches its limit, a change from one state to another occurs. As such, change achieves free flow, and with this free flow, it lasts forever. {If change is allowed to flow freely, it will never be exhausted. This is why it can last forever.} This is why "Heaven will help him as a matter of course; this is good fortune, and nothing will be to his disadvantage."[12] The Yellow Emperor, Yao, and Shun let their robes hang loosely down, yet the world was well governed. They probably got the idea for this from the hexagrams *Qian* and *Kun*. {By letting their robes hang down, they distinguished noble from base. This involves the concept that *Qian* is noble and *Kun* humble.[13]}

They hollowed out some tree trunks to make boats and whittled down others to make paddles. The benefit of boats and paddles was such that one could cross over to where it had been impossible to go. This allowed faraway places to be reached and so benefited the entire world. They probably got the idea for this from the hexagram *Huan* [Dispersion].[14] {*Huan* means to bring about a thoroughgoing dispersal by taking advantage of the principle involved.[15]}

They domesticated the ox and harnessed the horse to conveyances. This allowed heavy loads to be pulled and faraway places to be reached and so benefited the entire world. They probably got the idea for this from the hexagram *Sui* [Following].[16] {*Sui* means "to follow or be made to follow an appropriate course." By domesticating the ox and harnessing the horse to conveyances, one has them follow in the direction one would go, so in each case one gets what is appropriate.}

They had gates doubled and had watchmen's clappers struck and so made provision against robbers. They probably got the idea for this from the hexagram *Yu* [Contentment].[17] {This takes up the idea of being prepared beforehand.[18]}

They cut tree trunks to make pestles and hollowed out the ground to make mortars. The benefit of pestles and mortars was such that the myriad folk used them to get relief from want. They probably got the idea for this from the hexagram *Xiaoguo* [Minor Superiority].[19] {This refers to providing succor through the use of things that have minor functions.}

They strung pieces of wood to make bows and whittled others to make arrows. The benefit of bows and arrows was such that they dominated the world. They probably got the idea for this from the hexagram *Kui* [Contrariety].[20] {*Kui* means "recalcitrance." When people are recalcitrant, strife arises. The use of bows and arrows provides the means to gain dominance over recalcitrance and strife.}

In remote antiquity, caves were dwellings and the open country was a place to stay. The sages of later ages had these exchanged for proper houses, putting a ridgepole at the top and rafters below in order to protect against the wind and the rain. They probably got the idea for this from the hexagram *Dazhuang* [Great Strength].[21] {Proper houses are stronger and greater than cave dwellings, this is why they constructed proper houses, and they got the idea for this from *Dazhuang*.[22]}

In antiquity, for burying the dead, people wrapped them thickly with firewood and buried them out in the wilds, where they neither made grave mounds nor planted trees. For the period of mourning there was no definite amount of time. The sages of later ages had this exchanged for inner and outer coffins. They probably got the idea for this from the hexagram *Daguo* [Major Superiority].[23] {This takes up the idea of the coffins being exceedingly thick.}

In remote antiquity, people knotted cords to keep things in order. The sages of later ages had these exchanged for written tallies, and by means of these all the various officials were kept in order, and the myriad folk were supervised. They probably got the idea for this from the hexagram *Kuai* [Resolution].[24] {*Kuai* means "to decide." Written tallies were the means by which they decided and passed judgment on the myriad affairs.}

3. This is why the *Changes* as such consist of images. The term *image* means "the making of semblances," and the Judgments deal with their materials. {*Material* here means "the virtue inherent in the material." The Judgments address themselves to the material out of which the hexagrams are formed in order to deal comprehensively with the concepts involved.} The lines as such reproduce every action that takes place in the world, and this is why "good fortune" and "misfortune" come about and "regret" and "remorse" appear.

4. The yang trigrams have more yin than yang lines, and the yin trigrams have more yang than yin lines.[25] What is the reason for this? The yang trigrams are odd in number, and the yin trigrams are even in number.[26] {As the few are patriarchs of the many, so the One is he to whom the masses gravitate. Yang trigrams have two yin lines, thus the one odd one is the sovereign of it. Yin hexagrams have two yang lines, thus the one even one is the master of it.}

As for their virtues and actions, what are these? {The following passage distinguishes the virtues and actions of the yang trigrams from those of the yin trigrams.} The yang trigrams consist of one sovereign and two subjects; this denotes the Dao of the noble man. The yin trigrams consist of two sovereigns and one subject; this denotes the Dao of the petty man. {Yang represents the Dao of the sovereign, and yin represents the Dao of the subject. The sovereign, through taking no purposeful action, maintains unified control over the masses. This nonpurposeful action as such is a manifestation of the One. The subject, by engaging himself in matters, concludes them on behalf of his sovereign. But once he so engages himself, duality manifests itself. Therefore yang lines are drawn with a single stroke in order to show that the Dao of the sovereign must be one, and yin lines are drawn with two strokes in order to show that the substance of the subject must involve duality. This is how the yin and yang numbers provide a way to distinguish between sovereign and subject. If the sovereign is represented by a single-stroke line, this then is the virtue of the sovereign, but if a two-stroke line occupies the position of sovereign, this does not represent the Dao of the sovereign. This is why a yang trigram is referred to as "the Dao of the noble man" and a yin trigram is referred to as "the Dao of the petty man."}

5. The *Changes* say: "You pace back and forth in consternation, and friends follow your thoughts."[27] {All the activity that takes place in the world must revert back to the One. A person who has to resort to thought to seek friends is still incapable of the One, but when he elicits a response in others with the One, they will come to him without thinking.} The Master [Confucius] said: "What does the world have to think and deliberate about? As all in the world ultimately comes to the same end, though the roads to it are different, so there is an ultimate congruence in thought, though there might be hundreds of ways to deliberate about it. So what does the world have to think and deliberate about?" {If few are involved, it will mean success, but if many are involved, then it will mean perplexity. Although the roads to it differ, where they all go to is the same place. Although deliberations may take hundreds of different forms, what they all ultimately reach admits no division. If indeed one knows what the essential is—that it is not to be found in wide searching but something strung together by the One—then, without any deliberating, he will get it completely.}

When the sun goes, then the moon comes, and when the moon goes, then the sun comes. The sun and the moon drive each other on, and brightness is generated in this process. When the cold goes, then the heat comes, and when the heat goes, then the cold comes. The cold and the heat drive each other on, and the yearly seasons come into being in this process. What has gone is a contraction, and what is to come is an expansion. Contraction and expansion impel each other on, and benefits are generated in this process.

The contraction of the measuring worm is done in order to try to stretch itself out, and the hibernation of dragons and snakes is done in order to preserve their lives. Perfect concepts [*jingyi*] come about by entrance into the numinous [*ru shen*], which, once had, allows one to extend their application to the utmost. {*Perfect concepts* means "the profound subtlety of the principles of things." The numinous, being utterly still, does not act, but when it responds to something, that response is perfect and thoroughgoing. Thus one is able to take advantage of all the subtle secrets that underlie the world and gain unified and complete control over their applications.} The use of these applications comes about by making one's person secure, which allows for the subsequent exaltation of his virtue. {The Dao governing how to make use of applications means that one first makes one's position secure and only after that takes action. Perfect concepts derive from "entrance into the numinous, which, once had, allows one to extend their application to the utmost." The use of these applications derives from "making one's person secure, which allows for the subsequent exaltation of his virtue." As principles must derive from their progenitor, so each and every matter springs from the root. If one returns to the root of things, he will find quiescence there and discover all the world's principles available to him. However, if he enslaves his capacity for thought and deliberation just so he can seek ways to put things to use and if he disregards the need to make his person secure just so he can sacrifice himself to achievement and fine reputation, then the more the spurious arises, the more principles will be lost, and the finer his reputation grows, the more obvious his entanglements will become.} To go beyond this is something that no one has ever known how to do, for to plumb the numinous to the utmost and to understand transformation represent the very acme of virtue.

The *Changes* say: "This one suffers Impasse on rocks, so he tries to hold on to the puncture vine for support, and then he enters his home but does not see his wife. This means misfortune."[28] The Master said: "If it is not something by which one should be brought to grief yet one is brought to grief by it, one's name will surely be disgraced. If it is not something to hold on to for support yet one holds on to it, one's person will surely be put in danger. Not only disgraced but also in danger: the time of such a person's death will soon arrive, so how could he ever manage to see his wife!"

The *Changes* say: "The duke uses this opportunity to shoot at a hawk located atop a high wall, so he gets it, and nothing fails to be fitting."[29] The Master said: "The hawk is the quarry, the bows and arrows are the instruments, and he who does the shooting is a man. The noble man lays up a store of instruments in his own person and waits for the proper moment and then acts, so how could there ever be anything to his disadvantage! Here one acts without impediment; it is due to this that when one goes out, he obtains his catch. What this means is that one should act only after having first developed his instruments." {The *gua* [in "one acts without *gua* (impediment)] means "being tied up." The noble man waits for the right moment and only then acts. Thus he never has any trouble with impediments.}

The Master said: "The petty man is not ashamed of being unkind, nor is he afraid of being unjust. If he does not see an advantage in something, he does not act, and, if he is not threatened by force, he is not chastised. For small matters one chastises him, so that for great matters he takes warning. This is how the petty man prospers. The *Changes* say: 'Made to wear whole foot shackles, his toes are destroyed, but he will be without blame.'[30] This is what is meant here."

As for goodness, if one does not accumulate it, there will not be enough of it to make a name for oneself, and, as for evil, if one does not accumulate it, there will not be enough of it to destroy one's life. The petty man takes small goodness to be of no advantage and so does not do it, and he takes small evil to be of no harm, so he does not forsake it. This is why evil accumulates to the point where one can no longer keep it hidden and crimes become so great that one can no longer be exonerated. The *Changes* say: "Made to bear a cangue, his ears are destroyed, and this means misfortune."[31]

The Master said: "To get into danger is a matter of thinking one's position secure; to become ruined is a matter of thinking one's continuance protected; to fall into disorder is a matter of thinking one's order enduring. Therefore the noble man when secure does not forget danger, when enjoying continuance does not forget ruin, when maintaining order does not forget disorder. This is the way his person is kept secure and his state remains protected. The *Changes* say: 'This might be lost, this might be lost, so tie it to a healthy, flourishing mulberry.' "[32]

The Master said: "If one's virtue be meager but position noble, or knowledge little but plans grandiose, or powers few but responsibilities heavy, then it is rare indeed that such a one will not be outstripped. The *Changes* say: 'The Caldron breaks its legs and overturns all its pottage, so its form is drenched, which means misfortune.'[33] This speaks of someone who is unequal to his responsibilities."

The Master said: "To understand incipience [*ji*], is this not a matter of the numinous! The noble man is not fawning toward what is above and is not contemptuous of what is below. Is this not to understand incipience! {What is above [prior to] physical form is equivalent to the Dao, and what is below [subsequent to] physical form is equivalent to concrete objects [the phenomenal world].[34] If one is not in silent, passive communion with the Dao but instead consciously makes demands upon it, he will never be free of fawning. If one does not detach himself from the material world but instead maintains close relations with it, he will never avoid contempt. One who is touched by neither fawning nor contempt, is this not one who has plumbed principle to its depths![35]} As for incipience itself, it is the infinitesimally small beginning of action, the point at which the precognition of good fortune can occur. {*Incipience* is the point at which something leaves nonbeing and enters being. As it is still in the realm of principle, it lacks any phenomenal aspect, so one cannot pin it down by name, cannot perceive it by shape. It is the numinous alone that, not hurrying in the least but with all possible speed, allows perfect access to it [incipience] by just responding. Thus it is so bright and lucid that it can cast a mysterious light that finds a mirror in the prephenomenal. 'A tree as large as a man's embrace begins with the tiniest of shoots,'[36] so the manifestation of good fortune and misfortune begins with the most subtle of mantic signs. Thus they are the vehicles for the precognition of good fortune.} The noble man acts upon something as soon as he becomes aware of its incipience and does not wait for the day to run its course. The *Changes* say: 'Harder than rock, he does not let the day run its course. Constancy means good fortune.'[37]

As hard as rock in the face of it,
Why would he ever need to let the day run its course,
For he can perceive the way things will break.

{Since he determines how things will be right at their start, he does not have to wait for the day to run its course.}

The noble man grasps the infinitesimally small and what is manifestly obvious.
He understands the soft as well as the hard.
So the myriad folk look to him."

{This is an example of "to understand incipience, is this not a matter of the numinous!"}

The Master said: "The scion of the Yan clan [Yan Hui] is just about perfect![38] Whenever he had a misdeed, he never failed to realize it, and, realizing it, never committed it again." {When it was still in the realm of principle, it remained dark and hidden from him, but when it took shape, he realized what it was. Master Yan's capacity was such that he failed when it came to incipiency. This is why he had misdeeds. However, he was successful when it came to handling things the second time around. This is a matter of returning after not having gone far, so once he understood, he never committed them again.} The *Changes* say: 'This one returns before having gone far, so there will be no regret here, which means fundamental good fortune.'[39] {The terms *Good fortune* and *misfortune* relate to images of success and failure. The fact that one obtains the first line [of *Fu* (Return), Hexagram 24] here indicates that, in regard to principle, the situation is not fully developed and has not yet reached its mature form, and this is why one obtains the "this one returns before having gone far." The good fortune that comes of shunning misfortune allows one to avoid "regret here" and finally obtain "fundamental good fortune." *Zhi* ["here"; literally, "god of the earth," i.e., "great"] means "great."[40]}

"Heaven and Earth mesh together, and the myriad things develop and reach perfect maturity; male and female blend essences together, and the myriad creatures are formed and come to life. The *Changes* say: 'If three people travel together, one person will be lost, but when one person travels, he will find his companion.'[41] This refers to the achievement of perfect unity." {Only after perfect unity has been achieved will transformation fulfill itself.}

The Master said: "The noble man acts only after he has made his person secure, speaks only after he has calmed his heart and mind, makes requests only after making his relationships firm. The noble man cultivates these three matters and so succeeds completely. If one acts from a position of precariousness, the people will not join in; if one speaks out of anxiety, the people will not respond; if one has not established relationships and yet makes requests, then the people will not join with him. Since no one will join in with him, those who would harm him will surely draw near. The *Changes* say: 'This one brings Increase to no one, so there are those who strike at him. There is no consistency in the way he sets his heart and mind, so he shall have misfortune.' "[42] {If one empties oneself of self and preserves his sincerity, this will succeed in keeping the common folk free of defiance, but if one vexes them with his demands, this will succeed in making them uncompliant.}

6. The Master said: "*Qian* and *Kun*, do they not constitute the two-leaved gate into the *Changes*? *Qian* is a purely yang thing, and *Kun* is a purely yin thing. The hard and the soft exist as hexagrams only after yin and yang have combined their virtues, for it is in this way that the numbers of Heaven and Earth become embodied in them {*Zhuan* [enumeration or calculation] here means "numbers."[43]} and so perfectly realize their numinous, bright virtues. The names for them may be heterogeneous, but they stay in bounds. {As they cover all the way that change operates, their names have to be heterogeneous, but each one takes its place in order and does not transgress upon the scope of another, and this is even more true for the phrases that follow the hexagram lines.} However, in examining the categories involved, do we not find ideas associated with an age in decline?"[44] {It was only after they became concerned about calamities that the sages made the *Changes*. With an age in decline, failure and success become all the more obvious, and it was by means of the phrases that follow the hexagram lines that they [the sages] clarified failure and success. Could this be the reason why we understand that they [the *Changes*] imply an age in decline? *Ji* [examine] means something similar to *kao* [ponder, consider].}

The *Changes* make evident both that which has already happened and scrutinizes what is yet to come, thus subtlety comes to light, revealing what is hidden. {For the *Changes*, nothing of the past remains unexposed, and nothing of the future escapes scrutiny. It is through the *Changes* that subtlety comes to light and the hidden becomes exposed. *Chan* [expose, reveal] here means "bring to light."} The hexagrams are elucidated in such a way that they suit their names. These elucidations, in their differentiation of things and rectification of language, form decisive phrases. Thus they are perfect and complete. {The way the elucidations interpret the lines and the hexagrams allows each hexagram to suit its name. They differentiate and clarify things in terms of principle and category; this is why they are called "decisive phrases."} The way they [the hexagrams] are named involves insignificant things, but the analogies so derived concern matters of great importance. {They rely on the images to bring the concepts to light and use the insignificant to serve as metaphors for the great.} The meanings are far-reaching, and the phrasing elegant. The language twists and turns but hits the mark. {Change and transformation lack any consistency, so no definite paradigms can be made for them. This is why the text says: "The language twists and turns but hits the mark."} The things and events dealt with are obviously set forth, but hidden implications are involved. {Things and events are obvious, but the principles involved are subtle.} One uses the concept of the two to assist the common folk in the way they behave and to clarify the retribution and reward involved with failure and success.[45] {*The two* refers to failure and success. It is by using the concepts of failure and success that one may comprehensively assist the common folk in the way they behave. Thus it "clarifies the retribution and reward involved with failure and success." The way that this retribution and reward works is that when one is able to seize the right moment for something, he will enjoy good fortune, but if he goes against the principle involved, he will suffer misfortune.}

7. The rise of the *Changes*, was it not in middle antiquity?[46] Did not the makers of the *Changes* become concerned about calamities? {If they had not become concerned about calamities, then it would have been sufficient for them to deal with things through nonpurposeful action.} Thus, *Lü* [Treading, Hexagram 10] is the foundation of virtue. {A foundation is where one plants one's feet.} *Qian* [Modesty, Hexagram 15] is how virtue provides a handle to things. *Fu* [Return, Hexagram 24] is the root of virtue. {Action originates in repose, and speech begins from silence. *Return* signifies the beginning to which each thing reverts. Thus it is virtue in its aspect of root or origin.} *Heng* [Perseverance, Hexagram 32] provides virtue with steadfastness. {*Steadfastness* means "not to waver."} *Sun* [Diminution, Hexagram 41] is how virtue is cultivated. *Yi* [Increase, Hexagram 42] is how virtue

proliferates. {One who is able to bring increase to things is someone whose virtue is broad and great.} *Kun* [Impasse, Hexagram 47] is the criterion for distinguishing virtue. {The more impasse is encountered, the more virtue is apparent.} *Jing* [The Well, Hexagram 48] is the ground from which virtue springs. {Where a well is located does not change, so it is an image for being able to abide in one's proper place.} *Sun* [Compliance, Hexagram 57] is the controller of virtue. {Compliance is the way to issue commands and to clarify controls.}

Lü [Treading, Hexagram 10] demonstrates how by practicing harmony one reaches goals. {To practice harmony yet fail to reach the goal is a matter of just following where things lead one, but *Lü* means to practice harmony and yet manage to reach the goal. Thus it constitutes a way upon which one may tread.} "Modesty provides nobility and so allows one's radiance to shine."[47] *Fu* [Return] demonstrates how distinctions among things should be made while they are still small. {If one makes distinctions while things are still at the subtle stage, one will return "after not having gone far."[48]} *Heng* [Perseverance, Hexagram 32] demonstrates how, faced with the complexity of things, one yet does not give way to cynicism. {"Faced with the complexity of things, one yet does not give way to cynicism": this is how one is able to practice perseverance.} *Sun* [Diminution, Hexagram 41] demonstrates how things can first be difficult and easy later. {One leads a frugal existence in order to cultivate the self. Thus at first things are difficult. However, it is due to having cultivated the self that one stays free of calamities. Thus things are easy later.} *Yi* [Increase, Hexagram 42] demonstrates how one brings about growth and opulence while avoiding any contrivance to do so. {This involves procedures that are promoted to bring increase to things. This is why the text says "one brings about growth and opulence." One promotes what has to be done in accordance with things themselves and avoids any artificial contrivance.} *Kun* [Impasse, Hexagram 47] demonstrates how one who suffers tribulation still stays in complete control of himself. {One may find himself in poverty and misery but does not compromise his commitment to the Dao.} *Jing* [The Well, Hexagram 48] demonstrates how one stays in one's place and yet can transfer what one has to others. {One can change the location of a fief or district but not the location of a well. Although where a well is located does not change, yet it can transfer its benefactions elsewhere.} *Sun* [Compliance, Hexagram 57] demonstrates how one can weigh things while yet remaining in obscurity. {One weighs and promulgates orders and commands, yet the common folk do not know where they come from.}

Lü [Treading, Hexagram 10] provides the means to make one's actions harmonious. *Qian* [Modesty, Hexagram 15] provides the means by which decorum exercises its control. *Fu* [Return, Hexagram 24] provides the means to know oneself. {This means to seek for it [the cause of failure or success][49] within oneself.} *Heng* [Perseverance, Hexagram 32] provides the means to keep one's virtue one. {This means to keep virtue whole and intact.} *Sun* [Diminution, Hexagram 41] provides the means to keep harm at a distance. {As this does not go beyond the cultivation of one's own person, one can use it to do nothing more than keep harm at a distance.} *Yi* [Increase, Hexagram 42] provides the means to promote benefits. *Kun* [Impasse, Hexagram 47] provides the means to keep resentments few. {One may have encountered impasse but is not swept away by it, neither does he hold resentment against things.} *Jing* [The Well, Hexagram 48] provides the means to distinguish what righteousness really is. {Do good to others but have no selfish motives. This is the way righteousness works.} *Sun* [Compliance, Hexagram 57] provides the means to practice improvisations. {*To improvise* means "to violate accepted ways of doing things and yet stay in harmony with the Dao." One can only practice improvisation by staying in accord with the principle of compliance.}

8. As a book, the *Changes* is something that cannot be kept at a distance. {One should act only after he has drawn comparisons and discussed what is involved, so the *Changes* cannot be kept at a distance.[50]} As a manifestation of the Dao the *Changes* involves frequent shifts. Change and action never stand still but keep flowing all through the six vacancies. {"The six vacancies" are the six line positions.} Rising and falling without any consistency, the hard and the soft lines change one into the other, something for which it is impossible to make definitive laws, {That is, one cannot establish constant rules for it.} since they are doing nothing but keeping pace with change. {In dealing with change and action, the important thing is to keep in step with the moment, for whether one advances or remains still depends on how things come together.}

One uses the *Changes* as the standard to determine whether one should go forth or withdraw. The hexagrams make one feel caution about being abroad or staying in.[51] {This clarifies the standards for going forth and withdrawing so that one can understand the admonitions connected with being abroad and staying in. "Going forth" and "withdrawing" are like "acting" and "retiring." "Being abroad" and "staying in" are like "becoming prominent" and "going into seclusion." In *Dun* [Withdrawal, Hexagram 33], "a time when one distances himself from events" is taken to mean "good fortune." In *Feng* [Abundance, Hexagram 55], "secluded withdrawal" is taken to mean the "utmost misfortune." In *Jian* [Gradual Advance, Hexagram 53] "lofty prominence" is taken to mean "a fine thing." In *Mingyi* [Suppression of the Light, Hexagram 36] "living in obscurity" is taken to mean "it is advantageous to persevere." These are examples of admonitions connected with being abroad and staying in.} They also cast light on calamities as well as the incidents that underlie them. *Incidents* here means "the causes or reasons involved." Let them [the hexagrams] be there not as a teacher or guardian but rather as if it were one's parents who had drawn near! {"The noble man when secure does not forget danger, when enjoying continuance does not forget ruin,"[52] and "makes earnest efforts throughout the day,"[53] thus one cannot afford to become slack.} At first one follows their phrases and then appraises their prescriptions. After that one will find that the hexagrams do contain a constant law. {If one is able to follow their phrases and so get the measure of their concepts, if one is able to appreciate how they trace beginnings and sum up endings, then one will understand that "they are doing nothing but keeping pace with change" and that this is their "constant law." One who understands how change operates will retain its essentials. This is why the text says: "But if one is not such a person, the Dao will not operate in vain."} But if one is not such a person, the Dao will not operate in vain.

9. As a book, the *Changes* takes the plumbing of beginnings and the summing up of endings as its material. {*Material* here means "embodiment" [of change, i.e., the hexagrams]. A hexagram unites a concept as it progresses from its beginning to its end point.} The way the six lines mix in together is due to the fact that they are nothing other than momentary things. {Each line depends on the moment. *Things* here means "events."} The first lines are difficult to understand, but the top lines are easy, for these are the

roots and branches [i.e., causes and effects, origins and endings]. The phrases attached to the first lines draw comparisons with things, about which the ending ones formulate conclusions. {Events begin in subtlety and later develop into the obvious. First lines, as the beginnings of calculations, draw comparisons and discuss the first stages involved. Thus they are difficult to understand. Top lines are the endings of hexagrams, where the events involved have all matured and become obvious. Thus they are easy to understand.} As for complicated matters, the calculation[54] of the virtues and the determination of the rights and wrongs involved could not be complete without the middle lines. Ah! If one actually were to sum up the chances for survival or destruction and good fortune or bad in this way, he could, even without stirring, understand what they will be! One who has such understanding has but to look at the hexagram Judgments to have his thought cover more than half of what is involved! {The Judgments focus on the unifying principles that establish the images and discuss the concepts connected with the middle lines. It is by means of their tight grip that they preserve wide-ranging meanings, and it is by means of their simplicity that they bring together all the different aspects of things. When one calculates the virtues of complicated matters, it is by means of the One that one can string them together [i.e., discern the unity in them]. Things of the phenomenal world have for their progenitor the Dao, and what all such things revert back to is the One. The more complicated things are, the more prone one is to become bogged down in concrete objects [the phenomenal world], but the tighter the grip that one has on the principles involved, the closer one will shift toward the Dao. In the way they deal with concepts, the Judgments depend on the One, and in the way it functions, the One is identical to the Dao. It is in what is prior to physical form that one can discern the Dao, so is it not indeed appropriate that the Judgments provide one with more than a fifty percent advantage!}

The second and the fourth lines involve the same kind of merit {Their yin merit is identical.} but differ as to position, {There is the difference between inner and outer trigrams.} so the respective good of each is not the same. Second lines usually concern honor, {Second lines occupy positions of harmony and centrality. Thus for the most part they involve honor.} while fourth lines usually concern fear, this because they are near [fifth lines]. {Their positions are immediately next to the rulers of the hexagrams [the fifth lines].} Thus for the most part they involve fear. In terms of its Dao, the soft or yielding does not find it beneficial to be distant. Its main tenet is to remain "without blame," and its function is to be soft or yielding and be centrally placed. {That fourth lines often involve fear is because they are near to the rulers. In terms of its Dao, the soft or yielding has to provide aid and assistance. Thus there is no benefit for it to be distant. Second lines are able to be "without blame" by being soft or yielding and being centrally placed.}

The third and the fifth lines involve the same kind of merit {Their yang merit is identical.} but differ as to position. {There is the difference between nobility and servility.} Third lines usually concern misfortune, while fifth lines usually concern achievement, this because of the different levels involved, the one lofty and noble and the other lowly and servile. To be soft and yielding here surely involves danger, whereas to be strong and hard surely means success. {The third and the fifth being yang positions are not for the soft and yielding [yin lines], so if they locate themselves there, it will mean danger. But if instead these positions are occupied by the hard and strong [yang lines], they will be up to the responsibilities inherent in them. What imbues the hard and the strong with nobility is the way they ward off depravity and preserve sincerity, how they act in such a way that they never violate their moral integrity. What imbues the soft and yielding with nobility is the way they embrace things widely and sustain a position of centrality, how they submit to others in such a way that they never lose their perseverance. If one uses his hardness and strength to engage in criminality, this is not the true Dao of the hard and the strong. If one uses his softness and submissiveness to engage in ignoble servility, this is not the true Dao of the soft and the yielding.}

10. As a book, the *Changes* is something which is broad and great, complete in every way. There is the Dao of Heaven in it, the Dao of Man in it, and the Dao of Earth in it. It brings these three powers together and then doubles them. This is the reason for there being six lines. What these six embody are nothing other than the Dao of the three powers. {What Explaining the Trigrams [*Shuo gua*] has to say about this is indeed complete!}

Since the Dao consists of change and action, we refer to it in terms of the "moving lines" [*yao*]. Since the moving lines consist of different classes, we refer to them as "things." {Classes mean categories. *Qian* [Pure Yang, Hexagram 1] is a yang thing. *Kun* [Pure Yin, Hexagram 2] is a yin thing. The moving lines belong to either the yin or the yang category; it is in consequence of this that they acquire hard or soft functions. This is why the text says: "Since the moving lines consist of different classes, we refer to them as 'things.' "} Since these things mix in together, we refer to these as "patterns." {The hard and the soft intermingle just as black [the color of Heaven] and yellow [the color of Earth] form combinations.} When these patterns involve discrepancies, fortune is at issue there.[55]

11. The rise of the *Changes*, was it not just at the end of the Yin [Shang] era when the virtue of the Zhou had begun to flourish, just at the time when the incident between King Wen and King Zhou was taking place?[56] {It was due to King Wen's flourishing virtue that he suffered such hardship and distress and yet was able to make the Dao prevail. Thus the text here praises the virtue of King Wen in order to clarify the Dao of change.} This is why King Wen's phrases [i.e., the Judgments] are concerned with danger. {It was King Wen's experience with King Zhou that imbued his Judgments with danger.} Being conscious of danger allows one to find peace and security, but to be easy brings about downfall. {*Easy* here means "easygoing, careless."} The Dao involved here is so very great that its sustenance of everything never fails. It instills a sense of fearful caution about things from beginning to end, and its essential purpose is to permit people to be "without blame." This is what the Dao of the *Changes* means. {When patterns involve discrepancies, fortune becomes at issue there. Consequently, one who would have his continuance preserved shall perish, but one who remains mindful of the possibility of perishing shall survive, and one who would maintain his control over things shall end in chaos, but one who remains mindful of danger shall find security. By having "a sense of fearful caution about things from beginning to end," one is always brought back to where he is "without blame." The dynamics that give rise to security and danger are embodied in the sum and substance of the lines and images.}

12. *Qian* is the strongest thing in the entire world, so it should always be easy to put its virtue into practice. Thus one knows whether or not there is going to be danger. *Kun* is the most compliant thing in the entire world, so it should always be simple to

put its virtue into practice. Thus one knows whether or not there are going to be obstacles.[57] The one is able to delight hearts and minds, and the other is able to refine the concerns of the feudal lords.[58] {Feudal lords are proprietary masters who exercise power. This means: "The one is able to delight the hearts and minds of the myriad folk, and the other is able to refine the sense of responsibility of those in power."} The Dao of change is what determines all the good fortune and misfortune that take place in the world; it is that which allows the world to realize all its unceasing and untiring efforts. Therefore, as speech and deed are subject to change and transformation, auspicious endeavors result in blessings, matters rendered into images provide understanding of concrete things, and the practice of divination allows one to know the future. {The fact that speech and deed are subject to change and transformation means that if one engages in auspicious activities, he will reap a reward of blessings; if he observes the way matters are rendered into images, he will know the methods of constructing concrete objects; and if he savors the practice of divination, he will witness experiences that are about to happen in the future.}

Heaven and Earth established the positions of things, and the sages fully realized the potential inherent in them. {The sages availed themselves of the rightness of Heaven and Earth and so had each of the myriad things realize its potentiality.} Whether consulting with men or consulting with spirits, they allowed the ordinary folk to share in these resources. {"Consulting with men" is equivalent to discussing things with the mass of people in order to determine the chances for failure and success. "Consulting with spirits" is equivalent to resorting to divination in order to examine the possibilities for good fortune and misfortune. Without enslaving their capacity for thought and deliberation, failure and success thus came to light by themselves, and, without belaboring their capacity for study and examination, good fortune and misfortune made themselves known. They [the sages] categorized the innate tendencies of the myriad things and thoroughly explored the reasons that underlie the most obscure and most profound of things. This is why, as the ordinary folk were allowed to share in these resources, they "delighted in being their [the sages'] advocates and never tired of doing so."[59]} The eight trigrams make their pronouncements in terms of images, {That is, they express themselves to us by means of their images.} and the line texts and Judgments address themselves to us in terms of the innate tendencies of things. {The phrases[60] used involve either danger or ease, and in each case they get at the true innate tendency involved.} The hard and soft lines intermingle and take up positions, thus allowing good fortune and bad to be seen.

Change and action speak to us in terms of the expression "advantageous." {When change occurs, be thoroughly commensurate with it, for this will exhaust the advantage in it.} Good fortune and misfortune shift from one to the other in accordance with the innate tendencies involved. {There is nothing fixed about good fortune and misfortune, as they are only the results of how men act. If the tendency is to stay in accord with principle, this will result in a disposal toward good fortune, but if the tendency is to go against the Dao, this will result in a fall into misfortune. This is why the text says: "Good fortune and misfortune shift from one to the other in accordance with the innate tendencies involved."} Therefore, it is when the covetous and the hateful make their attacks that good fortune and misfortune are produced. {If things go along smoothly together without any differentiation, what good fortune or misfortune could possibly occur? "It is only after the covetous and the hateful make their attacks" that discord and accord differentiate from each other, and this is why the text says: "Good fortune and misfortune are produced."} It is when the distant and the contiguous try to seize each other that regret and remorse are produced. {"Seize each other" is like saying "make each the possession of the other." Only after lines that are distant and lines that are contiguous try to seize and possess each other do "regret" and "remorse" come into being.} It is when true innate tendencies and spurious countertendencies work their influence that advantage and harm are produced. {If things respond to true innate tendencies, "advantage" will obtain, but if things respond to spurious countertendencies, "harm" will prevail.} For all the tendencies inherent in change, whenever the contiguous do not serve each other's interests, this is termed "misfortune." {"The contiguous" is equivalent to "lines that form contiguous pairs." The tendencies inherent in change are such that when hard and soft lines stroke each other, it indicates a state in which change and action are in step, but "whenever the contiguous do not serve each other's interests," there is sure to be calamity brought about by conflicting interests. Cases where there is mutual opposition but no calamity mean that a harmonious response has been obtained after all. All occasions in which mutual accord exists but results in "misfortune" indicate an inherent untimeliness. If one examines all such occasions in terms of the matters that comprise them, what they mean will become readily apparent.} Even when something might have caused harm [but did not], this is still an occasion for remorse and regret. {If one does not set himself up in opposition to things and, as a consequence, manages perfectly to fulfill the Dao of compliance, how then could there ever be anything that might harm him? [If, however, one does not manage to do this,][61] even though he is able to extricate himself from such situations, he is sure to experience "remorse" and "regret." "Might have" expresses the idea that harm could potentially have happened.}

The words of someone who is about to revolt have a sense of shame about them; the words of someone who entertains doubts in his innermost mind tend to prevaricate; the words of a good person are few; the words of an impatient and impetuous person are many; the words of someone who tries to slander good people tend to vacillate; and the words of someone who has neglected his duty or lost his integrity tend to be devious.

NOTES

1. This and all subsequent text set off in this manner is commentary by Han Kangbo.

2. See section one of the Commentary on the Appended Phrases, Part One.

3. Cf. "The movement of the six hexagram lines embodies the Dao of the three ultimates," section two of the Commentary on the Appended Phrases, Part One.

4. *Laozi*, section 39, p. 106. *Constancy* (*zhen*) here is usually glossed as "correct" (*zheng*), or, more precisely, as "the provider of correctness," "the rectifier," i.e., the sovereign or true ruler.

5. Kong Yingda comments: "Here we have an explanation of what the term 'line' means. It says that the lines reproduce the change and actions that particular things undergo, and [for the images] . . . it says that they provide likenesses of the appearance and shape of particular things." See *Zhouyi zhengyi*, 8: 3b. It also may be possible to translate the text here as: "The lines reproduce the action of the one [*Qian*, Pure Yang, Heaven], and the images provide likenesses of shapes of the other [*Kun*, Pure Yin, Earth]," since change, action, and energy are associated with the former, and the nurturing, maturation, and shaping of things are aspects of the latter.

6. Bao Xi (or Fu Xi) is the mythological emperor of remote antiquity who, in addition to having invented the trigrams, is also supposed to have taught humans how to domesticate animals. See the Commentary on the Appended Phrases, Part One, note 53.

7. Hexagram 30, *Li* (Cohesion) ䷝, consists of trigram *Li* doubled and is supposed to resemble the pattern in the mesh of nets.

8. Shen Nong, literally "Divine Husbandman," is said to have taught humans agriculture.

9. Hexagram 42, *Yi* (Increase) ䷩, consists of trigrams *Zhen* (Quake) below and *Sun* (Compliance) above. The two top unbroken lines are supposed to represent the hands grasping the plow handle, the three middle broken lines the curve of the extended handle, and the one unbroken line at the bottom the plowshare itself. The top part penetrates the earth, and the bottom part moves through it.

10. Hexagram 21, *Shihe* (Bite Together) ䷔, consists of the trigrams *Zhen* (Quake) below, which here seems to signify the bustle of the marketplace), and *Li* (Cohesion), representing the sun, above.

11. "They allowed things to undergo the free flow of change" translates *tong qi bian*. However, perhaps *bian* here might also be translated as "develop": "They allowed these things [the implements invented by Bao Xi and Shen Nong] to develop to the full extent of their potentiality."

12. See Hexagram 14, *Dayou* (Great Holdings), Top Yang.

13. Kong Yingda is more specific: "Hitherto people clothed themselves in skins that were cut in a short and meager fashion. Now people wore garments woven from silk, hemp, and cotton cloth that were cut in a long and generous fashion. This is why the text says: 'Let their robes hang down.' . . . Clothing distinguishes the noble from the base. *Qian* and *Kun* refer to the fact that those above and those below are different in substance. This is why the text says: 'They probably got the idea for this from the hexagrams *Qian* and *Kun*.' " See *Zhouyi zhengyi*, 8: 6b. There are two implications here: (1) Yao and Shun, in contrast to an earlier primitive, coarse age, represent an age of culture and refinement, a noble age. (2) The truly noble can wear long robes, because they do not rush around in purposeful action, and it is this that distinguishes them from the mean and vulgar, who, in effect, have to "roll up their sleeves" to get things done. This second implication usually figures in later commentaries on this passage. Zhu Xi, for instance, says of it: "*Qian* and *Kun* undergo change and transformation, but they do not engage in purposeful action." See *Zhouyi zhezhong*, 15: 8b.

14. Hexagram 59, *Huan* (Dispersion) ䷺, consists of trigrams *Kan* (Sink Hole), representing water, below and *Sun* (Compliance), representing wood and wind, above.

15. Kong Yingda likens this to how "oars take advantage of water in order to bring about transport." See *Zhouyi zhengyi*, 8: 7a.

16. Hexagram 17, *Sui* (Following) ䷐, consists of trigrams *Zhen* (Quake), the initiator of movement, below and *Dui* (Joy) above. This arrangement

is supposed to convey the image of oxen and horses willingly submitting to human commands in front (above) to pull loads and passengers behind (below) and, by so submitting, pleasing those in command.

17. Hexagram 16, *Yu* (Contentment) ䷏, consists of trigrams *Kun* (Pure *Yin*), signifying the Earth and also "Closed Door," below and *Zhen* (Quake), signifying thunder, above. *Zhen* as thunder is supposed to suggest the sound of the watchman's clapper outside (above), and the "Closed Door" is supposed to suggest the secure household behind doubled doors inside (below).

18. The graphs for *Yu* (Contentment) and another character *yu* (beforehand) are often written for each other; this is the basis for Han's comment here.

19. Hexagram 62, *Xiaoguo* (Minor Superiority) ䷽, consists of trigrams *Gen* (Restraint), meaning "mountain," below and *Zhen* (Quake), "thunder," above. This suggests the movement of the pestle and the stillness of the mortar.

20. Hexagram 38, *Kui* (Contrariety) ䷥, consists of trigrams *Dui* (Joy) below and *Li* (Cohesion), "sun, fire," above. Fire is something that provokes fear (domination), and this provides the protection those below need to feel happy and secure.

21. Hexagram 34, *Dazhuang* (Great Strength) ䷡, consists of trigrams *Qian* (Pure Yang), "Heaven" and "the hard," below and *Zhen* (Quake), "thunder," "movement," above. Above wind and rain move, and below the hard (sturdy) house endures.

22. The *da* in *Dazhuang* means "great," and the *zhuang* means "strong." Han has simply taken the literal meaning of the two characters to explain how the sages got the idea of proper houses from the hexagram.

23. Hexagram 28, *Daguo* (Major Superiority) ䷛, consists of trigrams *Sun* (Compliance), "wood," below and *Dui* (Joy), "lake or marsh," above. The four unbroken lines in the middle and the top and bottom broken lines are supposed to suggest the hard (solid) coffins surrounded by soft (loose) earth.

24. Hexagram 43, *Kuai* (Resolution) ䷪, consists of trigrams *Qian* (Pure Yang), "Heaven," "the hard," below and *Dui* (Joy), "lake or marsh," above. It is because *Dui* supplies the phonetic element in *shui* (order)/*shuo* (speak) that it is associated with speech and communication—as well as with writing (*shu*). *Qian* suggests the hard and durable nature of a physical tally and the trust that it signifies.

25. The yang trigrams are *Zhen* ☳, *Kan* ☵, and *Gen* ☶; the yin trigrams are *Sun* ☴, *Li* ☲, and *Dui* ☱. Of course, *Qian*, which consists entirely of yang lines, and *Kun*, which consists entirely of yin lines, are not included in this consideration: *Qian* is a yang trigram, and *Kun* is a yin trigram.

26. Since a broken or yin line consists of two strokes and an unbroken line of one stroke, all the yang trigrams consist of five strokes, and five is an odd, yang number. All the yin trigrams consist of four strokes, and four is an even, yin number.

27. See Hexagram 31, *Xian* (Reciprocity), Fourth Yang.
28. See Hexagram 47, *Kun* (Impasse), Third Yin.
29. See Hexagram 40, *Xie* (Release), Top Yin.
30. See Hexagram 21, *Shihe* (Bite Together), First Yang.
31. See Hexagram 21, *Shihe* (Bite Together), Top Yang.
32. See Hexagram 12, *Pi* (Obstruction), Fifth Yang.
33. See Hexagram 50, *Ding* (The Caldron), Fourth Yang; see also notes 13 and 14 there for alternate interpretations of Fourth Yang.
34. This paraphrases section twelve of the Commentary on the Appended Phrases, Part One.
35. Kong Yingda's remarks on this passage simply expand upon Han's commentary and are in complete agreement with it. However, later commentators, notably Zhu Xi, do not interpret "the above" (*shang*) as equivalent to the Dao and "the below" (*xia*) as equivalent to the phenomenal world but, respectively, as "superiors" and "subordinates, inferiors": "In relations with one's superiors, it is best to be reverential and modest. However, if one is reverential, this is close to fawning. In relations with one's inferiors, it is best to be amiable and cordial. However, if one is amiable, this is close to contempt. As reverence and fawning, on the one hand, and amiability and contempt, on the other, are so close to each other, it only takes the slightest thing to have the one degenerate into the other." See *Zhouyi zhezhong*, 15: 21b. This slight difference is the *incipient* difference between them, and it takes the noble man to understand that difference, i.e., "to understand incipience."
36. *Laozi*, section 64, p. 166.
37. See Hexagram 16, *Yu* (Contentment), Second Yin. "Harder than rock" translates *jie yu shi*, which is how traditional commentators understand it, though *yu* (more than) is sometimes glossed as *ru* (like, as much as).
38. Yan Hui was the favorite disciple of Confucius; see *Lunyu* (Analects) 11:18.
39. See Hexagram 24, *Fu* (Return), First Yang.
40. This interpretation of *zhi* seems unlikely; see Hexagram 24, *Fu* (Return), note 8.
41. See Hexagram 41, *Sun* (Diminution), Third Yin.
42. See Hexagram 42, *Yi* (Increase), Top Yang.
43. Zhu Xi glosses *zhuan* as *shi* (phenomena). See *Zhouyi zhezhong*, 15: 24a. Kong Yingda, like Han Kangbo, also glosses *zhuan* as "numbers." See *Zhouyi zhengyi*, 8: 15b. Both Han and Kong probably base this interpretation on a passage in the first section of Wang Bi's General Remarks, in which the *zhuan* seems to mean "calculate," and on a later passage in section nine of this part of the Commentary on the Appended Phrases (see also note 54 below).
44. The *Changes*, composed apparently during the decline of the Shang and the rise of the Zhou, supposedly reflects—in its many pronouncements on avoiding disaster and finding good fortune—an age beset by insecurity and danger.

45. Zhu Xi regards this passage as corrupt and impossible to explicate completely. To make sense of it he glosses, *er* (two) as "doubt" or "the doubtful" (i.e., when one is of "two minds" about something). This is apparently where Wilhelm's "this is why in doubtful cases they may serve to guide the conduct of men" comes from. See *The I Ching*, p. 345.

46. I.e., the end of the Shang era.

47. See Hexagram 15, *Qian* (Modesty), Commentary on the Judgments.

48. See note 39 above.

49. Following Kong Yingda. See *Zhouyi zhengyi*, 8: 18b.

50. Quoted in section eight of the Commentary on the Appended Phrases, Part One.

51. Another tradition of exegesis suggests that the passage means something quite different: "The coming and going of change happen according to standards. The outer and inner trigrams make one feel caution." See *Zhouyi zhezhong*, 15: 35a.

52. See section five earlier.

53. See Hexagram 1, *Qian* (Pure Yang), Third Yang.

54. "Calculation" (or, in its verbal form, "calculate") translates *zhuan*. This follows both Zhu Xi's gloss of it as *ticha* (understand, reckon, estimate) (see *Zhouyi zhezhong*, 15: 34b) and Wang Bi's understanding of it as "number" or "calculation"/"to calculate." See the first section of his General Remarks, as well as note 2 there. Han Kangbo and Kong Yingda, apparently following Wang, also interpret *zhuan* in this way in their comments on an earlier passage here in Part Two of the Commentary on the Appended Phrases. See note 43 above.

55. Kong Yingda's subcommentary warrants notice here: "If the lines take up their places together and intermingle to form patterns in such a way that they do no harm to or do not interfere with each other, then fortune is not at issue there. If, however, as the result of pattern discrepancies, the lines take up their places together in such a way that they do not accord with the principles involved, then fortune does become at issue there." See *Zhouyi zhengyi*, 8: 22b. "Discrepancies" as such refer to the misplacement of lines: a yin line in a yang position, a yang line in a yin position, and so forth.

56. It was during the captivity of King Wen, founder of the Zhou, by the last Shang tyrant that he is said to have added the Judgments to the hexagrams.

57. The translation here follows the commentary of Kong Yingda: "The practice of the virtue of *Qian* should always be easy and simple, otherwise there is trouble, and this is how one knows the point at which danger occurs. If it is no longer easy and simple, this means danger. Thus it is by the ease with which it is practiced that one knows whether or not danger exists. The practice of the virtue of *Kun* should always be simple and calm, otherwise there is confusion. This is how one knows the point at which obstacles occur. If it is no longer simple, this means obstacles. Thus it is by the sim-

plicity with which it is practiced that one knows whether or not obstacles exist." See *Zhouyi zhengyi*, 8: 23b.

58. Zhu Xi radically changes the meaning of this passage by removing the two characters *hou zhi*, which he regards as later additions and not part of the original text. This changes the expression *zhuhou zhi lü* (the concerns of the feudal lords) to *zhulü* (the concerns of all). See *Zhouyi zhezhong*, 15: 41a.

59. *Laozi*, section 66, p. 170.

60. The text as given in Lou, *Wang Bi ji jiaoshi*, 2: 574, has *qing* (innate tendency) instead of *ci* (phrases); this is an error. See Kong, *Zhouyi zhengyi*, 8: 24a.

61. Kong Yingda's subcommentary indicates that this interpolation is necessary. See *Zhouyi zhengyi*, 8: 25a.

Providing the Sequence of the Hexagrams [Xugua]

Part One

1. Only after there were Heaven [*Qian*, Pure Yang, Hexagram 1] and Earth [*Kun*, Pure Yin, Hexagram 2] were the myriad things produced from them. What fills Heaven and Earth is nothing other than the myriad things. This is why *Qian* and *Kun* are followed by *Zhun* [Birth Throes, Hexagram 3]. *Zhun* here signifies repletion.

2. *Zhun* is when things are first born. {*Zhun* signifies when "the hard and the soft begin to interact,"[1] thus it is "when things are first born."[2]} When things begin life, they are sure to be covered [the literal meaning of *meng*—i.e., encapsulated in membranes, eggs, or seeds]. This is why *Zhun* is followed by *Meng* [Juvenile Ignorance, Hexagram 4]. *Meng* here indicates juvenile ignorance, that is, the immature state of things. When things are in their immature state, one cannot fail to nourish them. This is why *Meng* is followed by *Xu* [Waiting, Hexagram 5]. *Xu* here indicates the dao[3] of food and drink [i.e., nourishment taken while waiting]. Food and drink necessarily involve *Song* [Contention, Hexagram 6]. This is why *Xu* is followed by *Song*. {As soon as things have life, they are provided with a proprietary instinct. It is in consequence of their having this proprietary instinct that strife arises.}

3. When there is contention, there is sure to be an arising of the masses. This is why *Song* is followed by *Shi* [The Army, Hexagram 7]. An army as such is a mass of people. A mass of people necessarily involves closeness. This is why *Shi* is followed by *Bi* [Closeness, Hexagram 8]. {If the masses arise but do not

close ranks, there will be no reason for strife to cease. People have to feel friendly and close to each other before they can achieve peace.} Closeness as such means "a bringing together." Bringing together has to involve domestication. This is why *Bi* is followed by *Xiaoxu* [Lesser Domestication, Hexagram 9]. {*Bi* does not belong to the Dao of the great thoroughfare.[4] Thus it only involves what individuals have domesticated in order to take care of themselves. As this is domestication that derives from mere closeness, it is called "Lesser Domestication," something that cannot happen on a grand scale.} Only after things have been domesticated can there be propriety. This is why *Xiaoxu* is followed by *Lü* [Treading, Hexagram 10]. {*Treading* here means "propriety." Propriety is the means by which one uses things in a suitable way. Thus, once things are domesticated, they are then ready for use, and, when they are put to use, this must be done with propriety.[5]} It is by this treading that *Tai* [Peace, Hexagram 11] occurs. Only then will there be security. This is why *Lü* is followed by *Tai*.

4. *Tai* [Peace] means "smooth going." Things cannot forever go smoothly. This is why *Tai* is followed by *Pi* [Obstruction, Hexagram 12]. Things cannot forever be obstructed. This is why *Pi* is followed by *Tongren* [Fellowship, Hexagram 13]. {When obstruction occurs, people think about interaction or cooperation [*tong*], and everyone begins to share the same goal. Thus they go forth bonded in fellowship, brought together without conscious deliberation.} When one shares fellowship with others, things are sure to yield themselves to him. This is why *Tongren* is followed by *Dayou* [Great Holdings, Hexagram 14]. When one's holdings are great, he must not let himself become satiated. This is why *Dayou* is followed by *Qian* [Modesty, Hexagram 15]. To have great holdings and yet be capable of modesty means that one must be content. This is why *Qian* is followed by *Yu* [Contentment, Hexagram 16].

5. When there is contentment, there will be a following. {One whose actions are based on compliance [with the natural order of things][6] is someone whom the masses will follow.} This is why *Yu* is followed by *Sui* [Following, Hexagram 17]. One who gets people to follow him by making them happy inevitably will have problems. This is why *Sui* is followed by *Gu* [Ills to Be Cured, Hexagram 18]. *Gu* here means "problems." Only when one has had problems can he grow great. {Enterprises that allow one to

achieve greatness originate from such problems.} This is why *Gu* is followed by *Lin* [Overseeing, Hexagram 19]. *Lin* here means "to become great."[7]

6. Only after a thing becomes great can it be viewed. This is why *Lin* is followed by *Guan* [Viewing, Hexagram 20]. Only after something can be viewed is there the possibility to come together with it. This is why *Guan* is followed by *Shihe* [Bite Together, Hexagram 21]. {When it is viewed, a thing becomes differentiated, and this is just the moment to come together with it.} The *he* [in *Shihe*] means *he* [unite, i.e., join the jaws together]. But things may not be just recklessly united and left at that! This is why *Shihe* is followed by *Bi* [Elegance, Hexagram 22]. *Bi* here means "adornment." {When things are brought together, one must adorn them in order to groom their external appearances.} Adornment will become pervasive only after it has been pushed to the limit, but at that it will become exhausted. {When adornment has reached its ultimate limit, the real substance of a thing perishes.} This is why *Bi* is followed by *Bo* [Peeling, Hexagram 23]. *Bo* here means "peel off."

7. Just as things cannot remain exhausted forever, so with *Bo* [Peeling]: when they reach all the way to the top, they then return to the bottom.[8] This is why *Bo* is followed by *Fu* [Return, Hexagram 24]. With such a return, there is freedom from errancy. This is why *Fu* is followed by *Wuwang* [No Errancy, Hexagram 25]. Only when there is no errancy can there be domestication. This is why *Wuwang* is followed by *Daxu* [Great Domestication, Hexagram 26].

8. Only after things have been domesticated can nourishment be had. This is why *Daxu* is followed by *Yi* [Nourishment, Hexagram 27]. *Yi* here means "*yang*" [to nourish]. If there is no nourishment, there can be no action. This is why *Yi* is followed by *Daguo* [Major Superiority, Hexagram 28]. {If nourishment does not occur, one will be incapable of action, but if nourishment reaches superior proportions, one will be amply prepared for it.} One cannot stay forever in a state of superiority. This is why *Daguo* is followed by [Xi]*Kan* [(Constant) Sink Hole, Hexagram 29]. *Kan* here indicates a pit. {One whose superiority knows no limits will encounter a pitfall.} Once so entrapped, there is sure to be something to catch hold of. This is why *Kan* is followed by *Li* [Cohesion, Hexagram 30]. *Li* here means "*li*" [clinging].

{When something reaches its ultimate point, it undergoes change, so when such entrapment reaches its limit, it is converted into something to which one can cling.}

Part Two

1. Only after there were Heaven and Earth were there the myriad things. Only after there were the myriad things were there male and female. Only after there were male and female were there husband and wife. Only after there were husband and wife were there father and child. Only after there were father and child were there sovereign and minister. Only after there were sovereign and minister were there superiors and subordinates. Only after there were superiors and subordinates did propriety and righteousness have a medium in which to operate. {This addresses the concept underlying *Xian* [Reciprocity, Hexagram 31]. In general, what Providing the Sequence of the Hexagrams brings to light does not extend to the arcane source of the *Changes*, for it merely follows the sequence of the hexagrams and relies on the sequence to clarify what the hexagrams mean. *Xian* [Reciprocity ䷞] consists of a soft trigram above and a hard trigram below. "The two kinds of material force [*qi*] stimulate and respond and so join together."[9] Of all the images of husband and wife, none is more beautiful than this! Nothing in the Dao of human relationships is greater than the relationship between husband and wife. It is due to it that we have the earnestness and civility between father and son [and in the other relationships]. As this profoundly states the concept underlying *Xian*, it elevates the relationship between husband and wife to progenitor of all human relationships, and so one does not attach these remarks to *Li* [Cohesion]. Earlier Confucians regarded the text from *Qian* [Pure Yang, Hexagram 1] to *Li* [Cohesion, Hexagram 30] as the first half of the *Classic of Changes* and to be concerned with the Dao of Heaven and that from *Xian* [Reciprocity, Hexagram 31] to *Weiji* [Ferrying Incomplete, Hexagram 64] as the second half and to be concerned with the Dao of Mankind. In the *Changes*, the six lines form the hexagrams in such a way that the three powers [Heaven, Earth, and Man] all have to be complete in them. These replicate change and transformation by intricately weaving Heaven and Man together,[10] so how could it be possible to shunt apart the Dao of Heaven and the affairs of mankind to a first and a second half of the

work! To do so is to safeguard what the text says to the neglect of seeking what it means, an error that put them far wide of the mark!} The Dao of husband and wife cannot fail to be long enduring. This is why *Xian* is followed by *Heng* [Perseverance, Hexagram 32]. *Heng* here means "long enduring."

2. Things cannot long abide where they are located. This is why *Heng* is followed by *Dun* [Withdrawal, Hexagram 33]. *Dun* here means "retreat." {In the Dao of husband and wife, perseverance is esteemed, but a creature cannot exercise such perseverance about the place in which to abide, for its suitability goes up and down with worldly conditions; there are times when one should withdraw.} Things cannot be in withdrawal forever. {Withdrawal is the means by which the noble man distances himself from petty men. Only by withdrawing will he later prevail, so how could he remain in such a state forever! If he were to do so, petty men would thrive and superior men would daily diminish in number.} This is why *Dun* is followed by *Dazhuang* [Great Strength, Hexagram 34]. {With the waxing of yang, there is a waning of yin. Here we have the ascendancy of the Dao of the noble man.} Things cannot remain strong forever. This is why *Dazhuang* is followed by *Jin* [Advance, Hexagram 35]. {*Jin* means "to advance using soft methods."} *Jin* here means "to advance." {Although this is "advance using soft methods," the main thing is that this is still "advance."} Going forward is sure to involve getting wounded. This is why *Jin* is followed by *Mingyi* [Suppression of the Light, Hexagram 36]. {When the sun reaches mid-sky, it starts its decline, and it is at full strength when it suffers eclipse.} *Yi* here means "wounding." When one is wounded abroad, he is sure to return to his own home. This is why *Mingyi* is followed by *Jiaren* [The Family, Hexagram 37]. {When one is wounded abroad, he is sure to return to convalesce at home.}

3. When the Dao of the family is completely exhausted, there is sure to be discord. {If a family is very intimate and loving, its failure will be due to a neglect of integrity and honor. This is why *Jiaren* in conceptual terms only advocates strictness and reverence. However, "if the music is overwhelming, this will lead to laxity, but if decorum is overwhelming, this will lead to estrangement."[11] As *Jiaren* places exclusive emphasis on strictness, failure here is sure to stem from discord.} This is why *Jiaren* is followed by *Kui* [Contrariety, Hexagram 38]. *Kui* here means "discord." When there is

contrariety, there is sure to be adversity. This is why *Kui* is followed by *Jian* [Adversity, Hexagram 39]. *Jian* here means "trouble." Things cannot remain in trouble. This is why *Jian* is followed by *Xie* [Release, Hexagram 40]. *Xie* here means "*huan*" [go slow, take it easy].

4. With relaxation, there is sure to be neglect. This is why *Xie* is followed by *Sun* [Diminution, Hexagram 41]. If diminution keeps going on and does not stop, this is sure to lead to increase. This is why *Sun* is followed by *Yi* [Increase, Hexagram 42]. If increase keeps going on and does not stop, there is sure to be a breakthrough. {If something increases without ever stopping, surfeit will result. As a result of this, "there is sure to be a breakthrough."} This is why *Yi* is followed by *Kuai* [Resolution, Hexagram 43]. *Kuai* here means "breakthrough." With resolution, one is sure to encounter opportunity. {If one uses rightness to break through or resolve evil, one will be sure to encounter happy opportunities.} This is why *Kuai* is followed by *Gou* [Encounter, Hexagram 44]. *Gou* here means "to meet."

5. Only after things meet is there a gathering. This is why *Gou* is followed by *Cui* [Gathering, Hexagram 45]. *Cui* here means "to gather." To gather and build upward is called "climbing." This is why *Cui* is followed by *Sheng* [Climbing, Hexagram 46]. If climbing goes on and does not stop, there is sure to be impasse. This is why *Sheng* is followed by *Kun* [Impasse, Hexagram 47]. When impasse is met with above, there is sure to be a turnabout downward. This is why *Kun* is followed by *Jing* [The Well, Hexagram 48].

6. The Dao of wells cannot help but involve radical change. {After a long time, a well becomes fouled, so then one should renovate it completely.} This is why *Jing* is followed by *Ge* [Radical Change, Hexagram 49].

7. For effecting a radical change in things, there is nothing as good as a caldron. This is why *Ge* is followed by *Ding* [The Caldron, Hexagram 50]. {"*Ge* [Radical Change] means 'get rid of the old'; *Ding* [The Caldron] means 'take up the new.' "[12] Once one has gotten rid of the old, one ought to "fashion ceremonial vessels and establish laws"[13] in order to gain control over the new state of affairs. The caldron is the means by which one brings harmony to the living creatures and keeps them well regulated.[14] It is the vessel associated with the accomplishment of a new order, and this is why

one takes this image from it.[15] For taking charge of such vessels, no one is more appropriate than the eldest son. This is why *Ding* is followed by *Zhen* [Quake, Hexagram 51].[16] *Zhen* here signifies movement. Things cannot be kept in a state of movement forever but eventually are brought to a stop. This is why *Zhen* is followed by *Gen* [Restraint, Hexagram 52]. *Gen* here means "to stop." Things cannot remain in a state of Restraint forever. This is why *Gen* is followed by *Jian* [Gradual Advance, Hexagram 53]. *Jian* here means "to advance." Advance is sure to involve being restored to one's home. This is why *Jian* is followed by *Guimei* [Marrying Maiden, Hexagram 54].[17] When one manages to be restored to his proper place, he is sure to enjoy greatness. This is why *Guimei* is followed by *Feng* [Abundance, Hexagram 55]. *Feng* here means "to grow great."}

8. When one exhausts the potential to grow great, he is sure to lose his position. This is why *Feng* is followed by *Lü* [The Wanderer, Hexagram 56]. When one is a wanderer, he has nowhere to be taken in. This is why *Lü* is followed by *Sun* [Compliance, Hexagram 57]. {If "one is a wanderer" and "has nowhere to be taken in," he will only succeed in gaining entrance and egress by using compliance.} Compliance provides entrance. Only after gaining such entry will one find delight in it. This is why *Sun* is followed by *Dui* [Joy, Hexagram 58]. *Dui* here means "delight." Having found such delight, one now disperses it. This is why *Dui* is followed by *Huan* [Dispersion, Hexagram 59]. {Though delightful, one may not enter into biased relationships. This is why one here ought to disperse.} *Huan* [Dispersion] involves separation or estrangement. {*Huan* means "to start out and go along with facility free of all impediment." As a result, one here utterly transcends all restraints and does not turn back, but this inevitably leads to estrangement.}

9. People cannot remain in a state of estrangement forever. This is why *Huan* is followed by *Jie* [Control, Hexagram 60]. {If in the handling of affairs there is this control, it will be maintained together by people, who then will not become estranged and break up.} Once there is such control, people will have trust in it. This is why *Jie* is followed by *Zhongfu* [Inner Trust, Hexagram 61]. {*Fu* means "trust." Once control already exists, one ought then to have trust in it and so maintain it.} One who enjoys such trust will be sure to put it to use. This is why *Zhongfu* is followed by

Xiaoguo [Minor Superiority, Hexagram 62]. {If one just works at maintaining this trust, he will neglect the Dao of "practicing constancy without being stubborn."[18] Nevertheless, with this trust he should achieve some superiority.} This is why it is called "Minor Superiority." Once there is superiority over creatures [the masses, i.e., "subjects"], one is sure to ferry them [across troubles, i.e., "rescue them"]. {It is by conduct superior in its respect and by decorum superior in its economy that one can reform the world and encourage good customs. This is how one gains the wherewithal to become a ferry.} This is why *Xiaoguo* is followed by *Jiji* [Ferrying Complete, Hexagram 63]. Creatures [the masses, i.e., "subjects"] must never be hard-pressed. This is why *Jiji* is followed by *Weiji* [Ferrying Incomplete, Hexagram 64], with which the hexagrams come to an end. {If one must resort to purposeful action to try to ferry creatures [across troubles], that means that one has already made them hard-pressed. When creatures are hard-pressed, opposition occurs, and when one's achievements peak, chaos starts to ensue. How could anyone ever serve as a ferry that way? "This is why *Jiji* is followed by *Weiji* [Ferrying Incomplete]."}

NOTES

1. The quote is from Hexagram 3, *Zhun* (Birth Throes), Commentary on the Judgments.

2. This and all subsequent text set off in this manner is commentary by Han Kangbo.

3. When *Dao* is capitalized, it indicates the Cosmic Dao, the Moral Dao, the Dao of the noble man, the Way; *dao*, on the other hand, indicates the way things are or operate for ordinary, lesser, or even evil events and processes—for instance, the "dao of the petty man."

4. "Great thoroughfare" translates *datong*, as it appears in the *Zhuangzi*, where it is used to mean the Dao on a grand scale, the Great Dao in the perfection of its operation. As such, the expression in other texts—including the *Changes* and its commentaries—often seems to mean "everything (right) goes smoothly." See *Zhuangzi yinde*, 19/6/92.

5. *Lü* is the modern pronunciation; the *duyin* or reading pronunciation is *li*, which makes it a homonym of *li*, propriety (they were also apparently homonyms in antiquity). This may be the simple basis of identifying "treading" with "propriety," though *lü* (treading) as a noun also means shoe or

foot cover, and one theory is that such foot covers indicate propriety. The Song dynasty commentator on the *Changes*, Xiang Anshi (d. 1208, a contemporary of Zhu Xi) offers another suggestion: " 'Treading' is not directly equivalent to 'propriety,' but where one should tread is never outside the bounds of propriety. If it is outside its bounds, it is not a place where one ought to tread." See *Zhouyi zhezhong*, 18: 3a.

6. Following Kong Yingda's comments. See *Zhouyi zhengyi*, 9: 11b–12a.

7. The Song era commentator Xiang Anshi attempts to explain the connection between "oversee" and "great": "*Lin* is not to be glossed simply as 'great,' for 'great' here refers to those above overseeing those below, or the great overseeing the small. Whenever *Lin* [Overseeing] is involved, it always concerns the affairs of the great, and this is why the term *great* is used to explain it here. Only if *Lin* means greatness the way *Feng* [Abundance, Hexagram 55] means greatness, could one truly gloss it with the term *great* as such." See *Zhouyi zhezhong*, 18: 4a.

8. Hexagram 23, *Bo* ䷖, consists of one positive line in the top, sixth place and five negative lines; Hexagram 24, *Fu* (Return) ䷗, consists of one positive line in the bottom, first place and five negative lines. As a pair, these two hexagrams form a continuum in which the one positive line from the top of Hexagram 23 "returns" to the bottom of Hexagram 24.

9. See Hexagram 31, *Xian* (Reciprocity), Commentary on the Judgments.

10. This alludes to a passage in section ten of the Commentary on the Appended Phrases, Part One: "It is by interspersing numbers that change proceeds. The numbers are combined in the various ways, which exhaust all aspects of change, and, in consequence, the hexagrams form the patterns of Heaven and Earth."

11. *Liji* (Book of rites), 37: 11b.

12. See the Hexagrams in Irregular Order.

13. See Wang Bi's commentary on Hexagram 50, *Ding*, the Judgment.

14. "Brings harmony and keeps well regulated" translates *heji*, which often means "blend ingredients"—as in cooking or concocting medicines. However, it is likely that Han is using *heji* in another sense here, as it appears for instance in the *Xunzi* (The teachings of Master Xun [Xun Qing, ca. 300–230 B.C.]): "[The petty man] does not have it in him to follow the lead of an enlightened sovereign above, nor does he have it in him to bring harmony to the common folk and keep them well regulated below." See Wang, *Xunzi jijie*, 5: 56. Han's statement has *heji shengwu* (brings harmony to the living creatures and keeps them well regulated) and the statement in the *Xunzi* has *heji baixing* (brings harmony to the common folk and keeps them well regulated).

15. *Ding* are the bronze ceremonial vessels that were often cast to commemorate events in ancient China, including enfeoffment of nobles, successions or appointments of individuals to noble rank and office, ascensions to rulership, etc., all of which signify new beginnings. As a ceremonial ves-

sel, the *ding* also symbolized stewardship of the state. Although Han, following Wang Bi (see Wang's commentary to Hexagram 50), interprets *Ding* in these terms, later commentators (Cheng Yi and Zhu Xi, for instance) emphasize instead the fact that the *ding* are cooking vessels—the "renewal" they bring about is the new (cooked) form of the raw food prepared in them. See *Zhouyi zhezhong*, 7: 12a–12b.

16. *Zhen* (Quake) ䷲ consists of a doubling of the trigram *Zhen*, also Quake. It is associated with the Eldest Son. See section ten of Explaining the Trigrams.

17. Here "Marrying Maiden" might be construed as "Maiden who restores herself [goes] to her [husband's] home."

18. *Lunyu* (Analects) 15:36: "The noble man practices constancy without being stubborn."

The Hexagrams in Irregular Order [Zagua]

{Hexagrams in Irregular Order mixes all the hexagrams together and creates an intricate weave out of their concepts, in some cases establishing a mutual category on the basis of similarities and in others letting the concepts clarify each other on the basis of differences.[1]}

Qian [Pure Yang, Hexagram 1] is hard and firm, *Kun* [Pure Yin, Hexagram 2] soft and yielding; *Bi* [Closeness, Hexagram 8] involves joy, *Shi* [The Army, Hexagram 7] dismay. {Affability and closeness involve joy, and a mobilization of the masses involves dismay.} The concepts underlying *Lin* [Overseeing, Hexagram 19] and *Guan* [Viewing, Hexagram 20] in some cases mean "provide" and in others "seek." {If one stirs oneself to oversee others, this is referred to as "provide," but if others come to view oneself, this is referred to as "seek."} *Zhun* [Birth Throes, Hexagram 3] means "making an appearance in such a way that one does not lose one's place"; {With *Zhun*, "it is fitting to establish a chief,"[2] for "this is a time for the noble man to weave the fabric of government."[3] Although he has made his appearance, he hesitates before difficulties, but fittingly he practices constancy so does not lose his position.[4]} *Meng* [Juvenile Ignorance, Hexagram 4] indicates confusion first, followed by a coming to prominence. {Confused, one does not know how to become established. But if one seeks to come out of his juvenile ignorance, he will in the end find the means to establish himself. *Prominence* here means "to become established."} *Zhen* [Quake, Hexagram 51] means "a start," *Gen* [Restraint, Hexagram 52] "a stop." And *Sun* [Diminution, Hexagram 41] and *Yi* [Increase, Hexagram 42] are the beginnings of prosperity and decline. {When Diminution reaches its limit, Increase occurs, and when Increase reaches its limit, Diminution occurs.} *Daxu* [Great Domestication, Hexagram 26] is a matter of timeliness; {One domesticates when the time is right for it, thus it can be done in great measure.} *Wuwang* [No Errancy, Hexagram 25] exposes one to calamity. {In the world of No Errancy, errancy leads to calamity.} *Cui* [Gathering, Hexagram 45] means "to collect together," and *Sheng* [Climbing, Hexagram 46] means "not to come back." {*Come* [*lai*] here means "return." Since one is now engaged in climbing upward, it means he cannot return.} *Qian* [Modesty, Hexagram 15] involves taking oneself lightly, and *Yu* [Contentment, Hexagram 16] involves sloth. {A modest person does not engage in self-importance.} *Shihe* [Bite Together, Hexagram 21] means "eat up," and *Bi* [Elegance, Hexagram 22] does not involve particular colors. {In adornment, the important thing is overall harmony, something not restricted to particular colors.} *Dui* [Joy, Hexagram 58] means "show yourself," but *Sun* [Compliance, Hexagram 57] means "stay hidden." {When joy occurs, the important thing is to show that one is happy, but with compliance the important things are humility and withdrawal.} *Sui* [Following, Hexagram 17] involves no precedents, and with *Gu* [Ills to Be Cured, Hexagram 18], a cleanup occurs. {One should follow what is appropriate for the moment and not be tied to precedents. With such following, one will be responsible for affairs. This is why *Sui* is followed by *Gu*: *Cleanup* means "put things in order." *Gu* signifies putting those affairs in order.} *Bo* [Peeling, Hexagram 23] signifies decay; {When things become ripe, they begin to peel.} Fu [Return, Hexagram 24] signifies a coming back. *Jin* [Advance, Hexagram 35] indicates the daytime,[5] and *Mingyi* [Suppression of the Light, Hexagram 36] indicates castigation. {*Castigation* means "wounding."} *Jing* [The Well, Hexagram 48] indicates something accessible to all, and *Kun* [Impasse, Hexagram 47] indicates a clash of interests. {The Well is something that is for everyone's use, so regret never appears here. *Impasse* means that whatever the encounter, one feels at peace and so does not put aside scruples.} *Xian* [Reciprocity, Hexagram 31] means "things will go quickly"; {There is nothing faster than *Xian* when things respond to one another.} *Heng* [Perseverance, Hexagram 32] means "long lasting." *Huan* [Dispersion, Hexagram 59] indicates a dispersal, and *Jie* [Control, Hexagram 60] indicates a stop. *Xie* [Release, Hexagram 40] means "a relaxation," and *Jian* [Adversity, Hexagram 39] means "trouble." *Kui*

Contrariety, Hexagram 38] signifies a turning outward; {This means mutual coolness and rejection.} *Jiaren* [The Family, Hexagram 37] signifies a turning inward. *Tai* [Peace, Hexagram 11] and *Pi* [Obstruction, Hexagram 12] are opposed in kind. If it is *Dazhuang* [Great Strength, Hexagram 34], it means "a halt," but if it is *Dun* [Withdrawal, Hexagram 33], it means "withdrawal." {When great correctness prevails, petty men are brought to a halt, but when petty men prevail, the noble man withdraws.} *Dayou* [Great Holdings, Hexagram 14] indicates mass support, and *Tongren* [Fellowship, Hexagram 13] indicates affability. *Ge* [Radical Change, Hexagram 49] means "get rid of the old"; *Ding* [The Caldron, Hexagram 50] means "take up the new." *Xiaoguo* [Minor Superiority, Hexagram 62] indicates superiority, and *Zhongfu* [Inner Trust, Hexagram 61] indicates confidence. *Feng* [Abundance, Hexagram 55] often involves incident; {One who has risen high should fear danger, and one who is satisfied should guard against satiation. One who enjoys abundance in great measure will often have reason for worry.} When one has few kith and kin, this is *Lü* [The Wanderer, Hexagram 56]. {As "one has few kith and kin," he has to live the life of a wanderer.} *Li* [Cohesion, Hexagram 30] signifies ascent, and [*Xi*]*Kan* [(The Constant) Sink Hole, Hexagram 29] signifies descent. {Fire burns upward, and water flows downward.[6]} *Xiaoxu* [Lesser Domestication, Hexagram 9] results in few resources; {Here one is not up to saving everything together.[7]} *Lü* [Treading, Hexagram 10] means "not staying in one's position." {Wang Bi says that all such yang lines in the *Lü* hexagram signify good fortune because they do not occupy their own positions.[8]} *Xu* [Waiting, Hexagram 5] means "do not advance"; {Fearing danger here, one comes to a halt.} *Song* [Contention, Hexagram 6] means "not being affable." In *Daguo* [Major Superiority, Hexagram 28], collapse is inherent. {There is weakness at the beginning and end.[9]} *Gou* [Encounter, Hexagram 44] indicates a meeting in which the soft encounters the hard.[10] *Jian* [Gradual Advance, Hexagram 53] signifies a woman who would marry but waits for the man to act. {The woman follows the man.} *Yi* [Nourishment, Hexagram 27) means "the nurturing of correctness," and *Jiji* [Ferrying Complete, Hexagram 63] signifies stability. *Guimei* [Marrying Maiden, Hexagram 54] signifies woman's ultimate end; {Woman's ultimate end is to marry.} *Weiji* [Ferrying Incomplete, Hexagram 64] signifies man hard-pressed. {When both the hard and strong and the soft and weak are out of their proper positions, it signifies the Dao of Ferrying Incomplete. Thus the text uses the term *hard-pressed.*[11]} *Kuai* [Resolution, Hexagram 43] means "to act decisively," for here the hard wins decisively over the soft: the way of the noble man is in the ascendancy, and the way of the petty man is brought to grief.[12] {The noble man advances his Dao by dealing decisively with petty men. Petty men, suffering decisive defeat, are driven away and thus deeply brought to grief.}

NOTES

1. This and all subsequent text set off in this manner is commentary by Han Kangbo.

2. See Hexagram 3, *Zhun* (Birth Throes), the Judgment.

3. See Hexagram 3, *Zhun* (Birth Throes), Wang Bi's commentary on the Commentary on the Images.

4. See Hexagram 3, *Zhun* (Birth Throes), Judgment and First Yang, Commentary on the Images.

5. The component trigrams of *Jin* (Advance) ䷢, Hexagram 35, are *Kun* (Pure Yin, Earth) below and *Li* (Cohesion, Brightness, Fire) above. The resultant hexagram is supposed to represent the sun over the earth, that is, daytime.

6. *Li* (Cohesion), Hexagram 30, is associated with fire, and (*Xi*)*Kan* ([The Constant] Sink Hole), Hexagram 29, is associated with water.

7. "Saving everything together" translates *jianji*. This may be an allusion to the *Zhuangzi*: "He [the petty man] exhausts his spirit on lame and shallow matters and yet wants to save both the Dao and the world [*jianji daowu*]." In other words, it takes the resources of a noble man to "save everything" or "save the Dao and the world." See *Zhuangzi yinde* 89/32/20. Note that Han here takes *xu* to mean "garner" rather than "tame" or "domesticate."

8. *Lü* (Treading) ䷉, Hexagram 10, has yang lines in the second, fourth, and sixth positions. If one considers the first position to be yang and the top position to be yin (instead of both being nonpositions—Wang is somewhat ambiguous), then all these lines are in weak, yin positions improper for them, yet all are characterized by "good fortune" in their respective line statements. See Wang's comments on these lines in *Lü*.

9. *Daguo* (Major Superiority) ䷛, Hexagram 28, has weak, yin lines at beginning and end.

10. *Gou* (Encounter) ䷫, Hexagram 44, consists of one soft, yin line in the first place that "encounters" the other five hard, yang lines.

11. When one counts the first position as yang and the top position as

yin (cf. note 8 above), *Weiji* (Ferry Incomplete) ䷿, Hexagram 64, consists entirely of yang lines in yin positions and yin lines in yang positions .

12. *Kuai* (Resolution) ䷪, Hexagram 43, consists of one yin line in the top position and five yang lines. The hexagram, as such, signifies the yang principle gathering strength and moving upward, forcing out the yin principle. Note also that when this progress of the yang principle is complete and all lines are yang, the resulting hexagram is *Qian* (Pure Yang), Hexagram 1, and we are back at the beginning of the cycle of sixty-four hexagrams. This surely is the reason why *Kuai* is placed here at the end of the Hexagrams in Irregular Order.

Explaining the Trigrams
[Shuo gua]

1. In the distant past, the way the sage[1] made the *Changes* is as follows: He was mysteriously assisted by the gods [*shenming*, literally, "the numinous and the bright"] and so initiated the use of yarrow stalks. {*Mysteriously* means "profoundly," and *assisted* means "enlightened." The yarrow stalks respond to commands as if they were echoes. How they manage to do this defies understanding—it just happens![2]} He made Heaven three and Earth two and so provided the numbers with a basis. {*Three* signifies the odd numbers, and two signifies the even numbers; seven and nine are yang [odd] numbers, and six and eight are yin [even] numbers.} He observed the changes between yin and yang and so established the trigrams. {The trigrams constitute the images, and the yarrow stalks constitute the numbers. As for the trigrams, these render yin and yang into comparable images and so constitute embodiments of transformation and change, such as "Thunder and Wind give rise each to the other" or "Mountain and Lake reciprocally circulate material force."[3] As for the yarrow stalks, these constitute the odd and even numbers that intermingle the elements of Heaven and Earth. The yarrow stalks exhaust all the numbers and in so doing establish the images. The trigrams complete the images and in so doing use up all the numbers. This is why the yarrow stalks are referred to in the terms "He made Heaven three and Earth two and so provided the numbers with a basis," and why the trigrams are referred to in the terms "He observed the changes between yin and yang [and so established them]."} As the trigrams are begun and are dispersed through the movement of the hard and soft lines, he initiated the use of such lines. {The hard and the soft lines

begin and disperse them; it is the movement of change that brings them together.} He was in complete accord with the Dao and with Virtue, and the principles involved conform to rightness. He exhausted principles to the utmost and dealt thoroughly with human nature, and in doing so arrived at the workings of fate. {Fate is the ultimate reach of life. To exhaust principles to the utmost is to explore fate to the ultimate degree.}

2. In the distant past, the way the sages[4] made the *Changes* was as follows: It was to be used as a means to stay in accord with the principles of nature and of fate. It was for this reason that they determined what the Dao of Heaven was, which they defined in terms of yin and yang, what the Dao of Earth was, which they defined in terms of hard and soft, {"In Heaven this [process] creates images, and on Earth it creates physical forms."[5] Yin and yang are terms that address things as aspects of material force, and hard and soft are terms that address them as kinds of physical forms. Change and transformation begin with the images of material force and only then go on to create physical forms. The natural endowments of the myriad things begin in Heaven and take on physical forms on Earth. Therefore, when Heaven is involved, we refer to things in terms of yin and yang, and when Earth is involved, we refer to things in terms of soft and hard. One might refer to things that exist as physical forms as either yin or yang; this is to trace them back to their origins. One might refer to things that exist as material forces as either hard or soft; this is to sum up their endings.[6]} and what the Dao of Man was, which they defined in terms of benevolence and righteousness. They brought these three powers together and doubled them; this is why the *Changes* forms its hexagrams out of six lines. They provided yin allotments and yang allotments, so their functions alternate between soft and hard; this is why the *Changes* forms its patterns out of six positions. {They established the six lines in order to replicate the actions of the three powers; this is why it takes six lines. The six positions are the places that the lines occupy. The second and the fourth positions are yin, and the third and the fifth are yang. This is why the text says: "They provided yin allotments and yang allotments." As the six lines ascend or descend, sometimes they are in hard positions and sometimes in soft. This is why the text says: "Their functions alternate between soft and hard."}

3. As Heaven [*Qian*, Pure Yang] and Earth [*Kun*, Pure Yin] establish positions, as Mountain [*Gen*, Restraint] and Lake [*Dui*,

Joy] reciprocally circulate material force, as Thunder [*Zhen*, Quake] and Wind [*Sun*, Compliance] give rise each to the other, and as Water [*Kan*, Sink Hole] and Fire [*Li*, Cohesion] do not fail to complement each other, the eight trigrams combine with one another in such a way that, to reckon the past, one follows the order of their progress, and, to know the future, one works backward through them. {With the combination of the eight trigrams, all the principles involved with change and transformation are complete. In regard to the past, one gets to know it by going with the flow [up to the present], and, in regard to the future, one reckons it by working backward [to the present].} Therefore, the *Changes* allow us to work backward [from the future] and reckon forward [from the past]. {The sages made the *Changes* in order to gain a view back [from the future] and "to provide beforehand for the needs of the common folk."[7]}

4. It is by Thunder [*Zhen*, Quake] that things are caused to move, by Wind [*Sun*, Compliance] that they are dispersed, by the Rain [*Kan*, Sink Hole, i.e., Water] that they are moistened, by the Sun [*Li*, Cohesion, i.e., Fire] that they are dried, by Restraint [*Gen*] that they are made to stop, by Joy [*Dui*] that they are made happy, by Pure Yang [*Qian*, i.e., Heaven] that they are provided with a sovereign, and by Pure Yin [*Kun*, i.e., Earth] they are harbored.

5. The Divine Ruler [*shangdi*] comes forth in *Zhen* [Quake] and sets all things in order in *Sun* [Compliance], makes them visible to one another in *Li* [Cohesion, i.e., Sun, Fire], gives them maximum support in *Kun* [Pure Yin, i.e., Earth], makes them happy then in *Dui* [Joy], has them do battle in *Qian* [Pure Yang], finds them thoroughly worn out in *Kan* [Water Hole], and has them reach final maturity in *Gen* [Restraint].

The myriad things come forth in *Zhen* [Quake]; *Zhen* corresponds to the east. They are set in order in *Sun* [Compliance]; *Sun* corresponds to the southeast. "Set in order" means that they are fresh and neat. *Li* [Cohesion, Fire, i.e., the sun] here means brightness. That the myriad things are made visible to one another here signifies that this is the trigram of the south. The fact that the sage [king] faces the south to listen to the whole world and that he turns toward the brightness there to rule is probably derived from this. *Kun* [Pure Yin, Earth] here means the Earth. The myriad things all are nourished to the utmost by it. This is why it says: "gives them maximum support in *Kun*." *Dui* [Joy] here means autumn at its height, something in which the myriad things all find cause to rejoice. This is why it says: "makes them happy then in *Dui*." [As for] "has them do battle in *Qian*," *Qian* here is the trigram of the northwest, so this signifies where yin and yang exert pressure on each other. *Kan* [Sink Hole] here means water. It is the trigram of due north. It is the trigram of wearisome toil. It is here that the myriad things all find refuge. This is why it says: "finds them thoroughly worn out in *Kan*." *Gen* [Restraint] is the trigram of the northeast. It is here that the myriad things reach the end of their development, but it is also the beginning of that development. This is why it says: "has them reach final maturity in *Gen*."

6. As for *the numinous*, it is the term used for that which invests the myriad things with the marvel of what they are and do. {*The numinous* is introduced at this point to clarify the fact that no external agent is involved in the way the [primal forces of the] eight trigrams move and exert themselves so that things undergo change and transformation and exchange places with one another. *The numinous* thus does not exist as a thing but "is the term used for that which invests the myriad things with the marvel of what they are and do." Thunder as such is swift, Wind fleet, Fire burns, and Water is wet; each spontaneously and naturally undergoes change, transforming one into the other. This is how the myriad things acquire the capability to become all that they can be.} Of things that make the myriad things move, none is swifter than Thunder. Of things that make the myriad things bend, none is swifter than the Wind. Of things that make the myriad things dry, none is a better drying agent than Fire. Of things that make the myriad things rejoice, none is more joy giving than the Lake. Of things that moisten the myriad things, none is more effective than Water. Of things that provide the myriad things with ends and beginnings, none is more resourceful than Restraint. This is why Water and Fire drive each other on, why Thunder and Wind do not work against each other, and why "Mountain and Lake reciprocally circulate."[8] Only in consequence of all this can change and transformation take place, thus allowing the myriad things to become all that they can be.

7. *Qian* [Pure Yang] means strength and dynamism [*jian*]; *Kun* [Pure Yin] means submissiveness and pliancy; *Zhen* [Quake] means energizing; *Sun* [Compliance] means accommodation;

Kan [Water] means pitfall; *Li* [Cohesion] means attachment; *Gen* [Restraint] means cessation; *Dui* [Joy] means to delight.

8. *Qian* [Pure Yang] has the nature of the horse, *Kun* [Pure Yin] that of the ox, *Zhen* [Quake] that of the dragon, *Sun* [Compliance] that of the cock, *Kan* [Water Hole] that of the pig, *Li* [Cohesion] that of the pheasant, *Gen* [Restraint] that of the dog, and *Dui* [Joy] that of the sheep.

9. *Qian* [Pure Yang] works like the head, *Kun* [Pure Yin] like the stomach, *Zhen* [Quake] like the foot, *Sun* [Compliance] like the thigh, *Kan* [Water Hole] like the ear, *Li* [Cohesion] like the eye, *Gen* [Restraint] like the hand, and *Dui* [Joy] like the mouth.

10. *Qian* [Pure Yang] is Heaven, thus it corresponds to the Father, and *Kun* [Pure Yin] is Earth, thus it corresponds to the Mother. As for *Zhen* [Quake], [*Kun*] here seeks [*Qian*] for the first time and gets a son, thus we call it the Eldest Son,[9] and as for *Sun* [Compliance], [*Qian*] here seeks [*Kun*] for the first time and gets a daughter, thus we call it the Eldest Daughter. As for *Kan* [Water Hole], [*Kun*] here seeks [*Qian*] for the second time and gets a son, thus we call it the Middle Son, and as for *Li* [Cohesion], [*Qian*] here seeks [*Kun*] for the second time and gets a daughter, thus we call it the Middle Daughter. As for *Gen* [Restraint], [*Kun*] here seeks [*Qian*] for the third time and gets a son, thus we call it the Youngest Son, and as for *Dui* [Joy], [*Qian*] here seeks [*Kun*] for the third time and gets a daughter, thus we call it the Youngest Daughter.

11. *Qian* [Pure Yang] is Heaven, is round, is the sovereign, is father, is jade, is metal, is coldness, is ice, is pure red, is a fine horse, an old horse, an emaciated horse, a piebald horse,[10] is fruit of the tree.

Kun [Pure Yin] is Earth, is mother, is cloth, is a cooking pot, is frugality, is impartiality, is a cow with calf, is a great cart, is the markings on things, is the multitude of things themselves, and is the handle of things. In respect to soils, it is the kind that is black.

Zhen [Quake] is thunder, is the dragon, is black and yellow, is overspreading, is the great highway, is the Eldest Son, is decisiveness and impetuosity, a green, lush bamboo, and the reed plants. In respect to horses, it is those that excel at neighing, those that have white rear legs, those that work the legs [i.e., run fast], and those that have white foreheads. In respect to cultivated plants, it is the kind that grows back [i.e., pod-sprouting plants, legumes, etc.]. At the end point of its development, it is soundness and sturdiness [i.e., it turns into *Qian* (Pure Yang)] and is luxuriant and fresh growth.

Sun [Compliance] is wood, is the wind, is the Eldest Daughter, is the straightness of a marking cord, is the carpenter [or "carpenter's square"], is the spotless and pure, is the lengthy, is the high, is the now-advancing and now-receding, is the unresolved, and is odor. In respect to men, it is the balding, the broad in forehead, the ones with much white in their eyes, the ones who keep close to what is profitable and who market things for threefold gain. At the end point of its development it is the trigram of impetuosity [i.e., it turns into *Zhen* (Quake)].

Kan [Sink Hole] is water, is the drains and ditches, is that which lies low, is the now-straightening and now-bending, and is the bow [and] the wheel. In respect to men, it is the increasingly anxious, the sick at heart, the ones with earaches. It is the trigram of blood, of the color red. In respect to horses, it is those with beautiful backs, those that put their whole hearts into it, those that keep their heads low, those with thin hooves, and those that shamble along. In respect to carriages, it is those that often have calamities [i.e., breakdowns/accidents]. It is penetration, is the moon, and is the stealthy thief. In respect to trees, it is those that are strong with dense centers.

Li [Cohesion] is fire, is the sun, is lightning, is the Middle Daughter, is mail and the helmet, is the halberd and the sword. In respect to men, it is those with big bellies. It is the trigram of dryness. It is the turtle, is the crab, is the snail, is the clam, and is the tortoise. In respect to trees, it is the hollow ones with tops withered.

Gen [Restraint] is the mountain, is the footpath, is the small stone, is the gate tower, is the tree fruit and vine fruit, is the gatekeeper and the palace guard, is the fingers, is the dog, is the rat, is the black maws of species [of birds and beasts of prey]. In respect to trees, it is the kind that is sturdy and much gnarled.

Dui [Joy] is the lake, is the Youngest Daughter, is the shamaness, is the mouth and tongue, is the deterioration [of plant life], and the breaking off of what had been attached. In respect to soils, it is the kind that is hard and alkaline. It is the concubine, the sheep.

NOTES

1. Kong Yingda glosses *sheng* (sage/sages) as Bao Xi (or Fu Xi). See *Zhouyi zhengyi*, 9: 1b.

2. This and all subsequent text set off in this manner is commentary by Han Kangbo.

3. See section three.

4. It is likely that *sheng* now refers to the ancient sages collectively: Bao Xi, King Wen, and the duke of Zhou. Both Han Kangbo and Kong Yingda are silent on this point.

5. See section one of the Commentary on the Appended Phrases, Part One.

6. "Tracing origins" and "summing up endings" allude to a passage in section eight of the Commentary on the Appended Phrases, Part Two. *Endings* here seems to mean something like "final effects," the end results of yin and yang material force.

7. See section eleven of the Commentary on the Appended Phrases, Part One. This passage, along with Han's commentary, may well be the place where the word *ni* (go against, oppose, reverse, go upstream/against the current, etc.) comes to mean "anticipate" or "predict," as in the compounds *nidu* and *niliao*. The logic of this transformation seems to be as follows: Time like a river flows in one direction. The present (*jin*) stands midway between past (*wang*) and future (*lai*). To understand the past, we must follow events from their inception up to the present. The *Changes* provide us with the means to know when and how a situation has come about and to follow it up to where we are now. This process is defined as "going with the flow" (*shun*, literally, "compliance"). To understand the future, we must leap ahead in time and then work our way backward through future time to where we are in the present. This process is defined as "working backward" (*ni*), that is, one has to go against the flow of future time. The *Changes*, through the hexagrams, provides us with the means to do this, since they not only provide us with the means "to trace beginnings" but also to reckon the way things will end—to "sum up endings," to use terminology that appears in section eight of the Commentary on the Appended Phrases, Part Two. It should be noted that this interpretation depends on the terms *wang* and *lai* really meaning "past" and "future" respectively. Han Kangbo and Kong Yingda certainly understand them in this way (see *Zhouyi zhengyi*, 9: 4a–4b), as does the later exegetical tradition, but the modern scholar Qian Zhongshu has demonstrated that these terms often have the reverse meanings in a variety of texts over many centuries: *wang* means "what we go forth to" (i.e., the future, and *lai* means "what has come about" (i.e., the past). See *Guanzhui bian*, 1: 54–56, where he discusses this passage in the Explaining the Trigrams. If we follow his suggestions, the passage here means something like: "To reckon the future, we follow their [the hexagrams] flow, and to know the past, we work backward through them. Therefore the *Changes* allows us to work backward [to the past] and reckon forward [into the future]."

8. See section three.

9. The six children of *Qian* ☰ and *Kun* ☷ are created in the following way: *Zhen* ☳ replaces the bottom yin line of *Kun* with a yang line, and *Sun* ☴ replaces the bottom yang line of *Qian* with a yin line; *Kan* ☵ replaces the middle yin line of *Kun* with a yang line, and *Li* ☲ replaces the middle yang line of *Qian* with a yin line; *Gen* ☶ replaces the top yin line of *Kun* with a yang line, and *Dui* ☱ replaces the top yang line of *Qian* with a yin line.

10. Kong Yingda, referring to such works as the *Erya* (Elegant and correct writings in familiar terms), a third/second century B.C. lexicographic work, explains *boma* (piebald horse) as "a horse that has teeth like a saw and that can eat tigers and leopards—this captures a sense of its perfect strength and vigor." See *Zhouyi zhengyi*, 9: 8a, and *Zhouyi zhezhong*, 17: 20a.

The Sixty-Four Hexagrams, with Texts and Commentaries

䷀

乾

Qian [Pure Yang]
(*Qian* Above *Qian* Below)

Judgment

Qian consists of fundamentality [*yuan*], prevalence [*heng*], fitness [*li*], and constancy [*zhen*].

COMMENTARY ON THE JUDGMENTS

How great is the fundamental nature of *Qian*! The myriad things are provided their beginnings by it, and, as such, it controls Heaven. It allows clouds to scud and rain to fall and things in all their different categories to flow into forms. Manifestly evident from beginning to end, the positions of the six lines form, each at its proper moment. When it is the moment for it, ride one of the six dragons to drive through the sky. The change and transformation of the Dao of *Qian* in each instance keep the nature and destiny of things correct. {The term *tian* [Heaven] is the name for a form, a phenomenal entity; the term *jian* [strength and dynamism: *Qian*] refers to that which uses or takes this form.[1] Form as such is how things are bound together. To have the form of Heaven and be able to maintain it forever without loss and, as the very head of all things, stay in control of it, how could this be anything but the ultimate of strength and dynamism! This is manifestly evident in its Dao from beginning to end. Thus each of the six positions forms without ever missing its moment, its ascent or descent not subject to fixed rule, functioning according to the moment involved. If one is to remain in repose, ride a hidden dragon, and if one is to set forth, ride a flying dragon. This is why it is said: "When it is the moment for it, ride one of the six dragons." Here one takes control of the great instrument [*daqi*, Heaven] by riding change and transformation. Whether in quiescence utterly focused or in action straight and true, *Qian* is never out of step with the great harmony, so how could it fail to keep the innate tendencies [*qing*] inherent in the nature and destiny of things correct![12]} It is by fitness and constancy that one preserves the great harmony [*dahe*] and stays in tune with it. {If one does not so stay in accord, he will be hard and cruel.} So one stands with head above the multitudes, and the myriad states are all at peace. {The reason why the myriad states are at peace is that each one has such a one as its true sovereign.}

COMMENTARY ON THE IMAGES

The action of Heaven is strong and dynamic. In the same manner, the noble man never ceases to strengthen himself.

COMMENTARY ON THE WORDS OF THE TEXT

"Fundamentality" is the leader of goodness [*shan*]. "Prevalence" is the coincidence of beauty [*jia*]. "Fitness" is coalescence with righteousness [*yi*]. "Constancy" is the very trunk of human affairs. The noble man embodies benevolence [*ren*] sufficient to be a leader of men, and the coincidence of beauty in him is sufficient to make men live in accordance with propriety [*li*]. He engenders fitness in people sufficient to keep them in harmony with righteousness, and his constancy is firm enough to serve as the trunk for human affairs. The noble man is someone who practices these four virtues. This is why it says: "*Qian* consists of fundamentality, prevalence, fitness, and constancy."

Qian manifests its fundamentality in providing for the origin of things and granting them prevalence. It manifests its fitness and constancy by making the innate tendencies of things conform to their natures. {If it were not for the fundamentality of *Qian*, how could it comprehensively provide for the origin of all things? If nature did not control their innate tendencies, how could things long behave in ways that are correct for them? This is why the origin of things and their prevalence must derive from the fundamentality of *Qian*, and the fitness of things and their rectitude must be a matter of making the innate tendencies of things conform to their natures.} The power in *Qian* to provide origins is such that it can make all under Heaven fit by means of its own beautiful fitness. One does not say how it confers fitness; it just is great! How great *Qian* is! It is strong, dynamic, central, correct, and it is absolutely pure in its unadulteratedness and unsulliedness. The six lines emanate their power and exhaustively explore all innate tendencies. In accord with the moment, ride the six dragons to drive through the sky. Then clouds will move, and rain fall, and all under Heaven be at peace.

COMMENTARY ON THE APPENDED PHRASES

As Heaven is high and noble and Earth is low and humble, so it is that *Qian* [Pure Yang] and *Kun* [Pure Yin, Hexagram 2] are defined.

The Dao of *Qian* forms the male. . . . *Qian* has mastery over the great beginning of things.

Qian through ease provides mastery over things. . . . As [*Qian*] is easy, it is easy to know. . . . If one is easy to know, he will have kindred spirits.

When [the Dao] forms images, we call it *Qian*.

As for *Qian*, in its quiescent state it is focused, and in its active state it is undeviating. This is how it achieves its great productivity.

Opening the gate is called *Qian*.

Qian and *Kun*, do they not constitute the arcane source for change! When *Qian* and *Kun* form ranks, change stands in their midst, but if *Qian* and *Kun* were to disintegrate, there would be no way that change could manifest itself. And if change could not manifest itself, this would mean that *Qian* and *Kun* might almost be at the point of extinction!

All the activity that takes place in the world, thanks to constancy, is the expression of the One. *Qian* being unyielding shows us how easy it is.

The Yellow Emperor, Yao, and Shun let their robes hang loosely down, yet the world was well governed. They probably got the idea for this from the hexagrams *Qian* and *Kun*.

The Master said: "*Qian* and *Kun*, do they not constitute the two-leaved gate into the *Changes*? *Qian* is a purely yang thing, and *Kun* is a purely yin thing."

Qian [Pure Yang, Hexagram 1] is a yang thing.

Qian is the strongest thing in the entire world, so it should always be easy to put its virtue into practice. Thus one knows whether or not there is going to be danger. [It] is able to delight hearts and minds.[3]

PROVIDING THE SEQUENCE OF THE HEXAGRAMS

Only after there were Heaven [*Qian*, Pure Yang] and Earth [*Kun*, Pure Yin, Hexagram 2] were the myriad things produced from them. What fills Heaven and Earth is nothing other than the myriad things.

THE HEXAGRAMS IN IRREGULAR ORDER

Qian is hard and firm.

First Yang

A submerged dragon does not act.
{The Commentary on the Words of the Text says all that can be said!}

COMMENTARY ON THE IMAGES

"A submerged dragon does not act": the yang force is below.

COMMENTARY ON THE WORDS OF THE TEXT

"A submerged dragon does not act." What does this mean? The Master says: "This refers to one who has a dragon's virtue yet remains hidden. He neither changes to suit the world {One does not change for the sake of the profane world.} nor seeks fulfillment in fame. He hides from the world but does not regret it, and though this fails to win approval, he is not sad. When he takes delight in the world, he is active in it, and when he finds it distresses him, he turns his back on it. He who is resolute in his unwillingness to be uprooted, this is a submerged dragon."

"A submerged dragon does not act" because one is too far below.

"A submerged dragon does not act": the yang force is hidden in the depths.

The noble man performs deeds out of his perfected virtue. Daily one can see him performing them. The expression "submerged" means that one remains concealed and does not yet show himself, his conduct such that it is not yet perfected. Therefore the noble man does not act.

Second Yang

When there appears a dragon in the fields, it is fitting to see the great man.[4] {It has come out of the depths and abandoned its hiding place; this is what is meant by "there appears a dragon." It has taken up a position on the ground; this is what is meant by "in the fields." With virtue [*de*] bestowed far and wide, one here takes up a mean [*zhong*] position and avoids partiality [*pian*]. Although this is not the position for a sovereign, it involves the virtue of a true sovereign. If it is the first line, he does not reveal himself; if the third, he makes earnest efforts; if the fourth, he hesitates to leap; if the top line, he is overreaching. Fitness to see the great man [*daren*] lies only in the second and the fifth lines.}

COMMENTARY ON THE IMAGES

"There appears a dragon in the fields": the operation of virtue spreads widely.

COMMENTARY ON THE WORDS OF THE TEXT

"When there appears a dragon in the fields, it is fitting to see the great man." What does this mean? The Master says: "This refers to one who has a dragon's virtue and has achieved rectitude [*zheng*] and centrality [*zhong*, the Mean]. He is trustworthy in ordinary speech and prudent in ordinary conduct. He wards off depravity and preserves his sincerity. He does good in the world but does not boast of it. His virtue spreads wide and works transformations. When the *Changes* says, 'when there appears a dragon in the fields, it is fitting to see the great man,' it refers to the virtue of a true sovereign."

"When there appears a dragon in the fields," it is the time for it to lodge there.

"There appears a dragon in the fields": all under Heaven enjoy the blessings of civilization.

The noble man accumulates knowledge by studying and becomes discriminating by posing questions. {When one who has a sovereign's virtue occupies a position in the lower trigram, it is an occasion for him to draw on the resources of others.} It is magnanimity that governs his repose, and it is benevolence that guides his actions. The *Changes* say: "When one sees a dragon in the fields, it is fitting to see the great man." This refers to one who has the virtue of a true sovereign.

Third Yang

The noble man makes earnest efforts throughout the day, and with evening he still takes care; though in danger, he will suffer no blame. {Here one occupies the very top of the lower trigram and is located just below the upper trigram, situated in a nonmean position and treading on the dangerous territory of the double strong.[5] Above, he is not in Heaven, so cannot use that to make his exalted position secure, and below he is not in the fields [Earth] so cannot use that to make his dwelling place safe. If one were to cultivate exclusively here the Dao of the subordinate, the virtue needed to occupy a superior position would waste away, but if one were to cultivate exclusively the Dao of the superior, the propriety needed to fill a lower position would wither. This is why the text says such a one should "make earnest efforts throughout the day." As for "with evening he still takes care," this is equivalent to saying that there is still danger. If in occupying a high position one were free of arrogance, in filling a low position were free of distress, and were to take care appropriate to the moment, he would not fall out with the incipient force of things and, although in danger and beset with trouble, would suffer no blame. To be located at the very top of the lower trigram is better than being at the overreach connected with Top Yang. Thus only by making full use of one's intellect can one remain free from blame here. It is because the third line of *Qian* occupies the top position in its lower trigram that one is spared the regret of the dragon that overreaches [in the top line]. It is because the third line of *Kun* [Pure Yin, Hexagram 2] occupies the top position in its lower trigram that one is spared the disaster brought about when dragons fight [in the top line].}

COMMENTARY ON THE IMAGES

"He makes earnest efforts throughout the day": whether going back up or coming back down, it is a matter of the Dao. {In terms of an ascent, this is not something about which to be arrogant, and in terms of a descent, this is not something about which to be distressed. Thus, whether one goes back up or comes back down, he is always with the Dao.}

COMMENTARY ON THE WORDS OF THE TEXT

"The noble man makes earnest efforts throughout the day, and with evening he still takes care; though in danger, he will suffer no blame." What does this mean? The Master says: "The noble man fosters his virtue and cultivates his task. He fosters his virtue by being loyal and trustworthy; he keeps his task in hand by cultivating his words and establishing his sincerity. A person who understands what a maximum point is and fulfills it can take part in the incipiency of the moment. A person who understands what a conclusion is and brings it about can take part in the preservation of righteousness. {When one is located at the very top of a trigram, this is a "maximum point," and when one is at the very end point of a trigram, this is a "conclusion." One who, when he reaches the maximum point of a matter, manages to avoid blame for any transgression is someone who understands maximum points and thus can take part in the accomplishment of great affairs.[6] One who, when he finds himself at a conclusion, can bring that conclusion to perfect fulfillment is someone who understands conclusions. For speeding up the progress of things, righteousness is not as good as expediency, but for preserving the completion of things, expediency is not as good as righteousness. This is why "nothing is ever without a beginning, but only the rare thing can have completion."[7] Who else but someone who can take part in the preservation of righteousness could ever understand conclusions!} Thus when he occupies a high position, he is not proud, and when he is in a low position, he is not distressed. To be at the top of the lower trigram is still to be below the upper trigram. As one understands that lowness has merely concluded, he is not proud, but as he also understands that he has reached a maximum point and fulfilled it, he is not distressed either. This is why, making earnest efforts, he takes care when the moment requires it and, though in danger, will suffer no blame." {"To take care" means to be alert and fearful. When one is at the maximum point of a matter but neglects to take advantage of the moment, he will miss it, or if he is idle and remiss, it will be lost through neglect. This is why, when the moment requires it, one "takes care" and, though in danger, "will suffer no blame."}

"Make earnest efforts throughout the day" because this is how one should do things.

"Make earnest efforts throughout the day": act in step with the moment. {This means always be in step with the moment of Heaven without cease.}

Nine in the third place signifies a double strength but one that is nonmean.[8] It is neither in Heaven above nor in the fields [Earth] below. Thus one makes earnest efforts here and, in accordance with the moment, takes care; thus, though in danger, he will suffer no blame.

Fourth Yang

Hesitating to leap, it still stays in the depths, so suffers no blame. {To leave the topmost line in the lower trigram and occupy the bottom line of the upper trigram signifies the moment when the Dao of *Qian* undergoes a complete change. Above, one is not in Heaven; below, one is not in the fields [Earth]; and in between one is not with Man.[9] Here one treads on the dangerous territory of the double strong and so lacks a stable position in which to stay.[10] This is truly a time when there are no constant rules for advancing or retreating. Drawing close to an exalted position [the ruling fifth line], one wishes to foster the Dao involved, but, forced to stay in a lower position, this is not something his leap can reach. One wishes to ensure that his position here remains quiescent, for this is not a secure position in which to stay. Harboring doubts, one hesitates and does not dare determine his own intentions. He concentrates on preserving his commitment to the public good, for advancement here does not lie with private ambitions. He turns his doubts into reflective thought and so avoids error in decisions. Thus he suffers no blame.}

COMMENTARY ON THE IMAGES

"Hesitating to leap, it still stays in the depths": when it advances there will be no blame.

COMMENTARY ON THE WORDS OF THE TEXT

"Hesitating to leap, it still stays in the depths, so suffers no blame." What does this mean? The Master says: "Although there is no fixed rule for one's rise or fall, one should not engage in deviant behavior. Although there is no constant norm governing advance or withdrawal, one should not leave one's fellows and strike off on one's own. The noble man fosters his virtue, cultivates his task, and wishes to be ready when the moment arrives. Therefore he suffers no blame."

"Hesitating to leap, it still stays in the depths": this is because one should test himself.

"Hesitating to leap, it still stays in the depths": here the Dao of *Qian* is about to undergo change.

Nine in the fourth place signifies a double strength but one which is nonmean. It is neither in Heaven above, nor in the fields [Earth] below, nor with man in the middle.[11] Thus one regards it as a matter for hesitation. A matter for hesitation means that one should have doubts about it. This is why he will suffer no blame.

Fifth Yang

When a flying dragon is in the sky, it is fitting to see the great man. {Not moving, not leaping, yet it is in the sky. If it is not flying, how could it be done? This is what is meant by "a flying dragon." When a dragon's virtue is present in the sky, then the path of the great man will prevail.[12] A sovereign's position depends on his virtue to prosper, and a sovereign's virtue depends on his position to have practical expression. When this grand and noble position is filled by someone with such paramount virtue, all under Heaven will go to him and look up to him with hope—is this not indeed appropriate!}

COMMENTARY ON THE IMAGES

"When a flying dragon is in the sky": a great man takes charge.

COMMENTARY ON THE WORDS OF THE TEXT

"When a flying dragon is in the sky, it is fitting to see the great man." What does this mean? The Master says: "Things with the same tonality resonate together; things with the same material force seek out one another. Water flows to where it is wet; fire goes toward where it is dry. Clouds follow the dragon; wind follows the tiger. The sage bestirs himself, and all creatures look to him. What is rooted in Heaven draws close to what is above; what is rooted in Earth draws close to what is below. Thus each thing follows its own kind."

"A flying dragon is in the sky": rule on high prevails.

"A flying dragon is in the sky": it now takes a position amid the virtue of Heaven.

The great man is someone whose virtue is consonant with Heaven and Earth, his brightness with the sun and the moon, his consistency with the four seasons, and his prognostications of the auspicious and inauspicious with the workings of gods and spirits. When he precedes Heaven, Heaven is not contrary to him, and when he follows Heaven, he obeys the timing of its moments. Since Heaven is not contrary to him, how much the less will men or gods and spirits be!

Top Yang

A dragon that overreaches should have cause for regret.

COMMENTARY ON THE IMAGES

"A dragon that overreaches should have cause for regret": when something is at the full, it cannot last long.

COMMENTARY ON THE WORDS OF THE TEXT

"A dragon that overreaches should have cause for regret." What does this mean? The Master says: "Although noble, he lacks a [ruler's] position; although at a lofty height, he lacks a people's following. {Beneath there are no yin lines.} He has worthies in subordinate positions, but none help him. {Although there are worthies below filling appropriate positions, they provide no help to him.} Thus, when he acts, he should have cause for regret." {One is located at the top of the upper trigram and is not appropriate for the position he holds. Thus he thoroughly reveals all his deficiencies. Standing alone, he makes a move, and no one will go along with him. The Commentary on the Words of the Text for *Qian* does not first discuss Qian but begins instead to talk about "fundamentality" and only later does it say what *Qian* is. Why does it do that? *Qian* designates the unified control that governs the four entities [fundamentality, prevalence, fitness, and constancy]. "The noble man never ceases to strengthen himself"[13] as he puts these four into practice. This is why the text here does not first discuss *Qian* and only later says: "*Qian* consists of fundamentality, prevalence, fitness, and constancy." It explains the rest of the hexagram lines in terms of the dragon, except for Third Yang, for which it makes the noble man the topic. Why does it do that? This is because the *Changes* consist of images, and what images are produced from are concepts. One first has to have a particular concept, which one then brings to light by using some concrete thing to exemplify it. Thus one uses the dragon to express *Qian* and the mare to illustrate *Kun*. One follows the concept inherent in a matter and chooses an image for it accordingly. This is why at First Yang and at Second Yang the respective virtues of the dragon in each correspond to the concepts involved. Thus one can use discussions of the dragon in order to clarify them. However, at Third Yang, "the noble man makes earnest efforts" and "with evening he still takes care" are not references to the virtue of a dragon, so it is obvious that it employs the noble man to serve as the image here. As a whole, the *Qian* hexagram is a matter of dragons throughout, but when it is expressed in different terms, these are always formulated in terms of the concepts involved.}

"A dragon that overreaches should have cause for regret": this signifies the disaster that results from the exhaustion of resources.

"A dragon that overreaches should have cause for regret": it is at extreme odds with the moment. {This means to be at complete odds with the dynamics of the moment.}

The expression "overreaches" means that one knows how to advance but not how to retreat, knows how to preserve life but not how to relinquish it, knows how to gain but not how to lose. Could such a one ever be a sage? But if one knows how to advance, to retreat, to preserve life, and to relinquish it, all without losing his rectitude, how could such a one be but a sage?

COMMENTARY ON THE APPENDED PHRASES

The Master said: "One might be noble yet lack the position, might be lofty yet lack the subjects, and might have worthy men in subordinate positions who yet will not assist him. If such a one acts with all this being so, he will have cause for regret."[14]

All Use Yang Lines

When one sees a flight of dragons without heads, it is good fortune. {The nines [yang lines] all signify the virtue of Heaven. As we are able to use the virtue of Heaven [for all the lines], we see the concept of a flight of dragons in them. If one were to take up a position of headship over men by using nothing but hardness and strength, that would result in people not going along with it. If one were to engage in improper behavior by using softness and compliance, that would result in a dao of obsequiousness and wickedness. This is why the good fortune of *Qian* resides in there being no head to it, and the fitness of *Kun* [Pure Yin, Hexagram 2] resides in its perpetual constancy.}

COMMENTARY ON THE IMAGES

"All use yang lines": the virtue of Heaven is such that it cannot provide headship.

COMMENTARY ON THE WORDS OF THE TEXT

Here the fundamentality of *Qian* is expressed in all nines [yang lines], signifying the entire world well governed. {This entire section [of the Commentary on the Words of the Text] uses the affairs of men to clarify what is meant. Nine signifies the positive principle [yang], and yang is exemplified by things that are strong and inviolable. The ability to employ strength and inviolateness completely and to renounce and drive far away those who are good at toadying can never emerge except when the entire world is perfectly governed.[15] This is why the text says: "Here the fundamentality of *Qian* is expressed in all nines, signifying the entire world well governed." Once one recognizes how a thing acts, then all the principles of its existence can be understood. The virtue that a dragon signifies is such that it precludes doing anything inopportune. "Submerged" and "does not act," what do these mean? It means that it is sure to locate itself at the lowest possible place. "Sees" and "in the fields" mean that it is sure to lodge there because of the suitability of the moment. Regard the lines as signifying the ways there are to be a man and the positions among them to signify moments. If a man refrains from inopportune behavior, then all moments can be known by him. The fact that King Wen had to suffer suppression of his bright virtue allows us to know what kind of ruler there was then,[16] and the fact that Zhongni [Confucius] had to travel about among strangers allows us to know what his own state was like.[17]}

Here the fundamentality of *Qian* is expressed in all nines [yang lines], thus we see the law of Heaven. {This entire section talks about the material force of Heaven in order to clarify what is meant.

The nines [yang lines] signify something that is strong and inviolable. Only the *Qian* hexagram can use them throughout. If one observes Heaven from the point of view of this pure strength, the law of Heaven can be seen.}

NOTES

1. It is likely that Wang has used *jian* (strength) as a pun on *Qian* (both characters seem to have had the same pronunciation in the archaic Chinese of his day: **g'ian*), implying that as the two sound alike, so their meanings are similar if not identical. In his commentary on *Kun* (Pure Yin), Hexagram 2, Commentary on the Judgments, Wang uses almost the same sentence structure: "The term *Earth* is the name of a form, a phenomenal entity; the term *Kun* refers to that which uses or takes this form." We should note also that *Qian* is also identified with *jian* in section seven of Explaining the Trigrams.

2. This and all subsequent text set off in this manner is commentary by Wang Bi.

3. See sections one, five, six, eleven, and twelve of the Commentary on the Appended Phrases, Part One, and sections one, two, six, ten, and twelve of the Commentary on the Appended Phrases, Part Two.

4. "The great man" translates *daren*, a term used, like *junzi*, to designate the noble man, one worthy of being a sovereign.

5. I.e., the third line is on top of two yang lines.

6. Wang here seems to have had section ten of the Commentary on the Appended Phrases, Part One, in mind here: "It is a grasp of incipience alone that thus allows one to accomplish the great affairs of the world."

7. *Shijing* (Book of odes), no. 255.

8. Nine is a "positive" (yang) and "strong" number, and so is three. "Mean" refers to the middle line in a trigram; since the third line is at the top of the trigram, it is "nonmean."

9. Kong Yingda's subcommentary helps to clarify this passage: "The *Changes* forms its hexagrams in such a way that the third and fourth lines signify the Dao of Man, but what Man is close to is below him [Earth], not what is above him [Heaven]. This is why Fourth Yang is said to be 'not with Man' and differs from Third Yang." See *Zhouyi zhengyi*, 1: 5a. Note also that Wang's comment here is derived from a passage in the Commentary on the Words of the Text.

10. See note 5 above.

11. See note 9 above.

12. "Prevail" translates *heng*, consistent with the Judgment to *Qian*: "*Qian* consists of fundamentality, prevalence, fitness, and constancy" (respectively, *yuan*, *heng*, *li*, and *zhen*). Lou Yulie, however, glosses *heng* here

as "clear" (*tongda*), as in "the road is clear." See *Wang Bi ji jiaoshi*, 1: 220 n. 18.

13. See the Commentary on the Images for this hexagram.

14. See section eight of the Commentary on the Appended Phrases, Part One.

15. "Except when the entire world is perfectly governed" translates *fei tianxia zhizhi*. The text in *Zhouyi zhengyi*, has *zhili* (perfect principle), but this has been shown to be a Tang era alteration to avoid the taboo use of the personal name of Li Zhi, Emperor Gaotzung (reigned 650—684). There is good evidence to prove that the text originally was either *zhi* (well governed) or *zhizhi* (perfectly governed). See Lou, *Wang Bi ji jiaoshi*, 1: 224 n. 49. Wing-tsit Chan's translation of this passage as "only because there is ultimate principle in the world. . . ." apparently follows the later, altered text. See *Source Book*, p. 320.

16. King Wen, the father of King Wu who overthrew the Shang and founded the Zhou state (1122 B.C.), was supposedly the long-suffering vassal of Zhou, the wicked last Shang king.

17. Lu, the home state of Confucius, was so badly governed that he had to travel abroad to try to find a worthy sovereign to serve.

HEXAGRAM 2

䷁

坤

Kun [Pure Yin]
(*Kun* Above *Kun* Below)

Judgment

Kun consists of fundamentality, and prevalence, and its fitness is that of the constancy of the mare. {The constancy of *Kun* is fitting just in the way constancy is fitting for the mare. The horse is a creature that travels by staying down [on the ground], but even more important we have the female of it, so it is something that represents the acme of compliance [*shun*]. Here one will prevail only after becoming perfectly compliant, and this is why the text says that one will only achieve fitness in the constancy of the mare.[1]} Should the noble man set out to do something, if he were to take the lead, he would go astray, but if he were to follow, he would find a master. It is fitting to find friends in the southwest and to spurn friends in the northeast. To practice constancy with serenity means good fortune. {The southwest is the land of utmost nurturing and belongs to the same Dao as *Kun*.[2] Thus the text says "find friends." The northeast is the opposite of the southwest. Thus the text says "spurn friends." When yin is manifest in something, that something must distance itself from its own ilk and go to the opposite [yang] kind, for only then will it garner the good fortune derived from practicing "constancy with serenity."}

COMMENTARY ON THE JUDGMENTS

How great is the fundamental nature of *Kun*! The myriad things are provided their births by it, and in so doing it compliantly carries out Heaven's will. It is the generosity of *Kun* that lets it carry everything, the integrative force of its virtue that accounts for its limitlessness, and its vast power to accommodate that makes it glorious and great—so that things in all their different categories can prevail as they should. The mare is a metaphor for the Earth, for it travels the Earth without limit. {The way the Earth manages to be without limit is by acting with humility. *Qian* rides through Heaven as a dragon, but *Kun* travels the Earth as a horse.} For one who is yielding and compliant, it is fitting to practice constancy here, and the noble man who sets out to do something, if he takes the lead, will be in breach of the Dao, but if he follows and is compliant, he will find his rightful place. "To find friends in the southwest" means to travel with one's own kind, and "to spurn friends in the northeast" means that in the end one will have blessings. The good fortune that here derives from practicing constancy with serenity is a matter of resonating with the limitless qualities of the Earth. {The term *Earth* is the name of a form, a phenomenal entity; the term *Kun* refers to that which uses or takes this form.[3] Two males will be sure to fight, and two masters will involve peril. That which has the form of the Earth [*Kun*] joins together with the hard and the strong [*Qian*] to form a matched pair, by means of which things are preserved "without limit." Of course, to put *Kun* into practice will certainly achieve the utmost compliancy, but if this were to be done without regard to the qualities of the mare or if one were to try to achieve fitness without regard to the perpetual maintenance of constancy, the one approach would make him not just square and solid but also inflexible, and the other would make him not just compliant but also irresolute, so in either case his search for security would be difficult indeed!}

COMMENTARY ON THE IMAGES

Here is the basic disposition of Earth: this constitutes the image of *Kun*. {In physical form, Earth is not compliant; it is its basic disposition that is compliant.} In the same manner, the noble man with his generous virtue carries everything.

COMMENTARY ON THE WORDS OF THE TEXT

Kun is perfectly compliant, but the way it takes action is strong and firm; it is perfectly quiescent, but its virtue is square and solid. {Action that is square and straight is incapable of doing evil, but to be so compliant that one becomes irresolute will lead to the deterioration of the Dao. When the virtue involved is perfectly quiescent, that virtue must be "square and solid."}

It is by following that one obtains a master and finds a rightful place, and it is by accommodating the myriad things that the transformative power of *Kun* achieves its glory—both these facts surely indicate how the Dao of *Kun* consists of compliance: in carrying out Heaven's will, its actions are always timely.

COMMENTARY ON THE APPENDED PHRASES

As Heaven is high and noble and Earth is low and humble, so it is that *Qian* [Pure Yang, Hexagram 1] and *Kun* [Pure Yin] are defined.

The Dao of *Kun* forms the female. . . . *Kun* acts to bring things to completion.

Kun through simplicity provides capability. . . . As [it] is simple, it is easy to follow. . . . If one is easy to follow, he will have meritorious accomplishments.

When [the Dao] duplicates patterns, we call it *Kun*.

As for *Kun*, in its quiescent state it is condensed, and in its active state it is diffuse. This is how it achieves its capacious productivity.

This is why closing the gate is called *Kun*.

Qian and *Kun*, do they not constitute the arcane source for change! When *Qian* and *Kun* form ranks, change stands in their midst, but if *Qian* and *Kun* were to disintegrate, there would be no way that change could manifest itself. And if change could not manifest itself, this would mean that *Qian* and *Kun* might almost be on the point of extinction!

All the activity that take place in the world, thanks to constancy, is the expression of the One. . . . *Kun* being yielding shows us how simple it is.

The Yellow Emperor, Yao, and Shun let their robes hang loosely down, yet the world was well governed. They probably got the idea for this from the hexagrams *Qian* and *Kun*.

The Master said: "*Qian* and *Kun*, do they not constitute the two-leaved gate into the *Changes*?. . . *Kun* is a purely yin thing.

Kun [Pure Yin] is a yin thing.

Kun is the most compliant thing in the entire world, so it should always be simple to put its virtue into practice. [It] is able to refine the concerns of the feudal lords.[4]

PROVIDING THE SEQUENCE OF THE HEXAGRAMS

Only after there were Heaven [*Qian*, Pure Yang, Hexagram 1] and Earth [*Kun*, Pure Yin], were the myriad things produced from them. What fills Heaven and Earth is nothing other than the myriad things.

THE HEXAGRAMS IN IRREGULAR ORDER

Kun [Pure Yin] [is] soft and yielding.

First Yin

The frost one treads on reaches its ultimate stage as solid ice. {What starts out as frost that one might tread on ultimately becomes hard ice. This is what is meant when it [the Commentary on the Words of the Text] says, "*Kun* is perfectly compliant, but the way it takes action is strong and firm." Yin as a Dao is such that, although rooted in humble weakness, it thereafter brings about prominence through its accumulated effect. Thus the text chooses "frost one treads on" to clarify how *Kun* begins. Yang as physical manifestation does not involve things that first have foundations established so they can achieve prominence later. Thus the text clarifies yang things in terms of activity and inactivity, as, for instance, [a dragon] "submerged" in the first line [i.e., *Qian*, First Yang].}

COMMENTARY ON THE IMAGES

The frost one treads on becomes solid ice: This yin thing begins to congeal. Obediently fulfilling its Dao, it ultimately becomes solid ice.

COMMENTARY ON THE WORDS OF THE TEXT

A family that accumulates goodness will be sure to have an excess of blessings, but one that accumulates evil will be sure to have an excess of disasters. When a subject kills his lord or a son kills his father, it is never because of what happens between the morning and evening of the same day but because of something that has been building up for a long time and that should have been dealt with early—but was not. When the *Changes* say "the frost one treads on reaches its ultimate stage as solid ice," is it not talking about compliancy [with the Dao involved]?[5]

Second Yin

He is straight [*zhi*], square [*fang*], and great [*da*], so without working at it, nothing he does here fails to be fitting. {Here, finding oneself at the center and obtaining his correct position there, he perfectly realizes in himself the qualities inherent in the Earth: he allows things their natural course, so they produce themselves, and he does not try to improve upon and manage them, so success comes about by itself.[6] This is why the text says: "Without working at it, nothing he does here fails to be fitting."}

COMMENTARY ON THE IMAGES

Actions associated with Second Yin are straight and thus square. {When one reveals himself to be straight and square in his actions, it means that he has allowed these qualities free play here.} "Without working at it, nothing he does here fails to be fitting": here is the glory of the Dao of Earth.

COMMENTARY ON THE WORDS OF THE TEXT

"Straight" refers to the rectitude [*zheng*] of *Kun*, and "square" refers to its righteousness [*yi*]. The noble man keeps his inner self straight by means of reverence [*jing*] and keeps his outer life square by means of righteousness. With the establishment of reverence and righteousness, one keeps oneself free from isolation. "He is straight, square, and great, so without working at it, nothing he does here fails to be fitting." Thus he has no doubts about what he should do.

Third Yin

One who effaces his own prominent qualities here will be able to practice constancy. He might attend to his sovereign's business, and if he were to make no claim for its success, he should bring about a successful conclusion. {One who occupies the very top of the lower trigram yet does not excite the suspicions of yang personages [sovereign, superiors] is someone who stays in harmony with the meaning [*yi*] involved here. He does not involve himself in initiating anything but must respond to the lead of another and must wait for orders before he starts to act: this is someone who effaces his own excellence and in so doing keeps himself correct. Thus the text says: "One who effaces his own prominent qualities here will be able to practice constancy." If there is business to attend to, he should do it but must not dare take the lead. Thus the text says: "He might attend to his sovereign's business." He brings things to a successful conclusion by obeying orders. Thus the text says: "If he were to make no claim for its success, he should bring about a successful conclusion."}

COMMENTARY ON THE IMAGES

"One who effaces his own prominent qualities here will be able to practice constancy": this means that he starts to act when the moment is opportune. "He might attend to his sovereign's business": his wisdom is glorious and great. Here is someone whose "wisdom is glorious and great," so he does not take the credit for things.

COMMENTARY ON THE WORDS OF THE TEXT

Although a yin person has excellence, he effaces it in order to attend to his sovereign's business and does not dare take credit for its success. This is the Dao of Earth, the Dao of the wife, and the Dao of the minister. The Dao of Earth has one "make no claim for . . . success" but working on behalf of the other [*Qian*—Pure Yang, i.e., Heaven—husband, sovereign], "he should bring about a successful conclusion."

Fourth Yin

Tie up the bag, so there will be no blame, no praise. {Here, located in a yin hexagram, one has a yin position occupied by a yin line, so to tread here does not involve a mean [*zhong*] position, and those who fill it do not have "straight and square" qualities. These do not engage in yang [the sovereign's] business, for they lack that excellence whose prominence should be effaced. "Tie up" [*gua*] means "bind up" [*jie*]—to keep confined. A worthy person should stay hidden here, and only by exercising caution can he get by, for the Dao of *Tai* [Peace, Hexagram 11] does not operate here.}

COMMENTARY ON THE IMAGES

"Tie up the bag, so there will be no blame": if one exercises caution, he will suffer no harm.

COMMENTARY ON THE WORDS OF THE TEXT

When Heaven and Earth engage in change and transformation, the whole plant kingdom flourishes, but when Heaven and Earth are confined, the worthy person keeps hidden. When the *Changes* say "tie up the bag, so there will be no blame, no praise," is it not talking about caution?

Fifth Yin

A yellow lower garment means fundamental good fortune. {"Yellow is the color of centrality [*zhong*, the Mean], and a lower garment adorns the bottom half of the body."[7] *Kun* is the Dao of the subject, whose excellence is completely realized below in the position of subordinate. Someone without hard and strong substance can let things fully realize their innate tendencies only by thoroughly grasping their principles, and he can occupy a noble position with the virtues of compliancy and obedience only if he has the required civil graces and control over those principles. He garners fundamental good fortune by letting his yellow lower garment hang loosely down and not by using martial power. Here, he achieves the utmost nobility of the yin but does not go so far as to excite the suspicions of the yang, and this is due to "the civil graces abiding within," "the very acme of excellence."}

COMMENTARY ON THE IMAGES

"A yellow lower garment means fundamental good fortune": this refers to the civil graces abiding within. {That one wears a yellow lower garment and garners fundamental good fortune here is due to "the civil graces abiding within."}

COMMENTARY ON THE WORDS OF THE TEXT

The noble man, garbed in yellow and maintaining the Mean, thoroughly grasps the principles of things. The correct position for him is this place in the trigram. Excellence abides within him, emanating through his four limbs and expressed in his deeds—the very acme of excellence.

Top Yin

Dragons fight in the fields, their blood black and yellow. {Yin as a Dao means to be humble and obedient and to remain within one's limits—this is how its excellence is fully realized. Here, however, it has become all that it can be but does not stop and would take over yang territory, something that the yang principle will not permit. This is why the text says that they "fight in the fields."}

COMMENTARY ON THE IMAGES

"Dragons fight in the fields": the Dao of *Kun* has reached its limits.

COMMENTARY ON THE WORDS OF THE TEXT

As yin provokes the suspicions of yang, it must fight. {Not having taken appropriate steps beforehand, yang becomes suspicious of yin now at the peak of its strength and so takes action; this is why "it must fight."[8]} It is because yin calls into question the fact that it is totally lacking in yang. {It fights because it calls into question the fact that it is not yang, that it is referred to as a dragon here.[9] It is because it still has not abandoned its own kind.} It is because it has still not forsaken its yin-ness that it is exterminated by yang, that blood is mentioned here. {As it still fights with yang and because they wound each other, so there is mention of blood.[10]} Black-and-yellow refers to how Heaven and Earth are mixed together. Heaven is black and Earth is yellow.

All Use Yin Lines[11]

It is fitting to practice constancy perpetually here. What is fitting here at All Use Yin Lines is to practice constancy perpetually.

COMMENTARY ON THE IMAGES

"All Use Yin Lines" signifies that greatness and final success are achieved through the practice of perpetual constancy. {This refers to one who is able to achieve greatness and final success through the practice of perpetual constancy.}

NOTES

1. This and all subsequent text set off in this manner is commentary by Wang Bi.

2. This paraphrases section five of Explaining the Trigrams: "*Kun* [Pure Yin] here means the Earth. The myriad things all are nourished to the utmost by it."

3. See Hexagram 1, *Qian* (Pure Yang), note 1.

4. See sections one, five, six, eleven, and twelve of the Commentary on the Appended Phrases, Part One, and sections one, two, six, ten, and twelve of the Commentary on the Appended Phrases, Part Two.

5. Zhu Xi points out that since the characters *shun* (compliancy) and *shen* (caution) were used interchangeably in antiquity, *shun* ought to be read as *shen* here—referring to how one should deal with things when they have just barely begun. His version would read: "Is it not talking about caution?" See *Zhouyi zhezhong*, 16: 25b. This seems rather forced and unlikely, especially since *compliancy* figures so prominently in this and other sections of the text of *Kun*. "Compliancy with the Dao involved" makes

good sense from the context and obviously refers to the fact that once a thing starts, it will comply with the dictates of its inner nature—whether for good or for evil.

6. This is similar to Wang's comment on a passage in the fifth section of the *Laozi*: "Heaven and Earth are not benevolent; they treat the myriad things as straw dogs." Wang Bi's comment: "Heaven and Earth allow things to follow their natural course. They do not engage in purposeful action and create nothing, so the myriad things manage themselves. This is why the text says that they 'are not benevolent.' " See Lou, *Wang Bi ji jiaoshi*, 1: 13.

7. This quotes from a passage in the *Zuozhuan* (Zuo's commentary on the *Spring and Autumn Annals*), concerning the twelfth year of the reign of Duke Shao (529 B.C.). Cf. Legge, *The Chinese Classics*, 5: 640.

8. This translates *yin yi yu yang bi zhan*. This interpretation and the rendering of Wang's commentary follow Kong Yingda's subcommentary: "As yin has reached the peak of its strength, it comes under the suspicions of yang, which then takes action, wishing to extirpate this yin, but since yin is already at the peak of its strength, it is unwilling to take evasive action. This is why 'it must fight.' " See *Zhouyi zhengyi*, 1: 27b. However, it is also possible to interpret both differently: "When yin feels it can disparage yang, there is sure to be a fight" (for the Commentary on the Words of the Text); "As it was not dealt with before this, its disparagement reaches full measure, and so it takes action. This is why 'there is sure to be a fight' " (for Wang Bi's commentary). This second reading follows Itō Tōgai's (1670—1736) interpretation; see *Shūeki kyōyoku tsūkai*, 1: 28. It glosses *yi* as *naigashiro ni suru*—"treat with contempt, disparage," i.e., "call into question one's viability." Later commentators, notably Cheng Yi and Zhu Xi, ignore the remarks of Wang Bi and Kong Yingda and take *yin yi yu yang bi zhan* quite differently: "When yin is an equal match for yang, there is sure to be a fight," deriving the sense of "equal match" for *yi* from another of its basic meanings, "resemble, feign." See *Zhouyi zhezhong*, 16: 31a.

9. Following Kong Yingda's subcommentary: "Top Yin at the peak of its strength seems as if it were yang, and, because it calls into question the fact that it is pure yin and totally lacking in yang, 'it is referred to as a dragon' in order to make this clear." See *Zhouyi zhengyi*, 1: 27b.

10. Zhu Xi comments: "Blood belongs to the yin category. *Qi* [spirit, material force] is yang, and blood is yin. Black and yellow are the true colors of Heaven and Earth, so this means that yin and yang are both wounded here." This agrees with Cheng Yi's interpretation: "Although yin here is at the peak of its strength, it has not abandoned its yin-ness. As it fights with yang, we can be sure that it gets wounded. This is why 'there is mention of blood.' Yin has already reached the peak of its strength and even goes so far as to do battle with yang, so yang cannot avoid getting wounded. This is why the blood involved is black and yellow." See *Zhouyi zhezhong*, 16: 31a.

11. The All Use Yin Lines of Hexagram 2, the Commentary on the Images, and Wang Bi's commentary to both are all omitted in the *Wang Bi ji jiaoshi* edition; translation of these texts here follows Kong, *Zhouyi zhengyi*, 1: 25b.

HEXAGRAM 3

䷂

屯

Zhun [Birth Throes]
(*Zhen* Below *Kan* Above)

Judgment

Zhun consists of fundamentality [*yuan*], prevalence [*heng*], fitness [*li*], and constancy [*zhen*]. {"When the hard and the soft begin to interact," *Zhun* [Birth Throes] occurs. If such interaction fails to take place, *Pi* [Obstruction, Hexagram 12] results. This is why, when *Zhun* occurs, it means great prevalence. With great prevalence, one is free from danger, and this is why it is fitting to practice constancy.[1]} Do not use this as an opportunity to go forth. {The more one would go forth, the greater the *Zhun* [Birth Throes].} It is fitting to establish a chief. {Stability will come about only with the obtaining of a master.[2]}

COMMENTARY ON THE JUDGMENTS

Zhun [Birth Throes] means the difficulty of giving birth when the hard and the soft begin to interact. One who takes action in the midst of danger here will greatly prevail and so can practice constancy. {It starts in danger and difficulty but goes on to arrive at great prevalence and, after that, attains perfect rectitude. This is why the text says: "*Zhun* [Birth Throes] consists of fundamentality, prevalence, fitness, and constancy."} It is by the action of thunder and rain that the repletion of things occurs, something always brought about by the hard and the soft when they "begin to interact." At this primordial stage of Heaven's creativity, though it is appropriate to establish a chief, it will not mean stability. {The *Zhun* hexagram signifies instability. Thus the text says: "It is fitting to establish a chief." *Zhun* represents the initial stage in the creative activity of Heaven and Earth, the beginning of the creation of things that takes place in primordial obscurity. This is why the text says "primordial stage." When one finds himself located at such initial stages of creative activity, there is no more appropriate good to pursue than that of establishing a chief.}

COMMENTARY ON THE IMAGES

Clouds and Thunder: this constitutes the image of Birth Throes. In the same way, the noble man weaves the fabric of government. {This is a time for the noble man to weave the fabric of government.[3]}

PROVIDING THE SEQUENCE OF THE HEXAGRAMS

Only after there were Heaven [*Qian*, Pure Yang, Hexagram 1] and Earth [*Kun*, Pure Yin, Hexagram 2] were the myriad things produced from them. What fills Heaven and Earth is nothing other than the myriad things. This is why *Qian* and *Kun* are followed by *Zhun* [Birth Throes]. *Zhun* here signifies repletion.

THE HEXAGRAMS IN IRREGULAR ORDER

Zhun [Birth Throes] means "making an appearance in such a way that one does not lose one's place."

First Yang

One should tarry here. It is fitting to abide in constancy. It is fitting to establish a chief. {To be located at First Yang of *Zhun* means that any action taken would result in trouble, so one may not advance; this is why the text says: "One should tarry here." When one is located at this moment, what is the fit thing to do? Can it be anything other than to "abide in constancy" and to "establish a chief"? One brings cessation to chaos by means of quietude, and one maintains that quietude by means of a chief. Pacifying the people depends on the practice of rectitude, and the promotion of rectitude depends on modesty [*qian*]. In the world of trouble represented by *Zhun*, the yin seek out the yang, and the weak seek out the strong. It is a time when the people long for their master. First Yang is located at the head of *Zhun*, but it also lies at the bottom of it. Its line text perfectly expresses what is meant here, and how just is its way for winning over the people!}

COMMENTARY ON THE IMAGES

Although "one should tarry here," may his will be set on practicing rectitude. {One may not advance here; this is why the text says: "One should tarry." But this does not mean seeking one's own happiness and setting aside one's rightful duties. This is why the text says: "Although 'one should tarry here,' may his will be set on practicing rectitude."} It is by the noble subordinating himself to his inferiors that he wins over the people in large numbers. {Yang is noble, and yin is inferior.}

Second Yin

Here *Zhun* [Birth Throes] operates as impasse, as yoked horses pulling at odds. She is not one to be harassed into getting married but practices constancy and does not plight her troth. Only after ten years will she plight her troth. {Second Yin, its intent fixed on Fifth Yang, does not acquiesce to First Yang. At this time of difficulty in *Zhun*, the correct Dao does not function, so although Second Yin is contiguous to First Yang, it is not responsive to it. Here Second Yin is hampered by encroachment on the part of First Yang, and this is why *Zhun* is defined as "impasse." As this moment is just at a point of difficulty in *Zhun*, the correct Dao[4] is not yet open, so although a long journey is in order, it is difficult to make progress here. This is why the text says "as yoked horses pulling at odds." The one doing the harassing is First Yang. If it were not for the difficulty caused by First Yang, Second Yin would, of course, marry Fifth Yang. This is why the text says: "She is not one to be harassed into getting married." As Second Yin has its intent fixed on Fifth Yang and does not acquiesce to First Yang, the text says that she "does not plight her troth." This condition, of a world subject to *Zhun* as difficulty, will not last longer than ten years. After ten years, there will be "a return to the constant Dao," and once that happens, the object of one's original intent will be gained. This is why the text says: "Only after ten years will she plight her troth."}

COMMENTARY ON THE IMAGES

The difficulty that Second Yin suffers is due to the fact that it rides on a hard [yang] line. "Only after ten years will she plight her troth" refers to a return to the constant Dao.

Third Yin

To go after deer without a forester would only get one lost in the depths of the forest. The noble man, then, is aware that it would be better to refrain, for if he were to set out he would find it hard going. {Third Yin, having got close to Fifth Yang, is free from any difficulty stemming from harassment, and, although Fourth Yin is right next to Fifth Yang, its intention is fixed on First Yang, so there is nothing to block Third Yin's own path and it can thus advance, free from the impasse *Zhun* offers. It might see how easy is the path to Fifth Yang but neglect to reckon on what it is: since Fifth Yang resonates with Second Yin, if Third Yin were to set off for it, it would not be accepted by it. How would this be any different from trying to pursue a quarry without the help of a forester! Although one might sight the quarry, without the forester, he would merely "get . . . lost in the depths of the forest," so how could he ever catch it? *Ji* [then] is an interjection.[5] How could the noble man in his actions ever bring contempt and humiliation upon himself! This is why "it would be better to refrain" and "if he were to set out he would find it hard going"[6] and "find himself in dire straits."}

COMMENTARY ON THE IMAGES

"To go after deer without a forester": rather than pursuing quarry in this way the noble man refrains. "If he were to set out he would find it hard going" and would find himself in dire straits.

Fourth Yin

Although it involves yoked horses pulling at odds, one seeks to get married here. To set out means good fortune, and all will be fitting without fail. {Although Second Yin is right next to First Yang, it holds fast to constancy and does not acquiesce, as it is not one to harm its own intention. But here Fourth Yin seeks to marry First Yang, and when it sets forth, it surely will be accepted. This is why the text says: "To set out means good fortune, and all will be fitting without fail."}

COMMENTARY ON THE IMAGES

That one may seek and so go forth here is clear. {It has discerned the conditions pertaining to the other lines.}

Fifth Yang

Benefaction here is subject to the difficulty of *Zhun*. To practice constancy in small ways means good fortune, but to practice constancy in major ways means misfortune. {To be located in difficulties as represented by *Zhun* means that although one here finds himself in a noble position, he cannot extend great measures of largess and nobility to everyone, for his powers to succor others are limited by his own weakness and by obstacles: he may be a pervasive force among this petty crowd, but he is still tied as a matter of resonance to Second Yin. "Benefaction here is subject to the difficulty of *Zhun*." This means that this is not the place where one can extend himself to others in a grand way. He should keep his intention firmly fixed on his comrade [Second Yin] and not let others drive a wedge between them. Thus "to practice constancy in small ways means good fortune, but to practice constancy in major ways means misfortune."}

COMMENTARY ON THE IMAGES

"Benefaction here is subject to the difficulty of *Zhun*": this means that it is not yet the time to extend one's powers in a grand way.

Top Yin

As one's yoked horses pull at odds, so one weeps profuse tears of blood. {This is to occupy a place of the utmost danger and difficulty: below there is no one to respond with help, and ahead there is no place to which one may suitably advance. Although Top Yin is right next to Fifth Yang, Fifth Yang's "benefaction . . . is subject to the difficulty of *Zhun*," so the situation does not lend itself to their mutual response. To stand fast here will not gain security, and there is no suitable place to which one might move. Here one is trapped in the most dire of predicaments and has absolutely no one on whom to rely. This is why the text says: "So one weeps profuse tears of blood."}

COMMENTARY ON THE IMAGES

"So one weeps profuse tears of blood": how can one last long here!

NOTES

1. See Wang's remarks on this hexagram in section seven of his General Remarks. Note that this and all subsequent text set off in this manner is commentary by Wang Bi.

2. "Chief" translates *hou* (skilled archer, i.e., chief). Kong Yingda thinks (after Wang Bi, see below) that this refers to the time when "the Dao of the human world was first created, when things in it were not yet settled, so this is why it is appropriate to establish a chief in order to achieve stability." See *Zhouyi zhengyi*, 1: 28a. However, in his next comment on *hou*, Kong seems to have changed his mind and glosses it as *zhuhou* (feudal lords): "It is suitable that the sovereign take this *Zhun* hexagram as guide and appropriate that he establish feudal lords in order to extend his kindness to all creatures everywhere." See *Zhouyi zhengyi*, 1: 29a. Although Cheng Yi also glosses *hou* as *zhuhou* in his comment on this passage, Zhu Xi thinks that it refers to First Yang, the ruler of the entire hexagram, which lies beneath yin lines and thus is an image of a sovereign who emerges as a worthy from the common folk—something more in line with Wang's "master." For Zhu's and Cheng's views, see *Zhouyi zhezhong*, 1: 20b.

3. "Weave the fabric of government" translates *jinglun*, that is, *jingwei*, the warp and woof of fabric, a metaphor for order/ordering, government/governing. See Cheng Yi's and Zhu Xi's comments in *Zhouyi zhezhong*, 11: 7b.

4. This is playing on the literal meaning of *dao* as "way" or "path."

5. The translation of *ji* (then) in Third Yin follows this gloss of Wang Bi; Kong Yingda also takes *ji* this way. See *Zhouyi zhengyi*, 1: 30b. However, later commentators such as Cheng Yi and Zhu Xi take *ji* as a substantive noun *incipience* as it occurs in section ten of the Commentary on the Appended Phrases, Part One: "It is by means of the *Changes* that the sages plumb the utmost profundity and dig into the very incipience of things." *Junzi ji* (the noble man, then, . . .) is glossed by Cheng Yi as *junzi jian shi zhi jiwei* (the noble man discerns the incipient and imperceptible beginnings of things), and Zhu Xi glosses it as simply *junzi jian ji* (the noble man discerns incipience). See *Zhouyi zhezhong*, 1: 23b. In the light of these glosses, Third Yin would read: "The noble man, discerning what is incipient here, is aware that it would be better to stand fast."

6. "If he were to set out he would find it hard going" translates *wang lin*. Lou Yulie cites Sun Xingyan's (1753–1818) *Zhouyi jijie* (Collected exegeses on the *Changes of the Zhou*):

The *Shuowen* [*jiezi*] [Explanations of simple and composite characters], an etymological dictionary of Chinese compiled about 100 a.d. by Xu Shen], cites *wang lin* [using the *lin* that in various contexts means "regret" or "base"] as *wang lin* [another character], in which *lin* means "hard going." Whenever the expressions *wang lin*, *wang jian lin* [if he were to set out he would experience hard going], and *yi wang lin* [if he were to set out in this way he would find it hard going] occur, they all ought to be interpreted in this way, for *lin* here is not the *lin* in *huilin* [remorse and regret]. See *Wang Bi ji jiaoshi*, 1: 244 n. 14.

This interpretation seems to hold true for occurrences in Wang Bi's commentary, and Kong Yingda usually understands *lin* this way when it occurs together with *wang* (set out), but not always: here, for instance, he understands it as *huilin* (remorse and regret). See *Zhouyi zhengyi*, 1: 30b.

HEXAGRAM 4

䷃

蒙

Meng [Juvenile Ignorance]
(*Kan* Below *Gen* Above)

Judgment

Meng brings about prevalence. It is not I who seek the Juvenile Ignorant but the Juvenile Ignorant who seeks me. An initial rendering of the yarrow stalks should be told, but a second or a third would result in violation. If there were such violation, I should not tell him. {The yarrow stalks are things that resolve doubts. The reason why a youth beset by ignorance seeks me is that he wants me to resolve the uncertainties that he has. If I resolve them in more than one way, he will not know which solution to follow and would then be thrown back into uncertainty. This is why "an initial rendering of the yarrow stalks should be told, but a second or third would result in violation" and "the one who would bring about this violation is the Juvenile Ignorant." How could other than Second Yang ever manage "an initial rendering of the yarrow stalks"! It is due to its "strength and adherence to the Mean" that it can decide such doubts.[1]} It is fitting to practice constancy here. {The fitness associated with *Meng* means that it is fitting to practice rectitude here. None is more perspicacious than the sage, and none is more benighted than the Juvenile Ignorant. "To take Juvenile Ignorance and cultivate rectitude in it," in fact, "is the meritorious task of the sage." As this is so, if one were instead to try to achieve perspicacity by cultivating rectitude [in others], this would be to misconstrue the Dao involved.[2]}

COMMENTARY ON THE JUDGMENTS

Meng [Juvenile Ignorance] consists of a dangerous place below a mountain. In danger and brought to a halt: this is *Meng*. {If one retreats, he will come to grief in danger, but if one advances, he will find the mountain a shut door, so he does not know where to go. This is the meaning of *Meng*.[3]} "*Meng* brings about prevalence": *Meng* operates through prevalence and is a matter of timeliness and the Mean. {What this moment of *Meng* wants to achieve is nothing other than prevalence. One makes *Meng* work by means of prevalence, and this is a matter of obtaining both the right moment and a mean position. 'It is not I who seek the Juvenile Ignorant but the Juvenile Ignorant who seeks me": their intentions are in resonance. "I" refers to the one who is not the Juvenile Ignorant. The one who is not the Juvenile Ignorant is [Second] Yang. It is always one who does not know who seeks out and asks one who does know; the one who does know does not seek to have things told to him. The unenlightened seeks out the perspicacious; the perspicacious does not solicit the counsel of the unenlightened. Thus the meaning of *Meng* is such that "it is not I who seek the Juvenile Ignorant but the Juvenile Ignorant who seeks me." The reason the "Juvenile Ignorant" comes and seeks "me" is that "their intentions are in resonance."} "An initial rendering of the yarrow stalks should be told": this he can do because of his strength and adherence to the Mean. {This refers to Second Yang. Second Yang is the master of all the yin lines. If it both lacked strength and violated the Mean, what possibly could it draw upon for the telling of "an initial rendering of the yarrow stalks!"} "But a second or a third would result in violation. If there were such violation, I should not tell him." The one who would bring about this violation is the Juvenile Ignorant. To take Juvenile Ignorance and cultivate rectitude in it is the meritorious task of the sage.

COMMENTARY ON THE IMAGES

Below the Mountain emerges the Spring: this constitutes the image of Juvenile Ignorance. {"Below the Mountain emerges the

Spring," which is something that does not yet know where to go. This is the image of Juvenile Ignorance.} In the same way, the noble man makes his actions resolute and nourishes his virtue. {"Makes his actions resolute" is the meaning underlying "an initial rendering of the yarrow stalks." "Nourishes his virtue" is the "meritorious task" of "cultivating rectitude."}

PROVIDING THE SEQUENCE OF THE HEXAGRAMS

Zhun [Birth Throes, Hexagram 3] is when things are first born. When things begin life, they are sure to be covered [the literal meaning of *meng*—i.e., encapsulated in membranes, eggs, or seeds]. This is why *Zhun* is followed by *Meng* [Juvenile Ignorance]. *Meng* [covered] here indicates *Meng* [Juvenile Ignorance], that is, the immature state of things.

THE HEXAGRAMS IN IRREGULAR ORDER

Meng [Juvenile Ignorance] indicates confusion first followed by a coming to prominence.

First Yin

With the opening up of Juvenile Ignorance, it is fitting both to subject him to the awareness of punishment and to remove fetters and shackles, but if he were to set out in this way, he would find it hard going. {When one is located at First Yin of *Meng*, Second Yang provides illumination from above, so this is why "the opening up of Juvenile Ignorance" occurs here. "With the opening up of Juvenile Ignorance," one's hesitation to act is cleared up, so both the awareness of punishment and the removal are appropriate. "But if he were to set out in this way, he would find it hard going" means that the threat of punishment cannot long be used.[4]}

COMMENTARY ON THE IMAGES

"It is fitting to subject him . . . to the awareness of punishment": one does this by rectifying what the law is. {The dao of punishment is something that the true Dao finds despicable.[5] One attempts to control him by rectifying what the law is; thus there is this reference to "subjecting him to the awareness of punishment."}

Second Yang

To treat the Juvenile Ignorant with magnanimity means good fortune. To take a wife means good fortune. His child will be up to taking charge of the family. {It is due to Second Yang's strength and its abiding in centrality [the Mean] that it attracts the Juvenile Ignorant. As Second Yang is magnanimous and does not spurn them, those both near and far all arrive. This is why "to treat the Juvenile Ignorant with magnanimity means good fortune." A wife is someone who serves to complement him and so allows him to perfect his virtue. If one embodies the yang principle and yet can treat the Juvenile Ignorant with magnanimity, if one can abide in the Mean with one's strength intact, and if one takes a mate in this way, then no one will fail to respond positively to him. This is why "to take a wife means good fortune." Here one finds himself situated inside the lower trigram [i.e., the household]; with strength intact, he receives the weak, and, though kind and affable, he manages to maintain the Mean. As he is able to fulfill his duties in this way, he can pass them on to his child. This is what is meant by "his child will be up to taking charge of the family."}

COMMENTARY ON THE IMAGES

"His child will be up to taking charge of the family": the strong and the weak [generation by generation] accept [succeed] one another.

Third Yin

It will not do to marry this woman. Here she sees a man strong as metal and discards her self-possession, so there is nothing at all fitting here. {At the time of Juvenile Ignorance, the yin seek out the yang, and the benighted seek out the perspicacious, when each one seeks to have his lack of understanding alleviated. Third Yin is located at the top of the lower trigram, and Top Yang is located at the top of the upper trigram; they represent a woman and a man, respectively. It is not Top Yang that seeks Third Yin, but Third Yin who seeks Top Yang. This is a case of the woman taking the lead and seeking the man. The true embodiment of a woman is such that it is correct behavior for her to await commands. But here when she "sees a man strong as metal," she seeks him, and this is why the text says that she "discards her self-possession." If one were to extend himself to such a woman, he would find that her behavior is essentially disobedient. Thus the text says: "It will not do to marry this woman" and "there is nothing at all fitting here."[6]}

COMMENTARY ON THE IMAGES

"It will not do to marry this woman": her behavior is disobedient.

Fourth Yin

Here confounded by Juvenile Ignorance, one becomes base. {This is the only yin line that is distant from a yang line. It is located between two yin lines, so there is no one to alleviate its darkness. This is why one is "here confounded by Juvenile Ignorance." Confounded by the darkness of Juvenile Ignorance, Fourth Yin is unable to get close to a worthy and so start to develop the right kind of intentions, something that leads as well to meanness. This is why the text says "base."[7]}

COMMENTARY ON THE IMAGES

The baseness associated with being "confounded by Juvenile Ignorance" is due to being alone at a distance from the solid and the real. {Yang is referred to here as "the solid and the real."}

Fifth Yin

The Juvenile Ignorant here will find good fortune. {Here is someone with yin character who abides in a noble position. He does not take responsibility for supervising himself but instead relies on Second Yang for that. If he delegates authority so things can be done and if he does not belabor his own intelligence, efforts at achievement will be successful. This is why the text says: "The Juvenile Ignorant here will find good fortune."}

COMMENTARY ON THE IMAGES

The good fortune associated with Juvenile Ignorance here is due to compliant behavior achieved through an obedient mind. {He delegates authority so things can be done, neither takes the lead nor initiates action: this is "compliant behavior achieved through an obedient mind."[8]}

Top Yang

Strike at Juvenile Ignorance, but it is not fitting to engage in harassment; it is fitting to guard against harassment. {Here one is located at the end point of *Meng*. Occupying the top position with strength, he can strike at and drive away Juvenile Ignorance and so alleviate their [the yin lines'] darkness. Thus the text says: "Strike at Juvenile Ignorance." Juvenile Ignorance wishes to be alleviated, and Top Yang itself wishes to strike at it and drive it away. As this meets the wishes of those above and those below [all the yin lines], none fails to comply. If one were to provide protection for them, then all would attach themselves to him, but to try to take them over by force would make them all rebel. Thus the text says: "It is not fitting to engage in harassment; it is fitting to guard against harassment."[9]}

COMMENTARY ON THE IMAGES

"It is fitting to guard against harassment": For those above and those below will all comply.

NOTES

1. This and all subsequent text set off in this manner is commentary by Wang Bi.

2. See Wang's remarks on this hexagram in section seven of his General Remarks.

3. *Meng* consists of the trigrams *Kan* (Water, Sink Hole), the "danger," and *Gen* (Mountain, Restraint), the "shut door" of the mountain.

4. Kong Yingda comments:

> Once Juvenile Ignorance is dispersed, there is nothing to inhibit his actions, and this is why it is fitting to apply the threat of punishment to him. It is also fitting to remove the fetters and shackles of the criminal. As Juvenile Ignorance has been dispersed, matters about which he felt doubt have become clarified. In all such cases, it is

> appropriate that the criminal have his fetters and shackles removed. . . . If he were to set out imbued with the Correct Dao, the goodness of his actions would keep on increasing, but if he were to set out subject to the dao of punishment, there would be a mean-spirited aspect to what he does.

See *Zhouyi zhengyi*, 1: 33a.

"Mean-spirited" translates *bilin* and is thus a gloss on *lin* (hard going). Later Neo-Confucians interpret this passage differently. Although Cheng Yi seems to agree with Wang and Kong that punishment is inimical to the Dao and that what is really needed is the internalization of the sense of goodness, he differs from them in thinking that removing the "fetters and shackles" is a metaphor for the lifting of ignorance itself. Zhu Xi takes another view of how the lifting of ignorance should take place: "One first ought to punish severely and then for a time release him [from the fetters and shackles] in order to see how he behaves afterward. If one lets him set out but does not release him from them, this would result in the utmost shame and remorse." Wang Anshi and some others take an even different approach: If one does not use severe punishments right at the start to correct small faults but instead frees the ignorant youth from his fetters and shackles, this will inevitably lead to a "dao of remorse." See also Hexagram 62, Xiaoguo (Minor Superiority), Fifth Yin, and note 11 there.

5. Cf. *Laozi*, sections 36 and 49, pp. 89–90 and 129, where a similar idea is expressed.

6. "Man strong as metal" translates *jinfu*. Kong Yingda comments: "Top Yang is called *jinfu* because of its strength and yang-ness." See *Zhouyi zhengyi*, 1: 33b. Both Cheng Yi and Zhu Xi explain *jinfu* as "a wealthy man" whom the woman here wants for his money. Cheng also thinks that she has discarded the one she rightly ought to respond to (Top Yang) and instead chases after the nearby and convenient Second Yang; thus, in his view, she is both greedy and opportunistic. See *Zhouyi zhezhong*, 1: 29b.

7. "Base" translates *lin* (elsewhere "remorse" or "hard going"). For another such instance of *lin* (including "baseness" and "debase"), see Hexagram 40, *Xie* (Release), Third Yin, and note 9 there.

8. "Neither takes the lead nor initiates action" translates *buxian buwei*. Wang expresses a similar view in almost exactly the same language in his commentary to *Laozi*, sections 10 and 28, pp. 23 and 74. "Compliant behavior" translates *sun* (*shun*)—cf. *Sun* (Compliance), Hexagram 57—and "obedient mind" translates *shun*, following Kong Yingda's subcommentary; see *Zhouyi zhengyi*, 1: 34a.

9. Cheng Yi interprets this passage differently. He thinks that Top Yang represents Juvenile Ignorance at its worst and strongest, at the point where it leads one to banditry and rebellion. Thus one must strike hard at it. In the light of his commentary, the text would mean: "Attack the Juvenile Ignorant. It is not fitting that he engage in banditry. It is fitting to prevent such banditry." Zhu Xi's commentary, however, seems to agree with that of Wang Bi: one should strike at Juvenile Ignorance but avoid excessive force. He

also adds the remark: "All one can do is guard against enticements to evil from without, so that the Juvenile Ignorant can perfect his truth and purity." As such, Zhu provides a more specific gloss on "guard against harassment" than does Wang Bi (or Kong Yingda). See *Zhouyi zhezhong*, 1: 31a–31b.

HEXAGRAM 5

䷄

需

Xu [Waiting]
(*Qian* Below *Kan* Above)

Judgment

As there is sincerity in waiting, so prevalence shall be gloriously manifest, and constancy result in good fortune. It is fitting to cross the great river.

COMMENTARY ON THE JUDGMENTS

Xu means "waiting," as danger lies in front.[1] Hard and strong, one does not founder here, the meaning of which is, one will not find himself in dire straits. "As there is sincerity in waiting, so prevalence shall be gloriously manifest, and constancy result in good fortune": here one abides in the place of Heaven and does so with rectitude and within the Mean. {This refers to Fifth Yang. Here one abides in the place of Heaven[2] and practices rectitude and the Mean. It is by doing so that he makes provision against all contingencies. This is how the Dao of *Xu* is perfectly realized. Thus "prevalence shall be gloriously manifest, and constancy result in good fortune."[3]} "It is fitting to cross the great river": this means that if one were to set forth, he would gain meritorious achievement.

{When someone imbued with the virtue of *Qian* [Pure Yang] obtains the chance to move forward, he will prevail in whatever he sets out to do.}

COMMENTARY ON THE IMAGES

Clouds rise up to Heaven: this constitutes the image of Waiting.[4] In the same way, the noble man takes this opportunity to enjoy himself in drinking and eating. {As Juvenile Ignorance [Hexagram 4] has already faded away, replete virtue here gloriously prevails, so the time for "enjoying [oneself] in eating and drinking" has certainly arrived!}

PROVIDING THE SEQUENCE OF THE HEXAGRAMS

When things are in their immature state, one cannot fail to nourish them. This is why *Meng* [Juvenile Ignorance, Hexagram 4] is followed by *Xu* [Waiting]. *Xu* here indicates the Dao of food and drink [i.e., nourishment taken while waiting].

THE HEXAGRAMS IN IRREGULAR ORDER

Xu [Waiting] means "do not advance."

First Yang

When waiting in the countryside, it is fitting to practice perseverance, for then there will be no blame. {When one finds himself in a time of Xu, this is the farthest point away from difficulties, so one can stop his progress here. In so doing, he keeps far away from danger and waits for the right moment. Although such a one refrains from responding to opportunities, he can still in this way safeguard correct norms of conduct.}

COMMENTARY ON THE IMAGES

"Waiting in the countryside": this means that one does not risk engaging himself in difficult matters. "It is fitting to practice perseverance, for then there will be no blame": this means that one never neglects his rightful duties.

Second Yang

When waiting on the sand, it might slightly involve rebuke, but in the end, good fortune will result. {Here one gets moved closer to difficulties, and this is why the text says "waiting on the sand."[5] This does not go so far as to "attract . . . robbers to him,"[6] so the text merely says: "It might slightly involve rebuke." Here one is close but not so close that he is oppressed by danger and far but not so far that he will be too late for the moment when it happens. He treads on a place of strength and abides in the Mean and in this way awaits the right opportunity. "Although 'it might slightly involve rebuke,' he will finish up with good fortune."}

COMMENTARY ON THE IMAGES

"Waiting on the sand": it is with ease and generosity that he locates himself in this central position, so although "it might slightly involve rebuke," he will finish up with good fortune.

Third Yang

When waiting on the mud, it attracts robbers to him. {As a hard and strong person is oppressed with difficulties here, he wishes to advance along his way, but by doing so he comes to the attention of robbers and attracts enemies. Since he still has something for which to wait, he does not let his hardness and strength founder. That robbers have come is because he brought them upon himself, "but if he seriously takes the utmost precautions," this will allow him to avoid defeat.}

COMMENTARY ON THE IMAGES

"Waiting on the mud": calamity lies just beyond. It is he himself who has attracted robbers, but if he seriously takes the utmost precautions, he will not suffer defeat.

Fourth Yin

When waiting in blood, one has to come out of the pit. {Whenever mention is made of blood, it means that yin and yang have wounded each other. Here yin and yang are immediately contiguous but do not resonate together. Yang wishes to press forward, but yin blocks its way; thus they wound each other. The pit signifies the Dao of the yin principle. Here one is located at the first line of *Kan* [Sink Hole], which is to abide in a pit. Third Yang advances hard and strong, and Fourth Yin cannot ward it off. As it has been invaded, Fourth Yin has to fall back. This is a matter of "as he is compliant, he obeys" orders. This is why the text says: "When waiting in blood, one has to come out of the pit."}

COMMENTARY ON THE IMAGES

"Waiting in blood": as he is compliant, he obeys.

Fifth Yang

When waiting for wine and food, it means the good fortune that derives from constancy. {The waiting involved with *Xu* is done in order to achieve great success. As one here has already obtained the "place of Heaven" and freely practices the Mean and rectitude, there is nothing to wait for any longer. This is the reason why all one need be concerned about is "wine and food," for here one garners "the good fortune that derives from constancy."}

COMMENTARY ON THE IMAGES

"Wine and food" means "the good fortune that derives from constancy" because of adherence to the Mean and rectitude.

Top Yin

When entering the pit, one finds that three uninvited guests have arrived. If one treats them with respect, in the end, there will be good fortune. {The reason Fourth Yin "has to come out of the pit" is that, not being in resonance with Third Yang, it blocks its way, and if it does not fall back, it would suffer disaster. Thus it must abandon the pit and so avoid this confrontation with Third Yang. When one reaches Top Yin, he finds himself at the very end of this hexagram, so this cannot have anything to do with blocking the way. Top Yin is in resonance with Third Yang, so Third Yang's coming to Top Yin is done in order to render it assistance. Thus there is no falling back because of fear of disaster on Top Yin's part, but instead one takes a stand here by "entering the pit." The reason the three yang lines had not dared to advance is that this line represents the last stage of *Xu*'s difficulties, but with the actual end of these difficulties, they arrive without waiting to be summoned. It is because Top Yin itself is located at the end of these difficulties that they come of their own accord. Top Yin is located at a place where there is no position for it. Also it is one yin line and yet plays the host for three yang lines, thus it must "treat them with respect," for only then "in the end [will] there . . . be good fortune."}

COMMENTARY ON THE IMAGES

"Uninvited guests have arrived. If one treats them with respect, in the end, there will be good fortune." Although one is not in a proper position here, this is not a great mistake. {To be located in a place where there is no position for one is what "one is not in a proper position" means. It is by paying the guests respect that one obtains "good fortune in the end." This is why the text says: "Although one is not in a proper position here, this is not a great mistake."}

NOTES

1. Cheng Yi sums up the relationship between the constituent trigrams of *Xu*: "*Qian*'s nature being hard and strong means that it is something that must go forward, but here it is located beneath the danger of *Kan* [Sink Hole]. As this danger becomes an obstacle to *Qian*, it must now wait here and advance only later." See *Zhouyi zhezhong*, 1: 32a.

2. Kong Yingda glosses *tianwei* (place of Heaven) as *tianzi zhi wei* (position of the Son of Heaven, i.e., a true sovereign). *Zhouyi zhengyi*, 2: 1b.

3. This and all subsequent text set off in this manner is commentary by Wang Bi.

4. Kong Yingda comments: "The way Heaven has it rain is to wait for the right time to let it fall. In this way the text sheds light on how the great beneficence of *Xu* shall be dispensed and how its replete virtue shall also prevail." See *Zhouyi zhengyi*, 2: 2a.

5. Kong Yingda comments: "Sands are the lands at the edge of bodies of water, a bit closer to the water itself, so when one waits for the right mo-

ment on these sands, difficulties are consequently somewhat closer to him." See *Zhouyi zhengyi*, 2: 2a.

6. Cf. Third Yang here at *Xu*; Hexagram 40, *Xie* (Release), Third Yin; and section eight of the Commentary on the Appended Phrases, Part One.

HEXAGRAM 6

䷅

訟

Song [Contention]
(*Kan* Below *Qian* Above)

Judgment

In Contention, there should be sincerity. Exercise prudence in handling obstruction. To halt halfway means good fortune. {*Obstruction* means "hindrance" or "blockage." Only after one is able to exercise prudence, can he garner the good fortune involved with halting halfway.[1]} To persist to the end means misfortune. It is fitting to see the great man. It is not fitting to cross the great river.

COMMENTARY ON THE JUDGMENTS

Song [Contention] consists of strength in the upper trigram [*Qian*] and danger in the lower trigram [*Kan* (Sink Hole)]. To be in danger but still have strength, this is what *Song* means. "In Contention, there should be sincerity. Exercise prudence in handling obstruction. To halt halfway means good fortune": all this refers to the hard line [Second Yang], which arrives and takes up a middle position. "To persist to the end means misfortune":

this means that Contention does not allow for a successful conclusion. "It is fitting to see the great man": what one esteems is his adherence to the Mean and his rectitude. "It is not fitting to cross the great river": one would sink into the watery depths. {Whosoever gets involved in disagreement and enters into Contention will find that no matter what measures are taken, none will succeed, because the difficulties that he tries to traverse are too grave. Only someone who has sincerity and treats hindrance with caution will obtain good fortune here. But even he can no longer persist to the end; it is by halting halfway that one has good fortune. If one fails to stifle Contention at its inception and so prevent it from developing, even though in each instance one avoids any deviant behavior, Contention will continue to progress to its final stage, and this, indeed, would result in misfortune. Thus, although one has sincerity and treats hindrance with caution, he still cannot use these attributes to bring Contention to a successful conclusion. This is why the text says: "In Contention, there should be sincerity. Exercise prudence in handling obstruction. To halt halfway means good fortune. To persist to the end means misfortune." If there is not someone who is good at listening [i.e., capable of passing judgment on Contention, i.e., of litigation], even though the truth is on one's side, what means could ever bring it to light? So how could anyone who gets this command to have sincerity and to treat hindrance with caution ever obtain good fortune by halting halfway? For this to happen, there must be someone in charge who is good at listening, and is he not located at Second Yang? Here he arrives with his strength, makes all petty persons behave correctly, and avoids violating the Mean in making judgments. In so doing, he fulfills his responsibilities perfectly.[2]}

COMMENTARY ON THE IMAGES

Heaven and water operate in contrary ways: this constitutes the image of Contention.[3] In the same way, the noble man in conducting business carefully plans how such things begin. {"In listening to litigation [*song*], I am like other men. But what is really necessary is the prevention of litigation itself from happening!"[4] Avoidance of Contention [*Song*] depends on "carefully plan[ning] how . . . things begin," and "carefully plan[ning] how . . . things begin" depends on the setting-up of limitations and controls. It is lack of clarity in contracts that is the origin of Contention. If things have their proper allotment and responsibilities do not encroach upon each other, how could strife ever arise? The reason why Contention occurs is that people overstep the bounds of contracts. Thus those who have virtue tend to their contracts and do not lay blame on others.[5]}

PROVIDING THE SEQUENCE OF THE HEXAGRAMS

Food and drink necessarily involve *Song* [Contention]. This is why *Xu* [Waiting, Hexagram 5] is followed by *Song*.

THE HEXAGRAMS IN IRREGULAR ORDER

Song [Contention] means "not being affable."

First Yin

If one does not perpetuate the case involved, it might slightly involve rebuke, but in the end, good fortune will result. {Here one is located at the beginning of *Song* [Contention], but Contention can never be brought to a successful conclusion. Thus only when "one does not perpetuate the case involved" will good fortune follow. It is always yang that starts singing and yin that joins in. Yin is never the one to take the lead.[6] It should be Fourth Yang that gives the summons, to which First Yin then responds, but instead First Yin finds itself transgressed against, so Contention occurs.[7] It may be located at the beginning of *Song*, but First Yin is not the one that starts the Contention. Although it cannot help but finally get involved in Contention, First Yin should be sure to analyze clearly how the Contention comes about.}

COMMENTARY ON THE IMAGES

"If one does not perpetuate the case involved": that is, Contention cannot be protracted forever. Although "it might slightly involve rebuke," its analysis is clear.

Second Yang

Not victorious in Contention, one escapes by returning home. If his city consists of fewer than three hundred households, there will be no disaster. {As a hard [yang] line that finds a place in *Song*, Second Yang is an inferior entity that is not up to the task. From below it engages one that is above [Fifth Yang] in Contention, so it is appropriate that it is not victorious. If through caution such a one is able to escape by returning home to his own city, he can thereby avoid calamity. But if his city surpasses three hundred households, it will not be a place of refuge for him, for calamity is never avoided by escaping and then relying on strength.[8]}

COMMENTARY ON THE IMAGES

"Not victorious in Contention": one escapes by returning home. When from below one engages in Contention one that is above, calamity ensues as easily as if it were just picked up.

Third Yin

Subsist on old virtue. If one exercises constancy in the face of danger, in the end, good fortune will result. He might attend to his sovereign's business, but he has no opportunity to accomplish anything of his own. {The substance of Third Yin is soft and yielding, so it is obedient to Top Yang. It does not behave like Second Yang and "from below engage . . . in Contention one that is above." Not being encroached upon, it safeguards all that it has. Thus it manages to "subsist on old virtue"[9] and remain free from error. Here, located in the struggles of a time of Contention, it is located between two hard [yang] lines. Though contiguous with both, it forms a pair with neither. This is why the text says "if one exercises constancy in the face of danger." Being soft in substance, it is not one to struggle. Remaining closely tied in resonance with Top Yang, none of the other lines is able to deflect it from its course. This is why the text says: "In the end, good fortune will result." Top Yang is so strong that it will be victorious in any struggle, and it is impossible to defy it. This is why "he might attend to his sovereign's business" but does not dare accomplish anything in his own right.}

COMMENTARY ON THE IMAGES

"Subsist on old virtue": To follow the lead of Top Yang means good fortune.

Fourth Yang

Not victorious in Contention, {This is due to the fact that First Yin's "analysis is clear."} one returns to fulfilling Heaven's command and so changes course. Serene practice of constancy means good fortune. {Here one who occupies a superior position and contends with a subordinate [First Yin] is able to use this opportunity to change what he does. Thus the blame suffered is not great. If he can return to following fundamental principles, this will enable him to change his previous order [that led to Contention with First Yin][10], and by "practicing constancy with serenity" he will not commit transgression [against First Yin] or violate his own Dao but will "practice humaneness beginning with oneself."[11] Thus good fortune will follow him.[12]}

COMMENTARY ON THE IMAGES

"One returns to fulfilling Heaven's command and so changes course": by practicing constancy with serenity he remains free from error.

Fifth Yang

The way Contention is dealt with here results in fundamental good fortune. {By being located here one obtains a noble position and becomes the ruler of *Song*. Fifth Yang by its adherence to the Mean and its rectitude judges what is crooked and what is straight. As one here practices the Mean, he avoids excess, and, as such a one is correct, he does no evil. Fifth Yang is so hard and strong that it is not in the least subject to distractions and so just and fair that it is not at all prone to partiality. This is why the text says: "The way Contention is dealt with here results in fundamental good fortune."}

COMMENTARY ON THE IMAGES

"The way Contention is dealt with here results in fundamental good fortune": this is due to adherence to the Mean and to rectitude.

Top Yang

One might be awarded with a leather belt, but before the day is over he will have been deprived of it three times. {Here is someone located at the very end of *Song*. As he abides at this top position full of hardness and strength, whenever he engages in Contention he is victorious. Although he receives an award thanks to his success in Contention, how long can he safeguard this honor? This is why in the space of just one day he will be deprived of the belt three times.}

COMMENTARY ON THE IMAGES

To receive an item of apparel because of success in Contention is indeed not something worthy of respect.

NOTES

1. This and all subsequent text set off in this manner is commentary by Wang Bi. The text of Wang's comment reads *jie ti ranhou* (only after one in all cases exercises prudence). However, Lou Yulie cites critical editions of the *Changes* with Wang's commentary prepared by Sun Xingyan (1753–1818) and Jiao Xun (1763–1820) in which *jie* (in all cases) is replaced by *neng* (is able). As the characters *jie* and *neng* resemble each other, it is assumed that these editors thought that *jie* was a mistake and that *neng* was correct. Kong Yingda also reads Wang's text as if it contained *neng* rather than *jie*. See *Wang Bi ji jiaoshi*, 1: 251 n. 1, and *Zhouyi zhengyi*, 2: 4a.

2. "Is he not located at Second Yang?" translates *qi zai er hu*. As the ruler of the *Song* hexagram is Fifth Yang, there has been speculation that this phrase contains a copyist's error and should read *qi zai wu hu*: "Is he not located at Fifth Yang?" If this is so, the error must have occurred before the Tang era and Kong Yingda, for Kong accepts *er* as correct and has much to say about it in his subcommentary to Fifth Yang:

> Wang's commentary above says: "Someone in charge who is good at listening, and is he not located at Second Yang?" This means that Second Yang is a ruler, but his commentary here also says: "[Fifth Yang] becomes the ruler of *Song*. [It] by its adherence to the Mean and its rectitude judges what is crooked and what is straight." So this means that Fifth Yang is also a ruler. For one hexagram to have two rulers like this often occurs throughout the hexagrams as a whole. Fifth Yang is this hexagram's ruler by virtue of its noble position, but any of the other lines might be a ruler because of the way it represents the hexagram's meaning.

Kong then goes on to say that the same kind of thing happens, for instance, in *Fu* (Return), Hexagram 24. See *Zhouyi zhengyi*, 2: 7a–7b. Still, although the "meaning" of *Song*—its "moral" or general advice—does seem to be expressed in Second Yang, I am not entirely convinced and continue to think that "is he not located at Fifth Yang" is the more likely reading: it makes good sense for the passage as a whole and is, of course, a much simpler explanation. By the same token, "the great man" probably refers to Fifth Yang and not Second Yang.

3. Kong Yingda comments: "The Dao of Heaven is to rotate to the west, but the flow of water is such that it goes east. . . . This is an image of two people mutually acting at odds." See *Zhouyi zhengyi*, 2: 5a. All celestial bodies seem to rotate from east to west, and the waters of Chinese lakes and rivers all eventually flow east to the sea.

4. *Lunyu* (Analects) 12:13.

5. This paraphrases *Laozi*, section 79, p. 79.

6. Wang says the same thing in his commentary to *Laozi*, section 10, p. 23.

7. Kong Yingda comments: "First Yin should be the one to respond to Fourth Yang, but Fourth Yang is so filled with strong yang-ness that it comes first to First Yin. This is in violation of principle and a transgression against this one. First Yin, a weak yin entity that finds itself transgressed against, now enters into Contention." See *Zhouyi zhengyi*, 2: 5a–5b.

8. Kong Yingda comments:

> Zheng's [Zheng Xuan, 127–200] commentary on the *Liji* [Book of rites] says: "A small state involves the rule of a junior grand master [*xiadaifu*]." This location [in *Song*] is an expression of the meager and the weak, and this is why Second Yang can escape by returning home and hiding away there. But if this involves a city that surpasses three hundred households in population, it would be a strong, large state that one cannot use as a hideout.

See *Zhouyi zhengyi*, 2: 5b.

9. Kong Yingda glosses "subsist on old virtue" (*shi jiude*) as "subsist on the salary and rank of the virtuous of former days"—i.e., be content with the position inherited from one's virtuous forebears. See *Zhouyi zhengyi*, 2: 6a.

10. This is how Kong Yingda interprets the passage; see *Zhouyi zhengyi*, 2: 6b.

11. *Lunyu* (Analects) 12:1.

12. Both Wang Bi and Kong Yingda seem to invest *ming* (literally, "order" or "command") with a double meaning here: it refers both to "Heaven's command" (i.e., fundamental [moral] principle[s]) and to the specific command that Fourth Yang had given to First Yin that gave rise to the Contention between them. Kong, in fact, moves back and forth between these two positions throughout his remarks. See *Zhouyi zhengyi*, 2: 6b–7a. However, both Cheng Yi and Zhu Xi gloss *ming* as *zhenli* (true moral principles) and

understand the "change of course" not in terms of the course of action (orders given) undertaken by Fourth Yang but as a "fundamental change of the heart and mind" in the person so represented. See *Zhouyi zhezhong*, 1: 40b–41a.

HEXAGRAM 7

䷆

師

Shi [The Army]
(*Kan* Below *Kun* Above)

Judgment

If an army's constancy is subject to a forceful man, there will be good fortune and with this no blame. {A "forceful man" is a designation for someone who is stern and resolute. It is good fortune when there is such a forceful man to maintain the rectitude of an army. It would be a crime to raise soldiers and mobilize the masses and then have no success. This is why the text says: "There will be good fortune and with this no blame."[1]}

COMMENTARY ON THE JUDGMENTS

Army means "the masses." *Constancy* means "rectitude." If one is able to practice rectitude through using the masses, he can rely on this to become a true sovereign. Here one has strength and is in a mean position [Second Yang], but another is in resonance with it [Fifth Yin].[2] Army operations are dangerous, but they are carried out with compliance.[3] If one were to utilize the whole world in this way, one would get all the common folk to follow one. As this means good fortune, how could there also be any blame involved? {*Du* [poison/to poison] here means something like *yi* [utilize].[4]}

COMMENTARY ON THE IMAGES

The Earth holds water within itself: this constitutes the image of *Shi* [The Army]. In the same way, the noble man cherishes the common folk and so brings increase to the masses.

PROVIDING THE SEQUENCE OF THE HEXAGRAMS

When there is contention, there is sure to be an arising of the masses. This is why *Song* [Contention, Hexagram 6] is followed by *Shi* [The Army].

THE HEXAGRAMS IN IRREGULAR ORDER

Shi [The Army] [involves] dismay.

First Yin

The Army should campaign according to regulations. Otherwise, whether it fails or succeeds, it will result in misfortune. {This is the beginning of *Shi*, where one puts the Army in order. It is by means of regulations that mass troops are held in order. If such regulations are disregarded, the troops will come apart in confusion. This is why the text says: "The Army should campaign according to regulations." Regulations must not be disregarded, for if in spite of having disregarded them, success were still achieved, this would certainly not be any better than if outright failure had occurred. To achieve success at the expense of disregarding orders is not something that the law will forgive. Thus if an army campaigns but does not do so according to regulations, whether it succeeds or fails, it will result in misfortune in either case.[5]}

COMMENTARY ON THE IMAGES

"The Army should campaign according to regulations," for if it were to disregard regulations, misfortune would result.

Second Yang

Here in *Shi*, one practices the Mean, so he has good fortune and so suffers no blame. His sovereign confers a threefold commendation on him. {Here one abides in the Mean with strength intact and, as such, resonating with Fifth Yang. This is what it means when one finds oneself in *Shi* and obtains this mean position in it. Second Yang enjoys the favor of the sovereign above and is itself the ruler of the *Shi* hexagram. One's responsibility here is great, and his mission weighty, so failure to achieve success would mean misfortune. This is why the text has it that with good fortune there will be no blame. To obtain the good fortune that an army campaign offers, one can do no greater good than to win the support of the other states. To have the other states grant their support and the masses their submission, nothing is more important than how the sovereign confers his grace and favor, so this is why he [the general represented by Second Yang] obtains the perfect commendation here.[6]}

COMMENTARY ON THE IMAGES

"Here in *Shi*, one practices the Mean, so he has good fortune," in that he receives the trust and favor of Heaven [that is, the sovereign]. "His sovereign confers a threefold commendation on him," in order to win the support of the myriad states.

Third Yin

The Army will perhaps use carriages to transport corpses, and this would be misfortune. {Here a yang position is filled by a yin line, and a hard line is ridden by this soft line above it. If one advances, there is no one there to resonate with, and if one retreats, there is no one there to provide protection. When one uses an army in this fashion, it is appropriate that he garner the misfortune of having to use carriages to transport corpses.[7]}

COMMENTARY ON THE IMAGES

"The Army will perhaps use carriages to transport corpses": this means a very great failure occurs.

Fourth Yin

If the Army pitches camp to the left, there will be no blame. {Here one has obtained a position but has no one with which to resonate. As he has no one to resonate with, he cannot make a move, but as he has obtained a position, he can thus stay there. Thus he has the Army "pitch camp to the left" and so incurs "no blame." The rule for moving an army is such that one wants to keep high ground at his right and back,[8] this is why he has the Army "pitch camp to the left."}

COMMENTARY ON THE IMAGES

If one "pitches camp to the left, there will be no blame," for he has not violated the true Dao. {Although one here is unable to garner success, he is equal to avoiding any violation of the true Dao involved.}

Fifth Yin

When there is game in the fields, it is fitting to seize it then, and this will incur no blame. The elder son may take command of the Army, but the younger son would use carriages to transport corpses. Even if he practices constancy, it will result in misfortune. {This one finds himself here in a time of *Shi* [The Army], but it is a weak person who has obtained this noble position. However, being yin, he does not lead the singing,[9] and, being weak, he does not commit aggression against others. If he responds only after having suffered aggression, when he sets out to deal with it, the corrective measures he takes are sure to succeed. This is why the text says "when there is game in the fields." It is because these others have initiated aggression against him that he can "seize it then, and this will incur no blame." The weak are not ones to command armies, and the yin are not ones to make hard warriors, thus they should not personally involve themselves, but others must be appointed instead. If the one appointed does not obtain his sovereign's support, the troops will not obey him. This is why it is right that "the elder son take[s] command of the Army" and why the misfortune pertaining to the younger son is certainly appropriate.[10]}

COMMENTARY ON THE IMAGES

"The elder son takes charge of the Army," because of the way he practices the Mean. "The younger son would use carriages to transport corpses": the one appointed is unsuitable.

Top Yin

He whom the great sovereign orders is either to found a marquisate or to establish a lesser feudatory, but if it is a petty man, he must not so employ him. {To find oneself at the very top of *Shi* [The Army] means that one is at the end of the process of *Shi*. In the orders that the great sovereign issues, he does not overlook those who have achieved merit but has them "found marquisate[s]" or "establish . . . lesser feudator[ies]" in order to maintain the realm at peace. "If it is a petty man, he must not so employ him," for this task is incompatible with such a dao as his.[11]}

COMMENTARY ON THE IMAGES

"He whom the great sovereign orders": this is how he shows his rectitude toward the meritorious. "If it is a petty man, he may not so employ him," for he is sure to throw the realm into chaos.

NOTES

1. This and all subsequent text set off in this manner is commentary by Wang Bi.

2. Kong Yingda's subcommentary defines the basic approach to the meaning of this hexagram—here and for the majority of later commentators: Second Yang represents a strong general, and Fifth Yin represents a compliant sovereign who relies on his general's loyalty to get things done. Except for Second Yang, all other lines are yin. They, except for Fifth Yin, represent the masses or army that the general and sovereign, whose intentions are "in resonance," use rightly to good purpose. See *Zhouyi zhengyi*, 2: 8a–8b.

3. Kong Yingda glosses *shun* (compliancy/compliant) as *roushun* "yielding and compliant"—the way army operations must be carried out in order to obtain "good fortune." See *Zhouyi zhengyi*, 2: 8b. "Yielding and compliant" is, of course, characteristic of the Dao of *Kun* (Pure Yin),

Hexagram 1. See the Commentary on the Judgments for that hexagram.

4. Wang Bi's gloss of *du* as *yi* is further explained by Kong Yingda as *shiyi*: "servant/subordinate" or "to employ as servant/subordinate." See *Zhouyi zhengyi*, 2: 8b. Neither Wang nor Kong explain why *du*, whose literal meaning of "poison/to poison" is so different, can mean this. One possibility is that Wang has been influenced by Ma Rong (79–166), a Han era commentator, who suggests that *du* should be understood as *zhi* (control, manage); i.e., poison used in the right amount can control illness. See Lu Deming's *Zhouyi yinyi* (Pronunciation and meaning of terms in the *Changes of the Zhou*), included in the *Jingdian shiwen*, 2: 68. In this sense, an army is like poison: it is dangerous to use, but, when used correctly, it can have good results. However, both Cheng Yi and Zhu Xi gloss *du* as *hai* (harm); i.e., no matter how they are carried out, army operations always inflict harm on the world. In the light of their interpretation, this passage would read: "When harm is brought to the world in this way, the common folk will still follow one." See *Zhouyi zhezhong*, 9: 15b–16a.

5. "Otherwise, whether it fails or succeeds, it will result in misfortune" translates *pi zang xiong*. In this reading, the "otherwise" is only implied from the context—i.e., nothing in the Chinese text explicitly expresses it. Kong Yingda also understands the text this way and suggests that the unusual wording here is a more emphatic way of saying "even though it succeeds, it will result in misfortune." See *Zhouyi zhengyi*, 2: 8b–9a. However, there are two other possibilities. One is to read *pi* (obstruction, i.e., failure) as the graph for *fou*, a function word that actually means "otherwise." The text would then mean: "Otherwise, even if it succeeds, it would still result in misfortune." Here we have to supply an implicit "even," and this is exactly the way that Cheng Yi understands it; see *Zhouyi zhezhong*, 1: 43b. Zhu Xi suggests a third way. He thinks that *pi* should be read *fou* but that here *fou* functions as a simple negative prefix, used instead of *bu*. He also glosses *fou zang* as *bushan* (not good). His interpretation would translate as: "If it [the regulation] is not good, there will be misfortune." See *Zhouyi zhezhong*, 1: 43a.

6. "The perfect commendation" translates *chengming*. This is Wang's explanation for "his sovereign confers a threefold commendation on him." Kong Yingda cites a passage in the *Liji* (Book of rites) to support Wang's remark: "The first commendation is the conferral of a *jue* [a bronze ceremonial vessel, an emblem of noble rank], the second commendation is the conferral of clothing, and the third commendation is the conferral of horses and carriage. With these three conferrals and three commendations, the honor involved is perfectly realized." See *Zhouyi zhengyi*, 2: 9b. However, most later commentators, Cheng Yi among them, do not interpret *wang san xi ming* as "his sovereign confers a threefold commendation on him" but as "his sovereign confers commendations on him three times [that is, repeatedly]." Lou Yulie, it should also be noted, explains *chengming* (perfect commendation) as *cheng ming* (successfully carry out orders): "*Cheng ming* means 'to accomplish perfectly the task set for him by the sovereign.'"

See *Wang Bi ji jiaoshi*, 1: 259 n. 11. In the light of this, *de cheng ming* (obtains the perfect commendation) would mean "is able to have him successfully carry out his orders," i.e., it is by these awards/commendations that the wise sovereign encourages his general to use the Army with rectitude and compliance in order to win, as the Commentary on the Images states, "the support of the myriad states."

7. "Use carriages to transport corpses" translates *yu shi*. Zhu Xi's interpretation follows that of Wang Bi, but Cheng Yi explains *yu shi* differently, as "many leaders," which involves possible, secondary meanings for the two characters respectively. Cheng's reading of the passage would read something like: "If perhaps the Army has many leaders [i.e., no unified command], it would result in misfortune." See *Zhouyi zhezhong*, 1: 44b–45a.

8. Cf. Griffith, *Sun Tzu: The Art of War*, p. 117.

9. See Hexagram 6, *Song* (Contention), First Yin and note 6 there.

10. If we summarize Kong Yingda's comments, the explanation for all this is as follows: The "sovereign" is Fifth Yin (weak but centrally located in the upper trigram), the "elder son" is Second Yang (strong and centrally located in the lower trigram), and the "younger son" is Third Yin. It is Fifth Yin and Second Yang that are in resonance, so Second Yang, strong, centrally located, and in rapport with Fifth Yin, is the right one to lead the Army and not the weak, off-centered (unbalanced, skewed, prone to take the wrong action) Third Yin. See *Zhouyi zhengyi*, 2: 10a–10b.

11. Kong Yingda comments: "The Son of Heaven ennobles and enfeoffs the one at Top Yin. If his merit is relatively great, he has him found a marquisate or dukedom as one of the feudal lords, and if his merit is relatively small, he has him establish a lesser feudatory as a minister or grand master to a feudal lord." See *Zhouyi zhengyi*, 2: 10b.

HEXAGRAM 8

䷇

比

Bi [Closeness]
(*Kun* Below *Kan* Above)

Judgment

For Closeness to result in good fortune, plumb and divine for fundamentality, perseverance, and constancy, for only with them will there be no blame. Those in places not at peace then come, but the latecomer suffers misfortune.[1]

COMMENTARY ON THE JUDGMENTS

Closeness means good fortune. Closeness is a matter of help and support, of compliance and obedience on the part of those below. "Plumb and divine for fundamentality, perseverance, and constancy, for only then will there be no blame": this depends on the strength and the adherence to the Mean [of Fifth Yang]. {When located at a time of *Bi* [Closeness], if one would plumb and divine to seek how to be without blame, how could that involve anything other than fundamentality, perseverance, and constancy? Here a group of people band together in mutual Closeness, but if they do so without fundamentality, perseverance, and constancy, it will lead to the dao of misfortune and evil. Also, if they do not meet their rightful ruler, in spite of their fundamentality, perseverance, and constancy, they still will not be equal to the need to stay free of blame. The one who enables that perseverance and constancy to stay free of blame can be none other than Fifth Yang![2]} "Those in places not at peace then come": all in the upper and the lower trigrams respond to it [Fifth Yang]. {There is no other yang line in either the upper or the lower trigram to divide off the folk under separate sovereignty, and, since Fifth Yang alone occupies a position of nobility, none fail to pay it allegiance. Since all in the two trigrams are in resonance with it, they find both cordiality and security there. As Fifth Yang represents security, the insecure entrust themselves to it. This is why "those in places not at peace then come" and why "all in the upper and the lower trigrams respond to it." It is those who have not who seek out those who have; those who already have do not need to seek out others to provide for them. It is those who are in danger who seek out security; those who already enjoy security do not need to seek out others to protect them. Fire has its flame, so those suffering from cold draw near to it. Therefore it is because they would find security there that "those in places not at peace then come."} "The latecomer suffers misfortune" because the Dao [of *Bi*] is then already exhausted. {This one [Top Yin] would join the cordial company, but he alone had lagged behind. As the process of cordiality has now already completed its cycle, he is condemned. This is how he "suffers misfortune."}

COMMENTARY ON THE IMAGES

There is Water on the Earth: this constitutes the image of *Bi* [Closeness]. In the same way, the former kings established the myriad states and treated the feudal lords with cordiality. {It was thanks to the Dao of *Bi* [Closeness] that the myriad states were so established and that the feudal lords were treated with such cordiality.[3]}

PROVIDING THE SEQUENCE OF THE HEXAGRAMS

An army as such is a mass of people. A mass of people necessarily involves closeness. This is why Shi [The Army, Hexagram 7] is followed by *Bi* [Closeness].

THE HEXAGRAMS IN IRREGULAR ORDER

Bi [Closeness] involves joy, *Shi* [The Army, Hexagram 7] dismay.

First Yin

If there is sincerity, joining in Closeness will not lead to blame. If the sincerity one has keeps the earthenware pot filled, it will always exert an attraction, so there will be good fortune brought on by others. {To find oneself at First Yin of *Bi* [Closeness] means that one is at the head of the process of *Bi*. If one initiates Closeness without sincerity, nothing could create a worse calamity. Thus one "keeps the earthenware pot filled" with sincerity, for only then can one avoid the blame to which Closeness might lead. This is why the text says: "If there is sincerity, joining in Closeness will not lead to blame." Located at the head of *Bi*, there is no particular resonance residing in this first line, so with heart and mind free of any such partiality, this line achieves Closeness with all. The trust that one manifests and the sincerity that one has established keep one's plain and simple vessel filled to overflowing, thus, although this always keeps attracting others, it is inexhaustible.[4] If one treats the whole world with cordiality and keeps one's earthenware pot ever filled with manifest sincerity, how could those who come in response ever be limited to one single road? Thus surely "there will be good fortune brought on by others."}

COMMENTARY ON THE IMAGES

The Closeness joined by First Yin involves "the good fortune brought on by others."

Second Yin

Here one joins in closeness from the inner trigram. Constancy results in good fortune. {One who finds himself here at a time of Bi obtains a position located in the middle [of the inner or lower trigram] and thus, being closely tied in resonance with Fifth Yang, cannot attract any of the other lines. Therefore this one manages to bring about its Closeness from the inner trigram and can have nothing more than the good fortune derived from practicing constancy [toward Fifth Yang].[5]}

COMMENTARY ON THE IMAGES

"Here one joins in Closeness from the inner trigram": one does not neglect his own.[6]

Third Yin

Here one joins in Closeness but not with his own people. {Fourth Yin joins in Closeness [with Fifth Yang] from the outer trigram, and Second Yin maintains its constancy toward Fifth Yang, so Third Yin can neither find a partner nearby nor has it any line to resonate with at a distance. Of all those that this one can share Closeness with, none are its own people. This is why the text says: "Here one joins in Closeness but not with his own people."}

COMMENTARY ON THE IMAGES

"Here one joins in Closeness but not with one's own people": will this not indeed cause harm?

Fourth Yin

Here one joins in Closeness from the outer trigram. Constancy results in good fortune. {Here in the outer trigram Fourth Yin joins in Closeness with Fifth Yang. As it manages to keep its steps within the bounds of its own position, this Closeness for Fifth Yang does no harm to its own worthiness, and, as its location here is no violation of its position, Fourth Yang's "constancy results in good fortune."}

COMMENTARY ON THE IMAGES

Here in the outer trigram one joins in Closeness with a worthy, and in so doing he goes to follow his superior.

Fifth Yang

The way one manifests Closeness here is comparable to how the sovereign has game driven three times and forgoes those that come before him, thus his subjects need not guard against him, and this means good fortune. {As the ruler of *Bi* [Closeness], Fifth Yang is in resonance with Second Yin. This is what is meant by "the way one manifests Closeness here." To practice Closeness and manifest it in this way means that the scope of one's cordiality is quite narrow. However. if one shows no partiality to anyone but just subjects all to his worthiness, then neither those who run away nor those who run hither need be left out. The decorum connected with driving game three times is such that the game that doubles back and comes toward the sovereign will be spared, whereas the game that turns from him and flees will be shot. This is because he cherishes those that come to him but hates those that run away.

Thus the way this is done always involves "forgo[ing] those that come before him."[7] To manifest Closeness while occupying this position of ruler is comparable to the use of the Dao of driving game three times. This is why the text says: "The sovereign has game driven three times and forgoes those that come before him." Because of his adherence to the Mean and rectitude, whenever he launches a campaign, it always is done according to constant principles: when one attacks, it should never involve subjects unfairly blamed, and when one makes a move against someone, it must only be done in order to suppress rebellion. It is because his subjects have no need to worry that they do not guard against him. Although one does not obtain the good fortune of the great man here, there still is the good fortune associated with this manifestation of Closeness. One can use this [the Dao of *Bi*] to carry out the duties of a senior official, but it is not the Dao by which one becomes a true sovereign.[8]}

COMMENTARY ON THE IMAGES

The good fortune associated with the manifestation of Closeness here is due to the centrality and rectitude of the position involved. It is because one spares those that double back and takes only those that go with the drive that one "forgoes those that come before him."[9] "His subjects need not guard against him," because he, as their sovereign, rules with the Mean.

Top Yin

One who joins in Closeness here lacked the means to be a leader, so he will have misfortune. {This one who finds himself at the end of the process of *Bi* is "the latecomer." Here the Dao of cordiality has already run its course. As "there is nothing he can do to share in this its final stage," he finds himself shunted aside by the moment, and this, after all, is his misfortune.}

COMMENTARY ON THE IMAGES

"One who joins in Closeness here lacked the means to be a leader," so there is nothing he can do to share in this its final stage.[10]

NOTES

1. This reading of the Judgment to *Bi* is in accord with both Wang Bi's commentary and the subcommentary of Kong Yingda; see *Zhouyi zhengyi*, 2: 11a. However, Cheng Yi and Zhu Xi interpret parts of it differently. "Plumb and divine" translates *yuanshi*, which Kong glosses as *yuanqiong qi qing shijue qi yi*: "plumb one's inclinations to their depths and determine one's intention by divination." Cheng Yi explains *yuan* as *tuiyuan* (trace to the origins/plumb the fundamentals)—essentially the same meaning as Kong's *yuanqiong*, but he explains *shi* (divine) as *bujue* or *budu*, both of which, here at least, seem to mean "divine" in the sense of determining by self-examination or introspection, for he declares: "This does not mean that one does it with yarrow stalks or tortoise shells." His gloss for *yuanshi* then translates into "carefully undergo self-examination for." Zhu Xi seems to agree with Cheng but adds the notion that this "necessarily involves a second divination so that one can undergo self-examination to determine if he possesses the virtues of fundamental goodness, enduring perseverance, and persistence of rectitude." The "first divination" here would be the original divination that provided the seeker with the prognostication of *Bi* itself. Also, both Cheng and Zhu interpret *buning fang lai* not as "those in places not at peace then come" (*fang* being synonymous with *difang*) but as "people come at such times when they are not at peace" (*fang* meaning "*fangqie*," according to Cheng's gloss) and "people would come when they are not at peace" (*fang* meaning "*jiang*," according to Zhu's gloss). See *Zhouyi zhezhong*, 2: 1a–1b.

2. This and all subsequent text set off in this manner is commentary by Wang Bi.

3. Kong Yingda explains the image as follows: "There is water on the Earth just as there are the myriad states within the realm. The way each of them is allowed to share in a Closeness based on cordiality is just like the way the Earth has water flow about everywhere so that its life-given moisture reaches all things." See *Zhouyi zhengyi*, 2: 12a.

4. "Always keeps attracting" here and "will always exert an attraction" in the text of First Yin translate *zhonglai*, i.e, the earthenware pot, metaphor for one's capacity for sincerity, keeps attracting others throughout the process of *Bi* (Closeness), and this results in good fortune. Cheng Yi, however, interprets this differently: "In the end this can bring some other good fortune"—i.e., from people and places "outside" one's immediate sphere. See *Zhouyi zhezhong*, 2: 2b.

5. Cheng Yi interprets Second Yin in metaphoric terms: The inner trigram represents the "inner self" and this correct but weak central line represents the subject or minister who cultivates his rectitude and obedience while waiting for his sovereign's summons. See *Zhouyi zhezhong*, 2: 3a.

6. "Does not neglect his own" translates *buzishi*. Kong Yingda comments: "[Second Yin] does not neglect its own partner, with which it is

bound in resonance [Fifth Yang]." See *Zhouyi zhengyi*, 2: 12b. Zhu Xi interprets this differently: "It is by his ability to practice rectitude here that he avoids doing himself damage [*buzishi*]." Cheng Yi's interpretation is more elaborate but essentially the same as Zhu's. See *Zhouyi zhezhong*, 11: 19b.

7. "The sovereign has game driven three times and forgoes those that come before him" translates *wang yong sanqu shi qian qin*. Kong Yingda's subcommentary first expands slightly upon Wang's interpretation of this passage, saying that it is correct and we should follow it, and then summarizes the views of Chu Zhongdu (sixth century A.D.) and other commentators on the *Yijing*, which constitute a different, alternate reading: "The sovereign has game driven on three sides and forgoes those that go in front [the open side]." See *Zhouyi zhengyi*, 2: 13a–13b. Cheng Yi and Zhu Xi agree with this second reading and use it in their own commentaries. See *Zhouyi zhezhong*, 2: 4b–5a.

8. Both Cheng Yi and Zhu Xi disagree with the commentaries of Wang Bi and Kong Yingda and assert that Fifth Yang does represent the perfect, universal, and impartial Dao of the true sovereign. See *Zhouyi zhezhong*, 2: 4b–5a.

9. "One spares those that double back and takes only those that go with the drive" translates *she ni qu shun*. As Cheng Yi understands *shi qian qin* (forgoes those that come before him) to mean "forgoes those that go in front," he explains *she ni qu shun* differently as well: " 'Go away from one' is what *ni* means [i.e., resist/disobey], and 'run toward one' is what *shun* means [i.e., obey]." Thus his interpretation of *she ni qu xun* is: "Discard those that disobey, and accept those that obey." See *Zhouyi zhezhong*, 11: 20b.

10. The reading of Top Yin and the Commentary on the Images here follows suggestions made by Kong Yingda in his subcommentary to both texts. "Lacked the means to be a leader" translates *wu shou*. However, Cheng Yi interprets *wu shou* to mean "had no proper beginning," something consistent with his understanding of *zhong* (always) as "in the end" in First Yin. His reading of Top Yin would be something like: "If *Bi* [Closeness] had no proper beginning, it would result in misfortune here at the end." "Proper beginning" is suggested by his gloss of *wu shou* as *shi bi buyi dao*: "to disregard the Dao when beginning *Bi*." "There is nothing he can do to share in this its final stage" translates *wu suo zhong*, following Wang Bi. Cheng understands this as "there is no means to end it [*Bi*] properly." Zhu Xi's view is again different: "If one speaks of this in terms of the top and the bottom of the image involved, then this line lacks a proper head [i.e., there is a noncentral, weak, yin line in the top position], but if one speaks of this in terms of the ending and the beginning of the image involved, then this line lacks a proper ending. *Wu shou* [no head] simply means *wu zhong* [no end]." See *Zhouyi zhezhong*, 2: 6b and 11: 20b.

䷈

小畜

Xiaoxu [Lesser Domestication][1]
(*Qian* Below *Sun* Above)

Judgment

Xiaoxu is such that prevalence may be had. Here one can neither do great domestic garnering nor block the strong,[2] but by hardening one's will it will be possible to act, and this is how prevalence occurs.[3] Dense clouds do not rain but start off from our western suburbs.[4]

COMMENTARY ON THE JUDGMENTS

Here in *Xiaoxu* [Lesser Domestication] a weak line obtains an appropriate position [as a yin line in a yin position], so those above and those below respond to it. Such a situation is called *Xiaoxu*. {This refers to Fourth Yin. The meaning of the entire hexagram resides in this line. It is because in the whole hexagram there is not a second yin line to share the response of the yang lines that "those above and those below respond to it." And, as it has obtained this position so that "those above and those below respond to it," Third Yang is unable to encroach upon it. That is the meaning of *Xiaoxu*.} The lower trigram is strong [*jian*] whereas the upper trigram is *Sun* [Compliance] itself,[5] so thanks to this hardness and its adherence to the Mean, the will of Fifth Yang is carried out, resulting in prevalence. "Dense clouds do not rain" refers to how they [the yang lines] keep moving away. They "start off from our western suburbs" means that the power [of *Xiaoxu*] is less than effective. {The power of *Xiaoxu* [Lesser Domestication] is sufficient to produce dense clouds, which then "start off from our western suburbs," but it is insufficient to produce rain. How do we know that it is less than able to produce rain? What could produce rain would be the yang rising to exert pressure on the yin and the yin having the capability to hold its ground against it, after which the rising vapor would turn into rain. But here it is possible neither to gain control over the Dao [innate tendency] of First Yang to return upward nor to block Second Yang from being drawn along and returning, too. As Third Yang is even less effective because it is unable to return upward at all, and as the ones below "keep moving away," how could the power that *Xiaoxu* [Lesser Domestication] has ever prove effective enough? Thus the reason why these dense clouds are yet unable to produce rain is that "they [the yang lines] keep moving away." But how could we ever explain this in terms of how it would rain only if the yin were able to block these yang lines? Top Yang alone can block Third Yang's path. Thus Third Yang is not only prevented from advancing, its "carriage body would be separated from its axle housing" [i.e., "put out of commission"]. It is by blocking Third Yang's path that Top Yang brings security to its position. This is why Top Yang "not only achieves rain but also secures its place." If Fourth Yin and Fifth Yang were both capable of the same excellent domestication as that done by Top Yang, then it is obvious that rain could be made to fall. If we were to discuss this in terms of the hexagram as a whole, we would have to say that it is capable of nothing more than the Lesser Domestication of dense clouds. If indeed the yin line is not equal to blocking the yang lines, although their return itself might be the most splendid thing possible, as dense clouds they "start off from our western suburbs" and thus cannot produce rain. That rain does not fall signifies that "the power [of *Xiaoxu*] is less than effective." A Judgment discusses the body or substance of a hexagram as a whole; thus this one says: "Dense clouds do not rain." The Commentary on the Images addresses itself in each case to the particular virtue of a given line; thus at Top Yang it says: "This one not only achieves rain but also secures its place."}

COMMENTARY ON THE IMAGES

Wind moves through the Heavens: this constitutes the image of *Xiaoxu* [Lesser Domestication]. In the same way, the noble man cultivates his civil virtues. {Here one finds that he cannot yet exercise his power, and this is why one here can do nothing more than "cultivate his civil virtues."[6]}

PROVIDING THE SEQUENCE OF THE HEXAGRAMS

Closeness as such means "a bringing together." Bringing together has to involve domestication. This is why *Bi* [Closeness, Hexagram 8] is followed by *Xiaoxu* [Lesser Domestication].

THE HEXAGRAMS IN IRREGULAR ORDER

Xiaoxu [Lesser Domestication] results in few resources.

First Yang

In returning, one follows the appropriate Dao [path], so how could there be any blame involved? This means good fortune. {Located at the first position of the *Qian* trigram, First Yang uses it to rise to the first position of the *Sun* trigram, and as Fourth Yin is in resonance with First Yang, it does not try to resist it. Here a yang line rises to a yin line, and its return follows the path that is right for it, and as Fourth Yin remains compliant and does not oppose First Yang, what violation is there that could possibly incur blame? This results in the good fortune that happens when one achieves "proper behavior."}

COMMENTARY ON THE IMAGES

"In returning, one follows the appropriate Dao [path]": Proper behavior here results in good fortune.[7]

Second Yang

Drawn along, one returns, and this means good fortune. Located at the middle position of the *Qian* trigram, Second Yang uses it to rise to Fifth Yang of the *Sun* trigram. As Fifth Yang does not represent the ultimate degree of domestication [i.e., it is not Top Yang of *Xiaoxu*], it is not the one to block Second Yang. Although it is incapable of achieving the same degree of nonresistance as does the yin line, Second Yang still allows itself to be drawn along and so succeeds in returning. This is how it has good fortune.

COMMENTARY ON THE IMAGES

"Drawn along, one returns": One here both abides in a central position and also is himself without error.[8]

Third Yang

The carriage body would be separated from its axle housing, so husband and wife turn their eyes against each other. {Top Yang, representing *Xiaoxu* at its strongest, does not permit Third Yang to be drawn along and join in the march [with First and Second Yang]. If it were to try to go forward under these circumstances, it would be sure to have its "carriage body . . . separated from its axle housing." Third Yang may be the top line in the yang trigram [*Qian*], but Top Yang is the leader of the yin trigram [*Sun*], and, since *Xiaoxu* is led by its yin trigram, Third Yang cannot leave its position and make its return [with the others]. The text expresses the meaning of this as a metaphor in which "husband and wife turn their eyes against each other."[9]}

COMMENTARY ON THE IMAGES

"Husband and wife turn their eyes against each other": this means that it is not possible to put the house in order.[10]

Fourth Yin

If there is sincerity, blood will be kept away, and apprehension purged, and one will not incur blame.[11] {That blood is mentioned here is due to the transgression of Third Yang against Fourth Yin. Fourth Yin rides on top of Third Yang, and they are right next to each other but do not form a pair. Also, Third Yang labors to advance, but Fourth Yin gets in its way, for it seems that Fourth Yin fears that Third Yang would invade and conquer it. Top Yang also has enmity for Third Yang, but it can do something about controlling it. As Fourth Yin has the same goal as Top Yang, they equally trust in each other's sincerity. Although Third Yang puts pressure on Fourth Yin, it cannot succeed in its transgression. Thus Fourth Yin manages to keep blood away [i.e., avoids injury] and have its fear purged, and in protecting itself it incurs no blame.}

COMMENTARY ON THE IMAGES

"If there is sincerity, . . . apprehension [will be] purged": This is due to Top Yang sharing its goal with it [Fourth Yin].[12]

Fifth Yang

If there is sincerity, this one will lend a helping hand and enrich its neighbors. {Fifth Yang obtains this position of nobility and, harboring no suspicions against Second Yang, does not oppose its arrival. Second Yang's being drawn along is something to which Fifth Yang lends its own helping hand; it is not dedicated to securing just its own security. This is what the text means by "if there is sincerity, this one will lend a helping hand." Because this is a yang line in a yang position, to be here is to be located where the real power is. One who abides in such fullness and finds himself in this position of real power but yet is not dedicated to just his own security is someone who will "enrich [his] neighbors."[13]}

COMMENTARY ON THE IMAGES

"If there is sincerity, this one will lend a helping hand": this means that Fifth Yang will not keep its wealth to itself.

Top Yang

This one not only achieves rain but also secures its place. It is esteemed for the way it carries its virtue, but even a wife's constancy here means danger, and as the moon is almost full, so if the noble man goes forth and acts, it will mean misfortune. {Located at the very top of *Xiaoxu*, Top Yang is the line that is able to accomplish domestication. It is because Third Yang does not manage to prevail here that "this one not only achieves rain," and it is because the strong cannot invade it that it "also secures its place." As the very embodiment of *Sun* and located at the top, it is something that the strong dare not transgress against. This is what is meant by "it is esteemed for the way it carries its virtue." Top Yang is the leader of this yin trigram, and, as it is able to domesticate the hard and the strong, "it is a gatherer and carrier of virtue." When a wife controls her husband or when a minister controls his sovereign, although they practice constancy, they still place themselves on the edge of danger. This is why the text says: "Even a wife's constancy here means danger." There is no fuller waxing for yin than the way it waxes here, and this is why the text says: 'The moon is almost full." That which is full and yet keeps on advancing is sure to violate its Dao.[14] When a yin excites the suspicions of a yang, it is sure to be attacked. So even if it is a noble man who is making his return here, for him to "go . . . forth and act" as such will surely lead to misfortune. This is why the text says: "If the noble man here goes forth and acts, it will mean misfortune."}

COMMENTARY ON THE IMAGES

"This one not only achieves rain but also secures its place," for it is a gatherer and carrier of virtue. "If the noble man goes forth and acts, it will mean misfortune," for he will be the object of suspicion... {To be located in a lower trigram and succeed there at going forth and acting while still avoiding blame is something that only happens in *Tai* [Peace].[15] However, *Tai* is such that *Kun* as a trigram is something that originally should be located below, as it is compliant, weak, and unable to be a match for the hard and strong [the yang lines of *Qian*, the lower trigram in *Tai*]. This is why the lines in *Qian* can all fulfill the nature of their kind, set forth to act, and have it result in good fortune. However, from this point on in *Xiaoxu*, to try to advance would in every case result in trouble. Although the trigram *Sun* here is incapable of the excellence at domestication achieved by the trigram *Gen* [the upper trigram in *Daxu* (Great Domestication), Hexagram 26], it also is unwilling to behave with the compliancy and obedience of the trigram *Kun* [the upper trigram in *Tai* (Peace), Hexagram 11]. Thus it may be capable of some slight advance, but it is incapable of a full-scale campaign, which explains why First Yang and Second Yang succeed when they try to return and why, when it comes to Third Yang, its "carriage body would be separated from its axle housing." Great Domestication [䷙] represents the ultimate in domestication. Its domestic garnering as such keeps on without end, and at its furthest point it extends everywhere. This is why the fullness of its domestication takes place throughout Fourth Yin and Fifth Yin, and when it reaches Top Yang, its Dao [way] permits one to speed along without any hindrance. However, *Xiaoxu* is able to garner domestically only that which it manages to gather by the time it reaches its end point [Top Yang]. This explains why Fourth Yin and Fifth Yang can thus manage to advance but Top Yang would suffer the separation of axle housing and carriage body if it were to try a campaign here of its own.[16]}

NOTES

1. "Domestication" translates *xu*, which means "to pasture or tame," on the one hand, and, when it is used interchangeably with a similar character, *xu*, "to save, store up, or garner," on the other. Both Wang Bi and Kong Yingda largely seem to understand it to mean the former—Kong, in fact, glosses it as *xuzhi* or *zhixu* (block, bring to a halt); see *Zhouyi zhengyi*, 2: 14a—though in certain places both in the text and in their commentaries it seems to refer—at least in part—to the accumulation of the resources that lead to prosperity. In these cases, it is translated as "garner domestically." This ambiguity was noticed by Cheng Yi, who first glosses *xu* as *ju* (gather, collect) then glosses it as *zhi* (stop, halt), and finally adds the statement "when a stopping or halting occurs, a gathering happens" (*zhi ze ju*)—so he wants to have it both ways. See *Zhouyi zhezhong*, 2: 7a. The same ambiguity exists in the text of and the commentaries to *Daxu* (Great Domestication), Hexagram 26.

2. Kong Yingda comments:

> If it were *Daxu* [Great Domestication, Hexagram 26], *Qian* would be below, and *Gen* would be above. *Gen* is a yang trigram, and since it also can block things, it can block the hardness and strength of *Qian* here, so what it domesticates is great. This is why this hexagram is called "Great Domestication." However, this hexagram [*Xiaoxu*, Lesser Domestication] has *Sun* above and *Qian* below. *Sun* is yin and weak as well as harmonious and compliant by nature, so it is unable to block and domesticate the *Qian* trigram that is located below. As it is only capable of domesticating and blocking Third Yang, what it domesticates is very limited. This is why its name is "Lesser Domestication."

See *Zhouyi zhengyi*, 2: 14a.

3. This and all subsequent text set off in this manner is commentary by Wang Bi. Kong Yingda comments: "First Yang and Second Yang manage to act because of their hardness and strength. It is due to their hardness and strength that the sovereign [Fifth Yang] is able to have his prevalence spread wide." See *Zhouyi zhengyi*, 2: 14a.

4. Kong Yingda comments: "If the yang lines that are ascending were able to be blocked and domesticated by the yin line, the two different *qi* [vapors] would exert enough pressure on each other to produce rain. Here,

however, the yin line can only block and domesticate Third Yang, and its *qi* is garnered only as dense clouds. First Yang and Second Yang continue to escape freely upward, and this is why no rain can be produced." See *Zhouyi zhengyi*, 2: 14a. Wang Bi says something similar in his comments on the Commentary to the Judgments here at *Xiaoxu*. See also Hexagram 62, *Xiaoguo* (Minor Superiority), Fifth Yin, and note 11 there.

5. "Strong" (*jian*) is a pun on *Qian* (Pure Yang), the lower trigram, and *Sun* actually means "compliance."

6. Kong Yingda comments:

> One who is a noble man here can but cultivate his civil virtues and wait for the time when, as if it were a strong wind blowing, he begins to issue orders. Then his power will touch everything just as the wind does when moving across the Earth. At such a time one can no longer say that his power "is less than effective." Here, however, the wind is up in the Heavens, and, being far away from things, there is no way its power can reach them. This is why the text says: "Wind moves through the Heavens."

See *Zhouyi zhengyi*, 2: 15b.

7. "Proper behavior here" translates *qiyi*. Kong Yingda comments: "For yang to rise to yin and for the hard to resonate with the soft, this involves behavior that maintains its right course by adhering to principle, and this means good fortune." See *Zhouyi zhengyi*, 2: 15b.

8. Kong Yingda comments: "This strong line is drawn along to return, because here in the middle of the lower trigram it avoids being blocked up, thanks to the centrality it obtains, and also because in its own right it stays free of error. This is how [the Commentary on the Images] explains 'drawn along, one returns, and this means good fortune.' " See *Zhouyi zhengyi*, 2: 16a.

9. Kong Yingda comments: "It is because the husband and wife are at odds that they 'turn their eyes against each other' and glare." See *Zhouyi zhengyi*, 2: 16a. Note also that the trigram *Sun* (Compliance) is also considered the Eldest Daughter (see section ten of Explaining the Trigrams), but here the pairing of *Sun* with *Qian* (Pure Yang, the male, a husband) results in a marriage based on opposition. The contiguous lines, Third Yang and Fourth Yin, also represent the married couple, and they too "are at odds." See Cheng Yi's comments, in which he remarks that Fourth Yin's success in opposing and controlling her "husband" is due to his "not having obtained centrality" (i.e., the line is off center and thus in violation of the Dao); she could not do it otherwise. See *Zhouyi zhezhong*, 2: 10b.

10. Kong Yingda comments: "The husband represented by Third Yang is incapable of putting Top Yang's house [the *Sun* trigram] in order, and this is why they 'turn their eyes against each other.' " See *Zhouyi zhengyi*, 2: 16a. Here, the opposition seems to be that of Third Yang with Top Yang rather than with Fourth Yin, but, as Top Yang is the leader of a yin trigram, *Sun*, this is still a yin versus yang confrontation.

11. Cf. Hexagram 59, *Huan* (Dispersion), Top Yang.

12. "Top Yang sharing its goal with it" translates *shang he zhi*. The reading of *shang* as *shangjiu* (ninth in the top place, that is, Top Yang) follows both Wang Bi's interpretation and that of Kong Yingda; see *Zhouyi zhengyi*, 2: 16a–16b. Cheng Yi interprets *shang* as "the line above"—i.e., Fifth Yang—and his comment on this passage reads in part: "It is because Fourth Yin has sincerity that Fifth Yang has confidence in it and shares its goal with it." That is, Cheng emphasizes the fact that the contiguous Fifth Yang and Fourth Yin stand in relation to each other as sovereign and minister. Zhu Xi is silent as far as this passage is concerned, but his commentary to Fourth Yin differs from both the Wang/Kong and the Cheng interpretations in that he thinks that it is Second Yang, with which Fourth Yin is in natural resonance, that comes to Fourth Yin's assistance. See *Zhouyi zhezhong*, 2: 11a–11b and 11: 22a.

13. Both Cheng Yi and Zhu Xi think that the word *neighbors* (*lin*) here has nothing to do with Second Yang but refers to Fourth Yin and Top Yang, the lines contiguous with it and with which it makes up the upper *Sun* trigram. The joint purpose of these three lines, as Zhu Xi puts it, is to "pool their strength and garner the lower *Qian* trigram." Thus the "helping hand" is extended not to Second Yang but to the other two lines in *Sun*. See *Zhouyi zhezhong*, 2: 11b–12a.

14. Kong Yingda comments: "A wife trying to control her husband is like the moon trying to compete with the sun when it is waxing to its full." That is, such an attempt is ephemeral and futile. See *Zhouyi zhengyi*, 2: 17a.

15. See Wang's commentary to Hexagram 11, *Tai* (Peace), First Yang.

16. That is, *Xiaoxu* is worn out by the time it reaches its end point at Top Yang, and, like Third Yang, would suffer a breakdown.

䷉

履

Lü [Treading]
(*Dui* Below *Qian* Above)

Judgment

Even if one treads on the tiger's tail here, as it will not bite, so he will prevail.

COMMENTARY ON THE JUDGMENTS

Treading is a matter of the soft treading on the hard. It is because *Dui* responds to *Qian* with cheerfulness that "even if one treads on the tiger's tail, as it will not bite, so he will prevail." {A Judgment as such addresses itself to what it considers to be the controlling principle of the hexagram in question. That which governs this entire hexagram is to be found in Third Yin. To "tread . . . on the tiger's tail" refers to the danger involved here. Third Yin is the master of the *Lü* hexagram. Here, it walks with a yin's softness on top of the hardness of Second Yang, and this is to tread on danger. That it treads on the tiger's tail and yet is not bitten is due to the way "*Dui* responds to *Qian* with cheerfulness." As the *Qian* trigram embodies the virtues of strength and rectitude, one here uses cheerfulness not as a device to commit the evil of sycophancy but as the right means to respond to *Qian*. Thus it is appropriate that one who treads on the tiger's tail in such a way here will not be bitten but prevail.[1]} If one is strong, adheres to the Mean, and is correct, he may tread in the place of a supreme sovereign and yet do so without anxiety, for this is the measure of his brilliance. {This refers to the virtue of Fifth Yang.}

COMMENTARY ON THE IMAGES

Above is Heaven, and below is Lake: this constitutes the image of *Lü* [Treading]. In the same way, the noble man makes distinction between the high and the low and so defines how the common folk shall set their goal.[2]

COMMENTARY ON THE APPENDED PHRASES

Lü [Treading] is the foundation of virtue.

Lü [Treading] demonstrates how by practicing harmony one reaches goals.

Lü [Treading] provides the means to make one's actions harmonious.[3]

PROVIDING THE SEQUENCE OF THE HEXAGRAMS

Only after things have been domesticated can there be propriety. This is why *Xiaoxu* [Lesser Domestication, Hexagram 9] is followed by *Lü* [Treading].

THE HEXAGRAMS IN IRREGULAR ORDER

Lü [Treading] means "not staying in one's position."

First Yang

If one treads with simplicity, to set forth will bring no blame. {To be located at First Yang is to be at the beginning of the process of Treading. The Dao of Treading is adverse to extravagance, so this is why "simplicity . . . brings no blame." If one conducts himself with simplicity when he finds himself here at a time of *Lü* [Treading], whatever he might set out to do should never fail to attract a following, but in doing so he must be "devoted exclusively to the realization of his heartfelt goals," for only then will he avoid arousing the opposition of others.}

COMMENTARY ON THE IMAGES

To set forth in such a way that one treads with simplicity means that one is devoted exclusively to the realization of his heartfelt goals.

Second Yang

The path to tread on is level and smooth, and if one secluded here practices constancy, he will have good fortune. {In the Dao of *Lü* [Treading], modesty is esteemed, and worldly success is no object of delight. This is one who works hard at achieving perfect sincerity and is offended by external ornamentation. Thus Second

Yang as a yang line occupying a yin position finds itself treading the path of modesty. Here, abiding in the inner trigram and treading the Mean, this one regards obscurity and prominence as of equal value. The excellence embodied in the Dao of *Lü* [Treading] is at its peak with this line. This is why "the path to tread on is level and smooth" and free of dangerous obstacles. To practice constancy here in the midst of seclusion is something well deserving of good fortune.}

COMMENTARY ON THE IMAGES

"If one secluded here practices constancy, he will have good fortune": one who keeps to the Mean will not bring confusion on himself.

Third Yin

The one-eyed may still see, and the lame may still tread, but when such a one treads on the tiger's tail, it will bite him, and he shall have misfortune. Here, a warrior tries to pass himself off as a great sovereign. {When one finds himself located here at a time of *Lü* [Treading], it would be called immodest even if it were a yang line that occupied this yang position, so is it not much worse to have a yin line occupying this yang position, to have a soft and weak line riding on top of a hard and strong line? One who tries to achieve clarity under such circumstances would as well be one-eyed, and one who tries to make a move under such circumstances would as well be lame, so anyone trying to tread on danger here will certainly be bitten. Such a one has his will fixed on the hardness and strength [represented by Fifth Yang] and neglects to follow the path on which he should tread. He wishes to use aggression to intimidate others with his military prowess and would pass himself off as a great sovereign, but his actions cannot help but bring him misfortune. Thus to have his will focused on Fifth Yang's position in this way is the height of stupidity.}

COMMENTARY ON THE IMAGES

"The one-eyed may still see" but not well enough to achieve clarity. "The lame may still tread" but not well enough to keep up. The misfortune of being bitten here is due to one's being unsuited for the position involved. "A warrior tries to pass himself off as a great sovereign" because his will knows nothing but hardness and strength.

Fourth Yang

One who treads on the tiger's tail here should be fearfully cautious, so that in the end he will have good fortune. {This line is right next to the most noble line [Fifth Yang]. As a yang line that carries a yang line, it is located at a place that inspires much apprehension, and this is why the text says: "One who treads on the tiger's tail here should be fearfully cautious." However, since this is a yang line occupying a yin position, it takes modesty as its basic principle, so although it is located in a dangerous and fearful place, in the end it will achieve its goal. This is why the text says: "In the end he will have good fortune."}

COMMENTARY ON THE IMAGES

"Here [one] should be fearfully cautious, so that in the end he will have good fortune": this is a matter of his goal being realized.

Fifth Yang

Tread resolutely here, and practice constancy in the face of trouble. {One who obtains this place is located in the position of nobility. As such a one should use his strength to achieve resolute rectitude, the text says: "Tread resolutely here, and practice constancy in the face of trouble." The Dao of *Lü* is adverse to worldly success, and as Fifth Yang is located in this noble position, danger is thus inherent in it.}

COMMENTARY ON THE IMAGES

"Tread resolutely here, and practice constancy in the face of trouble": the position is correct and appropriate for this.

Top Yang

One should look where he has trodden and examine the omens involved. Here the cycle starts back, so it means fundamental good fortune. {Omens of good fortune and bad spring from where one treads. Here, one is located at the very end of *Lü*, so with this the Dao of *Lü* has completed its course. Thus one may look where he has trodden and examine the omens involved. If in abiding in this position at the very top of *Lü*, one achieves resonance with the cheerfulness [of First Yang], though at a lofty height, he should not be in danger, for here the cycle starts back.[4] As the great completion of the Dao of *Lü*, this place signifies "fundamental good fortune."}

COMMENTARY ON THE IMAGES

As "fundamental good fortune" inheres in Top Yang, this means that one shall have blessings in great measure.

NOTES

1. See Wang's remarks on this hexagram in section seven of his General Remarks. Note that this and all subsequent text set off in this manner is commentary by Wang Bi.

2. *Dui* is defined as "lake" in section three of Explaining the Trigrams. Kong Yingda comments:

> Heaven, being noble, is located above, and Lake, being humble, is located below. The noble man emulates this image of the *Lü* hexagram and "makes distinction between the high and the low and so defines how the common folk shall set their goal." This means that he has the noble and the humble keep to their proper order. However, the name for the *Lü* hexagram combines two meanings. In terms of the hexagram lines, it refers to the one on top treading on the one below it, that is, Third Yin treading on Second Yang, but in terms of the image comprised of the upper and lower trigrams, *lü* [treading] means *li* [decorum]: the low should perform services for the high with proper decorum.

See *Zhouyi zhengyi*, 2: 18b.

3. See section seven of the Commentary on the Appended Phrases, Part Two.

4. "The cycle starts back" translates *qi xuan* both here and in the text of Top Yang. This reading follows Kong Yingda's gloss of *xuan* (revolve, turn) as *xuanfan* (turn or start back—as a cycle, etc.). See *Zhouyi zhengyi*, 2: 20a. Both Cheng Yi and Zhu Xi gloss *xuan* as *zhouxuan*, which means "full cycle" or "come full cycle"—i.e., the entire process that something undergoes. In their view, Top Yang is the completion of the cycle of *Lü*,

the point at which one should examine what he has done throughout the process ("where he has trodden") to see the good or bad that he has done as well as the omens that such actions produce. See *Zhouyi zhezhong*, 2: 18b.

HEXAGRAM 11

䷊

泰

Tai [Peace]

(*Qian* Below *Kun* Above)

Judgment

Tai is such that the petty depart, and the great arrive, so good fortune will prevail.

COMMENTARY ON THE JUDGMENTS

"The petty depart, and the great arrive, so good fortune will prevail." That is, Heaven and Earth interact perfectly, and the myriad things go smoothly. Those above and those below interact perfectly, and their will becomes one. The inner trigram is yang, and the outer is yin. The inner signifies strength and dynamism, and the outer signifies compliance and obedience. Inside is the noble man, and outside is the petty man. The Dao of the noble man is increasing, and the dao of the petty man is deteriorating.

COMMENTARY ON THE IMAGES

"Heaven and Earth perfectly interact": this constitutes the image of Peace. In the same way, the ruler, by his tailoring, fulfills the Dao of Heaven and Earth and assists Heaven and Earth to stay on the right course; in so doing, he assists the people on all sides. {What is called *Tai* [Peace] refers to the time when things go smoothly on a grand scale. When what is above and what is below achieve interaction on such a grand scale, things lose their proper place and time.[1] This is why the ruler helps things along by his tailoring and, "in so doing, assists the people on all sides."[2]}

PROVIDING THE SEQUENCE OF THE HEXAGRAMS

It is by this treading that *Tai* [Peace] occurs. Only then will there be security. This is why *Lü* [Treading, Hexagram 10] is followed by *Tai*.

THE HEXAGRAMS IN IRREGULAR ORDER

Tai [Peace, Hexagram 10] and *Pi* [Obstruction] are opposed in kind.

First Yang

When one pulls up the rush plant, it pulls up others of the same kind together with it,[3] so if one goes forth and acts, there will be good fortune. {The rush plant is such that when one pulls it up by its roots, it pulls up others connected to it. The word *ru* [pull up] refers to the way things get pulled up together. Here the three yang lines share the same aim, for all have fixed it on the outer [upper] trigram. The first line is the leader of its kind, so when it initiates action, the others follow, just like the rush plants that get pulled up together. The lines of the upper trigram respond compliantly and do not become disobedient or contrary, so when the yang lines advance, all of them achieve their purpose. This is why to go forth and act here with others of the same kind means that "there will be good fortune."}

COMMENTARY ON THE IMAGES

"When one pulls up the rush plant" and "so if one goes forth and acts, there will be good fortune" mean that here one should keep his aim fixed on outer things [the public world].

Second Yang

One here embraces the uncouth, makes use of those who wade rivers,[4] and does not leave out those who are far away, thus cliques disappear, and he succeeds in being worthy of the practice of centrality [the Mean]. {It is one who embodies strength and dynamism and occupies a central position who puts these to use in *Tai* [Peace]. He is someone who can include among his circle the uncouth and rustic and take in those who wade rivers. As the way he uses his heart and mind is so very broad, there are none he abandons at a distance. This is why it says that he "does not leave out those who are far away." Free from personal considerations and utterly impartial, he abides in "the bright and the great [Dao]."[5] This is why "cliques disappear." In this way, he thus can "succeed in being worthy of the practice of centrality [the Mean]." The word *shang* [usually "esteem"] here means "be worthy of."[6] "Practice of centrality" refers to the fifth line [i.e., the middle line in the upper trigram].}

COMMENTARY ON THE IMAGES

"One here embraces the uncouth" and "succeeds in being worthy of the practice of centrality [the Mean]" by implementing the bright and great [Dao].

Third Yang

There is no flat that does not eventually slope; there is no going away that does not involve a return, but one who practices constancy in the face of difficulty will be without blame. Grieve not over your faithfulness, for there are blessings in the salary that sustains you. {Originally *Qian* [as Heaven] is above, and *Kun* [as Earth] is below, but when one obtains the hexagram *Tai*, one finds that the former has descended, and the latter has risen. Thus the third line occupies a position at the boundary of Heaven and Earth and [as a yang line] is about to return to its proper place [above, i.e., Heaven]. When it actually does return to its proper place, as a superior [Third Yang] will keep to noble station, and as a subordinate [Fourth Yin] will keep to a humble station.[7] This is why "there is no going away that does not involve a return" and "no flat that does not eventually slope." Here one is situated at the point where the route between Heaven and Earth is about to be blocked and where the level road is about to slope, things that signify that a moment of great flux is about to occur and the world is about to undergo radical change. Thus one does not neglect his uprightness while in repose and does not neglect the proper response while engaged in action. Here in the face of difficulty, if one is able to practice constancy, he will not lose his righteousness. This is why he "will be without blame." This is someone who faithfully practices righteousness and sincerity, so, free of any grief over his own faithfulness, he achieves spontaneous understanding of what is here involved. This is why it says: "Grieve not over your faithfulness, for there are blessings in the salary that sustains you."}

COMMENTARY ON THE IMAGES

"There is no going away that does not involve a return": this is at the boundary between Heaven and Earth. {This is the boundary at which Heaven and Earth are about separately to return, each to its proper place.}

Fourth Yin

Fluttering, one does not use riches to deal with his neighbors. Without admonishing them, he has their faithfulness. {*Qian* is happy to arise and return to its own place, and *Kun* is happy to descend and return to its own place. The fourth line occupies a place at the head of *Kun* but does not have a strong hold on this position, so it retreats when it is ordered to do so. This is why it is described as "fluttering."[8] The lines of *Kun* [i.e., the upper trigram] all happily descend; when this one line itself retreats, the rest all follow. Thus here one does not have to rely on riches to make use of his neighbors, for none fails to identify his ambitions and wants with those of Fourth Yin itself. This is why their faithfulness comes about spontaneously without having to rely on admonition to get it.}

COMMENTARY ON THE IMAGES

"Fluttering, one does not use riches": all [the yin lines] have lost solid footing. "Without admonishing them, he has their faithfulness": they desire it in their heart of hearts.

Fifth Yin

The sovereign Yi gave his younger sister in marriage.[9] As a result, there were blessings and fundamental good fortune. {Women say of their getting married that they "are returning." The *Tai* [Peace] hexagram indicates a time when yin and yang interact with each other. Here a female occupies a noble position, treading a central course [staying on the path of the Mean] and abiding in compliance. Lowering herself to resonate with Second Yang, she enters into a mutual relationship of effect and response. As she employs the virtue of centrality to carry out her wishes, she does not violate the propriety involved. The statement "the sovereign Yi gave his younger sister in marriage" is truly in accord with this concept. She treads the way of compliance and abides in centrality [the Mean], so when she carries out her wishes it results in blessings. Here the mutual matching of yin with yang is brought to the perfection appropriate to it, therefore "fundamental good fortune" occurs.}

COMMENTARY ON THE IMAGES

"As a result, there were blessings and fundamental good fortune": here wishes are carried out by following the precept of the Mean.

Top Yin

The city wall falls back into the moat. Do not use the army now, and only in one's own city issue commands, otherwise constancy will be debased. {To be located at the very top of *Tai* [Peace] always indicates a return to the position with which it resonates [Third Yang]. Here the Dao of *Tai* is about to perish, for those above and those below do not interact. Those in humble station no longer take orders from above, and those in noble station no longer extend benefaction to those below. Thus "the city wall falls back into the moat," for the Dao of the humble has collapsed. "Do not use the army now" means "do not launch any importune attacks." "Only in one's city issue commands, otherwise constancy will be debased," for the Dao of *Pi* [Obstruction, Hexagram 12] has already formed, and orders will not be carried out.}

COMMENTARY ON THE IMAGES

"The city wall falls back into the moat": commands here will result in confusion.

NOTES

1. At a time of such fructification, nature is, in effect, out of control, and it requires a true sovereign to bring order to things. Kong Yingda explained Wang's statement as: "When things lose their proper place and time, then winter is warm, and summer is cold; autumn begets things, and spring puts them to death." See *Zhouyi zhengyi*, 2: 21a. This view is based on a belief in the resonance between human rule and the course of nature.

2. This and all subsequent text set off in this manner is commentary by Wang Bi.

3. Cf. Hexagram 12, *Pi* (Obstruction), First Yin.

4. "Those who wade rivers" seems to refer to those utterly benighted folk beyond the pale of even rudimentary civilization— those who do not even know to straddle a log to cross a river, let alone know about boats.

5. "The bright and great [Dao]" translates *guangda*. Kong Yingda glosses this expression as *guangda zhi dao* (the bright and great Dao). See *Zhouyi zhengyi*, 2: 21b. Note that Wang's use of *guangda* here is borrowed from Commentary on the Images for the line.

6. *Shang* might also mean "assist." In his *Jingyi shuwen* (Accounts of what has been heard concerning interpretations of the *Classics*), the great Qing dynasty philologist Wang Yinzhi (1766–1834) comments on Wang Bi's gloss: "Wang Bi interprets *shang* [esteem] as *pei* [be worthy of], but among ancient exegetical writings there is no evidence for this." He then goes on to cite the *Erya* (Elegant and correct writings in familiar terms), a third or second century B.C. lexicographic work, to the effect that *shang* means *you* (assist). See Lou, *Wang Bi ji jiaoshi*, 1: 279 n. 12. In the light of this interpretation, Second Yang of *Tai* should end with "he can assist the exercise of centrality." Also, if we interpret *shang* in its usual sense of "esteem," it would end with "he obtains esteem for his exercise of centrality."

7. That is, when Third Yang moves "back" to the fourth position, it will become a Fourth Yang, and when Fourth Yin moves "back" to the third position, it will become a Third Yin. Likewise, all the yang lines in the lower trigram so change to yin lines, and all the yin lines of the upper trigram so change to yang lines, thus *Tai* becomes *Pi* (Obstruction), Hexagram 12.

8. "Fluttering" translates *pianpian*, which Lu Deming (556–627 A.D.) glosses as *qing ju mao* (an appearance of lightly fluttering on the air). See *Zhouyi yinyi* (Pronunciation and meaning of terms in the *Changes of the*

Zhou), included in his *Jingdian shiwen* 2: 71; see also Lou, *Wang Bi ji jiaoshi*, 1: 280 n. 17. From the way Wang interprets the context, it appears that *pianpian* here means "flutter down."

9. Traditionally, Sovereign Yi is identified as the father of Zhou, the last of the Shang kings; his traditional dates are 1191–1155 B.C. This identification was first proposed by Yu Fan (164–233 A.D.); his comments are quoted in the *Zhouyi jijie* (Collected exegeses on the *Changes of the Zhou*) of Li Dingzuo (eighth century A.D.), 4: 79, and seem to be based on evidence given in the *Zuozhuan* (Zuo's chronicles on the *Spring and Autumn Annals*), in a passage concerning the ninth year of the reign of Duke Ai (487 B.C.); see Legge, *The Chinese Classics*, 5: 819. However, "Yi" is included among a number of Shang kings' names, and it is by no means certain that the *Zuozhuan* and Yu Fan are correct. There is also controversy over whether it is a daughter or a younger sister who is given in marriage. "Gave in marriage" translates *gui*, which literally means "[caused to] return." This involves a "return" to the husband's family. Note that the phrase "Sovereign Yi gave his younger sister in marriage" also occurs in Hexagram 54, *Guimei* (Marrying Maiden), Fifth Yin.

HEXAGRAM 12

䷋

否

Pi [Obstruction]

(*Kun* Below *Qian* Above)

Judgment

Pi is such that the evil men associated with *Pi* [Obstruction] make it an unfit time for the noble man to practice constancy. Thus the great depart, and the petty arrive.

COMMENTARY ON THE JUDGMENTS

"The evil men associated with *Pi* [Obstruction] make it an unfit time for the noble man to practice constancy. Thus the great depart, and the petty arrive." That is, as Heaven and Earth are estranged, the myriad things do not interact, and as those above and those below are estranged, there is no true polity in the world. The inner [lower trigram] is yin, and the outer [upper trigram] is yang; the inner is soft, and the outer is hard. Inside is the petty man, and outside is the noble man. The dao of the petty man is increasing, and the Dao of the noble man is deteriorating.

COMMENTARY ON THE IMAGES

Heaven and Earth do not interact: this is the image of Obstruction. In the same way, the noble man holds back the practice of his virtue and thus avoids disaster. He must not allow himself to be honored with rank and salary.

PROVIDING THE SEQUENCE OF THE HEXAGRAMS

Tai [Peace, Hexagram 11] means smooth going. Things cannot forever go smoothly. This is why *Tai* is followed by *Pi* [Obstruction].

THE HEXAGRAMS IN IRREGULAR ORDER

Tai [Peace, Hexagram 11] and *Pi* [Obstruction] are opposed in kind.

First Yin

When one pulls up the rush plant, it pulls up others of the same kind together with it,[1] but if one practices constancy, good fortune will prevail. {Being located at the first position of *Pi* [Obstruction] is to be situated at the onset of compliancy; it is the head of this kind.[2] Compliancy is not strength and dynamism, so how could one here possibly go forth and initiate action? When one is located in Obstruction, action will lead to wickedness. Third Yin belongs to this same Dao: one cannot go forward with either of them. This is why "when one pulls up the rush plant, it pulls up others of the same kind together with it." Here one should practice constancy and not engage in flattery; this will result in good fortune and prevalence for him.[3]}

COMMENTARY ON THE IMAGES

"When one pulls up the rush plant," "one practices constancy," and "good fortune will result": one should keep his will fixed on his sovereign. {As one's will is fixed on his sovereign, he does not recklessly try to advance himself.}

Second Yin

Bearing up under orders here means good fortune for the petty man, but, although it means obstruction and stagnation for the great man, he will prevail. {When one lives in a world governed by Obstruction and yet obtains a position for himself, this is due to employing the utmost compliancy, by "bearing up under orders" from the ruler. Here the petty man's path is free and clear, for "the inner is soft, and the outer is hard," but if the great man deals with this as Obstruction, his Dao will prevail.}

COMMENTARY ON THE IMAGES

"Although it means Obstruction for the great man, he will prevail": this is because he does not form associations indiscriminately.

Third Yin

He bears his shame. {Both the petty man and the great man here utilize the lesser Dao in taking orders from the ruler, yet because this position is not appropriate for the great man, he has to bear his shame.}

COMMENTARY ON THE IMAGES

"He bears his shame": the position is not appropriate.

Fourth Yang

He who is issued commands here will be without blame, and his comrade will share in his blessings. {The reason one cannot issue commands while situated in Obstruction is that those who answer them will be petty men: when commands are issued to petty men, this deteriorates the Dao of the true sovereign. Now here for the first time is someone with his ambitions dedicated to his sovereign but situated in a humble and obscure position; thus he can be issued commands and remain without blame, and "his comrade will share in his blessings." "His comrade" refers to the first line.}

COMMENTARY ON THE IMAGES

"He who is issued commands here will be without blame": his ambitions will be realized.

Fifth Yang

He brings Obstruction to a halt, and this is the good fortune of the great man. This might be lost, this might be lost, so tie it to a healthy, flourishing mulberry.[4] {One who fills this noble position and is fit for it can bring the Dao of Obstruction to a halt. As he attributes *Pi* [Obstruction] to petty men, this means the end of *Pi*. Only with the arrival of the great man can this be so. This is why it says "the good fortune of the great man." Living at a time when the Dao of the true sovereign has been deteriorating, how can anyone occupying this noble position feel safe? It is his mindfulness that survival here is going to be dangerous that allows him to achieve stability.}

COMMENTARY ON THE IMAGES

"This is the good fortune of the great man": the position is correct and suitably filled.

COMMENTARY ON THE APPENDED PHRASES

The Master said: "To get into danger is a matter of thinking one's position secure; to become ruined is a matter of thinking one's continuance protected; to fall into disorder is a matter of thinking one's order enduring. Therefore the noble man when secure does not forget danger, when enjoying continuance does not forget ruin, when maintaining order does not forget disorder. This is the way his person is kept secure and his state remains protected. The *Changes* say: 'This might be lost, this might be lost, so tie it to a healthy, flourishing mulberry.' "[5]

Top Yang

Here one overturns obstruction. Before there was obstruction, but afterward happiness. {First there is the overturning,[6] after which things go smoothly. This is why the text says "afterward happiness." This is the start of dealing with Obstruction by overturning it,[7] after which things can go smoothly, and this results in happiness.}

COMMENTARY ON THE IMAGES

When Obstruction comes to an end, one "overturns" it: how could it last forever!

NOTES

1. Cf. Hexagram 11, *Tai* (Peace), First Yang.
2. First Yin here is the first line in the lower trigram, *Kun* (Pure Yin)—pure compliancy.
3. This and all subsequent text set off in this manner is commentary by Wang Bi.
4. The occurrence of *sang* (mulberry), instead of some other tree, is probably because it rhymes with *wang* (lost). Whether the mulberry has other significance here is uncertain.
5. See section five of the Commentary on the Appended Phrases, Part Two.
6. Note that *Pi* "overturned" is *Tai*, Hexagram 11.
7. This translates *shi yi qing wei pi*. Another possible rendering is: "This is the start of replacing *Pi* with its overturning [i.e., with its "opposite," *Tai*]." Itō Tōgai (1670–1736), in fact, glosses Wang's statement this way: *qing pi wei tai* (*kei hi i tai*), "turns *Pi* over to make *Tai*." See *Shūeki kyōyoku tsūkai*, 4: 10.

䷌

同人

Tongren [Fellowship]
(*Li* Below *Qian* Above)

Judgment

It is by extending Fellowship even to the fields that one prevails. Thus it is fitting to cross the great river and fitting for the noble man to practice constancy.[1]

COMMENTARY ON THE JUDGMENTS

Fellowship is expressed in terms of how a weak line [Second Yin] obtains a position such that, thanks to its achievement of the Mean, it finds itself in resonance with the [ruler of the] *Qian* trigram. Such a situation is called *Tongren* [Fellowship]. {Second Yin is the ruler of the *Tongren* hexagram.[2]} When the *Tongren* hexagram statement says that "it is by extending Fellowship even to the fields that one prevails" and "thus it is fitting to cross the great river," it refers to what *Qian* accomplishes. {This explains how "it is by extending Fellowship even to the fields that one prevails" and "it is fitting to cross the great river" can take place. These are things that *Qian* brings about and not what Second Yin can accomplish. Thus the text makes it a special point to say: "When the *Tongren* hexagram statement says. . . ."[3]} Exercising strength through the practice of civility and enlightenment, they [Second Yin and Fifth Yang] each respond to the other with their adherence to the Mean and their uprightness: such is the rectitude of the noble man. {The exercise of strength here should not be done through military force but through the use of civility and enlightenment. The two respond to each other not out of evil but out of adherence to the Mean and rectitude, thus "such is the rectitude of the noble man." This is why the text says: "It is . . . fitting for the noble man to practice constancy."} Only the noble man would be able to identify with the aspirations of all the people in the world. {The noble man takes civility and enlightenment as his virtues.}

COMMENTARY ON THE IMAGES

This combination of Heaven and Fire constitutes the image of *Tongren* [Fellowship]. {The Heaven [*Qian*] hexagram is on top and fire [the *Li* trigram][4] burns up to it; this is the meaning of the *Tongren* hexagram.[5]} In the same way, the noble man associates with his own kind and makes clear distinctions among things. {The noble man and the petty man each in his own way can only be what his fellows are.}

COMMENTARY ON THE APPENDED PHRASES

In the Dao of the noble man
There's a time for going forth
And a time for staying still,
A time to remain silent
And a time to speak out.
But for two people to share mind and heart,
Such sharpness severs metal,
And the words of those sharing mind and heart,
Such fragrance is like orchids.[6]

PROVIDING THE SEQUENCE OF THE HEXAGRAMS

Things cannot forever be obstructed. This is why *Pi* [Obstruction, Hexagram 12] is followed by *Tongren* [Fellowship].

THE HEXAGRAMS IN IRREGULAR ORDER

Tongren [Fellowship] indicates affability.

First Yang

One practices fellowship at his gate and so stays free of blame. {Located here at the beginning of *Tongren*, this line is the leader of the *Tongren* hexagram. As it does not have a resonant relationship with any line above, so one's heart and mind here should not be bound by particularism. Instead one thoroughly identifies with the great community,[7] so when one goes out of his gate, he treats all with fellowship. This is why the text says: "One practices fellowship at his gate." If one practices fellowship upon going out of his gate, who could possibly find him worthy of blame?}

COMMENTARY ON THE IMAGES

If upon going out of his gate one practices fellowship, would there still be anyone who could place blame on him?

Second Yin

To practice fellowship just with one's clan is base. {Its resonance being with Fifth Yang, this line only allies itself with it, the ruler of the hexagram. If it were instead to slight its ruler, this would cause obstruction. To apply one's heart and mind in such a partial and narrow way is characteristic of a dao of baseness.}

COMMENTARY ON THE IMAGES

"To practice fellowship just with one's clan" is a dao of baseness.[8]

Third Yang

Here one hides armed troops in a thicket and ascends his high hill, but even after three years he does not stage his uprising. {When one finds himself here at a time of *Tongren*, he treads on the territory belonging to the very top of the lower trigram. As it is impossible now to encompass those above and those below in the same wide embrace and to identify thoroughly with the great community, now each separates off into groups by kind. However, Third Yang wishes to go against its Dao and covets the line with which it forms a pair [Second Yin] and would usurp the position of the one it responds to above [Fifth Yang.] But its opponent [Fifth Yang] is so hard and strong that its strength is no match for it. This is why "here one hides armed troops in a thicket" and dares not reveal his arrogance. "One . . . ascends his high hill" refers to how he looks at things from a distance but dares not advance. Appraising the relative strengths involved, he spends three years unable to stage an uprising. That such a one is unable to stage an uprising for three years is due to the fact that the Dao of Fifth Yang has already been fulfilled [i.e., as a yang line in the central, yang position of the upper trigram, it has become the sovereign of this hexagram], so how could Third Yang ever proceed against it?}

COMMENTARY ON THE IMAGES

"One hides armed troops in a thicket" because one's opponent is strong. "Even after three years he does not stage his uprising," for how could he ever proceed?

Fourth Yang

Although he rides the top of the wall, he fails in his attack, but this means good fortune. {It is one who occupies high ground and attacks downward who has the strength to "ride the top of the wall." But this is not the right place for Fourth Yang to tread, and this is why it does battle with an opponent [Third Yang]. Second Yin of its own accord remains in resonance with Fifth Yang, and although Third Yang has not transgressed against Fourth Yang, Fourth Yang still attacks Third Yang as a way to try to get Second Yin. Although Fourth Yang condemns Third Yang's behavior, it still imitates it. As it is in violation of the norms of righteousness and does damage to moral principles, Fourth Yang does not gain the support of the masses, and this is why in spite of "rid[ing] the top of the wall," it fails in its attempt. Unable to succeed, it turns around, and with its return to right principles, it obtains good fortune. Here one makes a return once he has failed in his attempt, and the reason he obtains good fortune is that "when he found himself in such difficulties, he returned to principled behavior."}

COMMENTARY ON THE IMAGES

"Although he rides the top of the wall," the sense of righteousness [in others] denies him success. His "good fortune" is due to the fact that when he found himself in such difficulties, he returned to principled behavior.

Fifth Yang

For Fellowship here there is first howling and wailing, but afterward there is laughter, for with the victory of the great army, they manage to meet. {The Commentary on the Judgments says: "Fellowship is expressed in terms of how a weak line [Second Yin] obtains a position such that, thanks to its achievement of the Mean, it finds itself in resonance with the [ruler of the] *Qian* trigram. Such a situation is called *Tongren* [Fellowship]." As this is so, then one who is soft and yielding in substance but abides in the Mean will gain the support of the masses, but one who insists on rigidity and employs inflexible methods will not win a mass following. It is because immediately between them lie the two yang lines [Third and Fourth Yang] that Fifth Yang has not yet attained its goal [Second Yin], and this is the reason for there being "first howling and wailing." But since Fifth Yang abides in the Mean and is located in this noble position, it is sure to achieve victory in battle. Thus the text says: "Afterward there is laughter." Here one at Fifth Yang is unable to make his opponents ally themselves to him of their own accord, so he has to use his power directly on them. Thus it has to be a "victory of the great army" over them, and consequently "they [Fifth Yang and Second Yin] manage to meet."}

COMMENTARY ON THE IMAGES

What first happens in Fellowship is due to centrality and forthrightness. The "great army" and "they manage to meet" refer to their success.[9]

Top Yang

If one practices Fellowship in the countryside, he will remain free of regret. {"Countryside" indicates that this is the very top of the outer trigram. When one finds himself here at a time of *Tongren* [Fellowship], he is located as far as possible on the outside. Although this is not the place to find comrades, it is still far from the strife that is going on inside. Thus, though one here might stay free of remorse and regret, he also will never achieve his ambition [to achieve Fellowship in a major way.]}

COMMENTARY ON THE IMAGES

"If one practices Fellowship in the countryside," his ambition will never be achieved. {Whenever one finds himself located at a time governed by *Tongren* [Fellowship] and finds that things do not go smoothly, it means that it is necessary to use military force, for with a failure to bring about the great community, each one will form cliques on the basis of selfish interests and pursue his own personal advantage through them. Although the man of Chu lost his bow, he could not "lose" his Chu.[10] The more extreme one loves his own state, the more this will bring about calamity for others, and this happens because people do not pursue Fellowship on a grand enough scale. The hard and strong lines [of *Tongren*] all go so far as to involve the use of military force.[11]}

NOTES

1. Kong Yingda comments:

> Fields indicate broad and distant places. The text uses the word *fields* as a metaphor for this. It means that, in entering into congenial fellowship with people, one must do so far and wide and leave no one out and, in so applying one's heart and mind, one must be free of partiality. . . . Here one has so joined his heart and mind to his fellows that he has sufficient means to cross over troubles, and this is why the text says "it is fitting to cross the great river."

See *Zhouyi zhengyi*, 2: 25b.

2. This and all subsequent text set off in this manner is commentary by Wang Bi. Wang remarks elsewhere: "The rare is what the many value; the one that is unique is the one the multitudes make their chief. If one hexagram has five positive lines and one negative, then we have the negative line be the master. If it is a matter of five negative lines and one positive line, then we have the positive line be the master." See section one of the General Remarks. Second Yin is also master or ruler of the *Tongren* hexagram because it "represents the hexagram's meaning," but Fifth Yang is also its ruler by virtue of its "noble position." See Hexagram 6, *Song* (Contention), note 2.

3. "When the *Tongren* hexagram statement says" translates *Tongren yue*. Both Cheng Yi and Zhu Xi think these three characters are a later interpolation in the text. See *Zhouyi zhezhong*, 9: 22b.

4. The trigram *Li* (Cohesion) is also identified with Fire and Brightness; see sections three, five, and eleven of Explaining the Trigrams.

5. Kong Yingda comments: "The Heaven trigram is on top, and fire [the *Li* trigram] also burns upward as it strives to make its own nature the same." See *Zhouyi zhengyi*, 2: 26b.

6. See section eight of the Commentary on the Appended Phrases, Part One.

7. "Great community" translates *datong*, a term common to both the Confucian and the Daoist traditions. In Confucian thought, *datong* signifies that age of great peace and social harmony that supposedly existed at the time of the ancient sage kings, as, for instance, it occurs in the *Zhuangzi*;

see the *Liyun* (Evolution of rites), section nine of the *Liji* (Book of rites), 22: 1a–12b. In Daoist thought, *datong* might better be translated as "great unity," for the "community" involved is not restricted to human society but encompasses all of nature; see the *Zhuangzi*, 28/11/65.

8. "Baseness" translates *lin*; this reading follows both the commentary of Wang Bi and the subcommentary of Kong Yingda; see *Zhouyi zhengyi*, 2: 27a, and Lou Yulie's remarks in *Wang Bi ji jiaoshi*, 1: 287, n. 9. *Lin* is glossed in these commentaries as *linse*, *bilin*, etc., all of which suggest narrowness, bias, and miserliness. Cheng Yi instead glosses *lin* as *kelin*, "regrettable," and Zhu Xi seems to interpret it as "regret" (as in *huilin*, "remorse and regret"); see *Zhouyi zhezhong*, 2: 32a and 11: 30b.

9. Kong Yingda comments: "It is because one at Fifth Yang uses the Dao that has him practice a rectitude tempered by the Mean and a perseverance hardened by strength that others do not yet follow him. Thus the text says: 'First there is howling and wailing.' " See *Zhouyi zhengyi*, 2: 28a.

10. Kong Yingda cites the *Haosheng* (It is preferable to let people live) section of the *Kongzi jiayu* (The school sayings of Confucius) (a work that the annotator, Wang Su [195–256], is long thought to have forged but that may contain authentic material from the early Confucian tradition): "King Zhao of Chu when on an outing lost his 'Crow Caw' bow. His attendants requested that they be allowed to look for it, but the king said: 'A man of Chu lost a bow but someone in Chu will find it, so why should we also look for it?' When Confucius heard this, he said: 'What a pity his ambition is not greater. He did not say that a *man* lost it and a *man* would find it—why does it have to involve Chu?' " This same anecdote, worded slightly differently, is contained in the *Shuoyuan* (Garden of sayings), compiled by Liu Xiang (77–6 B.C.); see Lou, *Wang Bi ji jiaoshi*, 1: 289 n. 25, for a comparison of the two texts.

11. The "hard and strong lines" are Third, Fourth, and Fifth Yang but do not include First Yang and Top Yang. Kong Yingda notes that Wang's commentary here is not limited to a consideration of Top Yang and its image but is actually a general analysis of the *Tongren* hexagram as a whole. See *Zhouyi zhengyi*, 2: 28b.

HEXAGRAM 14

䷍

大有

Dayou [Great Holdings]
(*Qian* Below *Li* Above)

Judgment

Dayou is such that it provides fundamental prevalence. {If one does not effect a great mutual identification of interests that involves everyone, from what other source could Great Holdings be had? And once one has Great Holdings, fundamental prevalence is sure to follow.[1]}

COMMENTARY ON THE JUDGMENTS

Great Holdings is expressed in terms of how a weak [i.e., yielding] line [Fifth Yin] obtains the noble position and there practices the Mean and enjoys greatness, as those above and those below all respond to it. Such a situation is called *Dayou* [Great Holdings]. {Fifth Yin fills the noble position with its yielding nature and achieves greatness through abiding in the Mean. As there is no other yin line in the entire hexagram with which it has to share the resonance of the yang lines, all the lines above and below respond to it, and of these there is none that it does not welcome. This is the meaning of the *Dayou* hexagram.} The virtues of Great Holdings include hardness and strength but also civility and enlightenment. It is by resonating with Heaven's will that one achieves timely action, and this is how fundamental prevalence comes about. {As the virtues of Great Holdings work in response to Heaven's will, one's actions here do not fail to keep in step with the moment. Its hardness and strength allow him to stay free of impediment, and its civility and enlightenment keep him free of wrongdoing. As he is in resonance with Heaven, he emulates its greatness,[2] and, since he keeps his actions timely, things will not go against him, "and this is how fundamental prevalence comes about."}

COMMENTARY ON THE IMAGES

Fire on top of Heaven constitutes the image of *Dayou* [Great Holdings].[3] In the same way, the noble man suppresses evil and promulgates good, for he obeys the will of Heaven and so brings out the beauty inherent in life. {*Dayou* [Great Holdings] is an image of inclusiveness, thus it deals with the suppression of evil and the promulgation of goodness. Such a one brings out the beauty in things, that is, as he is commensurate with the virtue of Heaven, he brings out the beauty in the lives of all things.[4]}

PROVIDING THE SEQUENCE OF THE HEXAGRAMS

When one shares fellowship with others, things are sure to yield themselves to him. This is why *Tongren* [Fellowship, Hexagram 13] is followed by *Dayou* [Great Holdings].

THE HEXAGRAMS IN IRREGULAR ORDER

Dayou [Great Holdings] indicates mass support.

First Yang

Although one never encounters calamity here, to remain blameless he should bear up under difficulties, for only then will there be no blame. {Here we have a hard and strong line for the beginning of the *Dayou* hexagram, one that can neither tread a middle course nor, being so filled with strength, refrain from overflowing. If one were to keep to such a model when he sets out to do things, he is sure to bring calamity on himself later, but if one wishes "to remain blameless, he should bear up under difficulties, for only then will there be no blame."}

COMMENTARY ON THE IMAGES

First Yang of *Dayou* [Great Holdings] is such that one never encounters calamity here.

Second Yang

As there is a great wagon to carry things, {One's duties may be heavy here, but they present no danger.} one should set forth, for there will be no blame. {This indicates strength that does not violate the Mean, one entrusted with duties by Fifth Yin. Although the duties so borne are heavy, they present no danger, so this one can go as far as possible without getting stuck in the mud. Thus one may in this way "set forth, for there will be no blame."}

COMMENTARY ON THE IMAGES

When one has "a great wagon to carry things," he may keep storing things in it without making it break down.

Third Yang

When a duke uses this position, he enjoys prevalence along with the Son of Heaven, but a petty man is not equal to it. {When one finds himself here at a time of *Dayou* [Great Holdings], he is located at the very top of the lower trigram. This line rides on top of another hard and strong line while still managing to tread on the territory of its rightful position. As it shares with Fifth Yin the same merit,[5] it represents the utmost measure of martial force, which none can surpass. When a duke uses this position, he succeeds in sharing in the Dao of the Son of Heaven, but a petty man is not equal to this, and he can expect calamity to come of it.[6]}

COMMENTARY ON THE IMAGES

"When a duke uses this position, he enjoys prevalence along with the Son of Heaven," but it is a calamity for the petty man.

Fourth Yang

If one rejects such plenitude, there will be no blame. {Not only is this line already out of position [as a yang line in a yin position], but also, above, it is next to the awesomeness of the most noble one [Fifth Yin] and, below, it is contiguous with a subject minister who shares in that sovereign's might [Third Yang], so what it has to fear is indeed really dangerous! Only someone who has the wisdom of a sage can avoid suffering blame here. Although Third Yang is replete with power, Fifth Yin cannot be abandoned. If Fourth Yang is able to distinguish what his actual situation is here, devote his whole heart and mind to Fifth Yin, and constantly "reject . . . such plenitude [i.e., that of Third Yang], there will be no blame."[7]}

COMMENTARY ON THE IMAGES

"If one rejects such plenitude, there will be no blame." This means intelligence that is wise in making distinctions. {The term *intelligence* [*ming*] is equivalent to "talent" [*cai*].}

Fifth Yin

Trust in him makes him attractive, makes him awesome, and this means good fortune. {Here one abides in nobility with softness and yielding and occupies greatness while staying within the Mean. As he has no selfish designs on others, those above and below respond to him. "It is through trust in him that he inspires the ambition of others." Thus "trust in him makes him attractive." As he has no selfish designs on others, others are also fair-minded with him. As he harbors no suspicions toward others, others also trust in him. Since both fair-mindedness and trust prevail, what trouble or what need for precaution could there possibly be? Since such a one teaches people how to act without using words, whatever he does cannot help but be "awesome."[8] If one is the master of *Dayou* [Great Holdings] but does not deal with it in terms of this Dao, could good fortune ever be had by him?}

COMMENTARY ON THE IMAGES

"Trust in him makes him attractive": it is through trust in him that he inspires the ambition of others. The "good fortune" connected with his being "awesome" stems from the fact that he rules with ease and simplicity, with no need to take precautions.

Top Yang

Heaven will help him as a matter of course; this is good fortune, and nothing will fail to be fitting. {*Dayou* [Great Holdings] represents a world of riches and abundance. One who occupies Top Yang in *Dayou* but does not let himself get entangled in this place [of riches] has to be someone whose ambition is such that he admires and longs for worthiness. All the other lines ride on top of hard [yang] lines, but this one alone rides on top of a soft [yin] line, which indicates that it is in accord [with Heaven]. Fifth Yin is virtuous because it is trustworthy, and Top Yang treads thereon, that is, it "treads the Dao of trustworthiness." Although Top Yang is unable to embody a soft and yielding nature, yet it allows its hardness and strength to ride on top of a soft [yin] line, which means that it "keeps his thoughts in accord [with Heaven]." One who dwells in a world of rich holdings and yet does not allow his heart to be entangled by things but instead keeps his ambitions fixed on lofty things is someone who admires and longs for worthiness. This line possesses these three virtues,[9] so it finds the Dao helpful through and through, and this is why the Commentary on the Appended Phrases cites it all there.[10]}

COMMENTARY ON THE IMAGES

Top Yang of *Dayou* means good fortune, since "Heaven will help him as a matter of course."

NOTES

1. This and all subsequent text set off in this manner is commentary by Wang Bi.

2. "As one is in resonance with Heaven, he emulates its greatness" translates *ying tian ze da*. This reading follows the gloss of Lou Yulie, who interprets *ze* as *faze* or *xiaofa* (emulate); see *Wang Bi ji jiaoshi*, 1: 292 n. 4. However, it is also possible to take *ze* as a function word, "thus," which would result in "if one is in resonance with Heaven, he will thus achieve greatness."

3. See Hexagram 13, *Tongren* (Fellowship), note 4. Kong Yingda comments: "In substance Heaven is high and bright. The nature of fire is such that it burns upward. As a thing that casts light here, fire takes a position above in Heaven. This indicates the utmost brilliance, something that brings absolutely everything to light. Here we also have the sense of encompassing everything, and this is the principle underlying the promulgation of goodness." See *Zhouyi zhengyi*, 2: 29b.

4. "He obeys the will of Heaven and so brings out the beauty inherent in life" translates *shun tian xiu ming*, which follows the gloss provided in Wang Bi's commentary in Lou, *Wang Bi ji jiaoshi*. 1: 290 (see also 1: 292 n. 6). However, Cheng Yi interprets the same passage as *fengxun tian xiumei zhi ming* (he obeys the excellent will of Heaven). See *Zhouyi zhezhong*, 11: 32a. Kong Yingda's gloss supports Wang's interpretation, but the text of Wang's commentary in *Zhouyi zhengyi* (2: 29b) differs from the critical

text in *Wang Bi ji jiaoshi*, reading: "Such a one brings out all the potential in the nature of things. 'He obeys the will of Heaven and so brings out the beauty inherent in life' means that his actions are commensurate with [or "he is one with"] the lives of all things." Lou Yulie's version, based on good textual evidence of its own, seems to make more sense.

5. This paraphrases section nine of the Commentary on the Appended Phrases, Part Two: "The third and the fifth lines involve the same kind of merit [about which Han Kangbo comments: "Their yang merit is identical"] but differ as to position" (about which Han observes: "There is the difference between nobility and servility").

6. Wang's comments here are based upon reading *heng* (prevalence) as *heng* and not as *xiang* (to offer), an almost identical character with which it was used interchangeably in antiquity. Zhu Xi notes that citations of this and other similar passages in the *Changes* that occur in the *Zuozhuan* (Zuo's commentary on the *Spring and Autumn Annals*) write *xiang* for *heng*, and he glosses *xiang* as *chaoxian* (to make a court [sacrificial] offering) and *xiangxian* (to make a sacrificial offering). Therefore Zhu's reading of Third Yang would be: "A duke uses this opportunity to make offerings to the Son of Heaven." However, Cheng Yi, like Wang and Kong Yingda (see *Zhouyi zhengyi*, 2: 30a), reads *heng* as *heng* but interprets Third Yang differently:

> When this Third Yang finds itself at a time of *Dayou*, it occupies a position appropriate for one of the feudal lords, and, as it has such an abundance of riches, it must put them entirely at the disposal of the Son of Heaven. This means that one takes all he has and gives it over to the Son of Heaven, something that is a constant principle governing the relationship between sovereign and subject. If a petty man occupies this position, he will maintain exclusive control of his wealth for his own personal use, because he does not understand the Dao that has a duke take it and present it to his sovereign, and this is why the text says: "A petty man is not equal to it."

For Cheng's and Zhu's comments, see *Zhouyi zhezhong*, 2: 37b.

7. Kong Yingda glosses *peng* (plenitude) as *pang* (side) and says that it refers to the line "at the side" of Fourth Yang: i.e., Third Yang. See *Zhouyi zhengyi*, 2: 30b. In his commentary, Wang Bi also glosses *peng* as *pang*, but it seems obvious from what he says that *pang* does not simply mean "side." Note that both Cheng Yi and Zhu Xi also interpret *peng* as "plenitude"; see *Zhouyi zhezhong*, 2: 38a. The sense of "plenitude" for *peng* or *pang* is derived from *pengpeng* and *pangpang*: the sound of a drum roll, i.e., a "swelling," "overwhelming" sound. See Lou, *Wang Bi ji jiaoshi*, 1: 293–294 n. 17.

8. Cf. Wang's commentary to *Laozi*, section 17: "When a great man reigns as sovereign above, he occupies himself with things toward which he takes no purposeful action and practices a teaching that does not use words." See Lou, *Wang Bi ji jiaoshi*, 1: 40.

9. Kong Yingda lists them: "treading the way of trustworthiness," "keeping one's thoughts in accord [with Heaven]," and "admiring and longing for worthiness." See *Zhouyi zhengyi*, 2: 31a.

10. The quotations are from section twelve of the Commentary on the Appended Phrases, Part One, which reads:

> The *Changes* says: "Heaven will help him as a matter of course; this is good fortune, and nothing will be to his disadvantage." The Master said: "*You* [numinous help] means 'help.' " One whom Heaven helps is someone who is in accord with it. One whom people help is someone who is trustworthy. Such a one treads the Dao of trustworthiness, keeps his thoughts in accord [with Heaven], and also thereby holds the worthy in esteem. This is why "Heaven will help him as a matter of course; this is good fortune, and nothing will be to his disadvantage."

HEXAGRAM 15

䷎

謙

Qian [Modesty]
(*Gen* Below *Kun* Above)

Judgment

Qian [Modesty] is such that it provides prevalence, so the noble man has the capacity to maintain his position to the end.

COMMENTARY ON THE JUDGMENTS

"*Qian* [Modesty] is such that it provides prevalence": the Dao of Heaven provides succor to all below and so shines forth its radiance; the Dao of Earth consists of humility and so works in an upward direction. The Dao of Heaven is to make the full wane and to bring increase to the modest; the Dao of Earth is to transform what is full and to make what is modest flow and spread.[1] Gods and spirits harm what is full but enrich what is modest. And the Dao of Man is to hate the full and to love the modest. Modesty provides nobility and so allows one's radiance to shine; it provides humility and so prevents any transgression. This is how the noble man reaches his proper end.

COMMENTARY ON THE IMAGES

In the middle of the Earth, there is a mountain: this constitutes the image of *Qian* [Modesty].[2] In the same way, the noble man lessens what is too much and increases what is too little; he weighs the amounts of things and makes their distribution even. {Where he finds something too much, because of Modesty he decreases [*pou*] it, and where he finds something too little, because of Modesty he increases it. He provides things as they are needed and so ensures that their distribution never fails to be even.[3]}

COMMENTARY ON THE APPENDED PHRASES

The Master said: "To be diligent yet not to brag about it, to have meritorious achievement yet not to regard it as virtue, this is the ultimate of magnanimity. This speaks of someone who takes his achievements and subordinates them to others. As for his virtue, he would have it prosper ever more, and as for his decorum, he would have it ever more respectful. Modesty as such leads to perfect respect, and this is how one preserves his position."

Qian [Modesty] is how virtue provides a handle to things.

Qian [Modesty] provides the means by which decorum exercises its control.[4]

PROVIDING THE SEQUENCE OF THE HEXAGRAMS

When one's holdings are great, he must not let himself become satiated. This is why *Dayou* [Great Holdings, Hexagram 14] is followed by *Qian* [Modesty].

THE HEXAGRAMS IN IRREGULAR ORDER

Qian [Modesty] involves taking oneself lightly.

First Yin

The noble man is characterized by the utmost Modesty and because of that may cross the great river. This means good fortune. {To be located at the very bottom of the *Qian* hexagram signifies the most modest degree of all modesty. It is only the noble man who can embody the utmost modesty, and because of that he may cross over great difficulties, and nothing will harm him.}

COMMENTARY ON THE IMAGES

"The noble man is characterized by the utmost Modesty": he uses his humility to shepherd himself. *Shepherd* here means "nurture" or "care for."

Second Yin

One allows his Modesty to sing out here, and to practice constancy means good fortune. {"Sing out" refers to one's reputation being heard. Here one obtains his rightful position [as a yin line in a yin position] and abides in the Mean, practicing rectitude there with humility.}

COMMENTARY ON THE IMAGES

"One allows one's Modesty to sing out here, and to practice constancy means good fortune," for Modesty is attained in his innermost heart.

Third Yang

Diligent about his Modesty, the noble man has the capacity to maintain his position to the end, and this means good fortune. {Third Yang occupies the very top of the lower trigram and so manages to tread on the territory of its rightful position [as a yang line in a yang position]. There is no yang line either above or below to divide off one's people here, and Third Yang is venerated as master by all the yin lines. In nobility none takes precedence over this one. When one finds himself here in this world of Modesty, how can one keep his nobility secure? One carries those above and reaches out to those below, is diligent about his Modesty, and is not lazy: this is how he has good fortune.}

COMMENTARY ON THE IMAGES

A noble man who is "diligent about his modesty" is someone to whom the myriad folk will submit.

Fourth Yin

Nothing will fail to be fitting here, for he flies the banner of Modesty everywhere. {Fourth Yin rides on top of Third Yang and yet does it with Modesty. As such this expresses how from above one condescends to lower himself. Fourth Yin carries Fifth Yin and yet complies with Modesty. As such this is the Dao that "works in an upward direction." As one here devotes himself entirely to carrying out the Dao that governs how a superior should condescend to lower himself, "nothing will be to one's disadvantage here," and, as wherever he goes "he flies the banner of Modesty,"[5] "he never acts against its principle."}

COMMENTARY ON THE IMAGES

"Nothing will fail to be fitting here, for he flies the banner of Modesty everywhere": that is, he never acts against its principle.

Fifth Yin

One does not have to use wealth on them to gain access to neighbors here, and, as it is fitting to attack with military force, nothing will be to one's disadvantage. {Fifth Yin occupies the position of nobility and does so with Modesty and compliance, thus it can have access to its neighbors without using wealth on them. In spite of its Modesty and compliance, it still attacks with military force, but in all such cases those whom it attacks are scornfully rebellious.}

COMMENTARY ON THE IMAGES

"It is fitting to attack with military force," because it is a campaign against those who do not submit.

Top Yin

One may allow one's Modesty to sing out here, and it may be fitting therefore to have one's army make a move, but he should campaign only against a city-state. {Located here at the very extremity of the outer trigram, Top Yin does not share in inner governance. Thus one has nothing more than his reputation, and "one's ambition to accomplish things remains unfulfilled." It may tread the path of Modesty and compliance, but here at the outer extremity all this allows it to do is launch a campaign against a city-state.}

COMMENTARY ON THE IMAGES

"One may allow one's Modesty to sing out here," but one's ambition to accomplish things remains unfulfilled. It is possible "therefore to have one's army make a move, but he should campaign only against a city-state." {"Good fortune, misfortune, regret, and remorse are all generated from the way one acts."[6] The reason such action occurs is that it is provoked by what seems to be advantage. Thus "food and drink necessarily involve *Song* [Contention]. . . . When there is contention, there is sure to be an arising of the masses."[7] One who dwells in a place scorned by all is never harmed by those who are prone to act, and one who abides in a place that no one fights over never has it snatched away by those who are prone to fight. This explains how the six lines of this hexagram are either out of position [Fifth Yin is the ruler, and this position should have a yang line], have no resonance [First Yin should resonate with Fourth Yin, and Second Yin with Fifth Yin, but they are all yin lines and thus do not], or ride the wrong lines [Fourth Yin rides on top of Third Yang; a yin line should not ride on top of a yang line], yet none of them involve misfortune, blame, regret, or remorse. This is all due to the fact that they make Modesty their master. "Modesty provides nobility and so allows one's radiance to shine; it provides humility and so prevents any transgression." This is indeed something in which we can trust!}

NOTES

1. Kong Yingda comments: "Of hills and mountains, rivers and valleys, what is high is gradually brought low, and what is low is made higher. This

is what the text means by 'transform[ing] what is full and . . . mak[ing] what is modest flow and spread.' " See *Zhouyi zhengyi*, 2: 32a. That is, water and eroded soil work their way down and make streams swell and spread.

2. One of the attributes of the *Gen* (Restraint) trigram is Mountain, so the image is one of a mountain below, thrusting its way up through the middle of the earth.

3. This and all subsequent text set off in this manner is commentary by Wang Bi. Kong Yingda glosses *pou* (lessen/decrease) as "gather," thus his interpretation is somewhat at odds with Wang's commentary. See *Zhouyi zhengyi*, 2: 32b. Cheng Yi also reads *pou* as "gather": "Thus one who gathers together large quantities does so to augment what is too little. He weighs the relative abundance and scarcity of things and averages out their distribution so that fairness is achieved." However, Cheng's commentary also helps to explain the image: "The text does not say 'a mountain located at the middle of the Earth' but 'in the middle of the Earth there is a mountain.' This means that in the middle of what is humble and low there inheres something magnificent and lofty, that is, the magnificent and lofty is hidden within the humble and lowly." See *Zhouyi zhezhong*, 11: 35a.

4. The first quotation is from section eight of the Commentary on the Appended Phrases, Part One; the second and third quotations are from section seven of the Commentary on the Appended Phrases, Part Two.

5. In Fourth Yin, "flies the banner of Modesty everywhere" translates *hui qian*, which follows Wang Bi's gloss, *zhi hui jie qian*: literally, "when one directs [troops] with a banner, in all cases it is Modesty." Cheng Yi comments: "*Hui* [banner/flag] is an image for the display of something—just as a banner does when held in a man's hand. Whether in action or in restraint, in advance or in retreat, one must here display his modesty, for he abides in a place where he should be much afraid, especially since he is located above the worthy minister [Third Yang]." See *Zhouyi zhezhong*, 3: 3b. Lou Yulie explains *hui qian* the same way; see *Wang Bi ji jiaoshi*, 1: 297 n. 6.

6. Cf. section one of the Commentary on the Appended Phrases, Part Two. "Generated from the way one acts" translates *sheng hu dongzhe ye*. In the original passage, this phrase is translated as "generated from the way the lines move." The syntax and diction admit both readings, and the different contexts shape the meaning accordingly.

7. The quotations are from sections two and three of part one of Providing the Sequence of the Hexagrams.

HEXAGRAM 16

䷏

豫

Yu [Contentment]
(*Kun* Below *Zhen* Above)

Judgment

It is fitting to establish a chief and to send the army into action.

COMMENTARY ON THE JUDGMENTS

Yu [Contentment] is such that hardness [Fourth Yang] has its ambitions realized by getting others [the yin lines] to respond. When action occurs as a result of such compliance, there is *Yu* [Contentment]. Because *Yu* [Contentment] involves action done out of compliance, then even Heaven and Earth resemble it in this respect, so will it not prove all the more capable when it comes to establishing a chief or sending the army into action? Heaven and Earth act only out of compliance, thus the sun and the moon do not err, nor do the four seasons vary. The sage acts only out of compliance, thus by keeping to punishments that are clearly defined, his people remain submissive. The concept underlying moments of *Yu* [Contentment] is indeed great!

COMMENTARY ON THE IMAGES

Thunder bursts forth, and the Earth shakes: this constitutes the image of *Yu* [Contentment].[1] In the same way, the former kings made music in order to ennoble the virtuous and in its splendor offered it up to the Supreme Deity[2] so that they might be deemed worthy of the deceased ancestors.

COMMENTARY ON THE APPENDED PHRASES

They [the ancient sage kings] had gates doubled and had watchmen's clappers struck and so made provision against robbers. They probably got the idea for this from the hexagram *Yu* [Contentment].[3]

PROVIDING THE SEQUENCE OF THE HEXAGRAMS

To have great holdings and yet be capable of modesty means that one must be content. This is why *Qian* [Modesty, Hexagram 15] is followed by *Yu* [Contentment].

THE HEXAGRAMS IN IRREGULAR ORDER

Yu [Contentment] involves sloth.

First Yin

If one allows one's Contentment to sing out here, there will be misfortune. {As First Yin is located at the initial position of *Yu* [Contentment], it can only realize its ambitions above [with Fourth Yang]. When happiness goes to excess, licentiousness results, and when "ambitions are exhausted," "there will be misfortune," so how may Contentment be sung out here?[4]}

COMMENTARY ON THE IMAGES

If "one allows one's Contentment to sing out here," this means that one's ambitions are exhausted, so "there will be misfortune."

Second Yin

Harder than rock, he does not let the day run its course. Constancy means good fortune. {To be located here at a time of *Yu* [Contentment] means that one obtains a rightful position where one treads the Mean. This is someone who, being secure in his practice of constancy and rectitude, does not seek thoughtless Contentment. If one is compliant but does not follow thoughtlessly and is content without violating the Mean, he will therefore conduct relationships with superiors without sycophancy and with subordinates without insult. As such a one understands wherefrom misfortune and fortune arise, he does not take delight thoughtlessly, and as he distinguishes what constitutes ineluctable principles, he does not allow his behavior to vary from them—and so "harder than rock, he does not let the day run its course"![5]}

COMMENTARY ON THE IMAGES

"He does not let the day run its course. Constancy means good fortune": this is because of his adherence to the Mean and his rectitude.

COMMENTARY ON THE APPENDED PHRASES

The Master said: "As for incipience itself, it is the infinitesimally small beginning of action, the point at which the precognition of good fortune can occur. The noble man acts upon something as soon as he becomes aware of its incipience and does not wait for the day to run its course. The *Changes* say: 'Harder than rock, he does not let the day run its course. Constancy means good fortune.'

As hard as rock in the face of it,
Why would he ever need to let the day run its course,
For he can perceive the way things will break.
The noble man grasps the infinitesimally small and
what is manifestly obvious.
He understands the soft as well as the hard.
So the myriad folk look to him."[6]

Third Yin

Contentment, its eyes haughty with pride, means regret, but one too slow will also have regret. {Here one is located at the very top of the lower trigram, that is, at the boundary between the two trigrams. Where this one treads is not its rightful position [because it is a yin line in a yang position], yet it supports the actions[7] of the master of the *Yu* [Contentment] hexagram [Fourth Yang]. When one [Fourth Yang] enjoys Contentment with eyes so haughty with pride as this, regret will surely come of it [for Third Yin], but if he [Third Yin] is too slow to follow, he will suffer Contentment's [i.e., the master of Contentment's, or Fourth Yang's] ire. Third Yin's position is not one he can secure, yet he uses it to pursue Contentment, so it is perfectly appropriate that such a one here encounters regret whether he advances or retreats.[8]}

COMMENTARY ON THE IMAGES

"Contentment, its eyes haughty with pride, means regret": this is because [Third Yin's] position does not suit it.

Fourth Yang

As they pursue Contentment, this one obtains it in great measure, and if no one harbors suspicions, the formation [*he*] of a friendly association happens quickly [*zan*]. {Being located here at a time of *Yu* [Contentment], Fourth Yang resides where the action begins.[9] As it alone is a yang line, it is followed by all the yin lines, and because none fail to follow after it, this is how Fourth Yang obtains its Contentment. This is why the text says: "As they pursue Contentment, this one obtains it in great measure." If you do not have trust in someone, that someone also will harbor suspicions toward you. Thus when no one harbors suspicions, the formation of a friendly association happens quickly. *He* [why not?, i.e., surely] here should be read as *he* [form/come together], and *zan* [hair clasp] means *ji* [quickly].[10]}

COMMENTARY ON THE IMAGES

"As they pursue Contentment, this one obtains it in great measure": that is, his ambitions are realized in great measure.

Fifth Yin

Maintain constancy in the face of such harassment, and persevere in warding off death. {Fourth Yang acts with hardness and strength and is the master of the *Yu* hexagram. As Fourth Yang exercises control as absolute ruler, it is not something on which Fifth Yin can ride.[11] Thus it does not dare to contend with Fourth Yang for power. However, since it also abides in the Mean and occupies the noble position, it cannot possibly run away. This is why it is constantly forced to go so far as to do nothing but "maintain constancy in the face of such harassment" and just "persevere in warding off death."}

COMMENTARY ON THE IMAGES

Fifth Yin has to "maintain constancy in the face of such harassment" because it rides on top of a hard [yang] line. It has to "persevere in warding off death" because the Mean may never be abandoned.

Top Yin

Here the benighted pursuit of Contentment is complete, but if one changes course, there will be no blame. {Top Yin is located at the very end of *Yu* as action [i.e., the top of the *Zhen* (Quake) trigram]. To bring *Yu* to its end point means to exhaust the possibilities of happiness. Thus we have reached the point where "the benighted pursuit of Contentment is complete." If one were to push Contentment beyond its limits and just try to keep on going, "how could it ever last long"? Thus one must "change course," for only then "there will be no blame."}

COMMENTARY ON THE IMAGES

Here the "benighted pursuit of Contentment" is at its height, so how could it ever last long?

NOTES

1. Kong Yingda comments: " 'Thunder' is the sound of yang *qi* [material force], and 'shake' describes something when it quakes. Upon thunder bursting forth, the Earth quakes, and this is how the myriad things are begotten by the yang material force, each one without exception made content. This is why the text says: 'Thunder bursts forth, and the Earth shakes: this constitutes the image of *Yu* [Contentment].' " See *Zhouyi zhengyi*, 2: 35b. It was thought that spring thunder is responsible for rousing things (both plants and animals) to life, as is said in section five of Explaining the Trigrams: "The myriad things come forth in *Zhen* [Thunder, Quake]." *Yu* [Contentment], of course, consists of *Zhen* on top of *Kun* (Earth, Pure Yin). However, Cheng Yi explains this passage somewhat differently: "The yang force is, to begin with, imprisoned inside the Earth, but when it goes into action, it quits the Earth with shaking and quaking. It begins by being pent up, but when it shakes itself free, it expands and spreads freely and so finds

harmony and contentment. This is how *Yu* [Contentment] occurs." See *Zhouyi zhezhong*, 11: 38a.

2. "Supreme Deity" translates *shangdi. Shangdi*, or simply *di*, was the principal Shang deity, appropriated by the Zhou and identified with their *Tian* (Heaven). See Creel, *The Origins of Statecraft*, p. 44 n. 11 and pp. 493–506.

3. See section two and note 17 of the Commentary on the Appended Phrases, Part Two.

4. This and all subsequent text set off in this manner is commentary by Wang Bi.

5. Kong Yingda comments: "Aware of how fast incipiency works, he does not wait for a single day to reach its end before he banishes what is evil and cultivates what is good, and so constantly preserves his rectitude." See *Zhouyi zhengyi*, 2: 36a.

6. See section five of the Commentary on the Appended Phrases, Part Two.

7. "Supports the actions" translates *cheng dong. Cheng* also means "carry." (Third Yin, after all, "carries" [*cheng*] Fourth Yang.) As the master of the *Yu* hexagram, Fourth Yang controls the actions involved: it gets things done, realizes its ambitions, as the Commentary on the Judgments says, by getting the other lines (all yin) to respond. It is, in effect, the motive force underlying Contentment as such. Contiguous Third Yin is immediately below, so it has to guard against playing the sycophant to Fourth Yang, something that would be cause for regret.

8. "Eyes haughty with pride" translates *xu* in Third Yin and *suixu* in Wang Bi's commentary. This interpretation follows the comments of Lou Yulie. Lou cites the *Zhuangzi*—"He is so haughty and full of pride [*suisui xuxu*] that who could ever live with him!" (*Zhuangzi*, 76/28/27)—and Guo Xiang's (d. 312) commentary—"*Suisui xuxu* describes someone who is defiant and recalcitrant, a person whom one should be leery of and keep away from." Lou thinks that Wang read this statement in the *Zhuangzi* as Guo interpreted it later and glosses Wang's use of *suixu* accordingly:

> As the sole yang line, Fourth Yang is full of its own self-importance among all the yin lines. Eyes haughty with pride, its manner is impossible to live with, but here is Third Yin supporting [carrying] and following it, so it is sure to get insulted by it, and this will cause regret. However, since Third Yin is contiguous and carries it from below, if it is too slow in following Fourth Yang, it will also become the victim of its ire.

See *Wang Bi ji jiaoshi*, 1: 302 n. 9. However, *suixu* can also mean "wide-eyed with hope," and this seems to be how Kong Yingda interprets it: "*Xu* means *suixu*, and *suixu* describes delight [*xiyue*]." See *Zhouyi zhengyi*, 2: 36b. "Delight" in this case must refer to Third Yin—to someone over-anxious to gain Contentment through the agency of his superior (Fourth Yang). Cheng Yi and Zhu Xi agree with Kong Yingda and gloss *xu* as *shangshi*: "look upward" [toward Fourth Yang with hope]. See *Zhouyi zhezhong*, 3: 8a. Their reading of Third Yin would have to differ accordingly: "To be overanxious for Contentment will result in regret, but to be too slow will also mean regret."

9. As the master of *Yu*, Fourth Yang initiates its action, but it is also the master or ruler of the upper trigram *Zhen* (Quake), which as a whole signifies action.

10. Another rarely seen character, also pronounced *zan*, has this *zan* as the phonetic and the *shou* (hand) significant on the left side; it means "quickly." However, both Cheng Yi and Zhu Xi gloss *zan* (hair clasp) as *ju* (gather, come together), and, since they do not mention *he* (why not?, i.e., surely), this implies that they read *he* as it stands. Thus their reading of this part of Fourth Yang would be something like: "If no one harbors suspicions, why should not a friendly association come together?" See *Zhouyi zhezhong*, 3: 8b.

11. Lou Yulie glosses this as: "It [Fourth Yang] is not something that it itself [Fifth Yin] can drive [i.e., control, use for its own purposes]." See *Wang Bi ji jiaoshi*, 1: 302 n. 13.

HEXAGRAM 17

䷐

隨

Sui [Following]
(*Zhen* Below *Dui* Above)

Judgment

Sui is a time for the fundamental achievement of prevalence and the fitting practice of constancy and, as such, involves no blame.

COMMENTARY ON THE JUDGMENTS

The hard comes and takes a place below the soft; by its action delight occurs. This is *Sui* [Following]. By achieving great prevalence and through the practice of constancy, one stays free of blame: so it is when a time of Following prevails in the world. The meaning underlying a time of Following is indeed great! {*Zhen* [Quake] is hard [a yang trigram] and *Dui* [Joy] is soft [a yin trigram]. Here the hard takes a position below the soft, acts there, and so moves on to delight, thus achieving a Following. To deal with a time of Following and yet fail to get things to go smoothly on a grand scale means that one is acting contrary to the moment, and if one gets others to follow and yet does not deal with them in terms of the fitting practice of rectitude, this will result in a dao that leads to disaster. Thus it is by getting things to go smoothly on a grand scale and it is through the "fitting practice of constancy" that one here achieves a state that "involves no blame." To deal with a time of Following in such a way that one makes things go smoothly on a grand scale and also allows for the fitting practice of constancy means that one is successful at seizing the moment, and if one is successful at seizing the moment, the whole world will follow him. The way *Sui* [Following] operates depends only on the moment, so when the moment takes a different turning, and one does not follow it, this results in the Dao of *Pi* [Obstruction, Hexagram 12]. This is why "the meaning underlying a time of Following is indeed great!"[1]}

COMMENTARY ON THE IMAGES

Within the Lake, there is Thunder: this constitutes the image of *Sui* [Following].[2] In the same way, the noble man when faced with evening goes in to rest and leisure. {"Within the Lake, there is Thunder": this is the image of how the activation of delight takes place. When all follow one with delight, one can then avoid purposeful action [literally, "practice *wuwei*," *wuwei* meaning "avoid/no purposeful action"] toward them and not let them belabor one's bright mirror [i.e., mind]. Thus "the noble man when faced with evening goes in to rest and leisure."}

COMMENTARY TO THE APPENDED PHRASES

[The Lord Yellow Emperor, Lord Yao, and Lord Shun] domesticated the ox and harnessed the horse to conveyances. This allowed heavy loads to be pulled and faraway places to be reached and so benefited the entire world. They probably got the idea for this from the hexagram *Sui* [Following].[3]

PROVIDING THE SEQUENCE OF THE HEXAGRAMS

When there is contentment, there will be a following. This is why *Yu* [Contentment, Hexagram 16] is followed by *Sui* [Following].

THE HEXAGRAMS IN IRREGULAR ORDER

Sui [Following] involves no precedents.[4]

First Yang

This one's self-control has the capacity to change course, so his practice of constancy means good fortune, and, when he leaves his own gate, he relates to others in such a way that he achieves merit. {Here located at the very beginning of *Sui* [Following], First Yang has no line above with which it can resonate,[5] which means that it does not find itself with any partisan ties; thus, when it acts, it is able to follow the moment, and its intentions are not subject to the control of any particular master. Following should not be done to suit one's personal wishes, but it is one's personal wishes that should follow what is right and proper. Thus one's self-control[6] should have the capacity to change direction [i.e., be able to handle different circumstances], but the course it follows must never violate what is right. When this one leaves his own gate, he stays free of any contrary behavior, so what violation could ever occur?}

COMMENTARY ON THE IMAGES

"This one's self-control has the capacity to change course," and in so pursuing what is right, he has good fortune. "When he leaves his own gate, he relates to others in such a way that he achieves merit," for he commits no violation.

Second Yin

This one ties itself to the little child and abandons the mature man. {When a yin line as such finds itself in a world governed by *Sui*, it is unable to stand independently but must find ties elsewhere. This one located here at a time of *Sui* [Following] in substance is soft and weak but yet has to ride on top of the hard and the active [First

Yang], so how could it ever maintain its proper goal? It in fact acts contrary to it by going after the one to which it is near [First Yang]. If Second Yin follows this one, it has to abandon that one [Fifth Yang], and it cannot "give itself over to both." Fifth Yang is located above it, and First Yang is located below it, this is why the text says: "This one ties itself to the little child and abandons the mature man."}

COMMENTARY ON THE IMAGES

"This one ties itself to the little child" and cannot give itself over to both [i.e., to both the little child represented by First Yang and the mature man represented by Fifth Yang].

Third Yin

This one ties itself to a mature man and abandons the little child. By following in this way, one should obtain what one seeks, so it is fitting to abide in constancy. {When a yin line as such finds itself in a world governed by *Sui*, it is unable to stand independently but must find ties elsewhere. Although Third Yin in substance belongs to the lower trigram, since Second Yin has already been taken by First Yang, to what line shall Third Yin attach itself? This is the reason why it abandons First Yang and ties itself to Fourth Yang, and as such its will becomes fixed on "the mature man." Fourth Yang lacks proper resonance in either case,[7] but since it also wishes that Third Yin would follow it, Third Yin obtains what it seeks, and this is why the text says: "By following in this way, one should obtain what one seeks." Although the way Third Yin responds here is not correct for it, since it has attached itself to a man,[8] how could it ever go wrong? This is why the text says: "It is fitting to abide in constancy." First Yang is located below it, and Fourth Yang is located above it, this is why the text says: "This one ties itself to a mature man and abandons the little child."}

COMMENTARY ON THE IMAGES

"This one ties itself to a mature man," and its will is such that it [Third Yin] abandons the one below. {"The one below" refers to First Yang.}

Fourth Yang

This one has success at garnering a Following, but constancy will still result in misfortune. The sincerity he has is there in the path he follows, and, as it is brought to light in this way, what blame will he have? {Fourth Yang is located at the beginning of delight [i.e., *Dui* (Joy), the upper trigram]. Of the two yin lines below that Fourth Yang might take, Third Yin seeks a tie with it, and, since Fourth Yang does not oppose it, the text says: "This one has success at garnering a Following." Fourth Yang abides in the territory of the subject minister, so where it treads is not its rightful position [it is a yang line in a yin position]. To use this to seize control over the people is a violation as far as the Dao of the subject minister is concerned, and such a one is in violation of what is right. This is why the text says: "Constancy will still result in misfortune."[9] Its substance hard and strong, Fourth Yang abides here in delight [i.e., *Dui* (Joy)], and as such it wins the hearts and minds of the people. As one who can handle its duties, Fourth Yang achieves success. Although it is in violation of a constant moral norm, its ambition is to bring succor to others. One's heart and mind here harbors impartiality and sincerity, and such a one manifests his trustworthiness in the path he follows. As he brings his success to light in this way, how could he ever incur any blame?}

COMMENTARY ON THE IMAGES

"This one has success at garnering a Following," but the concept here involves misfortune. "The sincerity he has is there in the path he follows," and this brings his success to light.

Fifth Yang

This one's sincerity is manifest in his excellence, so he shall have good fortune. {Fifth Yang treads on rectitude and abides in the Mean, and as such when it occupies this place in a world of Following, it is the perfect fulfillment of what is appropriate for a time of Following and so obtains the trust of others. Thus its excellence results in good fortune.}

COMMENTARY ON THE IMAGES

"This one's sincerity is manifest in his excellence, so he shall have good fortune": his position is correct and central.

Top Yin

Seize and bind him, then so tied up make him follow. Thus the king should use this opportunity to extend his prevalence to the western mountains. {As a hexagram *Sui* [Following] is such that the yin lines obey the yang lines, but this one occupying the position at the very top will not be a follower. It is because the Dao of *Sui* at this point has already run its complete course that Top Yin alone does not follow. This is why it has to be seized and bound before it will follow. "Within the borders of all the land/None but is the subject of the king."[10] Thus because this one will not follow, he shall be chastised by the king, and this is why he will have him tied up. "The king should use this opportunity to extend his prevalence to the western mountains": *Dui* [Joy, the upper trigram] represents the west direction,[11] and "mountains" signify a road that is dangerous and full of obstacles. It is because Top Yin, located in the western mountains, will not follow that "the king should use this opportunity to extend his prevalence to the western mountains."[12]}

COMMENTARY ON THE IMAGES

"Seize and bind him," for with Top Yang it [the Dao of *Sui* (Following)] is exhausted.

NOTES

1. This and all subsequent text set off in this manner is commentary by Wang Bi.

2. Cf. section four of Explaining the Trigrams: "It is by Thunder [*Zhen* (Quake)] that things are caused to move, . . . by Joy [*Dui*] that they are made happy." See also section six of the same text: "Of things that make the myriad things move, none is swifter than Thunder. . . . Of things that make the myriad things rejoice, none is more joy giving than the Lake." Here the image consists, as Zhu Xi says, of "Thunder that lies hidden in the Lake and rests when the moment is right for it [literally, *suishi*, "following the moment"]." See *Zhouyi zhezhong*, 11: 40a.

3. See section two of Commentary on the Appended Phrases, Part Two, as well as note 16 there.

4. Han Kangbo comments: "One should follow what is appropriate for the moment and not be tied to precedents. With such following, one will be responsible for affairs."

5. First Yang should resonate with the fourth line, but this line is also a yang line, so there is no resonance.

6. In First Yang and here in Wang's commentary "self-control" translates *guan*, glossed by Kong Yingda as *renxin suo zhu*: "that which controls the human heart and mind." See *Zhouyi zhengyi*, 3: 2a.

7. "Either case" refers to Fourth Yang's pairing up with either First Yang or Third Yin. Proper resonance in hexagrams exists between fourth lines and first lines and between top lines and third lines—but only if the two lines in each respective pair are of opposite signs. Here Fourth Yang and First Yang are both yang, so there is no resonance, and Top Yin and Third Yin are both yin, so there is no resonance there either, so the fact that Fourth Yang and Third Yin pair up is a matter of expedience and not because they form a true resonate pair.

8. "A man" (Fourth Yang) is not "the man" (Fifth Yang), which is both yang and centrally located in "the noble position" of this hexagram.

9. Zhu Xi comments: "As its [Fourth Yang's] power is a threat to Fifth Yang, even though its behavior might be correct, it will still have misfortune." See *Zhouyi zhezhong*, 3: 14b.

10. *Shijing* (Book of odes), no. 205.

11. *Dui* is associated with the height of autumn, which in traditional Chinese cosmology is linked with the west. See section five of Explaining the Trigrams.

12. Kong Yingda comments: "If he wishes to bind up this Top Yin, the king must use military force to extend his rule to the dangerous territory of the western mountains, for only then will he succeed in seizing and binding him." See *Zhouyi zhengyi*, 3: 2b. However, Cheng Yi and Zhu Xi interpret Top Yin differently. Rather than seeing Top Yin represent the exhaustion of the Dao of *Sui* (Following), they regard it as the maximum point in its development, and Top Yin, as such, is the strongest, most devoted follower of all. Thus "seize and bind" is supposed to refer to the devotion with which Top Yin follows—as if it were seized and bound. Cheng and Zhu seem to read this part of Top Yin as: "He lets it [the Dao of *Sui* (Following)] seize and bind him and then follows as if tied up."

"The king should use this opportunity to extend his prevalence to the western mountains" translates *wang yong heng yu xishan*, which is how Wang Bi and Kong Yingda seem to interpret it, but this fits neither Cheng's nor Zhu's gloss. Cheng thinks that this refers to the story of King Tai, the grandfather of King Wen and great-grandfather of King Wu, who overthrew the Shang and founded the Zhou (traditionally dated 1122 B.C.):

> Long ago King Tai used this Dao to make his kingly enterprise prevail in the western mountains. King Tai, to avoid the harassment of

> the Di tribe, left Bin and went to [Mount] Qi. The people of Bin both young and old, supporting each other, followed him as if they were going to market. The heartfelt commitment to follow him was as firm as this, so he was able to make use of it to make his kingly enterprise prevail in the western mountains. "Western mountains" here refers to Mount Qi.

Cf. *Mengzi* (Mencius) 1B:15. Therefore Cheng's interpretation of *wang yong heng yu xishan* seems to be: "The king used it [the Dao of Following] to extend his prevalence to the western mountains." Zhu Xi's interpretation is again different: "*Heng* [make prevail/extend prevalence] here should be read as the *xiang* in *jixiang* [perform sacrifices]. In terms of the Zhou state, Mount Qi is in the west. Whenever one [the king] who divined concerning sacrifices to mountains and streams got this [Top Yang], if he made his intentions as sincere as this, he had good fortune." For Zhu, *wang yong heng (xiang) yu xishan* seems to mean: "The [Zhou] kings used it [the devotion and sincerity inherent in the Dao of Following] to sacrifice to the western mountains." See *Zhouyi zhezhong*, 3:15b–16a. Also cf. Hexagram 46, *Sheng* (Climbing), Fourth Yin, and note 7 there.

HEXAGRAM 18

䷑

蠱

Gu [Ills to Be Cured]
(*Sun* Below *Gen* Above)

Judgment

Gu is such that it provides the opportunity for fundamental prevalence, and so it is fitting to cross the great river, but let there be three days before a new law is issued and three days after a new law is issued.

COMMENTARY ON THE JUDGMENTS

Gu consists of a hard [yang] trigram above and a soft [yin] trigram below. {If the one above is hard, this will allow him to pass judgments, and if the one below is soft, this will allow him to carry out orders.[1]} Compliance [the trigram *Sun* below] as well as immovableness [the trigram *Gen* (Restraint) above] make up *Gu*. {Not only is the one compliant, but the other is immovable, so they do not contend. If when there are problems one can avoid the disastrous effect of contention, this will allow one to take action to solve them.} "*Gu* [Ills to Be Cured] is such that it provides the opportunity for fundamental prevalence," and if that happens the entire world will become well ordered. {When one takes action, and it results in great prevalence, what could happen except that the entire world should become well ordered?} "It is fitting to cross the great river": when one sets forth, there will be problems. "Let there be three days before a new law is issued and three days after a new law is issued": with its ending, one starts all over again: such is the way Heaven operates. {The hexagram *Gu* [Ills to Be Cured] signifies a time when there are problems that await someone capable of dealing with them. It is at such a time that this [the Dao of *Gu*] allows one to take action. When others are already following with delight, this means that they await someone to make laws in order to put their affairs in order. Here is the time to advance virtue and cultivate enterprise, so that when one sets forth he shall achieve prevalence. This is why the text says: "It provides the opportunity for fundamental prevalence, and so it is fitting to cross the great river." *Jia* [the first of the ten characters in the heavenly branches numbering system (*tiangan*)] here means "a newly initiated law." One cannot enforce a new law in the same way that one can enforce an old one. Thus, for the three days before [its initiation] and for the three days after, one works to make this law blend in, and only after that does one use it as the basis for punishment. It is in response to some difficult situation that a [new] law is issued, but "with its [the situation's] ending, one starts all over again"—just as Heaven operates employing the four seasons.}

COMMENTARY ON THE IMAGES

Below the Mountain, there is Wind: this constitutes the image of *Gu* [Ills to Be Cured].[2] In the same way, the noble man stirs the common folk and nourishes their virtue. {"The hexagram *Gu* [Ills to Be Cured] signifies a time when there are problems that await someone capable of dealing with them." Thus the noble man uses such opportunities to bring succor to the common folk and to cultivate their virtue.[3]}

PROVIDING THE SEQUENCE OF THE HEXAGRAMS

One who gets people to follow him by making them happy inevitably will have problems. This is why *Sui* [Following, Hexagram 17] is followed by *Gu* [Ills to Be Cured). *Gu* here means "problems."

THE HEXAGRAMS IN IRREGULAR ORDER

With *Gu* [Ills to Be Cured], a cleanup occurs.

First Yin

One straightens out Ills to Be Cured caused by the father. If there is such a son, a deceased father will be without blame. Although dangerous, in the end, there will be good fortune. {To be located here at the start of some problem signifies the time when one is first charged with the responsibility for it. This has to be someone who relies on a soft and compliant nature to straighten out his father's affairs, someone who can carry on in the tracks left by his predecessor and be equal to the responsibility involved. Thus the text says "if there is such a son." If one who takes responsibility for a situation right at the start is equal to that responsibility, his "deceased father will be without blame." To be in on the start of some problem means that one is here in danger, but if he is equal to dealing with that problem, "in the end, there will be good fortune."}

COMMENTARY ON THE IMAGES

"One straightens out Ills to Be Cured caused by the father": one intends to become one's deceased father's successor. {At the start of dealing with problems, the moment might be right for either diminution or increase, so it might not be possible to become a successor completely, and this is why the text only goes so far as to say that one intends to become a successor.}

Second Yang

One straightens out Ills to Be Cured caused by the mother, but constancy is not possible. {This line abides in the middle position of the inner trigram, and as such it is appropriate that it straighten out the affairs of the mother.[4] This is why the text says: "One straightens out Ills to Be Cured caused by the mother." The nature of woman is such that she is incapable of perfect rectitude, so it is appropriate to suppress one's own hardness and strength here, and one must not only straighten things out but also remain obedient [to the mother]; thus the text says: "But constancy is not possible."[5] In straightening things out here one avoids violating the Mean, which is what is meant by "manages to practice the Dao of the Mean."}

COMMENTARY ON THE IMAGES

"One straightens out Ills to Be Cured caused by the mother," and in so doing manages to practice the Dao of the Mean.

Third Yang

One who here straightens out Ills to Be Cured caused by the father has slight regret but incurs no great blame. {Third Yang straightens out problems with its hardness and strength, but because it has no responsive partner,[6] it "has slight regret." By treading here, it obtains its own proper position [as a yang line in a yang position], and it uses its rectitude to straighten out the father's affairs, so although it involves "slight regret," in the end, it "incurs no great blame."}

COMMENTARY ON THE IMAGES

"One who here straightens out Ills to Be Cured caused by the father" in the end "incurs no great blame."

Fourth Yin

Here one deals leniently with Ills to Be Cured caused by the father, but if he were to set out he would experience hard going.[7] {This is an appropriate position for a line whose substance is soft and yielding [it is a yin line in a yin position]. One who straightens things out not with hardness and strength but by using softness and accommodation is capable of dealing leniently with his predecessor's problems. Nevertheless, here one has no responsive partner,[8] so if he were to set out, that would surely result in discord. Thus the text says: "If he were to set out he would experience hard going."}

COMMENTARY ON THE IMAGES

"Here one deals leniently with Ills to Be Cured caused by the father," but if he were to set out he would never succeed.

Fifth Yin

One who here straightens out Ills to Be Cured caused by the father thereby gains a fine reputation. {Fifth Yin occupies the noble position with its softness and yielding, thereby staying within the Mean and maintaining a proper response [with Second Yang]. It is by using such means to carry on the affairs of one's predecessor that one thereby practices the Dao of gaining a fine reputation.}

COMMENTARY ON THE IMAGES

One who straightens out the father's affairs "thereby gains a fine reputation," because his succession is marked by virtue. {Fifth Yin abides in the Mean with its softness and yielding and does not put its trust in martial force.}

Top Yang

This one does not concern himself with the affairs of king or feudal lords but works to elevate his own higher pursuits. {Top Yang by being located at the very top of such matters [represented by *Gu* (Ills to Be Cured)] thus stays free of any entanglement with position, and so it "does not concern [it]self with the affairs of king or feudal lords but works to elevate its own higher pursuits."}

COMMENTARY ON THE IMAGES

"This one does not concern himself with the affairs of king or feudal lords," and his ambition as such can serve as a model for others.

NOTES

1. This and all subsequent text set off in this manner is commentary by Wang Bi.

2. The upper trigram *Gen* (Restraint) is associated with Mountain, and the lower trigram *Sun* (Compliance) is associated with Wind. See section three of Explaining the Trigrams.

3. Kong Yingda comments: "The wind is capable of working up and dispensing nourishing moisture. . . . So the noble man is capable of using his nourishing grace to stir up the common folk below and nurture them with his virtue." See *Zhouyi zhengyi*, 3: 5a.

4. Both Cheng Yi and Zhu Xi note that Second Yang is in resonance with Fifth Yin, which in this pairing is the "mother." See *Zhouyi zhezhong*, 3: 19b.

5. It is obvious from the context that Wang glosses *zhen* (constancy) as *zheng* (rectitude): that is, one cannot use untempered rectitude to deal with a woman, for whom perfect rectitude is impossible.

6. Third Yang needs a resonate yin line in the top position, but here in *Gu* that line is yang, so there is no resonance.

7. "Hard going" translates *lin*; see Hexagram 3, *Zhun* (Birth Throes), note 6.

8. Fourth Yin needs a resonate yang line in the first position, but here in *Gu* that line is yin, so there is no resonance.

HEXAGRAM 19

䷒

臨

Lin [Overseeing]

(*Dui* Below *Kun* Above)

Judgment

Lin [Overseeing][1] is such that in its prevalence it is fundamental, and in its constancy it is fitting, but by the eighth month there will be misfortune.[2]

COMMENTARY ON THE JUDGMENTS

With *Lin* [Overseeing], the hard gradually grows strong and joyfully practices obedience. The hard responds in such a way that it stays within the Mean. Great prevalence is achieved through rectitude, and this is the Dao of Heaven. {The yang cycle progressively waxes, and the Dao of yin daily wanes: the Dao of the noble man increases day by day, and the dao of the petty man increasingly comes to grief day by day.[3] This is what "great prevalence is achieved through rectitude" means.[4]} "But by the eighth month, there will be misfortune," because it [the yang principle, the Dao of the noble man] wanes and does not always last. {By the eighth month, yang has waned, and yin has waxed, so "the dao of the petty man is increasing, and the Dao of the noble man is deteriorating."[5] This is why the text says: "There will be misfortune."}

COMMENTARY ON THE IMAGES

Above the Lake, there is Earth: this constitutes the image of *Lin* [Overseeing].[6] In the same way, the noble man is both inexhaustible in his powers to edify others and feel concern for them and limitless in his practice of magnanimity and protection toward the common folk. {The very best aspect associated with the Dao of Overseeing is happy obedience. Here one does not rely on control by military might but instead obtains the trust of others. Thus no one disobeys. It is in this way that "the noble man is both inexhaustible in his powers to edify others and feel concern for them and limitless in his practice of magnanimity and protection toward the common folk."}

PROVIDING THE SEQUENCE OF THE HEXAGRAMS

Only when one has had problems can he grow great. This is why *Gu* [Ills to Be Cured, Hexagram 18] is followed by *Lin* [Overseeing]. *Lin* here means "to become great."

THE HEXAGRAMS IN IRREGULAR ORDER

The concepts underlying *Lin* [Overseeing] and *Guan* [Viewing, Hexagram 20] in some cases mean "provide" and in others "seek."[7]

First Yang

This one prompts Overseeing, and constancy here means good fortune. {*Xian*, "all," here should be read *gan*, "prompt" or "provoke,"[8] as in *ganying*, "provoke a response." First Yang has a resonate relationship with Fourth Yin and so provokes Fourth Yin to provide Overseeing. Fourth Yin treads on the territory of its rightful position [as a yin line in a yin position], and as First Yang is in resonance with it, its own "goal is pursued with rectitude." It is because the hard is moved to obey [Fourth Yin] that the pursuit of its ambitions remains so correct as this. When the Overseeing of things takes place in this way, one garners good fortune with such rectitude.}

COMMENTARY ON THE IMAGES

"This one prompts Overseeing, and constancy here means good fortune," for one's goal is pursued with rectitude.

Second Yang

This one prompts Overseeing, which means good fortune such that nothing fails to be fitting. {Second Yang has a resonate relationship with Fifth Yin and so provokes Fifth Yin to provide Overseeing. When the hard and strong is in the ascendancy, the soft and weak is placed in danger. But here, as Fifth Yin is weak, this means that Second Yang cannot share its goals, for if it were to practice obedience toward Fifth Yin, its hard and strong virtues would not last long. And from what source then could it possibly derive "good fortune such that nothing fails to be fitting"? However, if it were to oppose Fifth Yin completely, this would violate the resonance between them. So the fact that Second Yang has obtained the "good fortune such that nothing fails to be fitting" by getting Fifth Yin "to respond and provide Overseeing" must just mean that Second Yang "still refrains from obeying Fifth Yin's orders."}

COMMENTARY ON THE IMAGES

Here Second Yang has gotten Fifth Yin to respond and provide Overseeing, which results in "good fortune such that nothing fails to be fitting." This means that Second Yang still refrains from obeying Fifth Yin's orders.

Third Yin

This one does Overseeing with sweetness, about which there is nothing at all fitting, but once one becomes anxious about it, there will be no blame. {Sweet here refers to seductive, wicked flattery; it is a term for something wrong. Here where Third Yin treads is not the right position for it [it is a yin line in a yang position], and it abides in a world where the hard and strong grow strong, yet it tries to conduct the Overseeing of others with wicked flattery, so it is appropriate that about such behavior "there is nothing at all fitting." But if one here can become thoroughly anxious about this danger and reform the Dao that he practices, the hard and the strong will not harm such righteousness, thus "blame will not last long."}

COMMENTARY ON THE IMAGES

"This one does Overseeing with sweetness," for the position is not right for it. "Once one becomes anxious about it," blame will not last long.

Fourth Yin

Here perfect Overseeing is done, so there is no blame. {Fourth Yin occupies this position in such a way that it responds to First

Yang with obedience. It does not dread the growth of its [First Yang's] hardness and strength and so responds to it. By treading here, it obtains its rightful position, and this is how it realizes the full measure of perfection. When the hard and strong is in the ascendancy, the soft and weak is placed in danger, but here the soft and weak does not violate what is right, and it is this that allows for there to be "no blame."}

COMMENTARY ON THE IMAGES

"Here perfect Overseeing is done, so there is no blame," for the position is right for it.

Fifth Yin

This one does Overseeing with wisdom, which is the wherewithal for a great sovereign and means good fortune. {Fifth Yin is situated in the noble position, treading there in such a way that it manages to practice the Mean. It knows how to receive the hard and strong [Second Yang] with decorum and thereby strengthen its practice of rectitude. Fifth Yin does not dread the growth of Second Yang's strength and so is able to employ Second Yang in its service. It is by employing others in order to extend one's abilities, while doing no wrong in the process, that the perspicacious can extend his powers of sight and hearing to the utmost and the one empowered with wisdom can fulfill his ability to plan. This is how such a one accomplishes things without purposeful effort and reaches goals without having to take the steps himself.[9] The wherewithal of a great sovereign need be like this and nothing more, and this is why the text says: "This one does Overseeing with wisdom, which is the wherewithal of a great sovereign and means good fortune."}

COMMENTARY ON THE IMAGES

"The wherewithal of a great sovereign" consists of, in other words, the practice of the Mean.

Top Yin

This one does Overseeing with simple honesty, which results in good fortune and no blame. {Top Yin is situated at the very top of the *Kun* [Pure Yin] trigram and does Overseeing with simple honesty. Its will is focused on helping the worthy, and it makes simple honesty its virtue. Although it finds itself at a time when the hard and the strong grows stronger, the hard and the strong will not harm such honesty, and this is why the text says "no blame."}

COMMENTARY ON THE IMAGES

That good fortune is the result here of simple honesty in Overseeing is because Top Yin's will is focused on the inner trigram.[10]

NOTES

1. The basic meaning of *lin* is "look down on," from which is derived "oversee" (i.e., care for, manage, govern). "Approach" is another derived meaning, probably via *lin* (the same graph), the name of an ancient siege machine, "the approacher," apparently some kind of movable scaffold that allowed besiegers to fire projectiles down on and over walled fortifications. Wang Bi, Kong Yingda (see *Zhouyi zhengyi*, 3: 6a–6b), and Cheng Yi all take *lin* in the sense of "oversee," but Zhu Xi seems to read it as "make advances on," perhaps with the siege machine in mind: "*Lin* means 'advance and put pressure on something.' The two yang lines gradually grow strong and exert a coercive force on the yin lines." See *Zhouyi zhezhong*, 3: 22b–23a. Also see Wang's remarks on this hexagram in section seven of his General Remarks.

2. Kong Yingda comments: "*Lin* refers to the second lunar month [*jianchou*]. Seven months after the second lunar month, at the time of the *jianshen* month [the ninth lunar month], just when the Three Yin [*Kun*, Pure Yin] start to flourish, the Three Yang [*Qian*, Pure Yang] start to retreat. So with this the dao of the petty man waxes, and the Dao of the noble man wanes." See *Zhouyi zhengyi*, 3: 6b. As such, the *jianshen* month is the eighth month in sequence after the *jianchou* month. Other commentators usually start from other months to get to the "eighth month." Zhu Xi, for instance, follows what seems to be the majority view that identifies *Lin* with the twelfth lunar month: eight months after that brings us to *jianwei*, the eighth lunar month in the regular sequence, which is identified with Hexagram 20, *Guan* (Viewing), the reverse or opposite of *Lin*. See Zhu Xi's remarks in *Zhouyi zhezhong*, 3: 22b–23a. In either case, *Lin* (Overseeing), indicates the growth of the yang principle up to a certain point in a cycle (as in the year) and the weakening of it thereafter: prevalence and good fortune for the noble man before it, and misfortune for him afterward.

3. This paraphrases Hexagram 11, *Tai* (Peace), Commentary on the Judgments.

4. This and all subsequent text set off in this manner is commentary by Wang Bi.

5. Hexagram 12, *Pi* (Obstruction), Commentary on the Judgments.

6. The lower trigram *Dui* (Joy) is associated with Lake, and the upper trigram *Kun* (Pure Yin) is associated with Earth.

7. Han Kangbo comments: "If one stirs oneself to oversee others, this is referred to as 'provide,' but if others come to view oneself, this is referred to as 'seek.' "

8. "Prompts Overseeing" translates *xian (gan) lin*. *Xian* (all, in all cases) and *gan* (move; provoke) as graphs differ only in that *gan* has a heart (*xin*) significant added below. Kong Yingda also reads *xian* as *gan* (see *Zhouyi zhengyi*, 3: 7a), as does Cheng Yi, but Zhu Xi rejects this interpretation, leaving *xian* intact, and so explains First Yang differently: "This hexagram only has two yang lines, which make advances on all [*xian*] the four yin lines. This is why both yang lines have this image of *xian lin* [making advances on all]." See *Zhouyi zhezhong*, 3: 23b–24a. Of course, this means that Zhu's interpretation of subsequent lines also differs.

9. Wang here paraphrases the *Laozi*, section 47, p. 126: "Therefore the sage comes to know without having to travel, understands without having to see, and accomplishes things without taking purposeful action."

10. That is, its will is focused on First Yang and Second Yang—the "worthy," as Wang Bi puts it. Kong Yingda also interprets this passage in this way; see *Zhouyi zhengyi*, 3: 8b.

HEXAGRAM 20

䷓

觀

Guan [Viewing]
(*Kun* Below *Sun* Above)

Judgment

Viewing, as when the ablution has been made but not the offering, fills one with trust and makes for a solemn attitude.[1] {As far as the Dao of the true sovereign is concerned, there is nothing in it more worth Viewing than the ancestral temple sacrifice, and as far as the ancestral temple sacrifice is concerned, there is nothing more worth Viewing than the ablution. On reaching the offering, it is so simple and brief that it is no longer worth Viewing; this is why it is the ablution that involves the Viewing and not the offering. Confucius said: "The rest of the great sacrifice, once the ablution has occurred, is not something that I wish to view."[2] Here the subject of Viewing is rendered in all its dignity and grandeur, so those below who do the Viewing are morally transformed. This is why when the Viewing reaches the ablution, it "fills one with trust and makes for a solemn attitude."[3]}

COMMENTARY ON THE JUDGMENTS

The great subject of Viewing resides above. {Below is the place for the humble, and above the place for the noble.} Here Obedience [*Kun*] combines with Compliance [*Sun*], and, by holding to the Mean and imbued with rectitude, a model for Viewing is offered to the entire world.[4] "Viewing, as when the ablution has been made but not the offering, fills one with trust and makes for a solemn attitude," for those below are morally transformed by the Viewing. Viewing the numinous Dao of Heaven, one finds that the four seasons never deviate, and so the sage establishes his teachings on the basis of this numinous Dao, and all under Heaven submit to him! {To sum it up, the way the Dao of *Guan* [Viewing] works is to eschew the threat of criminal punishments to make people behave and instead to use Viewing as the means to arouse them to moral transformation. Anything numinous is without the form of concrete existence,[5] so we do not see Heaven making the four seasons behave, and yet the four seasons never deviate. In the same way, we do not see the sage make the common folk behave, and yet the common folk submit of their own accord to him.[6]}

COMMENTARY ON THE IMAGES

The Wind moves above the Earth: this constitutes the image of *Guan* [Viewing].[7] In the same way, the former kings made tours of inspection everywhere and established their teachings in conformity with their Viewing of the people.[8]

PROVIDING THE SEQUENCE OF THE HEXAGRAMS

Only after a thing becomes great can it be viewed. This is why *Lin* [Overseeing, Hexagram 19] is followed by *Guan* [Viewing].

THE HEXAGRAMS IN IRREGULAR ORDER

The concepts underlying *Lin* [Overseeing, Hexagram 19] and *Guan* [Viewing] in some cases mean "provide" and in others "seek."[9]

First Yin

This is the Viewing of the youth. If it be a petty man, he would suffer no blame, but if it be a noble man, it would be base. {To be located here at a time of *Guan* [Viewing] is to be the most distant from the ruler's court [Fifth Yang]. As First Yin is imbued with the weakness of the yin principle, it is unable to move forward by itself, so nothing can be observed by it. This is why the text says: "This is the Viewing of the youth." As its tendency is to do nothing other than obey, we have here "the dao of the petty man." Thus the text says: "If it be a petty man, he shall suffer no blame." But if a noble man were to find himself at a time of *Guan* [Viewing] and were limited as one is here by the "Viewing of the youth," would that not be despicable?}

COMMENTARY ON THE IMAGES

First Yin represents the "Viewing of the youth" and indicates the dao of the petty man.

Second Yin

This is Viewing as through the crack of a door, so it is fitting that a woman practice constancy here. {To be located here in the lower trigram, means that the range of one's Viewing is very meager, and as Second Yin is imbued with softness and weakness, it can do nothing more than be compliant and obedient. However, there still is resonance in it [with Fifth Yang], so it is not completely beset with ignorance. It is because what it sees is very narrow in scope that the text says: "This is Viewing as through the crack of a door." As Second Yin abides inside [i.e., in the lower trigram] and has obtained the right position for it and as it is compliant and obedient with only a meager view of things, the text says "it is fitting for a woman to practice constancy here," for this represents the Dao of the wife. This one is located at a time for Viewing the great. Although it abides in the Mean and has obtained a right position for itself [a central and yin position for a yin line], it cannot have a broad view of the great subject for Viewing but can only see as through the crack of a door, something that is truly contemptible.}

COMMENTARY ON THE IMAGES

"This is Viewing as through the crack of a door": a woman may practice constancy here, but this is still a contemptible thing to do.

Third Yin

Here one's Viewing is of his own activity: should it involve advance or retreat? {Third Yin abides at the very top of the lower trigram and is located at the juncture of the two trigrams. Nearby it is not contiguous with the noble one [the ruler, Fifth Yang], but it is not so far away that it is limited to the Viewing of the youth. It is at a place to do Viewing of which way the wind blows. To abide here at this moment allows one to do "Viewing of his own activity: should it involve advance or retreat?"}

COMMENTARY ON THE IMAGES

"Here one's Viewing is of his own activity: should it involve advance or retreat?": This is so one does not violate his Dao. {Third Yin is located at a time when one could either advance or retreat, so by Viewing the incipient trends inherent in such advance or retreat, one avoids violating his Dao.}

Fourth Yin

Here one's Viewing extends to the glory of the state, so it is fitting therefore that this one be guest to the king. {To abide here at a time of *Guan* [Viewing] means, since it is the very closest to the noble one [Fifth Yang], that it represents someone whose "Viewing extends to the glory of the state." One who abides in such close proximity and has so obtained the right position shall be very learned in state ceremonies, and this is why the text says: "It is fitting that this one be guest to the king."}

COMMENTARY ON THE IMAGES

"Here one's Viewing extends to the glory of the state," so he is honored as a guest.

Fifth Yang

Here one's Viewing is of his own activity: if it be a noble man, he shall be without blame. {Fifth Yang abides in the noble position and is the ruler of the *Guan* [Viewing] hexagram. Such a one widely propagates his great powers of moral transformation, casts his glorious light to the four ends of the earth, and so realizes the ultimate potential of Viewing. The sovereign morally transforms those below just the way the wind makes the grass bend when it blows. Thus he does Viewing of the customs of the people in order to find out how well he is practicing his own Dao. If the common folk commit crimes, the fault for them shall reside with this one person himself,[10] but if he touches them with the wind [i.e., moral influence] of the noble man, he shall find himself without blame. The sovereign is the master of moral transformation. If he would do Viewing of what he himself is, he should do Viewing of the people.}

COMMENTARY ON THE IMAGES

"Here one's Viewing is of his own activity," so one does Viewing of the people.

Top Yang

They view this one's activities: if it be a noble man, he shall be without blame. {"Here one's Viewing is of his own activity" refers to one's Viewing of how he practices his own Dao. "They view this one's activities" means that one is Viewed by the people. This one does not reside in the ruler's position but finds himself at the very top of the hexagram. There he loftily exalts his ambition for all in the world to view. As this one is located where he is viewed by all in the world, how could he fail to take care? In this way, he reveals his virtue as a noble man, and that is how he manages to be without blame. The term *activities* [*sheng*] is similar to "behavior" [*dongchu*].}

COMMENTARY ON THE IMAGES

"They view this one's activities," so he does not let his ambitions slacken. {Top Yang is located off by itself in this extraneous place, exposed there for all to view, so such a one cannot go easy with himself. He softens his own light and identifies with them completely[11] and thus "does not let his ambitions slacken."}

NOTES

1. See Wang's remarks on this hexagram in section seven of his General Remarks.

2. See *Lunyu* (Analects) 3:10.

3. This and all subsequent text set off in this manner is commentary by Wang Bi.

4. This is a reference to Fifth Yang, the noble ruler of the hexagram, which is central ("holding to the Mean") and correct ("imbued with rectitude").

5. Cf. the end of section four and beginning of section five of the Commentary on the Appended Phrases, Part One.

6. Wang Bi seems to have both Confucius and Laozi in mind here. See *Lunyu* (Analects) 17:19: "Confucius said: 'I would prefer to do without words.' Zigong replied: 'If you, Master, do not speak, what shall we dis-

ciples have to record?' Confucius then said: 'What does Heaven ever say? Yet the four seasons follow their courses because of it, and all the different things are produced by it. What does Heaven ever say?' " See also *Laozi*, section 57, p. 150: "Thus the sage says: 'I take no purposeful action, and the people by themselves are transformed. I love quietude, and the people by themselves behave with rectitude. I do not involve myself in what they do, and the people by themselves prosper. I am without desire, and the people by themselves cherish simplicity.' "

7. The lower trigram *Kun* (Pure Yin) indicates the Earth, and the upper trigram *Sun* (Compliance) is associated with Wind.

8. Wang Bi is silent here, and the translation follows the comments of Kong Yingda (*Zhouyi zhengyi*, 3: 9a–9b) and Cheng Yi (*Zhouyi zhezhong*, 11: 47a–47b). Both Kong and Cheng interpret the text to mean that the former kings went around "viewing" the people, and then on the basis of local custom established teachings and laws. Only Zhu Xi seems to have noticed the change here in meaning from *Viewing* as "provide a viewing" (i.e., offer a model) to *Viewing* as "do viewing" (i.e., find a model), and his commentary ingeniously tries to bridge this difference: "They made tours of inspection everywhere in order to view the people, and they established their teachings in order to serve as things to be viewed [i.e., to serve as models]." See *Zhouyi zhezhong*, 11: 47a.

9. Han Kangbo's comment, "If one stirs oneself to oversee others, this is referred to as 'provide,' but if others come to view oneself, this is referred to as 'seek,' " is relevant to both *Lin* (Overseeing) and *Guan* (Viewing). The same kind of dichotomy seems to exist for both hexagrams; regarding *Guan*, one either *provides* something for others to view or *finds* something to view in others. See note 8 above.

10. A number of passages in earlier texts express the same idea that Wang does in his statement here. For instance, *Lunyu* (Analects 20:3) purports to quote King Tang, founder of the Shang dynasty (according to tradition, reigned 1765–1760 B.C.): "If I myself commit crimes, they shall not be attributed to the people of the myriad regions, and if the people of the myriad regions commit crimes, these crimes shall lie with me alone." Other passages are to be found in the *Mozi* (The sayings of Master Mo) (fifth century B.C.), the *Guoyu* (Discourses of the states) (third century B.C.), and the *Lüshi Chunqiu* (The spring and autumn annals of Master Lü) (third century B.C.); see *Wang Bi ji jiaoshi*, 1: 320–321 n. 22.

11. "He softens his own light and identifies with them completely" translates *heguang liutong*. This recalls a similar expression in the *Laozi*, section 4, p. 10: *He qi guang tong qi chen* ("Soften [or "blend," "harmonize"] your light and become one with the dusty world"). Kong Yingda (*Zhouyi zhengyi*, 3: 10b) and Cheng Yi (*Zhouyi zhezhong*, 11: 46b–47a) seem to understand the text as Wang does. Zhu Xi simply says of "he does not let his ambitions slacken": "Although he fails to obtain the position of sovereign [or "the right position for himself"], he still cannot forget about self-discipline and vigilance." See *Zhouyi zhezhong*, 11: 46b.

☲☳

噬嗑

Shihe [Bite Together]
(*Zhen* Below *Li* Above)

Judgment

Bite Together means prevalence, for here it is fitting to use the force of criminal punishment. {*Shi* [bite] means "*nie*" [bite], and *he* [join the teeth] means "consolidate together." Whenever people fail to achieve togetherness, it is due to there being a gap or estrangement, and whenever they lack order, it is due to there being excesses or wrongdoing. To deal with such a gap or excess, one, as it were, bites down on it and joins the teeth together, and in this way brings about continuity or coherence. It is by using the force of criminal punishment that one brings about this continuity, and that is what is meant here by "criminal punishment" being "fitting."[1]}

COMMENTARY ON THE JUDGMENTS

When there is something between the cheeks, this is referred to as *Shihe* [Bite Together]. {"When there is something between the cheeks," one bites on it and consolidates it. This is the meaning of *Shihe* [Bite Together].} It is by biting together that prevalence comes about. {When something has gaps or discontinuities in it, if one does not bite on it, it will not consolidate, and there will be no way to achieve prevalence [i.e., for things to work together and go smoothly].} The hard and the soft achieve clarity by taking separate action; thunder and lightning make a vivid display by uniting together. {When the hard and the soft act separately, since they do not get muddled up, they achieve clarity; when thunder and lightning unite together, since they do not become confused, they make a vivid display. Both these cases express the idea of "it is fitting to use the force of criminal punishment."[2]} Here the soft one [Fifth Yin] obtains the central position and so moves upward, and although it does not suit the position, "here it is fitting to use the force of criminal punishment." {This refers to Fifth Yin. In order that it be possible to bite together so things go smoothly, there must be a ruler in charge, and this is none other than Fifth Yin. "Moves upward" means that the direction one takes is a matter of advancing. Whenever the phrase "moves upward" appears, it means that the direction taken leads to nobility. Although Fifth Yin does not suit the position [it is a yin line in a yang position], it does no harm here "to use the force of criminal punishment."}

COMMENTARY ON THE IMAGES

Thunder and Lightning: this constitutes the image of *Shihe* [Bite Together].[3] In the same way, the former kings clarified punishments and adjusted laws.

COMMENTARY ON THE APPENDED PHRASES

[Lord Shen Nong] had midday become market time, had the people of the world gather, had the goods of the world brought together, had these exchanged, had them then retire to their homes, and enabled each one to get what he should. He probably got the idea for this from the hexagram *Shihe* [Bite Together].[4]

PROVIDING THE SEQUENCE OF THE HEXAGRAMS

Only after something can be viewed is there the possibility to come together with it. This is why *Guan* [Viewing, Hexagram 20] is followed by *Shihe* [Bite Together]. The *he* [in *Shihe*] means *he* [unite, i.e., join the jaws together].

THE HEXAGRAMS IN IRREGULAR ORDER

Shihe [Bite Together] means "eat up."

First Yang

Made to wear whole foot shackles, his toes are destroyed, but he will be without blame. {First Yang abides in a place of no proper position.[5] As it is located at the start of punishment, it is one to receive punishment and not one to administer punishment. The start of any transgression necessarily begins in subtlety and only later reaches the blatant stage, so the beginning of punishment must begin with something light and only later go so far as to include execution. Here the transgression is light or the error mild, so "made to wear whole foot shackles, he has his toes destroyed," which means that he has his gait confined by shackles and that nothing more happens to him beyond suffering an adequate chastisement. Therefore he will not do anything more serious. To commit transgression and yet not change one's ways, now this we call a real transgression. "For small matters one chastises him, so that for great matters he takes warning,"[6] so this is how blessings are obtained here, and this is why "he will be without blame." The word *jiao* [whole foot shackle] here means a cage made by intertwining slats of wood; it is equivalent to the term *xie* [foot fetters]. *Jiao* is the generic term for such things.}

COMMENTARY ON THE IMAGES

"Made to wear whole foot shackles, his toes are destroyed": he goes no further. {His transgression stops here.}

COMMENTARY ON THE APPENDED PHRASES

The Master said: "The petty man is not ashamed of being unkind, nor is he afraid of being unjust. If he does not see an advantage in something, he does not act, and, if he is not threatened by force, he is not chastised. For small matters one chastises him, so that for great matters he takes warning. This is how the petty man prospers." The *Changes* say: "Made to wear whole foot shackles, his toes are destroyed, but he will be without blame." This is what is meant here.[7]

Second Yin

Biting through soft and tender flesh, he destroys the nose, but he will be without blame. {*Shi* [bite through] is the same as *nie* [bite]; here it refers to the effective use of punishment. Second Yin, located in a central position, obtains a proper position [as a yin line in a yin position], and the punishment that is meted out here is appropriate. This is why the text says "biting through soft and tender flesh." That Second Yin metes out punishment by "rid[ing] atop hardness and strength [First Yang]" [i.e., by relying on strength and harsh measures] means that it is not quite in complete accord with the Dao, so the "biting through" goes too far, and that is why the text says: "He destroys the nose." But the punishment is successful in dealing with the defect involved, and this is why even though "he destroys the nose," yet "he will be without blame." "Soft and tender flesh" [*fu*, literally, "skin"] indicates something soft and fragile [tender].}

COMMENTARY ON THE IMAGES

"Biting through soft and tender flesh, he destroys the nose," for this one rides atop hardness and strength.

Third Yin

Biting through dried meat, he encounters something poisonous. He will have small regret but be without blame. {Third Yin is located at the very top of the lower trigram, and where it treads is not the place of its proper position [because it is a yin line in a superior, yang position], so to eat something here under these conditions means that thing will be sure to be hard and tough. But how could it be limited to just the hardness and toughness? He should encounter its poisonous aspect as well. "Biting through" is a metaphor for meting out punishment to someone. "Dried meat" here is used as a metaphor for recalcitrance, and "poison" is used as a metaphor for the occurrence of anger. However, Third Yin provides carriage to Fourth Yang and does not itself ride atop hardness and strength [a yang line]. Although it falls short of what rectitude demands here, the punishment as such does not violate the dictates of the moment, and this is why although he "encounters something poisonous," "he will have small regret but be without blame."}

COMMENTARY ON THE IMAGES

"He encounters something poisonous," for the position is not suitable for this one.

Fourth Yang

Biting through dried bony gristle, he obtains a metal arrowhead. It is fitting that one have good fortune here in exercising constancy in the face of difficulties. {Although in substance this is a yang line that should be the ruler of the yin, its treading does not manage to stay within the Mean [i.e., it is not in a central position], nor is this position right for it [because it is a yang line in a yin position], so when it bites on someone, that one certainly will not submit, and this is why the text says "biting through dried bony gristle." "Metal" signifies hardness, and "arrowhead" signifies straightness. "Biting through dried bony gristle," one manages to be hard and straight, and whereas one can in this way derive benefit from the good fortune that obtains from "exercising constancy in the face of difficulties," this is inadequate as a means to fulfill the Dao that comprehensively covers the principles involved.}

COMMENTARY ON THE IMAGES

"It is fitting that one have good fortune here in exercising constancy in the face of difficulties," but one falls short of achieving splendor.

Fifth Yin

Biting through dried meat, he obtains yellow metal. Constancy here involves danger, but there will be no blame. {"Dried meat" signifies toughness; "yellow," centrality or the Mean; and "metal," hardness. Here a yin line occupies a yang position, a soft line rides atop a hard line, so when such a one bites on another, that other surely will not submit. This is why the text says "biting through dried meat." However, in occupying this place one obtains the noble position. Here one rides atop the hard and strong with softness and yet manages to stay within the Mean, and this is how punishment can be administered. Here one treads on a place that is not right for him and yet remains capable of administering the appropriate punishment, so this is the success derived from the hardness and strength [of Fourth Yang on which Fifth Yin rides]. Although the "biting" does not produce submission, this one achieves success thanks to how he manages to stay within the Mean. This is why the text says: "Biting through dried meat, he obtains yellow metal." Although Fifth Yin itself is not right here [because it is a yin line in a yang position], yet in the punishment administered such a "one achieves what is proper." Therefore, although "constancy here involves danger," "there will be no blame."}

COMMENTARY ON THE IMAGES

"Constancy here involves danger, but there will be no blame," for one achieves what is proper.

Top Yang

Made to bear a cangue, his ears are destroyed, and this means misfortune. {Top Yang occupies the very top of the punishment process; it signifies someone in whom evil has accumulated and who will not reform. His criminality is not something against which he takes warning, so punishment has to reach his head and goes so far as to destroy his ears. Even reaching his head, it is not an admonishment for him, and even destroying his ears, it is not a warning for him. No misfortune can be greater than this!}

COMMENTARY ON THE IMAGES

"Made to bear a cangue, his ears are destroyed," for his intelligence is not bright. {As "his intelligence is not bright," he pays no heed, and evil has accumulated in him to such an extent that he is incapable of being extricated from it.}

COMMENTARY ON THE APPENDED PHRASES

As for goodness, if one does not accumulate it, there will not be enough of it to make a name for oneself, and, as for evil, if one does not accumulate it, there will not be enough of it to destroy one's life. The petty man takes small goodness to be of no advantage and so does not do it, and he takes small evil to be of no harm, so he does not forsake it. This is why evil accumulates to the point where one can no longer keep it hidden and crimes become so great that one can no longer be exonerated. The *Changes* say: "Made to bear a cangue, his ears are destroyed, and this means misfortune."[8]

NOTES

1. This and all subsequent text set off in this manner is commentary by Wang Bi.

2. "The hard and the soft achieve clarity by taking separate action" translates *gang rou fendong er ming*, which reflects how Wang Bi and Kong Yingda parse the text; see *Zhouyi zhengyi*, 3: 11a–11b. However, Cheng Yi seems to understand it differently, as *gang rou fen, dong er ming* (the hard and the soft separate and signify action and perspicacity); see *Zhouyi zhezhong*, 9: 34b. Cheng's version seems to make more sense, since all the commentators seem to interpret the text here as a reference to the action signified by the lower *Zhen* (Thunder) trigram and the brightness signified by the upper *Li* (Fire, Light, Lightning) trigram. Neither Wang nor Kong Yingda clarify the connection between the separate or unified action of thunder and lightning and the exercise of criminal punishment. Cheng Yi, however, does just that:

> The hard [yang] lines and the soft [yin] lines are here interspersed. That they remain separate and do not get mixed up together provides an image of how clear distinctions are made, and such clear distinctions are the foundation of criminal investigation. "Action and perspicacity" refer to the lower *Zhen* [Thunder] and upper *Li* [Fire] trigrams—how the one signifies action and the other perspicacity. "Thunder and lightning make a vivid display by uniting together": thunder shakes and lightning flashes, and for an instant they appear as one and "make a vivid display by uniting together." Here bright illumination and awesome power act in concert, something that signifies the Dao by which one enacts criminal punishment. If one can brightly illuminate things, nothing can remain hidden, and if one has awesome power, no one will dare to remain unafraid.

3. The top and bottom lines are supposed to be the jaws closing on Fourth Yang, a solid object to bite through.

4. *Shihe* (Bite Together) consists of the trigrams *Zhen* (Quake) below, which here seems to represent the bustle of the marketplace, and *Li* (Cohesion), signifying Sun, above. See section two of the Commentary on the Appended Phrases, Part Two.

5. See the first paragraph of Considering the Line Positions, section five of Wang Bi's General Remarks.

6. This quotes section five of the Commentary on the Appended Phrases, Part Two.

7. See section five of the Commentary on the Appended Phrases, Part Two.

8. Ibid.

䷕

賁

Bi [Elegance]
(*Li* Below *Gen* Above)

Judgment

Elegance means prevalence, but it is fitting only for small matters, should one set out to do something.

COMMENTARY ON THE JUDGMENTS

Coming to it, the soft provides the hard with pattern, and this is why there is "prevalence." Separating itself out, the hard rises to the top, and in doing so provides the soft with pattern, and this is why "it is fitting only for small matters, should one set out to do something." {If the hard and the soft are not separate, how should pattern ever arise? Therefore, Top Yin of *Kun* comes to abide in the second position.[1] This is what is meant by "coming to it, the soft provides the hard with pattern." The soft comes to provide the hard with pattern in such a way that the position it takes obtains centrality [the Mean], and this is how prevalence occurs. Second Yang of *Qian* separates itself out and rises to the top position. This is what is meant by "separating itself out, the hard rises to the top, and in doing so provides the soft with pattern." But the hard rises to provide the soft with pattern in such a way that it does not obtain a central position [the Mean], so this is inferior to the way the soft comes to provide the hard with pattern. This is why "it is fitting only for small matters should one set out to do something."[2]} This is the pattern of Heaven. {Here the hard and the soft intersperse among each other and so form a pattern therefrom, and "this is the pattern of Heaven."[3]} It is by means of the enlightenment provided by pattern [i.e., culture] that curbs are set,[4] and this is the pattern of man. {One curbs people not with the coercive power of martial force but by means of the enlightenment provided by pattern [culture, the norms of social etiquette, etc.], and this is "the pattern of man."} One looks to the pattern of Heaven in order to examine the flux of the seasons, and one looks to the pattern of man in order to transform and bring the whole world to perfection. {It is by observing the pattern of Heaven that the flux of the seasons can be known, and it is by observing the pattern of man that the transformation and perfection [of the world] can be accomplished.}

COMMENTARY ON THE IMAGES

Below the Mountain, there is Fire: this constitutes the image of *Bi* [Elegance].[5] In the same way, the noble man clearly understands all the different aspects of governance and so dares not reduce it to a matter of passing criminal judgment. {When one finds oneself located at a time of *Bi* [Elegance], one should curb others by means of the enlightenment provided by pattern [culture]; one cannot use the coercive force of punishment to do this. This is why the text says: "In the same way, the noble man clearly understands all the different aspects of governance and so dares not reduce it to a matter of passing criminal judgment."}

PROVIDING THE SEQUENCE OF THE HEXAGRAMS

The *he* [in *Shihe*] means *he* [unite, i.e., join the jaws together]. But things may not be just recklessly united and left at that! This is why *Shihe* [Bite Together, Hexagram 21] is followed by *Bi* [Elegance]. *Bi* here means "adornment." Adornment will become pervasive only after it has been pushed to the limit, but at that it will become exhausted.

THE HEXAGRAMS IN IRREGULAR ORDER

Bi [Elegance] does not involve particular colors.

First Yang

He furnishes his toes with Elegance, discards carriage, and goes on foot. {At the very beginning of *Bi* [Elegance], there is this hard [yang] line occupying the lowest position. As it abides at a place of no proper position, it casts aside the opportunity for any unrighteousness and is content to go on foot in the pursuit of its goals. This is why "he furnishes his toes with Elegance." "Discards carriage, and goes on foot" means that "the righteous thing to do here is to refuse to ride in the carriage."}

COMMENTARY ON THE IMAGES

He "discards carriage and goes on foot," for the righteous thing to do here is to refuse to ride in the carriage.

Second Yin

He uses his cheek whiskers to provide Elegance. {Second Yin obtains a proper position but has no line with which to resonate. Third Yang also lacks such resonance. The two lines both find themselves without resonate partners and so pair up together here, for the fact that they are contiguous allows them access to each other. Cheek whiskers are such that they cling to that which is above them [the face], and so in following the path that it treads, Second Yin clings to the line above it. This is why the text says: "He uses his cheek whiskers to provide Elegance."[6]}

COMMENTARY ON THE IMAGES

"He uses his cheek whiskers to provide elegance," for this one rises together with the one above him.

Third Yang

Such consummate Elegance here, such perfect luster, so perpetual constancy means good fortune. {Third Yang occupies a position at the very top of the lower trigram and, in so abiding, obtains a proper position for itself [as a yang line in a yang position]. It forms a pair with Second Yin, and both tread a path that is right for them. Harmonizing perfectly together, they each bring luster to the other and, in doing so, bring their pattern to perfection. As such adornment as this is achieved, so a corresponding luster is obtained, and this is why the text says "such consummate elegance here, such perfect luster." One might preserve his constancy here forever, and no one should encroach upon him, and this is why the text says: "Perpetual constancy here means good fortune."}

COMMENTARY ON THE IMAGES

The good fortune here that stems from "perpetual constancy" happens because no one should ever encroach upon him.

Fourth Yin

Is it to be consummate Elegance or perfect simplicity? She keeps her horse white and, lingering there fresh and spotless, goes to marry only when the robber is no more. {Fourth Yin has its resonate partner in First Yang, but its way is blocked by Third Yang, which would take it by force, so although in their respective goals these two [Fourth Yin and First Yang] resonate together, they do not manage to have things go smoothly for them. Fourth Yin might want to remain still, but this would result in anxiety about whether or not First Yang would continue to respond; it might want to advance, but this would result in fear for the trouble that Third Yang would cause it. This is why, its being torn between Elegance and simplicity is a matter of harboring both anxiety and fear within. Fourth Yin keeps its horse fresh and spotless and, lingering there so white [*hanru*], waits.[7] Although it treads on the territory of its rightful position, it dares not try to realize its goal. Third Yang is so hard and fierce that Fourth Yin may not rashly give it offense, but if it " 'goes to marry [First Yang] only when the robber is no more,' in the end, there will be no mistake."}

COMMENTARY ON THE IMAGES

That Fourth Yin is in its rightful position is a matter of anxiety for it. But as it "goes to marry only when the robber is no more," in the end, there will be no mistake.

Fifth Yin

This is Elegance as from a hillside garden, so bundles of silk increase to great number. If one is sparing, in the end, there will be good fortune. {Fifth Yin has obtained the noble position and, as the ruler of the *Bi* [Elegance] hexagram, represents the acme of decorative beauty. Whereas when one applies adornment to something, the Dao of that thing becomes damaged, here one's application of adornment is like that of a garden to a hillside, and nothing can reach greater glory than this. Thus, when one's Elegance depends on bundles of silk, the hillside garden comes to grief, but when one's Elegance is derived from the hillside garden, bundles of silk increase to great number.[8] In using adornment, it is best to curtail extravagance and to be able to practice restraint. This is why its use here must be "sparing," for only then will one in the end obtain good fortune.}

COMMENTARY ON THE IMAGES

In the good fortune represented by Fifth Yin there is joy.

Top Yang

Here one turns Elegance into plainness, so there is no blame. {Top Yang is located at the furthest reach of adornment, and when adornment reaches its end point, it should revert to the plain and simple. Thus Top Yang allows this unadorned simplicity to happen. As it does not wear itself out on embellishment and adornment, it suffers no blame. Here one has to use plainness as if it were elegance and yet remains free of any regret that a terrible misfortune has occurred, for he has "realized his goal."}

COMMENTARY ON THE IMAGES

"Here one turns Elegance into plainness, so there is no blame": Top Yang represents one who has realized his goal.

NOTES

1. Lou Yulie draws our attention to the fact that when Top Yin and Second Yang of *Tai* (Peace), Hexagram 11, trade places, the hexagram becomes *Bi* (Elegance). This appears to be what Wang Bi had in mind here. See *Wang Bi ji jiaoshi*, 1: 329 n. 2.

2. This and all subsequent text set off in this manner is commentary by Wang Bi. Some commentators think that, instead of *xiaoli you youwang* (it is fitting only for small matters should one set out to do something), the texts of the Judgment and the Commentary on the Judgments of *Bi* should

read *buli you youwang* (it is not fitting should one set out to do something), since the graphs for *xiao* (small, small matters) and *bu* (negative prefix) can be easily confused. The Tang era scholar and author of the *Zhouyi juzheng* (Evidence for correct readings in the *Changes of the Zhou*), Guo Jing, for instance, uses this argument and adds:

> Second Yang discards the Dao of harmony embodied in the Mean and moves instead to a place of no proper position fraught with the utmost arrogance. This is why the subcommentary [of Kong Yingda] says: "Second Yang casts goodness aside and pursues evil." The casting aside of goodness and pursuit of evil is never something that one should want to do, and, since this involves great evil, how could it simply be a matter of "it is fitting only for small matters"? So it is perfectly obvious that a textual error is involved.

See Kong, *Zhouyi zhengyi*, 3: 14a, and Lou, *Wang Bi ji jiaoshi*, 1: 329 n. 4.

3. This passage seems to refer to the lower trigram, *Li* (Cohesion), which also signifies the sun, the most significant of the heavenly bodies that make up the pattern of Heaven. *Li* results when the middle line of the *Qian* (Heaven) trigram changes from yang to yin.

4. "Curbs are set" translates *zhi* (stop, make halt), an obvious reference to *Gen* (Restraint), the upper trigram. What distinguishes human culture is its capacity to cast light on the necessity of curbing individual behavior for the sake of the common good.

5. *Li* (Cohesion), the lower trigram, signifies fire as well as the sun, and *Gen* (Restraint), the upper trigram signifies "Mountain."

6. Kong Yingda comments: " 'Cheek whiskers' refer to the whiskers that cling to the face above. Second Yin always attaches itself above to Third Yang." See *Zhouyi zhengyi*, 3: 15a.

7. Lou Yulie glosses *hanru* as "not budging." This interpretation follows the gloss of *han* as *gan* (tree trunk[like], i.e., still, patient, stubborn, unmovable, etc.) by the Han commentator Zheng Xuan (127–200) (see Lu, *Jingdian shiwen*, 2: 78) and Jiao Xun's (1763–1820) *Zhouyi bushu* (Supplements to the commentaries and subcommentaries to the *Changes of the Zhou*), in which this remark on Wang Bi's commentary occurs: "Surely one should read *han* as *gan*. The *Guangya* [The *Erya* (Elegant and correct writings in familiar terms), expanded] [by Zhang Yi (fl. 227–232)] glosses *gan* as *an* [still, content, secure, etc.]. Although Fourth Yin has made its horse spotless, it continues to stay still and does not make a move, and this is why Wang Bi says 'not budging, so waits there.' " See *Wang Bi ji jiaoshi*, 1: 330 n. 15. Kong Yingda's own subcommentary on Wang's passage suggests that *hanru* refers to the fresh and spotless appearance of the horse; see *Zhouyi zhengyi*, 3: 15b. However, both Cheng Yi and Zhu Xi interpret *hanru* a third way, as a description of how the heart or will of Fourth Yin is so fixed on First Yang that it would "fly there" (*hanru*), a gloss that reads *han* as *han* in the sense of its other basic meaning, "feather" or "to feather," that is, "to soar or fly." This again seems forced and unlikely.

8. "Increase to great number" translates *jianjian*, which follows Kong Yingda's gloss of it as *zhongduo* (numerous, abundant). Kong interprets Fifth Yin and Wang's commentary to mean that if one runs a simple, honest government, one shall reap wealth and prosperity (i.e., much silk), but if one indulges in extravagant trappings, this will ruin the substance of government, and all will fail. See *Zhouyi zhengyi*, 3: 15b–16a. My translation of Fifth Yin tries to comply with these remarks. However, Cheng Yi and Zhu Xi suggest interpretations that differ from this and from each other. Cheng thinks that *jianjian* refers to the cutting and tailoring of silk material: as a tailor cuts and tailors it, so the hard and strong Top Yang line controls and guides the soft and weak ruler, Fifth Yin. Top Yang, in fact, being both "up high" and "near by" is represented by the "hill" and "the garden," respectively, and Fifth Yin is thus "made elegant" (adorned) by Top Yang. Cheng's interpretation suggests the following translation: "Here one takes Elegance from the hill and garden and, as if a bundle of silk, is cut and tailored. If one is sparing of this, in the end, there will be good fortune." Zhu Xi's interpretation is succinct enough to translate in its entirety:

> Fifth Yin as a weak but central line is the ruler of the *Bi* [Elegance] hexagram. It is by deriving honest simplicity from what is essential and by holding substance in high esteem that one perfectly realizes the Dao of Elegance. Thus there is the image of the hillside garden. However, the nature of the yin personality is such that it is miserly, and this is why there is the image of a poor, meager [*jianjian*] bundle of silk. A bundle of silk is a poor, inadequate thing. *Jianjian* has the meaning of "poor and meager" [*qianxiao*]. Although it is shameful for a person to be miserly, when it comes to decorum, restraint is preferred to extravagance, and this is how in the end one obtains good fortune here.

Zhu's interpretation suggests: "Here one derives Elegance from the hillside garden, poor and meager as a bundle of silk. But spare use [of Elegance] will lead to good fortune in the end." See *Zhouyi zhezhong*, 3: 41a–41b.

☶☷

剝

Bo [Peeling]
(*Kun* Below *Gen* Above)

Judgment

It would not be fitting should one set out to do something.

COMMENTARY ON THE JUDGMENTS

Bo means "*bo*" [peeling], for here the soft and weak are making the hard and strong change.[1] "It would not be fitting should one set out to do something," for the petty man is in the ascendancy. One should try to restrain things in such a way that one remains compliant with circumstances, for this is to observe the image. The noble man holds in esteem how things ebb and flow, wax and wane, for this is the course of Heaven. {*Kun* [Pure Yin, the lower trigram] indicates compliance, and *Gen* [Restraint, the upper trigram] indicates cessation or restraint, so here one should restrain things by complying with circumstances, but he should not dare to try to restrain them by using hardness and strength. By doing so, one observes the image involved. If one is too self-assertive and excessively outspoken, it will provoke such a negative reaction that it will mean his own downfall, and once his destruction is so brought about, all his efforts to achieve merit will also come to nothing, and this is not a course of action that the noble man should esteem.[2]}

COMMENTARY ON THE IMAGES

The Mountain is attached to the Earth: this constitutes the image of *Bo* [Peeling].[3] In the same way, those above make their dwellings secure by treating those below with generosity. {It is by treating those below with generosity that one avoids having one's bedstead suffer from Peeling.[4] "Make their dwellings secure" means that people will not lose their places or positions. To secure one's dwelling by treating those below with generosity is the Dao by which one controls Peeling.}

PROVIDING THE SEQUENCE OF THE HEXAGRAMS

Adornment will become pervasive only after it has been pushed to the limit, but at that it will become exhausted. This is why *Bi* [Elegance, Hexagram 22] is followed by *Bo* [Peeling]. *Bo* here means "peel off."

THE HEXAGRAMS IN IRREGULAR ORDER

Bo [Peeling] signifies decay.

First Yin

The bedstead has suffered Peeling to the legs; so does constancy meet with destruction. This means misfortune. {A bedstead is that in which a man finds his rest. "The bedstead has suffered Peeling to the legs," in other words, means that the bedstead's legs have been cut off or peeled away. "Meet with destruction" is another way of saying "peel off or cut away" [i.e., "deprive of"]. That the bedstead has been deprived of its legs signifies that the Dao of the subordinate has been destroyed, and the start of the destruction of the Dao of the subordinate signifies the fall of the hard and strong and the ascendancy of the soft and weak. Thus it is that with the deterioration of rectitude, misfortune arrives.[5]}

COMMENTARY ON THE IMAGES

"The bedstead has suffered Peeling to the legs": in the same way, destruction is visited on those below.

Second Yin

The bedstead has suffered Peeling to the frame; so does constancy meet with destruction. This means misfortune. {"Meet with destruction" seems to express something even more extreme here. "Frame" is what is on top of the legs. The Dao of Peeling has gradually grown stronger, thus it "has suffered Peeling to the frame." Little by little, Peeling has drawn close to the bed proper, so soon it will destroy the place where people stay in it. Peeling makes its weakness grow and its uprightness [i.e., "rectitude"] deteriorate, and as these now constitute its character, it is something that people will discard.[6]}

COMMENTARY ON THE IMAGES

"The bedstead has suffered Peeling to the frame," so there is no help for it to be had anywhere.[7]

Third Yin

This one does Peeling in such a way that it is without blame. {Third Yin is in resonance with Top Yang. All the other yin lines inflict Peeling on the yang, but this one alone renders assistance to it, so although Third Yin is located in Peeling, it manages in this way to be "without blame."}

COMMENTARY ON THE IMAGES

"This one does Peeling in such a way that it is without blame," for it breaks with those above and below it. {There are two yin lines both above and below Third Yin, but it is Third Yin alone that responds to Top Yang, and in doing so "it breaks with those above and below it."}

Fourth Yin

The bedstead has suffered Peeling to the skin. This means misfortune. {With First Yin and Second Yin, the Peeling just affects the bedstead, and as such the folk themselves still remain secure, for Peeling has not yet reached their bodies. But when we come to Fourth Yin, the Dao of Peeling has gradually grown so strong that not only has the bedstead suffered total Peeling, but Peeling also has reached their very bodies. The petty man consequently flourishes, and people are going to lose their bodies. How could this just be a matter of uprightness [i.e., "rectitude"] being destroyed? For misfortune holds sway everywhere.}

COMMENTARY ON THE IMAGES

"The bedstead has suffered Peeling to the skin," for here is disaster that draws increasingly near.

Fifth Yin

As if they were a string of fish, here court ladies enjoy favor, so nothing done here fails to be fitting. {Here located at a time of Peeling, Fifth Yin has obtained the noble position and is the ruler of the Peeling hexagram. The way that Peeling causes harm is that the petty man obtains favor and this consequently diminishes the noble man. However, if one were to grant favor to the petty in such a way that this would be strictly limited to palace ladies, no harm would be done to the upright. Thus, even though those who enjoy favor be numerous, "in the end, no mistake is made." "As if they were a string of fish" refers to this collection of yin lines. Head to head, they follow one upon the other, just like strung fish.[8]}

COMMENTARY ON THE IMAGES

"Here court ladies enjoy favor": in the end, no mistake is made.

Top Yang

Here the biggest fruit is not eaten. If it be a noble man, he shall obtain a carriage, but if it be a petty man, he shall allow Peeling to happen to humble huts. {Top Yang is located at the very end of this hexagram, and it alone has not fallen at all. Thus it is a fruit that has grown to reach great size and that has not been eaten. If a noble man abides here, then the common folk will obtain shade and protection, but if a petty man fills it, then he shall allow Peeling to happen to that which provides those below with shelter.}

COMMENTARY ON THE IMAGES

"If it be a noble man, he shall obtain a carriage," for he shall be borne along by the common folk. "If it be a petty man, he shall allow Peeling to happen to humble huts," for he never could fulfill it.[9]

NOTES

1. Kong Yingda glosses *bo* as *boluo*: "to peel off," as skin from fruit or vegetables, bark from a tree, etc. As such things so peel (and split), this indicates their "deterioration" or "decay," which is what *boluo* means by extension.

2. This and all subsequent text set off in this manner is commentary by Wang Bi. "Restrain things" translates *zhi zhi*. The second *zhi* is an indefinite object pronoun, and its referent here is uncertain, thus it is rendered "things." Kong Yingda thinks that it refers specifically to the noble man's sovereign and that "the image" mentioned in the Commentary on the Judgments and in Wang's remarks refers as much to the image—i.e., appearance—of that sovereign as to that of the *Bo* hexagram itself: "As one can but use softness and compliancy to restrain one's sovereign, all he can do is look to the image that his sovereign on high presents, take into account what his facial expression means, and so try to bring about restraint that way." See *Zhouyi zhengyi*, 3: 16b. Neither Cheng Yi nor Zhu Xi bring "the sovereign" into their discussions, and Cheng Yi seems to interpret *zhi* (restrain) as an intransitive verb "refrain from," so instead of "one should try to restrain things in such a way that one remains compliant with circumstances," Cheng's interpretation would suggest "being compliant, one should refrain from [doing] things." See *Zhouyi zhezhong*, 6: 38b.

3. *Kun* (Pure Yin), the lower trigram, signifies the Earth, and *Gen* (Restraint), the upper trigram, signifies "Mountain."

4. The significance of the bedstead is the subject of the following line statements and commentaries.

5. Kong Yingda here identifies *zhen* (constancy) with *zheng* (rectitude, righteousness). See *Zhouyi zhengyi*, 3: 17a.

6. Lou Yulie points out that the text here may be corrupt and, following the remarks of the Tang era commentator Guo Jing, suggests that it should read something like: " Little by little, Peeling has drawn close to where people are, so soon the bed itself will be destroyed. In this thing in which people stay, Peeling makes weakness grow and uprightness deteriorate, and as these now constitute its character, it is something that those people will discard." See *Wang Bi ji jiaoshi*, 1: 334–335 nn. 7 and 8.

7. Kong Yingda links this statement with Wang's last remark, "Peeling makes its weakness grow and its uprightness deteriorate, and as these now constitute its character, it is something that people will discard." That is, since people discard the bedstead, they will not help to stem its further deterioration. See *Zhouyi zhengyi*, 3: 17b.

8. Cheng Yi points out that fish and women are both yin creatures; see *Zhouyi zhezhong*, 4: 3a.

9. Zhu Xi interprets the Commentary to the Images differently: "It is only the noble man who can shelter the petty man. The petty man must rely on the noble man for the protection of his own person. Now here the petty man would inflict Peeling on the noble man [i.e., bring about his downfall], but then if the noble man perishes, the petty man also would lack all means to shelter his own person, and this would be just as if he let Peeling

happen to his own humble hut." See *Zhouyi zhezhong*, 11: 55b. Zhu's interpretation suggests a different translation: "If it be a petty man, he shall allow peeling to happen to his own humble hut, which then never can be used." However, Kong Yingda reinforces Wang Bi's interpretation: "If a petty man were to occupy this position as sovereign, he would allow Peeling to devastate the humble huts of the common folk. So this means that a petty man could never fulfill the role of sovereign." See *Zhouyi zhengyi*, 3: 18b.

HEXAGRAM 24

䷗

復

Fu [Return]

(*Zhen* Below *Kun* Above)

Judgment

Fu brings about prevalence. His going out and coming in are done without flaw, so when the friend arrives, he is without blame. The Dao [way] that he goes out and comes back on is such that he returns after seven days. It would be fitting should one set out to do something here.

COMMENTARY ON THE JUDGMENTS

"*Fu* [Return] brings about prevalence," for the hard and the strong [the yang principle] has returned. It takes action and makes its moves in compliance with the proper order of things, and this is how its "going out and coming in are done without flaw." {"Coming in" refers to the return that it makes, and "going out" refers to how "the hard and the strong [the yang principle] grows." Thus they are "without flaw." *Ji* [flaw] is equivalent to *bing* [fault, failing].[1]} "So when the friend arrives, he is without blame."

{"Friend" means the yang principle.} "The Dao [way] that he goes out and comes back on is such that he returns after seven days," {From the time the yang material force begins to undergo *Bo* [Peeling] until its completion and then on to the time it arrives in *Fu* [Return] is commonly seven days.[2]} for this is the course of Heaven. {As the course of Heaven involves a going out and coming back that does not exceed seven days, this means that the Return cannot involve a long time.} "It would be fitting should one set out to do something here," for the hard and the strong [the yang principle] grows. {This setting forth means that the dao of the petty man is now on the wane.} In *Fu* [Return] we can see the very heart and mind of Heaven and Earth! {*Return* as such means "to revert to what is the original substance [*ben*]," and for Heaven and Earth we regard the original substance to be the mind/heart. Whenever activity ceases, tranquillity results, but tranquillity is not opposed to activity. Whenever speech ceases, silence results, but silence is not opposed to speech. As this is so, then even though Heaven and Earth are so vast that they possess the myriad things in great abundance, which, activated by thunder and moved by the winds, keep undergoing countless numbers of transformations, yet the original substance of Heaven and Earth consists of perfectly quiescent nonbeing. Thus it is only when earthly activity ceases that the heart/mind of Heaven and Earth can be seen. If Heaven and Earth were to have had being instead for this heart/mind, then it never would have been possible for all the different categories of things to become endowed with existence.[3]}

COMMENTARY ON THE IMAGES

Thunder in the Earth: this constitutes the image of *Fu* [Return].[4] In the same way, the former kings closed the border passes on the occasion of the winter solstice, and neither did merchants and travelers move nor sovereigns go out to inspect domains. {"Domains" [*fang*] here refers to "matters" [*shi*, i.e., the conduct of government throughout a realm]. The winter solstice is the time when the yin principle commences its Return [begins to become quiescent], and the summer solstice is the time when the yang principle commences its Return [begins to become quiescent]. Thus to undergo Return as such means to reach perfect stillness and great tranquillity. The former kings behaved in such a way that they acted as do Heaven and Earth. For activity to be subject to Return means that it becomes quiescent; for movement to be subject to Return means that it comes to a halt; and for matters to be subject to Return means a disengagement from matters [*wu shi*].[5]}

COMMENTARY ON THE APPENDED PHRASES

Fu [Return] is the root of virtue.

Fu [Return] demonstrates how distinctions among things should be made while they are still small.

Fu [Return] provides the means to know oneself.[6]

PROVIDING THE SEQUENCE OF THE HEXAGRAMS

Just as things cannot remain exhausted forever, so with *Bo* [Peeling, Hexagram 23]: when they reach all the way to the top, they then return to the bottom.[7] This is why *Bo* is followed by *Fu* [Return].

THE HEXAGRAMS IN IRREGULAR ORDER

Fu [Return] signifies a coming back.

First Yang

This one returns before having gone far, so there will be no regret here, which means fundamental good fortune. {Located at the very first position of the *Fu* [Return] hexagram, First Yang represents the beginning of the process of Return. If one here did not make his Return with all haste, it would inevitably lead to the misfortune of getting lost, but this one makes his Return before he has gone far, which means that with the onset of regret he starts back.[8] If one were to "cultivate his person" in terms of what is meant here, disaster and trouble would indeed be kept far away! And if one were to utilize this in the conduct of one's affairs, would that not be just about the perfect way to act? This is why there is "fundamental good fortune."}

COMMENTARY ON THE IMAGES

"Return before going far" provides the way one should cultivate his person.

Second Yin

This one returns with delightful goodness, so there is good fortune. {Second Yin obtains its position in such a way that it is centrally located and is the very closest to First Yang. Above there are no other yang lines to bring this intimacy into question. The yang conduct themselves out of a sense of benevolence. Here Second Yin is located on top of First Yang, but it obeys First Yang as its adherent, and this is what is meant by saying that it "subordinates itself to benevolence." Once Second Yin has located itself in this central position, it has benevolence for its close companion and delights in the goodness of its neighbor. And this is what accounts for the "delightful goodness" of its Return.}

COMMENTARY ON THE IMAGES

The "good fortune" associated with "this one returns with delightful goodness" happens because Second Yin subordinates itself to benevolence.

Third Yin

This one returns with urgency, so although there is danger, there will be no blame. {"With urgency" [*pin*] refers to an anxious and hurried [*pincu*] manner.[9] Third Yin occupies a place at the very end of the lower trigram, so although it is superior to the confusion of Top Yin, it already has gone far off the way of Return, and this is the reason for the "urgency." As this one tries to Return with urgency, it never goes so far as to fall prey to confusion, and this is why, although in danger, it suffers no blame. As the way [Dao] of Return should be taken with all speed, so Third Yin makes its Return with urgency. Although what is meant here results in "no blame," if anything else were involved, such a one would find it impossible to maintain this [good fortune].[10]}

COMMENTARY ON THE IMAGES

As for the danger connected with "this one returns with urgency," the meaning is such that "there will be no blame."[11]

Fourth Yin

It is by traveling a middle course that this one alone returns. {Both above and below Fourth Yin there are two yin lines, and so it is located right in the middle of them. Where it treads is its rightful territory, and yet it also is in resonance with First Yang, so it alone obtains the wherewithal to effect the Return. It travels back by following the right way [or "by complying with the Dao"], and since there is nothing there to block its way, the text says: "It is by traveling a middle course that this one alone returns."}

COMMENTARY ON THE IMAGES

"It is by traveling a middle course that this one alone returns," for it follows the Dao [the right way].

Fifth Yin

This one returns with simple honesty, so there will be no regret. {Fifth Yin abides in magnanimity and yet treads a middle course [stays within the Mean]. As it abides in magnanimity, it is utterly free of any resentment, and as it stays within the Mean, it is able to use it "as the standard for [its own] self-examination." Although it has not sufficient means to attain to the good fortune that the Return "with delightful goodness" [Second Yin] has, since it effects its Return in accordance with the maintenance of magnanimity, "regret" can be avoided.}

COMMENTARY ON THE IMAGES

"This one returns with simple honesty, so there will be no regret," for the Mean is used as the standard for self-examination.

Top Yin

This one returns in confusion, which means misfortune. As it would involve utter disaster, if one were to set an army on the march here, it would in the end result in great defeat, and in terms of what it would do to the sovereign of one's state, it would mean misfortune. Even if it were as much as ten years, no attempt at recovery would ever succeed. {Top Yin is located at the very last position in the *Fu* [Return] hexagram, and this represents a condition of confusion. It is because one here tries to return while in confusion that the text says "this one returns in confusion." If one were to set an army on the march in such a condition, it would be impossible as such ever to have victory, so in the end there would surely be a great defeat. This condition being so, to use it for the sake of the state would be in violation of the Dao of the true sovereign. One might try a Return in the aftermath of such a great defeat, but if one were to evaluate such a situation, even trying to repair things with a Return of ten years would still leave the recovery unachieved.}

COMMENTARY ON THE IMAGES

The misfortune associated with "this one returns in confusion" is due to the way it violates the Dao of the true sovereign.

NOTES

1. This and all subsequent text set off in this manner is commentary by Wang Bi. For a very different translation of Wang Bi's commentary to *Fu* (Return), see Smith et al., *Sung Dynasty Uses*, pp. 240–245.

2. Why this process should take seven days is unclear. Kong Yingda's subcommentary cites several different, extremely complicated, and mutually contradictory explanations from the commentary tradition, none of which seems convincing enough to cite here. Also, the fact that both Cheng Yi and Zhu Xi avoid discussing this issue later in their own commentaries indicates that they had no satisfactory answer either. Lou Yulie suggests a simple explanation with which we shall have to remain content: " 'Seven days' is a general expression to indicate a period of time that does not last too long." See *Wang Bi ji jiaoshi*, 1: 340 n. 3.

3. Wang here seems to make a distinction between ontology and phenomenology: The heart/mind or original substance of Heaven and Earth is itself utterly quiescent and completely apart from phenomenal existence, nevertheless, it is the controlling mechanism through which Heaven and Earth generate and animate all phenomenal existence. Just as tranquillity and silence are not opposed to speech and activity, so the perfect quiescence and nonbeing of Heaven and Earth are not opposed to phenomenal existence with all its concomitant activity. If the mind of Heaven and Earth were instead to consist of being and activity, then *all* being and activity

would belong to Heaven and Earth, and there would be, in effect, no means by which—or place in which—the things of phenomenal existence could even exist. For various other interpretations of Wang's passage, see Lou Yulie, *Wang Bi ji jiaoshi*, 1: 340 nn. 5–9; Chan, *A Source Book*, pp. 320–321; and Fung, *A History of Chinese Philosophy*, 2: 180–181. We should also note that both Cheng Yi and Zhu Xi reject this quietist interpretation of Wang's—and other earlier commentators—and insist instead on regarding the heart/mind of Heaven and Earth as perfectly *active*—as Cheng says, "To cover it in a word, for Heaven and Earth we regard the generation of all things to be the heart/mind [i.e., intent]." See *Zhouyi zhezhong*, 9: 40a.

4. *Zhen* (Thunder) is the lower trigram, and *Kun* (Pure Yin), the upper trigram, signifies the Earth.

5. In the Daoist view, the sage-king ideally should govern *always* by a "disengagement from matters." See the *Laozi*, section 57, p. 149. Cheng Yi and Zhu Xi, as Confucians, stress instead that *Fu* (Return) signifies a *temporary* halt to activist government, a time to rest in order to nourish the yang principle so that it can grow into the basis for purposeful activity at appropriate times later. See *Zhouyi zhezhong*, 11: 56a.

6. See section seven of the Commentary on the Appended Phrases, Part Two.

7. Hexagram 23, *Bo* , consists of one positive line in the top, sixth position and five negative lines; Hexagram 24, *Fu* , consists of one positive line in the bottom, first position and five negative lines. As a pair, these two hexagrams form a continuum in which the one positive line from the top of Hexagram 23 "returns" to the bottom of Hexagram 24.

8. "The onset of regret" translates *ji hui*, which seems to be Wang's gloss for the "regret here" (*zhi hui*) in First Yang. Lou Yulie points out that as modal particles *ji* and *zhi* are interchangeable, and that, he says, is what accounts for their presence here. See *Wang Bi ji jiaoshi*, 1: 341 n. 11. If this is correct, one might translate both as "here" or "now." Kong Yingda cites Han Kangbo's commentary on First Yang, which appears in section five of the Commentary on the Appended Phrases, Part Two: "*Zhi* ["here"; literally, "god of the earth," i.e., "great"] means "*great*" (see note 40 there). This seems unlikely. Cheng Yi and Zhu Xi gloss *zhi* as *di* or *zhi* (arrive at, go so far as). *Wu zhi hui* (there will be no regret here) would instead mean "it will not happen that one will reach the point where one should regret it." See *Zhouyi zhezhong*, 4: 6a–6b. The *ji* in *ji hui*, on the other hand, also could mean "here," and "the onset of regret" might be rendered simply "with regret here." However, *ji* commonly occurs in the sense of "almost," "nearly," "on the point of," etc., and Wang might even have had the sense of "incipience" in mind here, since *ji* occurs with that meaning in the Commentary on the Appended Phrases in a passage just prior to the abovementioned discussion of *Fu* (Return), First Yang. Two recent commentators on Wang's statement, in fact, read it this way. See Kidder Smith's translation of Cheng Yi's commentary to *Fu* in Smith et al., *Sung Dynasty Uses,*

p. 248, and Bergeron, *Wang Pi*, p. 89. My "onset of regret" attempts a compromise among these interpretations.

9. *Pincu* itself is a difficult term to translate, for the *cu* can be written several different ways, and its meaning varies accordingly. That Wang Bi means *pincu* in the sense of "hurried," "urgent," or "with haste" is obvious from the rest of his comments on Third Yin. Since Kong Yingda paraphrases these in his gloss on *pin* and *pincu*, it is clear that he, too, understood it this way. See *Zhouyi zhengyi*, 3: 21a. However, Cheng Yi glosses *pin* as *lü* or *pinshuo*, both of which mean "frequent(ly)" and interprets Third Yin in terms of a frequent gain and loss of the Dao because of indecisiveness and lack of determination. See *Zhouyi zhezhong*, 4: 7a.

10. Kong Yingda comments: "This means that one here manages to stay free of blame because he takes care of himself as far as the Dao is concerned, but if in addition to taking care of himself he also had to deal with additional matters that might come along, then it would be impossible for him to maintain the good fortune of staying free of blame." See *Zhouyi zhengyi*, 3: 21a.

11. Kong Yingda comments: " 'The meaning is such that "there will be no blame" ' is equivalent to 'the meaning here is that it is by maintaining the constant Dao that one manages to be without blame.' " See *Zhouyi zhengyi*, 3: 21a.

无妄

Wuwang [No Errancy][1]
(*Zhen* Below *Qian* Above)

Judgment

Wuwang is such that in its prevalence it is fundamental, and in its constancy it is fitting. But if one is not righteous, it would mean disaster, and it would not be fitting should he set out to do something.

COMMENTARY ON THE JUDGMENTS

Wuwang [No Errancy] is such that the hard and strong comes from without and becomes the ruler within. {This refers to *Zhen* [the lower trigram].[2]} Being dynamic, it is strong. {*Zhen* signifies dynamism, and *Qian* signifies strength.[3]} The hard and strong attains centrality [the Mean] and resonance. {This refers to Fifth Yang [in resonance with Second Yin].} One here attains great prevalence through righteousness, as is the will of Heaven. {As "the hard and strong comes from without and becomes the ruler within," the more the action, the greater the strength. "The hard and strong attains centrality [the Mean] and resonance": awesomely hard and strong and squarely righteous, selfish desire plays no role here, so how could any errancy take place? With the suppression of the dao of errancy, the Dao of No Errancy is achieved, so what could happen here but great prevalence and fitting constancy? When "the hard and strong comes from without and becomes the ruler within," the dao of weakness and wickedness, of course, vanishes. The more the action, the greater the strength, so the Dao of hardness and straightforwardness works smoothly. "The hard and strong attains centrality [the Mean] and resonance," so virtue commensurate with Heaven shines forth. Thus "one here attains great prevalence through righteousness." As this is the declared will of Heaven, how could one possibly disobey? How could one possibly fall into error? This is why "if one is not righteous, it would mean disaster, and it would not be fitting should he set out to do something."} "If one is not righteous, it would mean disaster, and it would not be fitting should he set out to do something": If one were so to set out here in No Errancy, where, indeed, would he go? If one were not blessed by the will of Heaven, would he, indeed, accomplish anything? {If one is not righteous, it would mean disaster": Here one wants to set out to accomplish something without having first tried to alter course and so follow the path of righteousness. Although he dwells at a moment when one must not conduct himself with errancy, he still is going to set out to accomplish something without having first found the path of righteousness—so where is he going to go? How could anyone not blessed by the will of Heaven ever accomplish anything!}

COMMENTARY ON THE IMAGES

Thunder going on everywhere under Heaven: this constitutes the image of all things behaving with No Errancy.[4] {*Yu* [usually "with" or "together with"] here is a function word [grammatical particle] that means the same thing as *jie* [all, in all cases]. Here there is "thunder going on everywhere under Heaven," so it is impossible for anything to behave with errancy.[5]} In the same way, the former kings brought about prosperity, for they nurtured things in accord with the seasons. {*Mao* [lushly growing, lush growth] here means "*sheng*" [prosperity]. Once all things no longer dare to behave with errancy, each of the myriad things can fulfill its nature to perfection. "They nurtured things in accord with the seasons," and nothing can better bring about prosperity than this!}

PROVIDING THE SEQUENCE OF THE HEXAGRAMS

With a return, there is freedom from errancy. This is why *Fu* [Return, Hexagram 24] is followed by *Wuwang* [No Errancy].

THE HEXAGRAMS IN IRREGULAR ORDER

Wuwang [No Errancy] exposes one to calamity.

First Yang

If one has No Errancy here, to set out will result in good fortune. {Here one embodies hardness and strength but occupies the bottom position, filing this humble place with nobility. As this one acts in such a way that he does not fall into errancy, when he sets out, "he will achieve his ambitions."}

COMMENTARY ON THE IMAGES

When one sets out with No Errancy, he will achieve his ambitions.

Second Yin

If one here does not do the plowing but tends only to the reaping and does not develop new land but deals only with mature fields, it would be fitting for him to set out to do something. {To refrain from plowing but tend instead to the reaping and to refrain from developing new land but deal instead with mature fields means to work on behalf of another [the sovereign] to bring a matter to a successful conclusion and to refrain from initiating action oneself.[6] It is by not working for one's own credit that one perfectly realizes the Dao of the minister, and this is why the text here says: "It would be fitting for him to set out to do something."[7]}

COMMENTARY ON THE IMAGES

"One here does not do the plowing but tends only to the reaping," for it is never for his own wealth.[8]

Third Yin

Here calamity associated with No Errancy takes place, for someone has tied up one's ox. It is the traveler's gain and the townsman's calamity. {This involves a yin line occupying a yang position, behavior that is in violation of modesty and obedience, and herein lies the reason why calamity occurs in No Errancy here. An ox is a farmer's asset. In Second Yin "one does not do the plowing but tends only to the reaping," so "it would be fitting for him to set out to do something." However, Third Yin engages in disobedient behavior, so "someone has tied up [his] ox." And this is what is meant by the official enjoying gain and that person suffering loss. Thus the text says: "It is the traveler's gain and the townsman's calamity."[9]}

COMMENTARY ON THE IMAGES

The traveler gains the ox, and this means calamity for the townsman.

Fourth Yang

If one can practice constancy here, he will be without blame. {Located here at this time of No Errancy, we have a yang line occupying a yin position, the hard and strong riding atop the weak [i.e., atop Third Yin], a treading on the territory of the modest and the obedient [its yin position], and contiguity with the most honored one [Fifth Yang, the ruler of the hexagram], therefore it can practice righteousness with all its might and maintain secure control over the position in its charge—and still "be without blame."}

COMMENTARY ON THE IMAGES

It is because Fourth Yang signifies secure control over its position that one can practice constancy here.

Fifth Yang

If an illness strikes the one who practices No Errancy here, let him not resort to medication, for then there will be joy. {By managing to occupy the exalted position, Fifth Yang becomes the ruler of the No Errancy hexagram. Below the ruler, No Errancy holds true for all, so this is not a case of harm reaching the ruler this way. However, if one were to resort to medication to deal with it, the illness would become extremely bad. This is not a calamity brought about by errancy, so one should not take steps to deal with it in order to recover. To resort to medication when it is not a case of errancy will cause misfortune, and this is why the text says: "Let him not resort to medication, for then there will be joy."[10]}

COMMENTARY ON THE IMAGES

Under conditions of No Errancy medicine must not be tried. {One should use medicine to attack illness when there is errancy, but here, on the contrary, it would be used to attack illness when there is No Errancy, so this is why it must not be tried.}

Top Yang

If one were to act here in No Errancy, it would mean disaster, as there is nothing at all fitting here. {Here one is located under the most extreme conditions when one must not engage in errancy, so it is only appropriate to do nothing more than quietly safeguard his own person, and this is why he must not act.}

COMMENTARY ON THE IMAGES

If one were to undertake any action at this stage of No Errancy, he would suffer the disaster of being completely stymied.

NOTES

1. Zhu Xi comments that *Wuwang* is written with the *wang* meaning "hope" or "expectation" in Sima Qian's *Shiji* (Records of the grand historian) and says that the name of this hexagram might also mean "No Expectation" or "The Unexpected." Other earlier commentators have noted this same fact—Ma Rong (79–166), Zheng Xuan (127–200), and Wang Su (195–256), for example. See *Zhouyi zhezhong*, 4: 9b, and the biography of Lord Chunshen (third century B.C.) in *Shiji*, 78: 2397. Kong Yingda glosses *Wuwang* as an absence or avoidance of *zhawei xuwang* "deceitful and false behavior" (*Zhouyi zhengyi*, 3: 21b), so with him it would mean "No Pretension" or "No Fakery."

2. This and all subsequent text set off in this manner is commentary by Wang Bi. Zhu Xi suggests that *Wuwang* ䷘ is a transformation of *Song* ䷅ (Contention) , Hexagram 6—i.e., Second Yang trading places with First Yin (a movement from the outside toward the inside), thereby transforming the lower trigram from *Kan* to *Zhen*. The first yang line is considered the ruler of the lower trigram.

3. Cf. section seven of Explaining the Trigrams: "*Qian* [Pure Yang] means strength and dynamism; . . . *Zhen* [Quake] means energizing."

4. *Zhen* (Thunder, Quake) is the lower trigram, and *Qian* (Pure Yang) is the upper trigram.

5. Kong Yingda comments: " 'Thunder going on everywhere under Heaven': Thunder is a terrifying sound, and here we have 'thunder going on everywhere under Heaven.' The thunder stirs up the myriad things, and, sober with fear, none dares engage in deceitful or false behavior. This is why the text says: 'Thunder going on everywhere under Heaven: this constitutes the image of all things behaving with No Errancy.' " See *Zhouyi zhengyi*, 3: 22b.

6. Cf. Hexagram 2, *Kun* (Pure Yin), Third Yin, Commentary on the Words of the Text: "This is the Dao of Earth, the Dao of the wife, and the Dao of the minister. The Dao of Earth has one 'make no claim for . . . success,' but working on behalf of the other [*Qian*—Pure Yang, i.e., Heaven—husband, sovereign], 'he should bring about a successful conclusion.' "

7. Cheng Yi interprets this line with its agricultural metaphors differently, in terms of "doing things in accordance with the principles involved," "not making things happen before their time," and "not trying to force things to happen as one wants them to happen," and so he seems to understand the first part of Second Yin as: "One does not reap without first plowing, and one does not have a mature field without first clearing." Zhu Xi interprets it differently again:

> Here the compliant and obedient person finds himself in a central and correct position. He acts in accordance with the moment and is obedient to the principle involved, has freed his mind and heart of any selfish desires and expectations, so this is why there is this image of "not doing the plowing for the sake of the harvest, nor doing the clearing for the sake of having a mature field." This means that one should not take purposeful action at the beginning of something nor have expectation at its end.

See *Zhouyi zhezhong*, 4: 10a.

8. "Never for his own wealth" translates *weifu*. Although Wang Bi is silent here and Kong Yingda no help, both Cheng Yi and Zhu Xi interpret it this way, and I think Wang would have had no objection.

9. Lou Yulie, drawing largely on Kong Yingda's subcommentary, interprets Third Yin and Wang's commentary this way: "Here one does something on the order of taking an ox to start to plow up a new field, which is to initiate an activity and so, running up against the prohibition against it, has his plow ox tied up and led away—this is the calamity that this person suffers." See *Wang Bi ji jiaoshi*, 1: 346 n. 12.

10. "Illness" that one does not bring on oneself should not be treated, for it is accidental or brought about by the processes of nature. One should, in effect, wait it out, and health will return of its own accord. The same is true for the true sovereign and his good government—as they are exemplified here; cf. Kong Yingda, *Zhouyi zhengyi*, 3: 24a. Cheng Yi makes the same point; see *Zhouyi zhezhong*, 4: 13b–14a.

HEXAGRAM 26

䷙

大畜

Daxu [Great Domestication][1]
(*Qian* Below *Gen* Above)

Judgment

Daxu is such that in its constancy it is fitting. Not eating at home means good fortune. It is fitting to cross the great river.

COMMENTARY ON THE JUDGMENTS

In *Daxu* [Great Domestication] we find the hard and strong and the sincere and substantial gloriously renewing their virtue with each new day. {Any person who withdraws as soon as he achieves satisfaction is a weak person, and any person who falls as soon as he achieves honor is a person of meager worth, but those capable of "gloriously renewing their virtue with each new day" have to be "the hard and the strong and the sincere and substantial."[2]} By filling the highest position with the hard and strong, one honors the worthy. {This refers to Top Yang. With such a one occupying the top position, everything goes smoothly. Here the hard and strong come, but he [the ruler, Fifth Yin] does not reject such a one, and this is what is meant by "honors the worthy."} It takes great righteousness to be able to check the strong. {Nothing has greater strength than *Qian*, and only great righteousness has ever been able to check it.} "Not eating at home means good fortune," for here the worthy are nurtured. "It is fitting to cross the great river," for one is in resonance with Heaven. {Here assets garnered by Great Domestication are used to nurture the worthy, which frees them from having to eat at home, so this means good fortune. Here one honors the worthy and keeps the strong under check, and with righteousness so great that it resonates with Heaven, one does not have to worry about dangers and difficulties. Thus "it is fitting to cross the great river."}

COMMENTARY ON THE IMAGES

Heaven located within the Mountain: this constitutes the image of Great Domestication.[3] In the same way, the noble man acquires much knowledge of things said and done in the past and so domesticates and garners his own virtue. {It is one's capacity to domesticate and garner things in his bosom that allows him to prevent virtue from becoming dispersed and lost—nothing other than that.}

PROVIDING THE SEQUENCE OF THE HEXAGRAMS

Only when there is no errancy can there be domestication. This is why *Wuwang* [No Errancy, Hexagram 25] is followed by *Daxu* [Great Domestication].

THE HEXAGRAMS IN IRREGULAR ORDER

Daxu [Great Domestication] is a matter of timeliness.

First Yang

Here there is danger, so it is fitting to desist. {It is Fourth Yin that exerts domestic control over [blocks] First Yang, so at First Yang one cannot yet act in defiance. Thus, if one were to advance here, there would be danger, but if one were to desist, it would be fitting.}

COMMENTARY ON THE IMAGES

"Here there is danger, so it is fitting to desist." One should not defy calamity here. {First Yang is located at the first stage in the growth of strength, so it has not yet fully realized its true strength, and this is why it is possible to find desisting here a fitting thing to do.}

Second Yang

The carriage body would be separated from its axle housing.[4] {Fifth Yin is located where domestication is at its strongest, so at Second Yang one cannot yet act in defiance. To advance here under such circumstances would result, as the text says, in "the carriage body" getting "separated from its axle housing." This one manages to abide in centrality [the Mean] here and, because of that centrality, does not become one of "those who wade rivers,"[5] but rather one who would have no regrets even if he had to give up his life. Faced with difficulties, he is still able to hold his ground, thus "there will be no mistake."}

COMMENTARY ON THE IMAGES

"The carriage body would be separated from its axle housing," but if one abides in centrality [the Mean], there will be no mistake.

Third Yang

With fine horses to drive fast in pursuit, it is fitting to practice constancy in the face of difficulties. Even though it be said that there will be attempts to check one's carriage, he will defend himself, so it is fitting to set out to do something. {Whenever something reaches its point of furthest development, it will reverse itself, and this is why when domestication reaches its point of furthest development, there is a breaking out of it. The advance of First Yang and Second Yang was checked by the full power of domestication, thus they could not ascend. But with Third Yang, it ascends to Top Yang, and Top Yang abides in prevalence on the "highway of heaven." This route is such a great thoroughfare[6] that one can advance along it without any hindrance and so can drive at top speed. This is why the text says "with fine horses to drive fast in pursuit." Where Third Yang treads is the right place for it, and its advance occurs just at the right time, so there on its open road it is free from worry about danger or obstruction. Thus "it is fitting to practice constancy in the face of difficulties." *Xian* [train; restrain] here means "*he*" [detain, check, obstruct]. *Wei* [guard] means "*hu*" [defend; take care of oneself]. As one's advance here takes place at the right time, even though he has to cross over dangers and difficulties, no harm will result, and even though one's carriage might meet with attempts to check it, he will manage to defend himself. As Third Yang "shares the same goals as Top Yang," "it is fitting to set out to do something."[7]}

COMMENTARY ON THE IMAGES

"It is fitting to set out to do something," for Third Yang shares the same goals as Top Yang.

Fourth Yin

Here is a horn cover[8] for the young ox, so there is fundamental good fortune. {Fourth Yin is located at the beginning of the *Gen* trigram, and, as it treads on the territory that is right for it [it is a yin line in a yin position], it is able to check strong First Yang. However, the checking is not done with horns; Fourth Yin checks the hard and strong one with its compliancy and yielding. Here hard and strong First Yang does not dare defy Fourth Yin, and this is the start of warding off its sharp thrusts. As this prevents a violent struggle, how could it just be a matter of being "fitting"? In fact, "there will be joy."}

COMMENTARY ON THE IMAGES

Fourth Yin means "fundamental good fortune," so there will be joy.

Fifth Yin

Here one removes the boar's tusks, so there is good fortune. {The boar's tusks are wickedly and crookedly crossed, and it is an impetuous and vicious animal that is impossible to control. Here it refers to Second Yang. Fifth Yin has obtained the exalted position and has become the ruler of Great Domestication. Second Yang advances with its hardness and strength, but Fifth Yin is able to remove its tusks,[9] so the yielding and compliant manages to control the strong, nullifying its viciousness and preventing the growth of its power. How could this just be a matter of making its position secure? In fact, "there will be blessings."}

COMMENTARY ON THE IMAGES

The good fortune associated with Fifth Yin is such that there will be blessings.

Top Yang

What is the Highway of Heaven but prevalence! {Top Yang is located at the very furthest point in domestication, and when domestication reaches this, its furthest, point, there is a breakthrough, so now one arrives at the place in Great Domestication where there is great prevalence. "What" [*he*] is a function word [grammatical particle], and this line means: "What domestication there is, now that there is such prevalence here on the Highway of Heaven!"[10]}

COMMENTARY ON THE IMAGES

What could take place here on the Highway of Heaven other than moving with all grandeur in the Dao!

NOTES

1. For an explanation of *xu* as "domestication," see Hexagram 9, *Xiaoxu* (Lesser Domestication), note 1.

2. This and all subsequent text set off in this manner is commentary by Wang Bi.

3. The lower trigram, *Qian* (Pure Yang), also Heaven, is located below—i.e., "within" or "inside"—the upper trigram *Gen* (Mountain, Restraint).

4. Cf. Hexagram 9, *Xiaoxu* (Lesser Domestication), Third Yang.

5. See Hexagram 11, *Tai* (Peace), Second Yang.

6. See section three of part one of Providing the Sequence of the Hexagrams, as well as note 4 there.

7. Wang Bi's interpretation of Third Yang is supported by Kong Yingda's subcommentary (see *Zhouyi zhengyi*, 3: 26a–26b), but Cheng Yi and Zhu Xi interpret some of it differently. The part in question is read by Wang and Kong as *yue xian yu wei* (literally, say check carriage, one will defend), but by Cheng and Zhu as *ri xian yu wei* (daily practice/train carriage [driving] and guarding); see *Zhouyi zhezhong*, 4: 16b–17a. The graphs of *yue* (say) and *ri* (day/daily) are similar, and the basic meanings of *xian* (restrain; train) admit both possibilities—indeed, in some respects, *xian* has the same range of meaning as *xu* (domesticate, block).

8. "Horn cover" translates *gu*, a wooden guard placed over the point of each horn to prevent beasts from causing injury. See Cheng Yi's and Zhu Xi's remarks in *Zhouyi zhezhong*, 4: 17a–17b.

9. "Remove its tusks" translates *fen qi ya*. There is a great deal of controversy over what *fen* means here. Kong Yingda first examines the possi-

bility that *fen* means *jinzhi* (ban) or *sunqu* (cut down/away) and then rejects this in favor of *fangzhi* (ward off). See *Zhouyi zhengyi*, 3: 26b. See also *Wang Bi ji jiaoshi*, 1: 351 n. 14, where, among other possibilities, Lou points out that *fen*'s first meaning is "to geld an animal." This, in fact, is how Cheng Yi interprets it; see *Zhouyi zhezhong*, 4: 18a. Cheng would have read the text of Fifth Yin as *fenshi zhi ya* (the tusks of a gelded boar), whereas Wang apparently read it as *fen shi zhi ya* (remove the boar's tusks, or, as Kong understood it, ward off the boar's tusks). In Cheng's favor is the fact that his parsing of Fifth Yin parallels the only possible parsing of Fourth Yin, *tongniu zhi gu* (a horn cover for/of the young ox), something that Wang and Kong must have noticed but apparently rejected.

10. Kong Yingda's subcommentary supports Wang's interpretation of Top Yang; however, both Cheng Yi and Zhu Xi gloss it differently. Cheng addresses Top Yang in terms of the Commentary on the Images: " 'Highway of Heaven' is not a common expression, thus the Commentary on the Images makes a point of asking the question 'What could take place here on the Highway of Heaven' and then, by answering that it is 'moving with all grandeur in the Dao,' choosing something that seems infinitely expansive." The "what" *he*) in the Commentary on the Images, according to Cheng, wrongly got into the text of Top Yang and should be ignored. See *Zhouyi zhezhong*, 4: 18b and 11: 62b. So Cheng would read Top Yang as "The Highway of Heaven means prevalence" or "Here is prevalence worthy of the Highway of Heaven." Zhu Xi interprets *he* as a rhetorical particle, "How very open and free it [the Highway of Heaven] is!" See *Zhouyi zhezhong*, 4: 18b.

䷚

頤

Yi [Nourishment]
(*Zhen* Below *Gen* Above)

Judgment

Yi is such that constancy here means good fortune. Observe his nourishing and how he seeks to fill his own mouth.

COMMENTARY ON THE JUDGMENTS

"*Yi* [Nourishment] is such that constancy here means good fortune," for when Nourishment is correct, there will be good fortune. "Observe his nourishing" means "observe the nourishing [of others] that he does," and "[observe] how he seeks to fill his own mouth" means "observe how he nourishes himself." As Heaven and Earth nourish the myriad things, so the sage nourishes the worthy and thereby extends this nourishing to the countless common folk. A time of Nourishment is indeed great!

COMMENTARY ON THE IMAGES

Thunder going on under the Mountain: this constitutes the image of Nourishment.[1] In the same way, the noble man is careful with his language and practices restraint in his use of food and drink.[2] {As the noble man is even careful about the way he uses language and even practices restraint with food and drink, how much the more careful and restrained should he be about everything else![3]}

PROVIDING THE SEQUENCE OF THE HEXAGRAMS

Only after things have been domesticated can Nourishment be had. This is why *Daxu* [Great Domestication, Hexagram 26] is followed by *Yi* [Nourishment].

THE HEXAGRAMS IN IRREGULAR ORDER

Yi [Nourishment] means "the nurturing of correctness."

First Yang

You set aside your numinous tortoise shell and watch me move my jaw instead: this means misfortune. {"Move my jaw" means "chew food." Here a yang line occupies a subordinate position yet is the initiator of action. As such, it represents someone who is incapable of letting others get Nourishment from him, and when he takes action here, it is just to seek his own Nourishment. To ensure one's own safety, nothing is more important than refraining from contention, and for cultivating oneself, nothing is more important than self-preservation. If one keeps to the Dao, blessings will arrive, but if he seeks emolument for its own sake, disgrace will come instead. This one dwells in a world where one nourishes the worthy, yet he cannot practice constancy in the place where he treads and thereby perfect his virtue. Instead, he sets aside the obvious omen offered by his numinous tortoise shell, grows envious of the way I move my jaw, and so acts to satisfy his own desires. Thus he separates himself from the highest Dao and the route it offers to the best possible Nourishment. He stealthily keeps watch on the salary with which I am honored and contends for advancement, so he will suffer the worst possible misfortune.[4]}

COMMENTARY ON THE IMAGES

"You . . . watch me move my jaw": such a one certainly is not worth esteem.[5]

Second Yin

This one reverses the Nourishment process and so goes off the right path to the hill. If one practices Nourishment in this way and sets forth, there will be misfortune. {To provide Nourishment to one below is what is meant here by "reverses." *Fu* [be contrary, go off] here means "*wei*" [violate]; *jing* [warp in a fabric; by extension, immutable rule/right path] means the same thing as *yi* [moral principle]; and *qiu* [hill] signifies the place where this one should always tread [i.e., Second Yin should direct its efforts upward]. Second Yin occupies the central position in the lower trigram but is not in resonance with [Fifth Yin] above [two yin lines do not resonate], so instead it turns around and nourishes First Yang. Here is someone who, although dwelling below, does not serve and support the one above but instead nourishes someone below him. Thus the text says: "This one reverses the Nourishment process and so goes off the right path to the hill." If one provides Nourishment in this way, he will never see any blessings come of it. And if he acts in this way, he will never win any approval for it. Thus the text says: "If one practices Nourishment in this way and sets forth, there will be misfortune."[6]}

COMMENTARY ON THE IMAGES

It will mean misfortune if Second Yin sets forth, for such action will be in violation of the principles of its kind. {Its kind [i.e., yin] in all cases should provide Nourishment to those above, yet here Second Yin directs Nourishment below to First Yang.}

Third Yin

This one practices Nourishment in a contrary way, so even constancy here will mean misfortune, and he will have no employment for ten years, for nothing at all would be fitting. {Where Third Yang treads is not correct for it [because it is a yin line in a yang position], so Nourishment directed upward here is such that its provision to a superior becomes a form of sycophancy. As this is contrary to the correct principle of Nourishment, the text says: "This one practices Nourishment in a contrary way, so constancy here will mean misfortune." If one persists in behaving this way while so located in Nourishment, he will suffer rejection for ten years. If one decides to act in this way, "nothing at all would be fitting."}

COMMENTARY ON THE IMAGES

"No employment for ten years," for the Dao has been greatly violated.[7]

Fourth Yin

To reverse the Nourishment process here means good fortune. Such a one should stare down with the ferocious look of a tiger, and his will should be strong and persistent, for then he will be without blame. {In substance Fourth Yin belongs to the upper trigram, and it manages to dwell in a place proper for it [as a yin line in a yin position]; moreover it is in resonance with First Yang. This one above nourishes one below in such a way that Nourishment is provided in a correct, moral way. Thus the text says: "To reverse the Nourishment process here means good fortune." When one establishes a relationship with someone below him, he must not suffer disrespect. Thus "such a one should stare down with the ferocious look of a tiger," for he should inspire awe without being vicious, be stern without being cruel. Fourth Yin nourishes its own virtue and provides for the worthy, so how could there be any personal profit involved? Thus one's "will should be strong and persistent," for seriousness and dependability are to be esteemed. Only with the cultivation of these two traits [strength and persistence] will one manage to realize complete good fortune and be without blame. When one observes how this one nourishes himself, one sees that he treads the way of righteousness, and when one examines whom he nourishes, one sees that he nourishes the yang [i.e., the worthy and the positive]. Of all the lines in the *Yi* [Nourishment] hexagram, this one is the greatest.}

COMMENTARY ON THE IMAGES

"To reverse the Nourishment process here means good fortune," for the way this one above [Fourth Yin] provides is glorious.[8]

Fifth Yin

Here one goes off the right path, so to abide instead in constancy will mean good fortune. One must not cross the great river. {As this is a yin line that occupies a yang position, it signifies a violation of the principle of Nourishment. If such a one takes action here, it will be in violation of the principles of its kind [yin should be passive]. This is why it is appropriate for Fifth Yin to "abide in constancy." Fifth Yin has no line to resonate with in the lower trigram, but it is contiguous to Top Yang. Thus it is able to maintain its constancy in following Top Yang and so obtain good fortune here at a time of Nourishment. However, although it obtains this good fortune, its position here is an affront to modesty, so it could never cross over difficulties on its own.}

COMMENTARY ON THE IMAGES

That there is good fortune here associated with "abiding in constancy" is because Fifth Yin is obedient and so follows Top Yang.

Top Yang

They depend on this one for Nourishment. Severity will bring good fortune. It is fitting to cross the great river. {Here a yang line occupies the top position and treads on the four yin lines below. Fifth Yin cannot be the ruler just on its own, so homage must be paid to Top Yang [as the de facto ruler]. Thus none fail to depend on Top Yang in order to obtain Nourishment, and this is why the text says: "They depend on this one for Nourishment." As the ruler of all the yin lines, Top Yang must not suffer disrespect. Thus "severity will bring good fortune."}

COMMENTARY ON THE IMAGES

"They depend on this one for Nourishment. Severity will bring good fortune." So there will be blessings in great measure.

NOTES

1. *Zhen* (Thunder) is the lower trigram, and *Gen* (Mountain) is the upper trigram.

2. Although neither Wang Bi nor Kong Yingda interpret the image in terms of it, both Cheng Yi and Zhu Xi derive "Nourishment" from the basic meaning of *yi* as "jaw(s)." The hexagram consists of four yin lines bounded by one yang line at the top and one at the bottom—just as the hard teeth of the upper and lower jaw frame the empty mouth (filled with something "soft"). The upper jaw does not move (Mountain), but the lower one does (Thunder, i.e., movement). The noble man is careful about how he uses his jaws—either in speaking or in eating and drinking. See *Zhouyi zhezhong*, 4: 20b and 11: 62b. It should be pointed out, of course, that Wang

and Kong deal with Nourishment in terms of jaw(s) in their commentaries to First Yang.

3. This and all subsequent text set off in this manner is commentary by Wang Bi.

4. Cheng Yi and Zhu Xi interpret First Yang very differently. Cheng's is the more elaborate gloss:

> "Your" refers to First Yang: "You set aside your numinous tortoise and then, upon observing me, you drop your jaw. "Me" is used here in opposition to "you." The one that First Yang drops its jaw over is Fourth Yin. . . . A yang line embodies hardness and brightness, and it signifies the presence of enough talent and intelligence to nurture righteousness. The tortoise can breathe, but it does not eat. 'Numinous tortoise" serves as a metaphor for one's intelligence, the use of which frees one from having to seek Nourishment elsewhere. Although such a one has such talents, it is still a yang entity that dwells in a trigram that embodies activity [Thunder]—and this during a time of Nourishment. To seek Nourishment is something that a person desires to do. This one is in resonance with Fourth Yin. It is unable to look after itself here and instead has its ambitions fixed on moving upward. It takes delight in what it desires and so drops its jaw. With the heart and mind already moved in this way, it is certain that such a one will perish: befuddled by desire, he will lose himself. When a yang follows a yin, where will such a one not go? And this is how misfortune here comes about. "Drop the jaw" means "to drop or move the jaw or chin." When someone sees something to eat and wants it, he moves his jaw and drools—thus there is this image here.

See *Zhouyi zhezhong*, 4: 21a–21b.

5. Cheng Yi parses the text differently—"You watch me and drop your jaw"—to fit with his interpretation of First Yang. See *Zhouyi zhezhong*, 11: 63b.

6. Kong Yingda supports Wang's commentary here (see *Zhouyi zhengyi*, 3: 28b), but both Cheng Yi and Zhu Xi interpret Second Yin very differently, as they construe *yi* (nourishment) in its verbal form not as "provide nourishment" but as "get nourishment." Although Cheng's commentary is quite elaborate, most of its essentials are covered by Zhu's much briefer gloss:

> Here Second Yin seeks nourishment from First Yang. This is to turn things upside down and be in violation of the constant principle involved [as Cheng says, "those above nourish those below: this is correct in terms of principle"]. But to seek nourishment from above would result in misfortune when it sets forth to get it. A "hill" is a place where the earth is high, and here it serves as an image of "above."

Cheng adds that Top Yang, the only other yang line in the hexagram, is too far above for Second Yin to seek nourishment from it—that is why it would suffer misfortune if it tried to do so. See *Zhouyi zhezhong*, 4: 22b. Cheng and Zhu's interpretations of the Commentary on the Images to Second Yin also differ accordingly, as do their glosses on subsequent passages in the texts connected with this hexagram.

7. Cheng Yi and Zhu Xi say similar things in their commentaries, except that they are construed in terms of getting rather than giving Nourishment. See *Zhouyi zhezhong*. 3: 24b.

8. Following the gloss of Kong Yingda; see *Zhouyi zhengyi*, 3: 29a.

HEXAGRAM 28

大過

Daguo [Major Superiority]

(*Sun* Below *Dui* Above)

Judgment

Major Superiority is such that when the ridgepole sags, it is fitting to set out to do something, for this will result in prevalence.[1]

COMMENTARY ON THE JUDGMENTS

Major Superiority {*Guo* [superiority] should be read as the *guo* in *xiangguo* [surpass the other(s)].[2]} means that with a state of majority [greatness], superiority results. {It is only with majority [greatness] that one can attain superiority.} "The ridgepole sags," for the beginning and the end are weak. {First Yin represents the beginning, and Top Yin represents the end.} Here hardness and strength may be superior [i.e., "too strong"] but still stay within the Mean. {This refers to Second Yang.[3] As this one abides in a yin position, it is superior [to that position], but as it occupies the second position, it is central [abides in the Mean].} Here in a situation fraught with vicissitude, it saves the ridgepole from sinking—yet does not violate the Mean. As Compliance [*Sun*] and Joy [*Dui*] are at work here, {"Compliance [the lower trigram] and Joy [the upper trigram] are at work here," so if one uses them to rescue a difficult situation, that situation will surely be saved.} "it is fitting to set out to do something, for this will result in prevalence." {If when such danger occurs one does not offer his support, of what use would he possibly be? This is why setting out here will result in prevalence.} A time of Major Superiority is indeed great! {This means that it is a time for the noble man to take action.}

COMMENTARY ON THE IMAGES

The Lake submerges the Tree: this constitutes the image of Major Superiority.[4] In the same way, though the noble man may stand alone, he does so without fear, and, if he has to withdraw from the world, he remains free from resentment. {This is how Major Superiority is constituted, something to which the ordinary cannot attain.[5]}

COMMENTARY ON THE APPENDED PHRASES

In antiquity, for burying the dead, people wrapped them thickly with firewood and buried them out in the wilds, where they neither made grave mounds nor planted trees. For the period of mourning there was no definite amount of time. The sages of later ages had this exchanged for inner and outer coffins. They probably got the idea for this from the hexagram *Daguo* [Major Superiority].[6]

PROVIDING THE SEQUENCE OF THE HEXAGRAMS

If there is no nourishment, there can be no action. This is why *Yi* [Nourishment, Hexagram 27]is followed by *Daguo* [Major Superiority].

THE HEXAGRAMS IN IRREGULAR ORDER

In *Daguo* [Major Superiority], collapse is inherent.

First Yin

Use white rushes for a mat, and one will be without blame. {This bottom position is occupied by the soft and yielding. Can anything other than cautious and prudent behavior serve to keep one free of blame here at this time of superiority?}

COMMENTARY ON THE APPENDED PHRASES

The Master said: "Even if one were to place things on the ground, it would indeed still be permissible, so if one were to provide matting for it with rushes, how could there possibly be any blame attached to that! This is the extreme of caution. As things, rushes are insignificant, but their use can be very significant. If one makes caution a technique of this order and subsequently sets out to deal with things, such a one will never experience loss!"[7]

COMMENTARY ON THE IMAGES

"Use white rushes for a mat": something soft and yielding will be at the bottom.

Second Yang

A withered poplar puts forth new shoots. An old man gets a young wife for himself. Nothing done here fails to be fitting. {*Ti* [put forth new shoots from an old stem] here refers to the burgeoning [*xiu*] of the poplar. In Second Yang, a yang line occupies a yin position, so such a one can rise superior to his basic nature and save the ridgepole from sinking. Though there is no line in the upper trigram with which Second Yang can resonate [because there is a yang line in the fifth position], this one on his own keeps his heart free of any mean-spiritedness. To be situated in superiority and yet behave in this way means that no decline cannot be arrested. This is why its is possible here to have a withered poplar again put forth new shoots and an old man again get a young wife. As no line is more powerful than this one when it comes to saving the ridgepole from sinking at this time fraught with vicissitude, "nothing done here fails to be fitting." When something is too old, it withers, and when something is too young, it is immature, but if one takes what is too old and gives a part of it to what is too young, then the immature will mature, and if one takes what is too young and gives a part of it to what is too old, then the withered will flourish. This is what is meant by "tak[ing] what is too much on each side and shar[ing] it."[8] Here Major Superiority is at its weakest point, and yet Second Yang is something at its greatest strength, so when it uses this greatest strength to shore up things at this, the weakest, point, it is acting in accordance with the above concept.}

COMMENTARY ON THE IMAGES

An old man and a young wife take what is too much on each side and share it.[9]

Third Yang

The ridgepole sags, and this means misfortune. {Third Yang located here at a time of Major Superiority occupies the very top of the lower trigram and, as such, cannot keep the ridgepole high and so save a dangerous situation and prevent it from sinking. Instead, because it is a yang line occupying a yang position, it does manage to hold on to its own place, and, because it is in resonance with Top Yin, its heart and mind is committed there and nowhere else. Proper it is that the ridgepole sinks down here and that a decline fraught with misfortune occurs.}

COMMENTARY ON THE IMAGES

Misfortune connected with the ridgepole sagging here occurs because nothing can be had to shore it up.

Fourth Yang

The ridgepole is kept high, and this means good fortune, but there will be regret if there are ulterior motives. {Fourth Yang forms part of the upper trigram, and, as a yang line that occupies a yin position, is able to save the ridgepole from sinking and being bent down by the line below . This is why the text says: "The ridgepole is kept high, and this means good fortune." However, as Fourth Yang is in resonance with First Yin, it does not have a widespread commitment of mind and heart, and this is why the text says: "There will be regret if there are ulterior motives."}

COMMENTARY ON THE IMAGES

Good fortune connected with the ridgepole being kept high occurs because it is not made to sag by what is below.

Fifth Yang

A withered poplar puts forth blossoms. An old woman gets a young husband for herself. There is no blame, but there is no praise either. {Fifth Yang manages to occupy the exalted position, but because it is a yang line in a yang position, it can never save the ridgepole from danger. However, as it does occupy the exalted position, it also never lets the ridgepole sag down. And this is why blossoms can be put forth here but it is impossible to put forth new shoots, why it is possible to get a husband but impossible to get a wife. Here one is situated at a time when the ridgepole sags and behaves in such a way that "there is no blame, but there is no praise either," so how indeed could one long endure? This is why the blossoms put forth will not last long and a young husband here is really a disgrace.}

COMMENTARY ON THE IMAGES

"A withered poplar puts forth blossoms," but how could they last long, and "an old woman gets a young husband for herself," but how disgraceful that is!

Top Yin

If one tries to ford across here, he will submerge his head, and there will be misfortune, but there will be no blame. {Top Yin is located at the very top of Major Superiority, where superiority [the passage][10] is at its most difficult. To try to ford difficulties here where the passage is at its deepest inevitably would end in submerging one's head, and this means misfortune. However, as this one's ambition is fixed on saving the times, there cannot be any blame attached to him.}

COMMENTARY ON THE IMAGES

Although there is misfortune connected with trying to ford across here, one cannot be blamed for doing it. {Although there is misfortune, there is no blame, for such a one does no harm to righteousness.}

NOTES

1. See Wang's remarks on this hexagram in section seven of his General Remarks.

2. I.e., it should be read in the oblique falling tone and not in the level tone, in which case it would mean "mistake," "error," "crime," etc. See Lou, *Wang Bi ji jiaoshi*, 1: 359 n. 1. Note that this and all subsequent text set off in this manner is commentary by Wang Bi.

3. Cheng Yi thinks that it refers to both Second Yang and Fifth Yang, the two yang lines in central yin positions, where the Dao of the Mean prevails. See *Zhouyi zhezhong*, 9: 45a.

4. The lower trigram, *Sun* (Compliance), represents wood, and the upper trigram, *Dui* (Joy), is also called "Lake." See sections three and eleven of Explaining the Trigrams.

5. Kong Yingda expands upon Wang's commentary:

> There is no principle by which a lake would ordinarily submerge a tree, so here, when the text says that "the Lake submerges the Tree," it means that the Lake has grown to such an extreme size that it actually does submerge the Tree; this expresses the concept that something has the greatest superiority over something else. In *Daguo* [Major Superiority] there are two meanings. One refers to the natural world where something rises superior to its ordinary condition, as here where the Lake submerges the Tree, and the other refers to the great man who, by rising above the common run of humanity, manages to save difficult situations.

See *Zhouyi zhengyi*, 3: 30b.

6. See section two of the Commentary on the Appended Phrases, Part Two. The four unbroken lines in the middle of *Daguo* (Major Superiority) and the top and bottom broken lines are supposed to suggest the *hard* (solid) coffins surrounded by *soft* (loose) earth.

7. See section eight of the Commentary on the Appended Phrases, Part One.

8. "Too old" translates *laoguo*, and "too young" translates *shaoguo*. In both cases, the *guo* is the same as that in "Superiority." Wang here exploits the range of meaning in *guo*—"superior(ity)" on the one hand and "excessive(ness)" on the other—to explicate the text.

9. The commentaries of Cheng Yi and Zhu Xi instead emphasize that the strength derived from the bonding of Second Yang (the old man) and

First Yin (the young wife) is the result of how each rises "superior" to his or her situation, not due to the balancing of excesses. Their interpretation of the Commentary on the Images would therefore be something like: "An old man and a young wife provide for each other thanks to their respective superiority." They also emphasize the analogous relationship of the two constituent trigrams: *Sun* (Compliance) for the young wife and *Dui* (Joy) for the old man. See *Zhouyi zhezhong*, 4: 26b–27a and 11: 65b.

10. "Superiority" (*guo*) in the sense that one is superior to a distance—one can conquer a route, a passage—i.e., one can "cross over" (*guo*).

HEXAGRAM 29

䷜

習坎

Xikan [The Constant Sink Hole]
(*Kan* Below *Kan* Above)

Judgment

The Constant Sink Hole {"Sink hole" is the name for a dangerous pit, and "constant" refers to practicing something constantly.[1]} is such that if there is sincerity, then the heart and mind should prevail, {Hard and strong lines are correctly positioned inside [in the second and fifth places], so there is sincerity here. When the yang force is not expressed externally but stays within, this signifies a prevalence of heart and mind.} and one's actions will enjoy esteem. {Within there is prevalence, but one keeps this hidden from without; within there is hardness and strength, but one shows obedience and compliance without. If one faces danger in this way, "one's actions will enjoy esteem."}

COMMENTARY ON THE JUDGMENTS

The Constant Sink Hole signifies multiple dangers. {The Sink Hole serves to express danger, so this is why it is especially described in terms of "multiple dangers." The fact that it is called "The Constant Sink Hole" is due to its constant involvement with multiple dangers. As water flows in but does not fill it up, so one faces danger but does not violate his trust. Here there is an extreme of dangerous steepness, and this is why water flows but cannot fill it up. Though one is located in extreme danger, he does not neglect his strength and centrality, and though he faces such danger, he does not violate his trust: this is what "The Constant Sink Hole" means.} The reason "the heart and mind should prevail" is that one fills one's middle with hardness and strength, and the reason "one's actions will enjoy esteem" is that when one sets forth, he achieves merit. {One constantly practices [*xi*] how to deal with the Sink Hole, so when one goes to the land of the Sink Hole, he will be able to use every advantage against it, and this is why "when one sets forth," surely "he achieves merit." The strategic condition [literally, "danger"] of Heaven consists of there being no way to climb up to it, It is because one cannot manage to climb up to it that Heaven preserves its exalted majesty.} and strategic conditions on Earth consist of mountains, rivers, hills, and high ground. {If people have mountains, rivers, hills, and high ground, they can preserve their integrity.} Kings and dukes provide themselves with strategic conditions in order to protect their states. {States rely on strategic conditions to protect themselves. The conclusion is that from Heaven and Earth on down nothing can do without strategic conditions.} When the time comes for strategic conditions to play their role, their usefulness is indeed great! {It is not a matter of using them on a regular basis, but their use comes into play when the time demands it.}

COMMENTARY ON THE IMAGES

Water keeps coming on: this constitutes the image of the Constant Sink Hole.[2] In the same way, the noble man consistently practices virtuous conduct and constantly engages in moral transformation {With extreme danger unrelieved, moral transformation must not be neglected. This is why the text says: "Consistently practice . . . virtuous conduct and constantly engage . . . in moral transformation." Only when one is constantly practiced in how to deal with the Sink Hole will he manage to avoid being brought to grief by perilous situations and also remain constant in virtuous conduct. This is why the noble man takes the Constant Sink Hole as his model, for in so doing he "consistently practices virtuous conduct and constantly engages in moral transformation."}

PROVIDING THE SEQUENCE OF THE HEXAGRAMS

One cannot stay forever in a state of superiority. This is why *Daguo* [Major Superiority, Hexagram 28] is followed by *Kan* [Sink Hole]. *Kan* here indicates a pit.

THE HEXAGRAMS IN IRREGULAR ORDER

Li [Cohesion, Hexagram 30] signifies ascent, and *Kan* [Sink Hole] signifies descent.

First Yin

Here in the Constant Sink Hole one falls into the drain hole at the bottom, and this means misfortune. {The Constant Sink Hole signifies matters that are constantly perilous. To be located here at First Yin at the very bottom of the Sink Hole means that one has entered its drain hole. In addition to being located in the midst of multiple dangers, one here also enters the very bottom of the Sink Hole: this is a path fraught with misfortune. In such danger yet unable to save oneself, in the Sink Hole to begin with and then fallen into its very drain hole: this indicates someone who has lost the Dao [i.e., "his way"] and now lies exhausted at the bottom of the Sink Hole. There is no one above to resonate with [because there is a yin line in the fourth position] and who might help, thereby allowing one to save himself, and this is why there is misfortune.}

COMMENTARY ON THE IMAGES

Here at the Constant Sink Hole one falls into it, and to have so lost the Dao [one's way] means misfortune.

Second Yang

Here in the Sink Hole, where there is danger, one may only strive for small attainments. {Where Second Yang treads is out of its rightful place [it is a yang line in a yin position.], and this is why the text says "in the Sink Hole." There is no one above to resonate with [i.e., no responsive line in the upper trigram] and who might help, so it says: "There is danger." To be in danger at the Sink Hole signifies that this one is not yet able to extricate himself from danger. As Second Yang stays within the Mean [i.e., it is located in the middle position of the lower trigram] and as it gets on well with First Yin and Third Yin, so it can "strive for small attainments." But First Yin and Third Yin lack the wherewithal to be of help to Second Yang, and this is why the text says "small attainments."}

COMMENTARY ON THE IMAGES

"This one may strive for small attainments" but has not yet found his way out from inside [of the Sink Hole and danger].

Third Yin

Whether one comes or goes, there is a Sink Hole before him. In danger and stuck here too, it would not do to fall down the Sink Hole drain. {Not only does Third Yin tread on a place that is not its rightful position [it is in a yang position], it also is located at the juncture of the two Sink Holes. To set out would result in going to the one Sink Hole, but to stay would mean the other. This is why the text says: "Whether one comes or goes, there is a Sink Hole before him." *Zhen* [usually "headrest," "pillow"] here means to be "stuck" or "bogged down"[*zhenzhi*] in a precarious position.[3] One might set out, but there is nowhere to go. He might stay put, but no place offers security. This is why the text says: "In danger and stuck here too." "Whether one comes or goes," there is a Sink Hole in either case. Neither course of action can be employed here, for both would result in nothing but futile effort.}

COMMENTARY ON THE IMAGES

"Whether one comes or goes, there is a Sink Hole before him," so in the end there can be no meritorious outcome.

Fourth Yin

For a cup of wine and food bowls two, use plain earthenware. Provide this frugal fare through the window, and in the end there will be no blame. {Fourth Yin may be located amid multiple dangers, but its tread is correct. As a weak line in a weak position, it manages to tread on its rightful place, and in so doing it carries Fifth Yang. Fifth Yang also obtains its rightful place [because it is a yang line in a yang position]. Here a strong and a weak line each obtain their rightful places, so there is no question of mutually incompatible positions. Neither line is in resonance with any of the remaining lines, so here they fulfill this carrying and contiguous relationship. Expression of bright sincerity here has nothing to do with external ornamentation. Located in the Sink Hole under such circumstances, although Fourth Yin repays [the sovereign, Fifth Yang] with one cup of wine and two bowls of food, it is earthenware vessels that provide such extremely plain fare, and they are handed in through the window.[4] As such, they are worthy of presentation to princes or nobles and of offering at ancestral temple sacrifices. This is why the text says: "In the end there will be no blame."}

COMMENTARY ON THE IMAGES

"A cup of wine and food bowls two" signify the affiliation of the hard and the soft [or strong and weak—Fourth Yin and Fifth Yang].

Fifth Yang

The Sink Hole is not filled up, but here only when one is level with the top will there be no blame. {Fifth Yang is the ruler of the Sink Hole hexagram, but as it has no resonate supporting line from which it can get help for itself, it never is able to fill up the Sink Hole, and, as the Sink Hole does not get filled up, there is no end to the danger. *Zhi* [here] is a modal particle.[5] To be the ruler of the Sink Hole, one can be without blame only if he rises completely even with the top. This is why the text says: "Here only when one is level with the top will there be no blame." This means that only once one is level with the top will he escape blame, so it is obvious that Fifth Yang never manages to avoid blame here.[6]}

COMMENTARY ON THE IMAGES

"The Sink Hole is not filled up": because what is in the middle [the ruler] is not great enough.

Top Yin

Here it is as if for bonds two- and three-ply cords were used or as if one were put inside a bramble wall stockade. Such a one is not successful for three years, which means misfortune. {Here severe danger is at its highest point and can go no higher. As with the strictest of laws and the most rigorous of corrective measures, it is impossible to go against it. Proper it is that when one is arrested, he be put in a place to think over the error of his ways. Three years is the time for such danger to run its course, and when the danger has come to an end, the situation is reversed. This is why one here is unsuccessful for three years. But if one cultivates himself for these three years, he can thereby seek rehabilitation [literally, a "return"]. Thus the text says: "Such a one is not successful for three years, which means misfortune."}

COMMENTARY ON THE IMAGES

Top Yin has lost the Dao, so his misfortune will last three years.

NOTES

1. This and all subsequent text set off in this manner is commentary by Wang Bi. Kong Yingda notes:

> As Sink Hole represents great danger, the term *constant* [*xi*] is added to its name. *Xi* has two meanings here. In one sense it means repetitive, or "double," and as such refers to the fact that both the upper and the lower trigrams are *Kan* [Sink Hole], so "constant" here describes how dangerous it is—that is, what a multiplicity of danger is involved. In another sense, it refers to the fact than when someone is going to undertake something dangerous, he must first constantly practice how to deal with such matters, for only then might he be successful. And this too is why the term *constant* is used here.

See *Zhouyi zhengyi*, 3: 33a.

Note, however, that the hexagram is often referred to in the commentaries both as *Xikan* (Constant Sink Hole) and as simply *Kan* (Sink Hole).

2. *Kan* (Sink Hole, Water) is both the lower and the upper trigram.

3. This is Lou Yulie's gloss; see *Wang Bi ji jiaoshi*, 1: 367 n. 20.

4. Zhu Xi notes that a window is to let in light, and Cheng Yi adds to this the idea that a window allows for free passage: in spite of perilous times, there is enlightened and facile communication between minister and sovereign. See *Zhouyi zhezhong*, 4: 35b–36a.

5. See Hexagram 24, *Fu* (Return), note 8.

6. Cheng Yi follows Wang's interpretation here, but Zhu Xi reads it differently: "Although Fifth Yang is in the Sink Hole, because it is strong and central and because it has obtained the noble position, it will get out in a short time [and be without blame]." See *Zhouyi zhezhong*, 4: 37a–37b.

HEXAGRAM 30

䷝

離

Li [Cohesion]
(*Li* Below *Li* Above)

Judgment

Cohesion is such that it is fitting to practice constancy, for then it will result in prevalence. {The way Cohesion is constituted as a hexagram means that rectitude is expressed by the soft and yielding [yin] lines, and this is why one here must practice constancy first, for only then will prevalence be had. Thus the text says: "It is fitting to practice constancy, for then it will result in prevalence."[1]} To rear a cow will mean good fortune. {A soft and yielding line is located in the inner [lower] trigram and treads the path of rectitude and centrality [i.e., it is in the central position]. This signifies the goodness of the cow. To be strong on the outside yet obedient on the inside constitutes the goodness of the cow. The way Cohesion is constituted as a hexagram means that it makes the soft and yielding its ruler [Fifth Yin]. This is why one must not rear hard and fierce things here and why it is good fortune to rear a cow.}

COMMENTARY ON THE JUDGMENTS

Cohesion [*Li*] means "to cling" [*li*] {*Li* [cling] is similar to *zhu* [touch, be attached to], in the sense that each thing manages to find what is right for it to attach itself to.} The sun and the moon cohere to Heaven. Grain plants, shrubs, and trees cohere to Earth. By cohering to rectitude these double bright ones [the two constituent trigrams, *Li* (Fire, Cohesion)] transform and bring everything in the world to perfection. The soft and yielding [the yin lines] cohere to centrality and correctness, and so prevalence is had. And this is why "to rear a cow will mean good fortune." {It is when the soft and yielding adhere to centrality and correctness that things can go smoothly. The good fortune associated with such things going smoothly is at its very highest in the rearing of a cow, but it cannot include anything hard or fierce.}

COMMENTARY ON THE IMAGES

The bright ones act as a pair: this constitutes the image of Cohesion. In the same way, the great man continuously casts his brilliance in all four directions. {*Ji* [continue/continuously] here means "without cease." When these bright ones cast their light one after the other, the illumination never ceases.}

COMMENTARY ON THE APPENDED PHRASES

He [Bao Xi (Fu Xi)] tied cords together and made various kinds of snare nets for catching animals and fish. He probably got the idea for this from the hexagram *Li* [Cohesion].[2]

PROVIDING THE SEQUENCE OF THE HEXAGRAMS

Once so entrapped, there is sure to be something to catch hold of. This is why [*Xi*] *Kan* [(Constant) Sink Hole, Hexagram 29] is followed by *Li* [Cohesion]. *Li* here means "*li*" [clinging].

THE HEXAGRAMS IN IRREGULAR ORDER

Li [Cohesion] signifies ascent, and [*Xi*] *Kan* [(Constant) Sink Hole, Hexagram 29] signifies descent.

First Yang

This one treads with reverence and care. As he takes it seriously, there will be no blame. {*Cuoran* [usually "crosswise/confusedly"] here describes an attitude of reverence and care.[3] First Yang is located at the very beginning of Cohesion and is about to advance and begin to thrive, but its success is still not realized, and this is why it is appropriate for it to take care about where it treads. It is one's duty to be serious here, for this is how he avoids any blame.}

COMMENTARY ON THE IMAGES

It is due to the seriousness of one's reverential and careful treading that one avoids blame here.

Second Yin

It is to yellow that one coheres here, which means fundamental good fortune. {Second Yin abides in centrality [the Mean] and has obtained its rightful position. As it fills a yielding [yin] position with a yielding [yin] line, Second Yin treads upon the territory where the blessings of civilization flourish and in doing so manages to achieve centrality. This is why the text says: "It is to yellow that one coheres here, which means fundamental good fortune.[4]}

COMMENTARY ON THE IMAGES

"It is to yellow that one coheres here, which means fundamental good fortune," for such a one obtains the Dao of centrality [the Mean].

Third Yang

Cohesion here is as if it were that of the setting sun. If one does not beat the earthenware pot and sing, he will have only the wail of the very aged, which means misfortune. {*Jie* [wail] is an exclamation of sadness. Third Yang is located at the very end of the lower *Li* trigram, obviously at a place where it is about to perish, and this is why the text says: "Cohesion here is as if it were that of the setting sun." As such a one is about to reach his end, if he does not turn over his affairs to others, nourish his will, and practice nonpurposeful action [*wuwei*], then all he can do is wail when he reaches extreme old age. This is why the text says: "If one does not beat the earthenware pot and sing, he will have only the wail of the very aged, which means misfortune."[5]}

COMMENTARY ON THE IMAGES

"Cohesion here is as if it were that of the setting sun," so how could it ever last long?

Fourth Yang

Sudden is its arrival, now blazing, now dying, now being discarded. {Fourth Yang is located at the moment when the Dao of light and brightness begins to change: it had been dark but now begins to dawn; it had been submerged but now begins to emerge. This is why the text says: "Sudden is its arrival." As the brightness begins to propagate, its blaze begins to surge. Thus the text says "blazing." Fourth Yang is immediately next to the most exalted one [Fifth Yin, the ruler of the hexagram], and where it treads is not its rightful position [because it is a yang line in a yin position]. Wishing to bring its surge of brightness forward, it sets what is above ablaze, but its own fate is such that it surely will never carry this through to the finish. Thus the text says "dying." Fourth Yang acts against the concept underlying Cohesion. It does not have any line with which to resonate, nor is there one that it may carry.[6] As such it is not accepted by any of the other lines, so it finishes up, as the text says, "being discarded."}

COMMENTARY ON THE IMAGES

So "sudden is its arrival" that it finds no acceptance.

Fifth Yin

This one sheds tears enough to make a flood, is sad enough to wail, but he has good fortune. {Where Fifth Yin treads is not its rightful position [it is a yin line in a yang position; moreover, the ruling position of this hexagram], and it lacks sufficient means to deal with the place whereon it treads. As a weak line that rides upon a strong line, it is incapable of controlling the line below. That line is strong and advancing, and, as it is going to come and harm Fifth Yin, the grief that it [Fifth Yin] suffers is profound, so much so that there are floods of tears and wailing. The place to which it coheres is located at the exalted position, so even though Fourth Yang is the head of rebellion[7] and inflicts the profoundest grief upon Fifth Yin, as Fifth Yin is assisted by all the other lines, when it sheds floods of tears and wails, it reaps good fortune after all.}

COMMENTARY ON THE IMAGES

The good fortune of Fifth Yin resides in its cohering to the princely or noble position [i.e., the rulership of the hexagram].

Top Yang

It is right for the king to launch a punitive expedition with this one. It is praiseworthy to remove the head, and to take prisoner those who are not of the same ugly sort will spare one from blame. {"Cohesion means 'to cling.' " When each one manages to make secure that to which he clings, we call this Cohesion. Top Yang is located at the ultimate point in Cohesion, where the Dao of Cohesion has already reached perfection. So here one gets rid of those of a different sort in order to rid the common people of harm. It is the time for "the king to launch a punitive expedition with this one" [the hard and strong one represented by Top Yang]. Thus "it is praiseworthy to remove the head,"[8] and by "tak[ing] prisoner those who are not of the same ugly sort," one will manage to be spared from blame.}

COMMENTARY ON THE IMAGES

"It is right for the king to launch a punitive expedition with this one," in order to rectify the realm.

NOTES

1. This and all subsequent text set off in this manner is commentary by Wang Bi.

2. See section two of the Commentary on the Appended Phrases, Part Two. Hexagram 30, *Li* (Cohesion), consists of the trigram *Li* doubled ䷝ and is supposed to resemble the pattern in the mesh of nets.

3. Zhu Xi does not bother to gloss *cuoran*, but Cheng Yi reads it as *jiaocuo* (crosswise), i.e., one's footsteps crisscross over themselves: "Although one here has not yet begun to advance, he is already laying down footprints" (i.e., taking care about which way to go). See *Zhouyi zhezhong*, 4: 39b.

4. Kong Yingda comments: "Yellow is the color of centrality." See *Zhouyi zhengyi*, 3: 27b.

5. Cf. *Zhuangzi*, 46/18/15: "Zhuangzi's wife died, and when Huizi paid him a visit of condolence he found him beating on a tub and singing."

6. A yang line should not carry a yin line. See section three of Wang's General Remarks and note 23 there.

7. "Head of rebellion" translates *nishou*. *Shou* may be a corruption of *dao*; if so then the phrase should be translated "even though Fourth Yang rebels against the Dao." See Lou, *Wang Bi ji jiaoshi*, 1: 372 n. 14. However, the wording of the text of Top Yang and Wang Bi's interpretation of it suggest that "head of rebellion" is the more likely interpretation.

8. "Remove the head" (*zhe shou*) also means, of course, "decapitate," so there is probably a play on words here that suggests "decapitate the chief of the rebellion," represented by Fourth Yang.

HEXAGRAM 31

䷞

咸

Xian [Reciprocity]
(*Gen* Below *Dui* Above)

Judgment

Reciprocity is such that prevalence is had. It is fitting to practice constancy here. To marry a woman means good fortune.

COMMENTARY ON THE JUDGMENTS

Reciprocity is a matter of stimulation. Here the soft and yielding [*Dui* (Joy), here representing the Youngest Daughter] is above, and the hard and strong [*Gen* (Restraint), representing the Youngest Son] is below.[1] The two kinds of material force [*qi*] stimulate and respond and so join together. {This is how "prevalence is had."[2]} The one is passive, and the other joyous. {And this is how "it is fitting to practice constancy here."} The male takes a place below the female, {So "to marry a woman means good fortune."} and this is how "prevalence is had," how "it is fitting to practice constancy," and how "to marry a woman means good fortune." It is by the mutual stimulation of Heaven and Earth that the myriad things are created. {With the joining together of the two kinds of material force, creation takes place.} It is by the sage stimulating the hearts and minds of men that the entire world finds peace. If we observe how things are stimulated, the innate tendencies [*qing*] of Heaven and Earth and all the myriad things can be seen. {The innate tendencies of Heaven and Earth and the myriad things are seen in how they are stimulated. Whenever stimulation takes place, it is a realization of the Dao of Reciprocity, but if stimulation cannot take place, this means that the things involved do not belong to the same category of existence. Thus the text cites marrying a woman to illustrate the principle of common categories. When beings of the same category of existence do not stimulate and respond to each other, in each such instance it is because some overreaching of station occurs. Thus, although a woman is a creature who should respond to a man, it is necessary for the man to take a place beneath her, for only then will marriage to her result in good fortune.}

COMMENTARY ON THE IMAGES

The Lake is above the Mountain: this constitutes the image of Reciprocity.[3] In the same way, the noble man receives others with self-effacement [*xu*, literally, "emptiness"]. {If one receives others with self-effacement, they will certainly be stimulated and respond to him.[4]}

PROVIDING THE SEQUENCE OF THE HEXAGRAMS

Only after there were Heaven and Earth were there the myriad things. Only after there were the myriad things were there male and female. Only after there were male and female were there husband and wife. Only after there were husband and wife were there father and child. Only after there were father and child were there sovereign and minister. Only after there were sovereign and minister were there superiors and subordinates. Only after there were superiors and subordinates did propriety and righteousness have a medium in which to operate.

THE HEXAGRAMS IN IRREGULAR ORDER

Xian [Reciprocity] means "things will go quickly."

First Yin

Reciprocity is in the big toe. {First Yin is located at the very beginning of Reciprocity and represents the beginning of stimulation. Stimulation is located at the extremity [of the body]. Thus there is nothing more than an inclination involved. If one's basic person is solid and strong, this will not go so far as to damage one's equanimity.}

COMMENTARY ON THE IMAGES

When "Reciprocity is in the big toe," the inclination is directed to the outside. {Fourth Yang [with which First Yin is in resonance] belongs to the outer [upper] trigram.}

Second Yin

Reciprocity is in the calf of the leg, which means misfortune, but if one stays still, he will have good fortune. {Here the Dao of Reciprocity has moved forward a stage and has left the big toe and ascended to the calf. The substance of the calf is such that its movement is impetuous, but to act impetuously when stimulated by something is a dao of misfortune. So to follow impetuosity here would result in misfortune, but to stay still would mean good fortune. As Second Yin does not ride on top of a hard and strong [yang] line [i.e., it is not threatened from below], it can as a consequence stay still and garner good fortune.}

COMMENTARY ON THE IMAGES

Although beset by misfortune, to stay still here means good fortune. The compliant will come to no harm. {To be yin and so stay still realizes the Dao of compliance. Be not impetuous, and stay still, for compliance will let one avoid harm.}

Third Yang

Reciprocity is in the thigh, something that is compelled to follow along, so the inclination to set out here means hard going. {The thigh as such is something that follows the foot. When one advances, it cannot control the movement, and when one retreats, it cannot remain still in place. When stimulation is in the thigh, it indicates someone whose inclination is to follow others. Such a one's inclination is to follow others, and those that compel him to do so [First Yin, i.e., "Big Toe," and Second Yin, i.e., "The Calf"] also act out of baseness or vulgarity [i.e., impetuosity]. So it is because of this that such a one is made to set forth, and this makes what he should do [assert himself and stay still] hard going.[5]}

COMMENTARY ON THE IMAGES

"Reciprocity is in the thigh," and this one, too, tends not to stay still, for his inclination is to follow others. Those that compel him to do so are below [First Yin and Second Yin].

Fourth Yang

Constancy results in good fortune, and thus regret is avoided. You pace back and forth in consternation, and friends follow your thoughts. {Fourth Yang is located at the beginning of the upper trigram, is in resonance with First Yin, abides in the center of the body trigrams, and finds itself above the thighs. When two bodies [male and female, represented by the two constituent trigrams] begin to associate and stimulate each other, it is because they share the same inclination; it is a matter of their hearts or spirits being stimulated first. Whenever one begins to feel such stimulation yet fails to control it with rectitude, it will lead to disaster. This is why one must be sure to practice constancy here, for only then will good fortune result, and only with good fortune will one manage to avoid any possible regret. This one begins with a particular stimulation [Fourth Yang is in resonance with First Yin], but as he fails to realize perfectly the sum ultimate of all stimulations [i.e., enter into an impartial reciprocal relationship with the entire world], he is never able to reach the point where he is "without thought" [i.e., impartial][6] and so only obtains his own particular clique or faction. This is why the text has it that only when he paces back and forth in consternation do his friends follow his particular thoughts [i.e., he fails to achieve universal empathy].}

COMMENTARY ON THE IMAGES

"Constancy results in good fortune, and thus regret is avoided," for stimulation here has not brought about harm. {Stimulation has not been done to cause harm, thus it is possible to rectify matters and so manage to avoid regret.} "You pace back and forth in consternation," for this one has failed to achieve magnificence and greatness.

Fifth Yang

Reciprocity is in the upper back, which amounts to no regret. {The *mei* [upper back] is above the heart and below the mouth. Moving forward here does not involve great stimulation, and, whereas moving backward may not be without purpose, that purpose would be shallow or trivial. This is why the text says that there is merely "no regret" here.[7]}

COMMENTARY ON THE IMAGES

"Reciprocity is in the upper back," so the purpose is trivial.

Top Yin

Reciprocity is in the jowls, cheeks, and tongue. {The Dao of Reciprocity peters out at this stage. This is why it becomes nothing more here than words spoken by the mouth and tongue.}

COMMENTARY ON THE IMAGES

When "Reciprocity is in the jowls, cheeks, and tongue," it produces the speech of an overflowing mouth. {The jowls, cheeks, and tongue are the instruments by which speech is made. "When 'Reciprocity is in the jowls, cheeks, and tongue,' it produces the speech of an overflowing mouth." As even the "you pace back and forth in consternation" [of Fourth Yang] indicates that no magnificence or greatness has been achieved, so we understand here that things are so much more insubstantial at this stage of the "overflowing mouth."}

NOTES

1. See section ten of Explaining the Trigrams.

2. This and all subsequent text set off in this manner is commentary by Wang Bi.

3. *Gen* (Mountain, Restraint) is the lower trigram, and *Dui* (Lake, Joy) is the upper trigram. Kong Yingda comments: "The nature of the lake is such that it lets water flow down from it, so it can provide nourishing moisture to what is below. The substance of the Mountain is such that it accepts things from above, so it can receive this nourishing moisture." See *Zhouyi zhengyi*, 4: 2a.

4. Cf. *Laozi*, section 61, p. 160: "A small state can take over a big state by placing itself under a big state." Part of Wang Bi's commentary here is worth quoting: "It is only by cultivating humility that one will always get what he wants."

5. "Hard going" translates *lin*. See Hexagram 3, *Zhun* (Birth Throes), note 6. However, Cheng Yi glosses *lin* here as *xiulin* (humiliating), which suggests that Cheng would read the last part of Third Yang differently: "So when he sets out, it will be humiliating." See *Zhouyi zhezhong*, 5: 3b.

6. Cf. *Zhuangzi*, 32/12/74: "The man of virtue rests without thought [*wusi*] and acts without calculation."

7. Kong Yingda's commentary helps to make sense of Wang's pithy remarks:

> The upper back is above the heart and below the mouth. Fourth Yang already occupies the center of the body and is where the heart or spirit is stimulated. Fifth Yang has advanced to a point above Fourth Yang, thus its stimulation takes place in the upper back. With the upper back, one has gone beyond the heart, and this is why moving forward [i.e., moving further away from the heart] cannot involve great stimulation [as it is the heart that is the seat of greatest stimulation]. Due to the fact that Fifth Yang is located above the heart, to move backward [i.e., back toward the heart] would not be without purpose [as the *xin* (heart/mind) is also the seat of the will, and one is moving closer to it], but such purpose would be shallow or trivial.

See *Zhouyi zhengyi*, 4: 3b.

However, Cheng Yi and Zhu Xi read Fifth Yang quite differently. Cheng's commentary is the more detailed:

> Fifth Yang occupies the exalted position [it is the ruler of the hexagram], so it ought to stimulate the whole world with its perfect sincerity. However, it is in resonance with Second Yin and is contiguous with Top Yin. If it forms a relationship with the former and finds delight in the latter, it would be guilty of selfish partiality and shallow narrowness, which is not at all the Dao of a true sovereign of men, for how could such a one ever stimulate the whole world? *Mei* is the flesh of the back, something that is opposed to the heart and something that does not see things. This means both that it can oppose the selfish inclinations of the heart and that stimulation for it does not involve things that it might see and take delight in. Thus one may here obtain the rectitude with which the true sovereign of men stimulates the whole world and in so doing avoid regret.

See *Zhouyi zhezhong*, 5: 6b.

HEXAGRAM 32

恒

Heng [Perseverence]
(*Sun* Below *Zhen* Above)

Judgment

Perseverance is such that prevalence is had, and that means that there will be no blame and that it is fitting to practice constancy here. {That one has prevalence here because of Perseverance is due to achieving the three matters [i.e., avoiding blame, it being fit to practice constancy, and, as is stated in the next line of the Judgment, it being fit should one set out to do something]. As a Dao, Perseverance works in such a way that once prevalence is had, one can avoid blame, and once one achieves this avoidance of blame with the mastery of Perseverance, he will find it fitting to practice rectitude [i.e., constancy].[1]} It would be fitting should one set out to do something here. {Every successful state of Perseverance is a matter of practicing the constant Dao: "When something ends, there is always another beginning," a process that takes place in such a way that there is never any deviance. This is why it would be fitting should one set out to do something here.}

COMMENTARY ON THE JUDGMENTS

Perseverance means "long lasting." Here the hard and strong [the *Zhen* (Quake) trigram] is above, and the soft and yielding [the *Sun* (Compliance) trigram] is below. {The hard and strong is in the exalted position, and the soft and yielding is in the humble, which means that a proper order is maintained.} Here Thunder and Wind work together. {The Eldest Yang [*Zhen*, "the Eldest Son"] and the Eldest Yin [*Sun*, "the Eldest Daughter"] are here able to complement each other.[2]} Here action [i.e., the *Zhen* trigram] takes place in terms of *Sun* [Compliance], {Here is action without deviance.} and the hard [yang] and soft [yin] lines are all in resonance, {None is unmatched.} so Perseverance is had. {All of this deals with the Dao of everlasting duration.} "Perseverance is such that prevalence is had, and that means that there will be no blame and that it is fitting to practice constancy here." This means that duration inheres in the Dao as such. {It is through the Dao that one manages to achieve duration. Thus one always succeeds at avoiding blame and finds it fitting to practice rectitude.} The Dao of Heaven and Earth perseveres forever and never comes to a stop. {It is because they are in a successful state of Perseverance that their Dao never comes to a stop.} "It would be fitting should one set out to do something here," for when something ends, there is always another beginning. {As one has realized the constant Dao here, he will find that, with one ending, there will be another beginning, so he can carry on indefinitely.} The sun and the moon have found their places in Heaven and so can shine forever. The four seasons change one into the other and so can occur forever. The sage stays forever within the course of the Dao and so brings about the perfection of the entire world. {This means that as each of these succeeds at Perseverance, so they all are able to last forever.} If we observe how things manage to persevere, the innate tendencies [*qing*] of Heaven and Earth and all the myriad things can be seen. {The innate tendencies of Heaven and Earth and the myriad things are seen in how they manage to persevere.}

COMMENTARY ON THE IMAGES

Thunder together with Wind: this constitutes the image of Perseverance.[3] {The Eldest Yang and the Eldest Yin join here and work together, and this constitutes the Dao of everlasting duration.} In the same way, the noble man takes a stand and does not change his direction. {He succeeds at Perseverance, so does not change.}

COMMENTARY ON THE APPENDED PHRASES

Heng [Perseverance] provides virtue with steadfastness.

Heng [Perseverance] demonstrates how, faced with the complexity of things, one yet does not give way to cynicism.

Heng [Perseverance] provides the means to keep one's virtue one.[4]

PROVIDING THE SEQUENCE OF THE HEXAGRAMS

The Dao of husband and wife cannot fail to be long enduring. This is why *Xian* [Reciprocity, Hexagram 31] is followed by *Heng* [Perseverance]. *Heng* here means "long enduring."

THE HEXAGRAMS IN IRREGULAR ORDER

Heng [Perseverance] means "long lasting."

First Yin

This one takes Perseverance to mean "deep penetration," but even the practice of constancy here would mean misfortune, for there is nothing at all fitting here. {First Yin is located at the beginning of Perseverance, right at the very bottom of the hexagram, so it represents someone who tries "to gain deep penetration [i.e., profound success] right at the beginning." To seek deep penetration into something and so try to exhaust it completely would leave that thing bereft of any remaining resource. Even if one were to try to arrive at this point gradually, the thing involved would defy his efforts to overcome it, so how much the less successful should one be if he were to seek for deep penetration right at the beginning? To think that Perseverance works in such a way would be to turn right behavior into misfortune and virtue into something harmful, and no act would be fitting.}

COMMENTARY ON THE IMAGES

The misfortune connected with "tak[ing] Perseverance to mean 'deep penetration' " is due to the attempt to gain deep penetration [i.e., profound success] right at the beginning.

Second Yang

Regret vanishes. {Although Second Yang is out of position [it is a yang line in a yin position], it perseveres in maintaining its position in the center, and, in so doing, dissipates regret.}

COMMENTARY ON THE IMAGES

That Second Yang has regret vanish is because it is able to maintain itself in the center indefinitely.

Third Yang

This one does not persevere in maintaining his virtue, so he might have to bear the shame of it, for constancy would be debased. {Third Yang occupies the middle of three yang lines and the top position of the lower trigram and is situated immediately below the upper trigram. If it were to form a trigram with the lines above, that would not be completely noble; if it were to remain part of the trigram below, that would not be completely base; and if it were to stay in the middle, it would not actually be in the middle of a trigram. Such a trigram [Third, Fourth, and Fifth Yang] is within Perseverance as such, but as it is not fixed or certain, it does not have anything to do with Perseverance. When virtue is practiced without Perseverance, it is impossible to probe how much such a practice might result in deviancy or confusion, so that is why the text says: "He might have to bear the shame of it." If one extends virtue under such circumstances, no one else will accept it, something extremely contemptible, and this is why the text says: "Constancy would be debased."}

COMMENTARY ON THE IMAGES

"This one does not persevere in maintaining his virtue," so he will not be accepted by anyone.

Fourth Yang

In the field there is no game. {When one perseveres at a place that is not one's proper position [here there is a yang line in a yin position], regardless of how much such a one labors, he will never garner anything.}

COMMENTARY ON THE IMAGES

This one has been out of his proper place for a long time, so how could he get any game?

Fifth Yin

If one perseveres in virtue here and practices constancy, it would be good fortune for the woman but misfortune for the man. {Fifth Yang has achieved the exalted position. However, as the ruler of Perseverance, it is unable to "take charge and act according to moral principles," but instead, bound tightly in resonance with Second Yang and devotedly practicing a single-minded constancy to it, it can do nothing more than follow the lead of another. This may mean good fortune for the woman, but it is misfortune for the man.}

COMMENTARY ON THE IMAGES

For the woman to practice constancy here means good fortune, for to the end she should only follow one man, but, as the man should take charge and act according to moral principles, for him to behave like an obedient woman would mean misfortune.

Top Yin

This one takes Perseverance to mean "constant activity," which means misfortune. {Quietude is the sovereign of activity, and repose is the master of action.[5] Thus repose is the state in which the one at the top should reside, and it is through quietude that the Dao of everlasting duration works.[6] Here Top Yin is located at the very top of the Perseverance hexagram, which means that it abides in a state of utmost action [as it is at the top of the *Zhen* (Quake) trigram]. If one were to take this to be Perseverance, nothing that he ventures to do would ever result in success.[7]}

COMMENTARY ON THE IMAGES

Here someone who takes constant activity to mean "Perseverance" is at the top, and this will result in an enormous failure to achieve any merit.

NOTES

1. This and all subsequent text set off in this manner is commentary by Wang Bi. Kong Yingda thinks that Wang's is the most likely interpretation;

see *Zhouyi zhengyi*, 4: 4a, and Lou, *Wang Bi ji jiaoshi*, 2: 381 n. 1.

2. See section ten of Explaining the Trigrams.

3. *Sun* (Wind, Compliance) is the lower trigram, and *Zhen* (Thunder, Quake) is the upper trigram.

4. See section seven of the Commentary on the Appended Phrases, Part Two.

5. Cf. *Laozi*, section 26, pp. 69–70.

6. Cf. *Laozi*, section 16, pp. 35–36.

7. "Quietude" and "repose" are Daoist rather than Confucian virtues, so it is no surprise that Cheng Yi and Zhu Xi interpret Top Yin differently. They interpret *zhen* (constant activity) to mean "haste" or "insecure agitation" and emphasize the fact that Top Yin is a weak line, thus insecure, agitated, and prone to act unwisely and "in haste." See *Zhouyi zhezhong*, 5: 12a–12b.

HEXAGRAM 33

遯

Dun [Withdrawl]
(*Gen* Below *Qian* Above)

Judgment

Withdrawal is such that prevalence is had. It is fitting to practice constancy in small matters.

COMMENTARY ON THE JUDGMENTS

"Withdrawal is such that prevalence is had" means that it is through Withdrawal that one achieves prevalence. {The concept underlying Withdrawal is that only by withdrawing will one [eventually] prevail.[1]} When the hard and strong achieves a rightful position and finds resonance, such a one can act when the time is right. {This refers to Fifth Yang. As "the hard and strong achieves a rightful position and finds resonance [with Second Yin]," it is not obstructed and a victim of its own overreaching. One who practices Withdrawal and stays clear of obstruction and overreaching will be able to take action when the time is right.} "It is fitting to practice constancy in small matters," for it is only by gradual advancement that they [the forces of yin] grow in strength. {Here the Dao associated with yin forces [First and Second Yin] may tend to advance gradually and grow in strength, but the correct Dao [the Dao of rectitude] has not yet completely perished, and this is why the text says that "it is fitting to practice constancy in small matters."} The significance of a time of Withdrawal is indeed great!

COMMENTARY ON THE IMAGES

Below Heaven, there is the Mountain: this constitutes the image of *Dun* [Withdrawal].[2] In the same way, the noble man keeps at a distance the petty man, whom he does not overtly despise but from whom he remains aloof.

PROVIDING THE SEQUENCE OF THE HEXAGRAMS

Things cannot long abide where they are located. This is why *Heng* [Perseverance, Hexagram 32] is followed by *Dun* [Withdrawal]. *Dun* here means "retreat."

THE HEXAGRAMS IN IRREGULAR ORDER

If it is *Dazhuang* [Great Strength, Hexagram 34], it means "a halt," but if it is *Dun* [Withdrawal], it means "withdrawal."

First Yin

There is danger here at the tail of Withdrawal, so do not use this as an opportunity to go forth. {Withdrawal as an overall concept means that one should avoid the inner and go to the outer, but a tail as such is located at the rearmost point of something. Located here during a time of Withdrawal, "if one does not go forth [i.e., refrains from action], what calamity could there be?" As this is the tail of the Withdrawal, it means that one has already been overtaken by disaster. If one seeks to move away only after danger has actually arrived, it will prove impossible to avoid being threatened by that danger, and that is why the text says "do not use this as an opportunity to go forth."}

COMMENTARY ON THE IMAGES

There is danger here at the tail of Withdrawal, but if one does not go forth, what calamity could there be?

Second Yin

If one holds them with yellow ox hide, none will manage to break away. {As Second Yin abides in the inner [lower] trigram and occupies the middle position, it is the ruler of the Withdrawal hexagram,[3] but all the others [i.e., the other lines] try to withdraw from it, so what measures can such a one take to hold them fast? If one were able to hold to the Dao of principles and centrality [the Mean], of generosity and obedience, and use it to try to hold them fast, none would manage to break away.[4]}

COMMENTARY ON THE IMAGES

"Hold . . . them with yellow oxhide" means "to hold their wills fast."

Third Yang

To be so attached here at a time of Withdrawal is as if one were in pestilential danger, but a kept servant will have good fortune. {Third Yang is located in the inner [lower] trigram and is next to Second Yin. Here a yang line adheres to a yin line; it ought to withdraw but is attached, and this is why the text says "attached here at a time of Withdrawal." As a concept, Withdrawal means that one ought to keep petty men at a distance, but here a yang adheres to a yin, which means that such a one remains attached to the place where he is located. Not only is such a one unable to keep himself away from harm, he also has worn himself out in the process. So it is appropriate that he finds himself humiliated with shame and placed in great danger. To be so attached to where one finds himself is quite acceptable for a kept servant, but it is the way to misfortune for anyone who would apply himself to some great undertaking.}

COMMENTARY ON THE IMAGES

The danger of being attached at a time of Withdrawal renders one worn-out as with illness. Whereas a kept servant might have good fortune here, one may not engage in great undertakings.

Fourth Yang

Here one should withdraw from that of which he is fond, so the noble man will have good fortune, but the petty man will be obstructed. {Fourth Yang is located in the outer [upper] trigram but is in resonance with [First Yin in] the inner [lower] trigram. A noble man would withdraw from that of which he is fond, so [as Fourth Yang] he can discard it [First Yin], but the petty man remains attached to what he loves and so is obstructed.}

COMMENTARY ON THE IMAGES

The noble man withdraws from that of which he is fond, but the petty man is obstructed. {*Pi* [obstructed] should here be read as the *pi* in the expression *zangpi* [good and evil] [i.e., the petty man will "fall on evil times"].}

Fifth Yang

Here is praiseworthy Withdrawal, in which constancy brings good fortune. {Fifth Yang withdraws in such a way that it achieves rectitude, and it practices control back upon the inner trigram, where the petty man [Second Yin with which it is in resonance]—"whom [Fifth Yang] does not overtly despise but from whom he remains aloof"—obeys orders and rectifies his will completely. As good fortune stems from this achievement of rectitude, so Withdrawal here is praiseworthy.}

COMMENTARY ON THE IMAGES

"Here is praiseworthy Withdrawal, in which constancy brings good fortune," and this is due to rectifying the will.

Top Yang

This is flying[5] Withdrawal, so nothing fails to be fitting. {Top Yang is located at the very extremity of the outer [upper] trigram. It is not in resonance with any other line, so, transcendent and absolutely aloof, this one's heart and mind are free from any doubts or cares. No disaster can entangle him as no harpoon arrow can reach him. This is how there is "flying Withdrawal, so nothing fails to be fitting.}

COMMENTARY ON THE IMAGES

"This is flying Withdrawal, so nothing fails to be fitting," for there is nothing about which one should have hesitation or doubt.

NOTES

1. This and all subsequent text set off in this manner is commentary by Wang Bi. Wang also discusses this hexagram in section seven of his General Remarks.

2. The lower trigram *Gen* (Restraint) is associated with Mountain, and the upper trigram *Qian* (Pure Yang) is associated with Heaven.

3. One would expect Fifth Yang to be the ruler of this hexagram, but, as Cheng Yi says in his commentary to Fifth Yang,

> Withdrawal is not something a sovereign over men should get involved in, and this is why there is nothing said about this line filling the ruler's position. However, if a sovereign is caused to flee, it certainly amounts to Withdrawal. So Fifth Yang, too, [like Second Yin] merely manages to keep itself within the bounds of centrality and rectitude [i.e., it is not really a ruler].

See *Zhouyi zhezhong*, 5: 17b.

4. Cheng Yi construes the text of Second Yin to refer instead to the special strong and correct bond between Second Yin and Fifth Yang, which are in resonance, and adds: "Yellow is the color of the center, an ox is an obedient creature, and ox hide is something strong and sturdy." See *Zhouyi zhezhong*, 5: 15a.

5. "Flying" translates *fei* (rich/fat), as suggested by Wang Bi's commentary: "No harpoon arrow can reach him." Also, when other early writers such as Zhang Heng (78–139) and Cao Zhi (192–232) quote or paraphrase the text of Top Yang here, they use the character *fei* (fly/flying) instead of *fei* (rich/fat). However, Kong Yingda glosses *fei* as *raoyu*

(rich, abundant, wealthy), and later commentators such as Cheng Yi and Zhu Xi gloss it as *kuanyu* (rich; extremely resourceful), so all of them seem to take *fei Dun* as "resourceful Withdrawal" or "Withdrawal over which one has abundant control." See Lou, *Wang Bi ji jiaoshi*, 2: 386 n. 13; *Zhouyi zhengyi*, 4: 8b; *Zhouyi zhezhong*, 5: 18a.

HEXAGRAM 34

䷡

大壯

Dazhuang [Great Strength]

(*Qian* Below *Zhen* Above)

Judgment

Great Strength is such that it is fitting to practice constancy.

COMMENTARY ON THE JUDGMENTS

"Great Strength" means that the great are strong. {"The great" refers to the yang lines. Here the dao of the petty is about to reach its demise, and the great achieve rectitude, so the text says: "It is fitting to practice constancy."[1]} Strength is the result of action taken by the hard and strong. "Great Strength is such that it is fitting to practice constancy" means that the great behave with rectitude. In such rectitude and greatness the innate tendencies of Heaven and Earth can be seen. {"The innate tendencies of Heaven and Earth" can be characterized in no other terms than "rectitude and greatness." In such all-embracing rectitude and absolute greatness "the innate tendencies of Heaven and Earth can be seen."}

COMMENTARY ON THE IMAGES

Above Heaven, there is Thunder: this constitutes the image of *Dazhuang* [Great Strength].[2] {This signifies "action taken by the hard and strong."} In the same way, the noble man will not tread any course that is not commensurate with decorum. {To be strong but violate decorum would result in misfortune, and, with misfortune, strength would be lost. Thus the noble man with his great strength remains obedient to the demands of decorum.[3]}

COMMENTARY ON THE APPENDED PHRASES

In remote antiquity, caves were dwellings, and the open country was a place to stay. The sages of later ages had these exchanged for proper houses, putting a ridgepole at the top and rafters below in order to protect against the wind and the rain. They probably got the idea for this from the hexagram *Dazhuang* [Great Strength].[4]

PROVIDING THE SEQUENCE OF THE HEXAGRAMS

Things cannot be in withdrawal forever. This is why *Dun* [Withdrawal, Hexagram 33] is followed by *Dazhuang* [Great Strength].

THE HEXAGRAMS IN IRREGULAR ORDER

If it is *Dazhuang* [Great Strength], it means "a halt," but if it is *Dun* [Withdrawal, Hexagram 33], it means "withdrawal."

First Yang

Here strength resides in the toes, so to go forth and act would mean misfortune, in this one should be confident. {To obtain Great Strength one must be capable of fully realizing it on his own. It is by never allowing oneself to be rendered ineffective or helpless by others that one manages to realize all one's strength. First Yang is located at the bottom and there has its strength, and this is why the text says "strength resides in the toes." If one tries to move forward through the use of hardness and strength while still residing in a lowly position, one can be sure that it would result in the misfortune of being thoroughly frustrated, and this is why the text says:

"To go forth and act would mean misfortune, in this one should be confident."}

COMMENTARY ON THE IMAGES

"Here strength resides in the toes," so this one should be confident that he would be thoroughly frustrated. {This means that one can be sure here that he would be thoroughly frustrated.}

Second Yang

Constancy here means good fortune. {Second Yang manages to abide in a central position [the Mean], and, as a yang line in a yin position, it treads the path of modesty and does not overreach itself. Thus "constancy here means good fortune.}

COMMENTARY ON THE IMAGES

For Second Yang, constancy means good fortune, because of its centrality [adherence to the Mean].

Third Yang

The petty man considers this an opportunity for his strength, but the noble man considers it a trap, for even with constancy there would be danger, as when a ram butts a hedge and finds its horns deprived of power.[5] {Third Yang occupies a position of extreme strength, and, as a yang line that occupies a yang position, it represents one who would employ his strength. Thus the petty man considers this an opportunity to exercise his strength, but the noble man considers it a chance to get himself entangled. If one exercises his strength under such circumstances in which there is danger in spite of constancy, even if he were a ram that repeatedly used its strength to butt a hedge, would not his strength always be deprived of power?}

COMMENTARY ON THE IMAGES

"The petty man considers this an opportunity for his strength," but the noble man thinks it a trap.

Fourth Yang

Constancy means good fortune, so regrets vanish. The hedge is sundered and does not sap one's strength. This is the strength of an axle housing of a great carriage. {When one below advances with hardness and strength, he is going to have worry and concern, but, as Fourth Yang is a yang line in a yin position, it acts in such a way that it neither violates modesty nor loses its strength, and so this is how "constancy means good fortune, so regrets vanish" can be had here. Fourth Yang obtains its strength, and the yin lines above do not hem it in and deny it its path. This is why the text says: "The hedge is sundered and does not sap one's strength." "The strength of an axle housing of a great carriage" means that nothing has the capacity to separate carriage body from axle,[6] so that one may therefore set forth.}

COMMENTARY ON THE IMAGES

"The hedge is sundered and does not sap one's strength," so this one should still set forth.

Fifth Yin

One loses a ram in a time of ease, so he has no regret. {To be located at a time of Great Strength means that even yang lines that occupy yang positions do not manage to be free of blame, so is this not all the more true here where a yin line occupies a yang position, where one soft and yielding rides on top of one that is hard and strong? A ram means strength, but this one has to lose his ram-ness [strength] and forfeit the place that he occupies. It is possible to lose strength in times of ease but not when faced with danger and difficulties,[7] and this is how one here manages to have "no regret." Second Yang treads where constancy means good fortune, and, as it is capable of fulfilling its responsibilities, Fifth Yin entrusts itself to Second Yang and, as a consequence, is able to have "no regret." It is by entrusting itself to Second Yang that trouble fails to reach Fifth Yin, but if it had remained in its place, enemies and robbers would have arrived, and this is why the text says "loses a ram in a time of ease."}

COMMENTARY ON THE IMAGES

This one "loses a ram in a time of ease," for the position is not right for it.

Top Yin

This ram butts the hedge and finds that it can neither retreat nor advance. There is nothing at all fitting here, but if one can endure difficulties, he will have good fortune. {Top Yin is in resonance with Third Yang [where another ram butts the hedge], so it is unable to retreat; it is afraid of the growing power of the hard and strong, so it is unable to advance. Beset by doubt and paralyzed with hesitation, the will is utterly undirected, so if one were to decide matters under such circumstances, nothing fitting would ever come of it. Although Top Yin is located where the hard and strong are growing in power, those hard and strong ones will not harm the righteous. If one secures the position allotted to him here, keeps his will steadfastly on Third Yang, and in this way maintains his own place, disasters will vanish. This is why the text says: "If one can endure difficulties, he will have good fortune."[8]}

COMMENTARY ON THE IMAGES

That one can neither retreat nor advance means ill fortune, but "if one can endure difficulties," blame will not last long.

NOTES

1. This and all subsequent text set off in this manner is commentary by Wang Bi. Wang also discusses this hexagram in section seven of his General Remarks.

2. The lower trigram *Qian* (Pure Yang) is Heaven, and the upper trigram *Zhen* (Quake) is associated with Thunder.

3. Kong Yingda's comment helps to explain the connection between thunder and the proper behavior here for the noble man: "When one's power is at its peak, it tends to produce arrogance and high-handed behavior. This is why at a time of Great Strength one truly must take care not to

'tread any course that is not commensurate with decorum.' Thunder in Heaven, of course, suggests such power." See *Zhouyi zhengyi*, 4: 9b.

4. See section two of the Commentary on the Appended Phrases, Part Two, and note 21 there.

5. Two words in Third Yang seem problematic: *wang* (trap) and *lei* (deprived of power). The *wang* that Wang Bi glosses as *wang* (net, trap, to net, entrap, entangle, etc.), "get himself entangled" (*luo ji*), actually means "negate," "nullify," or simply "not." This is how Cheng Yi and Zhu Xi take it, and their interpretation would read something like: "The noble man considers that it is not so" (i.e., that he is not really strong here or that his strength is nullified by the circumstances). The basic meaning of *lei* is "worn out," "tired," "weak," "weakened." Wang seems to understand *lei* in this way in his commentary on First Yin of *Gou* (Encounter), Hexagram 44. Cheng Yi and Zhu Xi gloss it similarly as *leikun* (tired out) and *kun* (tired), respectively, but Kong Yingda glosses it as *julei chanrao* (ensnared and entangled). See *Zhouyi zhezhong*, 12: 8b–9a; *Zhouyi zhengyi*, 4: 10a; and Lou, *Wang Bi ji jiaoshi*, 2: 389 n. 4, which consists primarily of the views of the Qing era scholar, Jiao Xun (1763–1820).

6. Cf. Hexagram 9, *Xiaoxu* (Lesser Domestication), Third Yang.

7. Cheng Yi glosses *yi* (ease) as *heyi* (with peace and ease), i.e., "accommodatingly": Fifth Yin yields to the four advancing yang lines below with calm and good grace. Zhu Xi glosses *yi* as *rongyi* (easily), in the sense that Fifth Yin is lost so suddenly that it happens before it is aware of it. Zhu also thinks that it is possible that *yi* is written for *chang* (field), the only difference between the two characters being the additional *tu* (earth) significant on the left side, and in support of this he cites textual evidence showing that the *chang* in *jiangchang* (field boundary) is sometimes written *jiangyi*. In this sense, Fifth Yang would mean: "This one loses a ram at the field [boundary], but there is no regret." See *Zhouyi zhezhong*, 5: 21b–22a. Kong Yingda expands upon Wang's interpretation: "Fifth Yin must lose its ram-ness while it is still a time of ease before it is beset with robbers; it must not wait until a time of danger and difficulty when they have already arrived." See *Zhouyi zhengyi*, 4: 10b.

8. Kong Yingda comments: "If Top Yin is able to endure difficulties and keep his will steadfast so that it does not abandon itself to Third Yang, it will obtain good fortune." See *Zhouyi zhengyi*, 4: 11a.

HEXAGRAM 35

☲☷

晉

Jin [Advance]
(*Kun* Below *Li* Above)

Judgment

Advance is such that the marquis of peace and prosperity is thereby conferred horses in great numbers and received three times each day.[1]

COMMENTARY ON THE JUDGMENTS

Jin [advance] means *jin* [make progress, move forward]. Here brightness appears above the Earth. It is obedience that allows one to adhere to this great brightness, and it is a soft and yielding advance that allows one to move upward. {Whenever one says "move upward," the goal of that movement is a place esteemed.[2]} And this is what is meant by "the marquis of peace and prosperity is thereby conferred horses in great numbers and received three times each day." {"Peace and prosperity" is a term of praise. To adhere to brightness with obedience is the Dao of a true servitor or minister, and, when "it is a soft and yielding advance that allows one to move upward," things will be given to one. This is how one here obtains the conferral of horses in such large numbers. If one receives an article of clothing thanks to his success at contention, "before the day is over he will have been deprived of it three times,"[3] but when one comes to enjoy his sovereign's favor by advancing with softness and yielding, he will be "received three times each day."}

COMMENTARY ON THE IMAGES

Brightness appears above the Earth: this constitutes the image of Advance.[4] In the same way, the noble man illuminates himself with bright virtue. {It is through obedience that he adheres to brightness and in so doing realizes the Dao of self-illumination.}

PROVIDING THE SEQUENCE OF THE HEXAGRAMS

Things cannot remain strong forever. This is why *Dazhuang* [Great Strength, Hexagram 34] is followed by *Jin* [Advance]. *Jin* here means "to advance."

THE HEXAGRAMS IN IRREGULAR ORDER

Jin [Advance] indicates the daytime.[5]

First Yin

Now advancing, now retreating, constancy means good fortune. One is not yet trusted here, but if he were to let his resources grow rich, there would be no blame. {First Yin is located at the beginning of obedience [the *Kun* trigram] and is in resonance with the line at the start of brightness [Fourth Yang, the beginning of the *Li* trigram], and with this the virtues of brightness and obedience begin to thrive. Whether advancing in brightness or retreating in obedience, this one does not lose his rectitude, thus the text says: "Now advancing, now retreating, constancy means good fortune."[6] Located here at the beginning of the hexagram, one's achievements have not yet come to light, and others do not have confidence in him. This is why the text says: "One is not yet trusted here." This one has just stepped onto the beginning of the hexagram and has not yet reached a position where he might properly tread, so if one were to be content with this, he would, of course, forfeit his capacity for growth. Therefore, he must enrich his resources,[7] for only then will there be no blame.}

COMMENTARY ON THE IMAGES

"Now advancing, now retreating," one should do nothing but walk in righteousness. "If he were to let his resources grow rich, there would be no blame," for he has not yet received an appointment. {As First Yin has not yet reached a position where he might properly tread, "he has not yet received an appointment."}

Second Yin

Now advancing, now saddening, constancy means good fortune, and one receives here great blessings from his departed grandmother. {Second Yin advances, but there is no response [i.e., from Fifth Yin], so its virtue does not shine forth, and this is why the text says "now advancing, now saddening." Abiding in the center, Second Yin achieves a rightful position [as a yin line in a yin position]; treading the path of obedience, one here practices rectitude and does not let the will deviate because of any lack of response. This represents someone who is able to achieve perfect sincerity when situated in obscurity. This one cultivates his virtue in such a way that it is done even in extreme isolation and thereby achieves good fortune through righteousness, and this is why the text says: "Constancy means good fortune." A mother is someone who resides within and perfects her virtue. "A calling crane is in the shadows; its young answer it."[8] One establishes his sincerity in obscurity but even in obscurity would have a response to it. This is why at first it is "now saddening." It is because Second Yin treads the path of constancy and does not deviate that one "receives here great blessings from his departed grandmother."}

COMMENTARY ON THE IMAGES

"One receives here great blessings," because of his centrality [adherence to the Mean] and righteousness.

Third Yin

All trust, so regret vanishes. {This is not a rightful position for Third Yin [it is a yin line in a yang position], so there should be regret. As Third Yin's will is fixed on moving upward, it enjoys the trust of all the others [i.e., First Yin and Second Yin, which also want to move upward]. Obedient, it attaches itself to the bright [the upper trigram, *Li*, immediately above] and thus manages to have "regret vanish."}

COMMENTARY ON THE IMAGES

All trust this one, for his will is fixed on moving upward.

Fourth Yang

Now advancing like a flying squirrel, this one should practice constancy in the face of danger. {Where Fourth Yang treads is not its rightful position [it is a yang line in a yin position]. Above, it would provide carriage for Fifth Yin [a yang line should not carry a yin line], and, below, it would use the three yin lines for support, so where it treads is definitely not its rightful place.[9] Whether it carries the one on its back or rides on the others, on the one hand, no undertaking can be made secure, and, on the other, its ambitions have absolutely no support, so to try to advance under such conditions would justly lead to disaster. Someone who advances like a flying squirrel lacks the wherewithal to keep safe.[10]}

COMMENTARY ON THE IMAGES

As a flying squirrel, "one should practice constancy in the face of danger," for his position here is not right.

Fifth Yin

Regret vanishes, and one should not worry about failure or success, for to set forth here means good fortune, and nothing shall fail to be fitting. {Here the soft and yielding obtains the exalted position, and a yin becomes a bright ruler [i.e., the ruler of *Li*, the upper trigram]. Such a one can avoid recourse to scrutiny and need not supersede the duties of those beneath him. Thus, although he might not be suitable for the position, he does away with any need to regret it. "One should not worry about failure or success," because for each and every thing there is someone to look after it. So when one sets about doing things with such a method, "nothing shall fail to be fitting."}

COMMENTARY ON THE IMAGES

"One should not worry about failure or success," for when one sets forth here, he shall have blessings.

Top Yang

This one has advanced as far as he can go, so now all he can do is attack the city. Although there is danger, he shall have good fortune and so will have no blame, but such behavior regards baseness as constancy. {Top Yang is located at the very extremity of Advance and exceeds the Mean associated with the bright,[11] so the light is about to be suppressed accordingly.[12] One here is already as far as he can go[13] yet would still advance more, so if this be not overreaching, then what is it? As this one fails to deal with things as natural transformations of the Dao and in terms of no purposeful action [*wuwei*], he certainly must attack, for only then will he subdue the city. With danger he obtains good fortune, and with good fortune he frees himself from blame, but to use such a method to effect rectification is, of course, despicable.}

COMMENTARY ON THE IMAGES

When "all [one] can do is attack the city," the Dao never shines brightly.

NOTES

1. Kong Yingda comments: "Not only is he the recipient of large numbers of gifts, he also is frequently favored by his sovereign, that is, he has three court audiences each day." See *Zhouyi zhengyi*, 4: 11a.

2. This and all subsequent text set off in this manner is commentary by Wang Bi.

3. Cf. Hexagram 6, *Song* (Contention), Top Yang, and Wang's commentary to it.

4. The lower trigram is *Kun* (Pure Yin, i.e., Earth), and the upper trigram is *Li* (Cohesion, i.e., Fire, the Sun). Note also that *Kun* represents the utmost of obedience.

5. See note 4 above. The hexagram is supposed to represent the sun over the earth, that is, daytime.

6. Although Wang Bi and Kong Yingda gloss *cui* (oppress, repress, frustrate) as "retreat," both Cheng Yi and Zhu Xi take it in its basic, original sense, so their reading of First Yin would read: "Although advance here is frustrated, constancy will mean good fortune." See *Zhouyi zhengyi*, 4: 12a, and *Zhouyi zhezhong*, 5: 24a–24b.

7. Kong Yingda comments: "He ought to expand and enrich his virtue, which will enable his achievements to spread far and wide." See *Zhouyi zhengyi*, 4: 12a. Cheng Yi glosses *yu* (enrich) as *yongrong kuanyu* (at ease/poised and generous), as such a one here "should not be anxious about gaining the confidence of those above." See *Zhouyi zhezhong*, 5: 24b.

8. See Hexagram 61, *Zhongfu* (Inner Trust), Second Yang.

9. Kong Yingda comments: "The line above [Fifth Yin] is unwilling to have [Fourth Yang] carry it, and the lines below are unwilling to grant it support, so if one were to try to advance under such circumstances, no un-

dertaking would be secure, and no support so acquired could be kept intact." See *Zhouyi zhengyi*, 4: 13a.

10. "Flying squirrel" translates *shishu*. This interpretation follows the comments of Kong Yingda:

> The way one behaves here is just like the *shishu*, an animal that lacks the wherewithal for success. . . . In Cai Yong's [133–192] *Quan xue pian* [Encouragement to learning], there occurs the statement: "The five things of which the *shishu* is capable do not amount to one real skill." . . . [Xu Shen's (30–124)] *Shuowen jiezi* (Explanations of simple and composite characters) identifies the *shishu* with the *wujishu* (five-skills rodent): "It can fly but not so that it can pass over a roof; it can climb but not so that it can reach the top of a tree; it can swim but not so that it can cross a narrow valley stream; it can burrow but not so that it can cover itself; and it can run but not so that it can beat a man." . . . Zheng Xuan [127–200] cites the *Shijing* [Book of odes, no. 113]: "*Shishu* [big rat], *shishu*, don't eat our millet," etc., to explain *shishu* here, . . . but as Mr. Wang uses the expression, "lacks the wherewithal to keep safe," we ought to take *shishu* to mean the "five-skills rodent" [i.e., the flying squirrel].

See *Zhouyi zhengyi*, 4: 13a. Both Cheng Yi and Zhu Xi reject Wang's and Kong's interpretation and, following Zheng Xuan, read *shishu* as "big rat"—a rapacious rodent, frightened but stealthy. However, this interpretation presents problems for the way they understand the expression *zhenli* (practice constancy in the face of danger). Cheng takes it to indicate that one here should "start on the way to reform," and Zhu says: "If the diviner gets such a prognostication as this, even if he be righteous, he shall still be in danger." See *Zhouyi zhezhong*, 5: 26a.

11. That is, this one exceeds the Mean associated with enlightened rule—it literally has gone beyond the middle of *Li*, the upper trigram.

12. This alludes to the following hexagram, *Mingyi* (Suppression of the Light, Hexagram 36), in which *Li* (Fire, Cohesion, Brightness) becomes the lower trigram.

13. "Is already as far as he can go" translates *yi zai hu jue*. The character *jue* is usually read *jiao* (horn[s]), but the context of Wang's use of it suggests that it should be read *jue*, literally "southwest"—i.e., the last place where one in north China would see the sun before it finally sets. In fact, Kong Yingda glosses *jue* as *dongnan yu* (the farthest reaches in the southwest): "Here at the very extremity of Advance it is just like when the sun has passed the middle of its journey and is already at the southwest [*jue*], where it still keeps advancing." See *Zhouyi zhengyi*, 4: 13b. That Top Yang is, of course, also at the end of the upper trigram *Li* (Brightness, etc.) and the fact that Top Yang of *Jin* (Advance) leads to *Mingyi* (Suppression of the Light), the next hexagram, which deals with the demise of brightness (the Dao of good government), both suggest that Wang and Kong are correct in reading *jiao* (horn[s]) as *jue* (southwest)—the farthest point the sun reaches before it is gone. However, both Cheng Yi and Zhu Xi read the

character as *jiao* (horn[s]) and insist that it refers to the horns on the head (at the end) of a beast—male hardness and strength gone to an extreme. This, in turn, serves as an image of harsh government and its punitive policies. See *Zhouyi zhezhong*, 5: 27a–27b.

HEXAGRAM 36

䷣

明夷

Mingyi [Suppression of the Light]
(*Li* Below *Kun* Above)

Judgment

Suppression of the Light is such that it is fitting to practice constancy in the face of adversity.

COMMENTARY ON THE JUDGMENTS

When the light has gone into the earth, there is Suppression of the Light.[1] Inside all cultivation and light and outside all yielding and obedience, so should one be when beset with great adversity, as was King Wen.[2] "It is fitting to practice constancy in the face of adversity" means to keep one's brilliance in the dark. Though there is adversity within, yet one should be able to rectify his will, as did the viscount of Ji.[3]

COMMENTARY ON THE IMAGES

"The light has gone into the earth": this constitutes the image of Suppression of the Light.[4] In the same way, the noble man oversees the mass of common folk. {One who displays brilliance in overseeing the mass of common folk will harm them and make them false.[5] This is why one should take cover to nourish his rectitude and should keep his brilliance suppressed to oversee the masses.[6]} It is by keeping it dark that brilliance is had. {It is by keeping one's brilliance hidden within that one really achieves brilliance, for when one's brilliance is displayed without, it will be shunned as artfulness.[7]}

PROVIDING THE SEQUENCE OF THE HEXAGRAMS

Going forward is sure to involve getting wounded. This is why *Jin* [Advance, Hexagram 35] is followed by *Mingyi* [Suppression of the Light]. *Yi* here means "wounding."

THE HEXAGRAMS IN IRREGULAR ORDER

Mingyi [Suppression of the Light] indicates castigation.

First Yang

Suppression of the Light finds this one in flight, keeping his wings folded. This noble man on the move does not eat for three days. Whenever he sets off to a place, the host there has something to say about it. {The ruler of Suppression of the Light is located at Top Yin, which represents the darkest dark. First Yang is located at the beginning of the hexagram, the furthest from adversity. Wishing to put the utmost distance between him and adversity, Suppression of the Light makes him flee far. In order to conceal his movements completely, he does not follow well-worn roads. Thus the text says: "Suppression of the Light finds this one in flight." Filled with dread, he makes his way, his movements reflecting the fact that he dares not attract attention. This is why the text says "keeping his wings folded." His journey is prompted by his esteem for righteousness, thus the text says "this noble man on the move." His will is fixed anxiously on moving along, so, though hungry, he does not take the time to eat. Thus the text says "does not eat for three days." As this one differs from his fellow men to an utmost degree, when he approaches someone as such, that person is sure to be suspicious of him. Thus the text says: "Whenever he sets off to a place, the host there has something to say about it."[8]}

COMMENTARY ON THE IMAGES

When a "noble man is on the move," he does not eat out of a sense of righteousness.

Second Yin

Suppression of the Light finds this one wounded in the left thigh, but he is saved by a horse's strength and as a result has good fortune.[9] {To be "wounded in the left thigh" means that one cannot be strong in his movements. Second Yin fills a central position [adheres to the Mean] with softness and compliance. This one suppresses his brilliance, and, as a result, if he were to advance, he would not seem different from his fellow men, and, if he were to retreat, he would not draw closer to adversity. He is neither suspected nor feared, for he "takes compliance as his rule." Therefore "he is saved by a horse's strength and as a result has good fortune." Here one does not "keep . . . his wings folded," and only because of that does he manage to make his escape.}

COMMENTARY ON THE IMAGES

That Second Yin has good fortune is because such a one takes compliance as his rule.

Third Yang

Suppression of the Light finds this one on a southern hunt. He captures the great chief but must not be hasty to put constancy into practice. {Third Yang occupies the top position in the lower trigram, so it is located at the apex of cultivation and light. Top Yin represents the darkest dark, something that has gone into the earth. Therefore this one at Third Yang suppresses his brilliance so he can succeed in going on a southern hunt, where he captures the great chief [Top Yin]. With this southern hunt he manifests his brilliance.[10] Once he has killed the ruler, he can go on to rectify the people. But the people have been misled for such a very long time that their transformation ought to take place gradually; one must not try to rectify them quickly. Thus the text says: "He . . . must not be hasty to put constancy into practice."[11]}

COMMENTARY ON THE IMAGES

It was the will being fixed on the southern hunt that brought about this great success. {That is, it eliminated the ruler of darkness.}

Fourth Yin

This one enters into the left side of the belly and so obtains the heart of [him who effects] Suppression of the Light, this by leaving his gate and courtyard. {"Left" here indicates that this one takes compliance as his course of action, and by entering into the left side of [the ruler's] belly he gets at what is in his heart and mind. Therefore, though close to him, he is in no danger. To avoid adversity as the vicissitudes of the moment prompt, one need only repair to his gate and courtyard, but how could this not be taken for disobedience![12]}

COMMENTARY ON THE IMAGES

It is by "enter[ing] into the left side of the belly" that this one gets at what is in the heart and mind.

Fifth Yin

Suppression of the Light as a viscount of Ji experiences it means that it is fitting to practice constancy. {As Fifth Yin is closest to the darkness and is contiguous with adversity, there is no greater danger. Yet in the midst of this, even the darkness cannot drown him, and his brilliance cannot be extinguished. Such rectitude does not grieve at the danger, and this is why the text says: "It is fitting to practice constancy."}

COMMENTARY ON THE IMAGES

The constancy of a viscount of Ji is such that his brilliance cannot be extinguished.

Top Yin

Not bright but dark, this one first climbed up to heaven but then entered into the earth. {Top Yin is located at the most extreme reach of Suppression of the Light; it represents the darkest dark. In the beginning, the fundamental role of this one was to cast light but, gradually tending toward darkness, it eventually entered into the earth.}

COMMENTARY ON THE IMAGES

This one first climbed up to Heaven and cast light on states in all four directions. The reason such a one later entered into the earth [i.e., perished] was that he had lost the right way to rule.

NOTES

1. See Wang's remarks on this hexagram in section seven of his General Remarks.

2. King Wen, the father of King Wu who overthrew the Shang and founded the Zhou state (1122 B.C.), was, supposedly, the long-suffering vassal of Zhou, the wicked last Shang king.

3. The viscount of Ji was an uncle of Zhou, the wicked last Shang king. He first tried to remonstrate with his nephew and then, when he saw that it was to no avail, withdrew from court, here, the "within."

4. The lower trigram is *Li* (Cohesion, i.e., Fire, the Sun), and the upper trigram is *Kun* (Pure Yin, i.e., Earth): in other words, light is below the earth.

5. Cf. *Laozi*, section 65, p. 168: "Those of antiquity who excelled at practicing the Dao did not use it to enlighten the common folk but to keep them stupid." Wang Bi comments: " 'Enlightened' here means to have too much knowledge and to be artful and crafty, something that harms one's pristine simplicity. 'Stupid' means to preserve one's true nature unself-consciously and to be in accord with nature." "Enlightened" here translates *ming*, the "light" and "brilliance" of *Mingyi* (Suppression of the Light).

6. This and all subsequent text set off in this manner is commentary by Wang Bi.

7. Wang Bi again comments on *Laozi*, section 65, p. 168: "If one goes further and uses artful craftiness to prevent the common folk from being false, as they will see through this craftiness, they will thwart such efforts and shun him." Cheng Yi interprets the Commentary on the Images to *Mingyi* very differently:

> Brightness is the means by which illumination is had. The noble man never fails to illuminate things, but if he were to use an excess of brightness, it would do harm to his powers of scrutiny. When one uses too much scrutiny, though he may complete what has to be done, he will be deficient in the "vast power to accommodate" [see Hexagram 2, *Kun* (Pure Yin), Commentary on the Judgments]. Thus the noble man . . . does not utilize his powers of bright scru-

> tiny to the utmost but instead uses a muted approach, for only then will he be able to treat others with tolerance and bring harmony to the masses.

See *Zhouyi zhezhong*, 12: 12b.

8. Both Cheng Yi and Zhu Xi interpret First Yang somewhat differently. In particular, they gloss *chui qi yi* (keeping his wings folded) as "drooping" or "lowering his wings"—as a bird does when wounded. Cheng's comments are the more detailed:

> Whenever petty men harm a noble man, they harm his ability to act [literally, "that by which he moves/acts"]. . . . With his bright perspicacity, the noble man discerns the subtleties underlying trends and events. Although here at the beginning [of Suppression of the Light] there are clues as to why he gets wounded, they are not yet apparent, but the noble man can discern them, and this is why he goes away to avoid such things happening. . . . Awareness of the incipiency of things is a function of the unique vision of the noble man; it is not something that can be recognized by the mass of men. . . . So who among the common mass of men would fail to find his behavior suspicious and peculiar?

See *Zhouyi zhezhong*, 5: 29a–29b.

9. Cf. Hexagram 59, *Huan* (Dispersion), First Yin.

10. Cheng Yi expands upon the significance of the southern hunt: "The south is in front and in the direction of brightness. A hunt involves chasing down and eradicating that which causes harm, so a 'southern hunt' means to go forward and eliminate harm." See *Zhouyi zhezhong*, 5: 31a.

11. Both Cheng Yi and Zhu Xi remark that the meaning of Third Yang can be seen in how King Tang overthrew the Xia to found the Shang dynasty and how King Wu (and Wen) overthrew the Shang to found the Zhou.

12. Cheng Yi takes Fourth Yin differently and thinks that it concerns the way a petty man ingratiates himself with a corrupt ruler, and, once he has that ruler's confidence, "he can then go out and about." What I have translated as "this by leaving his gate and courtyard" (*yu chu menting*) Cheng would seem to interpret as "at this he may leave gate and courtyard." Zhu Xi's interpretation is again different. He rejects Cheng's reading and insists that all the lines represent the *junzi* (noble man) except Top Yin, and he seems to read *yu chu menting* much as Wang Bi reads it: "One obtains the heart . . . by leaving one's gate and courtyard." However, unlike Wang, who takes this to mean that one should not try to hide at home but come to court and survive there, in effect, by outwitting the ruler, Zhu thinks that one at Fourth Yin (the lowest position in the upper, *Kun* [Darkness] trigram—where the force of darkness is at its weakest) has enough integrity of purpose to see things from an external perspective (the perspective of those in the lower, *Li* [Brightness] trigram) and so knows that he dwells in the midst of Suppression of the Light and that he "should leave it and go far away." See *Zhouyi zhezhong*, 5: 31b–32b.

HEXAGRAM 37

☲

家人

Jiaren [The Family]
(*Li* Below *Sun* Above)

Judgment

The Family is such that it is fitting that the woman practice constancy. {The concept underlying the Family is that each family member cultivates the Dao of his own family and that he is incapable of understanding the affairs of other people outside the family. In terms of the general and unifying principle involved, constancy here is not the constancy of the noble man with its scope of fundamental prevalence, so this is why "it is fitting that the woman practice constancy." Her practice of it is properly only something for inside the family.[1]}

COMMENTARY ON THE JUDGMENTS

As far as the Family is concerned, the woman's proper place is inside it, {This refers to Second Yin.} and the man's proper place is outside it. {This refers to Fifth Yang. As a concept, the Family is based on what the inner [lower] trigram represents [of which Second Yin is the ruler], and this is why the text mentions the woman first.} Male and female should keep to their proper places; this is the fundamental concept expressed by Heaven and Earth. The Family is provided with strict sovereigns, whom we call Father and Mother [Fifth Yang and Second Yin]. When the father behaves as a father, the mother as a mother, the son as son, the elder brother as elder brother, the younger brother as younger brother, the husband as husband, and the wife as wife, then the Dao of the Family will be correctly fulfilled. When the Family is so maintained with rectitude, the entire world will be settled and at peace.[2]

COMMENTARY ON THE IMAGES

Wind emerges from Fire: this constitutes the image of the Family.[3] {It is a powerful action that starts from the inside [the inner trigram] and provides for their mutual generation.[4]} In the same way, the noble man ensures that his words have substance and his actions perseverance. {In the Dao of the Family, one should tend to familiar and little things and avoid any carelessness or rashness in doing so. Thus should the noble man "ensure . . . that his words have substance" and that he put nothing in his mouth that does not belong there; he should "ensure that . . . his actions have perseverance" and that he allow himself to do nothing that should not be done.}

PROVIDING THE SEQUENCE OF THE HEXAGRAMS

When one is wounded abroad, he is sure to return to his own home. This is why *Mingyi* [Suppression of the Light, Hexagram 37] is followed by *Jiaren* [The Family].

THE HEXAGRAMS IN IRREGULAR ORDER

Jiaren [The Family] signifies a turning inward.

First Yang

As this one maintains the Family with strict control, regret disappears. {It is generally true that teaching should take place from the first and that rules should be set right at the beginning. If one waits until the Family is embroiled in confusion before taking strict measures or if one waits until its goal turns to deviant purposes before taking corrective steps, then he shall surely have cause for regret. First Yin is located at the initial position of the Family hexagram, so it represents how one should deal with the Family in its beginning phase. Thus it is appropriate that the Family be maintained with strict control here, for only then will the cause for regret disappear.}

COMMENTARY ON THE IMAGES

When one strictly controls the Family, its goals will not become deviant.

Second Yin

This one has no matters to set off to and pursue but stays within and prepares food. Such constancy means good fortune. {Second Yin abides in the inner trigram in the central position [in the Mean], so it manages to tread on the territory of its rightful position, and, as a yin, it responds to a yang [Fifth Yang], so it fulfills perfectly the correct meaning of what it is to be a wife. This one has nothing else that she need pursue and so applies herself within to preparing food, free of all concerns save compliance and obedience. This is why "such constancy means good fortune."}

COMMENTARY ON THE IMAGES

The good fortune that Second Yin has is due to obedience and compliance.

Third Yang

If the Family is run with ruthless severity, one may regret the degree of it, yet there will be good fortune. But if wife and child overindulge in frivolous laughter, in the end it will result in baseness. {As this is a strong line in a strong position, it represents someone who is hard and strict. Third Yang occupies the topmost position in the lower trigram, so it represents the leader of one family. Rather than let one's actions be affected by carelessness, it is better to be too solemn; rather than let one's family be affected by confusion, it is better to be too strict. This is why even when "the family is run with ruthless severity," the degree of which one may regret, still it will fulfill the Dao proper to it. "But if wife and child overindulge in frivolous laughter," such a family violates basic rules and standards.}

COMMENTARY ON THE IMAGES

"If the Family is run with ruthless severity," no violation occurs, "but if wife and child overindulge in frivolous laughter," this violates the basic rules and standards of the family.

Fourth Yin

This one enriches the Family, so there is great good fortune. {Fourth Yin is able to use her riches and so fills her position with obedience. This is why "there is great good fortune." But if she is only able to enrich her Family, how is this enough to constitute "great good fortune"? Soft and yielding, she dwells in Compliance [*Sun*, the upper trigram] and treads on the territory of her rightful position [as a yin line in a yin position]. She is brilliantly successful at the Dao of the Family and, as such, stays close to the exalted position [Fifth Yang, the ruler of the hexagram]. This is how she is able to enrich her Family.}

COMMENTARY ON THE IMAGES

"This one enriches the Family, so there is great good fortune," for she fills her position with obedience.

Fifth Yang

Only when a true king arrives will there be a real Family,[5] so let him be without worry, for he shall have good fortune. {*Jia* [come/go] here means *zhi* [arrive]. Fifth Yang treads the path of righteousness and is responsive, occupies the exalted position, is the embodiment of Compliance [*Sun*, the upper trigram], and maintains his family as a true king who perfectly realizes the Dao involved. This one abides in the exalted position and is brilliantly successful at the Dao of the Family, thus none of those below fail to be transformed. As the father behaves as a father, the son as son, the elder brother as elder brother, the younger brother as younger brother, the husband as husband, and the wife as wife, the six familial relationships are harmonious and amicable, with each attending to the other with love and joy. As such, the Dao of the Family operates with perfect correctness. This is why "only when a true king arrives will there be a real family, so let him be without worry, for he shall have good fortune."}

COMMENTARY ON THE IMAGES

This one maintains the Family with the perfection of a true king, so each attends to the other with love.

Top Yang

This one inspires trust and is awesome, so in the end there is good fortune. {Top Yang is located at the end point of the Family hexagram and dwells where the Dao of the Family has reached full maturity. "He was an example to his wife" and thereby had an effect on those outside.[6] This is why the text says: "This one inspires trust." Whenever one's basic nature is characterized by fierceness, the main cause for worry will be his lack of mercy, and whenever one's basic nature is characterized by love, the main cause for worry will be that he lacks the means to inspire awe. This is why the Dao of the Family emphasizes awe and strictness above all else. The only way possible for the Dao of the Family to reach its end point of development is for it to work through trust and awe. If one acquires an aura of awe and respect for himself, others will react accordingly, and if one turns inward and reflects on this awe and respect, he will know how to use them to affect others.}

COMMENTARY ON THE IMAGES

That good fortune follows upon the inspiration of awe means that this one has reflected upon what awe means to himself.

NOTES

1. This and all subsequent text set off in this manner is commentary by Wang Bi.

2. Cf. *Lunyu* (Analects) 12:11.

3. The lower trigram is *Li* (Fire, Cohesion), and the upper trigram is *Sun* (Wind, Compliance).

4. Kong Yingda comments: "*Sun* is outside *Li*, so this means that the wind emerges consequent to the fire. When the fire first emerges, it becomes a powerful action, thanks to the wind, and once the fire is burning at full strength, this again produces more wind. There is in the way these inner and outer phenomena generate each other a resemblance to the concept that constitutes The Family." See *Zhouyi zhengyi*, 4: 16b.

5. Cf. the Judgment of *Cui* (Gathering), Hexagram 45, and that of *Huan* (Dispersion), Hexagram 59.

6. Wang quotes and paraphrases from the *Shijing* (Book of odes), no. 240, which describes how perfectly King Wen (the founder of the Zhou dynasty) filled his role as family head and how this had a salutary influence on the whole realm.

HEXAGRAM 38

䷥

睽

Kui [Contrariety]

(*Dui* Below *Li* Above)

Judgment

In small matters there is good fortune.[1]

COMMENTARY ON THE JUDGMENTS

The movement of fire is such that it goes up, whereas the movement of water is such that it goes down. Two daughters may live together, but their aspirations do not pursue the same path. It is by being joyous and clinging to the bright, by advancing softly and so moving upward, and by achieving centrality [the Mean] in responding to the hard and strong that one here manages to have good fortune in small matters. {When things always go against each other, this constitutes the dao of harm. So what is the means here by which one may have "good fortune in small matters"? It is by having these three virtues.[2]} Heaven and Earth may be contrary entities, but their task is the same. Male and female may be contrary entities, but they share the same goal. The myriad things may be contrary entities each to the other, but as functioning entities they are all similar. A time of Contrariety can indeed be put to great use! {A time of Contrariety is not something that can be put to use by the petty man.}

COMMENTARY ON THE IMAGES

Above Fire and below Lake: this constitutes the image of Contrariety.[3] In the same way, the noble man differentiates among things while remaining sensitive to their similarities. {His appreciation of similarities stems from his thorough grasp of the principles of things, and his appreciation of differences emerges in the course of his practical handling of affairs.[4]}

COMMENTARY ON THE APPENDED PHRASES

They strung pieces of wood to make bows and whittled others to make arrows. The benefit of bows and arrows was such that they dominated the world. They probably got the idea for this from the hexagram *Kui* [Contrariety].[5]

PROVIDING THE SEQUENCE OF THE HEXAGRAMS

When the Dao of the family is completely exhausted, there is sure to be discord. This is why *Jiaren* [The Family, Hexagram 37] is followed by *Kui* [Contrariety]. Contrariety here means "discord."

THE HEXAGRAMS IN IRREGULAR ORDER

Kui [Contrariety] signifies a turning outward.

First Yang

Regret disappears. If one here loses his horse, he need not pursue it, for it will come back as a matter of course. As he meets with evil men, he avoids blame. {First Yang is located at the beginning of the Contrariety hexagram, abiding at the bottom of the lower trigram. As it is without a line to resonate with and has to stand alone, one here should feel regret. But as it shares a common aspiration with Fourth Yang, it succeeds in having that regret disappear. A horse is something whose whereabouts will certainly be uncovered. When one here first finds himself among others, so much obstreperousness prevails that he "loses his horse." As none of the others can unite in purpose, self-interest ensures that each will uncover the other [as far as hiding the horse is concerned]. This is why "he need not pursue it, for it will come back as a matter of course."[6] This is just the time when estrangement prevails, and First Yang is positioned at the very bottom. There is no one above who can respond with help, and, here below, this one has no power on which he might rely. If he were to reveal his virtue and set himself apart, he would be harmed by evildoers, [but he does not do so] and this is how "he meets with evil men" and thereby successfully "avoids blame."[7]}

COMMENTARY ON THE IMAGES

"He meets with evil men" and in so doing "avoids blame."

Second Yang

This one meets his master in a narrow lane, so there is no blame. {Located here in Contrariety, Second Yang is in a wrong position for it [because it is a yang line in a yin position], so such a one here will experience insecurity in whatever he does. However, Fifth Yin is also in a position that is wrong for it, so they both go off to seek their own coterie, and, when they leave their gates and head in the same direction, they meet unexpectedly. This is why the text says "meets his master in a narrow lane." Located here in Contrariety, Second Yang obtains assistance, so, although it is in a wrong position, it "still never loses the Dao."[8]}

COMMENTARY ON THE IMAGES

"This one meets his master in a narrow lane," so still never loses the Dao.

Third Yin

Here one has his wagon hauled back and oxen controlled. This one has the forehead tattooed and nose cut off. But whereas nothing good here happens at the start, things end well. {Whenever creatures are close but do not get along together, there will be misfortune. Third Yin is located in Contrariety in such a way that it is not in a rightful position for it. As a yin, it abides in a yang position; as a soft and weak line, it rides atop a hard and strong line. As its aspiration is fixed on Top Yang, it is not in a harmonious relationship with Fourth Yang, and Second Yang is already in a resonate relationship with Fifth Yin; so, although contiguous with [these two yang lines], it must not form a pair with either of them. This is why the text says: "One has his wagon hauled back." That "his wagon is hauled back" means that where Third Yin treads is not the territory of its rightful position, so it loses its means of carriage. "Oxen controlled" means that this one is detained right here and so does not succeed in advancing. "This one has the forehead tattooed and nose cut off" refers to how Fourth Yang seizes Third Yin from above and how Second Yang seizes it from below, yet Third Yin, true to its resonance with Top Yang, holds fast to its goal and does not falter.[9] So, although at first Third Yin suffers difficulties, in the end it acquires the assistance of the hard and the strong [Top Yang].}

COMMENTARY ON THE IMAGES

That one here "has his wagon hauled back" is due to its position not being suitable. That "nothing good here happens at the start, [but] things end well" is due to meeting the hard and strong one [Top Yang].

Fourth Yang

Contrariety finds this one isolated, but he does meet a prime stalwart. They trust each other, so although there is danger, there is no blame. {Fourth Yang has no line with which to resonate and takes its place all alone. Fifth Yin is itself in resonance with Second Yang, and Third Yin is in a contrary posture with relation to Fourth Yang, so this is why the text says: "Contrariety finds this one isolated." First Yang also is without a resonate relationship and has to take a separate stand. Located here at a time of Contrariety, both find themselves standing alone, similarly occupying the bottom positions in their respective trigrams, and they are comrades. But Fourth Yang is located in a wrong position for it [because it is a yang line in a yin position]; it would form a pair with Third Yin or Fifth Yin, but these are both estranged from it. So its location lacks all means to provide security. This is why it seeks a companion of its own kind and so entrusts itself to it. Thus the text says: "He does meet a prime stalwart."[10] Comrades get along and harbor no suspicions about each other. Thus the text says: "They trust each other." Although one might find himself in the midst of estrangement, when the will is firm, it realizes its goals. Thus, in spite of danger here, "there is no blame."}

COMMENTARY ON THE IMAGES

"They trust each other," and "there is no blame," for the will realizes its goals.

Fifth Yin

Regret disappears. His clansman bites through skin, so if one were to set forth here, what blame would there be? {As this is not its proper position [it is a yin line in a yang position], there should be regret, but as Fifth Yin has a resonate relationship with Second Yang, it [regret] disappears. "His clansman" refers to Second Yang, and "bites through skin" means "to bite into something soft."[11] Although Third Yin would form a pair with Second Yang, once it has been bitten, it ceases to stand in the way of Second Yang responding to Fifth Yin. If one were to set forth under such circumstances, what blame could there possibly be? Setting forth here will surely result in union [between Fifth Yin and Second Yang].}

COMMENTARY ON THE IMAGES

"His clansman bites through skin," so if one were to set forth here, he would have blessings.

Top Yang

Contrariety finds this one isolated. He sees a pig covered with mud, a cart filled with demons. First he draws his bow but later unstrings it. If it were not for the enemy, there would be a marriage. He should set forth now, for once he encounters rain, there will be good fortune. {Top Yang is located at the end point of Contrariety, and, as the path through Contrariety is not open to this one, the text says: "Contrariety finds this one isolated." Whereas Top Yang abides where the blaze is most fierce, Third Yin abides where the marsh is most wet.[12] These are the extremes of Contrariety. To gaze upon the most filthy of things from the most cultured and enlightened vantage point is certainly Contrariety at its utmost. There is no more filthy thing than a pig covered with mud. But when Contrariety is brought to its most extreme, it means that things will then tend to unity, and when differences are at their most extreme, it means that things will then tend to harmony. "Things might be oversize, deviant, deceptive, or strange, but the Dao tends to make them all into one."[13] Before attaining to a well-ordered state, things will first appear very distinct from one another. This is why when "he looks upon [Third Yin as] a pig covered with mud," it seems the filthiest thing possible, and when "he looks upon [Third Yin as] a cart filled with demons," it seems strange enough to make him cry out in dismay. He first draws his bow and is about to attack what he takes to be harm, but later unstrings it, for the estrangement gives way to harmony. Fourth Yang has tattooed the one with whom Top Yang is in resonance [i.e., blocked Third Yin's way], thus Fourth Yang is the "enemy."[14] The determination [of Top Yang and Third Yin] here in the face of Contrariety is about to bring about their union. If it were not for the enemy [Fourth Yang], they would already be married, but to set forth now would not be untimely, for the suspicions generated by Contrariety should disappear. One places value on encountering rain, because it unites yin and yang. Once yin and yang are united, all suspicions will disappear.}

COMMENTARY ON THE IMAGES

The good fortune that stems from encountering rain means that all suspicions will disappear.

NOTES

1. See Wang's remarks on this hexagram in section seven of his General Remarks.

2. This and all subsequent text set off in this manner is commentary by Wang Bi.

3. The lower trigram is *Dui* (Lake, Joy), and the upper trigram is *Li* (Fire, Cohesion).

4. That is, just as the unity (sameness) of the *Kui* hexagram consists of contrary (different) parts, so the noble man appreciates how the unity of the whole Dao incorporates individual phenomenological differences. Cheng Yi offers a different interpretation: "In the same way, the noble man identifies [with the great moral principles that all men share] yet distinguishes himself [from the common errors of the vulgar]." He should be in but not of the common world. See *Zhouyi zhezhong*, 12: 16b.

5. See section two of the Commentary on the Appended Phrases, Part Two, and note 20 there.

6. Kong Yingda comments: "This is just the time when Contrariety takes hold, so estrangement is all too readily apparent. A horse is a kind of animal that can only be hidden with difficulty. Although one may perhaps lose one for a time, this is something that people here will not cover up for each other, and one need not go to look for it, for circumstances are such

that it will come back to him as a matter of course." See *Zhouyi zhengyi*, 4: 19b.

7. Cheng Yi identifies the horse with Fourth Yang: "A horse is the means by which one moves. A yang is something that moves upward. Only during a time of Contrariety is this denied to one so that he cannot move. This is what is meant by he 'loses his horse.' But once Fourth Yang combines forces with First Yang, then First Yang can move again. This is what is meant by 'he need not pursue it,' for his horse will be had again." Cheng then goes on to explain how the noble man must not cut off relations with the mass of petty men, for they would soon regard him as an enemy, and then he could never convert them to righteousness. See *Zhouyi zhezhong*, 5: 39b.

8. Both Cheng Yi and Zhu Xi emphasize that the meeting of Second Yang and Fifth Yin is irregular and roundabout, and takes place under straitened circumstances because of the prevailing circumstance of Contrariety. Nothing great can happen here; the best that can be hoped for is to be without blame. See *Zhouyi zhezhong*, 5: 40b.

9. Kong Yingda comments: "Tattooing the forehead is what is meant here by *tian* [usually Heaven, the sky]." See *Zhouyi zhengyi*, 4: 20a. Both Cheng Yi and Zhu Xi think that *tian* refers to having the hair cut off. See *Zhouyi zhezhong*, 5: 41a–41b. Tattooing and nose amputation were punishments designed to mark criminals permanently to prevent them from continuing their criminal ways. Here they seem to be metaphors for blocking Third Yin's advance.

10. "Prime stalwart" translates *yuanfu*. Kong Yingda comments: "*Yuanfu* refers to First Yang. As this is located at the beginning of the hexagram, it is referred to as 'prime' [*yuan*]. First Yang and Fourth Yang are both yang lines, and when one of them is referred to as '*fu*,' it means the *fu* in *zhangfu* [stalwart]; it is not the *fu* of *fufu* [husband and wife]." See *Zhouyi zhengyi*, 4: 20a–20b. Cheng Yi is not in disagreement with this, but he adds the idea that *yuan* here also means *shan* (morally good/just). See *Zhouyi zhezhong*, 5: 42a.

11. Kong Yingda comments: "Third Yin is a yin line, this is why it can be symbolized by 'skin,' something soft and fragile." See *Zhouyi zhengyi*, 4: 20b.

12. Top Yang is located at the top of the *Li* (Fire) trigram, and Third Yin is located at the top of the *Dui* (Lake—i.e., Marsh) trigram.

13. Wang here paraphrases the *Zhuangzi*, 2/4/35. Instead of "the Dao tends to make them all into one," the *Zhuangzi* reads, "the Dao gives them a common identity and makes them one." See also Lou, *Wang Bi ji jiaoshi*, 2: 409 n. 21.

14. Both Cheng Yi and Zhu Xi think that Top Yang initially mistakes Third Yin, its natural partner, as an enemy. So what I have translated (following Wang Bi) as "If it were not for the enemy, there would be a marriage," Cheng and Zhu would seem to read as "It is not an enemy, so he [Top Yang] should marry [Third Yin]." See *Zhouyi zhezhong*, 5: 43b.

HEXAGRAM 39

䷦

蹇

Jian [Adversity]
(*Gen* Below *Kan* Above)

Judgment

Adversity is such that it is fitting to travel southwest but not fitting to travel northeast. {The southwest consists of level ground; the northeast consists of mountains. If when one is afflicted with trouble, he goes toward flat land, such trouble will disappear, but if he goes toward mountains, "the way [Dao] will peter out."[1]} It is fitting to see the great man. {If one sets forth here, he will find succor.} To practice constancy will bring good fortune. {All the hexagram lines are in rightful positions, so each treads the path that is correct for it. To tread the path of righteousness though faced with trouble is the Dao of the rightly governed state. As long as the path [Dao] of righteousness remains unobstructed, one will be saved from trouble by righteousness. Thus "to practice constancy will bring good fortune." However, if one were to stray from the path of righteousness upon encountering trouble, how could good fortune ever be had that way?}

COMMENTARY ON THE JUDGMENTS

Jian [Adversity] means trouble, that is, to be faced with danger. To be able to stop when one sees danger, this is indeed wisdom! When in Adversity, "it is fitting to travel southwest," for to set forth there would gain one a central position. It is "not fitting to travel northeast," for in that direction the way [Dao] will peter out. "It is fitting to see the great man," for to set forth there will bring meritorious achievement. The practice of constancy by those in rightful positions is the way to bring about the rightly governed state. At a time of Adversity, one is indeed offered great opportunities! {Adversity is not a time that can be put to use by the petty man.}

COMMENTARY ON THE IMAGES

Atop the Mountain, there is Water: this constitutes the image of Adversity.[2] {"Atop the Mountain, there is Water": this is the image of Adversity.} In the same way, the noble man reflects upon himself and cultivates virtue. {To dispel trouble there is nothing better that one can do than "reflect . . . upon himself and cultivate . . . virtue."[3]}

PROVIDING THE SEQUENCE OF THE HEXAGRAMS

When there is contrariety, there is sure to be trouble. This is why *Kui* [Contrariety, Hexagram 38] is followed by *Jian* [Adversity]. *Jian* here means "trouble."

THE HEXAGRAMS IN IRREGULAR ORDER

Jian [Adversity] means "trouble."

First Yin

If one sets forth here, he shall have Adversity, but if he comes back, he shall have praise. {First Yin is located at the beginning of trouble and abides at the place where one should first come to a stop. This one's unique vision and advance knowledge allow him to see the danger and so desist in order that he may wait for the right moment. This is indeed wisdom! Thus if one were to set forth here, he should meet with Adversity, but if he were to come back, he should obtain praise.}

COMMENTARY ON THE IMAGES

"If one sets forth here, he shall have Adversity, but if he comes back, he shall have praise," so this means that one should wait.

Second Yin

This minister of the king suffers Adversity upon Adversity, but it is not on his own account. {Located here at a time of Adversity, Second Yin treads on the territory of its rightful position [as a yin line in a yin position], situated so that it does not stray from the

Mean, and as such is in resonance with Fifth Yang. If Fifth Yang were not beset with trouble, this one out of personal considerations would distance himself from harm. Instead he keeps a firm grip on his heart and mind and does not turn back, his will fixed on rectifying his sovereign's affairs. This is why the text says: "This minister of the king suffers Adversity upon Adversity, but it is not on his own account." It is by treading the path of centrality [i.e., the Mean] and practicing righteousness that Second Yin preserves his sovereign. If one behaves in such a way when located in Adversity, he shall never suffer blame for it.}

COMMENTARY ON THE IMAGES

"This minister of the king suffers Adversity upon Adversity" but in the end will give no cause for blame.

Third Yang

To set forth here would result in Adversity, so this one comes back. {To advance would be to fall into danger [i.e., into *Kan* (Sink Hole)], but if one were to come back, he would obtain his proper position. This is why the text says: "To set forth here would result in Adversity, so this one comes back." Third Yang is the ruler of the lower trigram; this is the one on whom those within [i.e., the two yin lines of the inner (lower) trigram] rely.}

COMMENTARY ON THE IMAGES

"To set forth here would result in Adversity, so this one comes back," and those within take delight in it.

Fourth Yin

To set forth here would result in Adversity, and to come back would mean involvement. {If this one were to set forth, there would be no response [because Fourth Yin does not have a resonate line], and were he to come back, it would result in his having to ride atop the hard and strong [Third Yang], so setting forth and coming back both lead to trouble. This is why the text says: "To set forth here would lead to Adversity, and to come back would mean involvement."[4] Fourth Yin obtains a position that is right for it [i.e., it is a yin line in a yin position] and treads the path of righteousness, so such a role suits his basic nature, and, although he encounters trouble, he will not be provoked into foolhardy action.}

COMMENTARY ON THE IMAGES

"To set forth here would result in Adversity, and to come back would mean involvement," but this one has the substance to fill such a position.[5]

Fifth Yang

To one in great Adversity friends will come. {Of those located at a time of Adversity, Fifth Yang is the only one situated right in the middle of danger, so it represents the greatest of troubles. This is why the text says "great Adversity." However, it abides in such a way that it does not stray from rectitude and treads a path that does not stray from the Mean. This one's grip on virtue is long lasting; he never lets his moral integrity vary. To such a person as this comrades will indeed gather, and this is why the text says: "Friends will come."}

COMMENTARY ON THE IMAGES

"To one in great Adversity friends will come," because of his adherence to the Mean and moral integrity.

Top Yin

To set forth here will result in Adversity, but to come back means great success and so good fortune. It is fitting to see the great man. {To set forth here would result in everlasting troubles, but if one were to come back, one's troubles would end. With the end of one's troubles, the mass of common folk are also entirely saved from their troubles, such a goal to be realized in all its greatness. This is why the text says: "To set forth here will result in Adversity, but to come back means great success and so good fortune." When danger is eased and troubles dispelled, the great Dao can prosper. Thus the text says: "It is fitting to see the great man."}

COMMENTARY ON THE IMAGES

"To set forth would result in Adversity, but to come back should mean great success," for the will here is fixed on one inside. {Top Yin has a resonate relationship in the inner [lower] trigram [with Third Yang],[6] so if it were to set forth, it would lose that, but if it were to come back, its ambitions would garner success, for its will is fixed on one inside. "It is fitting to see the great man," for in so doing he will follow that estimable person.[7]}

NOTES

1. This and all subsequent text set off in this manner is commentary by Wang Bi.

2. The lower trigram is *Gen* (Mountain, Restraint), and the upper trigram is *Kan* (Water, Sink Hole).

3. Kong Yingda comments:

> Lu Ji [Three Kingdoms era (222–280) figure] said: "Water actually should be situated below the Mountain. Although it is now above the Mountain, it should in the end return [*fan*] below, and this is why the text says: 'reflect upon himself [*fanshen*].' When one finds himself in a world beset with trouble, he must not use it as a time for action. All he can do is reflect upon himself, undergo self-examination, and so cultivate the potential of his virtue. In so doing he will get rid of trouble."

See *Zhouyi zhengyi*, 4: 22a–22b.

4. "Involvement" translates *lian*. That Wang Bi interprets this as a troublesome, adverse involvement is obvious from his commentary. Kong Yingda supports him in this, as do the remarks by Ma Rong (79–166) and Zheng Xuan (127–200) that Kong quotes in his subcommentary; see *Zhouyi zhengyi*, 4: 33a. However, both Cheng Yi and Zhu Xi understand *lian* as the correct union of Fourth Yin with Third Yang and (Cheng) through Third Yang to "those below" (i.e., "the masses"), something that signifies the correct way to deal with a time of Adversity. See *Zhouyi zhezhong*, 5: 48a.

5. "Substance" translates *shi*, as in *benshi* (basic nature, one's "real stuff"), which Wang used in his remarks on Fourth Yin; i.e., with danger threatening from every side, one has to have real strength of character to maintain righteousness and act correctly. As Cheng Yi interprets Fourth Yin to mean that one here should unite with Third Yang, he understands *shi* as *chengshi* (sincerity), i.e., Fourth Yang ought to enter into a relationship with Third Yang and unite with those below with all "sincerity." See *Zhouyi zhezhong*, 12: 20a–20b.

6. Both Cheng Yi and Zhu Xi apparently interpret *nei* (inner, inside) not as referring to the inner (lower) trigram and Third Yang, Top Yin's resonate line, but as inside the Adversity hexagram and/or the upper trigram, *Kan* (Sink Hole). They emphasize the pairing of Top Yin and Fifth Yang and identify the "great man" with the ruler of the entire hexagram, Fifth Yang. So "Top Yin may resonate with Third Yang, but it follows Fifth Yang." See *Zhouyi zhezhong*, 5: 49b and 12: 21a.

7. Kong Yingda identifies *gui* (estimable) with *yang* (the hard and strong), i.e., Third Yang.

HEXAGRAM 40

䷧

解

Xie [Release]
(*Kan* Below *Zhen* Above)

Judgment

Release is such that it is fitting to travel southwest. {The southwest indicates the mass of common folk. When one dispels trouble and rescues a dangerous situation, it is fitting to extend such a thing to the masses. The encounter with trouble here does not result in coming to grief in the northeast, so this is why nothing is said about "not fitting to travel northeast."[1]} When there is nothing to set forth for, let there be a return, which shall mean good fortune, but when there is something to set forth for, quick action shall mean good fortune. {Someone good at dispelling troubles never goes astray when it comes to securing a safe place for himself. As a concept, Release means release from troubles and deliverance from danger. When there are no troubles worth setting forth to deal with, as Release has occurred, one should return and thus not stray off the middle path [or "be in violation of the Mean"], but if there are troubles such that one should set forth and deal with them, then good fortune will come about only if quick action is taken. When there are no troubles, one may return to his "position of centrality," but when there are troubles, one should be able to bring about deliverance from the danger involved.}

COMMENTARY ON THE JUDGMENTS

Xie [Release] is such that when there is danger one should make a move, for by so moving one avoids danger, that is, Release occurs. {One moves outside danger; this is why the text uses the word *avoids*. Once one avoids danger, he finds Release from it; this is why the word *Release* is used.} "Release is such that it is fitting to travel southwest," for by setting forth there one shall obtain the masses. "Let there be a return, which shall mean good fortune," for one thereby obtains a position of centrality. "When there is something to set forth for, quick action shall mean good fortune," for by so setting forth one shall have meritorious achievement. When Heaven and Earth allow Release, thunder and rain play their roles; when thunder and rain play their roles, all the various fruits, shrubs, and trees burgeon forth. {When Heaven and Earth are stopped up, thunder and rain do not play their roles; it is only with intercourse between them, which moves them to free up, that thunder and rain play their roles. Once thunder and rain play their roles, what was dangerous and difficult will give way to a prevailing ease, and what was stopped up will give way to a freedom of process. This is why "all the various fruits, shrubs, and trees burgeon forth."} A time of Release is indeed great! {No boundary fails to open up.[2] A time when troubles give way to Release is not a time when one should take steps to control troubles, thus we do not say anything about how one should make use of it. Everything involved is embodied in the name "Release," and, as there is nothing hidden or secret about it, we do not call it a concept.}

COMMENTARY ON THE IMAGES

Thunder and rain perform their roles: this is the image of Release.[3] In the same way, the noble man forgives misdeeds and pardons wrongdoing.[4]

PROVIDING THE SEQUENCE OF THE HEXAGRAMS

Things cannot remain in trouble. This is why *Jian* [Adversity, Hexagram 39] is followed by *Xie* [Release]. *Xie* here means "*huan*" [go slow, take it easy].

THE HEXAGRAMS IN IRREGULAR ORDER

Xie [Release] means "a relaxation."

First Yin

There is no blame. {Release [*xie*] is *jie* [differentiate, break up, disperse]; that is, one buffeted with troubles and snarled in difficulties now finds Release from them here. Located at the start when Release from Adversity begins to take effect and situated at the borderline where the hard and the soft start to differentiate, First Yin is going to be spared the plight of the wrongdoer and, as such, finds danger quelled. Located here one does not find his position a cause for worry, and so "there is no blame."[5]}

COMMENTARY ON THE IMAGES

To be on the borderline between hard and soft as a concept means "there is no blame." {When something incurs blame, it means that it does not measure up to the principle involved. *Concept* [*yi*] here is the same thing as "principle" [*li*].[6]}

Second Yang

This one hunts down three foxes in the fields, obtaining a yellow arrow. Constancy here means good fortune. {The fox is a secretive creature. Second Yang responds with its strength and centrality and is given a position of trust by Fifth Yin. Although located in the midst of danger, such a one understands the character of danger. He uses this understanding to release others from it, for he can hunt down what lies hidden. This is why the text says: "This one hunts down three foxes in the fields."[7] "Yellow" refers to the cultivation of centrality [the Mean], and "arrow" signifies the straight. To "hunt down three foxes" there in the fields means that one achieves the Dao of cultivating centrality [the Mean], and one who so succeeds at not deviating from the straight and narrow is someone who can perfect his righteousness. This is why the text says: "This one hunts down three foxes in the fields, obtaining a yellow arrow. Constancy here means good fortune."}

COMMENTARY ON THE IMAGES

That constancy at Second Yang results in good fortune is because one here achieves the Dao of centrality [or "manages to stay on the path of the Mean"].

Third Yin

If one bears a burden on his back yet also rides in a carriage, it will attract robbers to him. Such behavior regards baseness as constancy.[8] {Where Third Yin is located is not its rightful position, and where it treads is not its correct path. In order to attach itself to Fourth Yang, it employs effeminate and underhand tactics to ingratiate itself. Third Yin rides atop Second Yang and carries Fourth Yang on its back to gain security for itself. If robbers come, it is because they are attracted by such a one himself, and even if he is fortunate enough to avoid them, this would involve a debasement of correct behavior.[9]}

COMMENTARY ON THE IMAGES

"If one bears a burden on his back yet also rides in a carriage," this, too, is despicable. As this one himself attracts robbers, who else should bear the blame?

Fourth Yang

Release your big toe, for a friend will come and then place trust in you. {Fourth Yang is out of position and incorrect, but as it forms a pair with Third Yin, Third Yin manages to become attached to it as its big toe, and with Third Yin as its big toe, Fourth Yang loses its resonate relationship with First Yin. This is why Fourth Yang must release [i.e., free itself from] this big toe before the friend [First Yin, its true resonate partner] will come and place trust in Fourth Yang.[10]}

COMMENTARY ON THE IMAGES

"Release your big toe" means that one here is not yet in a proper position.

Fifth Yin

Only the noble man could bring about Release here and have good fortune, for he would even inspire confidence in petty men. {Fifth Yin abides in the exalted position and treads the path of centrality [the Mean]; moreover it is in resonance with the hard and the strong [Second Yang]. As such, one here can achieve Release and so garner good fortune. It is through the Dao of the noble man that one effects Release from troubles and dispels danger. Although petty men might be in the dark about this, they still understand that they must submit and so harbor no resentment about it. This is why the text says "for he would even inspire confidence in petty men."[11]}

COMMENTARY ON THE IMAGES

The noble man brings about Release here, so petty men withdraw.[12]

Top Yin

The duke uses this opportunity to shoot at a hawk located atop a high wall, so he gets it, and nothing fails to be fitting.[13] {First Yin is located in such a way that it is in resonance with Fourth Yang, and Second Yang is in resonance with Fifth Yin. Third Yin is not in resonance with Top Yin and is out of position with its bearing a burden on the back and carriage riding. It occupies a place at the top of the lower trigram, and this is why the text says "high wall." A high wall is not the place for a hawk just as this high place is not where Third Yin should tread. Top Yin abides at the zenith of movement [the *Zhen* (Thunder) trigram] and designates the maximum development of Release. It represents one who will bring about Release from gross disobedience and do away with abominable revolt. Thus he uses this opportunity to shoot at it [the hawk, i.e., Third Yin, i.e., disobedience and revolt]. This one makes a move only after he has attained his greatest strength and acts only after he has attained full force, thus it is certain that "he gets it, so nothing fails to be fitting."}

COMMENTARY ON THE IMAGES

"The duke uses this opportunity to shoot at a hawk" so as to bring about a Release from disobedience.

NOTES

1. Cf. Hexagram 39, *Jian* (Adversity), Judgment. Note that this and all subsequent text set off in this manner is commentary by Wang Bi.

2. This translates *wu qi er bushi*. *Qi* (boundary) may be a textual corruption for either *che* (split, burst) or *suo* (place). The former would result in "no bursting forth fails to open up," which seems redundant, and the latter would be "no place fails to have its opening up"—i.e., "Release occurs everywhere." Lou Yulie prefers this last reading. See *Wang Bi ji jiaoshi*, 2: 418 n. 7.

3. The lower trigram is *Kan* (Sink Hole), where rain collects, and the upper trigram is *Zhen* (Thunder).

4. Kong Yingda interprets this to mean that the noble man forgives and pardons out of leniency. See *Zhouyi zhengyi*, 4: 24b.

5. Kong Yingda comments:

> As long as dangers and troubles remain unquelled, the humble will suffer harm. As this is so, during the time when Release from Adversity has not yet occurred, the soft and weak will be unable to avoid blame. But after disentanglement from obstruction has taken place, the hard and the strong will no longer be in a position to persecute [the humble]. . . . Although First Yin with its softness and weakness occupies a place other than a proper position, when it encounters such a moment as this, it need not worry about incurring blame, and this is why for First Yin "there is no blame."

See *Zhouyi zhengyi*, 4: 24b.

According to Wang Bi, the first place in a hexagram is not a proper position for either a yin or a yang line; it is, in effect, a "positionless" position—a "borderline" between yin and yang. See section five of Wang's General Remarks. Insignificant (weak), without responsibilities, and at a time when the strong can no longer bully, here one need not worry about incurring blame.

Cheng Yi and Zhu Xi interpret First Yin differently. For them the first place is a yang position, and thus First Yin is out of place, but because it is in a correct responsive relationship with Fourth Yang, it avoids blame.

6. That is, First Yin has no position with which to be commensurate, so, although no good fortune can come of this, no blame will come of it either.

"Borderline" translates *ji*. Cheng Yi (and Zhu Xi after him) takes *ji* as *jijie* (relate, form a relationship), in keeping with the idea that First Yin avoids blame by entering into a correct relationship with Fourth Yang. Cheng also reads *yi* (concept) as *yi* (it is appropriate that), so it seems that for him the text would mean: "When hard and soft relate as they should, it is appropriate that 'there be no blame.' " See *Zhouyi zhezhong*, 12: 21b.

7. Both Cheng Yi and Zhu Xi think that "three foxes" refers to the three yin lines in this hexagram other than Fifth Yin (its ruler)—"petty men," according to Cheng. See *Zhouyi zhezhong*, 6: 3a.

8. See the extensive comments on Third Yin that appear at the very end of section eight of the Commentary on the Appended Phrases, Part One.

9. "Debasement of correct behavior" translates *zheng zhi suo jian*, Wang's gloss of *zhen lin*. Kong Yingda glosses *zhen lin* similarly: "The man who bears a burden yet rides in a carriage regards the base behavior he engages in as something correct." See *Zhouyi zhengyi*, 4: 25b.

10. Kong Yingda agrees with Wang Bi that the "big toe" is Third Yin and that the "friend" is First Yin. However, both Cheng Yi and Zhu Xi think that the "big toe" is First Yin and that Fourth Yang must rid itself of its relationship with First Yin before "noble friends will come to and place their trust in him." They say that the relationship between Fourth Yang and First Yin, though a resonate relationship between yin and yang, is improper because both lines are out of position (Fourth Yang is in a yin position, and Cheng and Zhu consider the first position to be yang) and, what is more, First Yin represents a "petty man." See *Zhouyi zhezhong*, 6: 4b–5a.

11. "Inspire confidence in petty men" translates *you fu yu xiaoren*. Both Cheng Yi and Zhu Xi gloss *fu* differently, as "proof," and their interpretation of this line seems to be: "The proof of this [that Release has occurred] lies with petty men." Cheng and Zhu think that "Release" in Fifth Yin refers to how the noble man (sovereign) must rid himself of petty men (represented by the other three yin lines) before he can have "good fortune." Proof of this lies with how petty men behave. As the Commentary on the Images says, "Petty men withdraw." The fact that they withdraw from his presence proves that he is successful. See *Zhouyi zhezhong*, 6: 5a.

12. Kong Yingda comments: " 'Petty men' means 'those who cause trouble.' They believe in the sincerity of the noble man, so they withdraw and submit to him in fear." See *Zhouyi zhengyi*, 4: 26a.

13. See the extensive comments on Top Yin that appear in section five of the Commentary on the Appended Phrases, Part Two.

損

Sun [Diminution]
(*Dui* Below *Gen* Above)

Judgment

Although one suffers Diminution, if there is sincerity, he shall have fundamental good fortune, be without blame, and may practice constancy.[1] It would be fitting should one set out to do something here. And what should one use? Two *gui* [plain and simple vessels] may be used to make sacrifice.

COMMENTARY ON THE JUDGMENTS

Sun [Diminution] is such that it means Diminution for those below and increase for those above, so the Dao of *Sun* moves upward. {*Gen* is a yang trigram, and *Dui* is a yin trigram. In all cases, it is yin that should be obedient to yang. Here yang is stopped above, and yin is happy to defer to it. "It means Diminution for those below and increase for those above," and this is what "moves upward" means.[2]} "Although one suffers Diminution, if there is sincerity, he shall have fundamental good fortune, be without blame, and may practice constancy. It would be fitting should one set out to do something here." {As a Dao, *Sun* means Diminution for those below and increase for those above, Diminution for the hard and strong and increase for the soft and weak. But this Diminution for those below and increase for those above is not properly a way to make up deficiencies, and this Diminution for the hard and strong and increase for the soft and weak is not a way to further the Dao of the noble man. Garnering good fortune out of this time of Diminution can only take place if one has sincerity. For if upon encountering Diminution one has sincerity, "he shall have fundamental good fortune," "be without blame," and thus may "practice constancy [or "rectitude"]"[3] and "it would be fitting should one set out to do something here." Diminution for the hard and strong and increase for the soft and weak should not happen so that the hard and the strong become extinguished, and Diminution for those below and increase for those above should not happen so that those above wax fat and powerful. If one allows the hard and strong to suffer Diminution but remains free of evil purposes and if one allows those above to have increase but avoids all obsequious ends, what blame should ever befall such a one and what is there that he could ever rectify? Although it would not permit rescue from great troubles, still if one were to set out to do something in this way, he would not find things in opposition to him.} "And what should he use?" {*What* (*he*) is a grammatical function word. "What should he use" implies the meaning "what need is there to provide rich offerings here?"} "Two *gui* may be used to make sacrifice." {The "two *gui*" refer to plain and simple vessels. If one were to practice Diminution with sincerity, even though it is a matter of only two *gui*, they still may be used to make sacrifice.} The use of "two *gui*" is in response to the particular time involved. {This is a Dao of extreme frugality, and it cannot be made a constant rule.} This is a particular time when Diminution for the hard and strong and increase for the soft and weak takes place. {Those below do not dare exercise their hardness and strength and instead place value on directing their efforts upward. This is what "Diminution for the hard and strong and increase for the soft and weak" means. The "hard and strong" are those whose virtue is superior, so their diminishment cannot be a constant rule.} Diminution and increase or waxing and waning take place in tandem with their proper times. {The natural substance of things in each case determines the measure of the thing involved. "The short as such cannot be taken for insufficiency," and "the long as such cannot be taken for excess," so how could Diminution or increase enhance either state?[4] As neither are constant principles of the Dao, they must only "take place in tandem with their proper times."}

COMMENTARY ON THE IMAGES

Below the Mountain, there is the Lake:[5] Diminution. {"Below the Mountain, there is the Lake": this is the image of Diminution.} In the same way, the noble man checks his anger and smothers his desire. {No greater good comes from being able to diminish something than the good of dealing with anger and desire.[6]}

COMMENTARY ON THE APPENDED PHRASES

Sun [Diminution] is how virtue is cultivated.

Sun [Diminution] demonstrates how things can first be difficult and easy later.

Sun [Diminution] provides the means to keep harm at a distance.[7]

PROVIDING THE SEQUENCE OF THE HEXAGRAMS

With relaxation, there is sure to be neglect. This is why *Xie* [Release, Hexagram 40] is followed by *Sun* [Diminution].

THE HEXAGRAMS IN IRREGULAR ORDER

Sun [Diminution] and *Yi* [Increase, Hexagram 42] are the beginnings of prosperity and decline.

First Yang

Once one's own duties are finished, he should quickly set forth, for then he shall be without blame, but he should take careful measure of how much diminishment takes place. {As a Dao, *Sun* [Diminution] means Diminution for those below and increase for those above, Diminution for the hard and strong and increase for the soft and weak, and it is something that operates in response to the particular time involved. First Yang abides at the very bottom, and as this hard and strong one undergoes Diminution in providing for the soft and weak [Fourth Yin], so it would not do to dawdle here, and as it is located at the beginning of Diminution, so it would not do to maintain one's fullness. Once one's own duties are finished, he must set forth [to help Fourth Yin] and does not dare relax and linger, for only then shall he manage to "be without blame." As this one uses his hardness and strength to provide for the soft and weak, although he avoids blame, he still will not gain affection. This is why after he manages to "be without blame," he still "take[s] careful measure of how much diminishment takes place," for only then will one here obtain a convergence of wills. *Chuan* [be quick] means the same as *su* [quickly].}

COMMENTARY ON THE IMAGES

"Once one's own duties are finished, he should quickly set forth," so the one above will let his will converge. {It is in order that the one above [Fourth Yin] should bring about a convergence of wills between them that one here "quickly sets forth."}

Second Yang

It is fitting that this one practice constancy, but for him to set forth would mean misfortune. {The soft and weak must not be increased completely, and the hard and strong must not be completely whittled away. The one below here [Second Yang] must not act without rectitude. First Yang has already allowed its hardness and strength to be diminished in order to accommodate the soft and weak [Fourth Yin], but Second Yang treads the middle course, so if this one also diminishes itself in order to bring increase to the soft and weak, it would bring about the Dao of *Bo* [Peeling, Hexagram 23].[8] This is why Second Yang must not "quickly set forth" and instead "finds it fitting to practice constancy." If it were to let itself advance to the soft and weak one [Fifth Yin], it "would mean misfortune." Thus the text says: "to set forth would mean misfortune." That Second Yang does not undergo diminishment in order to apply itself to increasing [Fifth Yin] is because "it takes the middle path [the Mean] as the route for its will."}

COMMENTARY ON THE IMAGES

Second Yang finds it fitting to practice constancy, for it takes the middle path [the Mean] as the route for its will.[9]

Third Yin

If three people travel together, one person will be lost, but when one person travels, he will find his companion. {As a Dao, *Sun* [Diminution] means Diminution for those below and increase for those above, so it is a Dao that "moves upward." The "three people" refers to the three yin lines from Third Yin up.[10] If the three yin lines were to travel together in order to provide support for Top Yang, Top Yang would lose its companion, and among them [the three yin lines] there would be no master. One might call this increase, but in fact it would be Diminution. Thus it is by Heaven and Earth resonating one with the other that things develop and reach perfect maturity; it is by male and female mating that things are formed and come to life.[11] If yin and yang did not form pairs, could life ever be had? This is why Third Yin by traveling alone finds his companion [Top Yang] and why two yins traveling together would be sure to excite suspicion.[12]}

COMMENTARY ON THE IMAGES

Here one person should travel, for three persons would excite suspicion.

Fourth Yin

One here may diminish his anxiety, for if he were to act quickly, he should have cause for joy and so be without blame. {Fourth Yin manages to tread upon the territory of its proper position [it is a yin line in a yin position], and, as this soft and weak one accepts the help of one hard and strong [First Yang], it can thus diminish its anxiety.[13] How could Fourth Yin ever allow its anxiety to last long? Thus one here acts quickly so as to have cause for joy. One diminishes anxiety by distancing himself from his faults. It is by having cause for joy that one obtains forgiveness. This is why the text says that, if one were to act quickly, he should have cause for joy, and that, by having cause for joy, he should be without blame.[14]}

COMMENTARY ON THE IMAGES

"One here may diminish his anxiety," for indeed there is that which can give cause for joy.

Fifth Yin

There are those who increase this one. Of tens of coteries of tortoises, there are none that can act in opposition,[15] so this means fundamental good fortune. {Fifth Yin abides in the noble position with its softness and weakness and, as such, practices the Dao of Diminishment. The great river and the sea occupy lowly positions, yet countless streams return to them.[16] Here one manages to tread on the noble domain by practicing diminishment, so "there are those who increase this one."[17] *Coterie* [*peng*] means "clique, party" [*dang*]. The tortoise is a creature that settles doubts. A yin is not someone to take the lead, and one soft and weak is not someone to take charge on his own, but here we have one who can take up this position because of his nobility and who preserves it by practicing diminishment. Thus people utilize all their strength, and duties are fulfilled with the utmost merit. The wise ponder possibilities, the perspicacious ponder stratagems, and there are none who can act in opposition. Thus the utilization of all the talented is complete. In garnering increase in this way one obtains "tens of coteries of tortoises," something sufficient to exhaust all the help that could be rendered by Heaven and man.[18]}

COMMENTARY ON THE IMAGES

For Fifth Yin there is fundamental good fortune, as one here has blessings from above.[19]

Top Yang

This one suffers no Diminution but enjoys increase without blame. The practice of constancy means good fortune, and it would be fitting if he were set out to do something. He acquires subordinates and ministers, and private family interests cease. {Top Yang is located at the very end of the Diminution process. Above there is no one to support, and, with the end of Diminution, there is now a return to increase [in anticipation of Hexagram 42, *Yi* (Increase)]. The virtue of this hard and strong one does not suffer Diminution, so that converts the process to increase, with no worry about incurring blame. One has good fortune here because of his righteousness. He is not subject to the soft and weak, so the virtue of his hardness and strength endures. This is why the text says: "This one suffers no Diminution but enjoys increase without blame. The practice of constancy means good fortune, and it would be fitting if he were to set out to do something." Top Yang abides in the uppermost position and rides upon the soft and weak. Located at the very end of Diminution, how estimable is the virtue of this hard and strong one! As he is someone to whom others return, the text says: "He acquires subordinates and ministers." With this acquisition of subordinates and ministers, the whole world becomes one, which is why the text says: "Private family interests cease."}

COMMENTARY ON THE IMAGES

"This one suffers no Diminution but enjoys Increase without blame," so one here may carry out his will with great success.

NOTES

1. "Be without blame, and may practice constancy" translates *wujiu, kezhen*. Wang Bi may not have read these phrases this way, for in his commentary to the Commentary on the Judgments there occurs the phrase, "what blame should ever befall such a one and what is there that he could ever rectify?" Here Wang apparently glosses *zhen* (constancy) as *zheng* (rectify).

2. This and all subsequent text set off in this manner is commentary by Wang Bi.

3. See note 1 above.

4. Cf. Wang Bi's commentary to *Laozi*, section 20, p. 47: "Finches have mates, as do doves. People who live in wintry climes are sure to know one type of fur from another. That which by nature is already sufficient unto itself will only come to grief if one tries to add to it. Therefore, what is the difference between lengthening the duck's legs and cutting down the legs of the crane?" Here and in his remarks on the Commentary on the Judgments to Hexagram 41, Wang is alluding to a passage in the *Zhuangzi*: "The long as such cannot be taken for excess, and the short as such cannot be taken for insufficiency. This is why, although the duck's legs are short, to lengthen them would cause it grief, and, although the crane's legs are long, to cut them down would cause it distress. Therefore, what is by nature long is not something that should be cut down, and what is by nature short is not something that should be lengthened." See *Zhuangzi*, 21/8/8.

5. The lower trigram is *Dui* (Lake, Joy), and the upper trigram is *Gen* (Mountain, Restraint).

6. Neither Wang Bi nor Kong Yingda attempts to explain the image further, but Cheng Yi has this to say about it:

> The vapors [*qi*] [of the Lake] well upward and moisten what is above [the Mountain]. The depth of the one is decreased in order that the height of the other be increased, so both contribute to the image of Diminution of what is below. When the noble man observes the image of Diminution, he uses it as a guide to bring Diminution to himself. In the course of cultivating himself, the things that he ought to diminish are, of course, anger and desire.

See *Zhouyi zhezhong*, 12: 23b.

7. See section seven of the Commentary on the Appended Phrases, Part Two.

8. If First Yang undergoes Diminishment and becomes a yin line and then if Second Yang does so also, *Sun* (Diminishment) would be transformed into Hexagram 23, *Bo* (Peeling) ䷖.

9. Or, "one here keeps his will fixed on the Mean."

10. Both Cheng Yi and Zhu Xi interpret Third Yin differently. They think that *Sun* (Diminution) ䷨ is the result of a transformation of Hexagram 11, *Tai* (Peace) ䷊. In their view, the "one person lost" is the Third Yang of *Tai*, which has become the Top Yang of *Sun*—the three persons traveling together being the original three yang lines in *Qian*, the lower trigram of *Tai*—and the "companion" found is Top Yang of *Sun*, in resonance with Third Yin, formerly Top Yin of *Tai*. See *Zhouyi zhezhong*, 6: 10a.

11. This paraphrases section five of the Commentary on the Appended Phrases, Part Two: "Heaven and Earth mesh together, and the myriad things develop and reach perfect maturity; male and female blend essences together, and the myriad creatures are formed and come to life."

12. Kong Yingda expands upon Wang Bi's remarks:

> The "three persons" refers to the three yin lines from Third Yin on up. The first mentioned "one person" is Top Yang, and the one mentioned second is Third Yin. . . . Third Yin is in resonance with Top Yang, but above it there are two other yin lines, Fourth Yin and Fifth Yin. As the Dao of Diminution moves upward, this means that each line follows the other in succession, but if Third Yin joins with the other two yin lines and travels with them, even though it wants to provide increase for this "one person," Top Yang, they [the three yin lines], each one in turn, would cause Top Yang to feel suspicious, and once suspicion is aroused, it would destroy the sense that Third Yin was its proper mate. . . . This is why the text says: "If three persons travel together, one person [Top Yang] will be lost," but if the "one person" [Third Yin] travels alone, Top Yang will accept it without any suspicion, and so it [Third Yin] "will find his companion."

See *Zhouyi zhengyi*, 4: 2b.

13. "Anxiety" translates *ji*, which can also mean "sickness, fault, flaw," etc. This is how Cheng Yi and Zhu Xi understand it. Cheng glosses *ji* as *jibing* (illness) and *bushan* (not good, shortcoming, failing), and Zhu glosses it as *yinrou zhi ji* (the shortcomings of softness and weakness inherent in the yin). Their reading of Fourth Yin would be: "One here has the chance to diminish his shortcomings, so if he were to act quickly, he would find joy and be without blame." See *Zhouyi zhezhong*, 6: 10b. However, Kong Yingda glosses *ji* as *xiangsi zhi ji* (anxiety associated with longing), i.e., that of Fourth Yin for First Yang. See *Zhouyi zhengyi*, 4: 28b. My translation of Fourth Yin and Wang Bi's commentary to it follows Kong's subcommentary.

14. Kong Yingda comments:

> Fourth Yin has had its feelings stirred by First Yang but for a long time has been unable to unite with First Yang, thus it has suffered the grief of anxious expectation. Thus, by now acting quickly, it has cause for joy. First Yang diminishes itself in order to increase Fourth Yin. But if Fourth Yin did not quickly accept this help, then it would incur the blame of having missed this opportunity to enjoy increase. This is Wang Bi says: "By having cause for joy, he should be without blame."

See *Zhouyi zhengyi*, 4: 28b.

15. The text of Fifth Yin to this point is identical to that of Hexagram 42, *Yi* (Increase), Second Yin.

16. This paraphrases the *Laozi*, section 32, p. 82: "If one were to make an analogy for the way the Dao works in the world, it would be like the way all the rivulets and streams run into the great river and the sea." Wang's own commentary to this passage reads:

> The rivulets and streams seek the great river and the sea not because the great river and the sea summon them but because they return to them of their own accord without any summoning or seeking taking place. To practice the Dao in the world is to achieve equity spontaneously without issuing any orders about it, to realize the Dao spontaneously without consciously trying to do so. This is why the text says: "It would be like the way all the rivulets and streams run into the great river and the sea."

17. Cf. *Laozi*, section 42, p. 117: "What a person hates to be is an orphan, someone lonely without a spouse, or one without food, yet rulers and lords take these terms as names for themselves. It thus happens that at times things will enjoy increase by being diminished and at times suffer diminishment by being increased." Kong Yingda comments on Fifth Yin: "When one who abides in the noble position is yet able to restrain and diminish himself, there will be none in the world who fail to return to him and bring increase to him." See *Zhouyi zhengyi*, 4: 29a.

18. Both Wang Bi and Kong Yingda take "tortoises" to refer to the wise, the talented, and the worthy. As the heating and cracking of tortoise shells were a means to decide issues and foretell the future, so the tortoise could serve as a symbol or metaphor for a person who exercised such capabilities. Cheng Yi interprets the "tortoises" differently. He thinks that they represent the general consensus (*gonglun*) of the masses of common folk, something that is sure to accord with "right principles" (*zhengli*), which "even tortoise shell and yarrow stalk cannot oppose." Zhu Xi's interpretation is again different, for he takes the expression "tens of coteries of tortoises" to mean "ten pairs of tortoise shells," a great treasure, something of tremendous value, and Fifth Yin to mean: "Someone brings increase to him with these [i.e., such wealth], which he cannot refuse, so his good fortune is readily apparent." See *Zhouyi zhezhong*, 6: 11a–11b. This passage has prompted much controversy; see Lou, *Wang Bi ji jiaoshi*, 2: 427 n. 32.

19. Kong Yingda says that "above" refers to Heaven. See *Zhouyi zhengyi*, 4: 29a. This is hinted at in Wang Bi's commentary to Fifth Yin: "all the help that could be rendered by Heaven and man." Cheng Yi expands upon Wang's remark: "It is because one here can take over completely the views of the mass of common folk and stay in perfect accord with the principles of Heaven and Earth that blessings descend upon him from Heaven above." See *Zhouyi zhezhong*, 12: 25a.

HEXAGRAM 42

䷩

益

Yi [Increase]
(*Zhen* Below *Sun* Above)

Judgment

Yi [Increase] is such that it is fitting to set out to do something and it is fitting to cross the great river.

COMMENTARY ON THE JUDGMENTS

Yi [Increase] is such that it means diminution for those above and Increase for those below, so the delight of the common folk is without bounds. {*Zhen* [Thunder, the lower trigram] is yang, and *Sun* [Wind/Compliance, the upper trigram] is yin. *Sun* is not something to oppose *Zhen*. One located above and imbued with compliance does not set himself in opposition to those below. This is what "diminution for those above and Increase for those below" means.} That which proceeds downward from above to what is below is indeed a Dao that is both great and glorious.[1] "It is fitting to set out to do something": for one who practices centrality and correctness blessings are had. {Fifth Yang occupies a central and correct position [because it is a yang line in a middle yang position], and it "proceeds downward from above to what is below," thus "blessings are had." It is because such central, correct, and blessed virtue is involved that "it is fitting to set out to do something," so wherever such a one might go he will be sure to find it fitting.} "It is fitting to cross the great river," for it is the Dao of wood that one should employ here. {Wood is the usual means for crossing the great river, and as such it is something that does not sink. The way Increase is used to cross over difficulties is just like the way one uses wood to cross over the great river.} Increase involves action yet is a matter of compliance, so progress is achieved day after day without limit—just as Heaven actuates and Earth begets, Increase takes place infinitely. {*Sun* [Diminution] works upward, and *Yi* [Increase] works downward.} Whenever one practices the Dao of Increase, one should do so in tandem with the proper time. {Increase should be used to make up insufficiencies. If one were to keep on increasing something that is already full, this would be a Dao that leads to harm. This is why the text says: "Whenever one practices the Dao of Increase, one should do so in tandem with the proper time."}

COMMENTARY ON THE IMAGES

Wind and Thunder: this is the image of Increase. In the same way, the noble man shifts to the good when he sees it and corrects his errors when he has them. {Nothing greater comes from Increase than to shift to the good and to correct one's errors.}

COMMENTARY ON THE APPENDED PHRASES

After Lord Bao Xi perished, Lord Shen Nong applied himself to things. He hewed wood and made a plowshare and bent wood and made a plow handle. The benefit of plowing and hoeing he taught to the world. He probably got the idea for this from the hexagram *Yi* [Increase].[2]

Yi [Increase] is how virtue proliferates.

Yi [Increase] demonstrates how one brings about growth and opulence while avoiding any contrivance to do so.[3]

PROVIDING THE SEQUENCE OF THE HEXAGRAMS

If diminution keeps going on and does not stop, this is sure to lead to increase. This is why *Sun* [Diminution, Hexagram 41] is followed by *Yi* [Increase].

THE HEXAGRAMS IN IRREGULAR ORDER

Sun [Diminution, Hexagram 41] and *Yi* [Increase] are the beginnings of prosperity and decline.

First Yang

It is fitting to use this opportunity to accomplish some great undertaking, but only with fundamental good fortune will one be without blame. {First Yang is located at the beginning of Increase and abides at the start of action [*Zhen* (Thunder/Quake)]. It embodies the virtues of hardness and strength, which it uses to deal with matters, but it does so with compliance [in resonance with Fourth Yin], so if one were to address himself to some great undertaking in this way, he would be sure to have much meritorious success. Here below where First Yang abides is not a situation for substantial undertakings; this humble place is not a position where one should be entrusted with weighty matters, and a great undertaking cannot be got through with only a small amount of success. This is why the text has it that only "fundamental good fortune" here will enable one "to be without blame."[4]}

COMMENTARY ON THE IMAGES

"Only with fundamental good fortune will one be without blame," for here below one should not address himself to substantial undertakings. {The time is right for a great undertaking, but here below one should not deal with substantial matters. This one may be at the right time for such things, but it is not the right position for them. Thus only "fundamental good fortune" here will enable one "to be without blame."}

Second Yin

There are those who increase this one. Of tens of coteries of tortoises, there are none that can act in opposition.[5] The practice of perpetual constancy here will mean good fortune. If the king uses this opportunity to make offering of this one to the Divine Ruler [*di*],[6] there would be good fortune. {Second Yin abides in this central position [in the Mean] with its softness and weakness and so obtains a position that is right for it. It occupies a place in the inner [lower] trigram and treads a middle course. When such a one finds himself at a time of Increase, he conducts himself with emptiness.[7] Increase comes from the outer [upper] trigram [from Fifth Yang], which comes on its own without being called for. This one neither tries to take the lead nor to initiate action, thus "coteries of tortoises" offers him stratagems, just as it happens for one who finds himself at Fifth Yin in the *Sun* [Diminution] hexagram.[8] As this position is not appropriate for one of such nobility, the text has it that good fortune here depends on perpetual constancy. The Divine Ruler [*di*] is the master of all living things, the patriarch who sets Increase in motion and who "comes forth in *Zhen* [Quake] and sets all things in order in *Sun* [Compliance]."[9] Second Yin abides here in Increase in such a way that it embodies softness and weakness and suits the position in which it finds itself. Moreover, it is in a resonate relationship with *Sun* [Compliance] [the upper trigram—specifically Fifth Yang], so a perfect offering to the Divine Ruler can be found here at this time.}

COMMENTARY ON THE IMAGES

"There are those who increase this one," and it comes from the outer trigram.

Third Yin

This one brings about Increase, but if he were to use it to save a bad situation, he should be without blame. He has sincerity, and to report to the duke that he treads the path of the Mean he uses a *gui* [jade tablet]. {As Third Yin abides in a yang position as a yin, it represents someone who seeks Increase. This is why the text says: "This one brings about Increase." Increase does not come from the outer trigram [i.e., from superiors]; Third Yin itself makes it happen: one here is not given it by others. Therefore, in terms of modesty, such a one should be executed,[10] but if he were to use it [his Increase] to save a bad situation [famine or other emergencies], he should be forgiven. Third Yin as a yin line in a yang position is located at the top of the lower trigram, a place where its strength is at the utmost. If one here uses this strength to save others from the danger of dwindled resources, he will be someone on whom they will rely. This is why "if he were to use it to save a bad situation," he should then manage to "be without blame." If one here is able to enjoy Increase but avoid using it for private gain and instead keeps his will fixed on alleviating danger and difficulties, if he does not allow his strength to lead him to overreach himself and does not abandon the path of the Mean, and if he reports to the duke as such, he will be entrusted with duties by the sovereign of the state. The ceremonial act of using a *gui* [jade tablet (a symbol of sincerity and trust)] here expresses this Dao perfectly, and this is why the text says: "He has sincerity, and to report to the duke that he treads the path of the Mean he uses a *gui* [jade tablet]." A duke is the highest-ranking retainer. One who in all things possesses the wherewithal to administer the entire world is called a king. The one second in greatness to him in the entire world is called a duke. The talents and capabilities of Third Yin are insufficient to report to the king, but they are sufficient enough to report to the duke, and in doing so Third Yin manages to use a *gui* [jade tablet]. This is why the text says: "He has sincerity, and to report that he treads the path of the Mean he uses a *gui* [jade tablet]."}

COMMENTARY ON THE IMAGES

This one brings about Increase and uses it to save a bad situation, for he is the one who firmly has it. {One who uses Increase to deal with unfortunate matters must be one who manages firmly to have it.[11]}

Fourth Yin

If one treads the path of the Mean and so reports to the duke, he shall have his way. It is fitting to rely on such behavior to seek support to move the capital of the state. {Fourth Yin abides here at a time of Increase, located at the beginning of the *Sun* [Compliance] trigram. It embodies softness and weakness and so suits its position [it is a yin line in a yin position]. From its position above it resonates with one below [First Yang]. One here is not so humble that he could not be any lower and not so high as to occupy a place where he overreaches himself. Although such a one's position is not central, he is someone who here stays on the path of the Mean. If he reports to the duke as such, in what would he not be allowed to have his way? And if he were to rely on such behavior to seek support to move the capital of the state, who would not accede to his wishes?[12]}

COMMENTARY ON THE IMAGES

If this one "reports to the duke, he shall have his way," for he has a will dedicated to Increase. {His will is fixed on obtaining Increase.}

Fifth Yang

This one has sincerity and a heart full of kindness, so he should have no doubt that he shall have fundamental good fortune. As he has sincerity, his own virtue will be taken to be kindness. {Fifth Yang obtains this position where one treads upon the territory of the noble, for this one is the ruler of the *Yi* [Increase] hexagram. To make Increase grow, there is nothing greater than sincerity, and to make kindness grow, there is nothing greater than heartfelt affection. This one "brings benefit to the common folk through things that they find beneficial and so is kind to them without bestowing largesse."[13] This is someone who practices heartfelt kindness. If one practices sincerity and acts with a heart full of kindness, he will fulfill the wishes of others perfectly and so certainly should not delay because of doubts that he shall have "fundamental good fortune." As one here is sincerely kind to others, they respond to him, and this is why the text says: "As he has sincerity, his own virtue will be taken to be kindness."}

COMMENTARY ON THE IMAGES

"This one has sincerity and a heart full of kindness," so one should have no doubt about it. "His own virtue will be taken to be kindness," so he shall greatly achieve his ambitions.

Top Yang

This one brings Increase to no one, so there are those who strike at him. There is no consistency in the way he sets his heart and mind, so he shall have misfortune. {Top Yang occupies the very end of the Increase process, so it represents one who has a surfeit of Increase. This one seeks Increase without end; he is someone whose heart and mind do not remain fixed on anything. Such insatiable desires no one can provide for. He sings alone, and no one else joins in, for "his are self-serving words." It is the Dao of men to hate surfeit, and those who are angry with this one are more than one, so this is why the text says: "There are those who strike at him."}

COMMENTARY ON THE IMAGES

"This one brings Increase to no one," so his are self-serving words. "There are those who strike at him," and these are from the outside [i.e., the others to whom he might have brought Increase].

NOTES

1. This and all subsequent text set off in this manner is commentary by Wang Bi.

2. See section two of the Commentary on the Appended Phrases, Part Two, and notes 8 and 9 there.

3. For both, see section seven of the Commentary on the Appended Phrases, Part Two.

4. Kong Yingda, Cheng Yi, and Zhu Xi all emphasize that the success here of First Yang is due to the Increase it enjoys thanks to its resonate relationship with Fourth Yin, to which it is compliant and to which it dedicates its works. See *Zhouyi zhengyi*, 4: 31a, and *Zhouyi zhezhong*, 6: 14a–14b.

5. The text of Second Yin to this point is identical to that of Hexagram 41, *Sun* (Diminution), Fifth Yin. For "tortoises," see note 18 there.

6. See Hexagram 16, *Yu* (Contentment), Commentary on the Images, and note 2 there.

7. "Emptiness" translates *chong*, which Kong Yingda glosses as *qianchong* (modesty). See *Zhouyi zhengyi*, 4: 31a.

8. Cf. Hexagram 41, Fifth Yin, and Wang Bi's commentary to that line.

9. See section five of Explaining the Trigrams.

10. Kong Yingda comments: "If one were to censure him in terms of the Dao of modesty, it would be in accord with principle to have him executed." *Zhouyi zhengyi*, 4: 31b.

11. The meaning of the text is uncertain, and Wang's comments do not

really clarify it. Kong Yingda comments: "It is clear that because this one uses Increase to save a bad situation he cannot be seeking it for himself. As he uses Increase to deal with unfortunate matters, he thus manages surely to have meritorious success." See *Zhouyi zhengyi*, 4: 32a. Cheng Yi's interpretation is somewhat different:

> Third Yin is the only one in Increase that can be used to deal with unfortunate matters, for he "firmly has it." This means that he devotes himself firmly to fulfilling his responsibilities. He occupies a position below, so he ought to receive orders from above. Thus, in concentrating on his duties, he devotes himself exclusively to saving the common folk from disaster. This is only possible when one has to save a situation of current danger. Third Yin happens to be located at this time of crisis, and it is impossible to replace such a one, so it is right that this one be given authority to act. This is why Third Yin manages to "be without blame." But if it had been ordinary times, this would not be permitted.

See *Zhouyi zhezhong*, 12: 27a.

12. Kong Yingda, Cheng Yi, and Zhu Xi all cite *Zuozhuan* (Zuo's commentary on the *Spring and Autumn Annals*), concerning the sixth year in the reign of Duke Yin (716 B.C.): "The move of our state of Zhou to the east was due to the support of [the dukes of] Jin and Zheng." Cf. Legge, *The Chinese Classics*, 5: 21. See *Zhouyi zhengyi*, 4: 32a, and *Zhouyi zhezhong*, 6: 17b. Cheng and Zhu also say that such a move is in accordance with the wishes of the common folk and is done for their Increase.

13. *Lunyu* (Analects) 20:2.

䷪

夬

Kuai [Resolution]
(*Qian* Below *Dui* Above)

Judgment

Kuai [Resolution] is such that action is taken openly in the king's court, and a sincere call here means danger. One should issue one's own city a decree, for it would not be fitting to resort to armed force at once. It would be fitting if one were to set forth to do something. {*Kuai* [Resolution] is the opposite of *Bo* [Peeling, Hexagram 23].[1] By having soft and weak lines convert hard and strong lines, *Bo* [Peeling] almost goes so far as to finish off all hard and strong lines. By having hard and strong lines take decisive action against soft and weak lines, *Kuai* [Resolution] acts [to eliminate soft and weak lines] in the same way *Bo* [Peeling] does to eliminate hard and strong lines. When the hard and strong perish, the Dao of the noble man wanes, and when the soft and weak wane, the dao of the petty man perishes. When the Dao of the noble man wanes, his virtues of strength and rectitude are denied a straight path to action and the power that stems from the threat of punishments cannot be exercised with any ease. Here "action is taken openly in the king's court," for this Dao should be practiced in public.[2]}

COMMENTARY ON THE JUDGMENTS

Kuai [Resolution] means to take decisive action. Here the hard and strong take decisive action against the soft and weak. Here one should act with strength yet do so with joy, for this is the way to be decisive yet achieve harmony. {If one "acts with strength yet do[es] so with joy," he shall be "decisive yet achieve harmony." "Action is taken openly in the king's court," for one soft and weak one rides atop five hard and strong ones. The hard and strong [yang] lines all grow in strength, but the one soft and weak [yin] line acts waywardly. Such a one is condemned to death by all equally; none is averse to it. This is why it is possible for "action to be taken openly in the king's court."} "A sincere call here means danger": his danger is now obvious. {The strong and righteous proclaim their order sincerely and openly, so the soft and weak wicked one is put in danger. This is why the text says: "His danger is now obvious."} "One should issue one's own city a decree, for it would not be fitting to resort to armed force at once." {When the hard and strong decide and control things, commands may be proclaimed. "Issue one's own city a decree" means to proclaim a command. To take advantage of one's strength "to resort to armed force at once" is to emphasize brute force as the means to achieve victory, but such emphasis on brute force to achieve victory is something that all will equally find a cause for suffering.} "It would be fitting . . . to set forth to do something," for the more the hard and strong grow in strength, the more likely it is that a successful conclusion will be had. {The stronger the virtues of the hard and strong grow, the more the wickedness of the soft and weak will wane, and this is why "it would be fitting . . . to set forth to do something," for the Dao [way] is ready-made for success.}

COMMENTARY ON THE IMAGES

The Lake has risen higher than the Sky: Resolution. In the same way, the noble man dispenses blessings so they reach those below. He dwells in virtue and so clarifies what one should be averse to. {The Lake has risen higher than the Sky: this is the image of Resolution.[3] When the Lake rises higher than the sky, moisture is sure to come down, and this expresses the concept of "dispens[ing] blessings so they reach those below." "Averse to" [*ji*] has the sense of "prohibit" [*jin*]. Laws should be clear, and judgments strict; one must not be lax about them here. This is why "he dwells in virtue and so clarifies what one should be averse to."[4] The noble man dispenses blessings but can be strict, is strong but can be joyous, decisive but can achieve harmony: this is the Dao of Resolution in all its beauty.}

COMMENTARY ON THE APPENDED PHRASES

In remote antiquity, people knotted cords to keep things in order. The sages of later ages had these exchanged for written tallies, and by means of these all the various officials were kept in order, and the myriad folk were supervised. They probably got the idea for this from the hexagram *Kuai* [Resolution].[5]

PROVIDING THE SEQUENCE OF THE HEXAGRAMS

If increase keeps going on and does not stop, there is sure to be a breakthrough. This is why *Yi* [Increase, Hexagram 42] is followed by *Kuai* [Resolution]. *Kuai* here means "breakthrough."

THE HEXAGRAMS IN IRREGULAR ORDER

Kuai [Resolution] means "to act decisively," for here the hard wins decisively over the soft: The way of the noble man is in the ascendancy, and the way of the petty man is brought to grief.[6]

First Yang

This one put his strength into his advancing toes, went forth but was not victorious, and so incurs blame. {First Yang abides at the start of the strengthening process and serves to represent the beginning of decisiveness. This one should have carefully examined his plans before trying to carry out his endeavors. He put his strength into his advancing toes, went forth but was not victorious, so it is appropriate that he incurs blame.}

COMMENTARY ON THE IMAGES

To set forth without gaining victory is to incur blame. {The principle behind his failure to achieve victory lies in his going forward [when he should not have done so].}

Second Yang

Despite cries of alarm that there are armed men night after night, this one need not grieve. {Second Yang abides in strength and treads a middle course [the path of the Mean] and represents someone who, as he is capable of carefully examining his own measures, stays free from doubt. Thus, "despite cries of alarm that there are armed men night after night,"[7] one here remains free of worry and doubt, and so "this one need not grieve."}

COMMENTARY ON THE IMAGES

Despite there being armed men, "this one need not grieve," for he manages to tread the path of the Mean.

Third Yang

To put strength into the cheekbones would mean misfortune, but the noble man acts with perfect Resolution. But if one here were to travel alone, he should encounter such a rain that he should be as if sunk in water, and, though he feel anger, there will be no one to blame. {*Qiu* [cheekbones] means *mianquan* [cheekbones]. This refers to Top Yin, which occupies the very top of the body [i.e., hexagram]; thus it is referred to as "the cheekbones." Third Yin of *Bo* [Peeling, Hexagram 23] performs a good deed in responding to Top Yang. When the hard and strong grow in strength, the Dao of the noble man prospers, and when the yin flourish, the dao of the petty man grows strong. As this is so, to assist the yang when one finds oneself at a time when the yin grow strong is good, but to assist the soft and weak at a time when the yang grow strong will result in misfortune. *Kuai* [Resolution] is a time when the hard and strong grow in strength, yet Third Yang alone responds to Top Yin and in doing so assists the petty man. This is why it "mean[s] misfortune." If a noble man occupies the position of Third Yang, he will surely be capable of casting off any entanglement with Top Yin; that he should be decisive about this he has no doubt. This is why the text says that he "acts with perfect Resolution." However, if Third Yang does not associate with the other yang lines but instead travels alone in pursuit of different ambitions and responds to the petty man [represented by Top Yin], he will suffer hardship and distress by doing so. "He should encounter such a rain that he should be as if sunk in water," and he should feel resentment but would have no place to lay the blame.[8]}

COMMENTARY ON THE IMAGES

As "the noble man acts with perfect Resolution," in the end he is without blame.

Fourth Yang

This one's thighs are without skin, and his walking falters.[9] If he were to allow himself to be led by the ram, regret would disappear, but he might hear what is said but not trust it. {Those below advance with hardness and strength and are not to be warded off by Fourth Yang, so this one is sure to be encroached upon and wounded. He loses the means to keep himself secure, thus "his thighs are without skin, and his walking falters." A ram is so strong and sturdy that it is difficult to move; here it refers to Fifth Yang. As the ruler of the *Kuai* [Resolution] hexagram, Fifth Yang is not to be encroached upon by those below, so if one at Fourth Yang were to allow himself to be led by Fifth Yang, he could manage to have regret disappear—but nothing more. But this hard and strong one [Fourth Yang] might overreach himself to the extent that he becomes incapable of accepting what is said and instead might try to take charge of his own situation. This is what is meant by "he might hear what is said but not trust it." If he were to set forth in this way, we can know well that misfortune would befall him.[10]}

COMMENTARY ON THE IMAGES

"His walking falters," for the position is not right for him. "He might hear what is said but not trust it," for his perception is dim. {This is the same as the misfortune of having the ears destroyed in [Top Yang of] *Shihe* [Bite Together, Hexagram 21].}

Fifth Yang

The pokeweed is dispatched with perfect Resolution. If this one treads the middle path, he shall be without blame. {The *xianlu* [pokeweed] is a weak and fragile plant, so it is the easiest thing possible to deal with it decisively. Here we have the most noble matching itself against the most humble. Although victory is had here, it is really not worth very much. Fifth Yang is located in a middle position and treads that path, so one here is up to avoiding blame but nothing more than that; this is not enough to bring one glory.}

COMMENTARY ON THE IMAGES

"If this one treads the middle path, he shall be without blame," but this middle position is not enough to bring him glory.

Top Yin

As no cry will do here, it will end in misfortune. {Top Yin is located at the very end of Resolution and represents a petty man at the top. As the Dao of the noble man grows strong here, this one is rejected by all the others. Thus his situation is not something that a cry can prolong.}

COMMENTARY ON THE IMAGES

The misfortune connected with "no cry will do here" is that this one after all cannot last long.

NOTES

1. *Kuai* consists of all yang lines except Top Yin, and *Bo* consists of all yin lines except for Top Yang.

2. This and all subsequent text set off in this manner is commentary by Wang Bi.

3. The lower trigram is *Qian* (Pure Yang, i.e., Heaven, the Sky), and the upper trigram is *Dui* (Lake).

4. Although Cheng Yi admits that Wang Bi's interpretation here is possible and makes sense, he himself prefers to gloss *ji* (averse) as *fang* (guard against) or *fangjin* (guard against and prevent): "The noble man who dwells securely in virtue keeps a tight hold on it. . . . For if he keeps guard over it and prevents its slipping away, it will not be dispersed and lost." See *Zhouyi zhezhong*, 12: 26b.

5. See section two of the Commentary on the Appended Phrases, Part Two, and note 24 there.

6. See note 12 of the Hexagrams in Irregular Order.

7. "Night after night" translates *moye*. It is uncertain whether *mo* (no) should be read as such, making *moye* mean "no particular night" (hence, "night after night") or whether it should be read as *mu* (evening), so that *muye* means "evening(s) and night(s)." Wang Bi's text can be read either way, as can the commentaries of Kong Yingda, Cheng Yi, and Zhu Xi. See Lou, *Wang Bi jijiaoshi*, 2: 437 n. 9. Kong comments: "Despite the fact that people repeatedly give the cry of alarm, saying, 'night after night [or "evening and night"] there are sure to be armed soldiers who will come to harm us,' as this one can carefully examine his own measures [capabilities], he need be neither doubtful nor worried." See *Zhouyi zhengyi*, 5: 2b.

8. Cheng Yi and Zhu Xi interpret Third Yang differently. They agree that the "cheekbones" refer to Third Yang itself, which is "high" but not at the very top. They note that Third Yang exceeds the Mean (i.e., it is be-

yond the central position in the lower trigram), so it is too resolute and acts too harshly; this is why there is misfortune. Even a noble man here runs the risk of traveling alone and getting soaked by rain—an encounter with the "lake" of the upper trigram and the yin wetness of Top Yin. It is this that provokes the anger of the sovereign, but Resolution should finally carry the noble man through these trials, so that in the end one at Third Yang will "be without blame." See *Zhouyi zhezhong*, 6: 22b–23a.

9. Cf. Hexagram 44, *Gou* (Encounter), Third Yang.

10. Zhu Xi also interprets the *yang* (ram) as something in front of Fourth Yang, which Fourth Yang should follow to be able to advance, but Cheng Yi thinks the *yang* (sheep) refers to Fourth Yang itself—one here should allow himself to be led like a sheep (get himself under control) and advance together with the other yang lines upward; thus his "regret would disappear." But as Fourth Yin is in a yin position—soft, weak, but recalcitrant—one here will not listen and so comes to grief. See *Zhouyi zhezhong*, 6: 24a.

HEXAGRAM 44

䷫

姤

Gou [Encounter]
(*Sun* Below *Qian* Above)

Judgment

Gou [Encounter] is such that the woman is strong; it would not do to marry this woman.

COMMENTARY ON THE JUDGMENTS

Gou [Encounter] means "to meet"; here the soft and weak meets the hard and strong. {When we apply Encounter to humankind, it refers to a woman meeting men. Here there is but one woman, yet she meets five men, which signifies utmost strength; thus one must not marry her.[1]} "It would not do to marry this woman," for one could not stay with her long. When Heaven and Earth encounter each other, things in all their different categories are made manifest. {It is by this pairing that such success is achieved.} When the hard and strong meets the central and the correct, this worldwide process achieves cosmic effect. {The transformative process thus achieves cosmic effect.} The concept underlying moments of *Gou* [Encounter] is indeed great! {Whenever the text mentions the word *concept* [*yi*], what it means is not exhausted by what can be seen [in the image involved] but actually indicates the idea that inheres in [that image].[2]}

COMMENTARY ON THE IMAGES

Below Heaven, there is Wind: this is the image of Encounter. In the same way, the sovereign issues his commands and makes known his wishes to the four quarters of the world.[3]

PROVIDING THE SEQUENCE OF THE HEXAGRAMS

With resolution, one is sure to encounter opportunity. This is why *Kuai* [Resolution, Hexagram 43] is followed by *Gou* [Encounter]. *Gou* here means "to meet."

THE HEXAGRAMS IN IRREGULAR ORDER

Gou [Encounter] indicates a meeting in which the soft encounters the hard.[4]

First Yin

This one should be tied to a metal brake, and for him to practice constancy would mean good fortune. But if one here were to set forth to do something, he would suffer misfortune, for it would be like a weak pig [sow] that but strives to romp around. {Metal is a tough, hard substance. A brake [*ni*] is a governor that controls motion, which here refers to Fourth Yang. First Yin is located at the beginning of Encounter. It is a single soft and weak [yin] line, yet carries five hard and strong [yang] lines. Such a one embodies an impatient nature, so when he meets with opportunities, he tends to go through with them, to go every which way with no one in control, utterly at the mercy of his own inclinations. The soft and weak are persons who cannot do without someone else leading them, and the Dao of the servant woman and the subordinate is such that they cannot fail to practice constancy. This is why First Yin must be tied to the line with which it is in a correct resonate relationship, for only then can it practice constancy and have good fortune. "A weak [*lei*] pig" here means "a sow." In a group of pigs, the boar is strong, and the sow is weak, and this is why the text calls this one "a weak [*lei*] pig." *Fu* [sincere, trust] is like the *wu* in *wuzao* [strive (work at nothing but) to be frivolous, strive to indulge one's impatience]. One who is yin in nature and impatient in attitude is exemplified especially well by the "weak pig" [sow]. The text here talks about a yin person who does not practice constancy and thus breaks away from the one who should be doing the leading. To express the ugliness of this lascivious behavior, the text likens it to the willfulness of the "weak pig" that "but strives to romp around."}

COMMENTARY ON THE IMAGES

"This one should be tied to a metal brake," for the Dao of the soft and weak is to be led [i.e., controlled].

Second Yang

In this one's kitchen, there is a fish, about which there is no blame. It is not fitting to entertain guests. {First Yin is a yin line and is at the very bottom; thus it is referred to as "a fish." As a yin line in an incorrect position and located at the beginning of Encounter, First Yin cannot oppose the line contiguous to it [Second Yang], so on its own it is delighted to answer the call to come to Second Yang's kitchen; it is not a matter of its being taken there by force. Thus "there is no blame." To claim another's goods and consider them one's own largess to dispense is something the righteous would not do. Thus the text says: "It is not fitting to entertain guests."[5]}

COMMENTARY ON THE IMAGES

"In this one's kitchen, there is a fish," but the righteous does not allow it to reach guests.

Third Yang

This one's thighs are without skin, and his walking falters.[6] Though in danger, he incurs no great blame. {Third Yang occupies the very top of the lower trigram, but Second Yang is supported by First Yin, which thus does not provide carriage for Third Yang, so Third Yang does not obtain security here, and, were it to set forth, there would be no proper resonate line for it. As it cannot lead any line to come to its support, all it can do is keep tightly to its own place. This is why the text says: "This one's thighs are without skin, and his walking falters." However, it manages to tread on territory that is the right position for it; one does not occupy his place here recklessly. This represents someone who is out of step with the moment [through no fault of his own] and so is subject to danger. Disasters that might occur would not happen because he himself summoned them, so "he incurs no great blame."}

COMMENTARY ON THE IMAGES

"His walking falters," for he never finds anyone to lead.

Fourth Yang

In this one's kitchen, there is no fish, which gives rise to misfortune. {As Second Yang has this one's fish, Fourth Yang has lost it. For this one to make a move without the support of the common folk, that is, to act once he has lost resonance with them, would mean misfortune.[7]}

COMMENTARY ON THE IMAGES

The misfortune associated with "there is no fish" is a matter of one here finding himself at a distance from the common folk.

Fifth Yang

With his basket willow and bottle gourd, this one harbors beauty within, so if there is destruction, it will only come from Heaven. {The basket willow [*qi*] is such that it is a plant that grows in fertile soil, and the bottle gourd [*paogua*] is such that it is tied up and not eaten.[8] Fifth Yang manages to tread the territory of the noble position [it is the ruler of the Encounter hexagram], but it does not meet with any proper response [there is no line with which it is in a resonate relationship]. This one may have obtained land, but it does not provide him with a living; he may harbor beauty within but never has a chance to let that beauty shine forth. As one here does not meet with any proper response, his orders will never circulate. However, such a one manages to occupy a position that is right for him [because it is a yang line in a yang position], embodies hardness and strength, and abides in centrality [the Mean], so if "this one's will remains fixed on not giving up his mandate," he cannot be destroyed. This is why the text says: "If there is destruction, it will only come from Heaven" [as punishment for wrongdoing].[9]}

COMMENTARY ON THE IMAGES

Fifth Yang harbors beauty within and is central and correct, so "if there is destruction, it will only come from Heaven," for this one's will remains fixed on not giving up his mandate.

Top Yang

Here one encounters the horns, and, though this is a base situation, it does not incur blame. {One here has advanced to the very end, and there is nothing to meet in addition to this, nothing other than horns. This is why the text says: "Here one encounters the horns." This one advances, but there is no one to meet, so all such a one can do is suffer resentment in isolation, but, as he does not contend with others, his Dao here will not lead to harm, thus there is no misfortune or blame.[10]}

COMMENTARY ON THE IMAGES

"Here one encounters the horns": at the top one comes to the end and has to endure a base situation.

NOTES

1. Kong Yingda glosses *zhuang* (strong, strength) as *yinzhuang* (lascivious and strong). See *Zhouyi zhengyi*, 5: 4a. Note that this and all subsequent text set off in this manner is commentary by Wang Bi.

2. Lou Yulie suggests that the text of Wang's remarks here should be understood in light of the opening passage of Clarifying the Images, section four of his General Remarks: "Images are the means to express ideas. Words [i.e., the texts] are the means to explain the images." See *Wang Bi ji jiaoshi*, 2: 442 n. 2. Kong Yingda says that "the concept of one woman encountering five men is not at all sufficient to express the beauty and breadth involved here; it is only when the text discusses how Heaven and Earth encounter each other . . . that the concept underlying *Gou* [Encounter] achieves great stature." See *Zhouyi zhengyi*, 5: 4a–4b.

3. The lower trigram is *Sun* (Wind, Compliance), and the upper trigram is *Qian* (Heaven, Pure Yang).

4. See note 10 of The Hexagrams in Irregular Order.

5. Both Wang Bi and Kong Yingda gloss *bao* (wrap, wrapping) as *chu* or *paochu* (kitchen); see *Zhouyi zhengyi*, 5: 5b. However, Cheng Yi understands *bao* as *baoju* (straw for wrapping, i.e., wrapper):

> If Second Yang is able to hold First Yin securely, just as a wrapper keeps a fish, then its behavior in Encounter will be without blame. A guest is an outsider. "It is not fitting to entertain guests," for how could this wrapped-up fish be allowed to reach guests? This means that one must not allow it to go any farther and reach outsiders. The Dao of Encounter insists upon exclusivity, and if this is compromised, it would mean promiscuity.

Zhu Xi takes an even different approach: "If control over First Yin stays with Second Yang, Second Yang will as a consequence be without blame. But if Second Yang does not maintain control and instead allows First Yin to meet with all the rest, the harm that this would do would be far-reaching." See *Zhouyi zhezhong*, 6: 28b.

6. Cf. Hexagram 43, *Kuai* (Resolution), Fourth Yang.

7. Kong Yingda comments: "The yin [represented by First Yin] is the common folk of the yang. Here Second Yang has acquired their support, so the text says that Fourth Yang 'find[s] himself at a distance from the common folk.' " See *Zhouyi zhengyi*, 5: 6a.

8. Cf. *Lunyu* (Analects) 17:7: "How could I be a bottle gourd that is just hung up and not eaten?" Here Confucius complains that he is not just an empty ornament but someone who should be employed for the good of others.

9. Cheng Yi interprets Fifth Yang differently:

> Fifth Yang has no resonate relationship below, so this is not the time to have a meeting. However, as one has obtained the [hexagram that

> represents the] Dao of meetings [Encounter], one will be sure to have a meeting in the end. Meetings of those above and those below happen because people seek one another out. The basket willow [*qi*] is a tall tree, and its leaves are large. The basket willow occupies a lofty position, embodies greatness, and can be used to wrap things. A melon [*gua*] is a beautiful fruit that occupies a lowly place. Here we have something that is beautiful but abides in a lowly place, and this is an image of the worthy who remains out of the way and leads an insignificant life. Fifth Yang nobly abides in the position of ruler, but he seeks worthy talent below. To have the highest seek the lowest in this way is just like using willow leaves to wrap up a melon. One who can humble himself in this way also nourishes virtues of centrality and righteousness within, so he comes to perfect fruition and displays perfect beauty. If the sovereign of men is like this, he will never fail to meet those whom he seeks.

See *Zhouyi zhezhong*, 6: 30b.

10. Cheng Yi's interpretation differs:

> That which is both the hardest and the highest is the horns. Top Yang has the image of horns because it is hard and strong [a yang line] and abides in the top position. When people meet, they should come together with deference, mutual accommodation, and compliance, for only then will harmony ensue. Top Yang represents someone so high that he overreaches himself and moreover is hard and strong to an extreme degree, so who would ever want to get together with him? If one were to seek to meet someone in this way, he surely would find it hard-going or humiliating. It is because Top Yang behaves in this way that others keep him at a distance. And this is not anyone else's fault; this one brought it on himself. This is why Top Yang has no one upon whom he can lay blame for it.

See *Zhouyi zhezhong*, 6: 31b.

䷬

萃

Cui [Gathering]
(*Kun* Below *Dui* Above)

Judgment

Cui [Gathering] means prevalence. {When there is a gathering,[1] things go smoothly.[2]} Only when a true king arrives, will there be an ancestral temple. {*Jia* [come, go] here means "arrive." When a true king arrives, thanks to this time of gathering, there will an ancestral temple.[3]} It is fitting to see the great man [*daren*], and with prevalence it is fitting to practice constancy. {It is only when the gathering obtains a great man that things manage to go smoothly and it becomes fitting to practice constancy.} To use a great sacrificial beast means good fortune. {When the Dao of gathering is practiced perfectly, the use of a great sacrificial beast will result in good fortune, but if one were to use a great sacrificial beast when the Dao of gathering is not being practiced perfectly, the gods will not dispense blessings.} It is fitting to set out to do something.

COMMENTARY ON THE JUDGMENTS

Cui [Gathering] means *ju* [gathering]. Here compliance is practiced with delight, to which the hard and strong [ruler] responds by staying within the Mean. Thus Gathering is achieved. {If there is nothing but "compliance . . . practiced with delight," it would be but the dao of the evil sycophant, and if there were only hardness and strength so that it did violence to the resonance proper to centrality, this would be but power as exercised by a mighty overreacher. How could gathering ever be achieved by such means as these? But if the one practices compliance with delight, and the other practices stewardship with hardness and strength, that is, if the ruler were hard and strong yet trod the path of the Mean, and if resonance were maintained by him who so trod the path of the Mean, then true gathering would be achieved.} "Only when a true king arrives, will there be an ancestral temple," for then sacrifice will be achieved that is imbued with true filial piety. {Only the perfect practice of gathering will enable one to achieve sacrifice imbued with true filial piety.} "It is fitting to see the great man," for he achieves prevalence and gathering is had thanks to his righteousness. {A great man is someone who embodies centrality and righteousness. Such a one has great success at gathering because of his righteousness; thanks to it, gathering achieves perfection.} "To use a great sacrificial beast means good fortune," and "it is fitting to set out to do something," for one here obeys Heaven's commands. {One who "practices compliance with delight" and so does no harm to the hard and strong is someone who "obeys Heaven's commands." The virtue of Heaven is to be hard and strong, yet it does not do violence to centrality [or "does not violate the Mean"], so here the one finds delight in obeying Heaven's commands, while the other practices his stewardship with hardness and strength.} Observe how gathering takes place here, for in such gathering the innate tendencies of the myriad things can be seen. {"Those with regular tendencies gather according to kind, and things divide up according to group."[4] Only when innate tendencies are the same will things gather, and only when material forces are in harmony will things group.[5]}

COMMENTARY ON THE IMAGES

The Lake has risen higher than the Earth: this is the image of Gathering. In the same way, the noble man gets his weapons in order, so he may use them to deal with emergencies.[6] {If gathering comes about but does not have defenses, the common man will start to have a mind of his own.[7]}

PROVIDING THE SEQUENCE OF THE HEXAGRAMS

Only after things meet is there a gathering. This is why *Gou* [Encounter, Hexagram 44] is followed by *Cui* [Gathering]. *Cui* here means "to gather."

THE HEXAGRAMS IN IRREGULAR ORDER

Cui [Gathering] means "to collect together."

First Yin

If this one has sincerity but does not let it run its course, there would be confusion one moment then Gathering the next. But if one declares that it would be for a handclasp and were to make smiles, he should feel no grief, for setting forth would incur no blame. {First Yin has a resonate relationship with Fourth Yang, but Third Yin carries Fourth Yang, so First Yin might be beset with heartfelt suspicions. This is why the text says: "If this one has sincerity but does not let it run its course." If this one were unable to remain loyal to the Dao, which would bring about a union of utmost goodness [between First Yin and Fourth Yang], it would confuse his sense of duty and subject him to struggle and conflict. Thus the text says: "There would be confusion one moment then Gathering the next." "A handclasp" describes brevity, and "make smiles" describes someone who is malleable and feeble. First Yin is the correct partner for Fourth Yang, but, because of its proximity, Third Yin is the favorite [of Fourth Yang]. If one at First Yin were content to be submissive, to withdraw, and to take care of himself in all modesty, then "he should feel no grief, for setting forth would incur no blame."[8]}

COMMENTARY ON THE IMAGES

"There would be confusion one moment then Gathering the next," for the will is confused.

Second Yin

This one is summoned, so he has good fortune and is without blame. If one is sincere, it would be fitting to perform a *yue* sacrifice here.[9] {Second Yin abides here at a time of Gathering. It embodies softness and weakness and suits its position, for it occupies the center of the *Kun* [Pure Yin] trigram. It alone occupies a correct place here [in the lower trigram], and, in doing so, it differs from all the others. As one here conducts himself in a different way from the rest of the gathering, he is often shunned by the common folk. The one who alone practices rectitude puts himself in danger. As this one is incapable of altering the substance of what he is to distance himself from harm, he is sure to be summoned [by Fifth Yang], in consequence of which "he has good fortune and is without blame." "*Yue*" is the name of the Yin [Shang dynasty] spring sacrifice, the most frugal of the four seasonal sacrifices. This one abides at a time of gathering and occupies a central and correct position, and, as he conducts himself with loyalty and faithfulness, he can be sparing and frugal when it comes to sacrificing to spirits and gods.}

COMMENTARY ON THE IMAGES

"This one is summoned, so he has good fortune and is without blame," for his centrality is never altered [or, "he never deviates from the Mean"].

Third Yin

Now Gathering, now sighing, there is nothing at all fitting here, but one can set forth without blame, for it involves but a little baseness. {Where Third Yin treads is not the territory of its rightful position [it is a yin line in a yang position], and, because it pairs with Fourth Yang, Fourth Yang also has to give up its position. It is by improper gathering or by gathering the improper that disasters are born, and it is by interfering with the proper resonate relationships between people that harm arises. This is why the text says: "Now Gathering, now sighing, there is nothing at all fitting here." Top Yin also is without response and so stands alone, occupying a place at the very end and grieving about its danger. It longs for help and seeks a companion, and, "compliant," it waits for another. For such a one to gather with someone improper [Third Yin] is not as good as if he had gathered with a true comrade, [but still it is not too bad], thus "one can set forth without blame." For two yins to unite is not as good as the resonate relationship between a yin and a yang, [but still it is not too bad], thus "it involves but a little baseness."}

COMMENTARY ON THE IMAGES

"One can set forth without blame," for the one at Top Yin is compliant.

Fourth Yang

Only if this one were to have great good fortune would he be without blame. {Where Fourth Yang treads is not its rightful position [it is a yang line in a yin position]; moreover below it is supported by three yin lines, and in order to obtain that support it has to be out of its rightful position. Here such a one is at a time of gathering, not only incorrect but also dependent, and this is why he must have "great good fortune" and so achieve some great meritorious accomplishment, for only then will he manage to "be without blame."}

COMMENTARY ON THE IMAGES

"Only if this one were to have great good fortune would he be without blame," for his position is not correct.

Fifth Yang

Gathering is such that this one has his position. There is one without blame, but that is not because of his sincerity. Fundamentally and constantly does this one practice constancy, so his regret disappears. {Fifth Yang is so located at this time of Gathering that such a one obtains to the utmost a position of power and prosperity, and this is why the text says: "This one has his position." Fourth Yang acts without proper authority and also is dependent. It is the virtue of one there not to act; he merely protects himself and does nothing more, and this is why the text says: "There is one without blame, but that is not because of his sincerity." If one cultivates benevolence and maintains his rectitude, eventually his regret will surely vanish, thus the text says: "Fundamentally and constantly does this one practice constancy, so his regret disappears."}

COMMENTARY ON THE IMAGES

"Gathering is such that this one has his position," but he never has the opportunity to let his will shine forth.

Top Yin

This one wails and weeps, but is without blame. {Top Yin situated as it is at a time of gathering abides at this uppermost extremity. Fifth Yang is not one upon which such a one can ride, and within the lower trigram there is no one who will respond with help. He occupies the top and stands alone, with no one near or far to give him aid. There is no greater danger than this. "*Jizi*" [wail] is an expression for sighing or moaning, used, for example, when one is capable of knowing the extremity of his danger, of fearing the depth of the disaster threatening him, or of grieving over the severity of some illness—such that he even goes so far as to weep. This one does not dare take charge of his own security, yet he is not harmed by all the others, thus he manages to be "without blame."[10]}

COMMENTARY ON THE IMAGES

That "this one wails and weeps" is because he can never be secure here at the top.

NOTES

1. There are two words for "gathering" in the text of Hexagram 45; "Gathering" translates *cui*, and "gathering" translates *ju*, a more common expression.

2. This and all subsequent text set off in this manner is commentary by Wang Bi.

3. Kong Yingda comments: "When the world crumbles and falls to pieces, the common folk feel resentful, and the gods are angry. Although one might still make sacrificial offerings, there might as well be no ancestral temple at all. When a true king arrives at a time of great gathering, the virtue of filial piety will shine forth. Only then can one say that there is really an ancestral temple as such." See *Zhouyi zhengyi*, 5: 6b.

4. See section one of the Commentary on the Appended Phrases, Part One.

5. Cf. Hexagram 1, *Qian* (Pure Yang), Fifth Yang, especially the Commentary on the Words of the Text.

6. The lower trigram is *Kun* (Earth), and the upper trigram is *Dui* (Lake). Kong Yingda comments: "If the Lake rises higher than the Earth, then it could flood down on the mass of common folk." See *Zhouyi zhengyi*, 5: 7b. This implies the need to provide defense against possible dangers. Zhu Xi also interprets the Commentary on the Images to Gathering in this way. See *Zhouyi zhezhong*, 12: 33a–33b.

7. That is, the mass of common folk will disintegrate, with each person trying to protect himself against dangers.

8. Kong Yingda's commentary helps to elucidate Wang's remarks:

> If First Yin's mind were beset with suspicion, its thoughts and feelings would be thrown into confusion, to run every which way, and it would allows itself to gather with no reference to decorum [i.e., it would join in an unsuitable relationship with Second and Third Yin,

its neighboring fellow yin lines]. "A handclasp" describes brevity, that is, it is a simile for a very brief moment of time. "Make smiles" does not indicate sternness and resolution but weakness and malleability. First Yin is the correct partner for Fourth Yang, but Third Yin, because of its proximity, is the favorite. If First Yin were itself to declare that it would pair up with Fourth Yang but for a brief handclasp, this appearance of modesty and deference would spare it any conflict with others, so no grief would come to it from Third Yin. Thus if it were to set forth, it would be sure to achieve union and in doing so be without blame.

See *Zhouyi zhengyi*, 5: 8a.

9. Cf. Hexagram 46, *Sheng* (Climbing), Second Yang. A reference to the *yue* sacrifice also occurs in Hexagram 63, *Jiji* (Ferrying Complete), Fifth Yang.

10. Cheng Yi interprets this last part of Top Yin differently, saying that the person represented here is a "petty man" who does not at all belong in such an exalted position, but, as he himself is responsible for taking it up, he cannot blame others for it. The *wujiu* (be without blame) becomes "there is no one to blame" in Cheng's reading of the passage. See *Zhouyi zhezhong*, 6: 38a.

HEXAGRAM 46

䷭

升

Sheng [Climbing]
(*Sun* Below *Kun* Above)

Judgment

Sheng [Climbing] means fundamental prevalence, but only if one uses this opportunity to see the great man [*daren*] should there be no regret. {It is by being compliant and obedient that Climbing is possible. A yang line does not fill the noble position [the ruler here is the fifth line, in this case yin]; this means that there is no stern and strong person of rectitude here, so one cannot help but feel anxious. Thus "only if one uses this opportunity to see the great man should there be no regret.[1]} To go forth to the south means good fortune. {It is by the soft and weak going south that such a one shall cling to the great brightness there.[2]}

COMMENTARY ON THE JUDGMENTS

The soft and weak climb at their proper time. {When the soft and weak have their moment, they then have the chance to climb.} When obedience is practiced with compliance and when the hard and strong respond in such a way that the Mean is preserved, great prevalence is achieved. {If one is purely soft and weak, such a one cannot climb by himself, and, if one is overbearing, others will not follow, but here not only is the time right for Climbing, but also "obedience is practiced with compliance and . . . the hard and strong respond in such a way that the Mean is preserved." It is because Climbing comes about in this way that "great prevalence is achieved."} "Only if one uses this opportunity to see the great man, should there be no regret." This means that there will be blessings. "To go forth to the south means good fortune," for ambitions are realized. {The compliant manage to climb thanks to their obedience and, in doing so, attain to great brightness. This is what "ambitions are realized" means.}

COMMENTARY ON THE IMAGES

Within the Earth grows the Tree: this is the image of Climbing.[3] In the same way, the noble man lets virtue be his guide and little by little becomes lofty and great.

PROVIDING THE SEQUENCE OF THE HEXAGRAMS

To gather and build upward is called "climbing." This is why *Cui* [Gathering, Hexagram 45] is followed by *Sheng* [Climbing].

THE HEXAGRAMS IN IRREGULAR ORDER

Sheng [Climbing] means "not to come back."

First Yin

It is right that this one climbs, and he shall have great good fortune. {*Yun* [to trust, be trustworthy, sincerely] here means *dang* [ought, it is right that].[4] The three lines of the *Sun* [Compliance] trigram are all climbing. Although it lacks a resonate partner, First Yin, located here at the beginning of Climbing, combines its will with that of Second Yang and Third Yang, and they all climb together. As this is a moment suitable for Climbing, Climbing will be sure to result in great success, and this is why such a one here will have "great good fortune."}

COMMENTARY ON THE IMAGES

"It is right that this one climbs, and he shall have great good fortune," for this is the result of combining one's will with those above.

Second Yang

If one is sincere, it would be fitting to perform a *yue* sacrifice here.[5] Such a one will be without blame. {As Second Yang is in resonance with Fifth Yin, if one here were to set forth, he would be sure to be entrusted with office. Such a one embodies the virtues of hardness and strength, and his advance has nothing to do with seeking favoritism. He wards off evil, sustains his sincerity, and fixes his will on the great enterprise, and this is why it would be fitting for him here to use frugal offerings to the *shenming* [the numinous and the bright, i.e., the gods].}

COMMENTARY ON THE IMAGES

Due to the sincerity of Second Yang, there is joy.

Third Yang

This one climbs to an empty city. {Third Yang treads the territory of its rightful position, and, because it is a yang that climbs to a yin [Top Yin, its resonate partner] and because it rises up in this way, none oppose it. Thus it is just as if one were "climb[ing] to an empty city."[6]}

COMMENTARY ON THE IMAGES

"This one climbs to an empty city," and he need have no doubts. {If this one were to set forth, he would be sure to obtain the city.}

Fourth Yin

The king should use this opportunity to extend his prevalence to Mount Qi, for there would be good fortune and no blame. {Fourth Yin is located at such a place in Climbing that those below advance by climbing up; such a one can accept but cannot oppose them. If he were to try to prevent those below from advancing, if he willfully took it upon himself to obstruct acceptance of them, disastrous blame would befall him because of it. But if he were able to avoid such opposition and instead accepted them, if he complied with the innate tendency of these others, and by doing so facilitated realization of the will of the masses, he would obtain "good fortune and no blame." The assemblage at Mount Qi was such that he [King Tai] complied with the innate tendency of the situation and accommodated himself to all without exception.[7]}

COMMENTARY ON THE IMAGES

"The king should use this opportunity to extend his prevalence to Mount Qi," for to do so would be to comply with the situation.

Fifth Yin

Constancy results in good fortune, for this one has climbed in stages. {Fifth Yin has managed to climb to a noble position [as the ruler of the hexagram]. Such a one embodies softness and responded accordingly. He entrusted responsibilities to others and was not willful and arbitrary. Thus he achieved the noble position by the successful practice of constancy, with its good fortune, as he "climbed in stages."}

COMMENTARY ON THE IMAGES

"Constancy results in good fortune, for this one has climbed in stages," which is the way that one here can greatly realize his goals.

Top Yin

This one climbs in darkness, so it would be fitting if he were to practice unceasing constancy. {Top Yin is located at the very extremity of Climbing and represents someone who advances without stopping. As this one advances without stopping, even when he finds himself in darkness he still climbs. Thus, if he were to apply himself to unceasing constancy, it would be all right, but if he were to use this as the way to reign as master over others, he would be lost. To go on forever without stopping is the path to exhaustion.}

COMMENTARY ON THE IMAGES

The one who climbs in darkness may be at the top, but he shall find exhaustion there, not prosperity. {His labors here cannot sustain him long.[8]}

NOTES

1. This and all subsequent text set off in this manner is commentary by Wang Bi.

2. Kong Yingda comments: "Not only must one see the man of great virtue straight away, he also should go to the land of the bright yang force. If a yin here went in the yin direction, the more such a one traveled, the darker it would be. As the south is the land of the bright yang force, this is why the text says: 'To go forth to the south means good fortune.' " See *Zhouyi zhengyi*, 5: 9b.

3. The lower trigram is *Sun* (Compliance), i.e., Wood, and the upper trigram is *Kun* (Pure Yin), i.e., Earth.

4. Both Cheng Yi and Zhu Xi gloss *yun* differently from Wang Bi. Cheng interprets it as *xincong* (faithfully follow): First Yin carries Second Yang and, as its faithful follower, ascends along with Second Yang. Thus Cheng's reading of First Yang would be "this one faithfully climbs, so there is good fortune." Zhu Xi interprets *yun* as *xin* (we can trust that, i.e., surely): "First Yin abides here below with its compliance and obedience and is the ruler of the *Sun* [Compliance] trigram. It complies with the wishes of Second Yang. If the one who interprets this prognostication behaves likewise, he surely [*xin*] will be able to climb and achieve great good fortune." See *Zhouyi zhezhong*, 6: 39b.

5. Cf. Hexagram 45, *Cui* (Gathering), Second Yin, and Wang Bi's commentary. A reference to the *yue* sacrifice also occurs in Hexagram 63, *Jiji* (Ferrying Complete), Fifth Yang.

6. That is, it is as if one were entering an unguarded or "open" city.

7. "The king should use this opportunity to extend his prevalence to Mount Qi" translates *wang yong heng yu qishan*. Cf. Hexagram 17, *Sui* (Following), Top Yin and note 12. Kong Yingda and Cheng Yi have it that reference here is to an assemblage at Mount Qi involving King Wen, but, as Lou Yulie points out, there is no such event mentioned in ancient sources. It is most likely a reference to the story of King Tai, the grandfather of King Wen, as it seems to be in the passage in *Sui* (Following). Note also that Zhu Xi interprets *heng* (prevalence) as *xiang* (sacrifice), just as he does for its occurrence in Hexagram 17. See *Wang Bi ji jiaoshi*, 2: 452 n. 9, and *Zhouyi zhezhong*, 6: 41a.

8. Kong Yingda comments: "Although one here may practice government without cease, what he will get in exchange for it is danger and blame." See *Zhouyi zhengyi*, 5: 11a.

HEXAGRAM 47

䷮

困

Kun [Impasse]
(*Kan* Below *Dui* Above)

Judgment

Kun [Impasse] means prevalence. {When one encounters straitened circumstances, one must get free of them. It is the petty man who, when situated at a time of Impasse, cannot get himself free.[1]} With his constancy, the great man has good fortune and is without blame. {Such a one may be situated in straitened circumstances, yet he manages to be "without blame." As he has "good fortune," he can avoid it [blame].} If one has words, they will not be believed.[2]

COMMENTARY ON THE JUDGMENTS

Kun [Impasse] is such that the hard and strong are hindered. {The hard and strong suffer hindrance at the hands of the soft and weak.} But such a [hard and strong] one remains joyful in the face of danger and, though he encounters Impasse, does not lose that which shall allow him to prevail. {He may be situated in danger, but that does not alter his capacity for joy; he may have encountered Impasse, but he "does not lose that which shall allow him to prevail."} Who but the noble man can do this? "With his constancy, the great man has good fortune," for here he stays on the path of the Mean with his hardness and strength. {One who, when he encounters Impasse, uses his hardness and strength and does not stray from the Mean will tread the path of righteousness and can embody greatness. But one who can practice righteousness but cannot do so on a grand scale will never save himself from Impasse. This is why the text says: "With his constancy, the great man has good fortune."} "If one has words, they will not be believed," that is, if one were but to esteem what the mouth can do, it would only result in grief. {One might have recourse to words here in Impasse, but this is a time when they will not be believed. As this is not a time when words will have an effect, if one attempts to use words to avoid blame, it will surely lead to grief. The good fortune that can be had here resides in the great man with his constancy, so what can the mouth have to do with it?}

COMMENTARY ON THE IMAGES

The Lake has no Water: this is the image of Impasse. In the same way, the noble man would sacrifice his life in pursuit of his goals. {"The Lake has no Water" comes from the fact that the Water is below the Lake, which is the image of Impasse.[3] One who bends his will when he encounters Impasse is a petty man. "The noble man may certainly find himself in straitened circumstances," but could he ever forget the Dao?[4]}

COMMENTARY ON THE APPENDED PHRASES

Kun [Impasse] is the criterion for distinguishing virtue.

Kun demonstrates how one who suffers tribulation still stays in complete control of himself.

Kun provides the means to keep resentments few.[5]

PROVIDING THE SEQUENCE OF THE HEXAGRAMS

If climbing goes on and does not stop, there is sure to be impasse. This is why *Sheng* [Climbing, Hexagram 46] is followed by *Kun* [Impasse].

THE HEXAGRAMS IN IRREGULAR ORDER

Kun [Impasse] indicates a clash of interests.

First Yin

This one suffers Impasse in the buttocks here on the root of the tree, so he enters a secluded valley and does not appear for three years. {First Yin is located at the very bottom, is bogged down in the Impasse of the most miserable of positions, and where it abides there is no security or comfort whatsoever. This is why the text says: "This one suffers Impasse in the buttocks here on the root of a tree." It may wish to go to its resonate partner [Fourth Yang], but Second Yang blocks its path. Staying would result in "suffer[ing] Impasse . . . here on the root of the tree," and advancing would garner no relief either, so this one has to become a fugitive in hiding. This is why the text says: "He enters a secluded valley." As a Dao, Impasse does not last for more than a few years. It is because of Impasse that he spends years in this way, but when the Impasse dissolves, he then comes out. Thus the text says that he "does not appear for three years."}

COMMENTARY ON THE IMAGES

"He enters a secluded valley," for in such seclusion he will be inconspicuous. {*Seclusion* as an expression means "not bright" [i.e., inconspicuous]. Here one enters into an inconspicuous place in order to hide himself away.}

Second Yang

This one has Impasse in his food and drink, but as soon as the crimson ceremonial garment arrives, it would be fitting to offer sacrifice here but to set forth would lead to misfortune, and there would be no one to blame. {As this is a yang line that abides in a yin position, it represents one who esteems modesty. This one finds himself situated at a time of Impasse in such a way that he achieves centrality, and what he embodies is the stuff of hardness and strength. However, he practices the Mean, treads the path of modesty, and as he does not limit his response to any one partner, he remains free of any selfish designs whatsoever. As such, there is none who comes before him in plenitude of resources. It is because he treats things with modesty that they come to him, and it is because he occupies this place of danger with hardness and strength that its difficulties are conquered. As he treads the path of the Mean, he does not violate that which is proper to him; as he does not have a resonate partner, he is free of any private patronage. When one takes up a place at a time of Impasse in such a way as this, nothing fails to come to him, and his riches are inexhaustible. This is why the text says that "this one has Impasse in his food and drink," for it signifies the ultimate of sumptuousness. A crimson ceremonial garment is something associated with the southern direction. One who undergoes a time of Impasse in this way can attract others from foreign lands, and this is why the text says "as soon as the crimson ceremonial garment arrives." This one is overflowing with inexhaustible riches, thus the text says: "It would be fitting to offer sacrifice here." However, if one were to keep on advancing after one is already full, this would be a dao that leads to ruin. So if one were to set forth in this way, whom could one possibly blame for the misfortune that would ensue? Thus the text says: "To set forth would lead to misfortune, and there would be no one to blame."[6]}

COMMENTARY ON THE IMAGES

"This one has Impasse in his food and drink," for there are blessings for him who practices the Mean.

Third Yin

This one suffers Impasse on rocks, so he tries to hold on to the puncture vine for support, and then he enters his home but does not see his wife. This means misfortune.[7] {Rocks as such are hard and inhospitable things, and here they refer to Fourth Yang.

Third Yin occupies a yang position as a yin line, which represents one whose ambition it is to find someone with military power [as patron and protector]. However, as Fourth Yang has already accepted First Yin, it will not take Third Yin, and Second Yang is not one to provide support, for a strong [yang] line should not offer carriage to it [a yin line]. Above Third Yin might pair with the impasse-ridden rocks, and below it might "try to hold on to the puncture vine for support," but as such a one tries to go in without having a resonate partner there, where should he ever find a true mate?[8] When one finds himself in Impasse in such a place as this, it is to be expected that he should have misfortune.}

COMMENTARY ON THE IMAGES

Here one "tries to hold on to the puncture vine for support," that is, one tries to ride atop the hard and strong. "He enters his home but does not see his wife," which is inauspicious.

Fourth Yang

This one comes slowly, so slowly, for he suffers Impasse at the metal-clad cart. Although there is humiliation, he should bring about a successful conclusion. {The "metal-clad cart" refers to Second Yang. As it is hard and strong enough to carry others, it is referred to as "a metal-clad cart." *Xuxu* [slowly, so slowly] is an expression that suggests doubt and fear. Fourth Yang has his will fixed on First Yin but is blocked by Second Yang, and, as such a one treads on a territory that is not his rightful position [because this is a yin position], he might try awe-inspiring orders, but they will not be carried out. Fourth Yang is incapable of abandoning First Yin, and it might want to go to First Yin, but it fears Second Yang. This is why the text says: "This one comes slowly, so slowly, for he suffers Impasse at the metal-clad cart." One at Fourth Yang has a resonate partner but is unable to succor him, thus the text says: "There is humiliation." However, because it is a yang that abides in this yin position, such a one treads the Dao of modesty. This one gets the measure of his own powers and so stays put and does not do battle with Second Yang. "Although he is not in his rightful position, in the end, others give in to him." Thus the text says: "He should bring about a successful conclusion."}

COMMENTARY ON THE IMAGES

"This one comes slowly, so slowly," for his will is fixed on the one below. {"The one below" refers to First Yin.} Although he is not in his rightful position, in the end, others give in to him.

Fifth Yang

This one cuts off noses and feet and so has Impasse with the red ceremonial garment, and only when he takes things slowly does he have joy. It is fitting to offer sacrifice here. {As a yang line that abides in a yang position, this one is invested with all the power proper to him. However, he is unable to employ modesty to attract others, so others do not join him. Distressed that others will not join him, he uses his power, but the more he cruelly implements the awe-inspiring punishments at his disposal, the more foreign lands become obstreperous and the more those near and far rebel; the more he uses punishments in order to obtain these others, the more these punishments become the instruments of their loss. This is why the text says: "This one cuts off noses and feet and so has Impasse with the red ceremonial garment." Second Yang obtains the red ceremonial garment [i.e., the allegiance of those in foreign lands] because of his modesty, but Fifth Yang loses it because of his hardness and strength. But as this one is an embodiment of "centrality and perseverance," he is capable of not persisting in the error of his ways. Here is someone who first has to suffer Impasse before he uses his proper Dao. Success at attracting others to one does not lie in harsh measures; this is why the text says "takes things slowly." He "takes things slowly" only after he suffers Impasse, but when "he takes things slowly," he has joy. Thus the text says: "This one . . . has Impasse with the red ceremonial garment, and only when he takes things slowly does he have joy." It is by offering sacrifice that one receives blessings. One at Fifth Yang treads the territory of the noble position and is able to change his ways when he encounters Impasse and not persist in his errors. When he offers sacrifice under such conditions at this, he is sure to obtain blessings from doing so, and this is why the text says: "It is fitting to offer sacrifice here."[9]}

COMMENTARY ON THE IMAGES

As long as this one "cuts off noses and feet," his goals will never be realized, but when "he takes things slowly, he has joy," and this is due to his centrality and perseverance. "It is fitting to offer sacrifice," for he shall have blessings.

Top Yin

This one suffers Impasse either in creepers and vines or in danger and perplexity, so he should say to himself, "Take steps that you will regret," for even if it means regret, to set forth here will result in good fortune. {Top Yin resides at the apogee of Impasse and moreover rides on top of a strong [yang] line. Below there is no resonate partner for this one, so the more one here tries to go on, the more entangled in trouble he will become. Going would result in tangles of trouble, but staying put would result in no chance to have security. Thus the text says: "This one suffers Impasse either in creepers and vines or in danger and perplexity." The second phrase ["or in danger and perplexity"] lacks the word *Impasse*, but that is because it already appears in the first phrase. To be situated here at the end point of Impasse means both that there is no through road for one were he to try go on ahead and that there would be no means to make one secure if he were to stay put. This is Impasse at its worst. Whenever anything reaches the point where it can go no further, one should think about how it will change, so, when one finds himself at this point in Impasse, one should plan for a breakthrough.[10] As one is located at this place where Impasse is at its worst, it represents a moment that one should use to make plans. "So he should say to himself" is an expression that means that one should think over plans. When it comes to the realization of plans, one ought to have success if he acts when an opening occurs. If one were to address the question of what means one should use to break through this ultimate stage of Impasse, he should say to himself, "Take steps that you will regret," for even if there be regret, by setting forth here he shall rescue himself. This is why the text says: "'Take steps that you will regret,' for even if it means regret, to set forth here will result in good fortune."[11]}

COMMENTARY ON THE IMAGES

"This one suffers Impasse either in creepers and vines," for he has not yet situated himself correctly. {This one has not yet found the right place for himself, and this is why Impasse has come to him here.} "Take steps that you will regret," for even if it means regret, you will find good fortune in moving on.

NOTES

1. This and all subsequent text set off in this manner is commentary by Wang Bi.

2. Kong Yingda comments: "When one has encountered Impasse, one should seek deliverance in the rectification of self and the cultivation of virtue. If one were instead to use crafty words and artful phrases, which should not be believed by others, the more he pursued this path the more straitened his circumstances would become. This is why one is warned that 'if one has words, they will not be believed.' " See *Zhouyi zhengyi*, 5: 11b.

3. The lower trigram is *Kan* (Sink Hole), which also signifies Water, and the upper trigram is *Dui* (Joy), here representing Lake.

4. Cf. *Lunyu* (Analects) 15:1: "The noble man may certainly find himself in straitened circumstances, but it is the petty man who, when in straitened circumstances, will let himself go out of control." Kong Yingda comments:

> When the Water is below the Lake, the Lake itself will dry out, so that the myriad things will all encounter Impasse [grief, hard times, etc.]. . . . But the noble man would maintain his commitment to the Dao even if it meant his death. Thus, although he encounters a world of Impasse and danger, in which he might be expected to sacrifice his life, he surely will pursue his lofty goals, from which he will not deviate and which he will not alter.

See *Zhouyi zhengyi*, 5: 12a.

5. See section seven of the Commentary on the Appended Phrases, Part Two.

6. Whereas Kong Yingda's commentary agrees with and merely expands upon Wang's comments, Cheng Yi's interpretation of Second Yang is rather different:

> Food and drink are what people desire, but they are also things that one bestows as gifts on others. Second Yang with its resources of strength and centrality finds itself here at a time of Impasse. It represents the noble man who is content with what he encounters. Al-

> though he is subjected to straitened and dangerous conditions, nothing affects his heart and mind, and he does not regret that he has been placed in Impasse. The Impasse that he suffers is merely an Impasse concerning the things people desire. What the noble man desires is to shower benefits on the common folk and to rescue them from the Impasse that besets the world. Second Yang is not yet able to pursue this desire to shower such benefits. Thus he represents someone who "suffers Impasse in food and drink." Such a great man or noble man cherishes his Dao and so suffers Impasse here below. He must find a sovereign secure in the Dao who would seek him out and entrust him with duties, for only then will he be able to dispense what he has stored up. Second Yang with its virtues of strength and centrality suffers Impasse below, but above there is Fifth Yang, which represents a sovereign who is likewise imbued with strength and centrality. Their Daos are the same, and their virtues coincide, so they are sure to find each other. Thus the text says: "As soon as the crimson ceremonial garment arrives" [*zhufu fanglai*]. *Fanglai* means *fangqie lai* [as soon as it arrives, or only when it arrives]. A *zhufu* is a garment worn by a king; it is a knee covering, and it is used here to suggest the arrival of such a person. "It would be fitting to offer sacrifice here." When offering sacrifice, one uses the utmost sincerity to get through to the numinous and the bright [the gods]. When this one finds himself at a time of Impasse, it is fitting that he use the utmost sincerity in exactly the same way, for if his virtue be sincere, he shall then be able to move and get through to his superior above. . . . Just when one finds himself at a time of Impasse, if he does not wait for the command [from above], perfectly sincere and content with his place here, but instead sets forth in order to seek [his sovereign] on his own, the risk involved would result in misfortune and would be something he brought upon himself—who could he blame for it?

Cheng's reading of Second Yang would seem to be: "This one suffers Impasse in food and drink, and only when the crimson ceremonial garment arrives [i.e., only if he were perfectly sincere], would it be fitting to offer sacrifice. If he were to set forth [of his own volition], there would be misfortune, and there would be no one to blame [but himself]." See *Zhouyi zhezhong*, 6: 44b–45a.

7. See the extensive comments on Third Yin that appear in section five of the Commentary on the Appended Phrases, Part Two.

8. That is, as Kong Yingda comments, such a one "does not see his wife." See *Zhouyi zhengyi*, 5: 13a.

9. Cheng Yi has a different interpretation of Fifth Yang:

> To cut off the nose is called *yi*, a wound done to one's upper part. To cut off the feet is *yue*, a wound done to one's lower part. Fifth Yang is waylaid both above and below by yin lines, which inflict

these wounds. . . . Fifth Yang is in the sovereign's position. When the sovereign of men suffers Impasse, it comes from those above and below not giving in to him. A *chifu* [red ceremonial garment (knee covering)] is something worn by a retainer or vassal, and it is used here to suggest the arrival of such a person; this is why the text mentions the term *fu* [knee covering]. The sovereign of men suffers Impasse because all in the world do not come to him. If all were to come, it would not be Impasse. Although such a one at Fifth Yang finds himself in Impasse, he still possesses the virtues of strength and centrality. Below there is Second Yang, a worthy who also has strength and centrality. As their Daos are the same and their virtues coincide, eventually [*xu*, which means "slowly" in the Wang Bi and Kong Yingda commentaries] there is sure to be a response, and Second Yang will come to him, and together they will save the world from Impasse. This is what is meant by there first being Impasse but eventually joy.

As such, Cheng's reading of Fifth Yang would be: "This one has his nose and feet cut off, and there is Impasse as far as those with red ceremonial garments are concerned, but eventually there will be joy. It is fitting to offer sacrifice here." See *Zhouyi zhezhong*, 6: 47a.

10. Lou Yulie suggests that Wang here is paraphrasing a passage in section two of the Commentary on the Appended Phrases, Part Two: "As for [the Dao of] change, when one process of it reaches its limit, a change from one state to another occurs. As such, change achieves free flow, and with this free flow, it lasts forever." See *Wang Bi ji jiaoshi*, 2: 459 n. 21.

11. Kong Yingda's commentary makes these remarks by Wang Bi more intelligible: "When one addresses the question of what means one should use to break through this ultimate stage of Impasse, one should plan for it, saying: 'You must take the initiative and do that which could lead to regret, because even if regret were to happen, be assured that afterward you, located as you are here in Impasse and seeking deliverance, can thereby move on and so garner good fortune for yourself.' " See *Zhouyi zhengyi*, 5: 14b. Cheng Yi and Zhu Xi interpret this part of Top Yin somewhat differently. They say that one here should know that whatever he does before Impasse undergoes flux and passes away will result in regret, but once one acquires this sense of regret and after he waits for this time of Impasse to pass away, he then can set forth and obtain good fortune—not before. See *Zhouyi zhezhong*, 6: 48a.

䷯

井

Jing [The Well]
(*Sun* Below *Kan* Above)

Judgment

One might change a city, but one does not change a Well. {Invariability is considered to be the virtue of the Well.[1]} It neither loses nor gains. {Its virtue is constant.} People may come and go, but it remains the same Well, pure and still. {That is, it undergoes no change.} One may have almost got it there, but that is not the same thing as actually hauling it out of the Well. {One may have already got it [the well pot or bucket] there but has not yet brought it out of the Well.} And if one breaks the pot, there will be misfortune. {The merit of the Well is realized only after it [the pot of water] has emerged. To have it almost there and then have it pour back is the same as not having tried to draw it out at all.}

COMMENTARY ON THE JUDGMENTS

Here the trigram *Sun* [Wood] goes into the Water [the upper trigram, *Kan*] and raises the Water; such is the Well. {One should pronounce *shang* [up, above, upper, etc.] here as it appears in the compound *jushang* [raise up] [i.e., in a deflected tone, as the verb "raise."][2]} The Well nourishes yet is never exhausted. "One might change a city, but one does not change a Well," for this is to occupy a central position with hardness and strength. {When one "occupies a central position with hardness and strength," one can fix the place in which he dwells so that it never changes.} "One may have almost got it there, but that is not the same thing as actually hauling it out of the Well," that is, the merit remains unrealized. {The merit of the Well is realized only after it has fulfilled itself.} It is because one breaks the pot that there is misfortune.

COMMENTARY ON THE IMAGES

Above wood, there is water: The Well. In the same way, the noble man rewards the common folk for their toil and encourages them to help each other. {"Above wood, there is water": this is the image of the Well. One uses the water that is raised from it for nourishment. It provides nourishment but is never exhausted. *Xiang* [each other] is like the word *zhu* [help]. Of the means one might use to "reward . . . the common folk for their toil and encourage . . . them to help each other" nothing is better than to nourish them and to do so without ever being exhausted.}

COMMENTARY ON THE APPENDED PHRASES

Jing [The Well] is the ground from which virtue springs.

Jing [The Well] demonstrates how one stays in one's place and yet can transfer what one has to others.

Jing [The Well] provides the means to distinguish what righteousness really is.[3]

PROVIDING THE SEQUENCE OF THE HEXAGRAMS

When impasse is met with upward, there is sure to be a turnabout downward. This is why *Kun* [Impasse, Hexagram 47] is followed by *Jing* [The Well].

THE HEXAGRAMS IN IRREGULAR ORDER

Jing [The Well] indicates something accessible to all.

First Yin

As the Well here is fouled with mud, one should not partake of it. At such an old Well there are no birds. {First Yin is at the very bottom of the Well, moreover it has no resonate partner above, so here it is in the depths where it is choked with sediment. Thus the text says: "As the Well here is fouled with mud, one should not partake of it." The mud of the well is such that one cannot partake of it, so this means that it is an old Well that has not been kept in repair. An old Well that has not been kept in repair is a place where birds do not feed, so how much the less should people do so! So for a time it is a place that is abandoned by all. The Well may be a thing that does not change and may be a place where virtue dwells, but if such constant virtue were debased, none would partake of it.}

COMMENTARY ON THE IMAGES

"As the Well here is fouled with mud, one should not partake of it," for this is the bottom of it. "At such an old Well there are no birds," for it is abandoned for a time.

Second Yang

Here the Well shoots down valleylike for the little fishes, as if it were a water jar so worn out that it leaks. {A river valley brings forth its water in such a way that it pours below from above, so the water always shoots down it. The Dao of the Well is such that it provides for those above from below. But Second Yang has no resonate partner above, so it turns downward and instead responds to First Yin. This is why the text says: "Here the Well shoots down valleylike for the little fishes." The "little fishes" refers to First Yin. Second Yang violates the Dao of the Well, for water here does not go up and out but turns and pours downward instead. Thus the text says: "As if it were a water jar so worn out that it leaks." That which occupies a position above ought to go down, and that which occupies a position below ought to go up. The Well is already something below, yet it still pours downward, which means that the Dao [way] to the Well here does reach where it should. Thus "none responds to this one."[4]}

COMMENTARY ON THE IMAGES

"Here the Well shoots down valleylike for the little fishes," so none responds to this one.

Third Yang

The Well here is cleansed, but one does not partake of it, which makes this one feel pain in his heart, for one could use this opportunity to draw from it. If there be a bright sovereign, then this one shall receive all his blessings. {"Cleansed" means that it is not filled with dirt. Third Yang is located at the top of the lower trigram and treads on the territory of its rightful position [as a yang line in a yang position]; moreover it has a resonate partner in the upper trigram [Top Yin], so it realizes the principle of the Well. However, just as Third Yang fulfills the principle of the Well and yet is not partaken of, so one here at Third Yang repairs himself so he is perfectly clean and yet is not entrusted with duties. This is why the text says "which makes this one feel pain in his heart." *Wei* [makes] means the same as *shi* [cause]. This one does not pour downward but instead responds to one above. Thus "one could use this opportunity to draw from it." "If there be a bright sovereign," then this one at Third Yang will be brought to light; then not only shall his behavior be commended, he shall also be honored with duties. Thus the text says: "This one shall receive all his blessings."[5]}

COMMENTARY ON THE IMAGES

"The Well here is cleansed, but one does not partake of it," which provokes painful feeling, {As this provokes an emotional response in the sincere, the text says "provokes painful feeling."[6]} but if this one were to seek the brightness of a true sovereign, he should receive blessings.

Fourth Yin

If the Well were relined with bricks here, there would be no blame. {This one obtains a position that is right for him [it is a yin line in a yin position] but has no resonate partner, so although he can make himself secure, he cannot provide for anyone above. He can use this opportunity to repair the faults in the Well, that is, correct and amend his own errors, but nothing more than that.}

COMMENTARY ON THE IMAGES

"If the Well were relined with bricks here, there would be no blame," which means that one should repair the Well.

Fifth Yang

As the Well is icy clear, being from a cold spring, this one should partake of it. {*Lie* [icy clear] means *jie* [pure]. Fifth Yang abides in a central position and achieves rectitude. Embodying hardness and strength as it does, it will not bend, and one here does not partake of what is not right. This one is central, correct, lofty, and pure, thus only if "the Well is icy clear, being from a cold spring," should this one "partake of it."[7]}

COMMENTARY ON THE IMAGES

Here one may partake of a cold spring, for it is central and correct.

Top Yin

The Well gives its bounty here. Do not cover it, for if one has sincerity, he shall have fundamental good fortune. {Top Yin is located at the very top, where the water has already been taken out of the Well. The merit of the Well in all its "great perfection" is revealed precisely in this line. This is why the text says: "The Well gives its bounty here." *Mu* [cloak, curtain] here is used in the sense of *fu* [cover]. If one did not monopolize what he has and did not keep his advantages for his own exclusive use, others would come to him, so were such a one to set forth he would never be exhausted. This is why the text says: "Do not cover it, for if one has sincerity, he shall have fundamental good fortune."}

COMMENTARY ON THE IMAGES

Fundamental good fortune is to be found at Top Yin, for there is great perfection there.

NOTES

1. This and all subsequent text set off in this manner is commentary by Wang Bi.

2. Kong Yingda comments: "In this hexagram, *Kan* is water and is on top, and *Sun* is wood and is below. Also, *Sun* means 'enter,' as Wood enters into the Water and raises it up; such is the image of *Jing* [The Well]." See *Zhouyi zhengyi*, 5: 15a. Cheng Yi thinks that *Sun* as Wood means a well sweep: "The well sweep draws up the pot. Down it goes into the mouth of the wellspring, then it draws up the water and brings it out." See *Zhouyi zhezhong*, 10: 25a.

3. See section seven of the Commentary on the Appended Phrases, Part Two.

4. Cheng Yi notes that "if there were those above who responded to this one at Second Yang, then water should be drawn upward, and the merit of the Well would be accomplished." See *Zhouyi zhezhong*, 12: 41a.

5. "This one shall receive all his blessings" translates *bing shou qi fu.* Cheng Yi interprets this last part of Third Yang differently: "If above there is a bright sovereign, then he ought to use this one and allow him to realize his productivity. Once this worthy's talents are so used, he shall be able to put his Dao into practice, the sovereign shall be able to make his merit prevail, and those below shall be able to enjoy this benefaction. That is, those above and below 'will all receive such blessings' [*bing shou qi fu*]." See *Zhouyi zhezhong*, 7: 3b–4a.

6. "Provokes painful feeling" translates *xing ce*, which Wang Bi glosses as "provokes an emotional response in the sincere," and "the sincere" seems to refer specifically to the one here at Third Yang. However, Cheng Yi interprets *xing ce* differently: "Here one has talent and knowledge but is not trusted with responsibilities, and considers the fact that he cannot act [*xing*] to be reason for sadness and pain." Zhu Xi offers a third explanation for *xing ce*: "The expression *xing ce* means 'all persons who practice the Dao [*xing dao zhi ren*] find this painful.' " See *Zhouyi zhezhong*, 12: 41a.

7. Kong Yingda comments: "Clearness and coldness are the original characteristics of water; it is only after it encounters things does it become dirty and warm. This is why the text speaks of a 'cold spring,' for this expresses its purity." See *Zhouyi zhengyi*, 5: 17a.

HEXAGRAM 49

䷰

革

Ge [Radical Change]
(*Li* Below *Dui* Above)

Judgment

Radical Change is such that only on the day when it comes to an end does one begin to enjoy trust, and then he shall have fundamental prevalence and find it fitting to practice constancy, and his regret shall disappear. {The common folk may share in the practice of old and regular ways, but it is impossible that they should share in carrying out change; they may share in the enjoyment of accomplishments, but it is impossible that they should share in planning how to deal with beginnings.[1] Thus, as a Dao, Radical Change finds one without trust on the day itself [i.e., when it begins] and becomes trusted only on the day when it has come to an end. It is only after he has this trust that such a one obtains "fundamental prevalence," finds it "fitting to practice constancy," and has "regret . . . disappear." However, if on the day that it comes to an end, one were still not trusted, then such Radical Change was improper. The reason that regret and remorse would arise here is due to the drastic change involved, but "if Radical Change were to happen and be right, any regret should consequently disappear."[2]}

COMMENTARY ON THE JUDGMENTS

Radical Change is such that just as Water and Fire try to extinguish each other, so is it when two women live together and find their wills at odds. This we call "Radical Change." {Whenever it happens that things are incompatible, change consequently arises. The reason that such change arises is due to the incompatibility involved. This is why the text selects images of incompatible things to represent Radical Change. The word *extinguish* here refers to causing change. Fire wants to go up, and Water wants to go down.[3] Water and Fire fight each other, and this then causes change. When two women live together, it is as if they have the characteristics of Water and Fire, in that they reside in close proximity yet are incompatible.} "Only on the day when it comes to an end does one begin to enjoy trust," that is, once Radical Change has occurred, people trust him. Such a one brings about joy through the practice of civility and enlightenment, and he shall have great prevalence thanks to his practice of righteousness. If Radical Change were to happen and be right, any regret should consequently disappear. {The reason this one can achieve Radical Change and yet enjoy trust is that he "brings about joy through the practice of civility and enlightenment." Once he "brings about joy through the practice of civility and enlightenment," he can thus extend himself by treading the path of righteousness. To effect Radical Change in this way means that one acts both in accord with Heaven and in compliance with the needs of the common folk, that is, "he shall have great prevalence thanks to his practice of righteousness." When one brings about Radical Change in such a way that "he shall have great prevalence thanks to his practice of righteousness," how can it be anything other than "right"?} Just as Heaven and Earth make use of Radical Change so that the four seasons come to pass, so did Tang and Wu[4] bring about Radical Change in the mandate to rule in compliance with the will of Heaven and in accordance with the wishes of mankind. A time of Radical Change is indeed great!

COMMENTARY ON THE IMAGES

Inside the Lake, there is Fire: this is the image of Radical Change.[5] In the same way, the noble man orders the calendar and clarifies the seasons. {The time of the year and the coincidence of seasons are inherent in change.}

PROVIDING THE SEQUENCE OF THE HEXAGRAMS

The Dao of wells cannot help but involve radical change. This is why *Jing* [The Well, Hexagram 48] is followed by *Ge* [Radical Change].

THE HEXAGRAMS IN IRREGULAR ORDER

Ge [Radical Change] means "get rid of the old."

First Yang

To bind himself tight, this one uses the hide of a brown cow. {Here at the beginning of Radical Change, the Dao of Radical Change is not yet developed, so First Yang represents someone who makes himself secure inside old, regular ways, as he is incapable of response to change. Such a one may carry on established procedures but "may not attempt anything new on his own." *Gong* [leather thongs, bind tight] here means *gu* [strengthen, make secure]. *Huang* [yellow, brown] signifies centrality. The hide[6] of the cow is so tough and pliant that it is impossible to change its shape; in the same way, what is used to strengthen this one is the toughness and pliancy found inside old, regular ways, which do not allow for change.}

COMMENTARY ON THE IMAGES

"To bind himself tight, this one uses the hide of a brown cow," for he may not attempt anything new on his own.

Second Yin

This one should fall in with Radical Change only on the day it comes to an end, and if he were to set forth then, it would mean no blame. {The character of a yin is such that it is incapable of taking the lead and instead should be an obedient follower. One here at Second Yin must not initiate Radical Change on his own but can only follow along after Radical Change has finished its course. This is why the text says: "This one should fall in with Radical Change only on the day it comes to an end." Although Second Yin and Fifth Yang have differences based on their natures as fire and water, they are alike in that they occupy central positions [of their respective trigrams, *Li* (Fire) and *Dui* (Lake)] and, as yin and yang, they resonate with each other. So if this one were to set forth, he should surely find his will in harmony [with Fifth Yang], so he need not worry about blame. And this is what is meant by "if he were to set forth then, it would mean no blame."}

COMMENTARY ON THE IMAGES

"This one should fall in with Radical Change only on the day it comes to an end," for to set forth then would result in blessings.

Third Yang

For this one to go out and attack would mean misfortune, and though he were to practice constancy, he would cause danger. Addressing themselves to Radical Change, the three say that they will accede to it; in this he should trust. {Third Yang is located at the very top of Fire [i.e., the lower trigram, *Li*]. Although the three lines of the upper trigram embody the nature of Water [in that they constitute the trigram *Dui* (Lake)], they all heed Radical Change. From Fourth Yang to Top Yin, they all follow orders and change, and none dare to disobey. This is why the text says: "Addressing themselves to Radical Change, the three say that they will accede to it." Their words are really true, thus the text says "in this he should trust." "Addressing themselves to Radical Change, the three say that they will accede to it; in this he should trust." Thus if he were still to go out and attack them, misfortune would indeed be his proper reward.[7]}

COMMENTARY ON THE IMAGES

"Addressing themselves to Radical Change, the three say that they will accede to it," so what reason does this one still have to proceed?[8]

Fourth Yang

Regret disappears, and as this one changes the mandate to rule with sincerity, he has good fortune. {Whereas First Yang occupies the bottom position of the lower trigram, Fourth Yang occupies the lower position of the upper trigram, so it is capable of change. It is because it has no resonate partner, that there should be regret, but as this one is located at the point where water and fire are contiguous, he is someone who may effect change, and this is why "regret disappears." Located here at the border of water and fire, this one happens to abide where change may take place and so can act without being charged with obstinacy or baseness. This one does not doubt those below and believes that it is their will that the mandate to rule be changed. It is because he does not miss the opportunity to comply with this wish that "he has good fortune." As he acts "with sincerity," he is trusted, and as he is trusted to change the mandate to rule, others are placated, and no one defies him. This is why the text says: "Regret disappears, and as this one changes the mandate to rule with sincerity, he has good fortune." Fourth Yang occupies the bottom position of the upper trigram, so this one is the first to proclaim the new mandate.[9]}

COMMENTARY ON THE IMAGES

Changing the mandate to rule results in good fortune because this one trusts that it is so willed. {He trusts that it is so willed and acts accordingly.[10]}

Fifth Yang

When the great man does a tiger change, one can trust in the outcome before any divining is done. {"One can trust in the outcome before any divining is done," for this one is in accord with the disposition of the times.[11]}

COMMENTARY ON THE IMAGES

"When the great man does a tiger change," the markings are manifest.

Top Yin

Whereas the noble man here would do a leopard change, the petty man should radically change his countenance. {Top Yin abides at the end of the process of Radical Change, for by this time the Dao of change has already been fully realized. If a noble man occupies this position, he should be capable of perfecting his pattern [*wen*, meaning "culture, cultivation"], but if a petty man would enjoy this perfection, he should change his countenance and so obey his superior.} To set forth would result in misfortune, but to stay put and practice constancy would result in good fortune. {The mandate to rule has already been changed, and new laws have been initiated, so with such meritorious achievement matters that require attention have dwindled away, and as they have dwindled away, one should avoid purposeful action [literally, "practice *wuwei* (no purposeful action)"]. Therefore, if one here at Top Yin were to stay put and achieve rectitude, he would have good fortune, but if he were to set forth, he would bring trouble on himself and so have misfortune.}

COMMENTARY ON THE IMAGES

When the noble man does a leopard change, it means that his pattern [*wen*, meaning "culture, cultivation"] becomes magnificent. When the petty man radically changes his countenance, it means that he will follow his sovereign with obedience.

NOTES

1. Wang Bi here paraphrases a passage in the biography of the legalist thinker and statesman, Gongsun Yang, Lord Shang (Shang Yang) (d. 338 B.C.):

> Whenever a person of lofty character attempts to do something, he is sure to be impugned by the world, and whenever a person with unique insight plans something, he is sure to be regarded as arrogant by the common folk. The stupid are still in obscurity even when something is accomplished, but the wise are perspicacious even before something has barely begun. The common folk may not share in planning how to deal with beginnings, but they may share in the enjoyment of accomplishments. Just as one who discusses utmost virtue should not associate with the vulgar, so it is that one who would accomplish things of great merit should not deliberate with the masses.

See Sima Qian, *Shiji* (Records of the grand historian), 68: 2229.

2. This and all subsequent text set off in this manner is commentary by Wang Bi.

3. The lower trigram is *Li* (Fire), and the upper trigram is *Dui* (Lake).

4. King Tang, whose reign is traditionally dated 1765–1760 B.C., overthrew the Xia and founded the Shang dynasty. King Wu, who reigned 1121–1116 B.C., overthrew the Shang and founded the Zhou dynasty.

5. See note 3 above.

6. *Ge* (Radical Change) and *ge* (hide) are written with the same character. In its verbal sense *ge* (hide) means "skin," "get rid of"—certainly a radical change.

7. "Addressing themselves to Radical Change, the three say that they will accede to it" translates *ge yan san jiu*. Whereas Kong Yingda's remarks simply expand on what Wang Bi says, both Cheng Yi and Zhu Xi interpret this sentence and all of Third Yang differently. Cheng's commentary is the more detailed and explicit:

> Third Yang fills the top position of the lower trigram as a hard and strong yang line, but as it also abides at the top of *Li* [Fire], it fails to achieve centrality. Thus it represents someone who tries to bring about and manage Radical Change. This one is in a subordinate position and yet tries to handle major change. If he were to proceed in this way, he would have misfortune. However, as Third Yang abides at the top of the lower trigram, if it really is proper that things undergo Radical Change, how could one here fail to act? If such a one took care to guard his constancy and to have a healthy fear of the dangers involved, and if it were in compliance with the consensus, then he may act without hesitation. The expression *ge yan* [talk of Radical Change] means something like "discussion that one ought to engage in Radical Change," and *jiu* [yield] means *cheng* [it will do] or *he* [agree]. One here should carefully examine the talk that one ought to engage in Radical Change, and if one does so as much as three times and agreement is always had, then one can trust that it should be done. If the talk is done seriously and carefully enough that it reaches such a state as this, then it surely must reach a proper conclusion. As such, "there is trust." Third Yang can trust in it, and it is something that the masses can trust also. When it turns out like this, one can carry out Radical Change here.

In the light of Cheng's commentary, Third Yang would read: "For this one to set forth [on his own] would mean misfortune, and in spite of his constancy he would have danger. But if talk of Radical Change were to reach agreement three times, one should have trust in it." See *Zhouyi zhezhong*, 7: 8b.

8. "What reason does this one still have to proceed" translates *you he zhi*. Cheng Yi, of course, suggests a different interpretation: "This one has already carefully examined what everyone is saying, which has gone so far as to reach agreement three times, so he knows that it is something that is absolutely correct to do. So 'why go any further [*you he zhi*]'?" See *Zhouyi zhezhong*, 12: 43a.

9. Cheng Yi interprets Fourth Yang differently: "As Fourth Yang acts with sincerity, his superior [Fifth Yang, the ruler of Radical Change] trusts him and those below obey him, so his good fortune is assured." In his remarks on the Commentary on the Images, Cheng also says: "That Radical Change here results in good fortune is because those above and below trust his intentions [or, "in his will"]. When sincerity reaches such a point as this, those above and below will trust him." See *Zhouyi zhezhong*, 7: 9b and 12: 43a.

10. Kong Yingda comments: "This one believes in the will of those below and acts to carry out their mandate." See *Zhouyi zhengyi*, 5: 19b.

11. "Tiger change" translates *hu bian*. Kong Yingda comments:

> Fifth Yang abides in centrality and occupies the exalted position, so this one with his virtue of the great man is the ruler of Radical

> Change. Such a one may adjust the ways of former kings and establish laws on his own initiative. There is with him such beauty in the manifestation of culture [*wen*] that it scintillates and commands attention. In this he resembles a tiger changing [into its rich, luxuriant winter coat], whose patterns [*wen*] shine forth with great brilliance.

See *Zhouyi zhengyi*, 5: 19b.

HEXAGRAM 50

䷱

鼎

Ding [The Cauldron]
(*Sun* Below *Li* Above)

Judgment

The Caldron means fundamental good fortune, from which comes prevalence. {"*Ge* [Radical Change] means 'get rid of the old'; *Ding* [The Caldron] means 'take up the new.' "[1] One may take up new ways but only in such a way that they keep his person correct; one may change old ways, but only in such a way that laws and controls are free of bias and reflect clear understanding. It is only after such a one achieves this good fortune that prevalence will occur. Thus the text has it that someone with such fundamental good fortune must come before prevalence can be had. The Caldron is a hexagram concerned with the full realization of the potential in change. Once change has taken place in *Ge* [Radical Change], one should fashion ceremonial vessels and establish laws in order to fulfill its potential. However, if one allows change to proceed without control, chaos must be expected. Only when laws and controls are attuned to the needs of the time will there be good fortune, and only after the worthy and the stupid distinguish themselves one from the other and only after the noble and the base have their proper places in the social order will there be prevalence. Thus the text says that someone with such fundamental good fortune must come before prevalence can occur.[2]}

COMMENTARY ON THE JUDGMENTS

The Caldron is an image. {It simulates an image of an object.} It is by taking Wood and putting it in Fire[3] that one cooks food [*peng ren*]. {Cooking food is the purpose of the Caldron.} The sage cooks in order to sacrifice to the Supreme Deity[4] and does large-scale cooking to nourish other sages and worthies. {Cooking is the purpose of the Caldron. Whereas "*Ge* [Radical Change] means 'get rid of the old,' " *Ding* [The Caldron] means complete the new. Thus we have the Caldron here, for it is a vessel in which one cooks food and blends and adjusts its flavors. To get rid of the old and to take up the new, one cannot do without sages and worthies. *Ren* here means *shu* [well-done, cooked (food)], which is the purpose of the Caldron, something that everyone in the world uses. However, the sage uses it "to sacrifice to the Supreme Deity" above and to do "large-scale cooking to nourish other sages and worthies" below.} It is through *Sun* [Compliance] that the ear and eye become sharp and clear. {When sages and worthies receive nourishment, then the sage himself [i.e., the sovereign] accomplishes things without purposeful action [*wuwei*]. This is why "it is through *Sun* [Compliance] that the ear and eye become sharp and clear" [i.e., sage and worthy ministers become his eyes and ears].} The soft and weak advances and goes up, attains a central position, and resonates with the hard and strong; this is how fundamental prevalence comes about. {This refers to Fifth Yin. It is because this one possesses these two virtues [softness and weakness (Compliance) and centrality] that he can complete the new and so garner great prevalence.}

COMMENTARY ON THE IMAGES

Above Wood, there is Fire: this constitutes the image of the Caldron.[5] In the same way, the noble man rectifies positions and makes his orders firm. {*Ning* [make firm] refers to an appearance of severity and discipline. The Caldron is something that takes up the new and fully realizes the potential in change. Whereas "*Ge* [Radical Change] means 'get rid of the old,' " *Ding* [The Caldron] means completes the new. "Rectifies positions" means clarifying how the noble and the base should have their proper place in the social order. "Makes his orders firm" refers to how one should achieve severity in the issuance of directives and commands.[6]}

PROVIDING THE SEQUENCE OF THE HEXAGRAMS

For effecting a radical change in things, there is nothing as good as a caldron. This is why *Ge* [Radical Change, Hexagram 49] is followed by *Ding* [The Caldron].

THE HEXAGRAMS IN IRREGULAR ORDER

Ding [The Caldron] means "take up the new."

First Yin

The Caldron has its toes turned upward here, for it is fitting that any obstruction be expelled. One acquires a concubine for the sake of her son, so there is no blame. {In general, yang things are solid, and yin things are hollow. The Caldron as such is solid below and hollow above, but here there is yin below, and, as this is so, we have here a Caldron that has been turned upside down; when a Caldron has been turned upside down, it means that its toes have been turned upward. "Obstruction" here means things that are not good. When one takes a concubine as one's principal wife, this also signifies something that has its toes turn upward [i.e., the hierarchy of the household, in which the "low" concubine becomes the "high" wife]. First Yin is located at the initial stage of the Caldron. When one is about to put something new inside it, he immediately turns it upside down in order to expel the foul residue that remains. One acquires a concubine so that she may produce a son, thus the text says: "There is no blame."}

COMMENTARY ON THE IMAGES

Although "the Caldron has its toes turned upward here," nothing contrary has been done. {One has turned it upside down in order to remove any obstruction, thus "nothing contrary has been done."} "It is fitting that any obstruction be expelled," so that one may accommodate something noble. {One gets rid of any foul residue so that the new may be taken in.[7]}

Second Yang

The Caldron is replete here. This one's companion suffers anxiety and so cannot come to him, but this means good fortune. {Yang in substance, this line occupies a place in the middle of the Caldron, so it represents something replete. Something replete cannot be added to further, for if one were to try to increase it, the excess would overflow, and such fullness would be damaged instead. "This one's companion" refers to Fifth Yin, which, because it is troubled by anxiety brought on by riding on top of the hard and strong [Fourth Yang], is unable to come to this one. But, as a result, this one will not be made to overflow, and that is how such a one here manages to complete his good fortune.[8]}

COMMENTARY ON THE IMAGES

"The Caldron is replete here," so this one should take care where he goes. {When the Caldron is replete, one must not go and get anything further for it. When the responsibilities for which one's capabilities are appropriate have already been extended to the utmost, he must not have anything further added to them.} "This one's companion suffers anxiety," but in the end there will be no mistake.[9]

Third Yang

The Caldron's ears are radically changed, so progress is blocked here; though there might be pheasant fat, this one has no chance to eat it. But soon it will rain, and that will make regret wane, so in the end there will be good fortune. {The Caldron as such is something whose middle is kept empty in expectation of things. However, Third Yang is located at the top of the lower trigram, and it does so as a yang line in a yang position. It has to guard its own solidity without a resonate partner and so has nothing at all that it can receive here. The ears should be empty so they can accommodate the caldron lifters, but here instead they are completely blocked up and solid. This is why the text says: "The Caldron's ears are radically changed, so progress is blocked here; though there might be pheasant fat [considered a great delicacy], this one has no chance to eat it." Rain is something that happens when yin and yang engage in intercourse free from one-sidedness and arrogance. Although Third Yang in substance is a yang line, it still is an integral part of a yin trigram, so if one here can manage to free himself from entirely playing the role of hard overreacher and devote himself to such harmonious interaction, "soon it will rain, and that will make regret wane, so in the end there will be good fortune."[10]}

COMMENTARY ON THE IMAGES

"The Caldron's ears are radically changed," so it forfeits the reason for its existence.[11]

Fourth Yang

The Caldron breaks its legs and overturns all its pottage, so its form is drenched, which means misfortune.[12] {Fourth Yang occupies the bottom position in the upper trigram and also is in a resonate relationship with First Yin, so not only should it carry the one [Fifth Yin], it should also bestow benefaction on the other [First Yin], things that such a one is not willing to do. This is why the text says: "The Caldron breaks its legs." As any obstruction had been expelled at First Yin, when the Caldron comes to be filled at Fourth Yang, it is already clean. Thus the text says "overturns all its pottage."[13] *Drenched* [*wo*][14] describes something dripping wet. Not only has the Caldron overturned all its pottage, its form is dripping wet. This represents someone whose knowledge is small yet whose plans are great, someone who is unwilling to bear his responsibilities. Such a one here suffers the utmost disgrace, for disaster is inflicted upon his very person. Thus the text says: "Its form is drenched, which means misfortune."}

COMMENTARY ON THE IMAGES

This one overturns all his pottage, so how could one ever trust him?

Fifth Yin

The Caldron has yellow ears and metal lifters, so it is fitting to practice constancy. {Fifth Yin abides in centrality with its softness and weakness and thereby is capable of thoroughly implementing the principles of things. This one is the beneficiary of the strength and correctness [of Second Yang], so the text says: "[The Caldron has] yellow ears and metal lifters, so it is fitting to practice constancy." As the ears are yellow, it is able to receive what is strong and correct in order to have itself lifted up.[15]}

COMMENTARY ON THE IMAGES

"The Caldron has yellow ears," so their middles can be filled with what is solid. {To fill their middles with what is solid means that what one receives here is nothing rash or improper.}

Top Yang

The Caldron has jade lifters, which means great good fortune and that nothing will fail to be fitting. {Top Yang is located at the very end of the Caldron hexagram; here is where the Dao of the Caldron reaches perfection. Abiding as it does where the Caldron as such is perfectly complete, it embodies hardness and strength yet treads the path of softness and compliance, so it uses its strength to serve as lifters. As it occupies the top position in such a way, even though it is so high, it does not in truth represent an overreacher. Because such a one achieves a regulated balance of strength and compliance, he is able to lift up that which is his responsibility. And because his response is free of partiality, there are none that he does not lift up. Thus the text says that this means "great good fortune and that nothing will fail to be fitting."}

COMMENTARY ON THE IMAGES

Jade lifters are at the top, which means a regulated balance of strength and compliance.

NOTES

1. This quotes the Hexagrams in Irregular Order.

2. This and all subsequent text set off in this manner is commentary by Wang Bi.

3. The lower or "inner" trigram is *Sun* (Compliance, in this case, also Wood), so it is "inside" the upper or outer trigram *Li* (Fire). "Putting . . . in" translates *sun*, the same character as *Sun* (Compliance), which is glossed as "entrance" or "enter" in section eight of part two of Providing the Sequence of the Hexagrams. Here it is a causative verb, "made to enter," i.e., "put in."

4. See Hexagram 16, *Yu* (Contentment), Commentary on the Images and note 2 there.

5. See note 3 above.

6. Cheng Yi interprets the Commentary on the Images somewhat differently: "The Caldron is a vessel that exists as a simulated object, whose shape is upright and whose body is stable and weighty. The noble man emulates this image of uprightness and so rectifies his own position, that is, he rectifies the position in which he abides. Wherever the noble man resides, he behaves with rectitude. . . . He emulates this image of stability and weight and so makes his orders firm." See *Zhouyi zhezhong*, 12: 44a–44b.

7. "Accommodate something noble" translates *cong gui*, which Wang interprets as "so the new may be taken in," glossing *cong* (literally, "follow") as *na* (take in) and *gui* (something noble) as *xin* (the new). Kong Yingda comments: "But here this refers to the removal of the base name 'concubine' and conversion into the principal wife, for the nobility [*gui*] involved follows upon [*cong*] that of the son." See *Zhouyi zhengyi*, 5: 21b. Both Cheng Yi and Zhu Xi offer a different explanation; Cheng comments: "To get rid of what is evil and receive what is good is what *cong gui* means. First Yin responds to Fourth Yang, so above it becomes a follower [*cong*] of that noble one [*gui*]." See *Zhouyi zhezhong*, 12: 44b–45a.

8. Both Cheng Yi and Zhu Xi interpret Second Yang differently. Cheng Yi comments:

> When the Caldron is filled with something, it is only when that something emerges out of the top of it that it serves its purpose. Second Yang being hard and strong has a capacity that should be used to succor the world, and it is in a resonate relationship with Fifth Yin. If this one were to follow his sovereign, Fifth Yin, he would achieve rectitude, and his Dao would surely prevail. However, this one is closely paired with First Yin, so it is a case of a yin pursuing a yang. Second Yang abides in centrality and responds to one in another central position, so he never goes so far as to abandon his rectitude. Although he may keep guard over himself, the other one [First Yin] is sure to go after him, thus he is warned, so that he can keep his distance and prevent First Yin from reaching him, for then he shall

> have good fortune. *Companion* [*chou*] here means "counterpart" [*dui*], as a yin and a yang are entities that form pairs, and it refers to First Yin. If it is allowed to pursue Second Yang, it would be improper and would bring harm to this one, and this is why there is anxiety. Second Yang must protect himself with rectitude and prevent First Yin from reaching him. . . . And this is how he has good fortune.

See *Zhouyi zhezhong*, 7: 14b–15a. In the light of this commentary, Second Yin would read: "This one may have a filled Caldron, but his companion causes him anxiety. However, if he were to prevent him from reaching him, he should have good fortune."

9. According to Cheng Yi, the reason there is "no mistake" is that Second Yang fends off an improper relationship with First Yin and remains true to his sovereign and proper resonate partner, Fifth Yin. See *Zhouyi zhezhong*, 12: 45a–45b.

10. Cheng Yi and Zhu Xi suggest different interpretations; Cheng's is the more detailed:

> "The Caldron's ears" refers to Fifth Yin, the ruler of the Caldron hexagram. The third line occupies the top of the *Sun* trigram as a yang line, so it represents someone who, though hard and strong, can still be compliant, whose capacity is sufficient to apply to the succor of the world. However, it is not in resonate relationship with Fifth Yin and is dissimilar [*butong*]. Whereas Fifth Yin is central but is not correct [it is a yin line in a yang position], Third Yang is correct [it is a yang line in a yang position] but is not central. This is what "dissimilar" means. So Third Yang represents someone who never has success with his sovereign, and, as that is so, how could his Dao ever lead to Radical Change? Radical Change means great difference. Third Yang and Fifth Yin differ so greatly that no harmony is possible between them. As Third Yang's way is blocked, such a one cannot achieve prevalence, and, as he cannot achieve harmony with his sovereign, he does not obtain responsibilities that might be properly his. Thus he lacks the wherewithal to exercise his usefulness. Fat is a great delicacy; it is an image for salary and position. "Pheasant" refers to Fifth Yin. This one has the virtues of culture and enlightenment, so it is called a "pheasant." Third Yang has talents that might be used but does not obtain the salary and position that Fifth Yin could provide, and this is what is meant by being unable to get the pheasant fat and eat it. The noble man amasses his virtue, and after a long time it will be sure to manifest itself. He guards his Dao, and in the end he is sure to achieve prevalence. Fifth Yin has an image of perception and enlightenment, and Third Yang is something that in the end will rise and advance to it. When yin and yang have free intercourse, rain results. . . . This means that Fifth Yin and Third Yang are about to join in harmony.

See *Zhouyi zhezhong*, 7: 15b.

11. Kong Yingda comments: "It forfeits its purpose as something hollow that can take in things." See *Zhouyi zhengyi*, 5: 22b.

12. Cf. section five of the Commentary on the Appended Phrases, Part Two.

13. "Overturns all its pottage" translates *fu gong su*. Both Wang Bi and Kong Yingda seem to understand *gong* as *zhong* (all). See *Wang Bi jijiaoshi*, 2: 473 n. 17. However, Cheng Yi and Zhu Xi read it as *gong* (duke), so for them the phrase should mean "overturns the duke's pottage." See *Zhouyi zhezhong*, 7: 16a–16b.

14. "Its form is drenched" translates *qi xing wo* and refers to the form of the caldron, which serves as a metaphor for the petty man who occupies this position. Cheng Yi thinks *xing* refers to "the duke's form," i.e., he himself is soaked by the overturned pottage, and Zhu Xi glosses *xing wo* (form is drenched) as *xing wu* (punishment is applied severely): "His punishment is severe." Both Cheng and Zhu explain the disaster inflicted on one at Fourth Yang as stemming from his attraction to the petty man they think is represented by First Yin. As Fourth Yang employs this petty man, he brings disaster upon himself and the kingly way. See *Zhouyi zhezhong*, 7: 16a–16b.

15. Kong Yingda comments:

> "Yellow" here signifies centrality, and "metal" signifies hardness and strength. The "lifters" are what go through the ears and lift up the Caldron. It is because Fifth Yin is in a central position that the text says "yellow ears." Its resonate partner is located at Second Yang. As here someone weak is the beneficiary of someone strong, the text says "metal lifters." As what this one receives consists of hardness and correctness [rectitude], it says: "It is fitting to practice constancy."

See *Zhouyi zhengyi*, 5: 22b.

䷲

震

Zhen [Quake]
(*Zhen* Below *Zhen* Above)

Judgment

Quake means prevalence. {One accomplishes things here through fear, and with that prevalence is had.[1]} When Quake [Thunder] comes, people shiver and shake, but then they whoop it up with talk filled with laughter. {As a concept, Quake means that first one inspires awe, which then results in fear. Thus the text says: "When Quake [Thunder] comes, people shiver and shake," for this is the appearance of fear. Quake shocks the lazy in order to rid them of their indolence. Thus "when Quake comes people shiver and shake," but "such fear leads to prosperity." "But then they whoop it up with talk filled with laughter," "for later they have constant rules to live by."} If Quake can startle at one hundred *li*, one will not lose control over the ladle [*bi*] and the fragrant wine [*chang*]. {If the shock of the Quake caused by one's awesomeness extends as far as one hundred *li*,[2] one can thereby avoid losing control over the ladle and the fragrant wine. The ladle [*bi*] is what is used to convey the contents of the Caldron, and *chang* is the fragrant wine; this means the offering up of sacrificial bounty in the ancestral temple [the prerogative of state power and sovereignty].}

COMMENTARY ON THE JUDGMENTS

"Quake means prevalence." "When Quake [Thunder] comes, people shiver and shake," for such fear leads to prosperity. "But then they whoop it up with talk filled with laughter," for later they have constant rules to live by. "If Quake can startle at one hundred *li*" means that if one can startle those at a distance, he can bring fear to those close by. {If the shock of the Quake caused by one's awesomeness extends as far as one hundred *li*, then the indolent will feel fear close by.} When one goes forth, this one may thereby be entrusted with the maintenance of the ancestral temple, that is, by making him the master of sacrifices. {This clarifies the concept of how one empowers the eldest son. As "one will not lose control over the ladle and the fragrant wine," when he himself [the sovereign] goes forth, this one [the eldest son] may thereby be entrusted with the maintenance of the ancestral temple.[3]}

COMMENTARY ON THE IMAGES

Double Thunder: this constitutes the image of Quake.[4] In the same way, the noble man is beset with fear and so cultivates and examines himself.

PROVIDING THE SEQUENCE OF THE HEXAGRAMS

For taking charge of such vessels, no one is more appropriate than the eldest son. This is why *Ding* [The Caldron, Hexagram 50] is followed by *Zhen* [Quake].[5] *Zhen* here signifies movement.

THE HEXAGRAMS IN IRREGULAR ORDER

Zhen [Quake] means "a start."

First Yang

When Quake [Thunder] comes, this one shivers and shakes, but then he whoops it up with talk filled with laughter, and this means good fortune. {First Yang embodies the virtues of hardness and strength and is the leader of the Quake hexagram. This represents someone who is capable, being beset with fear, of cultivating his virtue.}

COMMENTARY ON THE IMAGES

"When Quake [Thunder] comes, this one shivers and shakes," but such fear leads to prosperity. "Then he whoops it up with talk filled with laughter," for later he has constant rules to live by.[6]

Second Yin

When Quake comes, there is danger, and this one, alas, loses his cowries. He might climb nine hills, but one need not pursue him, for in seven days he will be taken. {As a concept, Quake means that one's awesomeness shocks the lazy in order to rid them of their indolence. First Yang finds a proper occupation in fulfilling its responsibilities, but Second Yin rides atop it, so when Quake comes, such a one finds himself in danger, loses his wealth and goods, and forfeits the place where he is positioned. This is why the text says: "When Quake comes, there is danger, and this one, alas, loses his cowries." "Alas" [*yi*] is a rhetorical expression, and "cowries" [*bei*] serves as a collective term for wealth or goods. This one rises in revolt and gets killed. He sets forth without any response or support, and wherever he goes there is no shelter for him. As awesome severity holds great sway here, no one takes him in, and he has to move about without any provisions. Although he repeatedly crosses over strategic high ground, he surely will come to grief through exhaustion of resources and will not last more than seven days. This is why the text says: "One need not pursue him, for in seven days he will be taken."[7]}

COMMENTARY ON THE IMAGES

"When Quake comes, there is danger," for this one rides atop the hard and strong.[8]

Third Yin

When Quake comes, this one trembles, but if he acts in this quake-affected way, he should stay free of disaster. {Third Yin is not in its rightful position; this position is not where it should be located [because it is a yin line in a yang position]. Thus one here should tremble with fear. However, Third Yin does not engage in the rebellious behavior of riding atop a hard and strong line, so it is possible to take fearful [i.e., cautious] action and still stay free of disaster.}

COMMENTARY ON THE IMAGES

"When Quake comes, this one trembles," for the position is not right for him.

Fourth Yang

Quake comes, so this one gets mired. {Fourth Yang is located in the midst of the yin and, finding itself as it does here at a time fraught with fear, it becomes the ruler of all the yin lines. As such, one here should bravely assert himself in order to bring security to all. But if such a one were to suffer Quake himself [i.e., succumb to fear], he would fall into difficulties. If one were to tread this path of unrighteousness and fail to ward off fear and instead make others provide for his own security, his virtue would "never shine forth."}

COMMENTARY ON THE IMAGES

"Quake comes, so this one gets mired," which means that he shall never shine forth.

Fifth Yin

Quake comes, so both to set forth and to come back mean danger. Alas, do not fail, for this is the chance to take successful action. {If Fifth Yin were to set forth, it would have no response, and if it were to come back, it would have to ride atop the hard and strong. If it is afraid either to set forth or come back, it cannot avoid danger. This one may be located at a time of Quake, but as such a one obtains the noble position, it indicates an incipient situation in which he could initiate successful action. But if he were to fear either to set forth or to come back, he would lose his chance for success. This is why the text says: "Alas, do not fail, for this is the chance to take successful action."[9]}

COMMENTARY ON THE IMAGES

"Quake comes, so both to set forth and to come back mean danger." This means that it is dangerous for this one to move. His chance for success lies in abiding in centrality [or "staying within the Mean"]. If one has greatness, he should not fail.

Top Yin

Quake comes, so this one is anxious and distraught, his gaze shifty and unfocused. To set forth would mean misfortune. If Quake were not to reach one's own person but only that of one's neighbor, he would be without blame. Even those joined in marriage here will have words. {This one occupies the very top of the Quake hexagram, so it represents one who is the most subject to Quake. Finding himself here at the very top of Quake, this one keeps trying for centrality but never succeeds, so he is so afraid that he is "anxious and distraught" and keeps looking around so much that his gaze is "shifty and unfocused," for his gaze has nothing upon which to rest. He is already located at the end point of action, so if he were to try to set forth further from here, the misfortune that would befall him would be quite appropriate. If the fear here is not something that this one brought about on his own but instead is something that occurs because of some action that the other took, this one should take warning from his fearful neighbor and adopt appropriate preventive measures, for, if he were to do so, "he would be without blame." When people are in conditions of utmost fear, they tend to have doubts about each other. Thus, even though it be those joined in marriage, they will still have words.}

COMMENTARY ON THE IMAGES

"Quake comes, so this one is anxious and distraught," for centrality is never achieved. Although there is misfortune, there is no blame, for he fears for his neighbor and so takes warning.

NOTES

1. This and all subsequent text set off in this manner is commentary by Wang Bi.

2. Lou Yulie notes: "During the Yin [Shang] era, people regarded a hundred *li* [one-third mile] as the extent of a state or domain [*guo*]; here this expression is used to describe how one's awesomeness should make the whole state Quake." See *Wang Bi ji jiaoshi*, 2: 477 n. 6.

3. Both Zhu Xi and Cheng Yi interpret the text here to mean that it is the sovereign himself who goes forth to act as master of sacrifices, serving as a model for the eldest son. It is by such emulation that sovereignty will be preserved generation after generation. See *Zhouyi zhezhong*, 10: 29b–30a.

4. Both trigrams of *Zhen* (Quake) are *Zhen* (Thunder, Quake). "Double" (*jian*) is glossed by Kong Yingda as *chong* (repeated, double) and *yinreng* (persistent, continuous). See *Zhouyi zhengyi*, 5: 24a–24b.

5. *Zhen* is associated with the Eldest Son. See section ten of Explaining the Trigrams.

6. See the Commentary on the Judgments.

7. Both Cheng Yi and Zhu Xi interpret Second Yin differently. Although Zhu suggests that much of Second Yin is unintelligible, he nevertheless thinks that it represents "yielding, compliance, centrality, and rectitude, enough for this one to preserve himself." Cheng has more to say about it:

> Second Yin abides in centrality and achieves rectitude, so this is someone who positions [or "handles"] himself well [*shanchu*] in Quake. However, it rides atop the strength and hardness of First Yang, the ruler of Quake. Quake is strong and dynamic and so moves upward with great force. Who could ever resist it? . . . When its coming is as fierce as this, Second Yin's position becomes, of course, quite dangerous. *Yi* [glossed as "alas" by Wang Bi and Kong Yingda] means *duo* [reckon]. . . . Because of the danger brought about by Quake, Second Yin reckons that he cannot defy it, so he has to abandon what he has and then climb up as high as he can go in order to take refuge from it. . . . What Second Yin values is centrality and rectitude. Although this one, upon estimating his strength, compliantly takes refuge, he rightly preserves his centrality and rectitude, so he does not lose sight of what he should do. He reckons that he is sure to lose [his position, what he has], so takes refuge far away in order to preserve himself. After some time has past, he will recover the constant norm of his existence [*chang*]. He will obtain this as a matter of course without pursuing it. *Pursue* means "to go after things." If this one were to go after things, he would fail to protect himself. Thus one here is warned not to pursue things, to take refuge far away, and to preserve himself—to find a place for himself in the grand design [*dafang*] of Quake. . . . There are six positions in a hexagram, so *seven* refers to another beginning, once a situation has reached its end point. When such a moment occurs, change [*yi*] takes place. So one here should not neglect his own preservation, for, although for a time he might not be able to resist [Quake's coming], when this time passes, the situation will have come to an end. Then this one can recover the constant norm of his existence. This is why the text says: "In seven days he shall be successful as a matter of course."

See *Zhouyi zhezhong*, 7: 21a–21b. Following this, Cheng's reading of Second Yin would seem to be: "When Quake comes, there is danger, so this one reckons that he should abandon his cowries. He should climb to the ninth hill and not pursue things, for in seven days he shall be successful as a matter of course."

8. Kong Yingda comments: "It is exactly because this one rides atop a strong yang that he is in revolt, and this is the reason why he gets killed." See *Zhouyi zhengyi*, 5: 25a.

9. "Alas" translates *yi*, a rhetorical expression, just as it occurs in Sec-

ond Yin. However, Cheng Yi again glosses it as *duo* (reckon) (see note 7 above). "The chance to take successful action" translates *you shi*. Cheng Yi interprets this as *suoyou zhi shi* (that which one has to do, i.e., one's proper concern), which he glosses as *zhongde* (the virtue of centrality). His reading of Fifth Yin would seem to be: "Quake comes, so both to set forth and to come back mean danger. This one should reckon that he must not fail to do that which he has to do"—preserve his "virtue of centrality." See *Zhouyi zhezhong*, 7: 23b.

HEXAGRAM 52

䷳

艮

Gen [Restraint]

(*Gen* Below *Gen* Above)

Judgment

Restraint takes place with the back, {This leaves the eyes unimpaired.[1]} so one does not obtain the other person. {The one restrained[2] is located behind, so he does not obtain the other person.} He goes into that one's courtyard but does not see him there. {This is because they do not see each other.} There is no blame.[3] {Whenever people are face to face and yet do not interact, it is the Dao of *Pi* [Obstruction, Hexagram 12]. Restraint is the hexagram concerned with stasis and, through that, noninteraction. But how can there be no blame when all so come to a stop and none gets along with the other? This is only possible if they do not see [i.e., are not aware of] each other. If one has restraint operate through the back, it becomes the means by which one may apply restraint without separating the person involved from the object of desire. The back is something that is without sight. When one is without sight, one is naturally still and passive. If one is still and passive and moreover without sight, he will "not obtain the other person." As each keeps the back to the other, even though they are close, they do not see each other. Thus the text says: "He goes into that one's courtyard but does not see him there." If one were to apply restraint, not where it cannot be seen, which is how to restrain naturally, but instead were to apply restraint forcibly, this would give rise to both wickedness and perversity. To be close and yet not obtain each other should mean misfortune. That one manages to avoid blame here is because: "Restraint takes place with the back, so one does not obtain the other person. He goes into that one's courtyard but does not see him there."[4]}

COMMENTARY ON THE JUDGMENTS

Gen [Restraint] means "stop." When it is a time to stop, one should stop; when it is a time to act, one should act. If in one's activity and repose he is not out of step with the times, his Dao [path] should be bright and glorious. {The Dao of restraint cannot always be used; it is something that one must employ only when it is not possible to take any action. If used when it suits its moment, this Dao turns out to be bright and glorious.} Let Restraint operate where restraint should take place, that is, let the restraining be done in its proper place. {The text here changes "back" and instead says "where restraint should take place" in order to clarify that it is the back, in fact, where restraint should take place. In applying restraint, one must not do so at the front, for only when it is applied at the back can it work. One who applies restraint when restraint should occur and who avoids applying it when action should take place obtains the right place for it. Thus the text says: "Let Restraint operate where restraint should take place, that is, let the restraining be done in its proper place."} Those above and those below stand in reciprocal opposition to each other and so do not get along. This is the reason why, although "one does not obtain the other person" and "one goes into that one's courtyard but does not see him there," yet "there is no blame."

COMMENTARY ON THE IMAGES

Mountains linked one to the other: this constitutes the image of Restraint.[5] In the same way, the noble man is mindful of how he should not go out of his position. {Each one stops at his own place and does not encroach upon another office.}

PROVIDING THE SEQUENCE OF THE HEXAGRAMS

Things cannot be kept in a state of movement forever but eventually are brought to a stop. This is why *Zhen* [Quake, Hexagram 51] is followed by *Gen* [Restraint]. *Gen* here means "to stop."

THE HEXAGRAMS IN IRREGULAR ORDER

Gen [Restraint] [means] "a stop."

First Yin

Restraint takes place with the toes, so there is no blame, and it is fitting that such a one practices perpetual constancy. {First Yin is located at the beginning of a time of restraint. If this one were to set forth, there would be no place for him to go. Thus he restrains his toes and so manages to stay free of blame. He is perfectly still and settled, therefore "it is fitting that such a one practices perpetual constancy."}

COMMENTARY ON THE IMAGES

If "Restraint takes place with the toes," one shall never violate the bounds of rectitude [or, "stray off the correct path"].

Second Yin

Restraint takes place with the calves, which means that this one does not raise up his followers. His heart feels discontent. {"Followers" refers to the toes. As this one has his calves restrained, his toes do not get raised up.[6] The calves are embodiments of movement, yet this one is located in a moment of restraint. Not only is he unable to raise up his followers, he also cannot withdraw and obey the call to quietude. This is why "his heart feels discontent."}

COMMENTARY ON THE IMAGES

"This one does not raise up his followers," nor does he withdraw and obey the call.[7]

Third Yang

Restraint takes place with the midsection, which may split the back flesh, a danger enough to smoke and suffocate the heart. {The midsection [*xian*] is the middle of the body. Third Yang is situated between the two images [i.e., the two trigrams], and this is why the text says: "Restraint takes place with the midsection." The back flesh [*yin*] is the flesh right at the backbone. If restraint were applied to the body here, it would break apart at the middle. In thus splitting the back flesh, the distress and danger would smoke and suffocate the heart. As a concept, Restraint means that each one is restrained in his own place and that those above and those below do not interact, so when we reach the middle a split occurs. No more serious danger could befall one than to have one's back flesh suffer a split, and the grief felt at such danger of perishing would, of course, smoke and scorch the heart. If restraint were applied to the middle of the body, the body would split at that place, and if a body were to split so that it had two masters, the great vessel [*daqi*] would indeed perish.[8]}

COMMENTARY ON THE IMAGES

If "Restraint takes place with the midsection," the danger would "smoke and suffocate the heart."

Fourth Yin

Restraint takes place with the torso. There is no blame. {What is above the middle is called "the torso." This one manages to tread the territory of its rightful position [it is a yin line in a yin position], so when such a one demands that the torso be restrained, he obtains the right place for it. Thus this one does not fall into blame.}

COMMENTARY ON THE IMAGES

"Restraint takes place with the torso," which means that this one applies restraint to his own body. {This one himself applies restraint to his body [i.e., knows when to stop and does so] and does not split the whole apart [as Restraint does in Third Yang].}

Fifth Yin

Restraint takes place with the jowls, so this one's words have order, and regret vanishes. {This one applies restraint to the jowls and in so doing occupies a central position [or, "abides within the Mean"], thus his mouth stays free of arbitrary words, and he can banish his regret.}

COMMENTARY ON THE IMAGES

"Restraint takes place with the jowls," so this one is central and correct. {This one is capable of employing centrality and rectitude, thus his "words have order."}

Top Yang

This one exercises Restraint with simple honesty, which results in good fortune. {Top Yang abides at the apogee of restraint, so it represents one who practices the most extreme restraint. One who has honesty and weight here at the top shall not fall into evil and errancy, so it is appropriate that he should have good fortune.}

COMMENTARY ON THE IMAGES

The good fortune that springs from "exercis[ing] Restraint with simple honesty" means that one will reach his proper end because of that simple honesty.

NOTES

1. This and all subsequent text set off in this manner is commentary by Wang Bi.

2. "Restraint" (uppercase *R*) translates *Gen*, the name of the trigram and hexagram, and "restraint," "restrained," etc. (lowercase *r*), translate *zhi* (literally, "stop").

3. "Does not obtain the other person" translates *buhuo qishen*, and means that, not aware of the other person, one has no desire to obtain him and so makes no attempt to do so. Cheng Yi thinks that *buhuo qishen* refers to *wangwo* (forgets the self) and *wuwo* (no self), that is, the person involved should transcend his own self and its desires. Likewise, the person goes

into his own courtyard but does not see those that are there: if one spares himself contact with things, he shall not have desire for them. Thus Cheng would seem to read the Judgment as "Restraint takes place with the back, so one is spared having his own person. He may enter his own courtyard but sees no one there. There is no blame." In other words, if one keeps one's back to things, he shall be spared the needs and desires of the self—and so remain blameless. Zhu Xi thinks that "the back" refers to the one part of the body that does not move and that *gen qi bei* ("Restraint takes place with the back") actually means "Let Restraint be as the back," i.e., one should be restrained or exercise restraint where it is proper to do so—one should be still as the back is by nature still, and one should not follow the rest of the body and so move as it does. This is what it means by "not having one's own body" (*shi buyou qishen*). The fact that he goes into his courtyard but sees no one means that he goes where he should go and stops where he should stop—thereby avoiding blame. See *Zhouyi zhezhong*, 7: 25b.

4. Kong Yingda comments:

> *Gen* [Restraint] means "stop"; it represents the concept of stasis or passivity [*jingzhi*]. It is in this sense that the hexagram has Mountain for its image, and this is why it takes the name "Restraint." Applied to human beings, it means arresting the emotional response to things, that is, preventing the workings of desire. Thus it means "restraint." "Restraint takes place with the back" is a phrase that clarifies where it is that one should operate restraint. If in operating restraint one comes up with the right place for it, its Dao should be easily realized, but if in operating it one does not come up with the right place for it, it would be impossible for it to achieve success. This is why the *Laozi* [section 3, p. 8] says: "Do not display desirable things, so that the hearts of the common folk may be spared from turmoil." The back is something that lacks the power of sight, and when something lacks the power of sight, it is naturally passive. If one wishes to utilize this method of restraint, one should put it into effect before the first stirrings of desire occur, for if one does so only after such stirrings happen, it would result in wounding the feelings of the person involved. Thus, if one operates restraint in such a way that the person involved lacks the power to see, one should come up with the right place for it without forcibly separating him from the object of his desire. But if one were to operate restraint at the face, this would mean trying to prevent interaction when the person involved is already face to face with the other. If one subjected his emotions to such forcible restraint, it would give rise to both wickedness and perversity as well as a corresponding amount of misfortune and blame. But if the power to see is denied him, this would mean that the one restrained is located behind, where there will be no chance for them to face each other. . . . If restraint is operated in such a way that one cannot see, how could one see the other person? Thus the text says: "One does not obtain the other person."

> As "one does not obtain the other person," this means that each keeps the back to the other.

See *Zhouyi zhengyi*, 5: 26b.

5. Both the lower and the upper trigram are *Gen* (Mountain), the ultimate image of stasis.

6. "Raise up" translates *zheng*, which Wang Bi does not explain but which Kong Yingda glosses as *zhengju* (start up). This suggests that "this one does not raise up his followers" means that, as this one's calves are restrained, his toes cannot start to move—i.e., he cannot take action here. However, both Cheng Yi and Zhu Xi think that Second Yin is the follower here of Third Yang—as the calves follow (obey) the thighs. They also interpret *zheng* (raise up) as "rescue" (*zhengjiu*). Cheng comments:

> Second Yin abides in centrality and achieves rectitude, so it represents one who has obtained the Dao of restraint. Above, it lacks a resonate partner to assist it, which means that it does not attain a true sovereign. Third Yang abides at the top of the lower trigram; as such it constitutes the ruler of restraint, that is, it is master over those that are restrained. It may be hard and strong, but it is in violation of the Mean [or "loses the path of centrality"], so it does not manage to exercise restraint properly. This hard and strong one [Third Yang] that exercises restraint above is not able to descend and seek out the one below. Although Second Yin possesses the virtues of centrality and rectitude, it is unable to follow them. Whether Second Yin moves or stops is something controlled by the one who exercises rulership over it; it is unable to take the initiative on its own. Thus it has this image of the calves. When the thighs move, the calves follow, for moving or stopping depends on the thighs and not on the calves. As Second Yin cannot manage to use its Dao of centrality and rectitude to rescue Third Yang from its lack of centrality, it must force itself to follow Third Yang. Unable to rescue it, all it can do is follow it. Although blame does not fall on Second Yin, how could this ever be what it wanted?

See *Zhouyi zhezhong*, 7: 27b.

7. Kong Yingda comments: "*Ting* [listen] means *cong* [obey]. Not only is this one unable to start to move [*zhengdong*], he also cannot quietly withdraw and obey the order that he be restrained. Thus 'his heart feels discontent.' " See *Zhouyi zhengyi*, 5: 28a.

Both Cheng Yi and Zhu Xi, in keeping with their reading of Second Yin, read the Commentary on the Images differently: "Second Yin does not rescue the one he follows [Third Yang], for that one [Third Yang] never turns back and listens to this one [Second Yin]." See *Zhouyi zhezhong*, 12: 49b.

8. Kong Yingda comments: " 'The great vessel' refers to the relationship between the state and the person [of the ruler]. This line also clearly shows that restraint so exercised is misapplied here." See *Zhouyi zhengyi*, 5: 28a.

HEXAGRAM 53

䷴

漸

Jian [Gradual Advance]
(*Gen* Below *Sun* Above)

Judgment

Gradual Advance is such that when a maiden marries, there is good fortune and it is fitting to practice constancy. {*Jian* is the hexagram concerned with gradual advance. Restrained and compliant, to advance as one should in this way, this is what "gradual advance" means. One should advance with restraint and compliance, thus the text says: "When a maiden marries, there is good fortune." In advancing, one does so with rectitude, thus it says: "It is fitting to practice constancy."[1]}

COMMENTARY ON THE JUDGMENTS

Jian involves advancing. {It involves going in the direction of advance.} "When a maiden marries, there is good fortune," which means that when one advances, he obtains a position, or when one sets forth, he has meritorious achievement. If one advances with rectitude, he can thereby rectify the state. This is the position of one who achieves centrality through hardness and strength. {It is because one advances gradually that he obtains his position.} If there is restraint and compliance, one's actions will not founder.[2]

COMMENTARY ON THE IMAGES

Above the Mountain, there is the Tree: this constitutes the image of Gradual Advance.[3] In the same way, the noble man finds a place for his worthiness [*xian*] and virtue [*de*] to dwell and so manages to improve social mores [*su*]. {A worthy and virtuous person shall find a place to dwell if he acts with restraint and compliance, and social mores shall improve if such a one also deals with them with restraint [*zhi*] and compliance [*sun*].[4]}

COMMENTARY ON THE APPENDED PHRASES

In *Jian* [Gradual Advance] "lofty prominence" is taken to mean "a fine thing."[5]

PROVIDING THE SEQUENCE OF THE HEXAGRAMS

Things cannot remain in a state of Restraint forever. This is why *Gen* [Restraint, Hexagram 52] is followed by *Jian* [Gradual Advance]. *Jian* here means "to advance."

THE HEXAGRAMS IN IRREGULAR ORDER

Jian [Gradual Advance] signifies a woman who would marry but waits for the man to act.

First Yin

The wild goose gradually advances to the shore. The youngest son is the danger, for he has words, but there will be no blame. {The wild goose is a water bird, which here signifies appropriate advance, that is, that which starts out below and ascends from there. Thus the text uses the wild goose as the metaphor for this. At each of the six hexagram lines, one should regard advancing to a place and treading there as a matter of moral principle. Here one starts to advance and finds himself at the very bottom. Also, as there is no resonate partner for this one, he is just like a wild goose treading on the shore, a dangerous situation that can offer no security. One here at First Yin begins to advance but does not obtain a proper position for himself, so he finds himself hard-pressed by the youngest son, who creates troubles for him by malicious gossip.[6] This is why the text says: "The youngest son is the danger, for he has words." Difficulties that might stem from the slanderous words of the youngest son will never harm the moral principles of the noble man, thus the text says: "There will be no blame."}

COMMENTARY ON THE IMAGES

There may be danger from the youngest son, but as far as moral principles are concerned, "there will be no blame."

Second Yin

The wild goose gradually advances to the crag, so one drinks and eats with delight, which means good fortune. {A crag is a safe place on mountainous rocks. This one advances and so obtains an appropriate position, abiding in centrality, and is in a resonate relationship [with Fifth Yang]. Originally such a one lacked a salary to take care of his own, but now he has advanced and so has obtained it. That he celebrates the occasion is because there is nothing he wanted more than this.}

COMMENTARY ON THE IMAGES

"One drinks and eats with delight," for not before had he had his fill.[7]

Third Yang

The wild goose gradually advances to the highland. The husband sets forth but does not return, and the wife gets with child but does not raise it, which means misfortune. It is fitting here to guard against harassment. {A highland [*lu*] is the highest point in elevation. Third Yang advances and arrives at the highland, where it takes up with Fourth Yin. Here is someone who cannot bring himself to return, that is, the husband has set forth but does not return and takes delight in a licentious relationship. As such, the wife here [Fourth Yin] also cannot maintain her constancy. It is not her own husband who gets her with child, so she does not raise it. Third Yang is originally part of the *Gen* [Mountain, i.e., Restraint] trigram, but here it abandons its fellows and takes up with Fourth Yin. This results not only in this one not returning but also goes so far as to cause the wife [Fourth Yin] to get with child and then not raise it. To be so taken with personal advantage that one forgets moral principles and to be so greedy for advance that one forgets one's old responsibilities, such is the dao of misfortune. Third Yang bonds with a different trigram [i.e., with Fourth Yin], thus "this one is compliant and provides for the common defense," so no other can come in between. This is why it is "fitting here to guard against harassment."[8]}

COMMENTARY ON THE IMAGES

"The husband sets forth but does not return," which means that he has forsaken his fellows. "The wife gets with child but does not raise it," which means that she has abandoned her Dao. "It is fitting here to guard against harassment," so this one is compliant and provides for the common defense.[9]

Fourth Yin

The wild goose gradually advances to the tree. Perhaps it obtains a proper perch for itself, and, if so, there would be no blame. {For a bird to go to a tree is for it to obtain what is suitable for it.[10] "Perhaps it obtains a proper perch for itself" means that it should come upon a safe perch. Although Fourth Yin rides atop a hard and strong line [Third Yang], they find in each other a commonality of purpose.}

COMMENTARY ON THE IMAGES

"Perhaps it obtains a proper perch for itself," for it gets obedience because of its own compliance.[11]

Fifth Yang

The wild goose gradually advances to the hill. The wife for three years does not bear a child. But in the end none shall triumph over this one, and there shall be good fortune. {The hill [*ling*] means a secondary highland [i.e., second to the highland of Top Yang]. Fifth Yang has advanced to obtain a central position, but, separated by Third Yang and Fourth Yin, it cannot join with its resonate partner [Second Yin]. Thus it is that "the wife for three years does not bear a child." Each [Fifth Yang and Second Yin] treads the path of righteousness and abides in centrality, so Third Yang and Fourth Yin cannot forever block their road, so in not more than three years "he [Fifth Yang] shall obtain what he desires." If this one advances in order to rectify the state, in three years he shall have success, and with that success the Dao will be saved. Thus it will not take more than three years.[12]}

COMMENTARY ON THE IMAGES

"In the end none shall triumph over this one, and there shall be good fortune," for he shall obtain what he desires.

Top Yang

The wild goose gradually advances to the highland. Its feathers can be used as a model, for they mean good fortune. {This one advances to a place that is high and pure, where he is free of the trammels of position, so nothing can subdue his heart or confuse his will. Towering high above in the clear distance, such a one is a model that we may esteem. This is why the text says: "Its feathers can be used as a model, for they mean good fortune."[13]}

COMMENTARY ON THE IMAGES

"Its feathers can be used as a model, for they mean good fortune." This one cannot be confused.

NOTES

1. This and all subsequent text set off in this manner is commentary by Wang Bi.

2. Kong Yingda comments: "Restraint means that one does not engage in precipitous action, and compliance means that one is able to act with modesty. As one advances as one should in this way, none will be opposed to him, thus such a one's actions will gradually make progress and never founder." See *Zhouyi zhengyi*, 5: 29b.

3. The lower trigram is *Gen* (Mountain), and the upper trigram is *Sun* (Compliance), which is associated with Wood and hence Tree.

4. Kong Yingda comments:

> When trees grow atop a mountain, they achieve their lofty position because of the mountain, and it is not because they suddenly spring up from below. Thus the image expresses the concept of Gradual Advance. . . . Improvement is always a matter of the civilized and virtuous [*wende*] behaving with modesty and humility and making advances gradually, for if one precipitously were to employ intimidation and punishments instead, others would not obey.

See *Zhouyi zhengyi*, 5: 29b.

5. See section eight of the Commentary on the Appended Phrases, Part Two.

6. The lower trigram *Gen* (Restraint) is associated with the Youngest Son. See section ten of Explaining the Trigrams. Lou Yulie, considering the remainder of Wang Bi's comment, glosses "youngest son" (*xiaozi*) as "petty man" (*xiaoren*). See *Wang Bi ji jiaoshi*, 2: 486 n. 3. Both Cheng Yi and Zhu Xi, on the other hand, say that it is the "youngest son" himself who is in danger because of the slander of others but that he can avoid blame by holding to his moral principles. Their reading of First Yin would seem to be: "The wild goose gradually approaches the shore. The youngest son is in danger, for there are words, but he shall be without blame." See *Zhouyi zhezhong*, 7: 22b–23a.

7. "Not before had he had his fill" translates *busu bao ye*. This follows Kong Yingda's commentary, in which he glosses *su* as *gu* (in the past, before). See *Zhouyi zhengyi*, 5: 30a. However, Cheng Yi glosses *su* as *kong* (in vain, to no purpose): "What the text means by 'one drinks and eats with delight' is that this one has achieved the goal of his moral will and now enjoys peace and harmony; it does not mean that he does nothing more than enjoy his fill of drink and food to no purpose [i.e., as an end in itself]." Likewise, Zhu Xi glosses *su* as *tu* (merely, pointless) and seems to interpret the text in the same way as Cheng. See *Zhouyi zhezhong*, 12: 51a–51b.

8. "Guard against harassment" translates *yu kou*. Kong Yingda comments: "Here Third Yang bonds with [a line from] a different trigram. It fears that there will be strife caused by enemies who will try to come between them. However, Third Yang enters into this union with such compliance that it provides for their mutual security, and so no other can come between them." See *Zhouyi zhengyi*, 5: 30b. Cheng Yi interprets this differently: "What is fitting for one at Third Yang is for him to ward off bandits [*yu kou*]. To reach a certain point in an unprincipled manner is banditry. To maintain one's rectitude and so distance oneself from licentiousness is what is meant here by 'ward off bandits.' If one is unable to ward off bandits in this way, one will cause oneself to go astray and so have misfortune"; i.e., if "the husband sets forth," there will be misfortune, so one at Third Yang ought not set forth and should stay put and keep guard over his own rectitude. See *Zhouyi zhezhong*, 7: 34a.

9. Kong Yingda comments: "Because Fourth Yin rides atop a yang line [Third Yang], one should take aversion to its contrariness. However, Third Yang bonds and takes up with Fourth Yin in such a way that this union provides for mutual security. This is why the text says: 'So this one is compliant and provides for the common defense.' " See *Zhouyi zhengyi*, 5: 30b. Cheng Yi has a different interpretation:

> What it is fitting to do is to ward off bandits. This means that one should use the Dao of compliance and so provide mutual defense. When the noble man joins with the petty man, he preserves his rectitude by keeping guard over himself, but how can this be nothing more than just keeping himself whole? He also enables the petty

> man to avoid falling into unprincipled behavior. Thus he uses the Dao of compliance and so provides mutual defense. One wards off evil that might befall them, and this is why the text says "ward off bandits."

Cheng's reading of the text here would seem to be: "To ward off bandits means that one should provide for mutual defense by being compliant." See *Zhouyi zhezhong*, 12: 52a.

10. "Proper perch" translates *qijue*. A *jue* is a rafter or a level, stable branch on a tree. Both Cheng Yi and Zhu Xi take the opposite view and say that a tree is not a proper perch for a wild goose and that such a place is dangerous for it. But if it were to obtain a level branch (*jue*) for a perch, it might be safe after all. See *Zhouyi zhezhong*, 7: 34b–35a.

11. Kong Yingda comments: "Although Fourth Yin rides atop Third Yang, as it embodies compliance, it subordinates itself to the one below, and although Third Yang is ridden upon, as it obeys the one above, it provides mutual protection. This is how Fourth Yin obtains a safe perch for itself." See *Zhouyi zhengyi*, 5: 31a. Cheng Yi interprets this differently:

> A *jue* [level branch] is a place of safety and stability. The Dao by which one may seek security consists of nothing but obedience and compliance. If one's moral actions are centered on compliance and rectitude and if one positions oneself in such a way that he remains lowly and compliant, what place would ever be unsafe? If one at Fourth Yin exercises compliance out of a sense of obedience and rectitude, he will obtain a level branch.

See *Zhouyi zhezhong*, 12: 52b.

12. "The Dao will be saved" translates *dao ji*, a double entendre that also can mean "the road will be delivered"—i.e., the road between Fifth Yang and Second Yin will be cleared of obstacles.

13. "Model" translates *yi*, which Kong Yingda glosses as *yibiao*. Cheng Yi glosses it similarly as *yifa*, but Zhu Xi glosses it as *yishi* (ceremonial dress decoration). Both Cheng and Zhu read *lu* (highland) as *kui*: great thoroughfare, i.e., the sky, where birds fly. They also both take Top Yang to refer to the transcendent individual who has escaped the bounds of office and position. Cheng, like Wang Bi and Kong Yingda, says that such purity can serve as a model, but Zhu says: "Top Yang has reached a height far beyond the positions of the human world. Nevertheless, its feathers can be used as ceremonial dress decoration. This is the image of one who, though extremely aloof, is still not without his uses." See *Zhouyi zhezhong*, 7: 36a–36b.

䷵

歸妹

Guimei [Marrying Maid]
(*Dui* Below *Zhen* Above)

Judgment

The Marrying Maiden is such that to set forth would mean misfortune. There is nothing at all fitting here. {*Maiden* [*mei*, literally, "younger sister"] is a term for the youngest daughter. *Dui* [the lower trigram] is the youngest yin [i.e., "daughter"], and *Zhen* [the upper trigram] is the eldest yang [i.e., "son"]. Here the youngest yin carries [i.e., is subordinate to] the eldest yang, and it "acts out of joy," so this is the image of Marrying Maiden.[1]}

COMMENTARY ON THE JUDGMENTS

Marrying Maiden expresses the great meaning of Heaven and Earth. If Heaven and Earth did not interact, the myriad things would not flourish, so Marrying Maiden is an expression of humankind from beginning to end. {Not only do yin and yang unite here, the eldest and the youngest also interact, so this represents "the great meaning of Heaven and Earth" as well as the very beginning and end of human relations.} Here one acts out of joy, so the one who marries is a maiden/younger sister. {If a youngest daughter were to be wed to an eldest son, that should be a cause of unhappiness for such a youngest daughter, but here "one acts out of joy," so the one who marries must be a youngest sister. Although this one is wedded to an eldest son, she marries as a younger secondary wife [*di*] attached [to an older sister], and this is why she has joy.} "To set forth would mean misfortune," for one's position is not correct. {Treading where it is not correct and acting with joy, to advance in such a way indicates a dao [path] of wickedness and evil.[2]} "There is nothing at all fitting here," for the soft and weak ride atop the hard and strong. {Setting forth would result in the misfortune of behaving incorrectly, and staying still would result in the contrariness of riding atop the hard and the strong.[3]}

COMMENTARY ON THE IMAGES

Above the Lake, there is Thunder: this constitutes the image of Marrying Maiden.[4] In the same way, the noble man recognizes the flaw by following a thing through to its far-distant end. {Marrying Maiden is a Dao that shows how ends and beginnings are mutually related. Thus one "recognizes the flaw by following a thing through to its far-distant end."[5]}

PROVIDING THE SEQUENCE OF THE HEXAGRAMS

Advance is sure to involve being restored to one's home. This is why *Jian* [Gradual Advance, Hexagram 53] is followed by *Guimei* [Marrying Maiden].

THE HEXAGRAMS IN IRREGULAR ORDER

Guimei [Marrying Maiden] signifies woman's ultimate end.

First Yang

The Marrying Maiden marries as a younger secondary wife. If this one as a lame person can still keep on treading, to set forth here would mean good fortune. {For the youngest daughter to become the mate of the eldest son means that she does not become the principal wife but is a younger secondary wife who follows an older sister. *Maiden* is a term for a youngest daughter. Whatever a youngest daughter may do, she can do nothing more virtuous than become such a secondary wife. Here she is made second in succession as if she were the child of a sovereign. Although she is young, this is not a rash act.[6] As for making a youngest daughter the secondary wife here, although she is "a lame person," she can still keep on treading, so this indicates long-lasting perseverance. This is the Dao [path] of good fortune that allows one "to keep on giving support." If one advances in this way, good fortune is indeed appropriate.}

COMMENTARY ON THE IMAGES

"The Marrying Maiden marries as a younger secondary wife," and this should be done with perseverance. If such a lame one can keep on treading, it shall mean good fortune, for it is to keep on giving support.

Second Yang

As a one-eyed person who can keep on seeing, how fitting is the constancy of this secluded one. {Although Second Yang is out of its proper position [it is a yang line in a yin position], it abides in the inner trigram [i.e., remains "secluded" there] and keeps a place in the center. Just as the one-eyed can still see, so this one still has the wherewithal to maintain the proper norms of conduct. Such a one remains within and treads the path of the Mean and, as such, can maintain the norms of conduct, so "how fitting is the constancy of this secluded one."}

COMMENTARY ON THE IMAGES

"How fitting is the constancy of this secluded one": such a one never deviates from the norms of conduct.

Third Yin

The Marrying Maiden should take a waiting approach to marriage, that is, return and then marry as a younger secondary wife. {As the mistress of the household still exists, this one might try to advance to that position, but such advance would be premature, so that is why there should be waiting here. As no advance can be made here, this one should return and wait for the proper moment to marry, something that should be done only as a younger secondary wife.[7]}

COMMENTARY ON THE IMAGES

That "the Marrying Maiden should take a waiting approach" is because the time is not yet right.

Fourth Yang

The Marrying Maiden exceeds the allotted time and marries late, for that is the time for it. {For one at Fourth Yang to marry someone, being that it is in an incorrect position and without a resonate partner, it would be necessary for another's path to peter out without his ever finding anyone with whom he could mate—only then could this one set forth. Thus one here "exceeds the allotted time" and "marries late," for such a one has to wait for the right moment.}

COMMENTARY ON THE IMAGES

The resolve to exceed the time allotted is based on the fact that one has to wait for something before action can take place.

Fifth Yin

When Sovereign Yi gave his younger sister in marriage,[8] the sovereign's sleeves were not as fine as the sleeves of the younger, secondary wife. When the moon is almost full, it means good fortune. {In Marrying Maiden, Fifth Yin alone occupies the noble position, thus it is referred to with the phrase "Sovereign Yi gave his younger sister in marriage." *Mei* [sleeves] are the sleeves of a garment, things used to achieve decorous appearance. "The sovereign's sleeves" designate what Sovereign Yi cherishes, that is, Fifth Yin, which represents the one whom Sovereign Yi adores and dresses up. This is why the text refers to Fifth Yin as "the sovereign's sleeves." Fifth Yin's mate resides at Second Yang. *Dui* [the lower trigram] represents the youngest, and *Zhen* [the upper trigram] represents the eldest. For the eldest to follow the youngest is not as good as for the youngest to follow the eldest, and this is why the text says "were not as fine as the sleeves of the younger, secondary wife."[9] The position of Fifth Yin "is at the center," and, as "this one acts with nobility," it reaches the very fullness of yin virtue. As far as this one trying to get married with such attributes is concerned, although this would not be as good as what the youngest could do, were this one to set forth, it surely would result in a successful union. This is why the text says: "When the moon is almost full, it means good fortune."[10]}

COMMENTARY ON THE IMAGES

When "Sovereign Yi gave his younger sister in marriage," the sleeves "were not as fine as the sleeves of the younger, secondary wife," but here the position is at the center, and this one acts with nobility.

Top Yin

The woman might present a basket, but it would contain no fruit; the man might have a sheep cut up, but there would be no blood. There is nothing at all fitting here. {The "sheep" refers to Third Yin.[11] Top Yin is located at the very end of the Marrying Maiden hexagram. Up from here, there is no line to carry, and, down from here, there is no line to respond, so if this line were to represent a woman who should receive orders, then her basket would be empty, and so she could not provide anything, and if it were to represent a man who should give orders, then he "might have a sheep cut up, but there would be no blood." He "might have a sheep cut up, but there would be no blood" means that no one responded to his order. Nothing is given here, whether it involves advance or withdrawal, thus the text says: "There is nothing at all fitting here."[12]}

COMMENTARY ON THE IMAGES

At Top Yin there is no fruit, for this one presents an empty basket.

NOTES

1. This and all subsequent text set off in this manner is commentary by Wang Bi. "Acts out of joy" is an obvious reference to the two constituent trigrams, *Dui* (Lake, Joy) and *Zhen* (Thunder, Quake, i.e., action).

2. Kong Yingda comments:

> The text uses the fact that Second Yang, Third Yin, Fourth Yang, and Fifth Yin are all unsuited to their positions [because they are yin lines in yang positions or yang lines in yin positions] to interpret "to set forth would mean misfortune." As the "position is not correct," this clearly is not reference to the principal wife. This one acts out of joy [i.e., impulsively] and moreover seeks for advancement, which indicates a dao of wickedness and evil.

See *Zhouyi zhengyi*, 5: 32b.

3. Kong Yingda comments: "The text uses the fact that Third Yin and

Fifth Yin ride atop hard and strong lines [Second Yang and Fourth Yang] to interpret 'there is nothing at all fitting here.' Yang is noble, and yin base. To advance with the baseness of a concubine and seek special favor would mean that the base would humiliate the noble. This is why the text says: 'There is nothing at all fitting here.' " See *Zhouyi zhengyi*, 5: 32b.

4. The lower trigram is *Dui* (Lake), and the upper trigram is *Zhen* (Thunder).

5. Kong Yingda comments: "Thus the noble man emulates this image and in like manner follows a thing to its end in the far-distant future; this is how he knows that it has to have an ever-persistent flaw." See *Zhouyi zhengyi*, 5: 32b. Cheng Yi comments:

> Thunder quakes above, and the Lake heeds it and becomes agitated. Yang moves above, and yin follows it with joy. This is an image of the woman following the man; thus it represents Marrying Maiden. The noble man observes this image of man and woman mating and their continuous begetting of progeny and in like manner follows a thing through to its end and so recognizes that it has a flaw. "Follow through to the end" refers to how the begetting of progeny continues on and so perpetuates the transmission of the family. "Recognizes the flaw" refers to one's knowing that things have flaws that have a way of perpetuating themselves. When a woman marries, she has the opportunity to beget progeny, which here expresses the concept of following through to the end. Moreover, if the Dao of husband and wife is to achieve this enduring end, one must understand that there is an inherent tendency [literally, "principle" (*li*)] for flaws to occur and take warning accordingly. *Flaw* [*bihuai*] means "*lixi*" [rupture, break, rent (as in clothing)]. The Marrying Maiden is someone who "acts out of joy." . . . The joy of the youngest daughter is such that she is moved to act because of emotional response. To act in this way sets aside rectitude and has nothing to do with the correct and constantly enduring Dao of husband and wife, so in the long run a flaw is sure to occur. Knowing that such a flaw shall surely happen, one thus ought to think about the way it will end in the far-distant future. All those in the world who are prone to quarrel never manage to think of how things will end in the far-distant future, and this does not just apply to the Dao of husband and wife. No matter under Heaven is ever without an end or ever without a flaw, but neither is any ever denied a Dao [path or process] that allows it to endure. When one observes the Marrying Maiden, one ought to think about the way it will end in the far-distant future.

Apparently Zhu Xi found Cheng's lengthy explanation superfluous, for he simply says: "Thunder moves, and Lake follows, such is the image of Marrying Maiden. The noble man observes how incorrect this union is and so realizes that in the end it will suffer rupture. If one applies this to things in general, one sees that this is always so." That is, if something is wrong at the beginning, it will fail in the end. See *Zhouyi zhezhong*, 12: 53a–53b.

6. Kong Yingda comments: "Just as it is appropriate that the son of a sovereign become his successor, so ought the younger sister of a wife become the secondary wife. In establishing a succession one ought to select the most senior person. However, although the son of a sovereign might be young, to establish him as successor would not be a rash act." See *Zhouyi zhengyi*, 5: 33a.

7. Cheng Yi's view is slightly different from Wang Bi's:

> Third Yin abides at the top of the lower trigram, so it does not originally represent someone mean and lowly. But because of loss of virtue and because there is no correct resonate partner, this one wants to marry but never gets the chance to marry. *Xu* means "wait." That this one waits is because there is no chance yet to get married. Here a yin line occupies a third position, which indicates that it is out of its correct position. If a soft and weak person were to act as if he were hard and strong, it would indicate obstreperousness. Third Yin is the ruler of the *Dui* [Joy] trigram. If one here were to seek marriage out of joy, such an act would be in violation of decorum. Above, there is no resonate line, which indicates that there is no one to accept this one. As there is no chance to get married, this one should wait. When a woman finds herself in such a situation, who would ever marry her? Indeed, as such, she cannot ever become a principal wife. So the only thing suitable for her to do is to return and then marry by seeking to become a secondary wife—this because she lost the opportunity to do otherwise because of her incorrectness.

Zhu Xi, however, notes that "someone" (Lu Xisheng [d. ca. 905]) glosses *xu* as "a woman in a mean and lowly state [*jian*]"—i.e., a low-ranking concubine—which would result in the following reading of Third Yin: "Here the Marrying Maiden would marry as a lowly concubine, so this one should return and then marry as a secondary wife." See *Zhouyi zhezhong*, 7: 40a.

8. Cf. Hexagram 11, Peace (*Tai*), Fifth Yin.

9. Cheng Yi and Zhu Xi interpret Fifth Yin differently from Wang. Instead of interpreting "the sovereign's sleeves" (*qi jun zhi mei*) as a metaphor for the younger sister herself, they read it as "this princess's sleeves," i.e., her dress and adornment: "This princess's sleeves are not as fine as the sleeves of the younger, secondary wife." They go on to explain that such a princess, a noble woman who marries beneath herself, does not esteem ornament, the way a secondary wife does, but virtue. She cherishes modesty and compliance and, though a princess, does not act with arrogance toward her spouse. All this signifies the epitome of yin virtue. See *Zhouyi zhezhong*, 7: 41a.

10. Kong Yingda comments: "For the yin, we esteem fullness [of virtue], just as when the moon is nearly full." See *Zhouyi zhengyi*, 5: 34a.

11. The lower trigram *Dui* (Joy) is associated with the sheep. See section eight of Explaining the Trigrams. Third Yin is the ruler of *Dui*.

12. Cheng Yi interprets Top Yin differently, as a line that represents a woman whose attempts at marriage never reach a successful conclusion—and thus as a woman who fails to continue a family lineage. Family lineage involves the sacrifice of fruits (woman's duty) and blood (man's duty). Such sacrifice here would be barren. See *Zhouyi zhezhong*, 7: 41b.

HEXAGRAM 55

䷶

豐

Feng [Abundance]
(*Li* Below *Zhen* Above)

Judgment

Abundance means prevalence, which the true king extends to the utmost. {Prevalence through expanded greatness is something only the true king can extend to the utmost.[1]} Stay free from worry, and you shall be fit to be a sun at midday. {As a concept, Abundance signifies how the insignificant is made to grow great and the obscure allowed to break out. One who achieves mastery over the world and yet denies the insignificant and the obscure the chance to achieve prevalence shall have unending cause for worry. This is why such a one extends the prevalence of Abundance to the utmost and in so doing manages to stay free from worry. One who exercises his virtue in such a way that Abundance prevails and worry is avoided is fit to occupy a place in mid-sky and so cast light everywhere. This is why the text says: "You shall be fit to be a sun at midday."}

COMMENTARY ON THE JUDGMENTS

Abundance is a matter of greatness [*da*]. {*Da* here should be read as the *da* in *chanda* [expand, make great].} Here one acts with enlightenment [*ming*], and so Abundance results. The true king extends this to the utmost, for he esteems greatness. {Greatness is what the true king esteems, so he extends Abundance to the utmost.} "Stay free from worry, and you shall be fit to be a sun at midday" means that such a one shall be fit to cast his light over the entire world. {That such a one is "fit to cast his light over the entire world" is due to virtue that allows him freedom from worry.} When the sun is at midday, it begins to set, and when the moon is at its full, it begins to wane. As everything in Heaven and Earth waxes and wanes at the proper moment; is this not even truer for men, even truer for gods and spirits? {Abundance functions in such a way that one comes to grief due to setting or waning. If one were to operate in terms of it at a time when insufficiency prevailed, Abundance still ought to result, but if one were to do so at a time when repletion already existed, satiation would soon occur. As one must not use Abundance as if it were a constant rule, so the text mentions the Dao of how all things ebb and flow.}

COMMENTARY ON THE IMAGES

Thunder and Lightning arrive together: this constitutes the image of Abundance.[2] In the same way, the noble man decides legal cases and carries out punishments. {Such a one acts with civility and enlightenment [*wenming*] and so makes no error as to the reality and principles involved [*qingli*].[3]}

PROVIDING THE SEQUENCE OF THE HEXAGRAMS

When one manages to be restored to his proper place, he is sure to enjoy greatness. This is why *Guimei* [Marrying Maiden, Hexagram 54] is followed by *Feng* [Abundance]. *Feng* here means "to grow great."

THE HEXAGRAMS IN IRREGULAR ORDER

Feng [Abundance] often involves incident.

First Yang

This one meets a master who is his counterpart. Although they are alike, there is no blame. To go forth here would mean esteem. {First Yang is located at the beginning of Abundance, and its mate is at Fourth Yang. Here a yang goes to a yang, and action takes place with enlightenment, which means that each enhances the light of the other. Here *xun* [ten-day period] should be read as *jun* [equal, alike]. Although they are alike, there is no blame [i.e., even though they are not resonate partners], so if one were to go forth here, he would enjoy esteem. First Yang and Fourth Yang are both yang lines, and this is why the text says "they are alike."[4]}

COMMENTARY ON THE IMAGES

"Although they are alike, there is no blame," but if one here were to try to exceed this likeness, there would be disaster. {Were First Yang to exceed this likeness [i.e., try to be more than equal], there would be contention, for any such union would involve a divergence of interests.}

Second Yin

This one has his Abundance screened off, so the polar constellation could be seen at midday. If he were to set forth, he would reap doubt and enmity, but if he were to have sincerity and develop accordingly, he should have good fortune. {*Bu* [screen] is a thing that covers over and darkens, that wards off the light. One at Second Yin may be located at a time of brightness and action but is unable to manifest his own Abundance. Not only does this one have his bright and great virtue kept in an inner place, he also has to abide as a yin in a yin position. What Abundance he has is screened off, hidden away and seen by no one. This is why the text says: "This one has his Abundance screened off, so the polar constellation could be seen at midday." Midday represents the apex of brightness, and the fact that the polar constellation can be seen signifies that here darkness is absolute. This one is located at the apex of brightness and yet his Abundance is screened off. Thus the text says: "The polar constellation could be seen at midday." This one cannot initiate anything himself, so "if he were to set forth, he would reap doubt and enmity." Instead he should tread the middle path and stay in this his rightful place, abide in obscurity and do no evil—be one who has sincerity. *Ruo* [accordingly] is a rhetorical expression. One who has sincerity can use it to develop his will and shall not be troubled by obscurity. Thus he shall garner good fortune.[5]}

COMMENTARY ON THE IMAGES

"If he were to have sincerity and develop himself accordingly" means that he should use sincerity to develop his will.

Third Yang

This one has his Abundance shaded, so that even the dim could be seen at midday. If he should break his right arm, there would be no blame. {*Pei* [shade] is a pennant or curtain, something used to fend off extremely bright light. *Mei* [the dim] refers to luminaries that give off faint, muted light. The resonate partner for Third Yang is at Top Yin, so this one has his will fixed on a yin, so even though one is better off here than at a yin line that occupies a yin position [i.e., Second Yin], he still lacks the wherewithal to free himself from obscurity. This is what is meant when the text says that the Abundance that this one has is so much in shade that "even the dim could be seen at midday." If such a one were to try to shine his light, all this would do would be to let the dim still be seen [i.e., it would be so faint]. When it comes to this one trying to get employed, he should break his right arm instead. As such, he could then do nothing more than keep himself safe, for he would not be worth employing.}

COMMENTARY ON THE IMAGES

"This one has his Abundance shaded," so he must not try to attempt great matters. {His brightness is insufficient.} "He should break his right arm," for he must on no account be employed. {Although he would still have the left one, this would not be good enough for employment.}

Fourth Yang

This one has his Abundance screened off, so the polar constellation could be seen at midday. He meets a master who is his equal, which means good fortune. {Here a yang line occupies a yin position, which means that one here has his "Abundance screened off." However, one at Fourth Yang obtains a relationship with First Yang, which allows him to develop and manifest himself. Such an equal master means good fortune.[6]}

COMMENTARY ON THE IMAGES

"This one has his Abundance screened off," which means that this position is not right for him. "The polar constellation could be seen at midday," which means that this one is so hidden that he casts no light. "He meets a master who is his equal," so it is good fortune to set forth.

Fifth Yin

This one arrives here and manifests himself, which gains him blessings and praise, and this means good fortune. {Fifth Yin comes and fills this exalted, yang position with its yin qualities. Such a one is able to enhance his own light. He manifests his virtue and gains blessings and praise.[7]}

COMMENTARY ON THE IMAGES

The good fortune of Fifth Yin is such that he gains blessings.[8]

Top Yin

This one keeps his Abundance in his house, where he screens off his family. When he peers out his door, it is lonely, and no one is there. For three years he does not appear, which means misfortune.[9] {A house is something that provides seclusion. As Top Yin is located at the very end of Abundance, it is the one farthest out. One here does not tread the territory of any proper position but instead keeps himself hidden in deep seclusion, so Top Yin represents a total recluse who has hidden his tracks completely. Not only does he keep his Abundance in his house, he also screens off his family. With his house amply provided for and his family so sheltered, he can live in utmost obscurity. Although he might peer out his door, "it is lonely, and no one is there," because he is abandoned there where he locates himself and where he has sought profound seclusion. This one finds himself at a time of enlightened action and estimable greatness and yet hides himself in profound seclusion with the [mistaken] thought to keep his own conduct lofty. The great Dao already offers deliverance, but he still does not show himself. This recluse will not become a man of worth to the world but instead turns around and runs counter to the Dao. His misfortune is indeed appropriate! For three years the Dao of Abundance has been fully in place. As long as the Dao of good government cannot yet offer deliverance, seclusion is still permissible. But only someone who confuses good government with chaos will remain a recluse after it has begun to offer that deliverance.}

COMMENTARY ON THE IMAGES

"This one keeps his Abundance in his house," which means he soars at the edge of the sky. {This one hides away his light to the utmost degree.[10]} "When he peers out his door, it is lonely, and no one is there," for he keeps himself hidden. {"Keeps himself hidden" means that one can go out but does not go out; it is not a matter of hiding away because it is the right thing to do. When one does not leave his door and courtyard, he might find himself out of step with the moment [or "miss opportune moments"] and so bring misfortune on himself, so how much truer this would be for someone who "keeps himself hidden"! Misfortune for such a one would indeed be appropriate!}

NOTES

1. This and all subsequent text set off in this manner is commentary by Wang Bi. Wang also discusses this hexagram in section seven of his General Remarks.

2. The lower trigram is *Li* (Cohesion), here signifying Fire, Lightning, and the upper trigram is *Zhen* (Thunder).

3. Kong Yingda comments: "In deciding cases at law, one must get at what the true and false circumstances are, and in carrying out punishments, one must be sure to strike the balance between leniency and severity." See *Zhouyi zhengyi*, 6: 2a.

4. See Kong Yingda's subcommentary to Fourth Yang in note 6 below.

5. Both Cheng Yi and Zhu Xi interpret this part of Second Yin and the following Commentary on the Images differently: if this obscure one culti-

vates sincerity patiently, such example shall influence Fifth Yin, which represents a "weak, benighted, and unrighteous ruler," to develop his will and become a worthy sovereign—so that good fortune for all shall result. See *Zhouyi zhezhong*, 7: 44a–44b and 12: 56b.

6. Kong Yingda comments:

> The resonate partner of Fourth Yang should be at the first line, but both are yang lines, which means that each can enhance the other's development to prominence, so this one obtain good fortune here. Thus the text says: "He meets a master who is his equal, which means good fortune." This means that Forth Yang forms a relationship with First Yang in such a way that both are masters, in the sense of host and guest [taking turns]. If we take it that First Yang goes to Fourth Yang, we consider that Fourth Yang is the host or master. Thus the text [of First Yang] says: "This one meets a master who is his counterpart." If one goes from Fourth Yang to First Yang, then First Yang is considered the host or master. Thus the text [of Fourth Yang] says: "He meets a master who is his equal."

See *Zhouyi zhengyi*, 6: 3a–3b.

7. "This one arrives here and manifests himself" translates *lai zhang*. Both Cheng Yi and Zhu Xi interpret Fifth Yin differently; for instance, Cheng glosses *lai zhang* as "this one is able to attract those talents below who have manifested excellence and employ them." In this way Fifth Yin, the ruler of Abundance, gains a reputation for dispensing blessings to all. See *Zhouyi zhezhong*, 7: 46b–47a.

8. Or, in Cheng's and Zhu's view, "dispenses blessings."

9. Cf. section eight of the Commentary on the Appended Phrases, Part Two: "In *Feng* [Abundance, Hexagram 55], 'secluded withdrawal' is taken to mean the 'utmost misfortune.' "

10. Kong Yingda comments: "He is like a bird soaring at the edge of the sky [i.e., as high and remote from the world as possible]." See *Zhouyi zhengyi*, 6: 4a.

HEXAGRAM 56

䷷

旅

Lü [The Wanderer]
(*Gen* Below *Li* Above)

Judgment

The Wanderer is such that prevalence might be had on a small scale, that is, one here might have the good fortune that the constancy of the Wanderer might provide. {Here one lacks the wherewithal by which he might complete the Dao of constancy and its concomitant good fortune and only has enough resources to realize the good fortune that the constancy of the Wanderer might provide. Thus the text draws particular attention again to "the good fortune that the constancy of the Wanderer might provide."[1]}

COMMENTARY ON THE JUDGMENTS

"The Wanderer is such that prevalence might be had on a small scale": the soft and weak obtains a central position in the outer [upper] trigram and is obedient to the hard and strong. When stopped, one here should cling to the bright, and he can still use this opportunity to achieve prevalence on a small scale, which is what "one here might have the good fortune that the constancy of the Wanderer might provide" means. {When creatures lose their master, they go astray, and when the soft and weak ride atop the hard and strong, they become contrary. Creatures that have become contrary and also have gone astray always end up by having no fixed abode, so how could one here ever manage to achieve small-scale prevalence and the good fortune that stems from constancy? The yang is the leader of creatures, and the yin should always be obedient to the yang, but here Fifth Yin alone rides atop a hard and strong line [Fourth Yang]. Nevertheless, in addition, it achieves a central position in the outer [upper] trigram, and, in doing so, provides carriage for Top Yang. So all the yin lines are obedient to the yang and do not engage in obstreperousness. "When stopped, one here should cling to the bright,"[2] and when one acts, he should not tread the path of recklessness. Although such a one cannot go so far as a yang does when he achieves the exalted position and makes everything go smoothly on a grand scale, "he can still use this opportunity to achieve prevalence on a small scale." If the Wanderer attaches himself to others in such a way that he does no damage to his sense of rectitude, he shall obtain the means to make himself secure.} The meaning underlying a time of the Wanderer is indeed great! {The Wanderer means great dispersion, for it is a time when all creatures lose the place where they dwell. All creatures that so lose their dwellings desire a place to attach themselves, so is it not a time when the wise have this right thing to do as well?}

COMMENTARY ON THE IMAGES

Above the Mountain, there is Fire: this constitutes the image of the Wanderer.[3] In the same way, the noble man uses punishments with enlightenment and care and does not protract cases at law. {He pauses to gain clarity over things, so punishment is the product of careful scrutiny.[4]}

PROVIDING THE SEQUENCE OF THE HEXAGRAMS

When one exhausts the potential to grow great, he is sure to lose his position. This is why *Feng* [Abundance, Hexagram 55] is followed by *Lü* [The Wanderer].

THE HEXAGRAMS IN IRREGULAR ORDER

When one has few kith and kin, this is *Lü* [The Wanderer].

First Yin

If the Wanderer lets himself be occupied by trivial matters here, by doing so he shall bring disaster upon himself. {First Yin occupies the very lowest position, so the Wanderer who might seek a place to stay here would not obtain the means to make himself secure and moreover would be beset with menial tasks. The reason he should bring disaster upon himself is that once his will was exhausted, he would come to grief.}

COMMENTARY ON THE IMAGES

"If the Wanderer lets himself be occupied with trivial matters here," his will would become exhausted, which would be a disaster.

Second Yin

Here the Wanderer arrives at lodgings where he is so attracted by the wealth involved that he becomes capable of the constancy of a young servant. {"A lodging" [*ci*] is a place at which the Wanderer can find security. *Huai* [cherish] here means "to be attracted" [*lai*]. Second Yin obtains a rightful position [as a yin line in a yin position], abides in centrality, embodies softness and weakness, and upholds the one above [Third Yang]. When one seeks a wanderer's lodgings in such a way as this, no doubt he might obtain a temporary place in the palace hostel [*cishe*]. Attracted by the wealth there, he acquires the capability that a young servant might have to practice rectitude [*zheng*]. Such a Wanderer is incapable here of filling a position of great promise, thus all the goodness [*mei*] that he might have would be exhausted in merely achieving the rectitude of a young servant. If he were to set forth and try to achieve more than this, he would certainly suffer harm. His capacity for righteousness [*yi*] extends no further than the rectitude of a young servant.[5]}

COMMENTARY ON THE IMAGES

If "he should become capable of the constancy of a young servant," in the end there will be no mistake.[6]

Third Yang

The Wanderer has his lodging burn down and loses his young servant status, so even with constancy he would have danger. {Third Yang abides at the top of the lower trigram and forms a close relationship with Second Yin. As it represents a person who is a lodged Wanderer and yet takes a path [or "pursues a dao"] that takes him downward, it suggests that such a one here might be hatching a plot with Second Yin to usurp authority, something that would excite the suspicions of the ruler [whose guest he is]. Thus he "has his lodging burn down," his servant status is lost, and his person is put in danger.[7]}

COMMENTARY ON THE IMAGES

"The Wanderer has his lodging burn down," so such a one thereby should feel wounded. As the Wanderer here allies himself with the one below [Second Yin], his capacity for righteousness [*yi*] is lost.[8]

Fourth Yang

The Wanderer takes refuge where he can find it and so obtains a place where he has to use his axe, so this one's heart is not happy. {An axe is what one uses to chop away brambles and thorns, something to make one's stopping place secure. Although Fourth Yang is located at the bottom of the upper trigram and does not try to put itself in front of the others, it still does not obtain a position that is right for it [it is a yang line in a yin position]. Here is someone who fails to find a place on good, level ground, a traveler who takes refuge where he can find it, someone who does not obtain a proper place to stop but only obtains a place where he has to use an axe,[9] thus his heart is not happy.}

COMMENTARY ON THE IMAGES

"The Wanderer takes refuge where he can find it," which means that he has not obtained a proper position. He "obtains a place where he has to use his axe," which leaves his heart unhappy.

Fifth Yin

This one has but one arrow to shoot at a pheasant. Although it is lost, in the end, because of his reputation, he is given an appointment. {To shoot at a pheasant he has but one arrow but even so loses it. This clearly indicates that although he has the chance to get a pheasant, in the end he is unable to do so. The Wanderer lodges here in the course of his advance. Although such a one is located at the center of civility and enlightenment and abides in the exalted position, in the end this position is not his to have. As this one can recognize the first sprouts of misfortune and good fortune, he realizes that his place here is not secure because in doing so he has to ride on Fourth Yang below [a wrong relationship]. However, above he gives carriage to Top Yang [a right relationship], thus in the end, thanks to his good reputation, he receives an appointment to office.}

COMMENTARY ON THE IMAGES

"In the end, because of his reputation, he is given an appointment," for his efforts benefit the one above.

Top Yang

This bird gets his nest burnt. The Wanderer first laughs and then later howls and wails. He loses his ox in a time of ease, which means misfortune. {When one finds himself at a lofty and dangerous place and makes that his home, this is called a "nest."[10] The Wanderer in his travels obtains the top position, thus he "first laughs." As one here occupies the very highest place as the Wanderer, he is the object of envy by all, and because he is a person who eschews intimacy and because he occupies a position that provokes envy and harm, he surely is on the path to misfortune. Thus the text says: "[He] later howls and wails." An ox is the farmer's valuable property. It is because the Wanderer occupies the uppermost position that he is envied alike by all, and this is why "he loses his ox in a time of ease." This does not occur at a time of danger and difficulty but because no one identifies with him. In such a precarious state with no support, " 'he loses his ox in a time of ease,' for in the end he hears nothing about it" [i.e., no one warns him]. Thus those that might do him harm will surely get to him.}

COMMENTARY ON THE IMAGES

As the Wanderer is positioned at the very top, he rightly gets burnt up. "He loses his ox at a time of ease," for in the end he hears nothing about it.

NOTES

1. This and all subsequent text set off in this manner is commentary by Wang Bi.

2. This refers to *Gen* (Restraint), the lower trigram, and *Li* (Cohesion, Fire, Brightness), the upper trigram.

3. The lower trigram is *Gen* (Restraint), in this case, Mountain, and the upper trigram is *Li* (Cohesion), here, Fire.

4. Kong Yingda comments:

> When fire is on top of the mountain, it races through the grass and shrubbery, a condition that does not leave it in one place for long. Thus this provides the image for the Wanderer. Furthermore, the two trigrams above and below are *Gen* [Restraint] and *Li* [Brightness]. So it is that the noble man emulates this image in the way he pauses in repose to investigate things with clarity, uses punishments only after careful scrutiny of the facts, and does not allow cases at law to become protracted.

See *Zhouyi zhengyi*, 6: 5a.

5. Both Cheng Yi and Zhu Xi seem to interpret Second Yin differently. *Huai* for them means "cherish" in the sense of, as Cheng puts it, *huaixu*: "hold in readiness" (for needs, emergencies, etc.). They emphasize that the two things that the Wanderer (any traveler) needs are "wealth" (i.e., the money to cover travel expenses) and the constancy (loyalty) of servants (so they do not cheat him). Also, unlike Wang Bi and Kong Yingda, they do not say anything about the limitations one at Second Yin is supposed to have, so their reading of it seems to be: "When the Wanderer arrives at lodgings, he should cherish his wealth and obtain the constancy of a young servant." See *Zhouyi zhezhong*, 8: 2a.

6. Kong Yingda comments: "The Wanderer may not achieve a position of grandeur here, for if he were to do so, he would be harmed by others. But now he merely extends his capacity for rectitude to a young servant, so 'in the end there is no mistake.' " See *Zhouyi zhengyi*, 6: 5a–5b.

7. Wang Bi and Kong Yingda interpret Third Yang in light of their understanding of Second Yin (see *Zhouyi zhengyi*, 6: 5b), but Cheng Yi and Zhu Xi take quite a different approach. Cheng comments:

> Third Yang is both hard and strong and also not central [i.e., does not practice the Mean]. . . . If one who is located at a time of the Wanderer becomes excessively hard and strong as well as arrogant, he will find himself on the way to grief and disaster. Arrogance will lead him to be disobedient to his sovereign, thus his sovereign will become inimical and burn down his lodging—and his place of security would be lost. . . . If such a one were excessively hard and strong, he would be harsh to his subordinate, thus his subordinate would leave him—and he would lose the constancy and trust of his young servant.

Cheng's (and Zhu's) reading of Third Yang seems to be: "The Wanderer has his lodging burned down and loses his young servant, so in spite of constancy, he will have danger." See *Zhouyi zhezhong*, 8: 2b.

8. Cheng Yi interprets the Commentary on the Images in light of his understanding of Third Yang: "Here one at a time of the Wanderer is excessively hard and strong and treats his subordinate with arrogance, so he surely will lose his [servant's] loyalty and trust, that is, he will lose his heart [*xin*]. To lose one's young servant's heart while being a Wanderer can certainly be dangerous." Thus his reading of the second part of the Commentary on the Images seems to be: "The Wanderer relates to his subordinate in such a way that his [the servant's] righteousness [heart, loyalty] is lost." See *Zhouyi zhezhong*, 12: 59a.

9. "Obtains a place where he has to use his axe" translates *de qi zi fu zhi di*, which follows Kong Yingda's gloss of it as *de yong fu zhi di*. *Zi* (property, wealth) is, in fact, sometimes used as a verb meaning "rely on, employ, borrow, use, etc.," in texts roughly contemporary with Wang Bi, so Kong's reading is quite possible. See *Zhouyi zhengyi*, 6: 5b. However, Cheng Yi ignores this possibility and glosses *zi* as *huocai*: "funds." So his reading of *de qi zi fu* would be "obtains his funds and an axe." In later times, the expression *zifu* (funds and axe) simply meant "travel expenses." See *Zhouyi zhezhong*, 8: 3a–3b.

10. Kong Yingda comments: "Here one occupies the uppermost position, just like a bird does in a nest. As this top position is occupied by the Wanderer, he is sure to be overthrown, suffering the same fate as when a bird gets its nest burned up." See *Zhouyi zhengyi*, 6: 6a.

HEXAGRAM 57

䷸

巽

Sun [Compliance]
(*Sun* Below *Sun* Above)

Judgment

Compliance is such that prevalence might be had on a small scale. {It is because the virtue of this entire hexagram consists of Compliance that prevalence can only be had on a small scale. When both superiors and subordinates [represented by the upper and the lower trigram] are compliant, none will be opposed to orders, so once they are given, they should be carried out as a matter of course. Thus, at times when actions are to be carried out through reiterated commands, both superiors and subordinates cannot but be compliant.[1]} It would be fitting should one set out to do something here. {If one conducts himself with the Compliance of a younger brother, no one will ever oppose him.} It would be fitting to see the great man. {If a great man employs such a one, his Dao will prosper all the more.}

COMMENTARY ON THE JUDGMENTS

The repeated *Sun* [Compliance] trigrams express how commands are reiterated. {Once commands are given, they should be carried out as a matter of course. But it never happens that commands are so carried out unless those involved are compliant.} If the hard and strong can practice Compliance while adhering to centrality and rectitude, his will shall be realized, {If, though hard and strong, one can yet exercise Compliance while adhering to centrality and rectitude, it shall be the way to get others to identify with him.} for the soft and weak would all be obedient to such a hard and strong one. {This makes it clear that there is no disobedience, the consequence of which is that "prevalence on a small scale is achieved."} And this is why there is "prevalence on a small scale," "it would be fitting should one set out to do something here," and "it would be fitting to see the great man."

COMMENTARY ON THE IMAGES

Wind following wind: this constitutes the image of Compliance.[2] In the same way, the noble man reiterates commands and has endeavors carried out.[3]

COMMENTARY ON THE APPENDED PHRASES

Sun [Compliance] is the controller of virtue.

Sun [Compliance] demonstrates how one can weigh things while yet remaining in obscurity.

Sun [Compliance] provides the means to practice improvisations.[4]

PROVIDING THE SEQUENCE OF THE HEXAGRAMS

When one is a wanderer, he has nowhere to be taken in. This is why *Lü* [The Wanderer, Hexagram 56] is followed by *Sun* [Compliance]. Compliance provides entrance.[5]

THE HEXAGRAMS IN IRREGULAR ORDER

Sun [Compliance] means "stay hidden."

First Yin

This one now advances, now retreats, so the constancy of the warrior would be found fitting. {Situated as it is at the start of orders, First Yin represents someone who is unable to obey orders. Thus "this one now advances, now retreats." For carrying out a command and for delivering someone from evil, none is better than the warrior. Thus "the constancy of the warrior would be found fitting" to rectify such a person as this.}

COMMENTARY ON THE IMAGES

"This one now advances, now retreats," for his will is in doubt. {With such a compliant and docile will, this one "now advances, now retreats" in doubt and apprehension.} "The constancy of the warrior would be found fitting," for the will would be thus controlled.

Second Yang

This one practices Compliance as if he were beneath a bed, but if he were to use it in respect to invokers and shamans on a large scale, there should be good fortune and no blame. {Second Yang occupies the center of the lower *Sun* [Compliance] trigram, and both because it is in a low place and also because this yang line abides in a yin position, it represents the most extreme degree of servile Compliance. This is why the text says: "This one practices Compliance as if he were beneath a bed." If one were to lose his rectitude because of such an extreme of servility, he should fall into blameworthy error. But if he were able to abide in centrality and apply such utmost servility to minister to the gods of Heaven and of Earth and avoid using it for the sake of those who have might and authority, he should then extend the effect of it and achieve large-scale good fortune and stay clear of error. This is why the text says: "If he were to use it in respect to invokers and shamans on a large scale, there should be good fortune and no blame."[6]}

COMMENTARY ON THE IMAGES

That there is large-scale good fortune here is because this one achieves centrality [adheres to the Mean].

Third Yang

This one practices Compliance with a scowl, which means regret. {*Pin* should be understood as *pincu* [scowl], which signifies that one here is unhappy and exhausted, forced into something that he cannot avoid. As Third Yang, with all its strength and rectitude, is still ridden upon by Fourth Yin, one here finishes up by being compliant because his will is exhausted, and this is a matter for regret.[7]}

COMMENTARY ON THE IMAGES

The regret that stems from practicing Compliance with a scowl here is due to this one's will being exhausted.

Fourth Yin

This one's regret vanishes, for in hunting he catches the three categories. {Fourth Yin rides atop a hard and strong line, which is cause for regret. However, because it obtains its rightful position [as a yin line in a yin position] and because it carries Fifth Yang, its humility is such that it can deal with that with which it is charged. Although it has to use its softness and weakness to control the hard and strong [Third Yang], because it can rely on the exalted one [the ruler, Fifth Yang] and tread the path of righteousness [it is in its rightful position], it surely is capable of hunting down the violent brute [*qiangbao*] or keeping the inhumane [*buren*] at a distance. If in hunting one has a good catch, there could be none better than the three categories. This is why the text says: "This one's regret vanishes, for in hunting he catches the three categories." "The first is called 'dried meat for the *dou* sacrificial vessel' [*gandou*], the second is called 'meat for honored guests' [*binke*], and the third is called 'provisions for the sovereign's kitchens' [*chong jun zhi pao*]."[8]}

COMMENTARY ON THE IMAGES

This one "in hunting . . . catches the three categories," which means meritorious achievement.

Fifth Yang

Constancy here means good fortune. Regret vanishes, and nothing fails to be fitting. Whereas nothing good here happens at the start, things end well. If there be three days before a new law is issued and three days after a new law is issued, there will be good fortune. {As it is a yang line here that abides in a yang position, it signifies a deficiency in humility and Compliance [which is something to regret]. However, this one holds fast to centrality and rectitude in issuing his laws, so none disobeys him. This is why the text says: "Constancy here means good fortune. Regret vanishes, and nothing fails to be fitting." If one here does not try to transform people gradually but instead attempts to do so suddenly by applying hard corrective measures to them, in the beginning all will be unhappy. However, if one carries through to the end in centrality and rectitude, the dao of evil will thereby deteriorate, and, it will turn out that "things end well." "For an order to be given" is what *geng* [law issued] means. In rectifying and delivering the people, one must not be too sudden. If the common folk have been firmly entrenched in error for a long time, correction must not be attempted precipitously. This is why one should issue a law three days before it goes into effect, wait three days after it is so issued, and then issue it again. Only then will the punishments involved not provoke blame and resentment. *Jia* [the first of the ten characters in the heavenly branches decimal cycle (*tiangan*)] and *geng* [the seventh] both mean the issuance of orders.[9]}

COMMENTARY ON THE IMAGES

The good fortune that accrues to Fifth Yang is due to its position being correct and central.

Top Yang

This one practices Compliance as if he were beneath a bed and so loses the axe that he uses. Even were he to practice constancy, there would be misfortune. {Top Yang is located at the very apogee of Compliance, and such an extreme of Compliance is absolutely excessive. Thus the text says: "This one practices Compliance as if he were beneath a bed." An axe is something one uses to cut things. This one with his excessive Compliance loses his sense of righteousness, so he loses the means to cut [i.e., make decisions, pass judgments]. Thus the text says: "[He] loses the axe that he uses.[10] Even were he to practice constancy, there would be misfortune."}

COMMENTARY ON THE IMAGES

That "this one practices Compliance as if he were beneath a bed" means that this one at the top has utterly exhausted it [i.e., the limits of Compliance]. He "loses the axe that he uses," so how can he practice righteousness? This means misfortune.

NOTES

1. This and all subsequent text set off in this manner is commentary by Wang Bi.

2. *Sun* (Compliance) has *Sun* (Compliance, i.e., Wind) for both its upper and its lower trigrams.

3. Kong Yingda comments: "Two winds follow upon each other, thus the text says 'wind following wind.' Once winds follow upon each other, nothing withstands them, thus the text says: 'Wind following wind. . . . In the same way, the noble man. . . .'" See *Zhouyi zhengyi*, 6: 7b.

4. See section seven of the Commentary on the Appended Phrases, Part Two.

5. "Compliance provides entrance" translates *sun ru ye*, which more literally might also be translated: "As for Compliance, that is how entrance happens." This follows Han Kangbo's commentary to the passage involved in section eight of part two of Providing the Sequence of the Hexagrams: "If 'one is a wanderer' and 'has nowhere to be taken in,' he will only succeed in gaining entrance and egress by using compliance." Cheng Yi and Zhu Xi seem to understand the phrase *sun ru ye* as "*Sun* means [compliant] entrance/penetration," with such entrance or penetration referring to such things as making progress, getting ahead, influencing the course of events, etc. See *Zhouyi zhezhong*, 8: 5b.

6. Kong Yingda comments:

> *Shi* [secretary/scribe] means "*zhushi*" [invoker-secretary], and *wu* [shaman] means "*wuxi*" [shaman/prognosticator]; both refer to people who serve the gods and spirits. *Large scale* [*fenruo*] means "*shengduo*" [extensive, in great numbers]. . . . When people have might and authority, it is easy to treat them with respect, but the Dao of gods and spirits is without form and often causes inattention and neglect. If one were able to exercise his virtue, abiding all the while in centrality, and to practice the Dao of Compliance with the utmost servility and applied all this to the service of the gods of Heaven and Earth but refrained from using it in the service of those who have might and authority, he should be able to extend the effect of it and achieve large-scale good fortune.

See *Zhouyi zhengyi*, 6: 8a.

7. Both Cheng Yi and Zhu Xi gloss *pin* as *lüshi* (repeatedly fail). They seem to understand Third Yang as: "This one repeatedly fails to penetrate [get ahead], so there is regret/humiliation." Cheng notes that because it exceeds the center (violates the Mean), Third Yang represents someone who arrogantly tries to use his strength to force his way ahead but repeatedly fails, so feels regret and humiliation. See *Zhouyi zhezhong*, 8: 7b.

8. Wang Bi here cites the *Wangzhi* (Regulations of the former kings), section five of the *Liji* (Book of rites), 12: 5a.

9. See Hexagram 18, *Gu* (Ills to Be Cured), the Judgment, the Commentary on the Judgments, and Wang Bi's commentary to the latter.

10. "The axe that he uses" translates *zi fu*, which follows Kong Yingda's gloss. See *Zhouyi zhengyi*, 6: 9a. Cf. Hexagram 56, *Lü* (The Wanderer), Fourth Yang, and note 9 there.

䷹

兌

Dui [Joy]
(*Dui* Below *Dui* Above)

Judgment

Dui [Joy] is such that prevalence is had. It is fitting to practice constancy here.

COMMENTARY ON THE JUDGMENTS

Dui means "to give joy." It is by being hard inside and yet soft outside that one manages to give Joy and still fittingly practice constancy. {If one gives Joy in such a way that it violates the need to be hard and strong, this will result in ingratiation, but if one acts with hardness and strength so that it violates the need to provide Joy, this will result in cruelty. "It is by being hard inside and yet soft outside that one manages to give Joy and still fittingly practice constancy." As one is hard inside, "Joy is such that prevalence is had," and, as one is soft outside, "Joy is such that prevalence is had."[1]} This is how one can be obedient to Heaven and yet responsive to mankind. {Heaven, though hard and strong, does not neglect to provide Joy.} If one leads the common folk with Joy, they will forget their toil, and if one has them risk danger and difficulty with Joy, they will forget about dying. Great is Joy, for it is the motivating force of the common folk!

COMMENTARY ON THE IMAGES

Lake clinging to Lake: this constitutes the image of Joy.[2] In the same way, the noble man engages in talk and study with friends. *Clinging* [*li*] means "linked" [*lian*]. No more flourishing application of Joy can be found than this.[3]

PROVIDING THE SEQUENCE OF THE HEXAGRAMS

Sun [Compliance, Hexagram 57] provides entrance. Only after gaining such entry will one find delight in it. This is why Compliance is followed by *Dui* [Joy]. *Dui* here means "delight."

THE HEXAGRAMS IN IRREGULAR ORDER

Dui [Joy] means "show yourself."

First Yang

This one achieves Joy through harmony, which means good fortune. {First Yang abides at the beginning of Joy, and because its response is not limited to any one particular line [i.e., it has no resonate partner], one here stays free of factional affiliation. This is what "achieves Joy through harmony" means. This one gives Joy but does not engage in ingratiation. Anyone who treads such a path when he takes action will never have his motives suspected by others, so his good fortune is indeed appropriate!}

COMMENTARY ON THE IMAGES

The good fortune that comes to one who achieves Joy through harmony is due to the fact that his actions never provoke suspicion.

Second Yang

This one achieves Joy through sincerity, which means good fortune. Regret vanishes. {One who gives Joy here so it does not violate the Mean has to be a person of sincerity. Such a one may lose his position [this is a yang line in a yin position] but he still gives Joy. His sincerity leads to good fortune, so regret vanishes.}

COMMENTARY ON THE IMAGES

The good fortune that comes to one who achieves Joy through sincerity is due to the fact that he keeps his will trustworthy. {His will is kept trustworthy.}

Third Yin

This one comes after Joy, which means misfortune. {Where this one treads, with its yin character of softness and weakness, is not the territory of its rightful position [it is a yin line in a yang position], so it represents someone who comes in search of Joy. Not correct and yet seeking Joy, such is the way of evil sycophancy.}

COMMENTARY ON THE IMAGES

The misfortune that comes to one who comes after Joy here is due to his position not being right.

Fourth Yang

This one has to deliberate how to deal with Joy and so knows no peace, but because he wards off harm, he has happiness. {"To deliberate how to deal with" [*shang*] here includes both the meaning of "consider" [*shangliang*] and "control" [*caizhi*]. *Ward off* [*jie*] means "keep away" [ge]. Third Yin, engaging in sycophantic Joy, is about to draw near to the most exalted one [the ruler, Fifth Yang], so Fourth Yang uses its virtues of hardness and strength to control it and keep it away. One here must both solve inner problems and deal with exterior threats, so he "knows no peace." He situates himself near to the royal domain and keeps away evil and wards off harm, so it is appropriate that "he has happiness."}

COMMENTARY ON THE IMAGES

The happiness of Fourth Yang is due to the blessings that take place.

Fifth Yang

This one puts his trust in one who embodies deterioration, which means danger. {Fifth Yang is paired with Top Yin, with which it has entered into a congenial relationship. Although one here occupies the exalted and correct position [the rulership of the hexagram], he does not find Joy in trusting the yang but instead finds Joy in trusting the yin; this is what "this one puts his trust in one who embodies deterioration" means. What "deterioration" [*bo*][4] means is that the dao of the petty man is in the ascendancy.}

COMMENTARY ON THE IMAGES

"This one puts his trust in one who embodies deterioration," even though his position is correct and proper. {This one with his correct and proper position puts his trust in the petty man and distances himself from the noble man, thus the text says "even though his position is correct and proper."[5]}

Top Yin

This one achieves Joy though being led. {Top Yin with its yin character occupies the rearmost position in Joy, so it represents a passive and withdrawn person. Thus one here must be led forth before he can have Joy.[6]}

COMMENTARY ON THE IMAGES

Top Yin achieves Joy through being led, so no brilliance ever attends such a one.

NOTES

1. This and all subsequent text set off in this manner is commentary by Wang Bi.

2. *Dui* (Joy) has *Dui* (Joy, i.e., Lake) for both its upper and its lower trigrams.

3. "Friends" translates *pengyou*. Kong Yingda comments: "People who share the same tradition of teaching [*tongmen*] are called '*peng*,' and people who share the same goal [*tongzhi*] are called '*you*.' There is no greater Joy than the Joy that such *pengyou* provide one another when they gather together to talk about and study the meaning of the Dao." See *Zhouyi zhengyi*, 6: 9b.

4. *Bo* (deterioration) is an obvious reference to Hexagram 23, *Bo* (Peeling). See the Commentary on the Judgments and note 1 of that hexagram.

5. Kong Yingda takes this to be a rebuke (see *Zhouyi zhengyi*, 6: 10b), and Cheng Yi regards it as a warning (see *Zhouyi zhezhong*, 12: 64b).

6. Both Cheng Yi and Zhu Xi interpret Top Yin differently. Cheng comments:

> When other hexagrams reach the apogee of their processes, they undergo transformation, but *Dui* represents Joy, which when it reaches its limit tries to reach ever-greater Joy. Top Yin constitutes the ruler of Joy. It abides at the very apogee of Joy, so it represents someone whose Joy is insatiable. Thus, though his Joy may have already reached an extreme, he still wants to draw it out and increase it further. So how is it that such a thing does not lead to regret and blame? I have just said that his Joy is insatiable, but this is regardless of whether what gives him Joy is good or bad [i.e., such Joy may not necessarily be blameworthy]. Also, below Top Yin rides atop the centrality and correctness of Fifth Yang, so such a one lacks the wherewithal to exercise any evil penchant for Joy.

Cheng's reading of Top Yin would seem to be: "This one tries to draw out Joy further." On the other hand, Zhu Xi comments: "Top Yin constitutes the ruler of Joy. As it abides in the top position of Joy with its yin character, it entices the two yang lines beneath it to find Joy together with it, but it is unable to compel their obedience. Thus Fifth Yang ought to take warning. However, nothing is said about the good fortune or misfortune of this line itself." Zhu's reading would seem to be: "This one tries to achieve Joy by enticing others." See *Zhouyi zhezhong*, 8: 14b.

HEXAGRAM 59

䷺

渙

Huan [Dispersion]
(*Kan* Below *Sun* Above)

Judgment

Huan [Dispersion] is such that prevalence is had, but only when a true king arrives will there be an ancestral temple.[1] It would then be fitting to cross the great river and fitting to practice constancy.

COMMENTARY ON THE JUDGMENTS

That prevalence is had in Dispersion is because the hard and strong comes in yet is not hard-pressed and because the soft and weak obtains a position outside yet cooperates with the one above. {Second Yang, with its hardness and strength, comes to abide in the inner trigram [*Kan* (Sink Hole)] yet is not hard-pressed by the danger there. Fourth Yin, with its softness and weakness, obtains a position in the outer trigram [*Sun* (Compliance)] yet cooperates with the one above [Fifth Yang, the ruler of the hexagram]. The inner is so hard and strong that it is free from any dangerous trouble, and the outer is so compliant that it is free from any perverse disobedience. This is why "prevalence is had" and "it would be fitting to cross the great river and fitting to practice constancy." Whenever the hard and strong obtains unimpeded opportunity and yet avoids getting entangled in either fear or deviancy,[2] and whenever the soft and weak treads the path of righteousness and unites his will with the hard and strong, it always results in "prevalence" and in circumstances in which "it would be fitting to cross the great river and fitting to practice constancy."[3]} "Only when a true king arrives will there be an ancestral temple," that is, a true king would have to be located in the midst of this. {If a true king is located in the midst of this time of dispersal, his arrival will ensure that there will be an ancestral temple [i.e., good government will prevail].} "It would be fitting to cross the great river." This means that if one rides atop wood, there should be meritorious achievement. {"One rides atop wood" and so crosses over troubles. Wood here provides the sole means to cross the river. In like manner, if in attempting to cross over troubles, one were constant in his use of the Dao of Dispersion, he should surely have meritorious achievement.}

COMMENTARY ON THE IMAGES

The Wind moves atop the Water: this constitutes the image of Dispersion.[4] In the same way, the former kings made offerings to *di* [the Divine Ruler] and established ancestral temples.[5]

COMMENTARY ON THE APPENDED PHRASES

They [the ancient sages] hollowed out some tree trunks to make boats and whittled down others to make paddles. The benefit of boats and paddles was such that one could cross over to where it had been impossible to go. This allowed faraway places to be reached and so benefited the entire world. They probably got the idea for this from the hexagram *Huan* [Dispersion].[6]

PROVIDING THE SEQUENCE OF THE HEXAGRAMS

Having found such delight, one now disperses it. This is why *Dui* [Joy, Hexagram 58] is followed by *Huan* [Dispersion]. *Huan* [Dispersion] involves separation or estrangement.

THE HEXAGRAMS IN IRREGULAR ORDER

Huan [Dispersion] indicates a dispersal.

First Yin

This one is saved by a horse's strength and as a result has good fortune.[7] {*Huan* [Dispersion] means *san* [dispersal/separation]. First Yin is located at the beginning of Dispersion, when the dissension and dispersal are not yet severe, so one here can move away—this so that he might realize his ambitions and also avoid trouble. Once one is no longer in a dangerous situation, he can flee and take refuge somewhere. This is why the text says: "This one is saved by a horse's strength and as a result has good fortune."[8]}

COMMENTARY ON THE IMAGES

The good fortune that accrues to one at First Yin is due to his compliance. {This one sees trouble and moves away from it; he does not contend with danger. This is why the text says: "The good fortune . . . is due to his compliance."[9]}

Second Yang

Dispersion is such that this one uses his support as means to run away, so regret vanishes. {A *ji* [table, i.e., "support"] is something that carries things, and here it refers to First Yin. Second Yang has no resonate partner at all, but it gets along well with First Yin. However, when First Yin finds a way to scatter, this allows Second Yang also to disperse and, in doing so, to run away. One here thus obtains the means to make himself secure, and that is why "regret vanishes."}

COMMENTARY ON THE IMAGES

"Dispersion is such that this one uses his support as means to run away," which allows him to get what he desires.[10]

Third Yin

This one disperses his person, so there is no regret. {As a concept, Dispersion means that the inner is threatened by danger and the outer enjoys security. In scattering his person [*san gong*, i.e., "running away"], one at Third Yin has his will fixed on the outer. He does not stand fast in the position he now holds but instead joins his will to that of the hard and strong [Top Yang, the resonate partner of Third Yin], and that is how he manages to be without regret.[11]}

COMMENTARY ON THE IMAGES

"This one disperses his person [i.e., runs away]," for his will is fixed on the outer.[12]

Fourth Yin

This one disperses for all, so there is fundamental good fortune. But in a time of dispersion, there is a mountain of unsettled thoughts. {Fourth Yin has climbed out of danger and difficulty and has obtained a position here in the trigram *Sun* [Compliance], where it joins its will to that of Fifth Yang. This all signifies someone who within handles important affairs of state and without issues orders that will transform the public good. Thus he can disperse dangers that threaten all others and, in so doing, brings glory to his Dao [or, "the path he has chosen"]. However, as this one is located in a low position that demands obedience, even though he cannot take exclusive charge of things, he still has the responsibility for dispersing the danger. So he continues to have a mountain of unsettled and worrisome thoughts. Although he has obtained "fundamental good fortune," what concerns him cannot be forgotten.[13]}

COMMENTARY ON THE IMAGES

"This one disperses for all, so there is fundamental good fortune." He has greatness and glory.

Fifth Yang

Dispersing sweat, this one gives out great shouts. Only if a true king abides here in this time of Dispersion would there be no blame. {Fifth Yang occupies the exalted position, treads the path of rectitude, and abides in the center of Compliance. Scattering sweat and giving out great shouts, this is one who clears away the dangers. The rulership at a time of Dispersion must be filled by a true king, for only then can that ruler stay free of blame.}

COMMENTARY ON THE IMAGES

"A true king abides," so there is no blame, for his position is correctly filled.

Top Yang

This one disperses the threat of bloodletting. He departs and stays far out of things and so suffers no blame. {*Ti* [far out] means *yuan* [distant/keep at a distance]. Top Yang stays the farthest from harm and does not let any encroacher get close. The way to disperse worry and the threat of harm here is to keep far out of things. This one disperses the threat of disaster in a place far removed from harm, so who is going to lay blame against him?[14]}

COMMENTARY ON THE IMAGES

"This one disperses the threat of bloodletting" by staying far away from harm.

NOTES

1. Cf. Hexagram 45, *Cui* (Gathering), Judgment, and Wang Bi's commentary there.

2. "Fear or deviancy" translates *ji hui*, which Kong Yingda in his subcommentary glosses as *weiji huixie* "fear [as a restraint] and perversity/deviance". See *Zhouyi zhengyi*, 6: 11b.

3. This and all subsequent text set off in this manner is commentary by Wang Bi.

4. The lower trigram is *Kan* (Sink Hole, i.e., Water), and the upper trigram is *Sun* (Compliance, i.e., Wind).

5. Kong Yingda comments: "This is the image of the wind moving atop the water, stirring up waves, which then disperse [*sanshi*]. . . . [In like manner,] the former kings, at times when things were completely relaxed [*huanran*] and there were no troubles, made offerings to *shangdi* [the Divine Ruler on High] in order to report to Him that there was peace." See *Zhouyi zhengyi*, 6: 12a. Kong here associates *sanshi* (dispersion/dispersal) with *huanran* (completely relaxed), i.e., all trouble broken up and dispersed. Cheng Yi has also glossed *Huan* as *shusan* (relaxed, free of worry). See *Zhouyi zhezhong*, 8: 15a.

6. See section two of the Commentary on the Appended Phrases, Part Two, and note 14 there.

7. Cf. Hexagram 36, *Mingyi* (Suppression of the Light), Second Yin, and Wang Bi's commentary there.

8. Kong Yingda's commentary supports Wang's interpretation: "One can here use the horse to rescue and extricate oneself." See *Zhouyi zhengyi*, 6: 12a. However, both Cheng Yi and Zhu Xi say that one at First Yin uses the strength of the horse (Second Yang) to save the situation from disintegration—i.e., to reverse the process of Dispersion or at least prevent its bad effects. See *Zhouyi zhezhong*, 8: 15b–16a.

9. Instead of First Yin being compliant to the exigencies of the moment, Cheng Yi and Zhu Xi emphasize how the soft and weak First Yin must be compliant to the hard and strong Second Yang, which they identify with the strong horse that allows it to save the situation. See *Zhouyi zhezhong*, 8: 16a–17b.

10. Kong Yingda, following Wang Bi, says that what one at Second Yang desires is the "means to make himself secure." See *Zhouyi zhengyi*, 6: 12a.

11. Cheng Yi and Zhu Xi interpret Third Yin differently. Cheng comments:

> At a time of Dispersion, Third Yin alone has a resonate partner, so it is free from any regret as far as being dispersed or scattered is concerned. However, it has a soft and weak yin character, lacks a natural capacity for centrality and rectitude, and abides at the top [of the lower trigram] in territory that offers it no proper position, so how could one here ever rescue the times from Dispersion and so extend those benefits to people in general? This one stops at his own person and so can do nothing more than free himself from regret. At the beginning, the word *Huan* [Dispersion] is added; this indicates that "at a time of Dispersion, this one person himself is free of the regret associated with Dispersion."

Zhu Xi is again different: "Third Yin is both yin and weak and also not central and correct, which is an image for someone who is devoted to his own selfish interests. However, it manages to abide in a yang position, and its will is fixed on saving the world from the current situation. This is someone who can disperse [*san*] his selfishness and, in so doing, free himself from regret." See *Zhouyi zhezhong*, 8: 17a.

12. Cheng Yi's reading is different: "At a time of Dispersion, this person's will is fixed on the outer [Top Yang]." See *Zhouyi zhezhong*, 12: 65b.

13. Cheng Yi and Zhu Xi interpret Fourth Yin differently. They take *huan qiqun* (this one disperses for all) to mean "this one separates himself from his clique," *huan you qiu* (at a time of Dispersion there is a mountain of . . .) to mean "Dispersion results in [new] grouping or cohesion," and *feiyi suosi* (unsettled thoughts) to mean "it takes an extraordinary person to have such thoughts." Fourth Yin is supposed to break away from petty cliques and bond with the strong and correct ruler, Fifth Yang, which forms the basis of new, correct social bonding. Only an extraordinary person could think of doing such a thing during a time of Dispersion. See *Zhouyi zhezhong*, 8: 17b.

14. Although Wang Bi reads *ti* as it is written (far), both Cheng Yi and Zhu Xi read it as *ti* (alarm, apprehension). Zhu, in fact, says the text here should be read as the text in Hexagram 9, *Xiaoxu* (Lesser Domestication), Fourth Yin: "If there is sincerity, blood will be kept away, and apprehension purged, and one will not incur blame." See *Zhouyi zhezhong*, 8: 19b.

HEXAGRAM 60

䷻

節

Jie [Control]
(*Dui* Below *Kan* Above)

Judgment

Control is such that prevalence is had, but bitter Control cannot be practiced with constancy.

COMMENTARY ON THE JUDGMENTS

"Control is such that prevalence is had," for the hard and strong and the soft and weak are kept separate, while the hard and strong obtain central positions. {*Kan* [Sink Hole] is yang, and *Dui* [Joy] is yin; here the yang is above, and the yin is below, a division of the hard and strong from the soft and weak. As "the hard and strong and the soft and weak are kept separate," no disorderly conduct occurs. As "the hard and strong obtain central positions" [Second Yang and Fifth Yang], control is exercised accordingly. This is what it means to have Control in charge. Control at its greatest occurs when the hard and the soft are kept separate, when male and female are kept distinct.[1]} "Bitter Control cannot be practiced with constancy," for "such a Dao leads to exhaustion." {If in applying Control one goes too far and makes it bitter, it will become something the people cannot bear. If the people cannot bear it, one will no longer be able to correct their behavior.[2]} If one travels through danger with joy and executes the duties of one's office with Control, things will go smoothly thanks to such centrality and rectitude. {That is, the result of such actions will lead to prevalence. However, if one travels through danger without joy, or if one applies Control so that it is excessive and violates the Mean, "such a Dao leads to exhaustion."} As Heaven and Earth are governed by Control, so the four seasons fulfill themselves perfectly. In like manner, when Control is applied with measured control, it does no injury to wealth, nor does it harm the common folk.

COMMENTARY ON THE IMAGES

Above the Lake, there is Water: this constitutes the image of Control. In the same way, the noble man establishes limits and evaluates moral conduct.[3]

PROVIDING THE SEQUENCE OF THE HEXAGRAMS

People cannot remain in a state of estrangement forever. This is why *Huan* [Dispersion, Hexagram 59] is followed by *Jie* [Control].

THE HEXAGRAMS IN IRREGULAR ORDER

Jie [Control] indicates a stop.

First Yang

This one does not go out the door to his courtyard, so there is no blame. {This is the beginning of Control; it represents one who is about to bring order to dispersion and establish controls. Thus it has to be someone who clearly distinguishes between "what constitutes facility and what makes for blockage," someone who gives careful consideration to what might be dangerous and what spurious. "This one does not go out the door to his courtyard." That is, he never neglects to operate with great caution and secrecy, so that afterward, when the situation is saved, "there is no blame."}

COMMENTARY ON THE APPENDED PHRASES

The Master said: "As for how disorder arises, well, what one says is considered the steps to it. If the sovereign is not circumspect, he will lose his ministers; if a minister is not circumspect, he will lose his life; and if the crux of a matter is not kept circumspect, harm will result. This is why the sovereign takes circumspection as a caution and is not forthcoming."[4]

COMMENTARY ON THE IMAGES

"This one does not go out the door to his courtyard," for he understands what constitutes facility and what makes for blockage.

Second Yang

If this one does not go out the gate of his courtyard, there will be misfortune. {One at First Yang has already formulated controls, and now here we have reached the point where it is up to one at Second Yang to promulgate them. But if one here keeps himself hidden, he will fail to seize this most opportune moment, and, as a consequence, failure will ensue. This is why "if this one does not go out the gate of his courtyard, there will be misfortune."}

COMMENTARY ON THE IMAGES

"If this one does not go out the gate of his courtyard, there will be misfortune," for he will fail to seize this most opportune moment.

Third Yin

As this one is in violation of Control, so he should wail, for there is no one else to blame. {"As" [*ruo*] is a rhetorical expression. Here a yin occupies a yang position, and the soft and weak rides atop the hard and strong, so this one finds himself in such violation of the Dao of Control that it causes him to wail in lamentation. This is something that he has brought upon himself, and no one else can be blamed for it. Thus the text says "for there is no one else to blame."}

COMMENTARY ON THE IMAGES

This one who violates Control should wail, for who else is there to blame for it?

Fourth Yin

This one is content with Control, so prevalence is had. {Fourth Yin obtains its proper place [it is a yin line in a yin position] and is characterized by obedience, so it represents someone who does not try to alter the Control placed upon him and, in so doing, manages to achieve prevalence. By supporting the one above [Fifth Yang, the ruler] in this way, one here obtains his proper Dao.}

COMMENTARY ON THE IMAGES

The prevalence that is had here by this one who is content with Control is due to his following the Dao of supporting the one above [the ruler].

Fifth Yang

Sweet Control means good fortune. If one were to set forth to do something here, he would enjoy esteem {Fifth Yang obtains its rightful position [as a yang line in a yang position] and abides in centrality [i.e., stays within the Mean]. This is the ruler of Control, who never violates the Mean, so Control, as it is said [in the Judgment], "does no injury to wealth, nor does it harm the common folk." To make Control not bitter, what could be more effective than to make it sweet? If one were to emulate this principle when setting forth to do something here, he who so set forth "would enjoy esteem."}

COMMENTARY ON THE IMAGES

The good fortune that is had here by this one who makes Control sweet is a matter of his keeping his position central [i.e., by abiding within the Mean].

Top Yin

Bitter Control means misfortune for one who practices constancy, but for such a one regret will vanish. {Here the application of Control exceeds the Mean, overreaching it even to an extreme. Such is "bitter Control." If such Control were applied to people, none could bear it, so it would mean misfortune for the righteous, but if such a one were to use this opportunity to cultivate his person and walk the path of No Errancy [see Hexagram 25], he should manage to have regret vanish.}

COMMENTARY ON THE IMAGES

"Bitter Control means misfortune for one who practices constancy," for such a Dao leads to exhaustion.

NOTES

1. This and all subsequent text set off in this manner is commentary by Wang Bi.

2. Here is another example of Wang glossing *constancy* (*zhen*) as "correct behavior" or "rectitude/righteousness" (*zheng*).

3. The lower trigram is *Dui* (Joy, also Lake), and the upper trigram is *Kan* (Sink Hole, also Water). Kong Yingda comments:

> That is, Water is in the Lake, and that is how it gets its Control. . . . "Limits" [*shudu*] refers to the relative amount of personal caliber [*zunbei*] that one must have to be eligible for different honors [*liming*], and "moral conduct" [*dexing*] refers to the relative amount of personal talent [*rencai*] that one must have to be worthy of various offices [*kanren*]. The noble man emulates this image and consequently establishes levels of honor with which people are to be treated so that the differences involved are always under proper control; he also evaluates their moral conduct so that the way that they are employed is always appropriate.

See *Zhouyi zhengyi*, 6: 12a.

4. See section eight of the Commentary on the Appended Phrases, Part One.

HEXAGRAM 61

䷼

中孚

Zhongfu [Inner Trust]

(*Dui* Below *Sun* Above)

Judgment

Inner Trust is such that even fishes and swine have good fortune. It is fitting to cross the great river and fitting to practice constancy.

COMMENTARY ON THE JUDGMENTS

Inner Trust is such that the soft and weak stay within, and the hard and strong obtain central positions. Its constituent elements are Joy and Compliance. One who has such trust {Only after these four virtues exist can Trust be had.[1]} can morally transform the realm. {Only after trust has been established can the realm be morally transformed. "The soft and weak stay within, and the hard and strong obtain central positions," so each fills the place that is right for him. As the hard and strong obtain central positions, they are characterized by straightforwardness and rectitude. As the soft and weak stay within, they are characterized by passivity and compliance. With the joyous practice of such compliance, obstreperousness and contention do not occur. When such a state exists, none will engage in artful competition, and actions based on honesty and substance will be the rule. So it is when perfect sincerity wells up from within.} "Even fishes and swine have good fortune" means that the sense of trust reaches even fishes and swine. {Fishes are among the most secluded of larval creatures,[2] and swine are among the lowest and most insignificant of animals. When the Dao of Contention does not arise and the virtue of Inner Trust is manifested with such purity, even though it be the most insignificant and secluded of creatures, this sincerity will reach all.} "It is fitting to cross the great river," for in riding atop wood there is the emptiness of the boat. {"Riding atop wood" consists of using the emptiness of the boat, which will never let one sink as long as it lasts. One uses Inner Trust to cross over difficulties just as "in riding atop wood there is the emptiness of a boat."[3]}

COMMENTARY ON THE IMAGES

Above the Lake, there is Wind: this constitutes the image of Inner Trust. In the same way, the noble man evaluates criminal punishments and mitigates the death penalty. {When trust emerges from within, even one who makes mistakes can find exoneration.[4]}

PROVIDING THE SEQUENCE OF THE HEXAGRAMS

Once there is such restraint, people will have trust in it. This is why *Jie* [Control, Hexagram 60] is followed by *Zhongfu* [Inner Trust].

THE HEXAGRAMS IN IRREGULAR ORDER

Zhongfu [Inner Trust] indicates confidence.

First Yang

This one's devotion is such that he has good fortune, but if he were to extend it to others, he would suffer disquiet. {*Yu* [concern] here means *zhuan* [devotion]. First Yang represents the initial stage of trust, and, as its resonate partner is at Fourth Yin, it signifies someone who obtains good fortune thanks to this devotion. As one at First Yang will never let his will change, his heart should remain attached to one other alone. Thus the text says: "If he were to extend it [devotion] to others, he would suffer disquiet."[5]}

COMMENTARY ON THE IMAGES

The devotion of First Yang "is such that he has good fortune," but his will should never change.

Second Yang

A calling crane is in the shadows; its young answer it. I have a fine goblet; I will share it with you.[6] {Second Yang is located in the inner [lower] trigram and moreover is beneath two consecutive yin lines, nevertheless one here treads a path that never strays from the Mean [Second Yang is in a middle position] and seeks no help from outside. It represents someone who relies on the truth that is in him.[7] This one has established sincerity with such heartfelt perfection that, even though he finds himself here in total obscurity, others still respond to him. This is why the text says: "A calling crane is in the shadows; its young answer it." This one does not use his power and influence for personal benefit; his virtue is such that he would do nothing but share these with others—the very perfection of sincerity. Thus the text says: "I have a fine goblet; I will share it with you."[8]}

COMMENTARY ON THE IMAGES

"Its young answer it," that is, the longing involved comes from the inner heart.

Third Yin

This one acquires an enemy. Now there is drumming, now halting, now weeping, now singing. {Third Yin abides at the top of the Youngest Yin [Daughter], and Fourth Yin abides at the bottom of the Eldest Yin [Daughter],[9] so they face each other but do not form a pair. This means that they are enemies. When a yin line occupies a yang position [Third Yin], it indicates someone who wishes to advance. This one wishes to advance but is blocked by an enemy, thus the text says "now there is drumming" [i.e., a signal to attack]. Fourth Yin abides in its correct position [as a yin line in a yin position] and moreover gives carriage to Fifth Yang. This indicates that it cannot be conquered by Third Yin. Thus the text says "now halting" [i.e., Third Yin disengages]. Third Yin is not victorious and so retreats, fearing that it will have its territory invaded. Thus the text says "now weeping." Fourth Yin treads the path of obedience and does not engage in disputes with others, so it retreats, and Third Yin suffers no harm. Thus the text says "now singing." When one lacks an estimate of his own strength and is inconsistent in advance and retreat, it is obvious that he will exhaust himself.[10]}

COMMENTARY ON THE IMAGES

"Now drumming, now halting" indicates that this one's position is not correct.

Fourth Yin

The moon is about to wax full here, and, as this horse abandons its mate, there is no blame. {At this time of Inner Trust, one here finds himself at the beginning of the *Sun* [Compliance] trigram and in resonance with First Yang in the *Dui* [Joy] trigram. As Fourth Yin occupies a correct position [or "abides in righteousness," i.e., it is a yin line in a yin position] and treads the path of obedience, it gives carriage to Fifth Yang. This represents someone who within assists the primary head [or "His Majesty," i.e., Fifth Yang, the ruler of Inner Trust] and without spreads moral transformation through the force of his virtue. As such a one perfectly fulfills all the potential of yin virtue, the text says: "The moon [the "great yin"] is about to wax full." "This horse abandons its mate" means that one rejects the company of his own kind. Although this one occupies a position where he can realize his virtue to the fullest, if he were to engage in contention provoked by others, he would lose his chance to realize all that potential. Thus the text says: "One here should separate himself from his own kind and direct himself upward." It is only by treading the path of righteousness, supporting the exalted one [Fifth Yang], and refraining from contention with Third Yin that such a one shall manage to stay free of blame.}

COMMENTARY ON THE IMAGES

"This horse abandons its mate," which means that one here should separate himself from his own kind and direct himself upward.

Fifth Yang

If this one maintains trust secure as a tether, there should be no blame. {"As a tether" means to use trust to make attachments [i.e., bind people to one through trust]. Located as he is in centrality and sincerity, one at Fifth Yang finds himself at a time to form relationships. As this one abides in the exalted position, he is considered the ruler of all others, so how could he ever set trust aside? Thus "if this one maintains trust secure as a tether," he should manage to stay free of blame.}

COMMENTARY ON THE IMAGES

"This one should maintain trust secure as a tether," for his position is both correct and suitable.

Top Yang

This one's high flying sound climbs up to Heaven, but he should have misfortune even though he tries to practice constancy. {*Han* [soar] means "to fly high." "Flying sound" means the sound [reputation] flies, but the reality or substance does not follow it. This one abides at the top position of the hexagram, so it is located at the end of trust. When trust comes to an end, it deteriorates. Here integrity and honesty perish within, but an extravagant beauty struts without. Thus the text says: "This one's high flying sound climbs up to Heaven." "This one's high flying sound climbs up to Heaven," but his rectitude has indeed perished.}

COMMENTARY ON THE IMAGES

"This one's high flying sound climbs up to Heaven," but how could he ever last long?

NOTES

1. This and all subsequent text set off in this manner is commentary by Wang Bi. The four virtues refer to (1) the soft and weak staying within (i.e., keeping to passive, subordinate roles), (2) the hard and strong obtaining central positions (i.e., exercising authority but staying within the Mean), (3) Joy, and (4) Compliance.

2. "Larval" translates *chong*, which in traditional Chinese thought indicates a broad category of creatures creepy, crawly, scaly—everything from worms and insects to the majestic dragon.

3. "Emptiness of the boat" translates *zhou xu*. Cheng Yi notes that the center of the *Zhongfu* (Inner Trust) hexagram is "empty," and that the hexagram as a whole (looked down on from above) is the image of a boat. However, Cheng seems to read *zhou xu* as "the boat is empty": "When one uses Inner Trust to cross over dangers and difficulties, it is just as fitting as when one rides atop wood to cross a stream, that is, when one does this

with an empty boat, for if the boat is empty [*zhou xu*], there is no chance that some calamity such as sinking or capsizing will occur." See *Zhouyi zhezhong*, 10: 44b. We should also note that the constituent trigrams of Inner Trust are *Dui* (Joy, Lake) below and *Sun* (Compliance, here Wood) above: Wood riding atop the Lake.

4. Kong Yingda comments:

> When the Wind travels atop the Lake, there is no place that it does not reach. In the same way, when trust envelops all creatures, there is no place that it fails to reach either. . . . In a world governed by Inner Trust, it is certain that no deliberate crime would occur, and wrongdoing as such would be but the product of error, something that could be forgiven. Thus the noble man here should evaluate criminal cases that involve such error and mitigate those that ordinarily require the death penalty.

See *Zhouyi zhengyi*, 6: 16a.

Cheng Yi offers a different interpretation:

> When there is Wind above the Lake, it is felt inside the Lake. In substance, water is unstable [*xu*, literally, "empty"], thus wind can enter it. The heart of man is also unstable, thus external things can move or influence it. The Wind imparting movement to the Lake is like things having influence on one's inner self. . . . When the noble man evaluates criminal cases, he does not stop until he exhausts the resources of his personal integrity [*zhong*, literally, "loyalty," i.e., being true to one self], and when he passes the death sentence, he does nothing less than push his sense of compassion to the limit. Thus his sincerity of will [*chengyi*] always makes him look for ways to mitigate the punishment [*huan*]. *Huan* means "be lenient" [*kuan*].

See *Zhouyi zhezhong*, 12: 69a.

5. Both Cheng Yi and Zhu Xi gloss *yu* [concern] as *duo* [measure]. That is, one at First Yang should evaluate the trustworthiness of his resonate partner at Fourth Yin, and, if he finds him worthy of trust, he should trust him, for only then would he have good fortune. See *Zhouyi zhezhong*, 8: 25b–26a.

6. Second Yang is quoted and commented on in section eight of the Commentary on the Appended Phrases, Part One.

7. "Relies on the truth that is in him" translates *ren qizhen*. Lou Yulie suggests that Wang Bi here alludes to *Laozi*, section 28, p. 75, where the concept of "the uncarved block" (*pu*, also "pristine, unsullied selflessness") is discussed, a term Wang glosses as *zhen* (truth). See *Wang Bi ji jiaoshi*, 2: 519 n. 11.

8. "Goblet" translates *jue*, which Wang Bi regards as a reference to noble rank, as it does in the term *juewei*: rank (*wei*) involving investiture with a ceremonial goblet (*jue*).

9. See section ten of Explaining the Trigrams.

10. Both Cheng Yi and Zhu Xi interpret Third Yin differently. Cheng comments:

> *Di* [enemy] here means "partner," the person with whom one exchanges trust, that is, Top Yang, the true resonate partner of Third Yin. Because they make the center empty [i.e., imbue the inner with selflessness], Third Yin and Fourth Yin are both rulers of Inner Trust. However, their respective positions differ. Fourth Yin obtains its proper position and so abides where it is correct [it is a yin line in a yin position], thus it abandons the one with which it is paired [Third Yin] in order to follow the one above [Fifth Yang]. Third Yin is not central and has strayed from a position that is right for it [it is a yin line in a yang position], thus such a one tries to obtain a partner so that he may link his ambitions to another's. Because of the soft and weak character of *Dui* [Joy], once one here [in the top position of the trigram, i.e., Third Yin] has made such an attachment, he ends up following what this person does, him whom he so trusts. So now he drums and grows strong, now he ceases and wastes away; now he sadly weeps, now he sings about his happiness. His activity and repose, his grief and happiness, all are attached to the one whom he trusts. As this one does nothing more than attach himself to the one he trusts, he is never conscious of either good fortune or bad. However, this is not something a noble man of discernment would ever do.

See *Zhouyi zhezhong*, 8: 27b–28a.

HEXAGRAM 62

䷽

小過

Xiaoguo [Minor Superiority]
(*Gen* Below *Zhen* Above)

Judgment

Minor Superiority is such that prevalence may be had, if the fitting practice of constancy takes place. Small matters may be undertaken here, but great matters may not be undertaken. The flying bird is losing its voice, for it should not go up but should go down, because then there would be great good fortune. {"The flying bird is losing its voice" means that its voice is sad because it is trying to find a place to stop.[1] The higher it goes, the less likely that it would find anything suitable, but if it were to go down, it would find someplace safe. The higher something goes, the more exhausted it becomes, and nothing finds this more true than a flying bird.[2]}

COMMENTARY ON THE JUDGMENTS

Minor Superiority is such that one can achieve superiority in minor things and thereby achieve prevalence. {"Minor things" means any kind of small matter. Here one achieves superiority in small matters and in so doing manages to make things go smoothly.} Such superiority succeeds through the fitting practice of constancy and is something that can be exercised only when the times allow it. {One may achieve success by superiority through the fitting practice of constancy, and this can be done only in response to the exigencies of the times. When one exercises superiority in reverence and temperance, such a one is fit to practice constancy.} The soft and weak obtain central positions, and, because of this, there is good fortune in minor matters. The hard and strong stray from their proper positions and so are not central, and because of this, it is not possible to undertake major matters. {The accomplishment of major matters is surely a thing for the hard and strong. When the soft and weak insinuate themselves into major things, this forms the Dao that leads to *Bo* [Peeling, Hexagram 23].}

There is the image of a flying bird in it [the *Xiaoguo* hexagram]. {"It should not go up but should go down": such is the image of the flying bird.} "The flying bird is losing its voice, for it should not go up but should go down, because then there would be great good fortune." That is, to go above means insubordination, but to go below means obedience. {To go above means that one rides atop the hard and strong [as Fifth Yin rides atop Fourth Yang], but to go below means that one gives carriage to the yang [as Second Yin supports Third Yang]. No greater misfortune can befall one than when one tries to exercise superiority in insubordination, but if one exercises superiority in obedience, such superiority will work a thoroughgoing change and beget good fortune.}

COMMENTARY ON THE IMAGES

Above the Mountain, there is Thunder: this constitutes the image of Minor Superiority.[3] In the same way, the noble man in his actions is superior in reverence, in his bereavement he is superior in grief, and in his expenditures he is superior in temperance.[4]

COMMENTARY ON THE APPENDED PHRASES

They [the ancient sage kings] cut tree trunks to make pestles and hollowed out the ground to make mortars. The benefit of pestles and mortars was such that the myriad folk used them to get relief from want. They probably got the idea for this from the hexagram *Xiaoguo* [Minor Superiority].[5]

PROVIDING THE SEQUENCE OF THE HEXAGRAMS

One who enjoys such trust will be sure to put it to use. This is why *Zhongfu* [Inner Trust, Hexagram 61] is followed by *Xiaoguo* [Minor Superiority].

THE HEXAGRAMS IN IRREGULAR ORDER

Xiaoguo [Minor Superiority] indicates superiority.

First Yin

To be a flying bird here would mean misfortune. {At a time of Minor Superiority, "to go above means insubordination, but to go below means obedience," but the resonate partner of First Yin is above in the upper trigram [Fourth Yang]. Nevertheless, to advance would be to commit insubordination. To have no place to rest the feet is a misfortune for a flying bird.}

COMMENTARY ON THE IMAGES

"To be a flying bird here would mean misfortune," and nothing at all could be done about it.[6]

Second Yin

This one is superior to his ancestor and meets his ancestress. He does not go as far as his sovereign but does meet his minister, so there is no blame. {To exercise superiority and so obtain what one should have is what is meant by "meet." At a time of Minor Superiority, this one fills a position that is right for it [it is a yin line in a yin position], that is, by exercising superiority one here obtains what he should have. An ancestor is an initiator, and here it refers to First Yin, and an ancestress is someone who abides within, treads the middle path [follows the Mean], and so practices rectitude. This one is superior to First Yin and treads the territory of the second position. Thus the text says: "This one is superior to his ancestor and meets his ancestress." Second Yin exercises superiority but does not arrogate to himself that which belongs to another, so he finishes up at the position of minister and nothing more. Thus the text says: "He does not go as far as his sovereign but does meet his minister, so there is no blame."[7]}

COMMENTARY ON THE IMAGES

"He does not go as far as his sovereign," for he must not rise superior to the position of minister.

Third Yang

If this one does not exert his superiority and ward them off but instead follows along, they are likely to kill him, which means misfortune. {In a world governed by Minor Superiority, the great do not hold sway, so this allows the petty to achieve superiority over them [literally, "to manage to pass them (the great) by"]. Third Yang abides at the top of the lower trigram. As a yang, it is in its rightful [yang] position, yet it is unable to take the lead in asserting its superiority and so ward the petty off. This reaches such a state that Third Yang allows them all [i.e., First Yin and Second Yin] to pass it by, while it, in response [to Top Yin], also follows along behind them. But when it tries to follow them, Third Yang suffers the misfortune of being killed. Thus the text says: "If this one does not exert his superiority and ward them off but instead follows along, they are likely to kill him, which means misfortune."}

COMMENTARY ON THE IMAGES

"If this one . . . follows along, they are likely to kill him," and what can be done about such misfortune as that?

Fourth Yang

That this one is without blame is because he deals with circumstances in such a way that he does not exert his superiority. If he were to set forth, there would be danger, so he must take warning. One must not use this one where perpetual constancy is required. {Although the character of this line is yang, it does not abide in its rightful position [it is a yang line in a yin position], so it signifies one who can avoid becoming the object of blame, and this is how he manages to avoid blame here. Having lost a rightful position in the lower trigram,[8] this represents someone who cannot assert his superiority. As this one cannot assert his superiority, he therefore takes advantage of the opportunity to avoid blame. Thus the text says: "That this one is without blame is because he deals with circumstances in such a way that he does not exert his superiority." Contentment here is poisoned wine, something for which one must not yearn. Fourth Yang is located at this unsettled time of Minor Superiority, and, as it is a yang in a yin position, it is incapable of taking any action. By taking advantage of this situation, one may protect oneself and so find it possible to avoid blame. But if one uses this as an opportunity to set forth and undertake action, he will find it a dao [path] that leads to danger. This one does not form relationships with others, nor do others have anything to do with him, so there is no hand to offer him help. Thus, when danger threatens, he must do nothing but take warning, for there is no one he can apply to for rescue. Sunk in such timidity and weakness of will, all this one can do is try to protect himself. One with such characteristics who moreover is located in the midst of this clique of petty men does not measure up to the requirements of responsibility. Thus the text says: "One must not use this one where perpetual constancy is required." That is to say, he does not measure up to the requirements of being employed where perpetual constancy is needed.[9]}

COMMENTARY ON THE IMAGES

"He does not exert his superiority but does meet with the opportunity to do as he should," for the position is not right for him. "If he were to set forth, there would be danger, so he must take warning," for in the end he could not last long.

Fifth Yin

Dense clouds do not rain but start off from our western suburbs.[10] The duke shoots and captures that one there in the cave. {At a time of Minor Superiority, the small exercises superiority over the great. A six [yin line] here obtains the fifth position [the rulership of the hexagram], so this represents the culmination of yin potency. Thus the text has it that "dense clouds do not rain but start off from our western suburbs." Rain occurs when the yin are above and the yang exert pressure on the yin but are unable to break through, for then the resulting vapor turns into rain. But *Gen* [Mountain, i.e., Restraint] is stopped below, and so such interaction does not take place here, thus it does not rain. Thus it is that in *Xiaoxu* [Lesser Domestication, Hexagram 9] it is because they [the yang lines] keep moving away and so bring prevalence that no rain falls there and that in Minor Superiority it is because the yang lines do not interact [with the yin lines] above that no rain falls here either. Although a yin is at the height of its powers above, it is never able to exercise that power. The office of duke is the highest rank of all the sovereign's ministers. As Fifth Yin represents the apogee of yin potency, it is referred to here as "duke." *Yi* [harpoon arrow] here means "to shoot." Those that stay in caves are creatures that tend to secrete themselves and lie low. In Minor Superiority, as superiority is small, it is impossible for one to accomplish anything great, just as it is for someone who secretes himself and lies low. If Fifth Yin with its yin character gains control over a time of Minor Superiority, it can but garner Minor Superiority, thus the text says: "The duke shoots and captures that one there in the cave." Opening the Dao [route] to superiority has nothing to do with capturing, for such a course would but lead to "dense clouds" and never to rain.[11]}

COMMENTARY ON THE IMAGES

"Dense clouds do not rain," for one [Third Yang] is already at the top. {The yang is already on top, thus it stops.[12]}

Top Yin

This one does not meet with the opportunity to do as he should but rises superior to it. He is a flying bird that goes farther and farther away, which results in misfortune. Such a course means utter disaster. {Here the superiority of the petty man finally arrives at its highest point. As the Superiority of one here knows no limits, he goes so far as to overreach himself. As such a one pushes his superiority to the point of overreaching, what can he then ever meet with? If a bird were to keep on flying without ever stopping, where would it ever find a place to rest? Such a one brings disaster upon himself, so what more could be said about it?}

COMMENTARY ON THE IMAGES

"This one does not meet with the opportunity to do as he should but rises superior to it," which means that he has already overreached himself.

NOTES

1. "The flying bird is losing its voice" translates *feiniao yi yin*. Kong Yingda comments: "*Yi* means *shi* [lose]. That the bird is losing its voice can only mean that it is exhausted and hard-pressed because of not having found a safe place to stop. The *Lunyu* [Analects 8:4] says: 'When a bird is about to die, its call is sad.' Thus we know that 'is losing its voice' [*yi yin*] means that its sound is sad." See *Zhouyi zhengyi*, 6: 18a. Cheng Yi and Zhu

Xi both seem to interpret *yi yin* as "leave behind [transmit] a message." That is, "the flying bird transmits the message: one should not go up, but one should go down." See *Zhouyi zhezhong*, 8: 30b–31a.

2. This and all subsequent text set off in this manner is commentary by Wang Bi.

3. The lower trigram is *Gen* (Mountain), and the upper trigram is *Zhen* (Thunder).

4. Kong Yingda comments: "Thunder appears here not from within the Earth but from the Mountain above, so it is superior to its proper place of origin. Thus the hexagram is called 'Minor Superiority.' When a petty man is superior to his duties, he tends to fail because he is too rash and too extravagant. Thus the noble man serves as a model to correct him." See *Zhouyi zhengyi*, 6: 18b. It was the traditional view of the Chinese that thunder was produced inside the earth; this was "its proper place of origin."

5. See section two of the Commentary on the Appended Phrases, Part Two, and note 19 there.

6. "Nothing at all could be done about it" translates *buke ruhe ye*, an interpretation that follows the commentary of Cheng Yi; see *Zhouyi zhezhong*, 12: 72a. Kong Yingda offers a different interpretation: "When advance would be to commit insubordination, whoever understands that this must not be done [*buke*] yet still does it, brings misfortune and blame upon himself, and whatever could such a one wish to do then [*yu ruhe hu*]?" See *Zhouyi zhengyi*, 6: 19a. Kong's reading of the text would seem to be: "'To be a flying bird here would mean misfortune.' As one must not do such a thing, what could he ever do about it then?"

7. Cheng Yi and Zhu Xi interpret Second Yin differently. Cheng comments:

> When a yang is above, it provides the image of the father. One who is more exalted than the father should have the image of the ancestor. Fourth Yang is above Third Yang, thus it represents the ancestor. Second Yin and Fifth Yin abide in mutually resonate positions and both have the virtues of softness and centrality. It is the will of Second Yin not to follow either Third Yang or Fourth Yang, thus it rises superior to Fourth Yang and meets Fifth Yin. This is what is meant by "is superior to his ancestor." The fifth line is both yin and noble, so it provides the image of the ancestress. It has the same virtues as Second Yin and resonates accordingly with it. In other hexagrams, the yin and yang should try to find each other, but at a time of Superiority one must rise superior to one's ordinary condition, thus it is different here. As there are none that Second Yin cannot rise superior to, when it follows Fifth Yin, it gets a warning about its exercise of superiority: "He does not go as far as his sovereign but does meet his minister." This means that this one should advance upward but should not encroach upon his sovereign's position. However, if such a one were to fulfill the Dao of the minister, there would be no blame.

See *Zhouyi zhezhong*, 8: 33a–33b.

8. Fourth Yang, at the bottom of the upper trigram, is in a lowly, subordinate position: not a place from which to exert superiority. If this line were at the top of the lower trigram (i.e., in the third position), a lofty position of authority, it could, of course, exert that superiority.

9. Both Cheng Yi and Zhu Xi interpret Fourth Yang in a more positive light. They say that a yang line in a yin position indicates humility and reverence, qualities that allow this hard and strong one to suppress his superiority, refrain from advancing, and so stay free of blame. Also Cheng Yi interprets *wuyong yongzhen* (one must not use this one where perpetual constancy is required) differently: "Just now at a time when the yin enjoy superiority, this yang hard and strong one finds himself out of his proper position. Thus the noble man must get in step with the moment and comply with the exigencies of the place. He must not hang on tenaciously to constant principles." So for Cheng, *wuyong yongzhen* seems to mean "this one must not practice perpetual constancy." See *Zhouyi zhezhong*, 8: 34b–35a.

10. Cf. Hexagram 9, *Xiaoxu* (Lesser Domestication), the Judgment, and note 4 there.

11. Kong Yingda says that rain is a metaphor for the moral transformative power of virtue, which is how one gets others to submit of their own accord. However, he observes, "here one shoots and so captures them, which emphasizes military power; one who emphasizes military power will but make dense clouds and no rain"; i.e., external coercion never leads to great and good government—something that only emerges once the populace has been morally transformed by the ruler. See *Zhouyi zhengyi*, 6: 20b. Both Cheng Yi and Zhu Xi think that the one in the cave refers to Second Yin. They go on to say that Fifth Yin captures Second Yin in order that Second Yin will help, but, as Cheng says, "how could two yin ever manage to accomplish anything great? It would be just like dense clouds being unable to produce rain." See *Zhouyi zhezhong*, 8: 35b.

12. Kong Yingda comments: "Once the yang line in *Gen* [Mountain, Restraint] has climbed to the top position of this particular trigram, it comes to a complete stop. Thus it does not climb further to interact [with the yin lines of the upper trigram] and so make rain." See *Zhouyi zhengyi*, 6: 20b.

HEXAGRAM 63

䷾

既濟

Jiji [Ferrying Complete][1]
(*Li* Below *Kan* Above)

Judgment

Ferrying Complete is such that even the small enjoy prevalence.[2] It is fitting to practice constancy, for although in the beginning good fortune prevails, things might end in chaos.

COMMENTARY ON THE JUDGMENTS

Ferrying Complete is such that prevalence may be had, that is, even the small achieve prevalence. {Ferrying Complete means that all have been ferried across. The small have not been left out, so all are ferried. Thus the text mentions the small to clarify what Ferrying Complete means.[3]} "It is fitting to practice constancy," for both the hard and strong and the soft and weak behave correctly and thus stay in their rightful positions. {If "both the hard and strong and the soft and weak behave correctly and thus stay in their rightful positions," evil will have no chance to occur. Thus only when such rectitude prevails, is it "fitting to practice constancy."} "In the beginning good fortune prevails," for the soft and weak [Second Yin] obtains a central position [follows the Mean]. But if one ends up ceasing [to practice constancy and follow the Mean], chaos will ensue, for this Dao [path] will eventually peter out. {It is by the soft and weak obtaining a central position that such small persons should prevail, but if the soft and weak do not obtain a central position [i.e., practice the Mean], such small persons would never prevail. Although the hard and strong manage to practice rectitude, this would still result in Ferrying Complete remaining unrealized. Thus the essential requirement of Ferrying Complete lies in the soft and weak obtaining a central position. If one were to misconstrue Ferrying Complete to mean perfect security, its Dao would come to an end, and no progress would occur, so that in the end only chaos would ensue. This is why the text says:

"Although in the beginning good fortune prevails, things might end in chaos." That things end in chaos is not due to their becoming so on their own but happens because of one ceasing [to do as one should]. Thus the text says: "If one ends up ceasing [to practice constancy and to follow the Mean], chaos will ensue."[4]}

COMMENTARY ON THE IMAGES

Water positioned above Fire: this constitutes the image of Ferrying Complete.[5] In the same way, the noble man ponders the threat of calamity and takes steps beforehand to prevent it. {He who survives should not forget about the threat of perishing, and one who enjoys a time of Ferrying Complete should not forget about the threat of Ferrying Incomplete [Hexagram 64].[6]}

PROVIDING THE SEQUENCE OF THE HEXAGRAMS

Once there is superiority over creatures [the masses, i.e., "subjects"], one is sure to ferry them [across troubles, i.e., "rescue them"]. This is why *Xiaoguo* [Minor Superiority, Hexagram 62] is followed by *Jiji* [Ferrying Complete].

THE HEXAGRAMS IN IRREGULAR ORDER

Jiji [Ferrying Complete] signifies stability.

First Yang

This one drags his wheels and wets his tail, so there is no blame. {First Yang is located at the very first position in Ferrying Complete, so it represents one who is at the start of ferrying himself across. Here at the start of ferrying, this one has not yet engaged in the act of doing so, thus he drags his wheels and lets his tail get wet. Although he has not yet made it to where it is easy going, his heart is free of any longing for what lies behind him, for this is someone who has his will fixed on escaping trouble and danger. In respect to moral stature, there is nothing about him that deserves blame.[7]}

COMMENTARY ON THE IMAGES

"This one drags his wheels," for his moral stature is blameless.

Second Yin

This wife loses her headdress, but she should not pursue it, for in seven days she will obtain it. {Second Yin abides in centrality and treads the path of righteousness [it is a yin line in a central, yin position], so it occupies the highest point of civility and enlightenment. Moreover, it is in resonance with Fifth Yang [the ruler of the hexagram], which means that it achieves the greatest glory possible for a yin. However, it is located between First Yang and Third Yang, with which, though contiguous, it does not get along well. Above it will not give carriage to Third Yang, and below it will not form a pair with First Yang. Here this yin is in all its prominence and glory located between two yang, with which, though contiguous, it does not get along. So how could such a one not suffer assault? This is why the text says "loses her headdress." The reason this one is called a "wife" [*fu*] is to indicate clearly that she herself has a husband and that it is other men who assault her. A *fu* is a headdress.[8] One who treads the middle path, holds fast to constancy and rectitude, and yet suffers assault will find that all will come to his aid. One who finds himself at a time of Ferrying Complete will not be allowed to follow a dao [path] of evil. Not only is this a time clearly governed by strict law, it is also an occasion when all will come to this one's aid. So those who robbed her will flee, and none will dare return. If one takes stock of such a situation, it should not take more than seven days, with no need for her to pursue her loss herself, for she will get it back as a matter of course.}

COMMENTARY ON THE IMAGES

That "she will obtain it" is because she follows the middle path [practices the Mean].

Third Yang

When Exalted Ancestor attacked the Demon Territory, it took him three years to conquer it. The petty man must not be used here. {Here at a time of Ferrying Complete, Third Yang abides at the end of civility and enlightenment. However, this one manages to tread the territory of his rightful position [as a yang line in a yang position], so this represent one who, though he abides at a time of decline, is still able to do ferrying [i.e., rescuing, saving the world]. When Exalted Ancestor attacked the Demon Territory, he was able to conquer it only after three years.[9] As it was a noble man who held such a position then, he was able to prevail, but if it had been a petty man, he would have ended up losing his state.}

COMMENTARY ON THE IMAGES

That it took three years to effect the conquest was because things were in such a state of decline.

Fourth Yin

To deal with the wet there are rags, but throughout the day this one should takes warning. {*Xu* [gorgeous clothes] should be read here as *ru* [wet]. Rags are things to be used to stop up leaks in a boat. Fourth Yin manages to tread upon its rightful territory [as a yin line in a yin position], but though it is contiguous with Third Yang and Fifth Yang, it does not get along well with them. This one's escape boat has a rent in it, yet he manages to ferry himself across because he has rags to deal with it. In order to keep himself whole while in the presence of those uncongenial to him, "throughout the day this one should take warning."}

COMMENTARY ON THE IMAGES

"Throughout the day this one should take warning," for there are things about which he should have misgivings.

Fifth Yang

The neighbor in the east slaughters an ox, but this falls short of the *yue* sacrifice of the neighbor in the west, which really provides that one with blessings. {An ox is the most splendid of sacrifices, and the *yue* is the most meager [consisting as it does of lowly wild vegetation].[10] Fifth Yang abides at a time of Ferrying Complete and occupies the exalted position, with all creatures [subjects] successfully ferried [i.e., all has been made right with the world]. So what should he do now? What he should concentrate on is nothing other than the offering of sacrifices. No greater form of sacrifice exists than the cultivation of virtue. That is why even pond grasses and such vegetation as duckweed and mugwort can be offered [by the virtuous] to gods and spirits. Thus [the *Shujing* (Book of history) says]: "The millet is not what provides the pleasing fragrance; it is only bright virtue that does so."[11] And this is why "the neighbor in the east slaughters an ox, but this falls short of the *yue* sacrifice of the neighbor in the west, which really provides that one with blessings."}

COMMENTARY ON THE IMAGES

The neighbor to the east who slaughters an ox is not as timely as the neighbor to the west. {Success lies in being in accord with the times and not in the richness of the sacrifice.} "[Such sacrifice] really provides that one with blessings," for great good fortune comes his way.

Top Yin

This one gets his head wet, which means danger. {Top Yin is located at the very end of Ferrying Complete. As the Dao of Ferrying Complete has petered out, one here proceeds into Ferrying Incomplete [Hexagram 64]. As one here proceeds into Ferrying Incomplete, his head is the first to violate the bounds [of Ferrying Complete]. He does not stop but advances too far, so he encounters trouble and danger. Thus the text says: "This one gets his head wet." It will not be long before he drowns, and there is no greater danger than that.}

COMMENTARY ON THE IMAGES

"This one gets his head wet, which means danger," so how could he last long?

NOTES

1. "Ferrying" translates *ji*, which is how Wang Bi and Kong Yingda interpret it, in both this hexagram and in *Weiji*, Hexagram 64. Cheng Yi and Zhu Xi prefer extended or derived meanings of *ji* for both hexagrams;

Cheng seems to read it as *jiuji*, "rescue," making the hexagram name "Rescue Complete" (i.e., "All Saved"), and Zhu reads it as *cheng*, "perfection," so making the hexagram name "Perfection Complete" (i.e., "All Things Perfectly Realized"). Although Wang's and Kong's "ferrying" also implies these meanings, their commentaries suggest that they read the text more literally.

2. This follows the commentaries of Wang Bi and Kong Yingda. Cheng Yi reads it differently: "*Jiji* is such that prevalence will apply only to small matters [or "only be slight"]." Zhu Xi thinks that *heng xiao* (the small enjoy prevalence) is a textual error for *xiaoheng*, which results in the reading: "*Jiji* is such that only slight prevalence may be had." See *Zhouyi zhezhong*, 8: 37b–38a.

3. This and all subsequent text set off in this manner is commentary by Wang Bi.

4. Cheng Yi's comments help to clarify the nature of Ferrying Complete:

> The affairs of the world are such that they are either in a state of advance or of retreat, and there is no one fixed principle to cover them. At the end of Ferrying [i.e., after all has been put right with the world], one should not try to advance things but come to a halt. However, this does not involve a perpetual halt but should be done because things are now in decline and chaos ensues, for the Dao of Ferrying Complete has already begun to peter out.

Cheng adds that things now are in such a state of flux that only a sage can handle things so that they do not degenerate completely. Everyone else is advised to stop and wait to see how things turn out. See *Zhouyi zhezhong*, 10: 46b–47a.

5. The lower trigram is *Li* (Cohesion), here signifying Fire, and the upper trigram is *Kan* (Sink Hole), representing Water.

6. Kong Yingda comments:

> Water positioned above fire is the image of a cook stove, which is used to finish the preparation of food and drink and which thus ferries one through life [i.e., rescues one, gives one succor, etc.]. . . . However, the Dao of Ferrying Complete is such that "in the beginning good fortune prevails," but "things might end in chaos." Thus "the noble man ponders the threat of calamity and takes steps beforehand to prevent it."

That is, as a cook stove must be tended with care to obtain proper results, so must one cultivate rectitude and follow the Mean to avoid calamity. See *Zhouyi zhengyi*, 6: 21b.

7. Cheng Yi is more forthcoming concerning the connection between halting here at the start of Ferrying Complete and the avoidance of blame:

> First Yang abides in this lowest position with its yang character. Not only is it in resonance with Fourth Yin, it also has a fiery nature

[as a yang line in the *Li* (Fire) trigram], so its ambition to advance is acute. However, this is a time of Ferrying Complete. If this one were to advance without cease, he would certainly reach the point where he would be subject to regret and blame. . . . Wheels are the means that allow one to move, but here instead one makes them drag so that he cannot advance. When an animal crosses water, it is sure to lift up its tail, for if it were to let its tail get wet, it could not cross. Here just at the start of Ferrying Complete, this one is able to halt his advance, and that is why he manages to avoid blame. If he did not realize that he should stop, he would end up incurring blame.

Zhu Xi concurs with Cheng's interpretation and adds that one here should take warning accordingly. See *Zhouyi zhezhong*, 8: 38b.

8. Zhu Xi says that *fu* here means "a lady's carriage curtain." See *Zhouyi zhezhong*, 8: 39a.

9. "Exalted Ancestor" (Gaozong) is identified with King Wu Ding of the Shang, whose reign is traditionally dated 1324–1266 B.C. The "Demon Territory" (Guifang) seems to have been a region to the northwest of the Shang state inhabited by a division of the Di, a people the Chinese regarded as barbarians. A brief discussion of the historical sources involved appears in Lou, *Wang Bi ji jiaoshi*, 2: 529 n. 9.

10. Cf. Hexagram 45, *Cui* (Gathering), Second Yin, and Wang Bi's commentary there.

11. Quoted from the *Zhoushu* (Book of Zhou), section 21 of the *Shujing* (Book of history); see Legge, *The Chinese Classics*, 3: 529.

䷿

未濟

Weiji [Ferrying Incomplete][1]
(*Kan* Below *Li* Above)

Judgment

Ferrying Incomplete is such that prevalence may be had. The young fox uses dry conditions to ferry itself across, but it still gets its tail wet. There is nothing at all fitting here.

COMMENTARY ON THE JUDGMENTS

"Ferrying Incomplete is such that prevalence may be had," that is, if the soft and weak achieves centrality [i.e., can practice the Mean]. {As the soft and weak [Fifth Yin] abides in centrality, it does not oppose itself to the hard and strong [Second Yang]. It draws upon the strength of the hard and strong and thereby achieves prevalence.[2]} "The young fox uses dry conditions to ferry itself across," but does not come farther out than the middle. {The young fox is incapable of crossing a large stream, so it must have dry conditions[3] before it is able to cross it. Here one is at a time of Ferrying Incomplete, so one must have access to the strength of the hard and strong—which can extract one from danger and trouble—before one is able to cross it [danger and trouble]. With dry conditions, it may be possible to ferry oneself across, but one is never able to escape from the midst of such danger.} "It still gets its tail wet," and "there is nothing at all fitting here," for such a one cannot carry on to the end. {Although the young fox is able to cross, it has no surplus strength, so when it tries to cross, it gets its tail wet. It exhausts its strength in this attempt and is unable to carry on to the end. That is, this one still lacks the wherewithal to ferry himself across such danger and trouble. One who can ferry himself across a time of Ferrying Incomplete must have surplus strength.} Although they are not in their rightful positions, the hard and strong and the soft and weak all form resonate relationships. {It is because the lines are all out of position that Ferrying Incomplete occurs. However, the hard and strong and the soft and weak all form resonate relationships, thus Ferrying becomes possible.}

COMMENTARY ON THE IMAGES

Fire positioned above Water: this constitutes the image of Ferrying Complete.[4] In the same way, the noble man carefully distinguishes among things and situates them in their correct places. {"Distinguishes among things and situates them in their correct places" means that he has each thing find the place that is right for it.[5]}

PROVIDING THE SEQUENCE OF THE HEXAGRAMS

Creatures [the masses, "subjects"] must never be hard-pressed. This is why *Jiji* [Ferrying Complete, Hexagram 63] is followed by *Weiji* [Ferrying Incomplete], with which the hexagrams come to an end.

THE HEXAGRAMS IN IRREGULAR ORDER

Weiji [Ferrying Incomplete] signifies man hard-pressed.

First Yin

This one gets his tail wet, which means humiliation. {First Yin is located at the beginning of Ferrying Incomplete, abiding at the very bottom of danger [*Kan* (Sink Hole)], and represents one who thus cannot ferry himself across. However, this one desires to go to his resonate partner [Fourth Yang], so when it tries to advance, it gets its body soaked. Ferrying Incomplete begins in such a way that it starts where Ferrying Complete [Hexagram 63] leaves off with Top Yin, which, though it gets its head wet, will not turn back. Here it [Top Yin of Ferrying Complete now become First Yin of Ferrying Incomplete] goes so far as to get its tail wet. It represents someone who does not know that he has reached his own limits. However, as a yin that occupies this lowly position, First Yin is not one to advance to the point of overreaching but merely tries to fulfill its innate sense of purpose [in joining with Fourth Yang]. When such a one encounters difficulty, it is capable of turning back. This is why the text does not say "misfortune." One at First Yin finds the scope of his actions already determined, yet he only turns back when he encounters the inevitable difficulties involved. This is indeed the height of stupid obstinacy! Thus the text says "humiliation."}

COMMENTARY ON THE IMAGES

"This one gets his tail wet," for he does not know that he has reached his limits.

Second Yang

This one drags his wheels. Such constancy means good fortune. {The character of Second Yang is hard and strong, and it treads the middle path [practices the Mean]. Moreover, it is in a resonate relationship with Fifth Yin. Although the character of Fifth Yin is yin and weak, Second Yang identifies its interests with Fifth Yin and does not try to usurp responsibilities on its own. Here at this time of Ferrying Incomplete such a one finds himself in the midst of danger and difficulty. Imbued with strength and centrality, he is invested with responsibilities. As such, Second Yang represents someone who can rescue the times from danger and difficulty, someone who can put things in order and make them go smoothly again. One may use strength to save the world from trouble, but the way to deal with that trouble lies in rectifying things while at the same time avoiding any violation of the Mean. This is why the text says: "This one drags his wheels. Such constancy means good fortune."[6]}

COMMENTARY ON THE IMAGES

That the constancy of Second Yang results in good fortune is because he adheres to the Mean in carrying out the rectification of things.

Third Yin

Ferrying Incomplete is such that to set out to do something here would mean misfortune, but it is fitting to cross the great river. {Because of its yin character and because it is out of its rightful place [it is a yin line in a yang position] and so abiding in danger, Third Yin cannot ferry itself across. If such a one, with his incorrect character and lacking sufficient strength to ferry himself across, were to try to advance here, he would lose his life. Thus the text says: "To set out to do something here would mean misfortune." However, Second Yang can save others from danger and difficulty, so one at Third Yin pairs up with Second Yang, discards his own chances, and entrusts himself to Second Yang. If he rides atop Second Yang in this way, how could he ever drown? And why would he ever find Ferrying Incomplete a source of grief? Thus the text says: "It is fitting to cross the great river."}

COMMENTARY ON THE IMAGES

"Ferrying Incomplete is such that to set out to do something here would mean misfortune," for this one is not in his rightful position.

Fourth Yang

Constancy results in good fortune, and thus regret vanishes. As a burst of thunder, this one attacks the Demon Territory,[7] for which after three years he is rewarded with a large state. {Fourth Yang may find itself at a time of Ferrying Incomplete, but one here has emerged out of danger and difficulty [i.e., he is out of the *Kan* (Sink Hole) trigram] and abides at the beginning of civility and enlightenment [the *Li* (Cohesion) trigram, representing fire, brightness, intelligence, etc.]. This one embodies hardness and strength and, as such, draws near to the exalted one [Fifth Yin, the ruler of the hexagram]. Although where he treads is not his rightful position [it is a yang line in a yin position], his will is fixed on righteousness, and this is why "constancy results in good fortune, and thus regret [at being in the wrong position] vanishes." Here one's will can be realized, for no one withstands his use of martial force. Thus the text says: "As a burst of thunder, this one attacks the Demon Territory." This attack on the Demon Territory is a campaign that determines whether the realm rises or falls. Thus each time the realm reaches such a life or death crisis, such a one should choose this course as the right thing to do. Fourth Yang is located at the beginning of civility and enlightenment and has just begun to emerge from danger and difficulty, thus his virtue has not yet reached the peak of its powers. Thus the text says "after three years" [i.e., the conquest takes three years, after which he gets his reward]. Fifth Yin occupies the exalted position with softness and weakness and in character embodies the height of civility and enlightenment, so one here does not grab credit for the achievements of others. Thus he rewards Fourth Yang with a large state.}

COMMENTARY ON THE IMAGES

"Constancy results in good fortune, and thus regret vanishes," for this one's will is realized.

Fifth Yin

Constancy results in good fortune, and thus this one avoids regret. The glory of the noble man is due to the sincerity he has, which brings good fortune. {Fifth Yin occupies the exalted position with softness and weakness and is located at the height of civility and enlightenment, for this is the ruler of the Ferrying Incomplete hexagram. Thus it is that this one must behave with rectitude, for only then should he have good fortune. And only with such good fortune should he manage to avoid regret. Thanks to his character, which consists of softness and compliance, civility and enlightenment, this one occupies the exalted position in such a way that he entrusts responsibility to the capable and does not attempt to take charge of everything himself. He tempers military action with his civil virtues and modifies hardness and strength with his tenderness, all of which truly represents "the glory of the noble man." Such a one entrusts responsibility to another because of his ability and does not harbor suspicions about him. Thus that other [Fourth Yang] exerts himself to the utmost and achieves meritorious success in the conquest [over the Demon Territory, i.e., the world's troubles]. Thus the text says: "The sincerity he has . . . brings good fortune."}

COMMENTARY ON THE IMAGES

"The glory of the noble man" casts such light that it brings good fortune.

Top Yang

This one has confidence and so engages in drinking wine, about which there is no blame, but he might get his head wet, for this one with his confidence could do violence to what is right. {Here at the very end of Ferrying Incomplete there is about to be a return to Ferrying Complete [Hexagram 63]. The Dao of Ferrying Complete is such that positions are filled only with people proper to them. As positions are to be filled then only with people proper to them, this one can have confidence in his own chances without the least doubt. Thus he can take his ease here [and wait for the times to change]. This is why the text says: "This one has confidence and so engages in drinking wine, about which there is no blame." As one at Top Yang can place his trust in others, he manages to achieve a happy, carefree state of mind and does not grieve about the way things decline. However, he may not grieve about the way things decline, but if he were to overindulge himself in the pursuit of pleasure, he would eventually come to violate the rules of propriety, that is, through having too much confidence, he would do violence to what is right. Thus the text says: "He might get his head wet [i.e., fall into the world's troubles], for this one with his confidence could do violence to what is right."}

COMMENTARY ON THE IMAGES

If this one were to get his head wet because of drinking wine, it would be because he does not know enough to keep to the rules of propriety.

NOTES

1. See Hexagram 63, *Jiji* (Ferrying Complete), note 1.

2. This and all subsequent text set off in this manner is commentary by Wang Bi.

3. "Dry conditions" translates *qi*. Cheng Yi glosses *qi* as *yi* (standing upright, i.e., bold and brave), that is, the young fox lacks the caution of a mature fox, so it dares to cross a stream that it should not—and so comes to grief. Cheng adds that prevalence can be had here at a time of Ferrying Incomplete only if one exercises appropriate caution. Zhu Xi differs from both Wang Bi and Cheng Yi and glosses *qi* as *ji* (almost), so his reading of the text seems to be: "The young fox almost manages to ferry itself across but gets its tail wet. . . ." See *Zhouyi zhezhong*, 8: 42b–43a and 10: 49b.

4. The lower trigram is *Kan* (Sink Hole), signifying Water, and the upper trigram is *Li* (Cohesion), signifying Fire.

5. Kong Yingda comments:

> When Fire is above Water, it cannot be used to cook food and so ferry creatures [succor them]. . . . The noble man observes a time of Ferrying Incomplete, when the hard and strong and the soft and weak are all out of their proper positions, and, using the virtue of caution, carefully distinguishes among all creatures [subjects] and has each one take its [his] proper place. This allows them all to make their positions secure. In so doing, he achieves ferrying [saves the world].

See *Zhouyi zhengyi*, 6: 24a.

6. Kong Yingda says that "drags his wheels" refers to "his struggle against difficulty," i.e., his sincere devotion to the sovereign and to the fulfillment of his duty to save the world. See *Zhouyi zhengyi*, 6: 24b.

7. For an explanation of "Demon Territory," see Hexagram 63, *Jiji* (Ferrying Complete), Third Yang, and note 9 there.

Bibliography

Primary Sources

Jing Fang 京房. *Zhouyi Jingshi zhangju* 周易京氏章句 (Mr. Jing's sentence by sentence commentary on the *Changes of the Zhou*). Edited by Ma Guohan 馬國翰. *Yuhan shanfang jiyishu* 玉函山房輯佚書 ed.

Kong Yingda 孔穎達. *Zhouyi zhengyi* 周易正義 (Correct meaning of the *Changes of the Zhou*). In Ruan Yuan, ed., *Shisanjing zhushu* 十三經注疏 (Commentaries and subcommentaries on the thirteen classics). 1815 woodblock ed. Reprint. Taibei: Yiwen yinshuguan, 1955.

Laozi. See Wang Bi, *Laozi Daodejing zhu*.

Li Dingzuo 李鼎祚. *Zhouyi jijie* 周易集解 (Collected exegeses on the *Changes of the Zhou*). *Congshu jicheng chubian* 叢書集成初編 ed.

Li Guangdi 李光地, ed. *Yuzuan Zhouyi zhezhong* 御纂周易折中 (Compiled upon imperial Order: Equitable judgments on interpretations of the *Changes of the Zhou*). Woodblock ed. of 1715. In Yan Lingfeng 嚴靈峰, ed., *Yijing jicheng* 易經集成 (Collectanea of works on the *Classic of Changes*). Taibei: Chengwen, 1975.

Liji 禮記 (Book of rites). In Ruan Yuan, ed., *Shisanjing zhushu* 十三經注疏 (Commentaries and subcommentaries on the thirteen classics. 1815 woodblock ed. Reprint. Taibei: Yiwen yinshuguan, 1955.

Lou Yulie 樓宇烈, ed. *Wang Bi ji jiaoshi* 王弼集校釋 (Critical edition of the works of Wang Bi with explanatory notes). 2 vols. Beijing: Zhonghua shuju, 1980.

Lu Deming 陸德明. *Jingdian shiwen* 經典釋文 (Explication of the texts of the classics). *Congshu jicheng chubian* 叢書集成初編 ed.

Lunyu 論語 (Analects). *Lunyu yinde* 論語引得 (A concordance to the *Analects* of Confucius). Harvard–Yenching Institute Sinological Index Series Supplement No. 16. Reprint. Taibei: Chengwen, 1966.

Ma Rong 馬融. *Zhouyi Mashi zhuan* 周易馬氏傳 (Mr. Ma's commentary on the *Changes of the Zhou*). Edited by Ma Guohan 馬國翰. *Yuhan shanfang jiyishu* 玉函山房輯佚書 ed.

Mengzi 孟子 (Mencius). *Mengzi yinde* 孟子引得 (A concordance to the *Mencius*). Harvard–Yenching Institute Sinological Index Series Supplement No. 17. Reprint. Taibei: Chengwen, 1966.

Ruan Yuan 阮元, ed. *Shisanjing zhushu* 十三經注疏 (Commentaries and subcommentaries on the thirteen classics). 1815 woodblock ed. Reprint. Taibei: Yiwen yinshuguan, 1955.

Shijing 詩經 (Book of Odes). *Maoshi yinde* 毛詩引得 (A concordance to the Mao recension of the *Book of Odes*). Harvard–Yenching Institute Sinological Index Supplement No. 9. Cambridge: Harvard University Press, 1966.

Sima Qian 司馬遷. *Shiji* (Records of the grand historian) 史記. Beijing: Zhonghua shuju, 1958.

Sun Xingyan 孫星衍. *Zhouyi jijie* 周易集解 (Collected exegeses on the *Changes of the Zhou*). *Congshu jicheng chubian* 叢書集成初編 ed.

Wang Bi 王弼. *Laozi Daodejing zhu* 老子道德經注 (Commentary on the *Laozi* or *Daodejing*). In vol. 1 of Lou Yulie, ed., *Wang Bi ji jiaoshi*. Beijing: Zhonghua shuju, 1980.

——. *Zhouyi lueli* 周易略例 (General remarks on the *Changes of the Zhou*). In vol. 2 of Lou Yulie, ed., *Wang Bi ji jiaoshi*. Beijing: Zhonghua shuju, 1980.

——. *Zhouyi zhu* 周易注 (Commentary on the *Changes of the Zhou*). In vols. 1 and 2 of Lou Yulie, ed., *Wang Bi ji jiaoshi*. Beijing: Zhonghua shuju, 1980.

Wang Xianqian 王先謙. *Xunzi jijie* 荀子集解 (Collected commentaries on the *Xunzi*). *Zhongguo xueshu mingzhu* 中國學術名著 ed. Taibei: Zhonghua shuju, n.d.

Yu Yue 俞樾. *Qunjing pingyi* 群經平議 (Equitable discussions on the classics). *Huang Qing jingjie xubian* ed.

Zheng Xuan 鄭玄. *Zhouyi Zhengzhu* 周易鄭注 (Zheng's commentary to the *Changes of the Zhou*). *Congshu jicheng chubian* 叢書集成初編 ed.

Zhouyi zhezhong. See Li Guangdi.

Zhuangzi yinde 莊子引得 (A concordance to *Chuang-tzu*). Harvard–

Yenching Institute Sinological Index Series Supplement No. 20. Cambridge: Harvard University Press, 1956.

Secondary Sources in Chinese and Japanese

Gao Heng 高亨. *Zhouyi gujing jinzhu* 周易古經今注 (Modern annotations to the ancient classic, the *Changes of the Zhou*). 1934. Reprint. Beijing: Zhonghua shuju, 1984.

Itō Tōgai 伊藤東涯 (Itō Nagatane 長胤). *Shūeki kyōyoku tsūkai* 周易經翼通解 (Comprehensive exegesis on the classic text and wings of the *Changes of the Zhou*). *Kanbun taikei* 漢文大系 ed.

Qian Zhongshu 錢鍾書. *Guanzhui bian* 管龍 (The pipe-awl collection). 4 vols. Beijing: Zhonghua shuju, 1979.

Works in Western Languages

Bergeron, Maria-Ina. *Wang Pi: Philosophe du non-avoir*. Taibei/Paris: Ricci Institute, 1986.

Blofeld, John, trans. *I Ching: The Book of Change*. New York: Dutton, 1968.

Bodde, Derk. *Essays on Chinese Civilization*. Edited by Charles Le Blanc and Dorothy Borei. Princeton: Princeton University Press, 1981.

Chan, Wing-tsit. *A Source Book in Chinese Philosophy*. Princeton: Princeton University Press, 1963.

Creel, Herrlee G. *Origins of Statecraft in China: The Western Chou Empire*. Chicago: University of Chicago Press, 1970.

Fung, Yu-lan. *A History of Chinese Philosophy*. Translated by Derk Bodde. 2 vols. Princeton: Princeton University Press, 1953.

Griffith, Samual B., trans. *Sun Tzu: The Art of War*. London, Oxford, New York: Oxford University Press, 1971.

Kunst, Richard. *The Original "Yijing": A Text, Phonetic Transcription, Translation, and Indexes, with Sample Glosses*. Ann Arbor: University Microfilms International, 1985.

Lau, D. C., trans. *The Analects*. Harmondsworth, England: Penguin, 1979.

Legge, James, trans. *The Chinese Classics*. 5 vols. Oxford: Clarendon Press, 1893–95. Reprinted Hong Kong: Hong Kong University Press, 1970.

———. *I Ching: Book of Changes*. Edited with introduction and study guide by Ch'u Chai and Winberg Chai. New Hyde Park, New York: University Books, 1964.

———. *I Ching: Book of Changes*. 1882. Reprint. New York: Dover, 1965.

——. *The Yi King; or Book of Changes.* Oxford: Clarendon Press, 1882.

Liu Yiqing. *Shih-shuo Hsin-yü: A New Account of Tales of the World.* Translated by Richard B. Mather. Minneapolis: University of Minnesota Press, 1976.

Peterson, Willard. "Making Connections: 'Commentary on the Attached Verbalizations' of the *Book of Changes,*" *Harvard Journal of Asiatic Studies* 42 (1982): 67–116.

Shaughnessy, Edward. *The Composition of the* Zhouyi. Ann Arbor: University Microfilms International, 1983.

Smith, Kidder, Peter K. Bol, Joseph A. Adler, and Don J. Wyatt. *Sung Dynasty Uses of the* I Ching. Princeton: Princeton University Press, 1990.

Wilhelm, Richard, trans. *The I Ching or Book of Changes.* Translated by Cary F. Baynes. 3d. ed. Princeton: Princeton University Press, 1967.

——. *I Ging: Das Buch der Wandlungen.* Jena: Eugen Diederichs, 1924.

Glossary

an. safety, security; still, content 安
bagua. eight trigrams 八卦
baixing. the common folk 百性
bao. wrap, wrapping 包
baoju. straw for wrapping 包苴
bei. cowrie 貝
  back 背
ben. fundamental; original substance 本
benshi. basic nature, one's "real stuff" 本實
bi. well-disposed; pair(ed) 比
  ladle 匕
bian. change 變
bihuai. flaw 敝壞
bilin. mean-spirited, narrowness, bias, miserliness 鄙吝
bing. flaw, failing 病
bing shou qi fu. this one shall receive all his blessings 並受其福
binke. meat for honored guests (the second of the three categories) 賓客
bo. peel; deterioration 剝
boluo. peel off 剝落
boma. piebald horse 駁馬
bu. not 不
  screen 蔀
budu. to divine 卜度
buhuo qishen. does not obtain the other person 不穫其身
bujue. to divine 卜決
buke ruhe ye. nothing at all could be done about it 不可如何也
buli you youwang. it is not fitting should one set out to do something here 不利有攸往
buning fang lai. those in places not at peace then come 不寧方來
buren. inhumane 不仁

bushan. not good 不善
busu bao ye. not before he had had his fill 不素飽也
butong. dissimilar 不同
buxian buwei. neither take the lead nor initiate action 不先不爲
buzishi. does not neglect his own 不自失
cai. talent 才
caizhi. control 裁制
cang. withdrawal, disengagement 藏
canwu. intersperse 參伍
chan. expose, reveal 闡
chanda. expand, make great 闡大
chang. constant norm 常
 field 場
 fragrant wine 鬯
chaoxiang. make a court (sacrificial) offering 朝享
che. split, burst 坼
cheng. carry 承
 it will do; perfection 成
 ride; supersede 乘
cheng dong. supports the actions 承動
cheng ming. successfully carry out orders 成命
chengming. the perfect commendation 成命
chengshi. sincerity 誠實
chengyi. sincerity of will 誠意
chifu. red ceremonial garment (knee covering) 赤紱
chong. emptiness 沖
 larval 蟲
 repeated, double 重
chong jun zhi pao. provisions for the sovereign's kitchens (the third of the three categories) 充君之庖
chou. companion 仇
chouzuo. synchronize with things, harmonious relations 酬酢
chu. kitchen 廚
chu lei. correspond analogously 觸類
chuan. be quick 遄
chui qi yi. keeping his wings folded, drooped, lowered 垂其翼
churu. ins and outs 出入
ci. lodging 次
 phrases 辭
cishe. palace hostel 次舍
cong. follow; obey 從
cong gui. accommodate something noble 從貴
cui. oppress, frustrate; retreat 摧

cuoran. reverence and care; crosswise/confusedly 錯然
da. great, greatness, growth 大
dafang. grand design 大方
dahe. great harmony 大和
dang. clique, party 黨
  ought; it is right that 當
Dao, dao. Way, way; Path, path, route 道
dao ji. the Dao will be saved 道濟
daqi. great instrument, i.e., Heaven; great vessel 大器
daren. great man 大人
datong. great community 大同
  great thoroughfare 大通
daxu. great void 大虛
de. obtain 得
  virtue 德
de qi zi fu zhi di. obtain a place where he has to use his axe 得其資斧之地
de yong fu zhi di. obtain a place where he has to use his axe 得用斧之地
dexing. moral conduct 德行
di. arrive at; go so far as 抵
  Earth 地
  enemy 敵
  secondary wife 娣
difang. place 地方
dong. act, action 動
dongchu. behavior 動出
dongnan yu. farthest reaches in the southeast 東南隅
dou. ceremonial vessel 豆
du. poison/to poison 毒
dui. counterpart 對
dun ren. being genuine about benevolence 敦仁
duo. reckon; measure 度
duyin. reading pronunciation 讀音
er. two 二
fan. return 反
  violation 犯
fang. guard against 防
  square; place; domain 方
fangjin. guard against and prevent 防禁
fangqie. only when, as soon as 方且
fangqie lai. as soon as it arrives 方且來
fangzhi. ward off 防止

fanshen. reflect upon himself 反身
faze. emulate 法則
fei. fat; rich 肥
flying 飛
fei tianxia zhizhi. except when the world is perfectly governed 非天下至治
feiniao yi yin. the flying bird loses its voice 飛鳥遺音
feiyi suosi. unsettled thoughts 匪夷所思
fen. remove; geld 豶
fen qi ya. remove its tusks 豶其牙
fengshun tian xiumei zhi ming. he obeys the excellent will of Heaven 奉順天休美之命
fenruo. large-scale, the large scale 紛若
fenshi. gelded boar 豶豕
fou. otherwise; not 否
fou zang. not good 否臧
fu. be contrary; go off 拂
confidence; proof 孚
cover 覆
headdress 茀
knee covering 紱
sincere, trust 孚
skin 膚
wife 婦
fu gong su. overturns all its pottage 覆公餗
fufu. husband and wife 夫婦
gan. prompt, promote, provoke, move 感
tree trunk 幹
gandou. dried meat for the sacrificial vessel 乾豆
gang. hardness, strength; hard and strong 剛
gang rou fendong er ming. the hard and the soft achieve clarity by taking separate action 剛柔分動而明
ganying. prompt/provoke a response 感應
ge. hide, skin; to skin, to get rid of 革
keep away 隔
ge yan san jiu. addressing themselves to Radical Change, the three say that they will accede to it 革言三就
gen qi bei. Restraint takes place with the back 艮其背
geng. seventh of the heavenly branches; laws issued; issuance of orders 庚
gong. all, public; duke 公
leather thongs; bind tight 鞏
musical note 宮
gonglun. consensus 公論

gu. horn cover 梏
in the past, before 故
strengthen, make secure 固
gua. hexagram 卦
impediment; tie up 括
melon 瓜
guabian. trigram change (method) 卦變
guaci. hexagram statement 卦辭
guai. at odds 乖
guaming. hexagram name 卦名
guan. self-control 官
guangda. bright and great 光大
gui. exalted, superior, (something) noble, nobility, estimable 貴
give in marriage; (cause to) return 歸
jade tablet 珪
plain and simple vessel 簋
guishen. gods and spirits;
negative and positive spiritual forces 鬼神
guo. overreaching; superiority; mistake, error, crime; passage 過
state, domain 國
hai. harm 害
han. soar 翰
hanru. white; not budging; lingering there so white 翰如
he. detain, check, obstruct 閡
form, formation; come together; agree 合
join the teeth 嗑
what; what a/how (very much) 何
why not?, i.e., surely 盍
he qi guang tong qi chen. soften your light and become one with the dusty world 和其光通其塵
he weizhe ye. what does it do? 何爲者也
heguang liutong. he softens his own light and identifies with them completely 和光流通
heji shengwu. bring harmony to the living creatures and keep them well regulated 和齊生物
heng. prevalence 亨
heng xiao. the small enjoy prevalence 亨小
heyi. with peace and ease, i.e., accommodatingly 和易
hou. skilled archer; chief 候
hu. defend, take care of oneself 護
hu bian. tiger change 虎變
hua. transformation 化
huai. cherish; be attracted 懷
huaixu. hold in readiness 懷畜

huan. mitigate (the punishment) 緩
huan qiqun. this one disperses for all 渙其群
huan you qiu. at a time of Dispersion there is a mountain of . . . 渙有丘
huang. yellow; brown 黃
huangmen shilang. director of the Chancellery 黃門侍郎
huanran. completely relaxed 渙然
hui. banner, flag 麾
opportunity 會
remorse 悔
hui qian. fly the banner of Modesty 麾 [撝] 謙
huilin. remorse and regret 悔吝
huocai zhi zi. wealth in property and money 貨財之資
huti. overlapping trigrams (method) 互體
ji. averse to 忌
borderline 際
continue, continuously, ceaselessly 繼
examine 稽
ferrying; rescue 濟
good fortune 吉
incipience; almost; then 幾
quickly; anxiety; illness; fault,flaw 疾
table 几
ji hui. fear or deviancy 忌回
onset of regret; with regret here 幾悔
jia. beauty 佳
come/go 假
first of the heavenly branches; laws issued; issuance of orders 甲
jian. double 洊
inferior, humble, mean and lowly 賤
strong; strength and dynamism 健
jianchou. second lunar month 建丑
jiang. would . . . 將
jiangchang. field boundary 疆場
jiangyi. field boundary 疆埸
jianji. save everything together 兼濟
jianjian. increase to great numbers 戔戔
jianshen. ninth lunar month 建申
jianwei. eighth lunar month 建未
jiao. horn(s) 角
whole foot shackles 校
jiaocuo. crosswise 交錯
jibing. illness 疾病
jie. all; in all cases 皆
bind up 結

differentiate, break up, disperse 解
pure 潔
wail 嗟
subtle, intermediate stages; small matters/faults; ward off 介
jie ti ranhou. only after one has in all cases exercised prudence 皆惕然後
jie yu shi. harder than rock 介于石
jiexian. border, borderline 界線
jijie. relate, form a relationship 際接
jin. the present 今
make progress, move forward, advance 進
prohibit 禁
jinfu. man strong as metal; wealthy man 金夫
jinzhi. ban 禁制
jing. passivity, repose, quiescence 靜
reverence 敬
warp; immutable rule; right path 經
jinglun. warp and woof 經綸
jingqi. consolidation of material force into essence 精氣
jingwei. warp and woof 經緯
jingyi. perfect concepts 精義
jingzhi. stasis, passivity 靜止
jiu. blame 咎
yield 就
jiuji. rescue 救濟
jiwei. incipient and imperceptible beginnings of things 幾微
jixiang. perform sacrifices 祭享
jizi. wail 齎咨
ju. gather, come together 聚
jue. goblet, bronze ceremonial vessel, an emblem of noble rank 爵
juewei. noble rank 爵位
julei chanrao. ensnared and entangled 拘纍纏繞
jun. equal, alike 均
junzi. noble man 君子
jushang. raise up 舉上
kanren. worthy of office 勘任
kao. ponder, consider 考
kelin. regrettable 可吝
kezhen. may practice constancy 可貞
kong. in vain; to no purpose 空
kou. harassment; banditry, robbers, enemies 寇
kuan. lenient, leniency 寬
kuanyu. rich; resourceful 寬裕
kui. thoroughfare 逵
kun. tired 困

lai. come, the future; attract, to be attracted 來
lai zhang. arrives here and manifests himself 來章
laoguo. too old 老過
lei. deprived of power; weak 羸
leikun. tired out 羸困
li. principle, principles 理
fitness, advantage 利
propriety, decorum 禮
one-third mile 里
cling, clinging 麗
lian. involvement; linked 連
libu lang. director of the Ministry of Personnel 吏部郎
libu shangshu. president of the Ministry of Personnel 吏部尚書
lie. icy clear 冽
liming. eligible for honors 禮命
lin. look down on, oversee; approach 臨
neighbors 鄰
regret, remorse; base, baseness; hard going (遴) 吝
ling. hill 陵
linse. narrowness, bias, miserliness 吝嗇
lixi. rupture, break, rent (as in clothing) 離隙
longma. dragon-horse 龍馬
lu. highland 陸
lü. frequent 屢
major key 律
minor key 呂
luo ji. get himself entangled 羅己
lüshi. repeatedly fail 屢失
mao. lush; lushly growing, lush growth 茂
mei. dim 昧
sleeves 袂
splendid; goodness 美
upper back 脢
mianquan. cheekbones 面權
ming. name 名
dark 冥
destiny; order, command 命
intelligence; light; enlightened, enlightenment 明
moye. no particular night, i.e., night after night 莫夜
mu. cloak, curtain 幕
evening 暮
na. take in 納
nei. inside, inner; inner/lower (trigram) 內
neng. is able 能

ni. brake 柅
oppose, reverse, go upstream/against the current; predict, anticipate 逆
nidu. predict, anticipate 逆睹
nie. bite 齧
niliao. predict, anticipate 逆料
ning. make firm 凝
nishou. head of rebellion 逆首
pang. side 旁
pangpang. the sound of a drum roll, i.e., a swelling, overwhelming sound; fullness, plenitude 旁旁
paochu. kitchen 庖廚
paogua. bottle gourd 匏瓜
pei. be worthy of 配
shade, shelter 沛
peng. plenitude 彭
coterie; people who share the same tradition of teaching 朋
peng ren. cook food 烹飪
pengpeng. the sound of a drum roll, i.e., a swelling, overwhelming sound; fullness, plenitude 彭彭
pengyou. friends 朋右
pi. obstruction, obstructed 否
pi zang xiong. otherwise, whether it fails or succeeds, it will result in misfortune 否臧凶
pian. partiality 偏
pianpian. fluttering 翩翩
pin. with urgency; scowl 頻
pincu. anxious and hurried; scowl 頻蹙
pinshuo. frequent 頻數
pou. lessen, decrease; gather 裒
pu. uncarved block; pristine, unsullied selflessness 朴
qi. basket willow 杞
boundary 圻
dry conditions 汔
material force, spirit; vapors 氣
qi xing wo. its form is drenched 其形渥
qi xuan. the cycle starts back 其旋
qi yi. proper behavior here 其義
qi zai er hu. is he not located at Second Yang? 其在二乎
qi zai wu hu. is he not located at Fifth Yang? 其在五乎
qian. modesty 謙
qianchong. modesty 謙沖
qiangbao. violent brute 強暴
qianxiao. poor, meager 淺小

qijue. proper perch 其桷
qijun zhi mei. the sovereign's sleeves 其君之袂
qing. innate tendency; emotions 情
qing pi wei tai. turn *Pi* (Obstruction) over to make *Tai* (Peace) 傾否爲泰
qingju mao. appearance of lightly fluttering on the air 輕舉貌
qingli. reality and principles 情理
qingtan. pure conversation 淸談
qingyu. selfish desire 情欲
qiu. cheekbones 頄
  hill 丘
qu. inclination, tendency 趣
raoyu. rich, abundant, wealthy 饒裕
ren. benevolence, humaneness 仁
ren qizhen. relies on the truth that is in him 任其眞
rencai. personal talent 人才
renxin suo zhu. that which controls the human heart and mind 人心所主
ri. day, daily 日
rongyi. easily 容易
rou. softness, weakness; soft and weak 柔
roushun. yielding and compliant 柔順
ru. gorgeous clothes 繻
  like 如
  pull up 茹
  wet 濡
ru shen. entrance into the numinous 入神
ruo. accordingly; as 若
san. disperse, dispersal/separation 散
san gong. scattering his person, i.e., running away 散躬
san wu. by threes and fives 三五
sandi. dispersive ground 散地
sang. mulberry 桑
sanshi. disperse, dispersal/separation 散釋
shan. human/moral goodness; morally good/just 善
shanchu. positions/handles himself well 善處
shang. above, superior; up, upper 上
  esteem; be worthy of; assist 尙
  musical note; deliberate how to deal with 商
shang he zhi. Top Yang sharing its goal with it 上合志
shangdi. Supreme Deity; Divine Ruler on High 上帝
shangjiu. ninth in the top place 上九
shangliang. consider 商量
shangshi. look upward 上視

shangshu lang. Secretarial Court Gentleman 尙書郎
shaoguo. too young 少過
she ni qu shun. one spares those that double back and takes only those that go with the drive 舍 [捨] 逆取順
shen. caution 愼
numinous 神
sheng. activities 生
prosperity 盛
sage 聖
sheng hu dongzhe ye. generated from the way the lines move; generated from the way one acts 生乎動者也
shengduo. extensive, in great numbers 盛多
shengui. spirit-tortoise 神龜
shenmi zhuyi. arcane mysticism 神秘注義
shenming. the numinous and the bright, i.e., the gods; intelligence 神明
shenwu er busha zhe. who had divine martial power yet did not indulge in killing 神武而不殺者
shi. bite 噬
cause 使
lose 失
phenomena; matters 事
secretary/scribe 史
substance; sincerity 實
time, moment 時
shi bi buyi dao. to disregard the Dao when beginning Closeness 始比不以道
shi buyou qishen. this is what it means by not having one's own body 是不有其身
shi jiude. subsist on old virtue 食舊德
shi yi qing wei pi. this is the start of dealing with Obstruction by overturning it 始以傾爲否
shishu. flying squirrel; big rat 鼫鼠
shiyi. servant, subordinate/to employ as a servant or subordinate 使役
shou. hand 手
shu. well done, cooked (food) 熟
writing 書
shudu. limits 數度
shui/shuo. order/speak 說
shun. compliance, compliancy, compliant behavior 順
shun tian xiu ming. he obeys the will of Heaven and so brings out the beauty inherent in life 順天休命
shusan. relaxed, free of worry 舒散
si. here; then 斯
idea, thought; think to 思

su. quickly 速
social mores 俗
sui. years of age 歲
suishi. following the moment, when the moment is right 隨時
suisui xuxu. defiant and recalcitrant 睢睢盱盱
suixu. eyes haughty with pride; wide-eyed with hope 睢盱
sun. compliance, compliant behavior; put in, made to enter 巽
sun ru ye. Compliance provides entrance 巽入也
sunqu. cut down/away 損去
suo. place 所
suoyou zhi shi. that which one has to do, i.e., one's proper concern 所有之事
tai. facility 泰
taiji. great ultimate 太極
tailang. Court Gentleman 臺郎
ti. alarm, apprehension 惕
constituent trigram; substance 體
far, far out 逖
put forth new shoots from an old stem 稊
Tian, *tian.* Heaven; the sky 天
tiangan. heavenly branches decimal cycle 天干
tianwei. place of Heaven 天位
tianxia. all under Heaven, the world, etc. 天下
tianzi. Son of Heaven 天子
ticha. understand 體察
ting. listen; obey 聽
tizhi. material substance 體質
tong. commensuration; continuity; interaction, cooperation 通
tong qi bian. they allowed things to undergo the free flow of change 通其變
tongda. clear, free 通達
tongmen. same school of teaching 同門
tongniu. young ox 童牛
tongzhi. people who share the same goal 同志
tou hu. pitch (arrows) into the pot 投壺
tu. earth 土
merely; pointless 徒
tuan. Judgment 彖
tuiyuan. trace to the origins; plumb the foundation 推原
wai. outside, outer; outer/upper (trigram) 外
wang. hope, expectation 望
lost 亡
the past; set forth, set out 往
trap; negate; not 罔

wang jian lin. if he were to set out he would experience hard going 往見吝
wang lin. if he were to set out he would experience hard going 往吝
wang san xi ming. his sovereign confers a threefold commendation on him; his sovereign confers commendations on him three times (i.e., repeatedly) 王三錫命
wang yong heng yu xishan (Qishan). the king/sovereign should use this opportunity to extend his prevalence to the western mountains (Mount Qi) 王用亨于西山 (岐山)
wang yong sanqu shi qian qin. the king/sovereign has game driven three times and forgoes those that come before him 王用三驅失前禽
wanglai. alternation 往來
wangwo. forget the self 忘我
wei. contrariness; violate 違
danger 危
guard 衛
make; cause 爲
position, rank 位
small, subtle 微
spuriousness 僞
weifu. never for his own wealth 未富
weiji huixie. fear (as a restraint) and perversity/deviance 畏忌回邪
weixiao. small, subtle matters 微小
wen. pattern; culture 文
wende. civilized and virtuous 文德
wenming. civilization; civility and enlightenment 文明
wo. soak(ed), drench(ed) 渥
severe (punishment) 剭
wu. nonbeing 無
shaman 巫
wu qi er bushi. no boundary fails to open up 無圻而不釋
wu shi. disengagement from matters 無事
wu shou. lacked the means to be a leader 無首
wu suo zhong. there is nothing he can do to share in this its final stage 無所終
wujishu. five skills rodent, i.e., flying squirrel 五技鼠
wujiu. be without blame 無咎
wusi. without thought 無思
wuwei. avoid/no purposeful action 無爲
wuwo. no self 無我
wuxi. shaman/prognosticator 巫覡
wuxing. five elements 五行
wuyong yongzhen. one must not use this one where perpetual constancy is required 勿用永貞

wuzao. strive to be frivolous; strive to indulge one's impatience 務躁
xi. practice; constant 習
xia. below, inferior, subordinate 下
xiadaifu. junior grand Master 下大夫
xian. all; in all cases 咸
danger 險
midsection 限
restrain; train 閑
worthy, worthiness 賢
xiang. each other 相
image 象
offer; sacrifice 享
xiangde. partnership 相得
xiangguo. surpass the other(s) 相過
xiangshu. image and number 象數
xiangsi. longing; expectation 相思
xiangxian. to make a sacrificial offering 享獻
xiangying. mutual response 相應
xianjie. small, minor matters 纖介
xianlu. pokeweed 莧陸
xiao. small; pettiness; decrease 小
xiaofa. emulate 效法
xiaoheng. only slight prevalence may be had 小亨
xiaoli you youwang. it is fitting for small matters should one set out to do something 小利有攸往
xiaoren. petty man 小人
xiaozi. youngest son 小子
xie. cleanse 渫
foot fetters 械
release 解
xin. heart/mind 心
(the) new 新
trust, we can trust that, surely 信
xincong. faithfully follow 信從
xing. action, engagement; act, provoke 行
body, form 形
human nature 性
punishment 刑
xing ce. provokes painful feeling 行惻
xing dao zhi ren. all persons who practice the Dao 行道之人
xing wu. punishment is severe, punishment is applied severely 刑剭
xingqi. concrete form 形器
xiong. misfortune 凶

xiu. burgeoning 秀
xiulin. humiliating 羞吝
xiyue. delight 喜說 [悅]
xu. domestication 畜
  eyes haughty with pride 盱
  garner 蓄
  self-effacement; emptiness; empty, unstable 虛
  sequence 序
  slowly; eventually 徐
  wait, waiting 須
xuan. mysterious 玄
  revolve, turn 旋
xuanfan. turn back 旋反
xuanming. noumenon 玄冥
xun. ten-day period 旬
xuzhi. block, bring to a halt 畜止
yan. words; to talk 言
yang. nourish 養
  positive, positive principle 陽
  ram, sheep 羊
yao. hexagram lines; moving lines 爻
yaoci. line statements 爻辭
yi. alas 億
  appropriateness; it is appropriate that; fitting 宜
  change; ease, laxity 易
  concept, meaning; righteousness; moral principle 義
  cut off the nose 劓
  idea 意
  jaws; provide/get nourishment 頤
  lose 佚
  model 儀
  standing upright, i.e., bold and brave 仡
  utilize 役
yi zai hu jue. already as far as he can go 已在乎角
yi zhao. cast aside things in his care 遺照
yibiao. model 儀表
yifa. model 儀法
yin. back flesh 夤
  lascivious 淫
  negative, negative principle 陰
  what is hidden 隱
yin yi yu yang bi zhan. as yin provoked the suspicions of yang, it must fight 陰疑於陽必戰

ying. resonance, response 應
ying tian ze da. as one is in resonance with Heaven, one emulates its greatness 應天則大
yinreng. persistent, continuous 因仍
yishi. ceremonial dress decoration 儀飾
yong. function; exertion 用
yong zhen. perseverance and constancy, perpetual constancy, perpetually/constantly practice constancy 永貞
yongrong kuanyu. at ease; poised and generous 雍容寬裕
you. assist 佑
being 有
numinous help 祐
people who share the same goal, i.e., friends 友
you fu yu xiaoren. inspire confidence in petty men 有孚于小人
you he zhi. what reason does this one still have to proceed; why go any further 又何之
you shen. render service to the numinous 祐神
you shi. chance to take successful action 有事
youhun. dissipation of one's spirit 遊魂
yu. concern 虞
enrich 裕
with, together with 與
yu chu menting. this by leaving his gate and courtyard 于出門庭
yu kou. guard against harassment; ward off bandits 禦寇
yu shi. use carriages to transport corpses; many leaders 輿尸
yuan. distance; keep at a distance 遠
fundamentality; primordial generator 元
yuanfu. prime stalwart 元夫
yuanqiong qi qing shijue qi yi. plumb one's inclinations to their depths and determine one's intention by divination 原窮其情筮決其意
yuanshi. plumb and divine 原筮
yue. cut off the feet 刖
say 曰
(type of sacrifice) 禴
yun. trust, trustworthy; sincerely 允
zan. hair clasp 簪
zangpi. good and evil 臧否
ze. emulate; model; thus 則
mysteries 賾
zhangfu. stalwart 丈夫
zhawei xuwang. deceitful and false behavior 詐僞虛妄
zhe shou. remove the head 折首
zhen. constancy 貞
constant activity; haste; insecure agitation 振

headrest, pillow 枕
truth 眞
zheng. correct, correct behavior, rectitude, righteousness, uprightness 正
corroboration 徵
raise up, rescue 拯
zheng zhi suo jian. debasement of correct behavior 正之所賤
zhengdong. start to move 拯動
zhengjiu. rescue 拯救
zhengju. start up 拯舉
zhengli. right principle 正理
zhenli. practice constancy in the face of danger 貞厲
true moral principles 眞理
zhen lin. regard baseness as constancy 貞吝
zhenzhi. stuck, bogged down 枕枝
zhi. arrive at; go so far as 至
constraint, controlling factor, to control 制
here; god of the earth, i.e., great 祇
manage 制
purpose, intention, will, ambition 志
stop, halt; curbs are set; restraint 止
straight 直
well governed 治
wise, wisdom 知
zhi hui. regret here 祇悔
zhi zhi. restrain things; restrain from doing things 止之
zhili. perfect principle 至理
zhilue. general introduction 指略
zhixu. block, bring to a halt 止畜
perfect void 至虛
zhizhi. perfectly governed 至治
zhong. all 衆
end; in the end 終
mean, the Mean, centrality 中
personal integrity; loyalty 忠
zhongde. virtue of centrality 中德
zhongduo. numerous, abundant 衆多
zhonglai. always keeps attracting 終來
zhou xu. emptiness of the boat 舟虛
zhouxuan. come full cycle 周旋
zhu. help 助
ruler, master, controlling principle 主
touch, be attached to 著
zhuan. devotion 專
enumeration, calculation 撰

zhuang. strong, strength 壯
zhufu fanglai. as soon as the crimson ceremonial garment (knee covering) arrives 朱紱方來
zhuhou. feudal lords 諸候
zhuhou zhi lu. concerns of the feudal lords 諸候之慮
zhulu. concerns of all 諸慮
zhushi. invoker-secretary 祝史
zi. property, wealth; rely on, employ; borrow, use 資
zi fu. the axe that he uses 資斧
zifu. funds and axe, i.e., travel expenses 資斧
ziran. nature, the natural 自然
ziran zhi xing. the nature one has thanks to natural endowment 自然之性
zong. fundamental regulator 宗
zongheng. political strategies and alliances 縱横
zongzhu. chief controlling principle 宗主
zunbei. personal caliber 尊卑

List of Proper Nouns

Bao Xi 包犧 (also Fu Xi 伏犧 a mythical cultural hero)
Bi. 比 (Closeness, Hexagram 8)
賁 (Elegance, Hexagram 22)
Bian wei 辯位 (Considering the line positions)
Bo. 剝 (Peeling, Hexagram 23)
Cai Yong 蔡邕 (133–192)
Cao Cao 曹操 (155–220)
Cao Pi 曹丕 (187–226)
Cao Shuang 曹爽 (third century A.D.)
Cao Zhi 曹植 (192–232)
Cheng Yi 程頤 (1033–1107)
Chu Zhongdu 褚仲都 (sixth century A.D.)
Cui. 萃 (Gathering, Hexagram 45)
Daguo. 大過 (Major Superiority, Hexagram 28)
Dao luelun 道略論 (General discussion of the Dao)
Daxiang 大象 (Great images)
Daxu. 大畜 (Great Domestication, Hexagram 26)
Dayan yi 大衍義 (Meaning of the great expansion)
Dayou. 大有 (Great Holdings, Hexagram 14)
Dazhuan 大傳 (Great commentary)
Dazhuang. 大壯 (Great Strength, Hexagram 34)
Di 狄 a barbarian tribe inhabiting the northwest of the Shang state
Ding. 鼎 (The Caldron, Hexagram 50)
Ding Mi 丁謐 (third century A.D.)
Dui. 兌 (Joy, Hexagram 58); also one of the eight trigrams
Dun. 遯 (Withdrawal, Hexagram 33)
Erya 爾雅 (Elegant and correct writings in familiar terms)
Fei Zhi 費直 (ca. 50 B.C.–10 A.D.)

Feng. 豐 (Abundance, Hexagram 55)
Fu. 復 (Return, Hexagram 24)
Fu Jia 傅瑕 (205–255)
Fu Xi 伏犧 (also Bao Xi 包犧, mythical cultural hero)
Gaozong 高宗 (title of King Wu Ding, "Exalted Ancestor")
Ge. 革 (Radical Change, Hexagram 49)
Gen. 艮 (Restraint, Hexagram 52); also one of the eight trigrams
Gou. 姤 (Encounter, Hexagram 44)
Gu. 蠱 (Ills to Be Cured, Hexagram 18)
Gua lue 卦略 (Cursory remarks on some hexagrams)
Guan. 觀 (Viewing, Hexagram 20)
Guangya 廣雅 (The *Erya* expanded)
Guifang 鬼方 Demon Territory
Guimei. 歸妹 (Marrying Maiden, Hexagram 54)
Guo Jing 郭京 (Tang era [618–907], dates unknown)
Guo Xiang 郭象 (died 312)
Guoyu 國語 (Discourses of the states)
Han Kangbo 韓康伯 (died ca. 385)
Haosheng 好生 (It is preferable to let people live), section of the *Kongzi jiayu* (The school sayings of Confucius)
He Shao 何劭 (late third/early fourth century A.D.)
He Yan 何晏 (190–249)
He Zeng 何曾 (199–278)
Heng. 恆 (Perseverance, Hexagram 32)
Hetu 河圖 (Yellow River chart)
Huan. 渙 (Dispersion, Hexagram 59)
Huang Di 黃帝 (the Yellow Emperor, a mythical figure)
Jia Chong 賈充 (217–282)
Jian. 蹇 (Adversity, Hexagram 39)
漸 (Gradual Advance, Hexagram 53)
Jiaren. 家人 (The Family, Hexagram 37)
Jie. 節 (Control, Hexagram 60)
Jiji. 既濟 (Ferrying Complete, Hexagram 63)
Jin. 晉 (Advance, Hexagram 35)
Jing. 井 (The Well, Hexagram 48)
Jingyi shuwen 經義述聞 (Accounts of what has been heard concerning interpretations of the classics)
Jiao Xun 焦循 (1763–1820)
Kan. 坎 Sink Hole (one of the eight trigrams)
Kong Yingda 孔穎達 (574–648)

Kongzi jiayu 孔子家語 (The school sayings of Confucius)
Kuai. 夬 (Resolution, Hexagram 43)
Kui. 睽 (Contrariety, Hexagram 38)
Kun. 坤 (Pure Yin, Hexagram 2); also one of the eight trigrams
困 (Impasse, Hexagram 47)
Li. 離 (Cohesion, Hexagram 30); also one of the eight trigrams
Lin. 臨 (Overseeing, Hexagram 19)
Liu Tao 劉陶 (third century A.D.)
Liu Xiang 劉向 (77–6 B.C.)
Liu Yiqing 劉義慶 (403–444)
Liyun 禮運 (Evolution of rites), section of the *Liji* (Book of rites)
Lü. 履 (Treading, Hexagram 10)
旅 (The Wanderer, Hexagram 56)
Lu Deming 陸德明 (556–627)
Lu Ji 陸績 (Three Kingdoms [222–280] figure)
Lu Xisheng 陸希聲 (died ca. 905)
Lueli xia 略例下 (General remarks, part two)
Luoshu 洛書 (Luo River diagram)
Lüshi chunqiu 呂氏春秋 (The spring and autumn annals of master Lü)
Ma Rong 馬融 (79–166)
Meng. 蒙 (Juvenile Ignorance, Hexagram 4)
Ming gua shi bian tong yao 明卦適變通爻 (Clarifying how the hexagrams correspond to change and make the lines commensurate with it)
Ming tuan 明彖 (Clarifying the Judgments)
Ming xiang 明象 (Clarifying the images)
Ming yao tong bian 明爻通變 (Clarifying how the lines are commensurate with change)
Mingyi. 明夷 (Suppression of the Light, Hexagram 36)
Mozi 墨子 (The sayings of Master Mo)
Pei Hui 裴徽 (late second–early third century A.D.)
Pei Kai 裴楷 (237–291)
Pei Xiu 裴秀 (224–271)
Pi. 否 (Obstruction, Hexagram 12)
Quan xue pian 勸學篇 (Encouragement to learning)
Qian. 乾 (Pure Yang, Hexagram 1); also one of the eight trigrams
謙 (Modesty, Hexagram 15)
Ruan Yuan 阮元 (1764–1849)
Sanguozhi 三國志 (Chronicle of the Three Kingdoms)
Shang Yang 商鞅 (died 338 B.C.)

Shen Nong 神農 (mythical cultural hero)
Sheng. 升 (Climbing, Hexagram 46)
Shi. 師 (The Army, Hexagram 7)
Shihe. 噬嗑 (Bite Together, Hexagram 21)
Shishuo xinyu 世說新語 (A new account of tales of the world)
Shiyi 十翼 (Ten Wings)
Shun 舜 (sage king of remote antiquity)
Shuo gua 說卦 (Explaining the trigrams)
Shuowen jiezi 說文解字 (Explanation of simple and composite characters)
Shuoyuan 說苑 (Garden of sayings)
Siben lun 四本論 (Treatise on the four basic relationships between talent and human nature)
Sima Qian 司馬遷 (ca. 145–ca.85 B.C.)
Sima Shi 司馬師 (208–255)
Sima Yan 司馬炎 (236–290)
Sima Yi 司馬懿 (179–251)
Song. 訟 (Contention, Hexagram 6)
Sui. 隧 (Following, Hexagram 17)
Sun. 巽 (Compliance, Hexagram 57); also one of the eight trigrams
損 (Diminution, Hexagram 41)
Sun Xingyan 孫星衍 (1753–1818)
Sunzi bingfa 孫子兵法 (Master Sun's art of war)
Tai. 泰 (Peace, Hexagram 11)
Tongren. 同人 (Fellowship, Hexagram 13)
Tuanci 彖辭 (Words of the Judgment)
Tuanzhuan 彖傳 (Commentary on the Judgments)
Wang Anshi 王安石 (1021–1086)
Wang Bi 王弼 (226–249)
Wang Chen 王沈 (third century A.D.)
Wang Ji 王濟 (ca. 240–ca. 285)
Wang Li 王黎 (third century A.D.)
Wang Su 王肅 (195–256)
Wang Ye 王業 (late second/early third century A.D.)
Wang Yinzhi 王引之 (1766–1834)
Wang Yinglin 王應麟 (1223–1296)
Wangzhi 王制 (Regulations of the former kings), section of the *Liji* (Book of Rites)
Weiji. 未濟 (Ferrying Incomplete, Hexagram 64)
Weizhi 魏志 (Chronicles of Wei)

Wenyan 文言 (Commentary on the words of the text)
Wu Cheng 吳澄 (1249–1333)
Wu Ding 武丁 (Shang king, reigned 1324–1266 B.C.)
Wuwang. 無妄 (No Errancy, Hexagram 25)
Xian. 咸 (Reciprocity, Hexagram 31)
Xiang Anshi 項安世 (died 1280)
Xiangzhuan 象傳 (Commentary on the images)
Xiaoguo. 小過 (Minor Superiority, Hexagram 62)
Xiaoxiang 小象 (Little images)
Xiaoxu. 小畜 (Lesser Domestication, Hexagram 9)
Xici zhuan 繫辭傳 (Commentary on the appended phrases)
Xie. 解 (Release, Hexagram 40)
Xikan. 習坎 (The Constant Sink Hole, Hexagram 29)
Xing Shou 邢璹 (Tang era [618–907], dates unknown)
Xu. 需 (Waiting, Hexagram 5)
Xu Shen 許慎 (30–124)
Xugua 序卦 (Providing the sequence of the hexagrams)
Xun Rong 荀融 (third century A.D.)
Xunzi 荀子 (The sayings of Master Xun)
Yanzi 顏子 (also Yan Hui 顏回 or Yan Yuan 顏淵), disciple of Confucius (late sixth/early fifth century B.C.)
Yao 堯 (sage king of remote antiquity)
Yi. 益 (Increase, Hexagram 42)
頤 (Nourishment, Hexagram 27)
Yichuan Yizhuan 伊川易傳 (Yichuan's commentary on the *Changes*)
Yijing 易經 (Classic/Book of changes)
Yu. 豫 (Contentment, Hexagram 16)
Yu Fan 虞翻 (172–241)
Yu Yan 俞琰 (1258–1314)
Yu Yue 俞樾 (1821–1907)
Zagua 雜卦 (The hexagrams in irregular order)
Zhang Heng 張衡 (78–139)
Zhang Yi 張揖 (fl. ca. 227–232)
Zhen. 震 (Quake, Hexagram 51); one of the eight trigrams
Zheng Xuan 鄭玄 (127–200)
Zhong Hui 鍾會 (225–264)
Zhongfu. 中孚 (Inner Trust, Hexagram 61)
Zhouyi benyi 周易本義 (Original meaning of the *Changes of the Zhou*)
Zhouyi bushu 周易補疏 (Supplements to the commentaries and subcommentaries to the *Changes of the Zhou*)

Zhouyi juzheng 周易舉正 (Evidence for correct readings in the *Changes of the Zhou*)
Zhouyi yinyi 周易音義 (Pronunciation and meaning of terms in the *Changes of the Zhou*)
Zhu Xi 朱熹 (1130–1200)
Zhun. 屯 (Birth Throes, Hexagram 3)
Zigong 子貢 (disciple of Confucius [late sixth/early fifth century B.C.])
Zuozhuan 左傳 (Zuo's chronicles)

Index

Index

Index

Index

Other Works in the Columbia Asian Studies Series

TRANSLATIONS FROM THE ASIAN CLASSICS

Major Plays of Chikamatsu, tr. Donald Keene 1961

Four Major Plays of Chikamatsu, tr. Donald Keene. Paperback text edition 1961

Records of the Grand Historian of China, translated from the Shih chi of Ssu-ma Ch'ien, tr. Burton Watson, 2 vols. 1961

Instructions for Practical Living and Other Neo-Confucian Writings by Wang Yang-ming, tr. Wing-tsit Chan 1963

Chuang Tzu: Basic Writings, tr. Burton Watson, paperback ed. only 1964

The Mahābhārata, tr. Chakravarthi V. Narasimhan. Also in paperback ed. 1965

The Manyōshū, Nippon Gakujutsu Shinkōkai edition 1965

Su Tung-p'o: Selections from a Sung Dynasty Poet, tr. Burton Watson. Also in paperback ed. 1965

Bhartrihari: Poems, tr. Barbara Stoler Miller. Also in paperback ed. 1967

Basic Writings of Mo Tzu, Hsün Tzu, and Han Fei Tzu, tr. Burton Watson. Also in separate paperback ed. 1967

The Awakening of Faith, Attributed to Aśvaghosha, tr. Yoshito S. Hakeda. Also in paperback ed. 1967

Reflections on Things at Hand: The Neo-Confucian Anthology, comp. Chu Hsi and Lü Tsu-Ch'ien, tr. Wing-tsit Chan 1967

The Platform Sutra of the Sixth Patriarch, tr. Philip B. Yampolsky. Also in paperback ed. 1967

Essays in Idleness: The Tsurezuregusa of Kenkō, tr. Donald Keene. Also in paperback ed. 1967

Other Works in the Asian Studies Series

Other Works in the Asian Studies Series

Among the Flowers: The Hua-chien chi, tr. Lois Fusek	1982
Grass Hill: Poems and Prose by the Japanese Monk Gensei, tr. Burton Watson	1983
Doctors, Diviners, and Magicians of Ancient China: Biographies of Fang-shih, tr. Kenneth J. DeWoskin. Also in paperback ed.	1983
Theater of Memory: The Plays of Kālidāsa, ed. Barbara Stoler Miller. Also in paperback ed.	1984
The Columbia Book of Chinese Poetry: From Early Times to the Thirteenth Century, ed. and tr. Burton Watson. Also in paperback ed.	1984
Poems of Love and War: From the Eight Anthologies and the Ten Songs of Classical Tamil, tr. A.K. Ramanujan. Also in paperback ed.	1985
The Columbia Book of Later Chinese Poetry, ed. and tr. Jonathan Chaves. Also in paperback ed.	1986
The Tso Chuan: Selections from China's Oldest Narrative History, tr. Burton Watson	1989
Waiting for the Wind: Thirty-Six Poets of Japan's Late Medieval Age, tr. Steven Carter	1989
Selected Writings of Nichiren, ed. Philip B. Yampolsky	1990
The Book of Lieh-Tzŭ A Classic of the Tao, tr. A. C. Graham. Morningside ed.	1990
Saigyō, Poems of a Mountain Home, tr. Burton Watson	1990
The Cilappatikāram of Iḷaṅkō Aṭikaḷ, tr. R. Parthasarathy	1993
The Lotus Sutra, tr. Burton Watson	1993

STUDIES IN ASIAN CULTURE

1.	*The Ōnin War: History of Its Origins and Background, with a Selective Translation of the Chronicle of Ōnin*, by H. Paul Varley	1967
2.	*Chinese Government in Ming Times: Seven Studies*, ed. Charles O. Hucker	1969
3.	*The Actors' Analects (Yakusha Rongo)*, ed and tr. by Charles J. Dunn and Bungó Torigoe	1969
4.	*Self and Society in Ming Thought*, by Wm. Theodore de Bary and the Conference on Ming Thought. Also in paperback.	1970
5.	*A History of Islamic Philosophy*, by Majid Fakhry, 2d ed.	1983
6.	*Phantasies of a Love Thief: The Caurapañcāśikā Attributed to Bilhaṇa*, by Barbara Stoler Miller	1971
7.	*Iqbal: Poet-Philosopher of Pakistan*, ed. Hafeez Malik	1971
8.	*The Golden Tradition: An Anthology of Urdu Poetry*, ed. and tr. Ahmed Ali. Also in paperback ed.	1973
9.	*Conquerors and Confucians: Aspects of Political Change in Late Yüan China*, by John W. Dardess	1973

10. *The Unfolding of Neo-Confucianism*, by Wm. Theodore de Bary and the Conference on Seventeenth-Century Chinese Thought. Also in paperback ed. 1975
11. *To Acquire Wisdom: The Way of Wang Yang-ming*, by Julia Ching 1976
12. *Gods, Priests, and Warriors: The Bhṛgus of the Mahābhārata*, by Robert P. Goldman 1977
13. *Mei Yao-ch'en and the Development of Early Sung Poetry*, by Jonathan Chaves 1976
14. *The Legend of Semimaru, Blind Musician of Japan*, by Susan Matisoff 1977
15. *Sir Sayyid Ahmad Khan and Muslim Modernization in India and Pakistan*, by Hafeez Malik 1980
16. *The Khilafat Movement: Religious Symbolism and Political Mobilization in India*, by Gail Minault 1982
17. *The World of K'ung Shang-ren: A Man of Letters in Early Ch'ing China*, by Richard Strassberg 1983
18. *The Lotus Boat: The Origins of Chinese Tz'u Poetry in Tang Popular Culture*, by Marsha L. Wagner 1984
19. *Expressions of Self in Chinese Literature*, ed. Robert E. Hegel and Richard C. Hessney 1985
20. *Songs for the Bride: Women's Voices and Wedding Rites of Rural India*, by W.G. Archer, ed., Barbara Stoler Miller and Mildred Archer 1986
21. *A Heritage of Kings: One Man's Monarchy in the Confucian World*, by JaHyun Kim Haboush 1988

COMPANIONS TO ASIAN STUDIES

Approaches to the Oriental Classics, ed. Wm. Theodore de Bary 1959

Early Chinese Literature, by Burton Watson. Also in paperback ed. 1962

Approaches to Asian Civilization, ed. Wm. Theodore de Bary and Ainslie T. Embree 1964

The Classic Chinese Novel: A Critical Introduction, by C.T. Hsia. Also in paperback ed. 1968

Chinese Lyricism: Shih Poetry from the Second to the Twelfth Century, tr. Burton Watson. Also in paperback ed. 1971

A Syllabus of Indian Civilization, by Leonard A. Gordon and Barbara Stoler Miller 1971

Twentieth-Century Chinese Stories, ed. C.T. Hsia and Joseph S.M. Lau. Also in paperback ed. 1971

A Syllabus of Chinese Civilization, by J. Mason Gentzler, 2d ed. 1972

A Syllabus of Japanese Civilization, by H. Paul Varley, 2d ed. 1972

An Introduction to Chinese Civilization, ed. John Meskill, with the assistance of J. Mason Gentzler 1973

Other Works in the Asian Studies Series

An Introduction to Japanese Civilization, ed. Arthur E. Tiedemann — 1974
Ukifune: Love in the Tale of Genji, ed. Andrew Pekarik — 1982
The Pleasures of Japanese Literature, by Donald Keene — 1988
A Guide to Oriental Classics, ed Wm. Theodore de Bary and Ainslie T. Embree; third edition ed. Amy Vladeck Heinrich, 2 vols. — 1989

INTRODUCTION TO ASIAN CIVILIZATIONS

Wm. Theodore de Bary, Editor
Sources of Japanese Tradition, 1958; paperback ed., 2 vols., — 1964
Sources of Indian Tradition, 1958; paperback ed., 2 vols., 1964; 1988; 2d ed., 2 vols. — 1968
Sources of Chinese Tradition, 1960; paperback ed., 2 vols., — 1964

NEO-CONFUCIAN STUDIES

Instructions for Practical Living and Other Neo-Confucian Writings by Wang Yang-ming, tr. Wing-tsit Chan — 1963
Reflections on Things at Hand: The Neo-Confucian Anthology, comp. Chu Hsi and Lü Tsu-ch'ien, tr. Wing-tsit Chan — 1967
Self and Society in Ming Thought, by Wm. Theodore de Bary and the Conference on Ming Thought. Also in paperback ed. — 1970
The Unfolding of Neo-Confucianism, by Wm. Theodore de Bary and the Conference on Seventeenth Century Chinese Thought. Also in paperback ed. — 1975
Principle and Practicality: Essays in Neo-Confucianism and Practical Learning, ed. Wm. Theodore de Bary and Irene Bloom. Also in paperback ed. — 1979
The Syncretic Religion of Lin Chao-en, by Judith A. Berling — 1980
The Renewal of Buddhism in China: Chu-hung and the Late Ming Synthesis, by Chün-fang Yü — 1981
Neo-Confucian Orthodoxy and the Learning of the Mind-and-Heart, by Wm. Theodore de Bary — 1981
Yüan Thought: Chinese Thought and Religion Under the Mongols, ed. Hok-lam Chan and Wm. Theodore de Bary — 1983
The Liberal Tradition in China, by Wm. Theodore de Bary — 1983
The Development and Decline of Chinese Cosmology, by John B. Henderson — 1984
The Rise of Neo-Confucianism in Korea, by Wm. Theodore de Bary and JaHyun Kim Haboush — 1985
Chiao Hung and the Restructuring if Neo-Confucianism in Late Ming, by Edward T. Ch'ien — 1985
Neo-Confucian Terms Explained: Pei-hsi tzu-i, by Ch'en Ch'un, ed. and trans. Wing-tsit Chan — 1986

Other Works in the Asian Studies Series

Knowledge Painfully Acquired: K'un-chih chi, by Lo Ch'in-shun, ed. and trans. Irene Bloom 1987
To Become a Sage: The Ten Diagrams on Sage Learning, by Yi T'oegye, ed. and trans. Michael C. Kalton 1988
The Message of the Mind in Neo-Confucian Thought, by Wm. Theodore de Bary 1989

MODERN ASIAN LITERATURE SERIES

Modern Japanese Drama: An Anthology, ed. and tr. Ted Takaya. Also in paperback ed. 1979
Mask and Sword: Two Plays for the Contemporary Japanese Theater, Yamazaki Masakazu, tr. J. Thomas Rimer 1980
Yokomitsu Riichi, Modernist, Dennis Keene 1980
Nepali Visions, Nepali Dreams: The Poetry of Laxmiprasad Devkota, tr. David Rubin 1980
Literature of the Hundred Flowers, vol. 1: *Criticism and Polemics*, ed. Hualing Nieh 1981
Literature of the Hundred Flowers, vol. 2: *Poetry and Fiction*, ed Hualing Nieh 1981
Modern Chinese Stories and Novellas, 1919-1949, ed. Joseph S.M. Lau, C.T. Hsia, and Leo Ou-fan Lee. Also in paperback ed. 1984
A View by the Sea, by Yasuoka Shōtarō, tr. Kären Wigen 1984
Other Worlds, Arishima Takeo and the Bounds of Modern Japanese Fiction, by Paul Anderer 1984
Selected Poems of Sō Chōngju, tr. with intro. by David R. McCann 1989
The Sting of Life: Four Contemporary Japanese Novelists, by Van C. Gessel 1989
The Travels of Lao Ts'an, by Liu T'ieh-yün, tr. Harold Shadick. Morningside ed. 1990
Stories of Osaka Life, by Oda Sakunosuke, tr. Burton Watson 1990
The Bodhisattva, or Samantabhadra, by Ishikawa Jun, tr. with intro. by William Jefferson Tyler 1990

Designer: Teresa Bonner
Text: Fournier
Compositor: Birdtrack Press
Printer: Maple-Vail
Binder: Maple-Vail